INFORMATION SYSTEMS MANAGEMENT IN PRACTICE

Fourth Edition

Barbara C. McNurlin

Writer—Information Systems

Ralph H. Sprague, Jr.

University of Hawaii

 PRENTICE HALL, Upper Saddle River, New Jersey 07458

Senior Acquisitions Editor: Jo-Ann DeLuca
Editor-in-Chief: P.J. Boardman
Assistant Editor: Audrey Regan
Editorial Assistant: Marc Oliver
Executive Marketing Manager: Nancy Evans
Sales Specialists: Audra Silverie, Kris King
Production Editor: Lynda Paolucci
Managing Editor: Katherine Evancie
Production Coordinator: Cindy Spreder
Manufacturing Buyer: Alana Zdinak
Senior Manufacturing Supervisor: Paul Smolenski
Manufacturing Manager: Vincent Scelta
Senior Designer: Suzanne Behnke
Design Director: Patricia Wosczyk
Cover Design: Karen Salzbach
Composition: East End Publishing Services

10   9   8   7   6   5   4   3

ISBN: 0-13-847971-2

Library of Congress Cataloging-in-Publication Data
Information systems management in practice / [edited by] BARBARA C.
    MCNURLIN, RALPH H. SPRAGUE, JR. — 4th ed.
      p.   cm.
    Includes bibliographical references and index.
    ISBN 0-13-847971-2
    1. Management information systems. 2. Information resources
management. I. McNurlin, Barbara C. II. Sprague, Ralph H. Jr.
    T58.64.I54   1998
    658.4'038—dc21   97-1245

Prentice-Hall International (UK) Limited, London
Prentice-Hall of Australia Pty. Limited, Sydney
Prentice-Hall Canada, Inc., Toronto
Prentice-Hall Hispanoamericana, S.A., Mexico
Prentice-Hall of India Private Limited, New Delhi
Prentice-Hall of Japan, Inc., Tokyo
Simon & Schuster Asia Pte. Ltd., Singapore
Editora Prentice-Hall do Brasil, Ltda., Rio de Janeiro

This book is dedicated to our parents

Dick and Peggy Canning
and
Ralph and Virginia Sprague

for all their inspiration, guidance, and support.

Contents in Brief

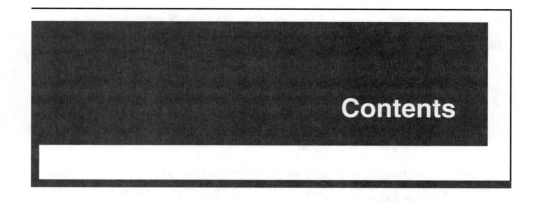

Contents

10 **MANAGEMENT ISSUES IN
SYSTEM DEVELOPMENT 292**

**PART IV   MANAGING THE EXPANDING UNIVERSE
OF COMPUTING 319**

11 **THE EXPANDING UNIVERSE
OF COMPUTING 321**

12 **SUPPORTING THE EXPANDING UNIVERSE OF COMPUTING   341**

PART V   SUPPORT SYSTEMS   363

13 **DECISION SUPPORT SYSTEMS AND EXECUTIVE INFORMATION SYSTEMS   365**

14 GROUP SUPPORT SYSTEMS 394

GLOSSARY 533

INDEX 545

Preface

This book deals with the management of information technology (IT) as it is being practiced in organizations today. Successfully managing IT has become crucial for several reasons:

- Information technology is now a strategic asset that is being used to mold competitive strategies and change organizational processes.
- The situations in which organizations are applying IT have increased in complexity, including more interorganizational environments.
- The capabilities of IT and the complexities of using the technologies are also growing at an accelerating rate.
- As IT and its uses become more complex, developing strategies and systems to deliver the technology has become more difficult.

The net result is a growing need for guidance on the issues, strategies, and tactics for managing the use of information technology. To partially satisfy this need, universities and colleges have developed courses that focus on the management of information technology. Textual material for these courses has been sparse for the following two particularly troublesome reasons.

First, the principles and strategies of effective management are evolving out of the experiences of practicing managers. Merely collecting reports from the current literature fails to provide the interaction to articulate and codify these principles. Current developments and experiences need interpretation and coalescence to provide the guidance that new and practicing managers need to further develop their knowledge and managerial skills.

Second, IT is changing so rapidly that textbook authors, technicians, practitioners, researchers, and academics are having a difficult time just staying current. For example, since the third edition of this book was published, two major developments stand out. One has been the surprise revolution of Internet-centric computing. This dramatic shift has come on the heels of the tumultuous move to client/server computing—which had not been fully absorbed by information systems (IS) departments before use of the Internet as a major computing platform became important. The second major development, which is much more subtle, but equally profound, is the movement toward knowledge management—which is a far different task from data management or information management. As a result of these and other changes, courses have often had to rely on periodicals to stay up-to-date.

CONTRIBUTION OF THIS BOOK

We believe this book makes a major contribution to both of these problems. The primary resource for this book is work we recently performed for several organizations—Wentworth Research's IT Management Programme, The Sourcing Interests Group, Andersen Consulting, and Ernst & Young's Center for Business Innovation. Our writing for these organizations does not merely report current developments and practices, it includes thoughtful interpretation to provide guidance, principles, and strategies for information systems executives.

Our objective in this book is to capture the material of most current importance to information systems executives, organizing it around a framework that provides guidance for the IS department. A key element of our writing continues to be examples of actual work in companies. This book includes over 75 company case examples.

USE OF THIS BOOK BY PRACTICING MANAGERS AND CONSULTANTS

In the management of information technology, this book is useful to several levels of managers:

1. Senior executives who want an overview of the issues and strategies in managing IT, with examples of what other companies are doing.
2. Information systems executives who must implement IT as a strategic resource to help their organizations attain their overall goals and objectives.
3. Information systems managers who are responsible for major technical areas, such as system development, technology planning, and operations.
4. Managers of functional units who (1) want to better understand the issues and processes of providing IT support for their areas of responsibility, or (2) are now responsible for overseeing the management of IT in their function.

We believe that practicing managers of all types will find this book valuable. By focusing on issues and strategies, while explaining technical concepts, this book provides an overview of information systems management for corporate executives and managers. By combining the experiences of successful executives in "the real world," this book provides a unique perspective for all information systems managers.

Consultants to executives and managers will also find this book a useful reference for staying up-to-date on important issues in the field.

USE OF THIS BOOK AS A TEXT

Future information systems managers who are graduate or undergraduate students will find that this book presents a view of what "the real world" has in store. As a text, it has been intended for students who have had at least one information systems course.

At the graduate level, it has been used since its first edition in 1986 for the second course, beyond the required IS course. It is especially well suited for the final course in a graduate curriculum on information systems management. In addition, as MBA students have become more computer literate in recent years, the book has been increasingly used as the text in the MBA IS core course. In both uses, the book gives students conceptual and practical guidelines for dealing with the management of today's information systems function.

At the undergraduate level, the book can serve as the text for a course dealing specifically with the management of IT, or in the capstone course that summarizes the practice of IT for students about to begin their careers. Most undergraduate majors in information technology take entry-level positions in the information systems department, and then proceed into management. In the short term, they work with information systems managers who are facing the problems and using the principles dealt with in this book.

Although this book has not been aimed at students majoring in other areas, non-IS majors are taking IS courses in increasing numbers to better understand the increasingly strategic IT arena. Most chapters in this book are pertinent to them because the theory is illustrated by real-life case studies, which are easily understood by non-IS majors.

At the end of each chapter are three types of questions and exercises to reinforce the material in the text.

- *Review questions* are based directly on the material in the chapter, allowing the reader to assess comprehension of the chapter's key principles, topics, and ideas.
- *Discussion questions* are based on a few topics in the chapter for which there is a legitimate basis for a difference of opinion. These questions focus discussion on these issues when the book is used in a seminar or classroom setting.
- *Exercises* provide an opportunity for the reader to put some of the concepts and ideas into practice on a small scale. In particular, one exercise in each chapter requires a student, or a team of students, to visit a local company and discover how the ideas in the chapter are being implemented in that company.

THE *INSTRUCTOR'S MANUAL*

We accompany this fourth edition with an *Instructor's Manual*, prepared by Jerry McBride of Marist College in Poughkeepsie, New York. Again, Jerry supplied the all-important critical questions in the guide. The purposes of the guide are (1) to help instructors prepare a strategy and outline for conducting an advanced systems course using this text and (2) to provide support materials and techniques to enhance the course.

We believe there are five approaches for using this text. The five course modes are:

- A lecture-based course
- A seminar-based course
- A directed study course
- An independent study course
- An action research course

In the *Instructor's Manual*, Jerry suggests some interesting resources to use in these different course approaches. For example, he explains how he has used a computer-based simulation game to help his students understand the consequences of their actions, as they try to introduce technology innovation into an organization.

The *Instructor's Manual* includes:

1. Outlines for the five course approaches
2. An overview for each chapter
3. Answers to the review questions in the text
4. Transparency masters for all the figures in the text
5. Suggestions on how to conduct site visit exercises
6. Several sample syllabi
7. An approach to using simulation software
8. Critical questions for each chapter, and how to create them

These critical questions deserve a short explanation. Like the discussion questions in the text, critical questions are designed to stimulate critical thinking and discussion among students. Some of the critical questions were prepared by Jerry's students as part of their homework. In the *Instructor's Manual*, we present critical questions for each chapter, as well as an explanation of how Jerry has helped his students create them, thereby stimulating their critical thinking.

A course in information systems management can be exciting—to teach and to take. We have provided the *Instructor's Manual* to make this one of those exciting courses.

FORMAT AND CONTENTS

This book is divided into six parts, each dealing with a major portion of the field of information technology. Chapter 1 precedes Part I because it serves as the framework around which the rest of the book is built. It traces the growing importance of information systems management and presents a conceptual model to show the key areas, how they fit together, and the principal issues for executives in each area. It also presents a very interesting longitudinal case example of how these ideas have been implemented in a company over the lifetime of this book—since 1986. In a nutshell, it presents a historical view covering more than the past ten years of the evolution of IS management.

Part I deals with *leadership issues*, including the role of information system executives, the strategic uses of the technology, and approaches to systems planning. Part II treats the all-important issues in *managing the essential information technologies*, distributed systems, telecommunications, information resources, and operations. Part III deals with *managing system development*; its evolution continues to present management with important, yet risky, challenges. Part IV explores the *expanding universe of computing*, including the technologies and the needed support from the systems department. Part V deals with *support systems*, that is, systems aimed mainly at supporting professionals and work groups. And finally, Part VI treats several aspects of *information technology's impact on people*.

Throughout the book, our objectives have been to keep the material practical, to give examples, and to derive guidance for today's and tomorrow's information systems executives based on the experiences of others. To that end, chapters are sprinkled with company examples. These are not so much case studies that require solutions or recommendations; rather, they are case examples that show how companies have put some of the ideas in a chapter into practice.

ACKNOWLEDGMENTS

We wish to acknowledge the contribution of Richard G. Canning, Barbara's father. His insight and foresight originally made this book possible in 1986. In the early 1960s, he recognized data processing executives' need for case studies, practical research findings, and thoughtful analysis. Through publishing and editing *EDP Analyzer* (now *I/S Analyzer*) from 1963 until his retirement in 1986, Dick Canning devoted a major portion of his professional career to that purpose. His legacy continues in this book.

We also wish to thank the organizations that have allowed us to draw on work we performed for them—Wentworth Research, the Sourcing Interests Group, Ernst & Young, and Andersen Consulting.

Finally, we thank Jerry McBride, Tracia McNurlin Barbieri, Jeff McNurlin, and R. Douglas Barbieri. Jerry was again instrumental in creating the all-important *Instructor's Manual*. Tracia acted as our secretary. Without her assistance, this fourth edition and the *Instructor's Manual* would not have been completed so quickly. And Jeff and Doug provided the technical know-how to implement the book's fine Web page at http://www.earthlink.net/~bmcnurlin.

Barbara Canning McNurlin
Ralph H. Sprague, Jr.

ONE

The Importance of Information Systems Management

INTRODUCTION

The use of information technology (IT)—computers and telecommunications—has been growing, at an increasing rate, ever since the invention of the computer in the 1950s. Now, with the widespread development of the Internet and the World Wide Web, the pace has picked up even more. We are well into the third stage of technology assimilation in which the technology makes pervasive changes in the structure and the operation of businesses, industries, work, and business practice. In the words of a *Business Week* cover story, "the Web changes everything." [1]

Although information technologies affect nearly all aspects of human endeavor, this book emphasizes their use in managing and operating enterprises. First known as business data processing and later as management information systems, the field is now called information systems (IS). The operative word is *systems*, because it combines the technologies, people, processes, and organizational mechanisms for the purpose of improving organizational performance.

Management has become the prime user of information technology. Although communication and computer technologies are used in space exploration, weapon systems, medicine, entertainment, and most other aspects of human activity, the majority of information technologies are used to manage organizations.

1

The process of managing technology in organizations is getting more complex as it becomes more important. To illustrate why, here are just a few of the major trends that will be discussed throughout this book.

- The initiative and responsibility for managing the technology is shifting from IS executives toward a collaborative effort, requiring a rich partnership among all senior executives.
- The role of the IS department is shifting from application delivery to system integration and infrastructure development.
- The growth of the Internet and in-company intranets provide worldwide connectivity and an emerging common user interface for all systems. No development in recent history has had the impact of the Internet and the World Wide Web.

The purpose of this book is to provide guidance to executives who manage the application of these technologies to improve organizational performance. This no longer means just IS executives. Historically, managing IT has been the job of technical managers, but it is increasingly becoming an important part of the responsibilities of top executives, line managers, and employees at all levels of an organization. Thus, this book is increasingly appropriate for chief executive officers, chief operations officers, business unit executives, and other managers who now have the responsibility, in partnership with the chief information officer, for using technology to improve the performance of the organization.

Note that this responsibility does not stop with just managing the technology. *Technology* is configured into systems which help manage *information* to improve *organizational performance.*

In this chapter, we first review the recent history of the growth of information systems and their management in organizations. Then we identify several technical and organizational trends that are having a major impact on IT management and organizational performance. Finally, we develop a framework for thinking about how information systems are used and managed in organizations. This framework serves as a road map for the rest of the book.

A LITTLE HISTORY

As we begin to consider the management in organizations, a little history provides some perspective [2]. Most people are surprised to find that the United States passed from the industrial era to the information era in 1957. In that year, the number of U.S. employees whose jobs were to primarily handle information (information workers) surpassed the number of industrial workers. During the 1970s, information workers exceeded 50 percent of the work force. See Figure 1-1.

In the late 1950s and early 1960s, however, information technology to support information work hardly existed. Only the telephone was widespread, and even it did not reach every desk. Computers were just beginning to be used in data processing applications, replacing the older electric accounting machines. Even where computers were in use, their impact was modest.

Most other information work was done in general offices without much support from technology. Xerographic office copiers existed but were only begin-

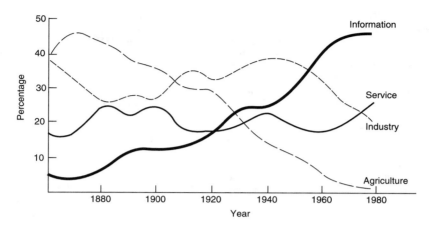

Figure 1-1   Percentage Aggregation of the U.S. Work Force
(from Porat [3])

ning to catch on. Electric typewriters were commonplace, but the first word processor would not arrive until 1964. Facsimile was used only in specialized applications and would not begin general office use until the 1970s. However, the future of technology support for information workers was extremely bright. Nearly all the foundations of information technology in the 1990s had been invented, and costs were beginning their steady long-term fall.

The Classic Infrastructure

As spending on IT began to grow in the 1960s, better ways to manage it became necessary. Since the various technologies were almost completely independent in their operations, a fragmented approach to information management generally evolved. Four major specializations emerged. As shown in Figure 1-2, each had its own products, authority center, and vendors. Furthermore, most offices that used IT heavily were served primarily by one of the four authority structures.

Business computing, for instance, meant data processing (i.e., records processing) almost exclusively, so computers usually were put under the controller, as electric accounting machines had been before them.

Telecommunications were basically outsourced to full-service vendors, which relieved user organizations of most administrative burdens. This approach prevented the growth of large staffs, except where internal teletypewriter networks were implemented. As a result, telecommunications had low visibility because the main responsibility of the telecom staff was locating and managing the equipment room and wiring corridors.

Specialized office products for mailrooms, reproduction centers, records management centers, and typing pools were generally purchased by the individual offices using them, although the administrative vice president usually had at

Figure 1-2   The Classic Infrastructure (from Panko and Sprague)

Typical Product/Service	Corporate Authority	Typical Users Vendors	(Markets)
Data processing management reporting	Director of Data Processing	IBM DEC Honeywell Bull Unisys	Accounting Payroll Reservations Check processing
Telecommunications PABX Telex Telephones	Telecommunications Administrator	AT&T GTE	Telex room General offices Switchboard
Specialized office products Mailing equipment Duplicators Microfilm Centralized word processing	Administrative Vice President	Frieden Bell & Howell Kodak 3M	Mailroom Reprographics Records management Word processing center
General office products Typewriters Copiers Convenience word processors	Administrative Vice President	Xerox Savin IBM	Various offices

Reprinted from: Panko, R. R. and Sprague, R. H., Jr., "Toward a New Framework for Office Support," *Proceedings of the ACM Conference on Office Information Systems*, June 1982, Copyright 1982, Association for Computing Machinery, Inc., by permission.

least nominal oversight responsibilities. Although spending on these products soon became quite large, their use in out-of-sight operations gave them far less visibility than their dollar spending would justify.

General office products were usually controlled by the administrative vice president. Consisting of small-ticket items such as typewriters, answering machines, facsimile terminals, and convenience copiers, general office products were usually controlled broadly, via the annual budgeting mechanism. This left considerable initiative to individual departments.

When this classic fourfold infrastructure emerged in the 1960s, it made considerable sense. It placed control fairly near users. Because the technologies were so diverse, there was no compelling reason to create a unified information management structure.

Pressures for Integration

Although this scattered infrastructure once served a useful purpose, strong pressures toward integrated management emerged in the late 1970s and continues today, for several reasons. First, spending grew so large that scattered management no longer satisfied basic corporate accountability. Recent figures show that more than half of all capital expeditions in America are for IT.

Second, technological barriers among various tools rapidly dissolved. Word processors and other intelligent office products became general-purpose computers that could handle many kinds of software. A number of office technologies that had contained no electronic logic were computerized. Many private branch exchanges (PBXs) could handle data communications and protocol conversion. Intelligent copiers served not only as copiers but also as printers and facsimile machines. Today, it has become difficult to find a significant piece of office equipment that does not contain a microprocessor and cannot be programmed to handle multiple tasks, thus cutting across old authority boundaries in the firm.

The networks began to eliminate the remaining barriers between traditional bailiwicks. Office products were combined to form integrated office systems using local area networks (LANs). Mainframe systems spawned distributed systems. Today, the network is the hub for all information technology use in organizations.

Clearly, the fragmented classical infrastructure has evolved to a more integrated approach. This is inevitable if we are to manage a pervasive technology, which is having a pervasive effect on the way organizations are managed and operate. To set the stage for discussing this more integrated approach, the next two sections explore the nature of the organizational environment and the technology environment, and the ways they interact.

THE ORGANIZATIONAL ENVIRONMENT

The way technology is used depends on the environment surrounding the organization that uses it. This environment includes the economic conditions, the characteristics of principal resources (especially labor), management philosophies, the social mores of the society, and other factors. This environment has been changing constantly. Simultaneously, technological advances affect the way technology can be used. There is an ongoing debate on whether the technology drives change in organizations or merely responds to it. This "chicken or egg" debate is giving way to the realization that IT and its use are evolving together. While academics discuss technology assimilation models, management practice themes and the technologies to implement them evolve simultaneously.

In this section, we explore two aspects of the organizational environment: the external forces that are causing executives to reexamine how their firms compete successfully, and the internal structural forces that affect the way organizations operate or are managed.

The External Organizational Environment

The changes taking place in the worldwide business scene have been widely discussed in both the public and technical press. The effects of the turbulence can be seen in the large number of corporate restructurings that have taken place since the mid-1980s. IT is contributing to these changes. It allows information to move faster, thus increasing the speed at which events take place and the pace at which individuals and organizations can respond to events. Following are the main changes we see taking place in the marketplace.

The Quality Imperative. Competition in international markets continues to focus on quality. Originally, quality meant reducing defects in product output. Now, the emphasis is on quality as defined by the customer. This customer satisfaction emphasis has, in turn, shifted management's attention to the key business processes in the organization—those that deliver the products and services to the customers. Information systems are a primary resource for examining and reengineering these key business processes to improve organizational performance and competitiveness.

Concern for the Environment. Ecology, recycling, and the "green" movement came to management attention in the early 1990s around the globe. Companies now tout their recycling efforts, environmental mutual funds have arisen, and "save the planet" concerns are voiced by a growing portion of the populace. The earth, and all its inhabitants, will be a major issue for executives throughout the 1990s, to reverse the destruction of past decades.

Consumer Computing. The 1990s have seen an increase in systems that let consumers access organizational computer systems. Bank automated teller machines (ATMs) are an early example of this trend, where customers can check account balances, determine whether or not certain checks have cleared, and establish automatic bill-paying processes. Companies are developing systems that will allow consumers to purchase products, inquire about the state of an order, and in general become a user of their internal information systems.

The World Wide Web is accelerating this process. Federal Express, one of the first companies to leverage the Web, got rave reviews from customers when it allowed them to directly access its package tracking system via its home page.

Deregulation. It has become easier for new companies to enter major industries such as airlines, banking, telecommunications, trucking and others because of deregulation. In the United States, for example, regional airlines have literally driven major carriers out of some short-haul, but lucrative, markets. And the U.S. banking industry has been fighting hard to get the U.S. Congress to limit the ability of non-banking firms to enter the banking field. While it is true that deregulation in the United States is more widespread than elsewhere in the world, this trend is underway in many countries.

Crossing Industry Boundaries. Deregulation has prompted companies to cross industry boundaries, such as major brokerage firms offering banklike services with their cash management accounts (loans, credit cards, etc.). Virtual malls on the Web compete with retail stores. Insurance companies are essentially in the securities business, with their single-payment life insurance policies in which owners can direct the investment of the policy cash values. Most of these boundary-crossing examples are led by IT-enabled products or services.

Globalization. Large U.S. banks, by trading securities on an around-the-clock, around-the-world basis, are also crossing boundaries. Formerly, companies in the "rich" United States created multinational operations by establishing foreign offices or by buying established firms in other countries. But the huge U.S. trade deficit has given foreign firms access to funds with which to buy U.S. businesses. Foreign banks have bought U.S. banks, foreign owners of newspapers and magazines have bought U.S. newspapers and magazines, and so on.

Multinationalism has become a two-way street. Firmly entrenched companies are suddenly finding powerful competitors from abroad entering their markets. The same globalization is happening in manufacturing. Parts and sub assemblies are being manufactured in many countries, and then shipped to other countries for final assembly, to cut overall labor costs.

Shorter Product and Service Development Cycles. Companies do not have as much time to develop new products or services and move them into the marketplace. Once they are in the market, their useful lives tend to be shorter. So time has become of the essence. Efforts to speed up "time-to-market" or reduce "cycle time" often depend on innovative uses of IT.

The Internal Organizational Environment

The work environment is also changing, so the art of managing people is undergoing significant changes. These changes are profound enough to change the structure of organizations. Here are some of the changes that are impacting how people work and how organizations operate.

Growth of Business Teams. There is a trend toward "working together." Rather than depending on chains of command and the authority of the boss, many organizations are emphasizing teams to accomplish major tasks and projects. In his landmark article, "The Coming of the New Organization," Peter Drucker [4] used the analogy of a symphony, where each member of the team has a unique contribution to make to the overall result. Task-oriented teams form and work together long enough to accomplish the task, then disband, perhaps to form another project team. This phenomenon is generating major interest in information systems called groupware, which support meetings, promote collaborative work, and enrich communications among far-flung team members.

Anytime, Anyplace Information Work. Information workers are increasingly mobile. Communication technology has developed to the point where information work can be done anywhere with a laptop computer, cellular telephone, and modem. Electronic mail, facsimile, and voice mail systems cross time zones in our global village to allow work to be done anytime, anywhere. People are sporadically working at home rather than commuting daily; and they are working in their preferred geographical location, even if it is remote from the main office.

Outsourcing and Strategic Alliances. To become more productive and more efficient, organizations are examining which types of work they should perform internally and which types of work can be done by others. Outsourcing may be a simple contract for services or a long-term strategic alliance. Between these two extremes is a variety of relationships that are redefining the way organizations work together.

Sets of strategic alliances built around an organization's core competences result in what is becoming known as the *virtual corporation*. IT is providing the information flows necessary to manage such a complex set of relationships.

The Demise of the Hierarchy. Until recently, most of us accepted our work style and work environment as givens. "It has always been this way" implied "it will always be this way." However, this is changing because the old styles are not functioning well in our faster-paced, global environment.

The traditional hierarchical structure, where employees at the bottom receive only enough training and feedback to perform one type of job, grouped several people performing the same type of work into a unit, overseen by a supervisor. The supervisor allocated the work, handled problems, enforced discipline, issued rewards, provided training, and so on. Management principles such as division of labor, unity of command, and chain of control defined this traditional work environment.

But it is no longer the most appropriate work environment in factories or offices. Self-managed groups, which work on assembly lines or in insurance firms, provide much of their own management, have lower absenteeism, yield higher productivity, produce higher-quality work, and are more motivated than workers in traditional settings.

A major reason for the demise of the hierarchy is that the more turbulent business environment—represented by the changes noted earlier—challenges the premises of a hierarchical structure because it cannot cope with rapid change. Hierarchies require a vertical chain of command where lines of responsibility do not cross and approval to proceed on major initiatives is granted from above. This communication up and down the chain of command takes too much time for today's environment.

IT enables team-based organizational structures by facilitating rapid and far-flung communication.

THE TECHNOLOGY ENVIRONMENT

The technology environment "enables" advances in organizational performance in the context of the organizational environment described previously. As we noted earlier, the two have a symbiotic relationship. IT and the organizational improvements it enables evolve jointly. The IT evolution is now described in the four traditional areas of hardware, software, data, and communication.

Hardware Trends

At first, the main hardware concerns of data processing managers were machine efficiency and tracking new technological developments. Batch processing was predominant, with on-line systems emerging later. As smaller machines came to market, distributing the processing to remote sites became feasible. That prospect was discussed in the mid-1970s, although few companies then had any distributed systems. At that time, hardware was centralized, often in large "showcase" data centers behind glass walls.

In the mid-1970s processing power began to move out of the central site— but only very slowly. Often, it was at the insistence of users who bought their own departmental minicomputers and word processors. In the 1980s—mainly due to the advent of personal computers (PCs)—this trend accelerated far beyond the expectations of most people, especially IS managers.

Now, this trend is well established. Desktop and portable laptop computers are faster and contain more memory than the centralized mainframes of just a few years ago. Client/server computing involves computers working together via networks with the "client" machine on the desktop providing the user interface and the "server" on the network holding the data and applications. The latest hardware advance, interestingly, appears to be a step backward toward recentralization. That is the network computer (NC), which contains only memory, processing power, and a browser (almost like mainframe terminals of old). There is no hard disk, no application programs, and no floppy disks. These "thin clients" act like a telephone in that they connect to the network to be able to work. All applications are pulled from the network where they are managed centrally.

These hardware trends are further distributing processing beyond organizational boundaries to suppliers and customers. The result is the movement of enterprisewide hardware and processing power out of the control—although perhaps still under the guidance—of the IS department. With the NC, it remains to be seen if that control is returned.

Software Trends

The early dominant issue in software and programming was how to improve the productivity of in-house programmers, those who created mainly transaction processing systems. Occasionally, the use of outside services was discussed—timesharing services, application packages, and contract programming from independent software houses, for example. The software industry was still underdeveloped, however, so in-house programming remained the concern of IS managers.

In the next phase, programming issues centered first around modular and structured programming techniques. Then the topic expanded to life cycle development methodologies and software engineering, with the goals of introducing more rigorous project management techniques and getting users more involved in the early stages of development. Eventually, prototyping (quick development of a mock-up) became popular. The first full report on prototyping appeared in 1981, although the subject had been discussed briefly earlier. Now prototyping is a way of life in most IS departments.

Then two other software trends appeared. First, purchased software became a viable alternative to in-house development for many traditional, well-defined systems. Second, IS managers began to pay attention to applications other than transaction processing. Software to support decision support systems (DSS), report generation, and database inquiry shifted some programming from professional programmers to end users. Today, many end users develop their own systems on their personal computers using such languages as Visual Basic.

The other major software trend in the 1990s has been the push for open systems, driven primarily by software purchasers who are tired of being "locked in" to proprietary software (or hardware) systems. The open systems movement demands that different products work together, that is, "interoperate." Vendors initially were accommodating this demand with hardware and software black boxes that perform the necessary interface conversions, but the cost is lower efficiency.

A major, yet subtle trend in the late 1990s is the shift from application-centered computing to document-centered computing. Announced as a Microsoft policy by president Bill Gates at COMDEX in 1991, this trend has picked up steam. Rather than launch an application, such as a word processor, users launch a document, which invokes the applications needed to perform the functions in the document. The appearance of the Web-centric language Java, from Sun Microsystems, further advanced this trend.

So while software development has moved to the Web, in intranets and the Internet, the installed base of legacy systems on which organizations depend for day-to-day processing is being outfitted with Web-based front-ends to broaden access and empower employees, customers, and suppliers. Like hardware, software is migrating to be network centric.

Data Trends

The evolution of the third core information technology area—data—has been particularly interesting. At first, discussions centered around file management and organizational techniques for files that served individual applications. Then generalized file management systems emerged for managing corporate data files. This more generalized approach led to the concept of corporate databases to serve several applications, followed a few years later by the concept of establishing a data administration function to manage these databases.

In the 1970s, the interest in data turned to technical solutions—database management systems. As work progressed, it became evident that a key element of these products was their data dictionary/directory. The early function of these dictionaries was merely specification and format, but that has expanded significantly. Dictionaries store more than data definitions: they store information about relationships between systems, sources and uses of data, time cycle requirements, and so on.

So for the first 20 years of information processing, discussions on data were about techniques to manage data in a centralized environment. It was not until the advent of fourth-generation languages and PCs that there was any interest in letting employees directly access corporate data. The users demanded it.

In addition to distributing data, the major trend in the early 1990s was expanding the focus from data resources to information resources, both internal and external to the firm. Data management organizes internal facts into data record format. Information management, on the other hand, focuses on concepts (as those ideas found in documents), from both internal and external sources. Thus information resources contain a much richer universe of digitized media, including voice, video, graphics, animation, and photographs.

In the late 1990s, yet another resource has been discerned a corporate asset in need of managing—knowledge. Here, the emphasis is on managing the intellectual capital of the organization. Some believe knowledge can reside in machines; others believe it only resides in people's heads. Knowledge *management* has become a hot topic. Meanwhile, data management continues to require attention, with the new areas of data warehousing and data mining, both aimed at providing more effective access to data and information.

Communications Trends

The final core information technology is telecommunications. This area has experienced enormous change, and has now taken center stage. Early use of data communications dealt with on-line and timesharing systems. Then interest in both public and private (intracompany) data networks blossomed. Telecom opened up new uses of information systems.

So telecom became an integral component of IS management. Communications-based information systems then began to link organizations to their suppliers and customers. In the early 1980s, there was a groundswell of interest in such interorganizational systems because some provided strategic advantage.

Communication technology is a crucial enabler for distributing computing and responsibility for its use. Local area networks (LANs) connected to wide area networks (WANs) allow computer connectivity to be at a level akin to that of voice connectivity provided by the worldwide telephone system. The growth of these network infrastructures within companies further shifted mainframe-centered computing to network-centric computing. The slogan "the network *is* the computer" has become the dominant view of information systems.

The Internet, and its dramatic growth for business computing and communications, primarily through electronic mail and the World Wide Web, has completed that shift. Development of the telecommunications infrastructure that interconnects organizations and individuals across the world promises to launch electronic commerce, communication, education, and entertainment on a global scale.

Networking of computer-based equipment is also blurring the boundaries between industries, and between private and working life. Cable TV provides Internet access, consumer electronic firms make hybrid PC/TVs, and telephone companies make smart phones, combining the functionality of PCs, cellular telephones, and a fax in small, portable products. The development of these and other "information appliances" is leading to the vision of an ever-present, ubiquitous "information window" through which people network [5].

Add to this the explosion of wireless communication and we can see that people are using wireless networks to do their jobs anytime, anyplace. The interleaving of the business and IT revolutions makes this an exciting time to live, perhaps too exciting for some.

THE MISSION OF INFORMATION SYSTEMS

With the organizational and IT environments as backdrops, we now turn to the mission of information systems. In the early days of transaction processing, systems acted as "paperwork factories"—to get employees paid, customers billed, products shipped, and so on. During that era, the objectives of information systems were defined by productivity measures, such as percentage of uptime for the computer, throughput (number of transactions processed per day), and lines of program code written per week.

Later, during the MIS era, the focus of information systems shifted to producing reports for "management by exception" or summary reports for all levels of management. This era gave us the classic information system objective to "get the right information to the right person at the right time."

In today's environment, missions and objectives such as these are limited and short-sighted. Even "the right information" objective fails to ensure that something useful results from the delivery of the information. We suggest as an appropriate focus, the following mission for information systems in organizations:

To improve the performance of people in organizations through the use of information technology.

The ultimate *objective* is performance improvement—a goal based on outcomes and results rather than a go-through-the-steps process goal. The *focus* is the people who make up the organization. Improving organizational performance is accomplished by the people and groups that comprise the organization.

Finally, the *resource* for this improvement is information technology. There are many intertwined contributors to performance improvement, but this book focuses on resources available from the development and use of IT: computers, software, machine-readable information, and communication technologies.

A SIMPLE MODEL

We propose a simple model to help define a new structure for the IS function in organizations. Figure 1-3 represents the process of applying IT to accomplish useful work. On the left is the technology; on the right are the users who put it to work. The arrow represents the process of translating users' needs into implemented systems that apply the technology. In the early days of information systems, this was conducted almost entirely by a systems analyst.

Figure 1-4 is a simple representation of what has happened during the past 30 years. Technology has become increasingly complex and powerful. At the same time, the uses have become increasingly sophisticated. Information systems are now viewed as system "products" and users have become "customers." The increased distance between the two boxes represents the increasingly complex process of specifying, developing, and delivering these system products. It is

Figure 1-3   A Simple Model of Technology Use

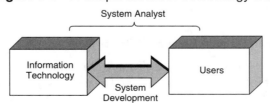

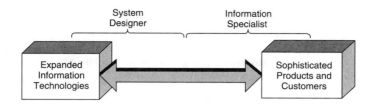

Figure 1-4   System Professionals Bridging the Technology Gap

no longer feasible for one system analyst to understand the fine points of the technologies needed in an application as well as the nuances of the application. More specialization is required of systems professionals to bridge this wider gap.

Systems professionals are not the only ones who can help bridge this gap between the technology and its users. Technology has become sophisticated enough to be used by many employees and consumers. At the same time, they are becoming increasingly computer literate; many employees even develop their own applications. Figure 1-5 represents this trend. Today, some of the technology is truly user friendly, and some applications, such as Web page development, database mining, and spreadsheet manipulation, are developed and used by employees. But it will be some time before end users handle this development of transaction systems.

The main point of this discussion is that the technology is getting more complex, the applications are becoming more sophisticated, and users are participating more heavily in the development of applications. The net result is that the management of the entire process is getting more complex and difficult as it is getting more important to do well.

A BETTER MODEL

Expanding the simple model gives us more guidance into the managerial principles and tasks. We suggest a model with four principal elements:

1. *A set of technologies* representing the technology infrastructure installed and managed by the IS department.
2. *A set of users* who use the technology to improve job performance.

Figure 1-5   End Users Bridging the Technology Gap

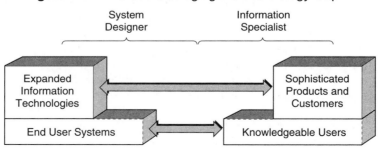

...livery mechanism for developing, delivering, and installing the applications ...d functions that serve the users.

...xecutive leadership to manage the entire IS function.

...s look more carefully at each of these elements.

...e Technologies

Several forces are contributing to the increased strength and complexity of IT. One, of course, is the inexorable growth in computing and communications capacity accompanied by significant reductions in cost and size of computers and telecom components. Another is the merging of the previously separate technologies of computers, telephones/telecom/cable TV, office equipment, and consumer electronics. Still a third is the ability to store and handle voice, image, and graphical data, and to integrate them. Here is a brief list of some rapidly growing technology areas:

- Personal computers
- The Internet
- Wireless and fiber-based networks
- Multimedia, integrating voice, image, text, graphics, and more
- Integration of consumer electronics and IT

These technologies can be combined and configured to form systems products that are useful to employees, customers, and consumers. No longer relegated primarily to automating transactions, information systems now fill major roles in management reporting, problem solving and analysis, distributed office support, and customer service. In fact, most activities of information workers are supported in some way by IT; the same is becoming true of suppliers, customers, and consumers.

The Users

As IT becomes pervasive, the old categories of users are no longer appropriate. The users of electronic data processing and management information systems were relatively easy to identify, and the functions of a system were defined to meet a set of their needs. Now, however, employees need integrated information systems to do their daily work, so new taxonomies are needed.

Panko and Sprague [1, 6] have developed a helpful dichotomy to describe activities of information workers supported by IT. It defines procedure-based activities and goal-based or problem-based activities. The value of the dichotomy is that it focuses on the important characteristics of information workers—their job procedures and goals—rather than on the type of data (for example, numbers versus text) or the business function (production versus sales), or even job title (managerial versus professional).

Procedure-based activities are large-volume transactions, where each transaction has a relatively low cost or value. The activities are well defined, so the principal performance measure is efficiency (units processed per unit of resource spent). For a procedure-based task, the information worker is told what to accomplish and the steps to follow. Finally, procedure-based activities mainly handle data.

Goal-based activities, on the other hand, handle fewer transactions, and each one has higher value. These activities, which can be accomplished in various ways, must therefore be measured by results, that is, attainment of the objectives or goals. Therefore, the information worker must understand the goals because part of the job is figuring out how to attain them. Finally, goal-based activities entail handling concepts, not data. Figure 1-6 summarizes these two kinds of information-based work, giving several examples from banking.

Some authors use the words *clerical* and *managerial* to refer to these two types of activities. Looking at the attributes, however, it is clear that managers often do procedure-based work, and many former procedure-based jobs now have goal-based components. Furthermore, the distinction between manager and worker is blurring in more and more companies. Likewise, many business problems are best described using a procedure-based approach.

The most important benefit of this dichotomy is that it reveals how much of a firm's information processing efforts have been devoted to procedure-based activities. This is understandable because computers are process engines that naturally support process-driven activities. As important as they are, it is clear that procedure-based activities are the "wave of the past." The wave of the future is applying information technology to goal-based activities, where the enterprise is more important than the process. For the task "pay the employees" or "bill the customer," the systems analyst can identify the best sequence of steps. For the task "improve sales of the Asian market," there is no best process. Decision makers will need to use a variety of support systems to leverage their judgment.

System Development

In our model, system development and delivery bridges the gap between technology and users, but there is a difference between systems for procedure-based activity and those for goal-based information work.

Figure 1-7 shows, on the left side, the set of technologies that forms the IT infrastructure. These are the technology resources that organizations can draw

Figure 1-6   A Dichotomy of Information Work

Procedure-Based	Goal-Based
• High volume of transactions	• Low volume of transactions
• Low cost (value) per transaction	• High value (cost) per transaction
• Well-structured procedures	• Ill-structured procedures
• Output measures defined	• Output measures less defined
• Focus on process	• Focus on problems and goals
• Focus on efficiency	• Focus on effectiveness
• Handling of "data"	• Handling of concepts
• Predominantly clerical workers	• Managers and professionals
• Examples	• Examples
"Back office"	Loan department
Mortgage servicing	Asset/liability management
Payroll processing	Planning department
Check processing	Corporate banking

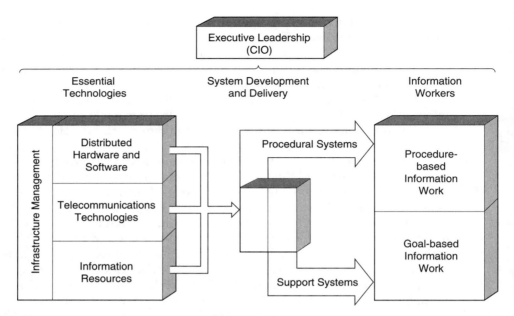

Figure 1-7   A Framework for IS Management

on to build systems to support both procedure-based and goal-based activities. Separate technical categories, such as mainframe, personal computer, office equipment, and telephone, are no longer relevant. Therefore, we show computer hardware and software, communication networks, and information resources as the three major categories. We call these "the essential technologies," and we call management of them "infrastructure management."

On the right are the two major kinds of information work that are supported by IT, using the procedure/goal-based dichotomy. These two categories are not distinct or separate, of course, but it is helpful to keep in mind the major differences between these two kinds of work. These differences lead to different approaches, and frequently different teams, in the bridging function of system development and delivery.

Figure 1-7 shows separate functions to deliver services to procedure-based users and goal-based users. Different technologies will be needed so that a full range of customer needs can be met with a full range of technologies.

Information Systems Management

The fourth component may be the most important of all—overall management of the IS function. The changes required to support the new organizational structures that are now emerging require a significant amount of well-coordinated business and IT executive leadership. The IT leadership comes from a chief information officer (CIO), who must be high enough in an organization to influence organizational goals, and have enough credibility to lead the harnessing of the technology to pursue those goals.

To summarize this model of the IS function in organizations, there are four major components:

1. The technology, which provides the electronic and information infrastructure for the enterprise.
2. Information workers in organizations, who use IT to accomplish their work goals.
3. The system development and delivery function, to bring the technology and users together.
4. The management of the IS function, with the overall responsibility to harness IT to improve the performance of the employees and the organization.

ORGANIZATION OF THIS BOOK

This book is designed to meet the needs of information systems managers—current ones and students who will become managers in the future. The organization of the book corresponds to the major parts of Figure 1-7. Part I (Chapters 2 through 4) deals with the strategic issues that are the responsibility of the top systems executive—the chief information officer (CIO) and the executive committee. Chapter 2 deals with the leadership components of the CIO's job; Chapter 3 looks at the strategic role of information systems; and Chapter 4 treats the subject of IS planning.

Part II (Chapters 5 through 8) deals with the management of the essential information technologies (on the left side in Figure 1-7). Respective chapters discuss the distributed systems architecture that is dominating the 1990s, building and managing the telecom system, managing the corporate information resources, and managing day-to-day operations.

Part III contains two chapters on the system development process used primarily to build procedural systems. Chapter 9 describes the evolution of system development and the tools and approaches used. Chapter 10 discusses important issues in managing system development.

Part IV, on the evolving computing arena, describes the exploding universe of information technologies—including mobile technologies, multimedia, and the Internet (Chapter 11). Chapter 12 discusses IS management's responsibilities for supporting this expanding universe of computing possibilities—many of which will be used for goal-based computing.

Part V consists of four chapters describing types of support systems—goal-based systems that support information workers. Included are decision support and executive information systems, group support systems, expert systems, and electronic document systems.

The final two chapters of the book, comprising Part VI, deal with people issues and information systems. Chapter 17 examines the all-important subject of organizational learning, while Chapter 18 discusses creating the new work environment.

To illustrate how an IS department has evolved over the years, as the technologies and their users have changed, consider the case of Mead Corporation. We have documented the evolution of the Mead IS organization since it appeared in the first edition of this book in 1985. Notice how this case example puts a number of the ideas discussed in this chapter into a real-life setting.

CASE EXAMPLE: Mead Corporation

Mead Corporation, with headquarters in Dayton, Ohio, is a paper and forest products company with more than 100 mills, plants, and distribution centers throughout the United States and Canada. The company is highly decentralized, with ten operating divisions—paper, packaging, paperboard, consumer, distribution, electronic publishing, and so on.

Corporate Information Services—1960s and 1970s

In the 1960s, Mead's corporate information services (CIS) department provided all divisions with data processing services. By 1967, the department's budget had grown so large that management decided to spin off some of the functions to the divisions. Divisions could establish their own data processing and process engineering groups, if they so desired. Or they could continue to purchase data processing services from CIS. Many of the divisions did establish their own IS departments, but all continued to use the corporate data center for their corporate applications.

In the late 1970s, the corporate information services department had six groups, as illustrated in Figure 1-8. The director reported to the vice president of operations services. The six groups under the director were

- Computer operations—to manage the corporate data center
- Telecommunications—to design the telecom network and to establish standards
- Technical services—to provide and maintain systems software
- Developmental systems—to handle traditional system development
- Operational systems—to maintain systems after they become operational
- Operations research—to perform management science analysis

The 1980s—Focusing on End User Computing

In 1980, management realized that its CIS organizational structure would not serve the needs of the rapidly growing end user community. Furthermore, to become an electronic-based organization, Mead needed a corporatewide network. Therefore, the department reorganized as shown in Figure 1-9 so that the director of corporate information resources (CIR) reported directly to the company president. This change signaled the increased importance of information resources to Mead.

CIR was responsible for creating hardware, software, and communication standards for the entire corporation; it ran the corporate data center; and it operated the network. All the divisions used the network and corporate data center, and they followed the corporate standards; some operated

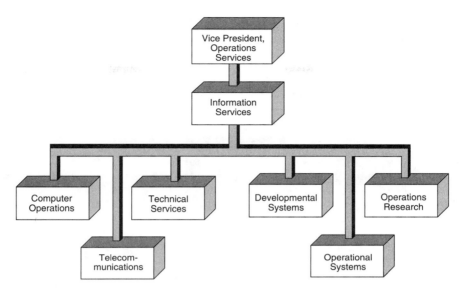

Figure 1-8   Mead Corporation's Pre-1980 Information Services Department
(from Mead Corporation)

their own small distributed systems as well, which linked into the corporate network. The three departments within the new group were as follows:

Decision Support Applications (DSA) provided all end user computing support for the company. It was the marketing arm, selling and training Mead employees on end user computing, while the information services department provided the technical support for the end user systems. At the time of the 1980 reorganization, DSA had no users, no products, no common applications among its multiple locations, and only five staff members in operations research and two in its office systems support group. By 1985, they were serving 1,500 users in some 30 Mead locations with ten staff members.

DSA offered 14 products and eight corporatewide applications. Its _interactive help center_ provided hotline support and evaluated new end user computing products. Its _office systems_ group supported the dedicated word processing systems and IBM's Professional Office System (PROFS)—which Mead used as the gateway to end user computing. Divisions were free to select any office system, but most followed the recommendations of this group to ensure corporatewide interconnection. Its _decision analysis_ group used operations research tools to develop linear programming models and simulations for users needing such sophisticated analysis tools. And it built a number of companywide decision support systems, such as a corporate budgeting model and a graphics software system. And the _financial modeling coordination and EIS_ group was in charge of Mead's integrated financial system. It also supported executive computing, through

Figure 1-9   Mead Corporation's 1980s Information Systems
Services Department (from Mead Corporation)

IBM PCs used by corporate executives and an executive information system (EIS) accessed through PROFS.

Information Services was responsible for most of the traditional information systems functions from the old information services department—companywide telecom support, data center operations, development of corporate-wide systems, database administration, system software support, and technical support for end user computing.

Most divisions developed their own applications, following the guidelines created by this department. The EDP steering committee—composed of the president and group vice presidents—established a policy that applications should be transportable among the various computing centers and accessible from any Mead terminal. The company's telecom network established the guidelines for making this interconnection possible.

Information Resources Planning and Control was responsible for planning future information systems and technology. This department grew out of the company's strong planning culture, and decentralization in the 1970s highlighted the need for an IT planning coordinating body. Although it was small, it had two important roles. First, it took the corporate perspective for IT planning to ensure that Mead's IT plans meshed with business plans. Second, it acted as planning coordinator, helping various groups and divisions coordinate their plans with corporate and CIR plans.

Late 1980s Adjustments

The 1980 reorganization separated the more people-oriented activities under DSA from the more technical activities under the information services department. The technology was better managed, and relations with users improved. However, this split caused two problems. First, traditional programmers and systems analysts felt that DSA received all the new and exciting development work. The second problem was coordinating the two departments. A matrix arrangement evolved to handle both problems, with both information services and DSA people staffing most projects.

The departmental structure implemented in 1980 remained essentially intact throughout the 1980s, with only two major changes. In early 1988, the vice president of information resources began reporting to Mead's chairman and CEO. Second, the DSA group was reorganized, as shown in Figure 1-10.

As users became more sophisticated and less generic, the department created small groups with expertise in specific areas. By the end of the 1980s they were supporting over 5,000 users corporatewide in three ways—service center help, application development consulting, and local area experts.

The *service center* people continued to introduce new users to technology and provide telephone hotline assistance to experienced users. The *application development consultants* helped users develop more sophisticated applications and guided maintenance of user-written applications, which had become a noticeable problem. They also updated traditional applications to permit end user systems to access the data. The *local area experts* worked in the functional departments supporting users in their area. They reported directly to their area manager and indirectly to the information resources department. Due to the growing number of user-written applications, they too helped users keep their applications up-to-date.

So, during the 1980s, Mead found its end user computing focus shifting from introducing new technology to making more effective use of the technology in place. By the end of the decade, they were concentrating on har-

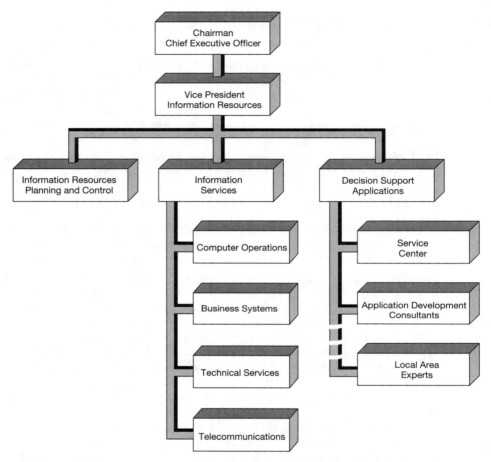

Figure 1-10   Mead Corporation's 1989 Corporate Information Resources Group
(from Mead Corporation)

vesting their investment in IT by using it as a lever to change the way they
were doing business.

1990—Leveraging the IT Infrastructure

In 1990, CIR underwent another reorganization to bring it in line with
a new strategy. We will first discuss the reorganization, then present the
strategy.

By 1990, management realized that end user systems and large-scale
business systems needed to cross-fertilize each other. Users needed one
place to go for help; therefore, application development was placed in one
group, which was renamed Information Services, as shown in Figure 1-11.

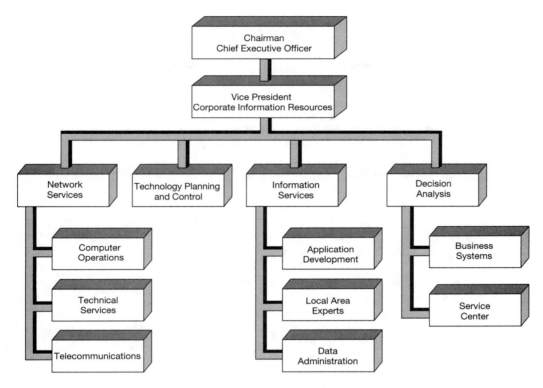

Figure 1-11   Mead Corporation's 1990 Corporate Information Resources Group
(from Mead Corporation)

The emphasis was to strengthen the mainframe-based electronic infrastructure of the company, of which the corporatewide network had become paramount. Although the network had been created in 1983, its value in connecting Mead to its vendors and customers had not been recognized until the late 1980s. Therefore, in 1990, CIR created a new group—network services—to handle computer operations, technical services, and telecom. The 1990 reorganization also consolidated administrative functions (such as chargeback) into the technology planning and control group.

So while the 1990 reorganization did not add new functions, it shifted emphasis from end user computing to building an infrastructure and integrating development of all sizes of applications.

1990 Strategy   In the early 1980s, Mead installed its first information resources business plan, which emphasized networking and end user computing. By the late 1980s, the objectives had been accomplished. In hindsight, management realized that the 1980 plan had been a technology plan, not a business plan, because its goal had been to get control of IT. Having accomplished this, Mead decided to create a true business plan, one that addressed how it would employ its IT resources.

Using the two-by-two matrix shown in Figure 1-12, management realized that Mead had only been building systems that fit into the lower right quadrant—systems that supported Mead's traditional products and internal business processes. Rather than focus on company operations, management decided to shift emphasis in two directions: (1) toward reengineering company operations and (2) toward using IT to work better with suppliers and customers.

Business process reengineering—that is, significantly restructuring the internal operations in a business—became a major strategic direction, with the companywide network playing a key role. Since IT removes many time and distance barriers associated with business processes, Mead decided to use IT to build new processes rather than simply accelerate existing ones. In rethinking all the major Mead processes, two were carved out to be recentralized and reengineered—people reimbursement and purchasing. The result has been very large savings. For example, the reengineering group discovered that the company had 240 people handling accounts payable, mainly reconciling mismatches between goods received and purchase orders. By reengineering purchasing, they realized they could eliminate the need to do such reconciliations. So they outsourced the function while they developed the new purchasing system.

The second emphasis involved doing business electronically by extending current business processes and products to suppliers and customers. The motto was: "It is easy to do business with us," using any means customers wanted—through electronic data interchange (EDI) for application-

Figure 1-12   Mead Corporation's Strategic Opportunities Framework
(from Mead Corporation)

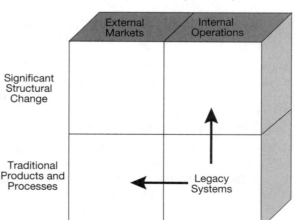

to-application transactions across company boundaries, through terminals at customer sites linked to Mead's computers, or even through the telephone using voice response. In essence, Mead installed various front-ends on its existing mainframe systems.

So, the basic strategy set forth in 1980 remained in force in 1990—to retain central control of the IT infrastructure and distribute responsibility for building and maintaining applications in the operating divisions. As the uses of IT changed, CIR reorganized to focus on those new uses—end user computing in the 1980s, business reengineering and customer-oriented systems in 1990.

1993 to Present—Vision 2000

In 1993, CIR management recognized that client/server computing was indeed a paradigm shift in computing, so that Mead's mainframe-based structure would (at long last) need to be changed, and changed significantly. So CIR launched Vision 2000 to develop a vision of what computing and communications will look like at Mead in the Year 2000.

Vision 2000 foresees computing to be three-tiered—mainframe, midrange servers, and desktops. Workstations will be users' "window to the world" of information access, analysis, and communication. Interfaces, data, and applications will be at the appropriate level. Applications will be of three types: enterprisewide, division, and local; and they will use a global network that reaches out beyond Mead.

CIR will continue to focus on shared services (providing the infrastructure and supporting enterprise applications), while divisions will tailor systems to their customers and business. Users will not need to worry about where processing occurs, where data is housed, or how the mechanics of information processing are handled; CIR will handle all this. Data will be viewed as a resource and managed accordingly, balancing access with integrity and security. And users will have greater geographic independence than in the past.

This vision is based on a "demanding partnership" in which the divisions "buy into" the infrastructure and its standards while CIR provides a flexible and responsive infrastructure.

CIR made the following five major assumptions when developing Vision 2000 in 1993:

1. The mainframe will continue to be the best platform for large-volume transaction systems or systems requiring massive computing power. In addition, it could become an enterprise server. This is consistent with the adoption of an enterprisewide client/server architecture.

2. Integration of voice, image, video, and so on will occur at desktops, servers, and portable devices; therefore, higher-capacity networks are needed to transmit and route these massive amounts of data.

3. Although unit costs of technology will continue to decline, overall IT usage at Mead will increase.
4. PCs present a hidden cost that is at least as large as the visible IT costs.
5. Technology advancements will increase; therefore, the challenge is to balance the need for standards while keeping up with the pace of change.

New Organizational Structure. In order to implement Vision 2000, Mead had two organizational options. One was to set up a skunk works to create the new infrastructure and systems. The other was to embed the new client/server paradigm into CIR's organizational structure. CIR chose the latter, so the entire corporate information resources group was reorganized to match the client/server model, as shown in Figure 1-13.

The core is the *Vision 2000 Project,* managed by a high-level CIR executive. Around this core is the technology layer of the CIR organization—the four core technologies that provide the IT infrastructure on which Mead operates. *Data Services* provides data and information. *Server Technology Services* handles all servers on the network, from mainframes on down. *Client Services* handles all devices that customers touch, which include desktop workstations, fax machines, and telephones. CIR defines its customers as Mead employees as well as others who interface with Mead. And *Network Services* handles everything that ties these other pieces together,

Figure 1-13   Mead Corporation's Current Corporate Information
Resources Structure (from Mead Corporation)

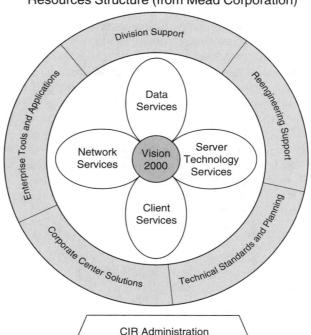

both voice and data communications as well as the Internet, intranets, gateways, firewalls, and working with their Internet service provider.

All four groups report to the vice president of CIR, John Langenbahn, who, by the way, has led Mead's IS department for the entire time we have been working on this book (since 1985). All four groups have two jobs: (1) to run current operations and (2) to build Vision 2000. Langenbahn notes that the move from mainframe to client/server has moved CIR from managing hundreds of components to managing thousands of them—an order-of-magnitude change.

On the outside layer of the organization chart, closer to the customer, are the application groups. They draw on Vision 2000 and the IT infrastructure provided by the inner layers to serve their constituencies. *Division Support* supports the applications developed by Mead's ten operating divisions. *Reengineering Support* is concerned with a few company-wide business processes that have been recentralized and reengineered to improve efficiency and lower costs. These include Mead's financial systems and purchasing system, all of which do not touch customers. *Enterprise Tools and Applications* provides a common desktop toolkit to all Mead staff. It consists of hardware as well as a suite of software products— spreadsheet, e-mail, word processing, graphics, browser, EDI, and knowledge tools (such as Notes). *Corporate Center Solutions* handles application development and maintenance of corporate applications. *Technical Standards and Planning* is a one-person think tank devoted to determining the standards that underlie Vision 2000—while everyone else works on the day-to-day issues. And finally, as shown below the circle, is *CIR Administration,* which handles contracting and financials.

Like other companies, Mead has encountered the typical staff problems of getting the mainframe staff to move into the client/server environment and getting new client/server talent to follow the discipline needed to develop enterprisewide systems.

Progress to Date. The Internet has had a large impact on Vision 2000 in that more and more of the elements of the vision can be served by it. For example, the vision foresaw storing lots of data on servers, so that CIR, not users, could handle backup. But now, with so much information on the Net, CIR does not need to acquire so much public information, install it, or maintain it in-house. For instance, CIR had planned to install the U.S. telephone directory on a CD-ROM server. Since that is available on the Net, CIR has simply added an icon to the standard desktop for quick access to the directory. So the Internet will reduce some Mead IT costs.

Client/server computing is not cheaper than mainframe computing. Mead realized that in 1993 (even though press articles were touting its lower cost). At that time, Mead placed the cost of a PC at $9,024 a year ($2,517 hard costs, $6,507 soft costs). However, since the company already had 6,000 PCs installed, it had already made a huge down payment on the new environment. And to reduce the soft costs, Mead has implemented its Vision 2000 standards so that those $6,507 in soft costs can be cut to $3,005 a year.

In all, CIR has made good progress in implementing Vision 2000. The vision was conceived in 1993, implementation began at the end of 1994, and by mid-1996, it had been rolled out to 2,000 Mead employees. The target population is 6,000, so CIR expects to be completed by the end of 1997.

QUESTIONS AND EXERCISES

REVIEW QUESTIONS

1. We define the information era in terms of information work and information workers. How has this sector of the U.S. work force changed during the past 100 years? What is the current status?
2. What was the nature of information technology in the late 1950s and early 1960s?
3. Summarize the four categories of the classic pattern of information technology.
4. What are some of the changes taking place in the marketplace?
5. Describe the traditional work environment. What changes are occurring in this traditional environment?
6. Give two or three characteristics of the technology trends in hardware, software, data, and communications.
7. What is the mission for information systems recommended by the authors? How does it differ from earlier perceptions of the purpose and objectives of information systems?
8. In the simple model of information technology and its uses (Figure 1-4), why are the two boxes moving apart? Why are end user systems not joining them completely?
9. Summarize the four components of the marketing model (Figure 1-7).
10. List several attributes of procedure-based and goal-based information activities. Which do you think are most important? Why?
11. Summarize the role of each of the ten groups in Mead's current information resources structure.

DISCUSSION QUESTIONS

1. While the PC dispersed control of processing power out of the IS department, the network computer will return control to the department. Do you agree or disagree? Discuss.
2. Do we really need a major change in the way the information systems function is structured? Aren't the necessary changes just minor modifications to accommodate normal growth in computer uses?
3. The procedure-goal dichotomy does not add much beyond the clerical-managerial distinction. Do you agree or disagree? Give reasons for your opinion.

EXERCISES

1. Drawing on current literature, redo Figure 1-2 (the classic infrastructure) to better represent the current situation in information systems.
2. Show how Mead's new organizational structure compares to the model in Figure 1-7 by entering Mead's functions on the figure.
3. Contact a company in your community and prepare a diagram and narrative to describe the organization of its information systems function. Compare it to Figure 1-7 and to Mead's current structure.

REFERENCES

1. "THE SOFTWARE REVOLUTION," *Business Week*, December 4, 1995, cover story.

2. Parts of this section are adapted from PANKO, R. R., and R. H. SPRAGUE, JR., "Toward a New Framework for Office Support," *Proceedings of the ACM Conference on Office Information Systems*, 1982, ACM (ACM Order Department, Box 64145, Baltimore, MD 21264), 1982.

3. PORAT, M. U., *The Information Economy* (Washington, DC: U.S. Department of Commerce, Office of Telecommunications Policy, 1977).

4. DRUCKER, P. F., "The Coming of the New Organization," *Harvard Business Review*, January/February 1988.

5. "THE INFORMATION APPLIANCE," *Business Week*, June 26, 1996, cover story.

6. PANKO, R. R., and R. H. SPRAGUE, JR., "Implementing Office Systems Requires a New DP Outlook," *Data Management*, DPMA (505 Busse Highway, Park Ridge, IL 60068), November 1984, pp. 40-42.

PART I

Leadership
Issues

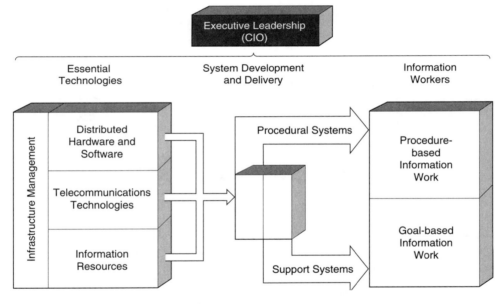

Executive Leadership
(CIO)

Essential
Technologies

System Development
and Delivery

Information
Workers

Infrastructure Management

Distributed
Hardware and
Software

Telecommunications
Technologies

Information
Resources

Procedural Systems

Support Systems

Procedure-
based
Information
Work

Goal-based
Information
Work

A Framework for IS Management

Part I of this book consists of three chapters that deal with the leadership issues of managing information, information systems, and information technology. To establish the context, Part I deals with the shaded portion of the figure above, which is based on Figure 1-7 from Chapter 1, the conceptual framework for this entire book.

Leadership of the information systems function is no longer limited to IS managers and professionals, or even to the chief information officer (CIO). Increasingly, this leadership role is shared with the chief executive officer (CEO) and other top line managers. Thus, the need for the management and nurturing of this shared relationship is one of the underlying themes of this book.

Chapter 2 identifies the major responsibility areas of the CIO, it suggests where the IS function is headed, and it discusses the leadership issues inferred by the evolution of the IS function. Chapter 3 explains the types of systems that are driving much of this change—systems that have a strategic impact on organizations. Chapter 4 completes the leadership section by focusing on the planning processes that are required to manage the technology and its impact on the organization over time.

TWO

Leadership Issues
in Information
Systems Management

INTRODUCTION

The management of information technology in organizations has changed drastically in the past 30 years. In the early years, the big job was to manage the technology—get it to work, keep it running, and thus reduce the cost of doing business. Later, the main thrust was to manage the information resources of the organization, particularly to support management decision making by delivering information when and where it was needed. Today, because IT has become pervasive in most organizations and affects every aspect of organizational performance, it is a driving force within which organizations operate; therefore, its proper deployment can determine an organization's growth, direction, structure, and viability.

    The responsibilities of the head of the IS function now go far beyond operating highly efficient production programming shops. These executives must understand the goals of the enterprise and work in partnership with line peers to deploy IT to attain the organization's goals. These partnerships require a much heavier involvement in IS leadership from the chief executive officer, the chief operations officer, and other members of the top-management team. The CIO is the focal point for the firm's IT deployment.

    We actually see two phenomena occurring simultaneously. While the top IS job is expanding into new areas of responsibility, the traditional portions of the job are shrinking. The traditional set of responsibilities for the IS executive has included

- Systems planning
- Data center management and operation
- Management of remote systems
- Identification of opportunities for new systems
- System analysis and design, and construction of new systems.

Several trends are moving those traditional responsibilities out of the IS department into other parts of the organization:

- *Distributed systems*—leading to the migration of software applications to user areas, operated under the control of the users, and generally purchased with their funds, sometimes following guidelines (but frequently not specified standards) from the IS department.
- *Ever more knowledgeable users*—who take on increased responsibilities. They are identifying the high-leverage applications and are frequently taking the initiative to acquire them. This trend has been accelerated by the Web, which puts nearly everyone directly in touch with a wide range of information resources.
- *Better application packages and development tools*—resulting in less need for armies of programmers and analysts to do brute-force system development. Head count and budget go down as a result.
- *Outsourcing*—at times the most effective strategy, based on fiscal and managerial considerations, for handling data center operations, application maintenance, network management, and PC support. Budget and head counts go down further.

Thus, as shown in Figure 2-1, the top IS executive is seeing the traditional job responsibilities "nibbled away." If he or she is unwilling or unable to take on expanded responsibilities, the job is downgraded or endangered. Fortunately, there are many new challenges that lead to expanded responsibilities for growth-oriented managers who aspire to become CIO.

In 1986, when the first edition of this book was published, the leading IS executives were talking about their new role as architects of the enterprisewide information systems infrastructure. There was much talk about the strategic use of information systems.

In 1989, attention shifted to helping formulate corporate policy, with an emphasis on creating a vision of the role of information systems in the future. In other words, from 1986 to 1989, the focus of the top information systems job had swung significantly toward addressing business issues.

In 1992, the challenge for IS executives was to use IT as a catalyst for revamping the way enterprises worked. To accomplish this task, they needed to be in a high enough position to influence the use of IT as a major underpinning of the enterprise of the future. Reflecting this higher level of responsibility, the title "vice president of MIS" or "information systems director" evolved to "chief information officer (CIO)," a position often occupied by someone with general management and expertise, rather than a traditional technology manager.

Today, the need to revamp business operations using information technology continues. And the Internet, in particular, now expands the CIO's horizon

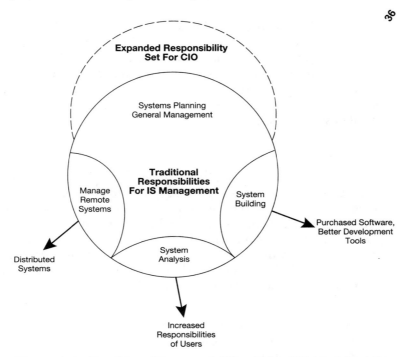

Figure 2-1   Traditional Responsibilities Being "Nibbled Away"
from Systems Executives

beyond company boundaries out to potential customers. IT now plays a more
"front office" role, especially in the rapidly changing Internet "marketspace."

In this chapter, we discuss the "what" and "how" of the top IS executive's
job, looking first at the top job itself by summarizing six major responsibilities,
and then exploring several ways the IS function is evolving in organizations.

THE CIO'S RESPONSIBILITIES

In order to take a leadership role in reshaping the way the enterprise works and
competes, we see IS executives having the following six primary responsibilities:

1. *Understand the business,* particularly the markets in which the firm sells its
   products and services.
2. *Establish credibility of the IS department,* thereby increasing the confidence of
   executive management in ideas presented by IS management.
3. *Increase the technological maturity of the firm,* making it easier for all employees
   to apply IT to their work.
4. *Create a vision of the future and sell it* by setting a goal for the use of IT by the
   organization and convincing others to embrace this vision.
5. *Implement an information system architecture* that will support the vision and the
   company in the future.
6. *Develop and nurture relationships* with senior management, line executives, suppliers, alliance partners, and customers (both external and internal).

Some of these responsibilities may be new to some IS executives, part of the expanding responsibilities we described earlier. Some have been in the job description but are taking on new dimensions. Item 6, for example, has always included getting top-management involvement, but today's shared leadership requires much richer relationships. Most IS executives will not need to start from scratch in all six areas, but many may find that they must work to move ahead in several of them.

Understand the Business

If IS executives are to play an important role in reshaping a business's use of IT—to improve operations as well as link to alliance firms and even reach out to the general public—they must understand the business. In the past, studying a business generally meant learning how part of it was run. However, studying internal operations is not enough. Today, it is also important to understand the environment in which the business operates because the rules of competition have changed and are likely to change even further with full-blown electronic commerce. Here are seven approaches CIOs are using to understand the business and its environment.

- Have project teams study the marketplace.
- Concentrate on lines of business.
- Sponsor weekly briefings.
- Attend industry meetings with line executives.
- Read industry publications.
- Hold informal listening sessions.
- Become a "partner" with a line manager.

Have Project Teams Study the Marketplace. To learn about the business, broaden the kinds of information that project teams seek in their study of the business, then have them describe their findings to IS management. For example, the project study might begin with a broad overview of the company, gathering the following information about the company and its industry:

- History and framework
- Current industry environment
- Business goals and objectives
- Major practices of competitors
- Pertinent government regulations
- The inputs, outputs, and resources of the firm

Such an overview study can be conducted for a business unit or a product in a few weeks. The study is apt to uncover some surprises, revealing things about the industry and company that even line people might not know—especially if, for example, a competitor is moving aggressively into electronic commerce. IS management can be briefed on the findings, thus becoming educated about the markets in which their firm participates.

Concentrate on Lines of Business. Robert Benson, of Washington University in St. Louis, Missouri, and Marilyn Parker of IBM have long been studying how to manage information on an enterprisewide basis [1]. They began their study thinking that they should develop data modeling tools. However, their thinking has broadened significantly. To help a company be successful, they found, IS needs to serve individual lines of business rather than the whole company. Planning for an entire enterprise without considering lines of business overlooks both competitive and performance matters. A line of business is where business and technology planning can be linked, they believe.

At the Enterprise-wide Information Management (EwIM) conference hosted by the two researchers a few years ago, Benson characterized a line of business as an organizational unit that conducts business activities with common customers, products, and market characteristics. For example, certain schools in a university have one line of business—undergraduate education. Other schools have two lines of business—undergraduate and graduate education. The customers, products, and market characteristics for the two are different; thus they are different lines of business.

Information technology can serve lines of business in two ways. One is by supporting current operations, which Benson and Parker call "alignment." The second is by using systems to influence future ways of working, which they call "impact" (Figure 2-2).

Benson and Parker suggest asking the following questions about each line of business to decide what each one needs.

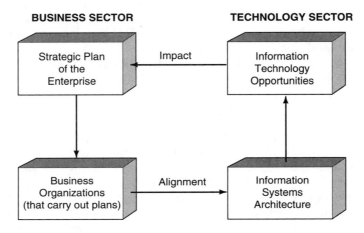

Figure 2-2   The Enterprisewide Information Management Model
(from Benson and Parker [1])

1. Are we organized to serve that line of business?
2. Do we have an "account manager" in IS who has responsibility for that line of business?
3. Is there someone within that line of business who oversees IT activity and talks the business language?
4. Do we have a sponsor in the line of business?
5. Do we have the attention of its management?
6. Does the line of business offer an opportunity to use systems in new ways?

By becoming familiar with lines of business, IS executives can better help them use IT to support current operations and influence the future, say Benson and Parker.

Sponsor Weekly Briefings. Another way to learn about the business is to sponsor short briefings each week for IS management and staff—presented by *line* management or staff. We have attended such meetings and found them most informative. They were about one-half hour long, with one speaker describing a part of the business. Managers and staff from different departments were invited to talk to a small group of IS managers and staff about their business and its marketplace—the products and services they offered versus what the competitors offered, the strengths and weaknesses of the firm and competitors, growth projections, possible changes in the market, and so on.

For example, in the aircraft industry an engineer could give the basics of the commercial aircraft business—sizes of planes, number of people they hold, lengths of flights, expected competition, how the field is changing, five-year and ten-year market projections, and so on. In the financial services industry, a manager could describe various types of customers and how they have changed, products now offered by the firm and competitors, changes in the world financial marketplace, and so on. At such briefings, it is helpful if the presenter provides a written summary of the ideas presented, so attendees can take something away with them. A brief question and answer period is also very useful.

To understand the business, one needs to understand the marketplace. Few employees get exposed to this breadth of knowledge. Through sponsoring short presentations by the people closest to a business, IS management can help fix that problem without cutting into working time too greatly.

Attend Industry Meetings with Line Executives. Another way to learn about the business is to accompany a line executive to an industry conference—not a computer conference. We have found that attending a conference is one of the quickest ways to uncover issues currently facing an industry. These conferences contain the jargon used in the industry and the approaches others have used to market products, handle regulations, respond to competition, and so on. Attending with a line executive can be even more enlightening because he or she can explain what the company is or is not doing in areas discussed by the speakers. Such joint attendance is also likely to foster a new friendship.

Read Industry Publications. One of the best ways to stay abreast of an industry is to read its publications. Getting a well-rounded view of an industry may require reading several publications a month. For example, news publications can provide information on new products, current issues, company changes, and so on. Newsletters, reports, and research journals generally provide better analyses of industry trends, discussions of ongoing research, and projections about the future.

One information systems executive we know spreads this job around in his department. Every systems person is responsible for reading certain periodicals and routing interesting articles to others.

Hold Informal Listening Sessions. In his book, *Thriving on Chaos* [2], consultant Tom Peters presents hundreds of suggestions on how managers can learn to not just cope with a chaotic business environment but thrive in it. In numerous places in the book, Peters urges people to simply listen and learn. His ideas are appropriate for IS managers in their dealings with their customers— both internal to the firm and external.

Yogi Berra, the famous baseball player, once said, "You can see a lot by observing." Similarly, Peters urges employees to listen to customers to determine their needs. Since product life cycles are shrinking, companies need to spot new trends earlier. Becoming a listening-intensive organization can help here.

Peters recounts several instances where people have created informal meetings to break down barriers among people who usually do not talk with one another. These get-togethers are held in a setting that is not charged with tension, participation is voluntary, and their purpose is to "just chat." For instance, one hospital administrator set aside one early morning each week to have coffee and rolls available in her office, with an open invitation for doctors and administrators to drop by and chat. She had some lonely breakfasts at first, she told Peters, but they have evolved into the "real staff meeting" of the week. Another hospital administrator held an informal staff meeting at lunch time every two weeks at a local pub and invited some doctors. The doctors felt honored to be invited and their attendance helped break down stereotypes on both sides and improve communications.

Become a "Partner" with a Line Manager. In 1987, the Society for Information Management [3] initiated its Partners in Leadership Award. Each year, the award is presented to two organizations, honoring one IS and one business executive in each enterprise who, through their alliance, have achieved significant business results. This award has been well received and is highly sought. It reinforces the partnering needed to successfully guide and deploy IT these days. We discuss partnering in more depth later in this chapter.

Summary. These, then, are several ways that CIOs and their staff can learn the businesses of the organization. With this knowledge, CIOs are in a better position to create a vision of using IT in their firm. It is important that specific steps or mechanisms, such as these, be implemented in the department; otherwise, the job of learning the business will be displaced by urgent but less important day-to-day work.

Establish Systems Department Credibility

The second major responsibility of the CIO is to establish and then maintain the credibility of the IS organization. Before the IS executive and the IS department can be viewed as an important force in the future of the organization, they must be viewed as successful and reliable today. This suggests that the IS departments have two missions, says Joseph Izzo [4], management consultant. One is to maintain today's systems, the other is to work on tomorrow's systems.

These two missions have very different goals and, therefore, need to be managed separately and quite differently. The "today" operation should concentrate on providing service, says Izzo, while the "tomorrow" operation needs to focus on helping the business to operate better. The first job of IS management is to get the "today" operation in shape. Until that is done, CIOs will have little credibility with top management, says Izzo.

Managing the "Today" Organization Better. The "today" organization includes computer operations, technical support (including telecom network support), and maintaining and enhancing existing applications. Since its main mission is service, the service levels of these various operations need to be measured.

To run the "today" operation, Izzo suggests hiring managers for each of these functions who are like factory supervisors—that is, they are delivery oriented and demand a high level of service from their department. Many IS organizations have a poor response rate, said Izzo, because they do not staff their organization correctly.

He recommends the following staffing levels, based on the workloads he has seen at over 20 companies. About 80–90 percent of requests for system development take less than one month to complete, he says. Most are one- or two-day projects; Izzo calls them *minor requests*. A department needs 25–35 percent of its work force to handle these requests, he believes. Another 9–15 percent of the requests take up to one work-year to fulfill; Izzo calls them *intermediate requests*. This workload requires 50–65 percent of the department's work force. The remaining 1–5 percent take more than one work-year. These *major requests* require 10–25 percent of a development work force.

Of these three types of development, Izzo points out that most departments only manage the majors. To more professionally manage the full range, Izzo recommends separating them into these three categories and handling each differently. Complete all minor requests within 30 days, on average, he recommends; don't prioritize them, just do them. To handle the intermediates, establish user committees to determine the merit of the requests. Let the line people prioritize this work by determining which projects get implemented and when. For the majors, follow the elaborate procedures that companies already have in place.

Once the "today" organization is in shape, then IS management has the credibility to propose its new ideas for the future. In Chapter 8, we further discuss running today's operations.

Increase the Technological Maturity of the Firm

Technologically mature organizations are those where management is comfortable *managing* the use of IT and employees are comfortable *using* the technology. These organizations are the ones most likely to take advantage of new uses of IT.

How can IS management help others in the firm become comfortable with IT? Managers can provide education—to make others aware of uses of IT as well as their role in either using or managing the technology. These days, IS departments are getting more help than they want familiarizing others with computers because IT "breakthroughs" are featured in the news media, computers are used in almost all areas of everyday life, and younger employees have literally been "brought up" on computers. In fact, IS executives now face "airline magazine syndrome," where the CEO or other top executives send a memo to the CIO that says, "What are we doing on this?" and attaches an article from an airline magazine about a "hot new technology" or a competitor's use of a new technology. So in many cases, IS departments are scrambling to keep up with the technology and users' expectations.

IS management also has the job of helping end users adapt to changes caused by IT, and encouraging innovative uses of the technology. In Chapter 17, we discuss some ways that IS departments can increase their firm's technological maturity, and put the company in a better position to use new information technologies for strategic purposes.

Create a Vision of the Future and Sell It

IS executives are no longer reactive, providing only support. They manage some of the most important tools for influencing the firm's future; therefore, they are becoming more proactive by helping to create a vision of the firm's future and its use of IT, and then selling those ideas to others.

What Is a Vision? A vision is a statement of how someone wants the future to be or believes it will be. It is used to set a direction for an organization. One of the most often-cited examples is the compelling statement U.S. President John Kennedy made in 1961: "We will put a man on the moon, and return him safely to earth, by the end of the decade." And it did come to pass. On July 21, 1969, the United States landed a man on the moon. His vision provided a direction for the U.S. space program for a decade.

Professors Cynthia Beath and Blake Ives [5], presented the following visions from chief executives.

- George Davis, chief operating officer at Otis Elevator, wants any salesperson in his company to be able to completely order an elevator in a day.
- Robert McDermott, president of USAA—an insurance company for current and retired military officers—wants policyholders to accomplish their objective in a single phone call.
- Mim Eschenbaum, vice president of Rittenhouse Homes, wants customers to be able to get a house designed and built from a retail store.

- Edward Johnson II, president of Fidelity Investments, wants to reprice mutual funds on an hourly, rather than a daily, basis.

Why Develop a Vision? The word *vision* is seen everywhere today because in turbulent times such as we now face, people are looking for some stability. A vision of a desirable future can provide stability when it sets the direction for an organization. In his book, *The Renewal Factor* [6], Robert Waterman discusses the difference between vision and strategy. A strategy tells how someone is going to get somewhere. It is a plan for the future. Strategies are fine as long as the future is relatively predictable, says Waterman. But we are now in turbulent times. No one can predict some of the most important events that will affect companies, he says, because these events are likely to be random, not linear or rational. Since IT is important to the success of many firms, their visions need to include use of IT.

Who Should Create the Vision? A growing number of CEOs are relying on their IS executives to create the corporate vision for using IT because innovative uses of computers provide ways to significantly change the manner in which companies do business. Where can CIOs come up with such inspirations? Listen to all ideas, no matter how crazy they sound, recommends Joel Barker [7], a futurist.

At a conference hosted by the Dooley Group [8], a management consulting firm, Barker asked the question: What types of people are most likely to find new ways to solve problems? His answer: people who anticipate dramatic shifts that might occur in the future. These types of people are generally outsiders, he says, because they see things in different ways. They have faith in themselves but they are unpracticed in the field under question. So they bring a fresh viewpoint to problems in that field. They do not know what cannot be done, so they try many new things. These visionaries are generally young people just entering a field or older people who are changing careers, and they love to tinker.

Insiders have an investment in maintaining the status quo because they understand the way a field operates. Outsiders do not have this investment, so they are more likely to come up with new solutions, says Barker.

Getting a Vision. We found two ways to create visions. One is to explore the present. Think about how it might be improved. For example, study the problems CEOs face today and look for ways to solve those problems. A second approach to create a vision is to "scout" the future. Look at trends that appear likely to continue as well as changes that might disrupt current trends. The Internet has just disrupted the computer field. What other disruptions lie ahead? People who uncover such shifts and take advantage of them early can give their firm a competitive edge.

Exploring the present. Peters [2] suggests four approaches. One is to ask: What bothers you most about the organization? When people are (or are not) working well with one another, what seems to be going on? Based on answers to these and similar questions, fix things that are wrong. Second, try participation, by involving people inside and outside the firm to uncover their top-ten irritants and their ten best experiences. Their ideas might inspire a vision. Third, clarify the vision over time, perhaps by holding a two- to three- day meeting with subordinates to study the data and stories in detail in order to refine shared views and values. And fourth, remember to listen. Visions are seldom original, Peters notes. A visionary may be the person who focuses attention on an idea at a point in time, but that visionary is likely to have heard it from someone else.

Scouting the future. The Institute for the Future [9] studies trends and publishes a ten-year forecast. The institute helps organizations plan their long-term futures by discussing near-term and long-term outlooks in numerous areas—such as the U.S. economy, demographics of the United States, U.S. labor force, technology, U.S. government, and international situations. They present issues that they see arising from the trends.

Another way to scout the future is to look for discontinuities, or shifts in trends. The people at the Institute for the Future call them "wild cards." Joel Barker calls them "paradigm shifts." By whatever name, they create major changes in the way people think about the world. The cellular telephone is such a shift, concern for the earth's environment is another, and the Web is another.

Barker encourages people to scout the future looking for discontinuities by listening to screwy ideas and new ways to solve existing problems. The more people a company has scouting the future, the better off they are, says Barker, because the future is more likely to be revolutionary than evolutionary. By spotting a revolutionary event early, a company has an advantage over competitors that are not thinking about the future.

At the Dooley Group conference, attendees offered the following ideas on possible shifts that could change the way people think in the next 15 years:

- Decline in the growth of cities
- Holograms to replace travel
- Small is better than big
- Personalized products (a market of one)
- Portable and personal two-way communication
- Small but very powerful batteries
- Manufacturing in outer space
- A power shift from a manufacturing base to a knowledge base
- Deterring the aging process

Selling a Vision. Once you have a vision about how you think the business should operate in the future, you need to sell that idea to others. Webb Castor [10], an independent consultant whose job has always been selling, irrespective of his job description, has a number of recommendations for selling an idea.

To sell an idea requires understanding the marketplace, says Castor, meaning, what the potential customers *want* rather than what they *should have.* To find out what they want, listen. Listening is actually a potent form of selling. By understanding and fulfilling someone's needs, you help them be successful, says Castor. And, by making the buyer successful, the seller becomes successful.

Often, personal relationships are the key to successfully selling an idea, says Castor, because people like to do business with people they know and trust. But if you believe you will not be effective, bring in a spokesperson. And finally, to be a successful salesperson, keep your customers informed, says Castor. If you can do nothing else to ease a bad situation, at least keep the other party informed. Customer care is very important in selling—products or ideas.

The following case example illustrates how one company developed and used a vision of IT to enhance its business performance.

CASE EXAMPLE: The Boeing Company

The Boeing Company, a major U.S. aerospace company with headquarters in Seattle, Washington, has three major components.

- Boeing Commercial Airplane Group manufactures the 747, 757, 767, and 777 airplanes.
- Boeing Defense and Space Systems manufactures missile systems, space systems, military airplanes and helicopters, and other military systems.
- Boeing Computer Services supplies information system support to Boeing and government agencies, offers commercial computing services, and does research and application development in new information technologies.

At an annual conference of the Society for Information Management [3] in the mid-1980s, the president of Boeing Computer Services described two visions—one Boeing had achieved and another it was developing. In 1991, Boeing developed a third vision—one intended to carry the company into the year 2010.

Vision 1: The Right Part in the Right Place at the Right Time. In the late 1960s, business was good at Boeing, but the company had a severe parts shortage that was hindering production. If a part was unavailable when needed, a tag—called a "traveler"—was affixed to the aircraft in place of the missing part. At that time, the company had 2,500–5,000 travelers per month attached to planes under construction.

To correct this situation, management created this vision: *the right part in the right place at the right time.* From 1966 to the mid-1980s, Boeing installed 15 major information systems as well as dozens of smaller ones to implement this vision. The parts shortage problem used to be greatest when a new aircraft was being introduced. For example, in 1966 when the 737 was rolled out, the number of travelers jumped to more than 8,000 a month. But by the mid-1970s, parts shortages had been reduced to fewer than 100 a month. And in the early 1980s, introduction of the 757 and 767 models caused barely noticeable increases in parts shortages.

Information systems helped Boeing solve the parts shortage problem and implemented its vision. In doing so, however, Boeing created islands of automation; systems had trouble passing information back and forth to one another. Meanwhile the company's marketplaces changed. So Boeing needed a new vision.

Addressing the Changing Marketplace. In the aerospace and defense markets, ways of doing business changed. There were tighter budgets in the U.S. Department of Defense—one of Boeing's major customers—and the U.S. government shifted up-front development costs to suppliers. Therefore, Boeing experienced pressure to use rapidly changing technologies in its products.

In the commercial aircraft market, deregulation led air carriers to expand hub-and-spoke operations where shorter flights and smaller planes were the norm. Fluctuating fuel prices made fuel economy a major concern in aircraft design. Boeing also faced more intense competition from foreign as well as domestic aircraft companies.

Boeing believed its competitiveness in the commercial airplane market depended on its use of information systems in three ways:

1. *To increase Boeing's responsiveness to the market.* Systems would help Boeing "design to cost"—meaning, design planes with the aircraft purchaser's operational costs in mind. Information systems would also help Boeing keep aircraft delivery schedules flexible, so it could deliver products earlier than competitors. Boeing also believed information systems would help tailor an existing aircraft for a customer without having to completely redesign it.

2. *To help the company gain a competitive advantage by making after-sale support more efficient.* With IT, Boeing would be able to create airplane documentation based on original design data. It would be better able to manage spare parts inventories worldwide. And Boeing could use artificial intelligence in embedded diagnostics systems to do troubleshooting during maintenance.

3. *To help Boeing streamline its design and build process.* The company's vision was based on this third use of IT.

Vision 2: An Enhanced Information Stream. Boeing's vision in the mid-1980s was to create an *enhanced information stream* because building and supporting an aircraft is really an information process. An enhanced information stream means that every step in designing and building an aircraft uses, adds to, and enhances a continuing stream of information.

First, a product is defined using a computer-aided design/computer-aided manufacturing (CAD/CAM) system. Then each succeeding step in the design, build, and support process uses that digital information, adds to it, and enhances it. The various islands of automation feed into one seamless information pipeline. Even after-sale support information is based on this enhanced digital description of a product.

This vision required a number of significant changes in the company. One was organizational. Boeing had to break down traditional organization barriers. Thirty years of computing had led to islands of automation based on organizational structure. If information was to be used better, it had to cross organizational lines. One way Boeing restructured itself was to establish design/build teams composed of people from engineering and manufacturing as well as other disciplines.

Boeing also streamlined its design and manufacturing processes *before* it automated, rather than automate its traditional ways of doing business. Finally, Boeing is using computers for as many jobs as possible, such as tracking engineering changes.

Vision 3: A Strategic Business Process Architecture. In the early 1990s, Boeing reassessed its position and undertook a long-range study to develop a new vision—for both the company's business processes and information systems in the year 2010. The team found that Boeing had often put the cart before the horse, in that IS plans drove business plans. The company had a clear vision for IT but no vision for business processes. The study therefore defines the world-class production processes that both the commercial airplane group and the defense and space group need to succeed in 2010, as well as the computing infrastructure to support those processes.

The study began with Boeing defining its existing business process architecture to understand how the company conducts business and to compare it to how it wants to conduct business in 2010. The 2010 strategic business process architecture provides the basis for its IT architecture, as shown in Figure 2-3. To define this business vision, Boeing asked the following fundamental questions:

- What business processes should we use?
- What information do we need to accomplish these processes?
- How are the processes and information related?
- How is the data managed?
- Which hardware, software, and networks are required?

Once the 2010 business processes were defined, Boeing developed them with the same intensity its uses to design and develop a new airplane. This has required changing its legacy systems. "Owners" of business processes have been established to develop the migration plans, for both the business processes as well as the supporting computing environment.

Although Boeing is currently the dominant airplane manufacturer in the world, the company must make changes to maintain that position. Airbus, the European consortium, has grown from zero to 25 percent market share. Toyota, the most efficient manufacturer in the world, is also expected to enter the business in the near future. Boeing management believes that instituting change from its position of strength is the only way to ensure success in this more competitive future.

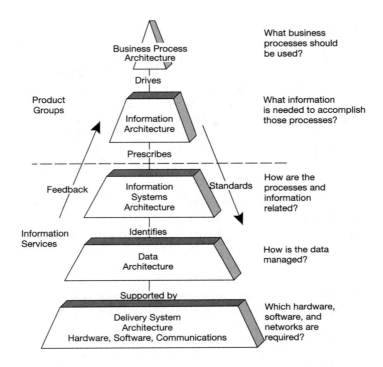

Figure 2-3   The Boeing Information Services 2010 Study
(reprinted courtesy of the Boeing Company)

Implement an Information System Architecture

Although it used to be considered strictly a technical issue, implementing an IT architecture has really occurred in tandem with rethinking company operations—how it works, what it does, with whom it works, and so on—because the architecture should support new ways of operating.

What kinds of attributes should the systems architectures have? Peter Keen [11], a true guru in the field, believes that large organizations—both in industry and government—are reaching the limits of complexity to the point that their complex organizational structures are impeding their mission. IT planning therefore needs to focus on simplifying organizations to ensure their health, says Keen. CEOs should look to IT to help them simplify their organizations.

Organizations can be simplified by increasing direct contact between people, Keen believes. IT can help by reducing the need for intermediaries, thereby flattening organizational hierarchies. IT can also help organize information for easier access. This is particularly needed for document-based information, where complex organizational structures have emerged just to process documents.

It is interesting to note that use of Web technology is doing just this. It allows increased direct contact between people (via e-mail) and it is permitting easier access to information (via Web servers and browsers). For example, it is being used to *significantly* reduce corporate accounting data complexity by placing much of this company information on *one* in-company Web server and allowing people in all parts of the company worldwide to draw on it. As a result, operations in France use the same data as those in Germany, Japan, the United States, Brazil, and so on—replacing *many* former regional databases and systems.

Developing a systems architecture is no longer a technical exercise; it is now a strategic business issue. Various approaches to developing architectures are presented throughout this book, especially in Part II where we discuss architectures for distributed computing, telecom, and information resources respectively.

Nurture Relationships

An increasingly important role for CIOs is to develop and nurture relationships. Leadership in the development and use of IT now requires a "partnering." Three sets of partnerships are of particular importance:

- Relationships with senior management—the chief executive officer, the chief operating officer, the chief financial officer, division presidents, and other members of the top-management team.
- Relationships with customers—both internal and external.
- Relationships with suppliers and other external partners.

Relationships with Senior Management. The relationship between the CIO and senior managers has often left a lot to be desired. At a meeting of the Chicago Chapter of the Society for Information Management, Diane Wilson [12], of MIT's Sloan School, reported on a research study that delved into CEOs' preconceived notions about the benefits of IT. The researchers interviewed 84 CEOs in ten industries for two hours each, asking them about the competence of their IS department and what they personally expect of IT and from their systems department. The majority of the CEOs interviewed—52 percent to be exact—were neutral, believing they did not have enough knowledge to direct IT investments. They are difficult to partner with, says Wilson, because they do not provide the necessary leadership.

The other 48 percent of the CEOs fell into four quadrants, depending on whether they took an optimistic or pessimistic view of the benefits of IT, and whether they had high or low confidence in their IS department. See Figure 2-4.

Quadrant 1. CEOs in this category (12 percent) have a high degree of confidence in receiving benefits from IT investments, as well as confidence in their IS department's ability to deliver those benefits. The main challenge in managing IT under this type of executive, says Wilson, is that the CEO generally takes a hands-off attitude and delegates the entire job to the CIO.

Quadrant 2. While still having a positive belief in the benefits of applying IT, CEOs in this category (26 percent) are well aware that implementation problems can destroy that potential. These executives can tell war stories to back up their beliefs. So they take a hands-on approach to managing IT. They believe they must establish the standard for using information in decision making

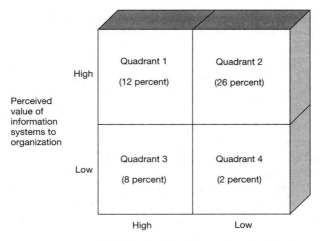

Figure 2-4   CEOs' Attitiudes Toward Information Systems
(based on Wilson [13])

throughout the firm, they review all important IT decisions, and they step in when problems arise to minimize the risk of IT not delivering on the promised benefits. They generally see their CIO as the technologist and the IT visionary.

Quadrant 3. CEOs counted here (8 percent) are pessimistic about IT, believing that all systems will be delivered over budget. Although they have confidence in their IS department, they manage mainly on cost to protect the enterprise from the risks.

Quadrant 4. CEOs in this category (2 percent) believe that IT is harmful because it introduces chaos and too much change for people to cope well. Generally these executives have gotten their skepticism from a bad experience, so they have little or no confidence in the IS group. They see their role as keeping a lid on the demand for IT and they discourage others from adopting IT.

Fortunately, there is evidence that the situation is getting better than their data indicates. Since IS is becoming so important in corporate strategy, the mission and vision of the use of IT need to be understood by, and even initiated by, senior management. This job cannot be delegated to IS management. Senior management needs to be aware that it is its role to direct the use of IT, and CIOs need to develop this awareness as part of their partnership with senior management.

Relationships with Customers. A major set of partnerships revolves around internal and external customers of the IS function. Line managers and other users are the internal customers. Increasingly, the organization's customers, who buy services and products, are becoming customers of the IS function also, a trend we discuss later in the book.

Peter Keen [11] believes that companies need to establish specific structures to instill mutual trust and respect among systems professionals and end users, and to focus the motivations of these groups. As an example, he cites a bank that developed a letter of credit product in response to a surprise offering by a foreign competitor. The bank undertook the unusual step (for it) of including marketing people and clients on the development team. The team rapidly prototyped a PC-based product, tested it with selected clients, and fended off the competitive product.

To make this partnership work, the bank had to redefine the boundaries between the team's work groups, giving each one access to the others' resources. This meant going against some established practices. The team met the challenge of the competitor, and at the same time significantly improved relations between the IS and marketing groups.

Federal–Mogul provides an example of a company that is improving relationships between information systems and line departments, and moving responsibility for managing the use of IT out to the line at the same time.

CASE EXAMPLE: Federal–Mogul

Federal-Mogul makes engine bearings, oil seals, ball bearings, fuel systems, electronics, and other parts for cars, light trucks, and heavy trucks. About one-half its parts are sold to original equipment companies—such as Ford, General Motors, and Chrysler. The other half goes to the after market, that is, to repair businesses. Most of the effort at the corporate IS department goes toward supporting the after-market portion of the business.

The challenge in the IS department was to change its orientation from cost reduction to customer service. In the mid to late 1980s, cost containment was emphasized, so development groups were centralized to cut costs. More recently, however, new business executives emphasized the need to have the right information technology in place to succeed in the future. Thus, the company is planning a significant increase in IT investments—not only to create new systems but to replace old ones.

As they looked to the future, IS managers realized they would have to know as much about each line of business as the people in these business units. They decided to model their department after an independent sales organization, even though they would not actually be an independent unit. This meant getting IS managers to know each line executive and his or her team. So, IS management created a new position—account executive.

Account Executives. The departments of sales and marketing, logistics, corporate staff and world trade each have one account executive; manufacturing has two. They each report directly to their respective line executive and indirectly to the CIO. These account executives supervise the members of the systems staff who specialize in building systems for that function. In effect, the line executives have their own IS manager and IS staff. The line executives are also in charge of their own IS budget for that group. Thus, each month, the functional executives see what they are spending on IS support, and they can reallocate resources as they choose.

Besides managing their functional IS staff, the account executives are also responsible for keeping their function's IT plans coordinated with corporate direction. Decisions on which user requests to implement are frequently based on how well the requested work matches the firm's strategic direction. IS staff formerly filled all user requests and were measured on user satisfaction. That measure was appropriate because users were the mid-level managers. Now, however, the users are top management, so the focus has shifted to strategic issues.

Although the reporting structure has been decentralized, the physical location of most of the IS staff has not changed. They still reside in the central IS department. The development staff is resisting being moved physically out into user departments, we were told. They fear they will be stranded among non-IS professionals and that they will be constantly "bothered" by users to make little changes and fix things. They want to be with other developers. IS management has not forced them to move, but that will come eventually.

All but one of the account executives are also still physically located in the IS department. Interestingly, the one account executive who has moved into his line area really likes being with the end users. Being on-site helps him solve their problems much faster.

Benefits. Federal–Mogul is deriving several benefits from this organizational structure.

1. Users accept systems changes more readily. They sense the desire of the IS department to be of better service.
2. Line executives more clearly understand their IT responsibilities. Since they now are in charge of their own IT budget, they are more involved in systems planning.
3. This change has told the rest of the IS organization that a change in culture is taking place. IS professionals are expected to become more of a partner with business unit staff.
4. IS executives have spurred line management to plan further ahead because they need longer lead times to put the supporting information systems in place.

Challenges. One challenge in this structure is encouraging the account executives to broaden their thinking beyond the function they serve. Since the account executives also report indirectly to the IS vice president, they are expected to include companywide considerations in their own systems planning—which they have been doing. They get together to discuss cross-functional implications of future plans. Other challenges in this new arrangement are career paths and training. Since there are only two levels of IS professionals in each functional area, there is little career growth in that area, except to move back into corporate IS management or into the line group.

One key to making this approach work is getting the support of the business executives, the vice president told us. He got them to see the need for this closer working relationship, but he had to push it. This will help the IS staff better support its business, he told them. Interestingly, one account executive who did seek out the priorities in the business unit found that the priorities of the top executive and the middle managers did not agree. This discrepancy encouraged the group to reexamine its priorities, and led to a meeting with the company president, who, in turn, explained his priorities.

Another key to this structure is learning to say "no." The operational managers are no longer the top-priority users; therefore, some of their requests need to be turned down—when they do not align with company strategy. It is not possible to satisfy many masters, they have learned.

The third key to success is having very senior people in these account executive positions. Federal-Mogul has people who have had 15 to 20 years of IT experience, understand the business, have credibility with the users, and have bought into the philosophy of the job. In all, the vice president of information services is optimistic that this step toward partnering will pay off in even better use of IT resources.

Relationships with Suppliers and Alliance Partners. Due to the dynamic changes in many industries, and the huge investments needed to react to these changes, IS departments are establishing cooperative external relationships, says Keen. In such relationships, both vendor and customer know more about each other's future plans, they work more closely on projects, and they may even undertake some joint ventures. This has not been the traditional mode of working between IS departments and vendors, so some new forms of partnering mechanisms need to be developed.

Yet another trend that has required IS executives to forge partnerships or alliances with other companies is the move to reduce the number of suppliers. Many companies have reduced their suppliers from thousands to tens. And the same is happening in the IS department. IS departments not only outsource their help desks, PC acquisition-maintenance-disposal, data center, network management, and other functions, they also often shrink their supplier base in other areas. Then they establish deeper relationships with these remaining suppliers. They tell them of future plans, do joint planning, perhaps work together on projects, and so forth. They treat these suppliers more as partners than as

suppliers. In Chapter 8 we explain what Eastman Kodak h
working procedures with one of its outsourcers, ISSC.

Summary. Of these six areas of responsibility, se
new. Running efficient operations to develop credibility *ε*
tems architecture have been part of the top systems job for some
executives have also long held an important role in training and educatio
increase the organization's ability to assimilate IT. However, only recently has
it become clear that CIOs must know as much about the business processes
and goals as they know about IT, maybe more. Moreover, the concept of creating an overall vision of the role of IT, and selling it throughout the organization, was quite foreign to many CIOs until recently. Finally, the need to partner with a wide variety of managers, suppliers, and customers is broadening
the managerial scope of the CIO role.

THE EVOLVING INFORMATION SYSTEMS FUNCTION

The changing roles and responsibilities of the CIO just discussed are largely
the result of the evolution of the IS function. In the second part of this chapter
we discuss several dimensions of this evolution, beginning with the escalating
benefits derived from IT. This, in turn, changes the way managers view information technology and its role. Recent research shows that there is a wide dis-
persion of views among top executives on this subject. In this context, we
explore the likely changes coming in IS departments.

The Escalating Benefits of Information Technology

The authors of *Strategic Choices* [13], Kenneth Primozic, Edward Primozic,
and Joe Leben, describe the evolution of IT and the escalating benefits it provides to organizations. The authors introduce the notion of "waves of innovation," which they define as how IT is used, by industry and by enterprise. They
identify five waves of innovation, as shown in Figure 2-5. They are

- Wave 1: Reducing cost.
- Wave 2: Leveraging investments.
- Wave 3: Enhancing products and services.
- Wave 4: Enhancing executive decision making.
- Wave 5: Reaching the consumer.

Wave 1: Reducing cost began in the 1960s when use of IT focused on
increasing the productivity of individuals and business areas. The goal was to
achieve clerical and administrative savings.

Wave 2: Leveraging investments, which began in the 1970s, concentrated on
making more effective use of corporate assets to increase profitability. Systems
were justified on return on investment and increasing cash flow.

The authors note that the focus in both of these waves was saving money,
not making money—by better managing processing and assets. Systems were
developed mainly for administration, finance, and manufacturing.

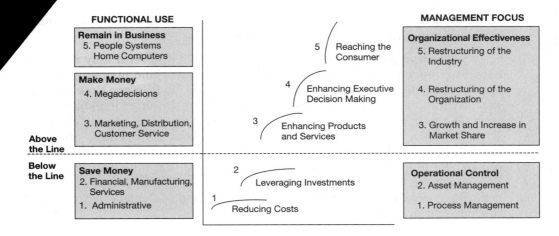

FUNCTIONAL USE

| Remain in Business |
| 5. People Systems |
| Home Computers |

| Make Money |
| 4. Megadecisions |

| 3. Marketing, Distribution, |
| Customer Service |

Above the Line

Below the Line

| Save Money |
| 2. Financial, Manufacturing, |
| Services |
| 1. Administrative |

5 / Reaching the Consumer

4 / Enhancing Executive Decision Making

3 / Enhancing Products and Services

2 / Leveraging Investments

1 / Reducing Costs

MANAGEMENT FOCUS

| Organizational Effectiveness |
| 5. Restructuring of the Industry |

| 4. Restructuring of the Organization |

| 3. Growth and Increase in Market Share |

| Operational Control |
| 2. Asset Management |

| 1. Process Management |

Figure 2-5   Waves of Innovation (from Primozic et al. [13])

Wave 3: Enhancing products and services began in the 1980s and was the first time attention shifted to using IT to produce revenue—by gaining strategic advantage or creating entirely new businesses.

Wave 4: Enhancing executive decision making began later in the 1980s and focused on changing the fundamental structure of the organization as well as creating real-time business management systems.

The authors point out that Waves 1 and 2 could be implemented at any time—because of their internal focus—but Waves 3 and 4 must be implemented once an industry leader sets a new direction. Companies that do not follow suit cease to remain competitive.

Wave 5: Reaching the consumer began in the 1990s, say the authors. It uses IT directly with consumers, leading to new marketing, distribution, and service strategies. In essence, it changes the rules of competition, which is precisely the focus of leading-edge firms—to restructure their industry by focusing on creating new businesses using the Internet, Web technology, and electronic commerce.

In this framework, Waves 1 and 2 are "below the line," in that they focus on saving money. Waves 3, 4, and 5 are "above the line" because they concentrate on making money and staying in business. Most organizations are just at the top of Wave 2, say Primozic et al., they have not yet begun to build information systems that make money—even though the leaders in their industries may have crossed the line quite some time ago.

Once companies do cross the line, top executives must be involved in guiding IT use because they must steer the company in the new business environment. The risks of inappropriately using IT for competitive purposes are too great for top management to abrogate leadership. So joint planning by top management and IS management must take place, say the authors.

To illustrate how one company has maneuvered through these five waves, consider the example of the American Airlines SABRE system.

CASE EXAMPLE: The SABRE System

The American Airlines computer reservation system—SABRE—represents a prime example of a system that has progressed through the five waves of innovation.

Waves 1 and 2. The system was built in the mid-1960s to reduce the costs of making airline seat reservations and to leverage the reservation-making assets of the airline. The system moved American from a manual-based reservation operation to a computer-based one.

Wave 3. In the mid-1970s, American offered the system to travel agents, giving them a way to make reservations directly through on-line terminals. American also enhanced the offering by adding functions of importance to travel agents, such as preparing trip itineraries. SABRE was a win-win proposition—the travel agents liked the direct access and American increased barriers to agents switching to other carriers' systems.

Wave 4. In the late 1970s, American expanded its reservation service to hotels and rental cars through alliances with these suppliers. In so doing, American was transforming itself, and perhaps the entire industry, from an airline company to a travel company. At about the same time, American also added a yield management component to SABRE, which allowed the company to more dynamically reprice seats to maximize revenue.

Wave 5. In the 1980s, American extended its reach to the consumer in two major moves. First, American introduced EAASY SABRE, the computer reservation system that consumers can access directly from their PCs. Second, American introduced its frequent flyer program, AAdvantage, thereby stimulating frequent business flyers to fly American and gain points for free trips. Furthermore, it allied the program with Citibank's credit card and MCI, giving their AAdvantage members free miles by using the credit card and the telephone company.

This example makes it very clear that top management had to be involved as soon as SABRE moved into the money-making Wave 3, when the airline began offering the system to its customers, the travel agents. That was a heart-of-the-business move, and it had to be led by the business executives of the organization, not the information system executives.

Where Are IS Departments Headed?

A recent report from the IT Management Programme (ITMP) [14], a CIO subscription research service in the United Kingdom, provided useful insight into the structure of IS organizations and where they are likely to be headed. A key argument of the report is that IS is not a single monolithic organization, but a cluster of four functions:

- *Run operations*: running the computers and networks
- *Develop systems:* developing and maintaining systems, designing new systems and updating existing ones
- *Develop architecture*: setting a strategy and maintaining an architecture for both IT and information, providing a framework or standard for systems operations
- *Identify business requirements:* helping to articulate what the business needs from information technology

The report argues that each of these functions requires a different set of skills and a different management strategy. Figure 2-6 shows the four functions on a matrix with two dimensions: the type of impact the technology has on the organization (from cost efficiency to added value), and the balance between required expertise—technical or business.

Failure to recognize the differences in these four areas has led, in some cases, to misplaced resources and/or underdeveloped expertise, notes the report. Organizations have historically invested heavily in computer operations and system development/maintenance, while neglecting the other two (developing architectures and identifying business requirements). Unfortunately, operations and systems development can often be purchased as commodities, while architecture development and business requirements identification are crucial and unique to the organization. Even if the IS organization recognizes and pursues all four areas, the future may see a "squeeze" similar to the "nibbling" concept we discussed at the beginning of the chapter. Figure 2-7 shows how external services—in the form of outsourcing—are competing well in the lower left, while

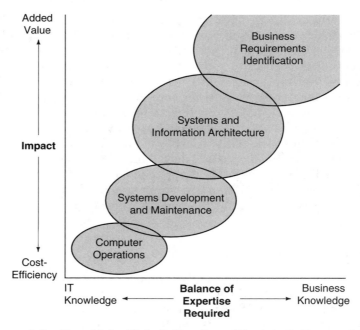

Figure 2-6   Four Major IS Activities (from Wentworth Research [14])

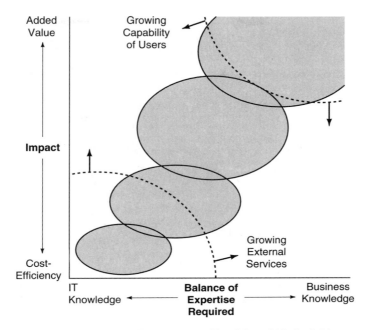

Figure 2-7   The Squeeze on Traditional IS Activities
(from Wentworth Research [14])

increasingly knowledgeable users are assuming more of the responsibility and initiative in the upper right area of the matrix.

Will these trends continue? Will the IS organization be squeezed into oblivion—outsourced on one end and absorbed into business units on the other? ITMP thinks not! Two roles will emerge as dominant for the IS function in the future. First, it is not reasonable to expect an outsourcing service provider to understand and satisfy all the needs of the organization without active management and counsel. They sell commodities. The IS organization needs to develop and manage these contract relationships with a variety of external suppliers.

Second, a crucial role for the IS organizations will be the development and management of the information technology to support the business systems infrastructure. This is perhaps the biggest challenge in the future, especially given the systems development and operations heritage. As the ITMP report puts it, "the precious baby of a coherent framework for systems should be differentiated from the bath water of system delivery and operation."

Figure 2-8 shows these two crucial functions and their relationship to the four traditional activity areas, including the overlap of the past and the future roles. Figure 2-9 shows how the old activities are evolving to the new roles.

The ITMP report concludes with the following four points:

- The four activity streams are different, and may well need to be treated differently.
- There are certain capabilities that should be preserved and developed, while other IT capabilities will simply become commodities.

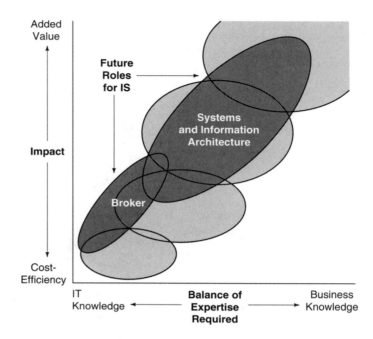

Figure 2-8   Future Roles for IS (from Wentworth Research [14])

	Stage 1 ⟶	Stage 2 ⟶	Stage 3 ⟶	Stage 4 ⟶
Business Requirements Identification	Specifics of Computer Programs	Analysis of Information Flows and Business Systems	Contributor to Multidisciplinary Analysis Team	Partner in the Team Looking at Business Processes
Systems and Information Architecture	Technology Guru and Implementor of Standards	Custodian of Technical Standards for the Business	Specialist in IT Trends	Information Systems Strategist
Systems Development and Maintenance	Computer Systems Programmer	Software Product and Method Specialist	Systems Integrator	Broker and Contract Manager
Computer and Network Operations	Sole Provider of Computer Operations	Preferred Supplier	Competing Supplier	Broker and Contract Manager

Figure 2-9   The Evolution of IS Activities and Functions
(from Wentworth Research [14])

- The spread of desktop computing has equipped everyone to become a better system user—not a skilled systems designer.
- Understanding the direction in which IS is heading does not mean it is sensible to attempt to reshape the whole of IS in one jump.

CONCLUSION

The transformation that IS departments are grappling with these days, says Dick Dooley [8], is learning how to create organizations where IT decision making is shared. The main responsibility for managing the *use* of IT needs to pass to senior line executives, while the management of the IT infrastructure is retained by the IS group. This transformation is reflected in the following saying attributed to Du Pont, says Dooley:

- "We used to do it *to* them"—meaning, IS required end users to obey strict rules for getting changes made to systems, submitting job requests, and so on.
- "Next, we did it *for* them"—meaning, IS moved to taking a service orientation.
- "Now, we do it *with* them," which reflects partnering.
- "We are moving toward teaching them how to do it themselves."

To achieve this transformation, CIOs must play a leadership role in their enterprise and develop partnerships with senior management, internal and external customers, and suppliers.

QUESTIONS AND EXERCISES

REVIEW QUESTIONS

1. Briefly summarize each of the six responsibility areas in the leadership role for CIOs.
2. The text suggests seven ways to "learn the business." Briefly summarize these seven ways.
3. What is the difference between a vision and a strategy?
4. Give several steps or actions for creating or building a vision for each of the two approaches given in the text.
5. Describe Boeing's three visions.
6. What are the three kinds of partnership that must be developed by the IS executive? How are they similar and how are they different?
7. Briefly describe the five attitudes CEOs take toward IT, according to Wilson's study.
8. Describe the job of account executive at Federal-Mogul.
9. Describe the five waves of innovation from Primozic, Primozic, and Leben.
10. What are the four areas that make up the overall responsibility of the IS function?
11. What are the two major roles that systems departments are likely to play in the future?

DISCUSSION QUESTIONS

1. The definition of a vision is not the responsibility of the CIO. It is the responsibility of the CEO and the other senior executives. Do you agree or disagree? Why?

2. Do you agree that the "rules of the game have changed" enough to warrant redefinition of the CIO's role? Won't the primary responsibility continue to be managing IT? Aren't there other executives that are better prepared and perhaps better motivated to know the business and its vision?

3. Discuss the disturbing question asked by Primozic, Primozic, and Leben. As we move into the knowledge management age, what is going to happen to organizations whose senior executives do not yet appreciate the value of data processing, let alone information or knowledge processing?

EXERCISES

1. There is considerable discussion of the evolving role of the chief information officer. At one time, CIO was said to mean "career is over." Find at least two articles on the role of CIOs that make conflicting arguments and summarize the differences.

2. There is also much discussion about partnering between IS and line organizations. Find at least two articles that discuss such partnering and summarize the factors they mention that contribute to successful partnering.

3. Contact the CIO in an organization. What is his or her title? How does he or she perceive the leadership role of the job? How do these characteristics relate to those in the text? How is he or she encouraging partnering with line departments?

REFERENCES

1. PARKER, MARILYN, ROBERT BENSON, with ED TRAINOR, *Information Economics: Linking Information Technology and Business Performance,* Prentice Hall, 1988. European edition 1989. Japanese edition 1990.

2. PETERS, TOM, *Thriving on Chaos: Handbook for a Management Revolution,* Alfred A. Knopf Inc., New York, 1987, 561 pages.

3. SOCIETY FOR INFORMATION MANAGEMENT, 401 N. Michigan Ave., Chicago, IL 60601.

4. JOSEPH IZZO, The Teton Group, 13428 Maxella Ave, #414, Marina del Rey, CA 90292.

5. BEATH, CYNTHIA and BLAKE IVES, "The Information Technology Champion: Aiding and Abetting, Care and Feeding," *Proceedings of the Twenty-First Annual Hawaii International Conference on System Sciences,* Vol. IV, pp. 115–123. Available from the IEEE Computer Society, Los Alamitos, CA.

6. WATERMAN, ROBERT, *The Renewal Factor: How the Best Get and Keep the Competitive Edge,* Bantam Books, New York, 1987, 338 pages.

7. BARKER, JOEL, *Discovering the Future: The Business of Paradigms,* Infinity Limited, 831 Windbreak Trail, Lake Elmo, MN 55042, 1985.

8. THE DOOLEY GROUP, 1380 Kenilwood Lane, Riverwoods, IL 60015.

9. THE INSTITUTE FOR THE FUTURE, 2740 Sand Hill Road, Menlo Park, CA 94025.

10. WEBB CASTOR, 19 Georgeff Road, Rolling Hills Estates, CA 90274.

11. ELAM, JOYCE, MICHAEL GINZBERG, PETER KEEN, and BOB ZMUD, *Transforming the IS Organization,* International Center for Information Technologies, Washington, DC, 1988.

12. DIANE WILSON, Sloan School of Management, M.I.T., 1 Amherst St. Room E40-146, Cambridge, MA 02139.

13. PRIMOZIC, KENNETH, EDWARD PRIMOZIC, and JOE LEBEN, *Strategic Choices: Supremacy, Survival, or Sayonara,* McGraw-Hill, New York, 1991, 272 pages.

14. COX, GEORGE, "Time to Reshape the IS Department?," IT Management Programme Report, Wentworth Research, Park House, Wick Road, Egham, Surrey TW20 OHW England, June 1994, http://www.wentworth.co.uk.

THREE

The Strategic Role of Information Technology

INTRODUCTION

The impact of computing on business operations finally appears to be taking hold. Witness the number of middle-management layers that have been exorcised from organizations, the decreasing employment levels in certain prospering industries (such as financial services), the incredibly fast pace of business these days, and the changing makeup of the labor force in developed nations—with large organizations downsizing significantly, alliances among companies far more common, and small firms effectively competing against their larger brethren, even in global markets. The "workscape" is definitely changing. We are in the midst of a business revolution. And much of that revolution can be attributed to the use of computers.

As we see it, computers play three strategic roles in business today, where we define *strategic as* meaning "having a significant, long-term impact on growth rate, industry, and revenue." These three roles are:

ng inward: To improve company processes and structure
ıg outward: Incorporated in products and services
ʒ across: Linking to other organizations

re 3-1 illustrates, these three roles take an internal/external view of
ıɔıness world. Internally, computers are used to improve business processes, and, more recently, to even change organizational structure. Externally,
more and more products and services are becoming computer based. Furthermore, to compete more effectively (or even compete at all), companies are allying
with others, including competitors. Those relationships are reinforced with electronic linkages.

It is interesting to note the changing emphasis on the strategic use of IT,
just over the lifetime of this book. The hot topic in the first edition (1986) was end
user computing (an internal use of computing). IS departments were gung-ho in
establishing end user computing departments and helping employees learn
about PCs and end user computing languages, such as Focus. The second edition
(1989) emphasized the then-hot subject of using IT for competitive advantage
(an external focus). Several companies gained worldwide notoriety for their
innovative use of computing to change the basis of competition in their industry.
The two most notable examples were American Hospital Supply (now Baxter
Healthcare) with its on-line hospital supply system and American Airlines with
its SABRE computer reservation system. The thrust in the third edition (1993)
was the hot topic of using IT to reengineer outmoded business practices (again,
an inward-looking topic, but with the goal of impacting a company's competitive
stance). That trend is still continuing because revamping corporate culture
takes years. But it is no longer the "in" subject in the strategic use of IT. Rather,
in this fourth edition, the hot topic is the Internet (looking outward), its equally
important inward-looking use (intranets), and its looking-across use in linking
organizations (extranets). The Internet represents another step toward fulfilling
the following on-line vision of the future.

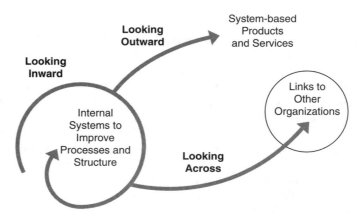

Figure 3-1   Strategic Uses of Information Systems

Where Are We Headed?

In his book *Shaping the Future,* [1] Peter Keen, a long-time insightful observer in the IT field, made eight prognostications about future businesses; see Figure 3-2.

Every large firm in every industry will have from 25 percent to 80 percent of its cash flow processed on-line, stated Keen. Many were above 50 percent in 1990, through computer reservation systems and on-line ordering, distribution, point-of-sale, and customer service systems. He foresees the future being *the on-line company* (our emphasis) where uninterrupted communication links are a business necessity.

Electronic data interchange (EDI) will be the norm. Just as customers do not transact business without telephones, some large organizations now require their suppliers to use EDI—the computer-to-computer transmission of business transactions using industry standard formats. EDI will become as central to global operations as the fax, he projects. The economics are too compelling to ignore: error rates cut in half, delays reduced by days, and costs saved from $5 to $50 per document.

Point-of-sale and electronic payments will be core services, just like EDI, airline reservation systems, just-in-time (JIT) inventory systems, and computer-integrated manufacturing. It makes no sense to have JIT and other zero-delay operations without accompanying on-line payment systems. JIT inventory is sure to lead to JIT payment.

Image technology will be an operational necessity. Paper documents have become the enemy because they cause organizational complexity and administrative overhead. Image processing applies IT to the cost-intensive operations of document processing.

Work will be distributed and reorganization will be commonplace. Whenever enterprises reorganize, work and information are redistributed. Since many corporate changes will take place, information, communications, and processing must be able to move with the work.

Figure 3-2 Peter Keen's Prognostications for the Mid-1990s (from Keen [1])

1. Every large firm in every industry will have from 25 to 80 percent of its cash flow processed on-line.
2. Electronic data interchange will be the norm.
3. Point-of-sale and electronic payments will be core services.
4. Image technology will be an operational necessity.
5. Work will be distributed, and reorganization will be commonplace.
6. Work will increasingly be location independent.
7. Electronic business partnerships will be standard.
8. Reorganizations will be frequent, not exceptional.

Work will increasingly be location independent. When work is on-line, it can be brought to people using workstations rather than vice versa. Therefore, IT can lead to new sources of organizational advantage.

Electronic business partnerships will be standard. Every large firm will extend its IT infrastructure to encompass customers and suppliers, predicts Keen; therefore, alliance partners may be chosen based on the quality of their IT facilities.

Reorganizations will be frequent, not exceptional. Furthermore, the flexibility of a firm's IT platform will significantly affect how quickly it can reorganize. In short, this platform will be the major determinant of its "business degrees of freedom." The infrastructure determines what products can be sold and which markets and locations can be addressed.

What's interesting about this vision is how much emphasis is placed on electronic communication. The Internet can move this vision closer to reality. But, for that to happen, companies need to work on all three levels: looking inward, looking outward, and looking across.

LOOKING INWARD

As we just noted, looking inward in the early 1990s meant business process reengineering (BPR). Originally, it meant a cross-functional initiative focused on achieving dramatic (that is, 10 to 50 times) performance improvements in one or more business processes. It generally entailed making simultaneous changes in organizational design and culture, and there was heavy emphasis on the use of IT.

Today, however, to many people, the word *reengineering* has a much different meaning. It has come to mean heartless layoffs, massive downsizing, and gut-wrenching restructuring—all in the name of cost reduction. Cost reduction was never the main intent of reengineering, notes Tom Davenport, author of one of the leading reengineering books [2a], in a retrospective article [2b]. What went wrong, says Davenport, was that reengineering forgot the people element. It treated people as if they were just bits and bytes, interchangeable parts that could be reengineered. The result has been widespread fear and anxiety in the workplace. Not a pleasant picture. And thus, a once-promising idea became an inhumane fad. Companies have, indeed, streamlined, but at a tremendous cost.

Redesign Business Processes

Although the term *BPR* has fallen into disrepute among consulting firms—many no longer use the term to sell their services—the basic tenets are still sound. The need still exists to significantly revamp inflexible paper-based processes and hierarchical structures. So it is appropriate to present an overview of the lessons learned from reengineering, beginning with a case of a successful reengineering effort.

CASE EXAMPLE: Prudential Insurance Company of America

Prudential Insurance Company of America, the largest insurance company in the world, was in strong financial shape, yet the insurance business was changing. Management foresaw the need to find new ways to sell insurance and increase customer value.

As described in a Harvard Business School case study prepared under the supervision of Assistant Professor John Sviokla [3], Prudential aimed to double sales by introducing a completely new way of selling insurance, accompanied by a new computer package.

To improve productivity, the agents said they needed more customer contact. Management also wanted to switch from product-based selling to need-based selling. The new approach encompassed both of these goals.

The new approach—called profiling—revolves around obtaining a financial profile of a prospective client, rather than selling the client a specific insurance product. Profiling requires gathering detailed client information and a longer selling process—neither of which is favored by insurance agents.

The agents transmit the client information to a regional computer, where a profiling software package generates a report for each potential client. The report describes the client's financial objectives, current financial situation, and Prudential's recommendations. In addition, the system generates an agent report, which matches the client's goals and needs with Prudential's products.

This new selling approach was rolled out office by office in one region; all new agents were indoctrinated in profiling. The project was driven by a senior sales manager known as a high-volume, high-quality producer; he was held in high esteem by the sales force.

Prudential's transformed approach to selling insurance did double productivity and increase sales. In an early study of 40 agents, commissions averaged $3,053 per call, compared to the company average of $1,700 per sale. Management estimated an overall 10 percent to 30 percent increase in sales. More importantly, the new process got potential clients to think about their financial situation rather than just buy an insurance policy. In short, it added customer value. Finally, time with customers increased—by a large margin, in fact. Formerly, only 30 percent of sales involved two or more client interviews. With profiling, that percentage jumped to 70 percent, and many sales involved three interviews.

Implementation of this reengineered core business process was considered a success; its use steadily increased within Prudential.

What Factors Lead to Success in Reengineering?   Success is not predestined, especially when changing a core business process. But there are conditions that predispose change projects to success or failure, note Barbara Bashein of California State University at San Marcos, Lynne Markus of Claremont Graduate School, and Patricia Riley of the University of Southern California [4]. The three performed a major study on success factors in reengineering projects.

Management's viewpoint is one success factor. Projects that are framed in terms of growth and expansion have a higher chance of success than those aimed at downsizing and cost cutting. People will rally around important strategic initiatives. Not so with cost cutting. A strategic growth perspective generates more enthusiasm and less resistance—both of which are key success factors in reengineering. Full-time team membership is a second precondition for success. The team members should come from both inside and outside the affected process. Insiders help define the current situation, while outsiders, such as customers and suppliers, bring a fresh viewpoint.

In addition to preconditions for success, preconditions for failure also exist. Unfortunately, these are often more numerous and prevalent than the success factors, state Bashein, Markus, and Riley. One such failure factor is choosing the wrong sponsor, that is, someone who is too low in the management ranks, or is getting ready to retire or change jobs, or will not take risks, and so on. Using technology to drive the effort also predisposes failure. Projects that replace an old process rather than address a new market opportunity have a lower success rate, unless they are backed by a highly visible senior line executive and are tied to an important strategic thrust. IT should be viewed as an enabler, not as a key driver, state Bashein, Markus, and Riley.

These preconditions need to be handled before a business process change project is initiated, and before an approach is selected.

Two Approaches: Revolutionary and Evolutionary.   Reengineering has had two main approaches. The radical cross-functional redesign of business processes was espoused by Michael Hammer and James Champy [5]. It stated that companies should start with a clean sheet of paper and redesign the new processes from scratch. This was revolutionary, they admitted, and therefore had only a 30 percent to 50 percent chance of success. But it was the only way to overcome organizational inertia and truly get a significant jump on the competition, they argued.

An oft-cited example was how Ford Motor Company significantly revamped its accounts payable department by instituting "invoiceless payments." (See Figure 3-3.) Rather than pay suppliers when an invoice was received (which required matching 14 data items), Ford switched to paying when goods were received (which required only matching three data items)—as long as those goods were recorded as on order in the company's database. This radical change reduced head count in the accounts payable department by 75 percent and significantly simplified the payment process.

The evolutionary approach, on the other hand, which was espoused by Davenport [2a], somewhat followed the continuous improvement tenets of the total quality management movement. It said, "build on what is currently in place."

Donna Stoddard of Harvard Business School and Sirkka Jarvenpaa of the University of Texas at Austin [7] studied the two opposing views, noted how they

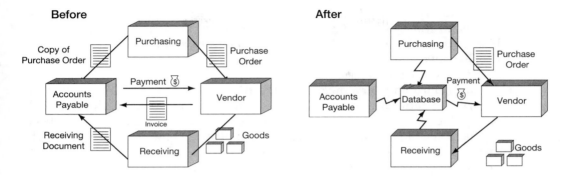

Figure 3-3   Ford's Reengineered Accounts Payable Process (from Hammer [6])

differed, and discussed what actually happened in practice. They uncovered differences between the two approaches in three areas:

- Leadership tactics
- The driving force for significant change
- The attitude toward changing the current structure

Leadership tactics. Evolutionary tactics use insiders. On the other hand, revolutionists say, "bring in outsiders," because insiders are too comfortable with the status quo and they may fear losing power or control. Yet, using leaders who are newcomers to the organization may not be the best approach because they may not have the ear of senior executives and they may underestimate the organization's politics. Using outside consultants also may not work. Too much of the leadership may be delegated to them, leaving a void in the organization. And the consultants may not have more experience than management in fostering change.

No matter which leadership approach was used, Stoddard and Jarvenpaa found that success depended on (1) the sponsor, who must buffer the reengineering team from the rest of the organization, and (2) the champion, who must be cheerleader, coach, and referee. Both must remain intact for the duration of the project.

The driving force for significant change. Evolutionists stress self-improvement tactics; revolutionists believe a crisis is mandatory for people to change. Crises help break inertia, thereby allowing new rules to be created. However, crises can supply their own seeds for failure. If no crisis exists, and management invents one, employees may just see it as another "program of the month." If, on the other hand, a crisis really does exist, the organization may not have the time nor the resources to take on the multiyear effort. So the revolutionary approach is problematic.

The attitude toward changing the current structure. Incremental approaches adapt changes to the current organization, while revolutionary approaches state that the "deep structure" must be changed. Stoddard and Jarvenpaa cite the research of Connie Gersick of UCLA [8], who states that deep structures are an organization's basic assumptions, business practices, culture, and structure. If these do not change, people's behaviors migrate right back to the status quo. People only create new solutions when the problems they face cannot be solved with the existing deep structure.

Stoddard and Jarvenpaa point out that changing such intrinsic elements as an organization's assumptions, values, and practices in a short time may only be possible by starting a new business. Unlearning takes years, at best, and may not happen at all if people can continue their old ways of working. Therefore, the "greenfield approach" (starting from scratch) may be the only viable way medium-size and large firms can make broad changes, surmise the two researchers. Yet, how do they divest the old and invest in the new? It may not be an option.

What actually happened in practice? In their initial study of three firms, Stoddard and Jarvenpaa found that all three combined revolutionary and evolutionary tactics. The broader and more radical the initiative, the more the organization needed revolutionary tactics to keep the project on target. However, although all the reengineering projects in these three companies began with a revolutionary bent, use of revolutionary tactics decreased as the projects moved toward implementation. These projects may be successful, but they may not achieve their full objectives, surmise Stoddard and Jarvenpaa, because radical change probably cannot be expected unless revolutionary tactics are used throughout the change life cycle.

The paradox of managing change is that the keys to success may simultaneously be the breeding grounds of failure. For example, since business processes are generally cross functional, changing these processes tends to encourage large-scope projects. But large-scope projects are likely to be left uncompleted, succumbing to pressures for short-term results. This appears to be what happened in all three of their cases.

Implementation Is the Real Issue. Lynne Markus of Claremont Graduate School does not believe that the key change management issue is deciding whether to take a revolutionary or evolutionary approach. The two may be equally effective, or not.

In an interview, she cited the case study of Rank Xerox written by Thomas Davenport [2c]. Rank Xerox wanted to know if radical change was better than continuous improvement, so one high-priority project followed a radical change approach while another used an incremental change approach. The result? The continuous improvement approach looked better than expected. It was not outperformed by the radical change approach, and it was not as risky.

If you start with a clean sheet of paper, says Markus, you run the risk of designing a structure that cannot be implemented. On the other hand, if your design takes today's structure into consideration, it is more likely to be implementable; although it may not be sufficiently radical to improve business significantly. The most important questions, says Markus, are: How much of the plan gets implemented and how much does the organization have to change to implement the plan?

To address implementation, we return to John Sviokla's study of insurance companies. In addition to Prudential Insurance, he studied three other insurance companies that used the same software package to implement profiling—obtaining financial profiles of prospective clients. Of the four projects, two were successful, two were not. The most striking difference across the organizations, states Sviokla, was how the implementation was managed.

The two firms that eventually dropped profiling after initial experimentation followed a *laissez-faire* approach. Their projects were championed by the head office, a few agents in each office were the initial users, and management allowed agents to adopt the new approach on their own, based on its merits.

In contrast, the two firms that successfully implemented profiling followed a focused approach. Profiling was spearheaded by field sales agents, it was rolled out office by office, management used external events as a lever to encourage use, and, most importantly, management "framed" profiling as the company's way to transform its business.

Framing (or positioning) is a crucial factor in creating success, notes Sviokla, because it "colors" the effort. In the two successful projects, the "owners" were sales agents rather than headquarters staff. And implementation was by office, not by individual agent. People need to learn how to make a new tool or process work in their local environment. Expecting individuals to do this on their own can be too much to ask. Much of the culture on how to use profiling revolved around storytelling, Sviokla observes, which led to the new culture spreading more quickly when everyone in an office began using it together.

In short, the implementation approaches that viewed profiling as a core business process succeeded. Those that viewed it as just another new product did not.

The message that comes through is that although the revolutionary approach ignites imaginations, it may be too risky to succeed in many organizations. Companies that successfully reach their objectives do so with as little risk and employee turmoil as possible.

Lessons Learned. In a speech at a UCLA colloquium sponsored by professor Burt Swanson [9], Michael Vitale, then at Ernst & Young [10] and now at the University of Melbourne, looked back at the lessons learned from reengineering and noted that it worked, even dramatically, in a number of companies. Generally, it has worked when the goal is to redesign work in the "case management" mold—that is, where the division of labor of functional specialists is undone and the people are reorganized into multifunctional teams. Each team is responsible for managing specific cases, generally with some IT support. At the Internal Revenue Service, this change increased the number of cases handled by one group by 100 percent, decreased staff by one-half, increased collections by one-third, and closed two-thirds of the offices.

It is important to match the approach to the desired goal, he notes. Figure 3-4 illustrates four options. The change can either be broad or narrow in scope, and the firm may have the time to make the change or need to make it quickly.

If the change needs to be done quickly and dramatically, and the scope is narrow (lower left), use focused restructuring. This idea came from Ernst &

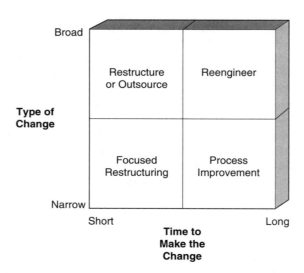

Figure 3-4 Options for Restructuring (adapted from Ernst & Young [10])

Young, said Vitale, and is part of its approach to organizational change. Spinning off a division and acquiring another company are examples of this approach. If the change must be made quickly and is broad in nature (upper left), restructure, recommends Vitale. One way to restructure quickly is to outsource.

If, on the other hand, there is time to make the change and the scope is narrow (lower right), use process improvement. For instance, use total quality management techniques to improve manufacturing. This is a bottom-up approach, so it requires time to analyze the current processes and implement changes. Finally, only a broad-scoped change that can be done slowly (upper right) is a candidate for reengineering, where a fundamentally different approach is needed. This takes several years. Companies that tried to change several major processes all at once failed, as have those who tried to reengineer quickly. Both used the wrong approach.

If reengineering has only been partially successful, yet the need for redesigned business processes still exists, what is a better solution? We believe it is in the emerging field (without a definitive name) where companies redesign processes as if knowledge and expertise matter. Some call it knowledge management; others call it establishing communities of practice. We explore these promising ideas in Chapters 14 and 18. At this juncture, we instead deal with a technology that seems to be moving the ideas of knowledge management further along. It is the intranet.

Capitalize on a Company Intranet

An intranet is an internal company network that takes advantage of the Internet's infrastructure, telecommunication protocols, and browsers.

The benefits of intranets are actually quite phenomenal. By drawing on these standard elements, companies can significantly decrease the cost of providing companywide information and connectivity. One of the most important attributes of intranets is that they support any make or brand of user device—from high-end workstations to desktop PCs, to laptops, to hand-held devices—as well as existing databases and software applications. Such interconnectivity has been the promise of open systems for many years. The Internet provides the connecting standard protocols to make the open system promise real.

Furthermore, investments in a companywide electronic infrastructure are significantly less than building a proprietary network. Companies only need the servers, firewall software on the servers to keep the public from accessing the intranet, modems (the higher speed the better), local links to the Internet, and browser software. The worldwide electronic infrastructure to link disparate machines, as well as the local area networks and workstations, are already in place. Companies also do not have to train employees on different products because the browsers are the standard interface. In fact, because the World Wide Web portion of the Internet basically has one standard authoring language (HTML—HyperText Markup Language), and vendors offer point-and-click tools to easily create Web pages, employees can easily create their own Web pages for whatever purpose they need. As a result, all employees are potentially Web site creators, reducing the IS department's programming bottleneck, while adhering to companywide standards. And companies only need to record information in one place, where it can be kept up-to-date, for access by all employees, no matter where in the world they are located.

Companies are using intranets to provide information on demand for increasing kinds of information: employee directories, procedure manuals, travel and purchasing forms, training guides, technical information, company updates, and so on. As *Business Week* [11] reports, employees are using them to make changes in benefits plans, design cars, share scientific data and research findings, fill out forms, find out about others' projects, "bid" on jobs, schedule meetings, and so on. So not only are intranets being used to put information online, they are being used to provide easier access to existing on-line data.

Although the initial uses were for text and graphics, intranets also support animation and video, interactive forms, links to existing in-house systems, and so on. Generally, the portion of the Internet used for intranets is the Web because its graphical interface and hypermedia links to other Web sites are the easiest to use. Here is a case in point: Home Box Office.

CASE EXAMPLE: Home Box Office

Home Box Office (HBO) licenses and produces movies and other programming for its television subscribers. As Netscape describes in a case study on its home page [12], HBO is using an intranet to give employees access to data for making television programming decisions and to help its sales force sell its programs. It runs Netscape server software on a Silicon Graphics parallel processor system and has a site license for Netscape's Navigator browser.

HBO's Oracle database contains information on every movie ever made (no matter whether it has been shown on HBO or not) or in the process of being made. And it has two to three years of play histories for all the networks. The database tracks a movie's cast, director, distributor, how much money it made, HBO's rights to sell the product, whether or not it is on videocassette, and when it is scheduled to play for the next two years.

In addition, this database is tied to a Nielsen database that tracks ratings of shows on HBO and the other networks. In fact, HBO tracks the entire life cycle of a show, from the time it is released in theaters through when it plays on television, all with audience sizes.

HBO researchers, programmers, and executives need this information to follow their intuition or a set of associations that lead them down a path. Before the Web site, it was only available on paper. Now, with the Web browser, they can easily traverse the entire database. In fact, the Web pages are beginning to reflect the way they think about this information. For more quantitative analysis, HBO employees can use the browser to make SQL queries to the Oracle database and dynamically build a graphical representation of the requested statistics to see trends. They can create a graph of their ratings for a day against the ratings of other networks to quickly see how they did.

Every month, HBO's marketing department rolls out its latest marketing campaign to its 200 to 300 sales representatives, to sell the programs to cable operators around the United States. The department also used to send out large boxes of marketing materials for each campaign, including video promos on cassettes, postcards, ad slicks, billboards, artwork, and marketing reports.

Now all that information is on HBO's intranet, which all its regional sales offices can access with Netscape's browser. As a result, HBO's sales reps can take the art work, ad text, post cards, ad slicks, and QuickTime clips of video promos directly to clients. Costs for printing, duplication of videocassettes, and distribution have been eliminated. But, more importantly, all that information is now at people's fingertips. HBO has increased productivity and employees have more control and flexibility. Furthermore, once the campaign materials are approved, they are immediately on-line. Hence, salespeople know the direction of a campaign earlier and can get to their customers sooner.

Furthermore, HBO is using Web technology as the common interface in its mixed Mac/PC environment for its disparate types of information. Using the browser, employees are able to access increasing amounts of corporate information—network programming, human resources policy manuals, the employee database, organization charts, the cafeteria menu, conference room availability, and the in-house newspaper. With information in a centralized area with a common interface, it is much more exploitable.

Improve Organizational Structure

Besides improving business processes, another internal use of IT is to improve organizational structure. To achieve the electronically based world mentioned earlier by Keen, and to successfully function in it, companies are restructuring themselves to take advantage of the new organizational options afforded by IT. One of Harvard Professor Warren McFarlan's favorite stories is Otis Elevator. He notes that IT allows companies to organize the way they choose. It does not favor centralization or decentralization. Otis Elevator takes advantage of IT organizationally and does both.

CASE EXAMPLE: Otis Elevator

Otis Elevator, with headquarters in Hartford, Connecticut, is the largest U.S. manufacturer of elevators. Although manufacturing is the heart of its business, it makes its money in after-sales service. Traditionally, its 122 branch offices interfaced with customers because mechanics were dispatched from these sites. These offices reported to 20 districts, which created monthly summaries of performance. These districts, in turn, were organized into three zones, which produced total performance reports for the Hartford headquarters one month after receiving reports from districts.

Thus, Otis had a bottom-up structure with autonomy at the branches. The problem with this structure was that some of the branches were well run while others were not. Some dispatched repairmen within 15 minutes, others took 2 to 3 hours and required two or three visits to finish a repair. Furthermore, quality control problems were not visible; they were hidden in the branches.

Centralizing Customer Service. To rectify this situation, all requests for service in the United States were directed to OtisLine—a centralized dispatch center with a database containing a description of each of the 500,000 installed Otis elevators, along with each one's service record for the past year. When a service request is made, the operator displays that elevator's record on the screen and then uses an expert system to choose a mechanic. Within 2 seconds time, the "brick" (beeper) on that mechanic's belt rings (softly, so as not to disturb his or her work), the mechanic views the message on a five-line liquid crystal display, and uses the radio phone to find out more about the problem.

As a sidelight, these "bricks" have had an unexpected effect on company camaraderie. The mechanics have a fairly lonely job; therefore, a radio phone was included with the beeper. Thus, the mechanics can talk to each other; and talk they do—about the line-up for the upcoming softball game, the bowling league,and so on. These phones have facilitated communications, especially informal communications, which the company has wisely allowed to continue.

Due to this centralized information management, Otis can consolidate information about elevator repairs, identify design problems, and redesign its product line faster. Otis also uses the centralized information to flag mechanics' problems and identify who needs more training on repairing certain types of elevators.

Between 1986 and 1990, Otis was able to decrease elevator service problems by 50 percent due to its centralized tracking system. Information technology allowed it to organize this way.

Decentralizing Decision Making. The next iteration in Otis's transformation addressed the question: Why do we need branches, districts, zones, and a corporate office? Why not consolidate districts and zones? These sites were originally established to maintain control, but with the centralized system, the company can allow the branches to manage their own mechanics, while headquarters maintains centralized control over dispatching. Otis thus considered moving more decision making down to the branches. Otis can consider such a reorganization because its control mechanisms have changed—from people to IT. This shift understandably upset company personnel. Therefore, in order to institute further organizational changes, the chairman had to lead because the process of getting buy-in was large.

Otis is continuing its long-term program of architecture development, so as not to give competitors a chance to catch up. In addition to focusing on providing better service, it has reduced its cost structure and moved decision making downward in the organization.

Otis Elevator could be categorized as taking an evolutionary approach to changing its organizational structure using IT. Other companies have been bolder and taken a revolutionary approach. These companies are called *virtual corporations*, by which we mean "there is no there there." Theoretically, they have no headquarters and employees work wherever they happen to be (at home, in a hotel, at a customer site, etc.). In reality, they usually have a headquarters of some sort, and some employees (generally support staff) may work in offices, but most of the employees work wherever they happen to be. Nathaniel Borenstein and 14 others [13] present an interesting example of this approach at First Virtual Holdings.

CASE EXAMPLE: First Virtual Holdings

First Virtual Holdings was formed in early 1994 to facilitate Internet commerce, write Borenstein et al [13]. Its first product, which hit the market in late 1994, was an Internet payment system. The system is unusual because it does not rely on encryption to safeguard transactions; rather it separates nonsensitive information (which may travel over the insecure Internet) from sensitive information (which never travels over the Net because it cannot guarantee proof of identity). Furthermore, its buyer e-mail callback mechanism discourages fraud.

When a buyer submits a transaction to First Virtual to buy something, generally over the Net, First Virtual verifies the buyer's Virtual personal identification number (PIN) in its database. It then sends the buyer an e-mail message asking him or her to confirm the transaction and commit to pay the bill. The buyer need only answer "yes," "no," or "fraud." If the buyer says "yes," First Virtual initiates a financial transaction using the buyer's credit card number, which is stored in First Virtual's database.

As interesting as this first product is, the operation of the company is even more interesting because it began as a purely virtual corporation. Its four founders lived in San Diego, Orange County, Silicon Valley, and northern New Jersey. And its first hires lived in even different places. So, for its first 15 months (a full eight months after it offered its first product), First Virtual had no offices, report Borenstein et al. Employees worked out of their homes. Furthermore, the first services were located all over the United States as well. Marketing was in Washington, DC, public relations in San Diego, the servers were at a secure EDS site in Cleveland, the 800 data number was answered in Atlanta, and the voice 800 number was initially answered in Portland, but now moves around the country. And, to top it off, First Virtual is a Wyoming corporation.

As Borenstein et al. report, it was not easy for the initial staff (and one founder) to adjust to the company's "virtualness" because they were not Internet veterans. And the larger the company grew, the more productivity suffered from communication difficulties among the dispersed staff—not hearing about a meeting, not knowing about an important discussion or its results, not being able to informally brainstorm at a moment's notice, not speaking as a unified voice in public statements, and so on.

In addition, they found it difficult to integrate new hires into this environment, especially if they were not independent people who worked best in the virtual setting. And it was also difficult to supervise people remotely and ensure that they understood "the big picture." Also, First Virtual learned that supervisors had to pay special attention to employee morale, because remote employees can easily feel out of touch.

Despite these problems, its virtual origins were the only way this company would have been formed because none of the founders wanted to move for this speculative venture. Furthermore, since it is an international company, its operations are bound to be spread around; so it can not exist without being virtual.

The employees have found that the best work environment involves projects carried out by small, highly motivated, teams. Teams have created the firm's technologies. And although none of them shared offices, they did meet regularly. Currently, two-day staff meetings are held once a month.

Finally, since it basically operates over the Internet, it performs all customer service via e-mail, which has allowed First Virtual to hire at least one bright but physically handicapped person in the function and allow the reps to live in any part of the United States.

Borenstein et al. report that it is absolutely not necessary to have everyone at one site for doing business on the Internet. However, employees do need to make special efforts in the areas of communication, efficiency, and motivation.

LOOKING OUTWARD

The basis for competing in more and more industries has become sophisticated computer systems. For airlines, hotels, and rental car companies, a computer reservation system is a must—either their own or someone else's. In the drug and hospital wholesaling industries, those with an automated order entry and distribution system have gobbled up those without these systems. In financial markets, computerized trading and settlement systems are replacing open outcry systems. In manufacturing, computer-aided design and engineering, and electronic data interchange are mandatory to compete. And the list goes on. As industry leaders increasingly turn to computerization to concurrently address the four hallmarks of competitiveness—quality, service, innovation, and speed—their competitors must do the same, or find themselves at a disadvantage. Using IT (or any technology) as the basis for a product or a service can, in some cases, be viewed as moving up a series of experience curves.

Jump to a New Experience Curve

Traditionally, an experience curve states that the cost of using a new technology decreases as the firm gains more experience with it. But in *Strategic Choices* [14], Kenneth Primozic, Edward Primozic, and Joe Leben present a new view, which consists of a set of connected curves rather than one continuous learning curve; see Figure 3-5.

Each curve represents fundamentally different technologies—in a product or service as well as in its manufacturing and support processes. Deciding to move to a new curve requires substantial investment, but that decision must often be made among competing technologies, none of which is yet the clear win-

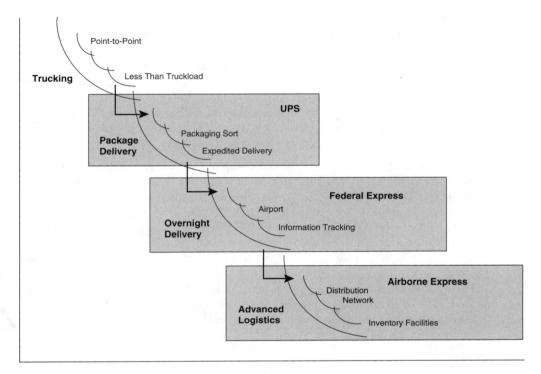

Figure 3-5   The Shipping Industry (adapted from Primozic et al. [14])

ner. A firm that correctly identifies a new market, and the technologies to exploit it, can shift to the new experience curve and successfully open up a new industry segment. However, management sometimes has such an emotional attachment to the current experience curve that it fails to see the next one and loses its market share to swifter competitors. This has repeatedly happened in the computer field. Mainframe manufacturers ignored minicomputer firms. Then minicomputer firms ignored PC manufacturers. Then PC manufacturers ignored operating system firms. And they, in turn, initially ignored the Internet.

To demonstrate this principle of experience curves, and the need to keep up or lose out, consider the authors' example of the shipping industry.

CASE EXAMPLE: The Shipping Industry

Primozic et al. [14] present an intriguing discussion of the shipping industry to illustrate their concept of experience curves. As shown in Figure 3-5, the trucking industry initially shipped two types of truckloads of goods: full truckloads point-to-point and less-than-truckloads (LTL).

One New Industry: Package Delivery. When United Parcel Service (UPS) based its entire business on LTL shipping, a new industry segment was born: package delivery. As a result of this new experience curve, the shipping industry changed, and UPS actually became much larger than the trucking companies because it served a market with far more customers. The new technology that was key to UPS's success—and thus represented this particular experience curve—was efficient package sorting at distribution centers to maximize use of the trucks.

A Second New Industry: Overnight Delivery. UPS, however, did not guarantee a delivery time nor track packages. Federal Express capitalized on these two missing functions, jumped to a new experience curve, and started yet another new industry segment: overnight delivery. Again, Federal Express became larger than UPS because it tapped an even larger market. And in order for UPS and other package carriers to compete, they too had to invest in the technologies to guarantee delivery and track packages.

Needless to say, IT played a crucial role in this experience curve. In fact, the Internet began playing a role when UPS allowed customers to order package pickup and when Federal Express created a Web page that allowed customers to query the whereabouts of a package directly from FedEx's package-tracking database. That Web site, which went live in November 1994, had 12,000 customers a day doing their own package tracking, thus saving FedEx $2 million a year [11].

A Third New Industry: Advanced Logistics. Within the past few years, yet a third industry has emerged: advanced logistics. Due to their distribution network and inventory facilities, overnight delivery services now handle inventory for large corporate clients, and guarantee overnight delivery of these inventoried items. On this experience curve, client companies outsource not only their inventory but also distribution to Federal Express, Airborne Express, and other carriers. Clients include parts suppliers, manufacturers, distributors, retailers, even movie studios (see later in this chapter). Again, as in the other two industries shown, IT plays an integral part in the offered services.

Embed IT in Products and Services

The smaller chips get, the more they are included in products—credit cards, vehicles, pacemakers, you name it. Furthermore, an increasing number of the products now have an important computer-based service component. The shipping industry, again, is a case in point. Information about the location of a package is now a vital, and presumed, part of the package delivery service, and IT is an integral part of that product/service. Here is the well-known case of Federal Express and its strategic underlying system, COSMOS.

CASE EXAMPLE: Federal Express

Federal Express, with headquarters in Memphis, Tennessee, is the leading overnight package carrier in the world. In fact, it started the industry in 1973. Soon after the firm was founded, a companywide computer system was installed as its operational backbone. That system, which has been continually enhanced, is now called COSMOS IIB. As described by Walter Carlson and Barbara McNurlin [15], it runs at the Memphis data center, which is linked to 75 dispatch centers and 24 call centers, which handle customers' calls requesting package pickup (Figure 3-6).

Use of COSMOS IIB starts when a Federal Express courier or station employee scans the bar code on an envelope using the company's hand-held SuperTracker device when a package is picked up. This initial scan automatically time and date stamps the package. When the courier returns to the delivery truck and places the SuperTracker in its "shoe," this information is transmitted to the Memphis data center. The average elapsed time from scanning to posting in the Memphis database is 4 minutes.

From this point on, each time the package changes hands—loaded in the truck, loaded on a plane, unloaded at a distribution center, and so forth—the bar code is scanned, thereby updating the package's location. At

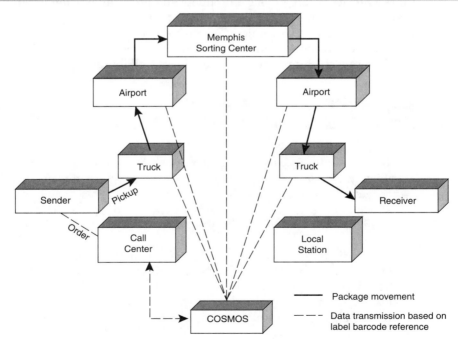

Figure 3-6   COSMOS IIB – Federal Express

any time, the sender or receiver of the package can obtain a status report by calling Federal Express. When the package is delivered and signed for, its delivery time and proof of delivery are recorded.

This entire operation is supported by COSMOS IIB, which gave the company its competitive edge for many years. Over the years, it increasingly has extended its system outward, providing software for large customers to inquire about the location of a package, request pickups, create their own packing labels, and so forth. In 1994, FedEx extended its reach even further by creating a Web site on the Internet. Through that site, any customers, large or small, can query against FedEx's package-tracking database to find out the status of a package. Thousands of customers access that site each day, and not only get the information they need faster but help FedEx save millions of dollars a year.

Make Strategic Use of Marketspace

In this section we will discuss how a company can develop strategic uses of IT on the Internet, or to put it more generally, in marketspace. This intriguing term, *marketspace*, came to our attention in two articles by Jeff Rayport and John Sviokla [16] both of Harvard Business School. They distinguish between market*places*, where physical products and physical location are important, and market*spaces*, where information substitutes for physical products and physical location. Here's an example of a marketspace. It comes from the Wentworth Research Sourcebook, which accompanies Roger Woolfe's IT Management Programme report "Supporting Inter-business Collaboration" [17a].

CASE EXAMPLE: An Automobile Manufacturer

This auto manufacturer has dealerships around the United States, many of which have a satellite dish, as does headquarters. In addition to other uses, these dishes are used by the firm's rental car subsidiary to auction used vehicles to the dealers. These vehicles, which have less than 10,000 miles, are made available to the company's dealers so that they have good, clean used cars to sell.

For 30 minutes at a specified time, an auctioneer is able to sell 60 vehicles on-line. As a car comes up for bid, the dealers view it on the monitors at their premises. They can see it from several directions, read its ratings (on cleanliness and condition), and use a mouse to bid against the other dealers on-line. Headquarters staff monitors the progress of the auction and advises the auctioneer on, say, lowering minimum bids to ensure that every vehicle is sold. The auctions are held once or twice a month.

The dealers have been extremely satisfied with the system because it saves them from having to travel to auctions and they can get good-quality used cars without much effort. And the manufacturer guarantees satisfaction. If, after taking delivery of a vehicle, the dealer decides he or she does not want it, the dealer can send it back.

Rayport and Sviokla, who give numerous marketspace examples, ask several stimulating questions, such as, "How can companies create value in marketspace?" and "How can they create value in marketspace and marketplace concurrently, leveraging off each other?" Their answers revolve around two frameworks. One involves three components that create value. The other is the virtual value chain. We discuss these to stimulate thinking on how companies might take strategic advantage of their information assets and marketspaces, such as the Internet.

Creating Value in Marketspace. Value is created by three components, in either the marketplace or marketspace: content (what is offered), context (how it is offered), and infrastructure (what enables the transaction to occur). For example, a newspaper has content (news, business, sports, and so on), context (format, editorial style, logo), and infrastructure (printing plant, home or office delivery, newsstands). Newspapers bind all three components together to create value.

That's the marketplace. But, argue Rayport and Sviokla, in marketspace, these three elements can be separated, as has been done by America On-Line (AOL). The content of AOL's on-line news service is supplied by national newspapers. The context is provided by AOL's front-end, which allows customers to create their own personal news service by selecting what they want to read. And the infrastructure is composed of telephone lines, networks, PCs, and modems, none of which AOL owns. When you get down to the basics, AOL's "brand" is simply the context.

The point, note Rayport and Sviokla, is that finding strategic uses of IT in marketspace means finding new combinations of content, context, and infrastructure in a world where the interface with the customer has radically changed. A world where customer loyalty (i.e., brand identification) is most likely to be associated with the context deliverer. Once consumers are loyal to that context (brand), any number of kinds of transactions are possible.

To move into this world, managers must shift their thinking from markets defined by physical places to those defined by information spaces, and decide which of the three components they want to address (singly or in combination). For instance, Disney might choose to only address content, as it has with its movies and characters. MasterCard might continue to choose infrastructure and enhance its global presence. The key is to decide where the company adds value and then exploit it.

Virtual Value Chains. The second framework proposed by Rayport and Sviokla for exploiting marketspace is the virtual value chain, which mimics the physical value chain espoused by Michael Porter in the mid-1980s [18]. As shown in Figure 3-7, a value chain for a product or service consists of the major activities that add value during its creation, development, sale, and after-sales service. According to Porter, there are primary activities and support activities in every value chain.

The five primary activities deal with the creation of the product or service, getting it to the buyer, and servicing it afterward. The following activities form the sequence of the value chain:

- Inbound logistics—receiving and handling inputs
- Operations—converting inputs to the product/service
- Outbound logistics—collecting, storing, and distributing the product/service to buyers
- Marketing and sales—offering the means/incentives for buyers to buy the product/service
- Service—enhancing or maintaining the value of the product/service

Four supporting activities underlie the entire value chain:

- Organizational infrastructure
- Human resources management
- Technology development
- Procurement

By studying how a firm performs primary and support activities for each product/service, a firm could, for example, explore how it could add more value at every activity. Alternatively, it could determine where another company adds more value and team up with that firm, essentially outsourcing that activity to a partner.

In the value chain, note Rayport and Sviokla, companies treat information as a support element, not as a source of value itself. To compete in marketspace, however, they need to take a different perspective: use information to create new value for the customer (such as FedEx did in opening up its tracking system to consumers via its Web site). Creating value in marketspace also involves a value chain, but it is a virtual value chain, they say, because the steps are performed with information and through information. At every step in the chain, there are five ways to add value via information: gather it, organize it, select it, synthesize it, or distribute it.

Needless to say, the IS organization should be playing a huge role in marketspace. And in some cases it does. Rayport and Sviokla have observed that companies seem to follow an evolution in using information to add value. First, they create ways to see their physical operations through information. That is, they foster *visibility* of operations, generally through their production systems that allow employees to coordinate activities across the physical value chain,

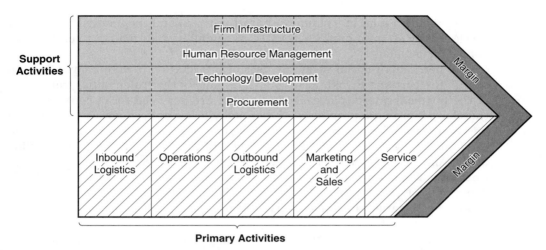

Figure 3-7   The Generic Value Chain (from Porter [5b])

sometimes in ways that lead to competitive advantage. Frito Lay's field employees input information on sales store by store as well as information about competitors' promotions and new competitive products. With all this field data, managers could better schedule production to match demand, route trucks most efficiently, and tailor promotions to suit local buying patterns. Frito Lay could react very quickly to events. This sort of visibility, say Rayport and Sviokla, lays the foundation for a virtual value chain.

Second, companies begin to substitute virtual activities for physical ones; note our preceding automobile manufacturer example. Another example of substituting space for place is demonstrated by companies that institute virtual worldwide teams, such as design teams in the United States, Europe, and Asia that work on designs and prototypes in a virtual information space. Time and space no longer become limitations. The teams can be located anywhere and work can be performed 24 hours a day. And many more designs can be created and tested in a shorter time and for less cost than if created in the physical world. This *mirroring of capabilities*, say Rayport and Sviokla, marks the beginning of creating a parallel virtual value chain.

Third, companies draw on their flow of information to deliver value to customers in new ways. In essence, they create new *space-based customer relationships*. USAA, the insurance company for military officers, exemplifies this third step, say Rayport and Sviokla. For many years, USAA has collected lots of information about its customers, and made it available companywide so that employees could provide advice and answer questions anytime a customer called (visibility). It then discovered it could create customer risk profiles and customize policies. And from that, USAA created new product lines, such as insurance for boat owners (mirroring capabilities). From there, it has expanded beyond insurance, to, say, offer financing to boat purchasers. And, in fact, it even offers to replace a stolen item in a claim theft, rather than send the insured a check—a service many seem to prefer. USAA is managing its information to create new value for customers.

When searching for strategic uses of information (or their virtual value chain), Rayport and Sviokla point out that many of the "rules" differ from those of the physical marketplace. Digital assets are not used up in consumption; therefore, information can be reused in many forms at very low cost. There are new economies of scale, so small companies can effectively compete against large companies, due to lower overhead, while still covering very large geographic areas. And there are new economies of scope, so insurance companies can offer financing and even discount buying programs to policy holders (as USAA is doing). Finally, transaction costs are lower in marketspace; thus, companies can capture information that was not possible to capture in the past (as Frito Lay is doing).

To take advantage of these four changes, however, requires a significant mindshift from supply-side thinking to demand-side thinking, say Rayport and Sviokla. That is, companies need to "sense and respond" rather than "make and sell" products and services. That appears to be a significant strategic opportunity for companies, and IS should play a role in identifying and helping their company take advantage of it.

LOOKING ACROSS

In more and more instances, companies cannot go it alone because the investments are too high and the needed competencies too broad. They must form alliances to compete. One example is the collaboration of the three largest Swiss banks, the three regional Swiss stock exchanges, the national settlement house, and wire services. They built SOFFEX (Swiss Options and Financial Futures Exchange), the world's first fully computerized options and futures exchange. Part of their motivation was to offer Swiss investors a market for Swiss financial instruments. Another motivation was to remain one of Europe's financial centers—that is, to stay competitive with London, Bonn, and Paris. SOFFEX is described in more detail in Andersen Consulting's *Trends in Information Technology* [19].

Another example is the Internet itself. Alliances are becoming the norm because the competencies needed to offer services on the Net include consumer-friendly software, telecommunications, brand-name recognition, banking expertise, and marketing savvy—core competencies not likely to all reside in one company.

Although most such alliances aim at regional, ethnic, or country markets, more of them reach out to other countries. This will be especially true of Internet-based services because the distribution network is in place (at least in developed countries). Furthermore, the fast pace of business is pushing suppliers, companies, and customers to form even tighter supply chains to keep pace with competitive supply chains. And finally, the reengineering of fundamental busi-

ness processes often requires changes in the information flo·
zations, as in the case of Ford's accounts payable syster
require interlinked information systems. Thus, the third ⸝
for interorganizational systems.

Characteristics of Interorganizational Systems

We define interorganizational systems (IOS) as those that require at least
two parties with different objectives to collaborate on the development and operation of a joint computer-based system. Generally, each party develops and operates its portion of the system, but each portion will not work without the other
parts. We see seven characteristics of interorganizational systems that distinguish them from other types of systems (see Figure 3-8).

IOS Require Partners. The main distinguishing characteristic is that it
takes at least two parties to create an IOS. Thus, the partners in the venture
must have a *willingness* to cooperate. This is not always as easy at it sounds,
especially if the resulting new business arrangement requires changing the way
a company operates or is expensive to implement.

The partners must also have the *ability* to perform the work. For example,
the in-house systems in some companies are not able to accept EDI transactions
without a substantial programming effort. EDI is the computer-to-computer
exchange of standard business transactions, including payment/remittance
advice, request for quotations, receiving advice, purchase order change requests,
and even corporate trade payments. Some banks' systems are not able to easily
process the corporate-to-corporate electronic payments that sometimes accompany EDI transactions.

So the partnership required in interorganizational systems is not only
based on readiness but also on willingness and ability.

Standards Play a Key Role. Standards play a major role in permitting
many IOS efforts to get off the ground. Companies want to leverage their system
development investment as much as possible. If they develop a system to work
with one trading partner, they want to reuse portions of that system for other
trading partners.

Figure 3-8 Characteristics of Interorganizational Systems

1. They require "partners."
2. Standards play a key role.
3. Education is important. *nature of partnership*
4. Third parties are often involved.
5. The work must be synchronized.
6. Work processes are often reevaluated.
7. Technical aspects are not the major issue.
8. Efforts often cannot be secretive.

Data and communication standards permit companies to reuse systems they build. If standards are available, companies are willing to build systems that would not be economically feasible for a single use. For internally built systems, the standards can be company policies. For intercompany systems, the standards need to be industry, national, or international standards. Due to the global reach of the Internet, its standards will become increasingly popular for intercompany information exchange.

Education Is Important. The education of potential partners is often more of a hurdle than the technology. In EDI, education of potential trading partners is far and away the biggest problem. While the EDI technology is straightforward, many information systems people (and corporate executives) are not familiar with EDI. In a cooperative effort, the more advanced partner often must pull the other partners along through education.

Third Parties Are Often Involved. Coordination of joint systems often entails using a third party—perhaps to educate people, probably to develop and maintain the standards, and often to provide the links between the separate company systems.

As an example, suppose that you decide to send purchase orders to your suppliers electronically. How are you going to do that? Are you going to have your operations people create a schedule for dialing each supplier's computer at a specified time each day to deliver those orders? What happens if one of those computers is down at the time you are to make the call? What procedure will you use to retransmit the order?

Instead of working out all these details, it might be easier to use a third-party service that provides electronic mailboxes to all these suppliers. You make one call a day to deliver the orders, and the service distributes the purchase orders to the proper mailboxes. When benefits come from volume, the greater the number of trading partners, the more complex interconnecting the systems becomes. Third parties reduce this complexity.

The Work Must Be Synchronized. Another distinguishing feature of interorganizational systems is that the various efforts need to be synchronized. For instance, suppose a number of companies are using a data format standard to exchange invoices electronically. What happens when the standard is updated? How do the companies synchronize their switch to the new version? Synchronization can be achieved by the standards body issuing the updated standard along with a predetermined cut-over date. Then all trading partners know when others will be ready to accept the new version.

There is also the need to synchronize communication schedules, pilot tests, recovery procedures, and the like. Although these are not new problems, the magnitude of the cooperative effort can increase the complexity of the problem, so new solutions may be required.

Work Processes Are Often Reevaluated. IOS appear to nudge companies to reexamine their work procedures. Often, computer systems have been developed to mimic the paper systems they replaced. In IOS, this may be less appropriate. For instance, companies have discovered that sending EDI shipping notices electronically completely eliminates the need to send invoices. Once a shipping notice has been received, and the merchandise has been accepted, the recipient company can issue a payment without an invoice. Obviously, such a change must be acceptable to both trading partners, and both must alter their company procedures.

The element that causes the most changes in company procedures is time. Consciously or unconsciously, most people factor in waiting time when they deal with paper media. For example, the engineers in one company requested paper purchase orders knowing that they had ten days to make changes before the purchase orders would be sent. When the company moved to electronic purchase orders, that ten-day "information float" time disappeared. This caused havoc in the company until the employees adjusted to the new time element. So companies need to be careful when they significantly change the timing in a business process.

Technical Aspects Are Not the Major Issue. In interorganizational systems, technical issues are minor compared to the relationship issues. The major challenge is building the new electronic relationships. As mentioned earlier, this often requires reevaluating current practices and educating many levels of employees.

These, then, are some of the major dimensions added by IOS.

What are companies doing in this area today? The most common answer has been EDI. Increasingly, it will be use of the Internet. Here are two cases to illustrate each. Airborne Express's innovative use of EDI is described in a case that accompanies Wentworth Research's "Sharpening the Customer Focus" report [17b]; Mobil Oil's is a case study that appeared on Netscape's home page [20].

CASE EXAMPLE: Airborne Express

Airborne Express, with headquarters in Seattle, Washington, specializes in providing customized express air service to businesses worldwide. Its hallmark is flexibility. Rather than offer a standard service, it tailors its services to a customer's needs. It offers customer-specific—and even location-specific—pricing. And it offers customer-specific delivery deadlines, such as 9 a.m. delivery to certain locations.

EDI plays a big role in the business. Data for some 55 to 60 percent of its 1 million shipments a day are received electronically from customers. And invoicing for about 70 percent of the shipments is covered by e-invoicing or self-invoicing. Customers that use Airborne's shipping system, or link computer-to-computer, do self-invoicing. They have Airborne's rates in their systems, so, at the end of the day, they print the manifest and pay Airborne without receiving a bill. Only 30 percent of its customers have to be sent a bill.

For large-volume customers, Airborne even does custom system development. A notable example is an alliance with Technicolor. Three years ago, Technicolor decided to branch out beyond film print reproduction and get into film distribution. National Film Service (NSF) had monopolized this business since the 1930s. But its service was slow because it trucked film canisters to movie theaters from 32 antiquated warehouses.

Airborne, its wholly owned subsidiary Advanced Logistics Services (ALS), and Technicolor developed a new system with just two warehouses, one near Hollywood and one colocated with its hub operation and sort facility in Ohio. The new service was introduced in 1993. Today, it has 40 percent of the film distribution market.

This new service draws on a number of IT capabilities. One is an easy-return airbill. When a film is shipped to a theater from a distribution center, a two-way airbill is applied to the film canister. It has a preset return date and the return-to distribution center already printed on it. When the return date arrives, Technicolor's computer sends ALS an electronic pickup request, and it dispatches a driver. (With the competitor, NSF, theaters call for pickup.) When the driver picks up the film, its easy-return airbill is scanned, which automatically updates the canister's previous outbound record in the tracking system and triggers a revenue record in the billing system.

With this two-way distribution capability, Airborne can offer Technicolor "proactive monitoring"—by periodically scanning all Technicolor shipments in its tracking system to find distressed records (records of film deliveries that have, for example, no return deadline). Airborne then notifies Technicolor of these potential problems so that Technicolor can take action to prevent these problems from actually occurring.

There is heavy interaction between the companies' computers. Traditionally, EDI has focused on invoicing and remittance. In this case, however, the schedule is more like real-time EDI, even though the transmissions are batched. The transmissions must occur during narrow time frames, which correspond to the movement of goods. If Technicolor is late in sending the electronic pickup request, the film is not picked up on time nor can it be delivered on time to the theater awaiting it. So there is a narrow window of opportunity that must be met.

The customized cross-company systems have been crucial in allowing Technicolor to compete successfully in this film distribution market. It can offer studios a distribution system that is more dependable and more trackable than the NFS system—and at competitive rates.

CASE EXAMPLE: Mobil Oil

Mobil Oil Corporation is using the World Wide Web to forge closer relationships with employees, customers, business partners, and the general public. In addition to its internal and external Web sites, Mobil is using the Web to develop new channels of communication and commerce with its business partners.

Its external Web site uses Netscape server software running on an IBM AIX system because the company likes Netscape's security features. For its internal Web sites, it also uses Netscape servers. The company is rolling out Netscape Navigator to its employees as part of a standard "common computing environment" for the desktop.

Mobil's internal Web provides employees with three general types of information. The first is employee information such as announcements, reference material, and news posted by individual departments, divisions, and organizations. The second is Internet guidelines and procedures, such as style guides, security guidelines, frequently asked questions, how to get software, how to access the Internet, and how to identify business opportunities to port to a Web server. Third, the intranet provides a platform for divisions and affiliates to put up their own Web applications, maintain bulletin boards, and collaborate on projects. The Exploration Group in New Orleans, for example, puts its daily operations status report on-line for the team to access. Geophysicists, geologists, and reservoir engineers use the Net to share knowledge on research, software, or to point to where information can be found.

Mobil Oil believes that corporate use of the Web will evolve over time. The first phase has been to provide information. The second phase is for running rudimentary electronic commerce. The third is business-to-business commerce, an important use, because it has the ability to reengineer how Mobil conducts business. For example, one Web application provides timely data to Mobil's North American distributors for heavy product lubricants. These distributors are able to access information via a Netscape server, which is fed by Mobil's mainframe applications. This approach saves Mobil money formerly spent on reports and phone calls. It also gives Mobil a way to provide a relatively inexpensive, yet valuable, service to its partners. The company does not need a proprietary network or propriety application. Putting up an application in HTML is very forgiving, Mobil has found, and changes are easy to make. Sophisticated Web applications can be built for thousands of dollars, versus millions for proprietary systems, and in a fraction of the time.

Mobil believes that successful companies will reengineer their business by taking advantage of Internet technology. Companies that do not experiment will be left behind.

Information Links

Speaking at a UCLA symposium [9], Yannis Bakos of the University of California, Irvine, distinguished between two kinds of interorganizational systems: information links and electronic markets.

An *information link* is a value-added chain between two organizations, such as between a manufacturer and a dealer, or a supplier and a buyer, said Bakos. Information links are used after the two organizations have established a relationship.

Two important reasons for creating this form of IOS are (1) to increase *by orders of magnitude* the amount of information passing between the two organizations and (2) to decrease response time between the two enterprises. Operating efficiencies can be increased by reducing the costs of coordination between the parties. Reduced inventory may allow the organizations to migrate to just-in-time operation.

Electronic data interchange (EDI) fits into this information link category. EDI is the computer-to-computer exchange of standard business transactions, including payment/remittance advice, request for quotations, receiving advice, purchase order change requests, and even corporate trade payments, often using the EDI X12 standard.

The most basic EDI level is a *computer-to-computer* link. It causes the least disruption to corporate procedures but it also produces the least benefits. The second level is *application-to-application* EDI, where each trading partner links one or more of its in-house systems to the EDI interface so that there is no manual intervention between transactions that pass between the various company applications. This level disrupts current corporate procedures but can provide greater benefits. The most advanced use of EDI is *changing the way work is performed* in order to gain the greatest benefits. One possible change that some companies are making is to centralize EDI-based functions, such as purchasing. An example of a strategic use of EDI is illustrated by Singapore's TradeNet, which is described in *Trends in Information Technology* [19].

CASE EXAMPLE: TradeNet

In trading, time is money. Given a choice, trading companies will use whichever regional trading city handles their products faster. Singapore is the island national at the tip of the Malaysian peninsula—at the intersection of the Indian and Pacific Oceans. Trading is their lifeblood. They handle $85 billion in trade annually. To remain world-class, the government created TradeNet, an EDI network, to electronically handle all customs transactions in Singapore. It has become a crucial piece of the information communication infrastructure in their nation.

Prior to TradeNet, obtaining customs approvals for shipments from the various Singaporean agencies took days. Couriers stood in line at the agencies to get paper declarations stamped by hand. With TradeNet, approvals take 15 minutes and are available 24 hours a day. TradeNet acts as a hub between government and industry. The government agencies all agreed on one electronic declaration document for import and export control. This form is filled in by importers and exporters on a personal computer and transmitted to the TradeNet computer, which issues the appropriate approvals if the requirements set forth by the agencies are fulfilled. TradeNet has been extremely successful. It went into operation in January 1989, and by mid-1990 it was handling 64 percent of all trading.

The prime motivation for TradeNet was increasing business efficiency to position Singapore as a global business hub. Trading companies now generally get the customs approvals before their shipments arrive in Singapore, so that they do not need to warehouse their goods. Thus, TradeNet has, in some ways, changed how the shippers operate.

Is EDI the Correct Paradigm for the Future? EDI is not a technical issue; it is a managerial and organizational issue. Therefore, when designing a company's electronic intercompany infrastructure, IS management needs to team up with executive and line management. To illustrate this point, at a 1996 colloquium at UCLA [9], John King [21], a professor at the University of California at Irvine, asked the provocative question: Is EDI the right paradigm for intercompany working? As shown in Figure 3-9, traditional EDI links a supplier (on the left) to a retailer (on the right) via a third-party, value-added network. The supplier receives orders from the retailer and then ships the merchandise to the retailer.

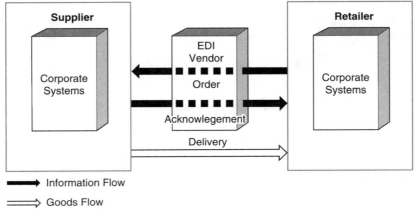

Figure 3-9   Wholesale Electronic Commerce:
The Traditional EDI Model (from King [21])

The new integrated supply chain model, however, is not the same at all. In fact, it is different in kind. As Figure 3-10 illustrates, a customer (A) buys a product and then checks out (G). The point-of-sale system registers the customer's purchase and sends the information about the purchase to the corporate system (B). This retailer corporate system then automatically relays that purchase information to the supplier's corporate computer (C), which it forwards to a manufacturing site and a distribution center. The supplier's manufacturing plant uses the data to produce more of the product (D), and the distribution center uses the data to restock the retailer's shelves (E and F).

The difference, says King, is that the retailer never touches the product. Furthermore, it never owns the product. The arrangement is actually a form of consignment. This point is important, he says, because it has redefined retailing. If retailing is defined as "the engagement in selling goods to ultimate consumers for personal or household consumption," then the retailer is not "the retailer," the supplier is. The retailer becomes the point of presence for consumers to access the supplier's products, and for this the retailer charges an access fee. This is not traditional EDI. It is a new kind of relationship. And it has different fundamentals.

Therefore, says King, companies that plan to enter the world of electronic commerce need to make sure they have the fundamentals right so that they build systems that carry out their business goals. Thus, IS management must work with executive management to get the paradigm right.

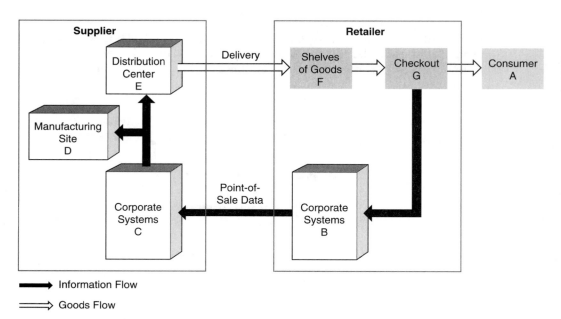

Figure 3-10   Wholesale Electronic Commerce: The Integrated
Supply Chain Model (from King [21])

Design Collaboration. An intriguing and increasingly common information link occurs in the design and delivery of complex products, such as airplanes
and automobiles. As Bakos points out, it links two organizations in a supply
chain. A case in point is Rockwell International's link to Boeing, as described in a
case study accompanying Wentworth Research's "Supporting Inter-Business
Collaboration" report [17a].

CASE EXAMPLE: Rockwell International

Rockwell is a U.S.-based engineering company with interests in the aerospace and automotive industries with a spectrum of interbusiness applications. It is, for example, a subcontractor to Boeing for the new-generation
777 airplane. Boeing decided from the outset that it would design the entire
airplane electronically, so all contractors have had to adhere to Boeing's chosen platform—the CATIA 3-D CAD system. Boeing helped to set up the
CAD system at Rockwell so that Rockwell engineers' designs, which were
subsets of Boeing designs, would be resident on the CATIA workstations
and would interact with Boeing's large CATIA mainframe system in Seattle.

Rockwell, like all the other 777 subcontractors, had to install the workstations, put in high-speed circuits to Seattle, and ensure they remained on
the same version of CATIA as Boeing. Rockwell was as responsive as Boeing needed because it wanted its own engineers to feel they were extensions
of Boeing's development team. Boeing wanted the same thing. As a result,
parts of Rockwell look more like Boeing than Rockwell—they became like a
virtual extension of Boeing. The improvement in performance is vast.
Rockwell can now probably turn around designs in an afternoon; formerly
it took 30 to 40 days.

With such "intimate" interbusiness applications, the two companies
use the same database simultaneously. Data integrity is obviously a concern, but so is performance because people from both companies contend
for access to the same database. Furthermore, Rockwell has had to change
its processes. It is not just a question of getting the right computers and
software; it requires Rockwell to spend enough time with the other company to understand its processes and adapt to them—in essence, to become
an extension of them. This means it must have many different IT platforms
and be flexible so it can adapt to customers' requirements. Rockwell takes
the view that it will do whatever the customer says it wants. Its goal is to be
the easiest and most flexible supplier to deal with.

Tight versus Loose Linkage

As Roger Woolfe of Wentworth Research [17a] points out, the actions of the
IS department in the information-linking type of IOS depend on the tightness of
the integration between the two organizations (see Figure 3-11). Loose integra-

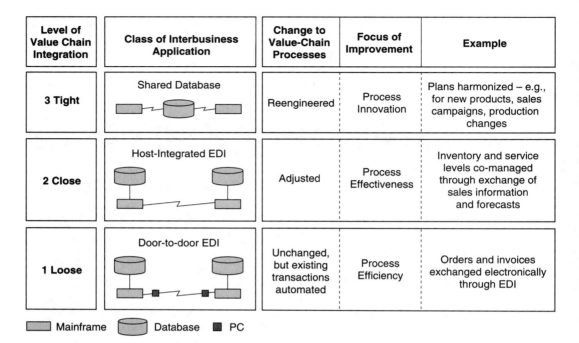

Level of Value Chain Integration	Class of Interbusiness Application	Change to Value-Chain Processes	Focus of Improvement	Example
3 Tight	Shared Database	Reengineered	Process Innovation	Plans harmonized – e.g., for new products, sales campaigns, production changes
2 Close	Host-Integrated EDI	Adjusted	Process Effectiveness	Inventory and service levels co-managed through exchange of sales information and forecasts
1 Loose	Door-to-door EDI	Unchanged, but existing transactions automated	Process Efficiency	Orders and invoices exchanged electronically through EDI

▭ Mainframe   ⬭ Database   ■ PC

Figure 3-11   Spectrum of Value Chain Integration (from Wentworth Research [17a])

tion occurs when companies only want to increase efficiency of their processes, probably by exchanging orders and invoices via EDI. In these cases, PC connections between the two can suffice. There need be no changes to their processes and no direct links into each other's systems, just door-to-door delivery of data.

Close integration moves one step higher and aims at improving process effectiveness, perhaps through exchanges of sales information and forecasts, so that the supplier and company can, in some ways, comanage inventory and service levels. The job for the IS department at this level requires creating interfaces between the affected applications, which are probably on the corporate mainframe, and laying down rules for passing data to each other. This level of information linking is fairly common in some industries, and the requisite interface software is available.

Tight integration depends on database sharing, which aims at creating new processes and emphasizes sharing of data, not just passing data between two companies. In fact, companies collaborate in new ways. For instance, retailers and manufacturers might collaborate on product introductions or promotions. Or, as in the case of Rockwell and Boeing, companies may collaborate in design. These relationships require a high level of trust. The job for IS is to jointly design the database to be shared, and perhaps even use identical platforms, as Rockwell has done. Furthermore, the processes within both companies probably need to be reengineered to work well together. Since information technology plays an integral part in these new processes, the IS department needs to be involved in the redesign effort.

Electronic Markets

An *electronic market,* said Bakos, is a computerized marketplace with several buyers and several sellers. Generally, someone acts as the market intermediary. Examples of these intermediaries are airline reservation systems and computerized security trading systems.

The goals of electronic markets are (1) to reduce the search costs of buyers so they can more easily compare offerings, and (2) to create a critical mass—the more organizations connected, the more valuable the system to each participant.

Electronic markets threaten the monopolistic power of suppliers and promote price competition as well as product differentiation. Competitive advantage for suppliers in an electronic market depends on their bargaining power and their operating efficiency—as compared to their competitors.

Most interorganizational systems are hybrids of these two forms, says Bakos, information links and electronic markets.

Following is an example of an electronic market, Telcot, with many buyers and sellers.

CASE EXAMPLE: Telcot

The Plains Cotton Cooperative Association (PCCA), in Lubbock, Texas, was founded in 1953 to buy cotton from its member growers in Texas and Oklahoma, and resell it to textile mills. By the late 1960s, PCCA was buying over 90 percent of its members' cotton because it had assumed the risk of reselling the cotton, according to Lindsey, Cheney, Kasper, and Ives [22].

In other parts of the country, the growers shouldered the risk by selling their cotton in pools and receiving the average price of a type of cotton once it had been sold. This arrangement allowed everyone to compete equally. But the majority of U.S. cotton growers dealt with independent brokers.

By the early 1970s, PCCA was in significant trouble, handling only 20 percent of its members' cotton, because the members could obtain higher prices by dealing directly with independent brokers. To survive, PCCA had to provide better service than these dealers. To do this, PCCA installed a computerized market-making system for cotton: Telcot. Telcot acts much like a stock exchange. The venture was risky because telecommunications-based systems were in their infancy in 1975, especially in rural areas. Furthermore, PCCA's users were computer novices. However, the system was a success due to the enhanced marketing features it offered.

Previously, growers called gin operators to figure out asking prices for specific lots of cotton. These telephone negotiations were time consuming and not always fair because (1) gin operators received commissions for arranging sales, and (2) buyers would call gin operators about their crops without intending to sell, just to compare price quotes. Telcot eliminated this telephoning by providing an electronic market where the growers could offer their cotton using several options:

- Regular order—offer their cotton for 15 minutes on the exchange and accept the highest bid about the preset minimum price,
- Firm offer—offer their cotton for a firm price,
- Loan advance—receive a cash advance based on a government standard price.

Since 1975, Telcot has continued to enhance the marketing features, such as permitting buyers to make counteroffers or describe the cotton they want to buy.

Telcot has transformed the cotton business in Texas and Oklahoma. Over 200 cotton gins, 40 buyers, and 20,000 cotton growers use PCs to access PCCA's IBM 3090 mainframe to execute some 115,000 on-line transactions a day. From 1975 to 1990, due to the success of Telcot, PCCA grew from a $50-million to a $500-million business.

In 1990, Telcot

- Began communicating to gins via FM radio and satellite, to overcome land-line transmission problems,
- Implemented an electronic title exchange, similar to electronic funds transfer, making a warehouse receipt a legal document,
- Started utilizing bar codes on cotton bales for EDI, to transfer information between gins, warehouses, and cotton mills.

In short, it has continued to innovate, demonstrating that the strategic use of IT is more important than the technology itself, providing ever-increasing flexibility to both cotton buyers and sellers.

CONCLUSION

Information technology is a strategic asset that can be used in three ways: looking inward to redesign business processes to improve competitiveness, looking outward to incorporate products and services, and looking across to link with other organizations. The most exciting development in this arena is the realization that a new world is emerging out there, the world of the marketspace. It is increasingly giving companies new options in all three arenas, allowing them to communicate in new ways with customers, add valuable information services to their products, and work in virtual spaces across organizational boundaries. This new world also presents the IS department with an entirely new workspace and a greater role in company success, if it takes advantage of the opportunity.

QUESTIONS AND EXERCISES

REVIEW QUESTIONS

1. List Keen's projections for the mid-1990s.
2. How did Prudential redesign its insurance-selling process?
3. What two approaches to reengineering have companies taken? What actually happened in practice, according to Stoddard and Jarvenpaa?
4. When should reengineering be used, according to Vitale?
5. How is Home Box Office using an intranet?
6. How has Otis Elevator restructured itself?
7. What are experience curves, according to Primozic et al.?
8. What three components create value in marketspace, according to Rayport and Sviokla?
9. What are the nine components in Porter's value chain?
10. What are the characteristics of interorganizational systems?
11. What are two kinds of interorganizational systems, according to Bakos?
12. Describe the new integrated supply chain model of electronic commerce as defined by King.
13. What are the three levels of links between companies, according to Woolfe, and what does the IS department need to do for each one?

DISCUSSION QUESTIONS

1. Using systems for competitive purposes is no different from traditional systems. Do you agree or disagree? Discuss.
2. Reengineering business processes is no different from installing systems traditionally. Do you agree or disagree? Discuss.
3. When companies work in collusion with each other, they may violate antitrust laws. How might such laws impede the development of interorganizational systems?
4. John King is right, EDI is the old paradigm. It is also not appropriate for electronic commerce on the Internet. Do you agree or disagree? Discuss.

EXERCISES

1. Find three articles or descriptions in journals, business periodicals, or the Internet that describe how three companies use the Internet for competitive purposes. Describe these uses to the class. Why do you find them interesting?
2. Find two articles on reengineering business processes. What principles and lessons do they present that differ from the ones in this chapter? What roles did the information systems department play?
3. Find an article about an electronic marketplace. Describe it to the class. How does it differ from a physical marketplace?
4. Visit the chief information officer of a local firm. What systems has the company developed for competitive purposes? Is it reengineering any of its business processes? Does it have an intranet? Does it have any interorganizational systems? If so, briefly explain what the company is doing in each of these four areas. How has the IS department teamed up with executive management or line management to design either an interorganizational system or a new business process?
5. View the Web version of this chapter at http://www.earthlink.net/~bmcnurlin. Find three Websites to link to the chapter and explain in a short paragraph why each

should be incorporated into the Web version. Submit to your professor, who may submit the three best link recommendations from the class to the authors along with the names of the people (or class) who should be given credit for the suggestions.

REFERENCES

1. KEEN, PETER G. W., *Shaping the Future: Business Design Through Information Technology*, Harvard Business School Press, 1991.
2. DAVENPORT, THOMAS, University of Texas at Austin:
   a. *Process Innovation*, Harvard Business Press, 1993.
   b. "Why Reengineering Failed: The Fad That Forgot People," *Fast Company,* Premier Issue, 1995, pp. 70–74.
   c. "Rank Xerox," HBS Case Study, #9-192-071 and 072, Harvard Business School, Cambridge, MA.
3. "CLIENT PROFILING: The Prudential Insurance Company of America," HBS Case Study N9-193-084, February 19, 1993, Harvard Business School, Cambridge, MA and "Managing a transformational technology: A field study of the introduction of profiling," HBS Working Paper 93-059, March 25, 1993.
4. BASHEIN, BARBARA, M. LYNNE MARKUS, and PATRICIA RILEY, "Business Process Reengineering: Preconditions for Success (and Failure)," *Journal of Information Systems Management*, Summer 1995.
5. HAMMER, MICHAEL and JAMES CHAMPY, *Reengineering the Corporation*, HarperBusiness, New York, 1993.
6. HAMMER, MICHAEL, "Reengineering Work: Don't Automate, Obliterate," *Harvard Business Review*, July–August 1990, pp. 104–112.
7. STODDARD, DONNA and SIRKKA JARVENPAA, "Business Process Reengineering: Tactics for Managing Radical Change," Working Paper, September 9, 1993.
8. GERSICK, CONNIE, "Revolutionary Change Theories: A Multilevel Exploration of the Punctuated Equilibrium Paradigm," *Academy of Management Review*, 16, 1, 1991, pp. 10–36.
9. UCLA IS COLLOQUIUM, coordinated by E. Burton Swanson, is held (basically) every other Thursday during the school year at the Anderson School at UCLA.
10. ERNST & YOUNG, Center for Business Innovation, One Walnut St., Boston, MA 02108.
11. "SPECIAL REPORT: HERE COMES THE INTRANET," *Business Week*, February 26, 1996, pp. 76–84.
12. "HOME BOX OFFICE GETS FASTER ACCESS TO CRUCIAL INFORMATION WITH NETSCAPE," adapted from a case study on Netscape's Web site: http://www.netscape.com, March 1996. Netscape, 501 E. Middlefield Rd., Mountain View, CA 94043.
13. BORENSTEIN, NATHANIEL ET AL., "Perils and Pitfalls of Practical Cybercommerce," *Communications of the ACM*, June 1996, pp. 36–44.
14. PRIMOZIC, KENNETH, EDWARD PRIMOZIC, and JOE LEBEN, *Strategic Choices: Supremacy, Survival, or Sayonara*, McGraw-Hill, New York, 1991, 272 pages.
15. CARLSON, WALTER and BARBARA MCNURLIN, *Uncovering the Information Technology Payoffs*, United Communications Group, 11300 Rockville Pike, Suite 1100, Rockville, MD 20852, 1992.

16. RAYPORT, JEFFREY and JOHN SVIOKLA, "Managing in the Marketspace," *Harvard Business Review*, Cambridge, MA, November/December 1994, pp. 141–150, and "Exploiting the Virtual Value Chain," November/December 1995, pp. 75–85.

17. IT MANAGEMENT PROGRAMME REPORT, Wentworth Research, Park House, Wick Road, Egham, England TW20 OHW, http://www.wentworth.co.uk.

   a. Woolfe, Roger, "Supporting Inter-Business Collaboration," September 1995, with accompanying Sourcebook cases of Rockwell International and the automobile manufacturer.

   b. Flint, David, "Sharpening the Customer Focus," March 1996, with accompanying Sourcebook case of Airborne Express.

18. PORTER, MICHAEL, *Competitive Advantage*, The Free Press, New York, 1985.

19. McNURLIN, BARBARA (ED.), *Trends in Information Technology,* Andersen Consulting (69 W. Washington, Chicago, IL 60602), Fall 1991.

20. "THE WEB FORGES NEW LINKS BETWEEN MOBIL AND ITS CUSTOMERS, PARTNERS, AND EMPLOYEES," a case study on Netscape's Web site: http://www.netscape.com, March 1996. Netscape, 501 E. Middlefield Rd., Mountain View, CA 94043.

21. KING, JOHN L., "High-Level Requirements for Electronic Commerce Support Systems," Technical Report, Information and Computer Science Department, University of California, Irvine, CA 1996.

22. LINDSEY, D., P. CHENEY, G. KASPER, and B. IVES, "Telcot: An Application of Information Technology for Competitive Advantage in the Cotton Industry," *MIS Quarterly*, December 1990, pp. 347–357.

FOUR

Information
Systems
Planning

INTRODUCTION

We noted in Chapter 1 that IS management is getting more difficult and more important at the same time. In systems planning, especially strategic systems planning, that is true in spades. On the one hand, the technology is changing so fast that it is tempting to say, "Why bother?" On the other hand, organizations' survival is becoming so dependent on technology that planning its effective use is a matter of organizational life and death.

How can this apparent paradox be resolved? The good news is that a variety of approaches, tools, and mechanisms has been developed to assist in systems planning. The bad news is that there is no recognized "best" way to go about it. The result is that most organizations use more than one approach or tool to assist in this very important information systems management function.

It is important to establish the appropriate mindset for planning. Some managers feel that planning means determining what decisions to make in the future. But that is not the correct mindset. Rather, planning means developing a view of the future that guides decision making today. This seemingly subtle difference turns out to be significant in the way that managers approach and execute the planning process.

In this chapter we first consider some of the characteristics and issues in planning in general, and systems planning in particular. We notice the difference in planning for operational, tactical, and strategic purposes, and emphasize

Figure 4-1 Three Types of Planning

Horizon	Focus	Issues	Primary Responsibility
3–5 Years	Strategic	Vision, Architecture, Business Goals	Senior Management CIO
1–2 Years	Tactical	Resource Allocation, Project Selection	Middle Managers IS Line Partners Steering Committee
6 Months–1 Year	Operational	Project Management, Meeting Time and Budget Targets	IS Professionals Line Managers Partners

that our concern is primarily with the latter. Finally, we examine several tools and approaches that have been used for strategic systems planning.

Types of Planning

Planning is usually defined in three forms, corresponding to three planning horizons. Figure 4-1 summarizes these three planning types and some of their characteristics. Our emphasis in this chapter is strategic planning—the top row. In Chapter 3 we defined strategic as "having a significant, long-term impact on the growth rate, industry, and revenue" of an organization. Strategic systems planning deals with planning for the use of information systems and technology for strategic purposes.

Generally strategic planning is thought to have a longer planning horizon than operational or tactical planning, as shown in Figure 4-1. Although this is usually true, some shorter-term developments can have a strategic impact. The World Wide Web has a strategic impact on many organizations in just one to two years. Nevertheless, strategic planning attempts to form a view of the future three to five years out, in order to help determine what should be done now.

Although system planning efforts are usually called strategic, there has been a definite shift in the emphasis over the past several years. Figure 4-2 illustrates some of these shifts. The basic trend is to move from a tactical midrange focus to a truly strategic effort.

Figure 4-2 Shifts in Systems Planning Emphasis

Then	Now
Tactical	Strategic
Project Selection	Project Integration
Building Infrastructure as a Project	Building Infrastructure as a Process
Steering Committees	CIO/Senior Executive Partnership

Why Is Planning So Difficult?

There are some fundamental reasons why systems planning is so difficult. Here is a laundry list of the issues in strategic systems planning.

Aligning Business Goals and Systems Plans. Obviously, the strategic systems plan needs to support and align with business goals. Unfortunately, strategic business goals are often thought to be extremely sensitive. As a result, the CIO, who is often not felt to be a full member of the top-management team, is left out of the inner circle which develops these plans. Fortunately, there is a strong trend for the systems planning responsibility to be shared among the CIO and other members of senior management. A recent article in the *Harvard Business Review* entitled "The End of Delegation" [1] contains statements from several CEOs asserting the importance of direct involvement by CEOs in the systems planning processes.

Rapidly Changing Technologies. How can you plan when the technology is changing so rapidly? One answer is continuous planning. Gone are the days of an annual planning cycle done in the last few months of the year, then put aside until the following year. The planning process first forms a best-available vision of the future on which to base current decisions. Then the technology is monitored to see if that future vision is changing. When it does, adjustments in current decisions are made. Some organizations have an advanced technology group charged with the responsibility for watching and evaluating new technologies.

Projects versus Portfolios. Another issue is the shift in emphasis from project selection to portfolio development. This requires a more sophisticated form of planning because projects must be evaluated on more than their individual merits. How they fit into other projects and how they "balance" the portfolio of projects become more important measures. The investment strategy analysis approach described later is an example of this approach.

Infrastructure Development. Everyone knows intuitively that the development of infrastructure is crucial. It is extremely difficult, however, to get funding *just* to develop or improve infrastructure. Often it must be done under the auspices of a large application development project. The challenge then is to develop improved applications over time so that the infrastructure improves over time. In the most recent major infrastructure development, some organizations converted to a client/server architecture as part of a major funded project. But one CIO told us he could not convince the board of directors to fund the conversion to client/server directly; he had to do it as part of a series of systems development projects. Obviously, this requirement increases the difficulty of the systems planning process.

Joint Responsibility. It is often easier to do something yourself than to get a coalition to do it. But systems planning initiated by and driven by the CIO is not proving as effective as systems planning done by a full partnership among the CIO, CEO, and other senior managers.

Other Planning Issues. There are several other characteristics of planning in general that make strategic systems planning difficult. There is always a tension between top-down and bottom-up approaches. The planning must strike a balance between radical change and continuous improvement. Most organizations have developed a planning "culture" with which systems planning must be compatible. Taken together, this sampling of issues clearly illustrates why systems planning is a difficult but crucial task.

TOOLS AND APPROACHES FOR SYSTEMS PLANNING

Due to the importance and the difficulty of systems planning, it is valuable to have a framework or methodology to guide the process. Over the years, a number of approaches have been proposed to help information systems managers do a better job of planning. The approaches presented here take different views of information systems planning. Some look at the assimilation of IT in organizations, some focus on defining information needs, and others discuss categorizing applications systems. The seven planning approaches and techniques we will discuss are:

- Stages of Growth
- Critical Success Factors
- Investment Strategy Analysis
- The Scenario Approach to Planning
- Linkage Analysis Planning
- Creative Problem-Solving Approaches
- Enterprise Modeling

Stages of Growth

Richard Nolan and Chuck Gibson published a landmark paper in 1974 entitled "Managing the Four Stages of EDP Growth " [2]. In it they observed that many organizations go through four stages in the introduction and assimilation of new technology. Since that time, Nolan has elaborated on the theory by adding two more stages [3]. Although the bases of the theory have come under some criticism [4], the basic ideas still provide a useful framework for information systems planning. Here is a brief description of the four stages.

Stage One: Early Successes. The first stage is the beginning use of a new technology. While some stumbling generally occurs, early successes lead to increased interest and experimentation.

Stage Two: Proliferation. Based on the early successes, interest grows rapidly as new products and/or services based on the technology come to the marketplace. These are tried out in a variety of applications. This proliferation stage is the learning period for the field, both for uses and for new products and services.

Stage Three: Control of Proliferation. Eventually it becomes apparent that the proliferation must be controlled. Management begins to feel that the costs of using the new technology are too high and the variety of approaches generates waste. The integration of systems is attempted but proves difficult, and suppliers begin efforts toward standardization.

Stage Four: Mature Use. At this stage, the use of the particular new technology might be considered mature. The stage has been set for introducing still other new technologies, wherein the pattern is repeated. In fact, an organization can be in several stages simultaneously, for different technologies.

Stages of Growth Modified. Cash et al. [5] discuss a somewhat modified version of the four stages. Their four phases (stages) are

1. Identification and initial investment
2. Experimentation and learning
3. Management control
4. Widespread technology transfer

This version of the four phases casts the important second phase in a somewhat different light. Nolan and Gibson gave a negative name—proliferation—to this phase, leaving the impression that users are being almost irresponsible by adopting the new technology too rapidly. Cash et al. point out that this is the stage when experimentation and learning take place; it is a trial-and-error phase. If too much control is exerted too soon, important new uses of the technology can be killed off.

They believe that the value of this "stage theory" approach is that it gives a better understanding of the factors that affect the formulation of information systems strategy and, therefore, it will allow managers to do a better planning job. Since the management principles differ from one stage to another, and since different technologies are in different stages at any point in time, the stage model is an important aid to the systems planning process.

Critical Success Factors

John Rockart is the director of the Center for Information Systems Research (CISR) at the Sloan School of Management, Massachusetts Institute of Technology. In 1977, Rockart and his colleagues began developing a method for defining executive information needs. The result of their work is the Critical Success Factors (CSF) method [6]. It focuses on individual managers and their current information needs, be it factual or opinion information. The CSF method can be used to help companies identify information systems they need to develop.

For each executive, critical success factors are the few key areas of the job where things must go right in order for the organization to flourish. There are usually fewer than ten of these factors that any one executive should monitor. Furthermore, they are very time dependent, so they should be reexamined as often as necessary to keep abreast of the current business climate. These key areas should receive constant attention from executives, yet CISR research found that most managers had not explicitly identified these crucial factors.

Rockart finds that there are four sources for these factors. One source is the *industry* that the business is in. Each industry has CSFs that are relevant to any company in it. A second source is the *company itself* and its situation within the industry. Actions by a few large, dominant companies in an industry will most likely provide one or more CSFs for small companies in that industry. Furthermore, several companies may have the same CSFs but, at the same time, have different priorities for those factors.

A third source of CSFs is the *environment*, such as consumer trends, the economy, and political factors of the country (or countries) that the company operates in. A prime example used by Rockart is that, prior to 1973, virtually no chief executive would have listed "energy supply availability" as a CSF. Following the oil embargo, however, many executives began monitoring this factor very closely. The fourth source is *temporal* organizational factors—areas of company activity that normally do not warrant concern but which are currently unacceptable and need attention. A case of far too much or far too little inventory might classify as a CSF for a short time.

In addition to these four sources, Rockart found two types of CSFs. One he calls *monitoring*—that is, keeping abreast of ongoing operations. The second he calls *building*—tracking progress of "programs for change" initiated by the executive. The higher an executive is in the organization, the more "building" CSFs are usually on his or her list. Rockart sees CSFs varying from organization to organization, from time period to time period, and from manager to manager.

One way to use the CSF method is to list the corporate objectives and goals for the year. These are then used to determine which factors are critical for accomplishing the objectives. Then two or three prime measures for each factor are determined. Discovering the measures is the most time-consuming portion of this stage, he says. Some measures use hard, factual data; these are the ones most quickly identified. Others use softer measures, such as opinions, perceptions, and hunches; these take more analysis to uncover their appropriate sources.

Investment Strategy Analysis

Another framework to support systems planning is based on somewhat traditional techniques of portfolio planning and investment analysis. David Norton, one of the founders of Nolan, Norton & Co., describes one approach his company uses to help its clients plan their investment strategy for information systems [7]. Norton believes there are four major types of applications:

1. Institutional procedures—the processing of internal transactions, as represented by many of today's mainline systems
2. Professional support systems, such as engineering support, managerial decision-making support, and similar activities
3. Physical automation
4. Systems that serve users outside the company, such as customers and suppliers

In addition, there will continue to be expenditures to provide the basic technical infrastructure to permit the development and use of these applications. Network protocols, database standards, and computing platforms are prime examples.

To build a framework for an investment strategy, set up a two-dimensional table, suggests Norton, with these four types of systems, plus the infrastructure, as the column headings. The rows are the main functional components of the business, such as research and development, manufacturing, marketing, and other service and support functions. Figure 4-3 illustrates this approach.

To demonstrate how the analysis works, Norton uses figures from two aerospace manufacturing firms. In the base year, each spent about 3.5 percent of sales on information systems. For an aerospace manufacturing company, the functional components might be engineering, quality assurance, manufacturing, finance, and administration.

As shown in Figure 4-4, seven years later, Company Alpha was spending 6.0 percent of sales on all information systems, with 2.4 percent of sales for professional support. Company Beta's overall expenditure had dropped to 2.3 percent of sales, with only 0.4 percent of sales for professional support. These patterns evolved because Company Alpha had decided that its strategic advantage lay in increasing the productivity of its key resource—its engineers and other professionals. The company gave substantial IT support to the engineers. Company Beta gave much less support to its engineers. (Since neither company spent

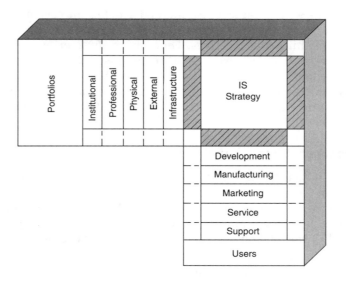

Portfolios: Describe the allocation of information systems resources
             for different classes of applications.

Users: Describe the allocation of information systems resources
             to different classes of users.

Figure 4-3   Information Systems Products and Customers (from Norton [7])

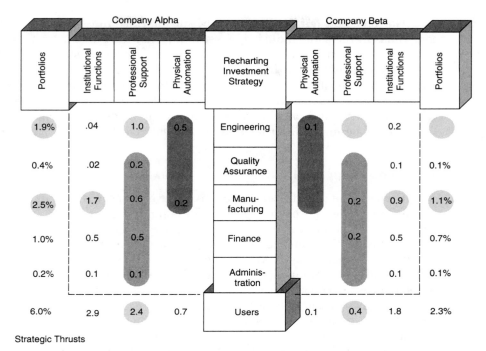

Portfolios	Institutional Functions	Professional Support	Physical Automation	Recharting Investment Strategy	Physical Automation	Professional Support	Institutional Functions	Portfolios
1.9%	.04	1.0	0.5	Engineering	0.1		0.2	
0.4%	.02	0.2		Quality Assurance			0.1	0.1%
2.5%	1.7	0.6	0.2	Manufacturing		0.2	0.9	1.1%
1.0%	0.5	0.5		Finance		0.2	0.5	0.7%
0.2%	0.1	0.1		Administration			0.1	0.1%
6.0%	2.9	2.4	0.7	Users	0.1	0.4	1.8	2.3%

Strategic Thrusts

1 Alpha is investing heavily in refurbishing its manufacturing systems around integrated database technology.

2 Alpha is investing heavily in the productivity of its engineers.

3 Alpha is investing generically in the productivity of all professional groups.

4 Alpha is investing heavily in CAD/CAM technology to improve the linkage between engineering and manufacturing.

Figure 4-4   Patterns of Spending by Portfolio Segment (from Norton [7])

much for external systems or for building a technical infrastructure, these categories are omitted from the columns in Figure 4-4).

As Norton points out, Company Alpha believed IT was a strategic tool, so the company encouraged its innovative use in four ways:

1. Renovate existing manufacturing systems around database technology.
2. Invest heavily in increasing the productivity of the engineers.
3. Foster innovation among the professional staff.
4. Invest heavily in computer-aided design and manufacturing technology.

Company Beta, on the other hand, viewed IT as an overhead item. Its use of IT followed three strategies:

1. Create new systems only when the old ones fail.
2. Let others prove the value of new uses of IT before we start doing things differently.
3. Invest in IT only when it will have a direct bottom-line impact.

Norton points out that there can be substantial differences in the ways that companies in the same industry invest in information systems, as this example illustrates. The strategies of these two companies were not stated explicitly, yet they were clearly evident in conversations with the company executives. Also, such an analysis of current expenditures helps bring out the true "intensity of beliefs" about the use of technology, says Norton. It allows managers to stand back, see where investments are currently being made, and then decide where they *should* be made, in order to align the IT investments with the business strategy.

The Scenario Approach

Professional planners and executives have often used a scenario approach to planning. The approach is gaining in popularity, supported by computer-based decision support systems, and driven by the key words "what if." In systems planning, the scenario approach provides a way to manage the planning assumptions by creating scenarios that combine trends, events, environmental factors, and the relationships among them. The scenarios help to identify some problem areas that could arise if some factors change, such as the amount and type of competition or changes in wage rates. Once these scenarios have been generated, managers choose several that *could* happen. Then one "most likely" scenario is selected as the basis for long-range plans.

Scenarios also provide flexibility in plans and a means of escape, should it be necessary. This is the role of the other scenarios that are less likely but still feasible. They identify the leading-edge indicators that management should monitor. In these times of rapid change, about the only thing that is certain is that some of the views of the future will prove to be quite wrong. The selected scenario of the future is used to develop a phased schedule for achieving the desired ends. Projects required to implement the scenario are divided into phases, and the commitment to proceed is given for the next phase of each project over time. The goal is to highlight unexpected changes and require reassessments of the continued feasibility of the scenario.

Another role that scenario creation can play is to protect against errors of judgment by management, by flushing out management mindsets (basic assumptions) that are no longer relevant. In this period of major change, many old rules based on things that commonly happened in the past may no longer apply.

Some people will reject the idea of ten-year or twenty-year future scenarios as being not worth the trouble because no one is able to forecast the future with any consistency. There is some validity in this view. Companies are being acquired and merged. There are changes in the business environment due to foreign competition and government regulations. Changes in technologies are accelerating; witness the Internet. However, the type of strategic approach discussed here *expects* things to change, so midcourse corrections are part of the scenario process. As scenarios of the future are regenerated at later points in time, they will certainly show new pictures of the future. That is the time for management to assess the changes, to determine if plans must be modified, and to decide if a new approach is needed.

Elements of a Scenario. So many variables come into play when attempting to visualize the future that no simple theories, based on just a few variables, will be adequate. Following are some of the elements that should be considered in information systems plans.

The business environment. It is not difficult to think of many factors that affect the general business environment, which in turn can affect information systems. These include

- The environment
- Shifting toward a service economy and away from mass production
- Mergers, acquisitions, and alliances
- Regional trading blocks
- National budget deficits
- Shortened product development cycles
- Changes in the strength of different currencies

Then there is the impact of new technology on the business environment. For instance, what will be the impact of the increased use of "digital money" and the increased use of the Internet, EDI, and other forms of electronic commerce?

Government and society. Possible new government regulations and new social attitudes are other important considerations when developing scenarios. At an International Conference on Information Systems (ICIS), Richard Mason of Southern Methodist University talked on emerging issues in information systems. He identified some ethical issues that are likely to affect organizations and their information systems department.

One issue is *information accuracy,* said Mason. If significant societal problems emerge because of data errors, government regulations are almost sure to follow. A related issue is *privacy,* said Mason. Any database with information about people runs the risk of invading personal privacy.

A third issue is the potential for inequalities in *access to information.* Being literate is the first step in accessing written information, but accessing information in computer systems needs additional skills. Thus, larger budgets for training and education may be required to help employees become more computer literate.

A fourth issue is *property,* particularly the rights to intellectual property. For instance, it is relatively easy and inexpensive to make copies of computerized files, thus possibly compromising the property rights of the information creators. Perhaps even more threatening are expert systems that can capture experts' knowledge and embed it in computer programs. Do those people need to be compensated for this use of their knowledge?

The scenario approach makes it possible to factor in the possibility of government regulations in one or more of these areas as one extrapolates today's trends of computer use into the future.

"People" changes. It would be a mistake, when setting up scenarios of the future, to think that employees in ten years will be like they are today. With

today's turbulent conditions, employees may well come to expect that employers will train them in new skill areas, so that they (the employees) do not become job-obsolete. At present, many employers seem to treat this as an employee responsibility, but that may change.

Another major people factor in scenario building is the distribution of ages. In the early 1990s, relatively fewer young employees were in the work force, but a surge of young workers into the work force started about 1995.

Then there are changes in the attitudes and expectations of employees. For instance, Florence Skelly, of the firm of Yankelovich, Skelly & White [8], at a conference of the Information Industry Association, discussed how the environment that exists when people are just reaching working age affects their attitudes and expectations for much of their working lives. In the 1950s young people in the United States were influenced by the then-popular attitude of acquiring material things. These people are now in the 50 to 55 age bracket and represent much of middle management. During the 1960s and 1970s, affluence was more taken for granted, and the attitudes of young people turned toward fixing society's ills. The people who reached their working age during that period have recently entered the work force. So the current entrants into the work force might have expectations for "curing ills."

Finally, in the 1980s, the attitude was more pragmatic: "You cannot be, do, or have everything, so select what it is you desire and lay out your plans for getting it. Win by wit and wisdom. Be competitive." This may well be the attitude of young people entering the work force in the next five to ten years.

Financial considerations. An important element in scenarios is the financial dimension. For instance, technology costs will be substantial. Companies will require benefits from these sizable IT investments. The main problem is the definition of *benefits* and *return on investment* The benefits that derive from straightforward cost displacements, such as increased productivity or reduced staffing, will be only moderate in the future. The significant benefits will come from using IT to create more "high producers" in companies, or gain competitive advantages, or radically change the way technology is used. The real management challenge is perceiving these as benefits in order to justify the cost of new uses of technologies.

Technology. Technology forecasting is a particularly tenuous activity. Scenarios that make assumptions about not-yet-developed technologies are even more dangerous. There are few experts who, back in the mid-1970s, accurately predicted the explosive growth of the microcomputer technology or those in the late 1980s who predicted the Internet's dominance in networking.

Creating Scenarios. Paul Schoemaker of the Wharton School at the University of Pennsylvania [9] believes that the process of developing scenarios has a sequence of ten steps.

1. *Define the scope.* Set the time frame and scope of analysis in terms of products, markets, geographical areas, and technologies.

2. *Identify the major stakeholders.* Who will have an interest in these issues? Who will be affected by them? Who could influence them? Obviously, stakeholders include customers, suppliers, competitors, employees, shareholders, government, and so forth.

3. *Identify basic trends.* What political, economic, societal, technological, legal, and industry trends are sure to affect the issues you identified in step one? For example, a company concerned with the future of environmental issues might identify trends such as increasing environmental regulation, continuing growth of environmental interest groups, scientific advances in molecular biology, and an increasingly liberal judiciary.

4. *Identify key uncertainties.* What events (whose outcomes are uncertain) will significantly affect the issues you are concerned with? Again consider economic, political, societal, technological, legal, and industry factors.

5. *Construct initial scenario themes.* Once you identify trends and uncertainties, you have the main ingredients for scenario construction. A simple approach is to identify extreme worlds by putting all positive elements in one and all negatives in another. Another method for finding initial themes is to select the top two uncertainties and cross match them. Naming the scenarios is also important. A scenario is a story. By capturing its essence in a title, you make the story easy to follow and remember.

6. *Check for consistency and plausibility.* The first set of scenarios may have internal inconsistencies. Ask if the trends are compatible with the time frame, whether or not scenarios combine outcomes that are indeed compatible, and whether or not stakeholders are placed in untenable positions.

7. *Develop learning scenarios.* From this process of constructing simple scenarios and checking them for consistency, some general themes should emerge. The initial scenarios provide future boundaries, but they may be implausible, inconsistent, or irrelevant. The goal is to identify themes that are strategically relevant and then organize the possible outcomes and trends around them.

8. *Identify research needs.* The learning scenarios might reveal blind spots that require additional research. Look especially for trends and uncertainties that are outside your industry that might need additional understanding.

9. *Develop quantitative models.* After completing additional research, you should examine the internal consistencies of the scenarios and assess whether certain interactions should be formalized by way of a quantitative model.

10. *Evolve toward decision scenarios.* Finally, in an iterative process, you must converge toward scenarios that you will eventually use to test your strategies and generate new ideas.

There are four tests to determine if your scenarios are good, says Schoemaker. First is relevance. The scenarios should make sense to users, such as senior executives and managers. Second, the scenarios should be internally consistent. Third, they should describe different futures rather than variations on one theme. Fourth, they should be scenarios that seem to describe a stable state instead of a transient situation.

In summary, Schoemaker says, scenarios should cover a wide range of possibilities and highlight competing perspectives while focusing on interlinkages and the internal logic between each future. As an example of a company that has used scenarios in systems planning, consider Denny's.

Denny's Inc., with headquarters in La Mirada, California, is in the food services industry. The company has five divisions. On the retailing side are Denny's restaurants, Winchell's Donut houses, and El Pollo Loco chicken restaurants—with over 2,000 restaurants and fast-food locations throughout the United States and in five other countries. Proficient Food Company distributes food products to these retail outlets. And in the area of food manufacturing, Portion-Trol Foods produces some of the food products used by the retail stores.

The vice president for information services believes that information systems directors need to do more than introduce new technology into their companies. They need to *anticipate* what their companies will need in the future.

To put an information systems strategic plan in place, the vice president coordinated meetings with the company and division presidents to find out their views of Denny's future. He found that the company was growth oriented, and that it might grow through acquisitions, mergers, or cooperative ventures. But it was likely to stay in the food services business. With this knowledge in hand, he realized that his department had to ready itself for such growth. So he brought in managers who understood how large companies function.

The company and its various departments and divisions use a five-year rolling plan. In planning five years ahead, the department managers go off-site for several days to generate company and systems scenarios. Using business scenarios from the past—and determining how accurate these have been—the managers try to anticipate what the company will look like in five years. They generate several possible scenarios. Some seem very probable, while others seem highly unlikely; they try to cover the gamut. Then the group concentrates on the four or five most likely scenarios. For each one, they develop a high-level systems plan.

The information services controller takes these plans and looks for the common elements in each from a systems perspective. Which systems elements are in all the plans? Which are in 80 percent (or 60 percent or 40 percent, etc.) of the plans? Which of the plans require relational databases? Which require networks? Which require voice workstations? And so on. The group then reconvenes to discuss the plans and scenarios and choose one system plan. They attempt to fully support the most likely scenario, cover 70 percent of the needs of the next most likely scenarios, and cover 30 percent of the least likely ones.

Their more near-term plans are refinements of these five-year plans. Plans for the year ahead for each division are presented to the 200 top managers of the company once a year, where each major group describes its plan to the others. This one-day meeting creates a common level of understanding of the changes that each company area is initiating.

Linkage Analysis Planning

Kenneth Primozic, Edward Primozic, and Joe Leben [10], in their book *Strategic Choices,* explain their planning methodology, linkage analysis planning. Briefly, it means examining the links that organizations have with one another with the goal of creating a strategy for utilizing electronic channels. Their planning methodology has five basic parts:

1. Understand "waves of innovation."
2. Exploit experience curves.
3. Define power relationships.
4. Map out your "extended enterprise."
5. Plan your electronic channels.

Understand "Waves of Innovation." We discussed these waves in Chapter 2, along with the example of American Airline's SABRE system. Briefly, the authors explain the first two waves, which yield low returns on IT investment, as concentrating on saving money. Waves 3 through 5, which have steeper sloping lines signifying greater potential returns on investment, focus on making money. Most companies are at the top of Wave 2, say the authors, because they do not yet build systems that make money.

Exploit Experience Curves. As we noted in Chapter 3, along with the example of the shipping industry, Primozic et al. detail a set of experience curves rather than one continuous learning curve. Each of their curves represents fundamentally different technologies, both in the product and in the process to make and support it. Switching from one curve to another requires substantial investments, but a firm that correctly identifies a new market, and installs the technologies to exploit it, shifts to the new experience curve and is very successful.

Define Power Relationships. In order to create a strategy for building electronic links among enterprises, Primozic et al. believe that management must first understand the power relationships that currently exist among these various players. For this analysis, they begin with Michael Porter's classic model of competitive forces [11], which include competitors, buyers, substitutes, suppliers, and potential entrants. To this model they add: technology, demographics, global competition, government regulations, and "whatever is important in your environment." The goals of this step are to: (1) identify who has the power, and (2) determine what threats and opportunities exist for the company in the future.

The analysis begins by identifying *linkages,* which are relationships the organization has with other entities. Figure 4-6 in the upcoming case example is a good illustration. The links are represented by lines between organizations (shown in boxes). Once identified, management needs to determine who is managing each link. Oftentimes, no one is—which should be of concern. From here, the team picks the most important link and decides how the firm can control that link. The authors believe that winning organizations in the 1990s will be those that control the electronic channels—that is, the electronic linkages among enterprises.

The discussion of how to gain power within one's world of linkages brings up a host of questions. Two important ones are: How might alliances with other firms—across industries or even with competitors—help us? How do we need to restructure ourselves to seize an opportunity, or ward off a threat?

Map Out Your "Extended Enterprise." These questions lead to the fourth step in their approach to planning—the extended enterprise. An extended enterprise includes all of one's own organization plus those organizations with which one interacts—such as suppliers, buyers, government agencies, and so forth. (See Figure 4-5.)

The purpose of this step is to get management to first recognize the existence of this extended enterprise, and then to begin to manage the relationships that exist in it, because Primozic et al. believe that successful 1990s managements will focus on the extended enterprise. According to the authors, there are two fundamental principles for managing these relationships:

1. The enterprise's success depends on the relationships among everyone involved, which includes employees, managers, suppliers, alliances, distribution channels, and so forth.
2. Some 70 percent of the final cost of goods and services is in their information content; therefore, managing information as a strategic tool is crucial.

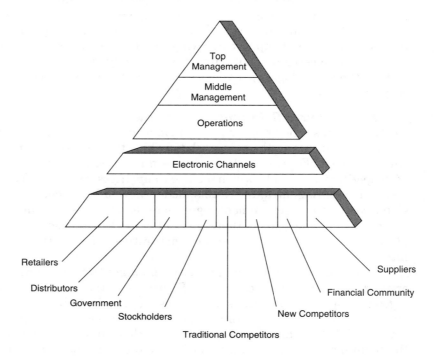

Figure 4-5   The Extended Enterprise (from Primozic et al. [10])

An extended enterprise diagram might deal only with external players, such as the government, stockholders, traditional competitors, the financial community, and so forth. Such a chart includes everyone whose decisions affect the organization or who are affected by its decisions. The analysis then moves on to discuss how the links might change and how each link should be managed. In the extended enterprise, each relationship will prosper only when it is "win-win," say the authors. For example, in return for maintaining a buyer's parts inventory and providing just-in-time delivery, the supplier may be paid electronically upon delivery of goods. Such an arrangement profits both parties.

Competitive advantage will depend increasingly on being able to exploit the collective resources of one's extended enterprise, say Primozic et al. Such enterprises often require electronic channels to exchange business transactions, which leads to the fifth step in their planning approach—planning the electronic channels.

Plan Your Electronic Channels.   An electronic channel is an electronic link used to create, distribute, and present information and knowledge—as part of a product or service or as an ancillary good. These channels focus on the information component of products, which is mainly in marketing, administration, distribution, and customer service. The authors believe that those who control the electronic channels in the 1990s will be the winners because they will be able to address new niche markets as they arise. Furthermore, as use of IT leads to a smaller, faster-paced world, organizations with the longest electronic reach into their extended organization will have an advantage.

The authors use linkage analysis charts to help management conceptualize the key issues they face in an extended enterprise, and focus on the factors that are critical to their future success. This methodology has been used by the Electric Power Research Institute, whose story we tell next.

CASE EXAMPLE: Electric Power Research Institute

The Electric Power Research Institute (EPRI), with headquarters in Palo Alto, California, is a large private research firm serving over 700 electric member utilities. Their 350 staff scientists and engineers manage some 1,600 R&D projects at any one time. The projects—which study such subjects as power generation, superconductivity, electronic and magnetic fields, and acid rain—are conducted by over 400 utility, university, commercial, government, and other R&D contractors, on behalf of the members. For an in-depth discussion of EPRI, see Mann et al. [12].

EPRI's Challenge. EPRI's mission is to deliver the information and knowledge from its research projects to the 400,000 employees in the 768 member utilities—to help them be more competitive. In 1983, management realized EPRI had to compress the "information float"—the elapsed time from the availability of research findings to the use of those results in industry.

The institute was suffering from "infosclerosis"—the hardening and clogging of their information arteries. Due to the volume of research findings—8 gigabytes of information in 1991—moving information in and out of EPRI was extremely difficult. In addition, because of the documentation and publishing process, the results often were *unavailable* for up to 24 months, so the reports were not as timely as they could be. Nor were they accessible because they were published in massive reports. Solving this information delivery challenge was critical to EPRI's survival.

EPRI's Vision. The institute's vision was to assist its members in exploiting EPRI's product—knowledge—as a strategic business resource, whenever and from wherever they choose. To accomplish this vision, EPRI is building state-of-the-art electronic information and communication services.

The delivery vehicle is EPRINET, an electronic "channel" that includes

- A natural-language front-end for accessing on-line information
- Expert system-based products that contain the knowledge of their energy experts
- Electronic mail facilities for person-to-person communications
- Video conferencing to foster small-group communication.

Using Linkage Analysis Planning. To focus the EPRINET effort, and to identify the services and products that would offer strategic business advantages to its members, EPRI used the linkage analysis planning methodology in a three-day workshop led by Kenneth Primozic. The workshop began with management stating that (1) EPRI was both an R&D organization and a knowledge provider, and (2) the goal was to leverage knowledge as a strategic asset.

From this starting point, Primozic asked, "Who is linked to EPRI in creating and distributing knowledge?" The participants identified the cocreators as contractors, research firms, universities, the government, and technology. They identified the recipients as the utility industry, universities, research labs, government policies, and knowledge as capital—as shown in Figure 4-6. Each of these represented a link to EPRI, so the group then studied the present and future power relationships in each buyer-seller link. During these discussions, they saw how some current customers (such as universities or research labs) could become future competitors and change the power relationship in a link.

Since management's goal was to leverage knowledge, the group listed all the ways this could be achieved. Then they focused on the most important way, which turned out to be treating knowledge as capital. During this

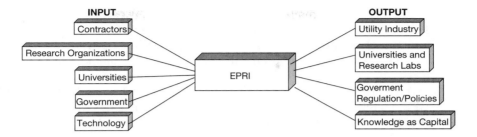

Figure 4-6   EPRI's Linkage Analysis (from Mann et al. [12])

analysis, management defined the following critical success factors for giving EPRINET a sustainable competitive advantage:

- Establish the "right" mix of product offerings, a mix that allows people to pick, choose, and combine at the lowest possible cost.
- Keep all customers in mind, which include utility executives, research engineers, and operations people.
- Use IT—specifically expert systems and natural language—to make the system easy to use and access.
- Create a range of "knowledge packages" targeted to specific audiences.
- Establish a timely, reliable, secure, global distribution channel.

EPRINET was made available in May 1990, and a marketing campaign began soon thereafter. The number of users has climbed steadily since then. Frequent users report that the system is indeed broadening the number of people they can stay in contact with and allowing them to uncover EPRI research findings that they would not have found otherwise.

Creative Problem Solving

Creative problem solving (CPS) approaches are procedures and techniques designed to solve complete problems in creative ways. Evolving over the past two or three decades, CPS techniques are proving useful to enhance several of the IS planning approaches discussed earlier. We discuss it here because, with modern variations, it is proving to be extremely valuable in leveraging combinations of other techniques. We will illustrate this in the final case example.

A major reason for the increased value of the CPS approach in systems planning and development is the recent work by J. Daniel Couger at the University of Colorado at Colorado Springs. Couger [13] has developed a variant to the CPS model that can facilitate IS planning. He has also formed the Center for Research on Creativity in Information Systems (CRCI), sponsored by a group of organizations interested in supporting the development of theory and insight on this subject.

CPS has evolved from several analytical approaches. The most widely used framework for problem solving was originated by Herbert Simon [14], who proposed a three-stage approach: intelligence, design and choice. *Intelligence* involves recognizing the problem and analyzing problem information to develop a useful problem definition; *design* is the generation of solutions; and *choice* involves the selection and implementation of a solution. The most widely used CPS model, developed by Sidney Parnes [15], contains five phases: fact finding, problem finding, idea finding, solution finding, and acceptance finding.

A unique feature of CPS is its use of divergence-convergence activities in each phase of the problem-solving process, represented by a diamond-shaped symbol. Each phase begins with a divergent activity (idea generation, where the alternatives are expanded) and concludes with a convergent activity (in which only the most promising ideas are selected for further exploration).

The Couger variant to the CPS model is shown in Figure 4-7. It contains three refinements. One, which he calls "creative opportunity delineation and problem solving," is the addition of an opportunity identification step.

The second refinement is his emphasis upon nonlinearity and recursiveness of the model; that is, the steps are not really linear, although the graphical

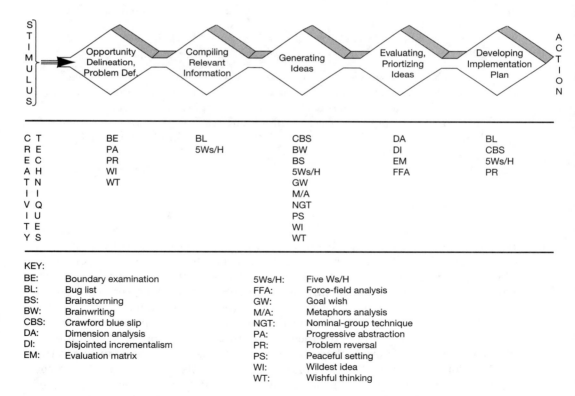

Figure 4-7   Couger Variant of the Creative Problem-Solving Model (from Couger [13])

representation implies that one step follows another. Furthermore, the problem solver may need to revisit prior steps (recursion). For instance, it may not be possible to define the problem until the second phase—reviewing all the relevant data—has been performed. Or the idea generation phase may uncover the need for more data before the problem solvers are able to fully attack the problem or opportunity. Or the problem solvers may decide in the evaluation phase that the generated ideas are not an optimal solution, requiring recursion back through phase three, the idea generation phase. There are also situations where not all of the phases are necessary, such as when the problem is clear to everyone, so phase one is unnecessary. On the other hand, the literature is replete with cases where the problem solvers assumed they understood the problem and spent time solving the wrong problem.

The third refinement is the most significant. Couger converted the CPS model into a methodology by identifying creativity techniques for each of the five phases, not just the idea generation phase. This approach operationalizes the static model, converting it to a dynamic methodology. For example:

- In phase one, creativity techniques can be used to help generate multiple problem/opportunity definitions.
- In phase two, creativity techniques can be used to identify other salient facts.
- In phase three, creativity techniques can assist in generating a variety of solutions.
- In phase four, creativity techniques can help identify various evaluation approaches.
- In phase five, creativity techniques can be used to identify alternative approaches for ensuring a successful implementation.

The brainstorming technique, generally used in phase three, may be the only technique listed that is familiar to most persons in the IS field. Use of other techniques is illustrated in the upcoming UTMC case example.

Couger believes that the CPS model is useful in a variety of IS activities. He has shown in a recent article [16] how it can be incorporated into the system development life cycle to ensure that more creative alternatives are considered at each stage of the life cycle. He believes it is especially effective in IS planning. At United Technologies Microelectronics Center (UTMC), its use led to an innovative approach of integrating Hoshin planning techniques (HPT) with enterprise modeling (EM) and business process redesign (BPR). The power of CPS for IS planning is illustrated in the UTMC case.

Enterprise Modeling

The UTMC case that follows illustrates some techniques that can be called *enterprise modeling*. As described by Snow [17], UTMC's story suggests that there is a need for focus at the enterprise level, and that several techniques and approaches may need to be used together.

UTMC's enterprise model development methodology used general planning techniques as its foundation; therefore, it can be applied by any organization. The issues addressed by UTMC's enterprise model are important to virtually all businesses today. Work on the enterprise model has positioned UTMC to address four of these most important issues:

- Reshaping business processes through IT
- Aligning IS and corporate goals
- Instituting cross-functional systems
- Utilizing data

United Technologies Microelectronics Center, Inc. (UTMC), headquartered in Colorado Springs, Colorado, is a subsidiary of United Technologies Corporation (UTC). Established in 1980, UTMC helps other UTC divisions integrate custom and semicustom microelectronics into its military and defense systems. In 1985, UTMC opened a wafer fabrication facility and expanded its charter to marketing semicustom and military-standard VLSI circuits to high-reliability military and aerospace companies outside of UTC. This significant shift in business focus had a dramatic effect on UTMC's marketing, manufacturing, engineering, and design activities. Today, UTMC also engages in government and customer-funded research and development.

The shifts in business objectives and the associated changes in management information needs strained UTMC's information architecture. In early 1990, senior management decided to operate the business more efficiently by using real-time integrated data. With this goal in mind, management tasked the MIS department with developing a computer systems integration strategy and identifying opportunities to reengineer UTMC's business processes. MIS management proposed the development of an enterprise model to achieve these objectives.

While the MIS department investigated different enterprise modeling techniques, UTMC's CEO attended a seminar on the Hoshin planning technique—a set of Japanese planning tools used to solve general business problems. After the seminar, he was excited about the prospect of creating a UTMC culture that utilized these planning techniques. Acknowledging his interest, MIS management modified and integrated the Hoshin planning techniques into an enterprise model methodology. Creativity techniques were used to design the methodology and incorporated into it.

Rather than taking the data focus inherent in many modeling methodologies, UTMC's methodology used a process focus, which meant that the resulting model would not be biased toward the current systems and databases. Instead, it would represent ideal or target business processes, which would identify opportunities to reengineer current business practices.

UTMC's CEO fully supported the project's goals and methodology because the newly defined methodology not only promised to address his systems and process concerns, but its Hoshin orientation was compatible with his cultural objectives for UTMC.

Enterprise Modeling Methodology

The methodology's focus on target business processes meant that the entire enterprise needed to be subdivided into functional units, which are depicted by the seven levels of business process hierarchy in Figure 4-8.

With the business processes understood, the methodology called for understanding and documenting the target process interrelationships. Next, the implementation viewpoint was linked to the process view by mapping the processes to information systems and then defining the inter-relationships between systems via a target system architecture. Finally, UTMC identified and ranked the differences between its current environment and the target model. The step identified the environmental changes UTMC would need to reengineer the business.

Assembling Business Segment Teams

The reengineering work would be performed by business segment teams. To choose these teams, MIS collaborated with the vice president of operations to prototype the new methodology and functionally decompose the company's overall business activity into major enterprise and business segments. Figure 4-9 depicts the resulting four enterprise segments and 15 business segments.

Senior management organized a team of six to ten employees for each of the 15 business segments. Team members represented a diverse cross-

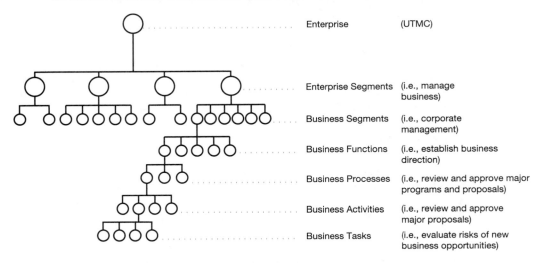

Figure 4-8   UTMC Business Process Hierarchy

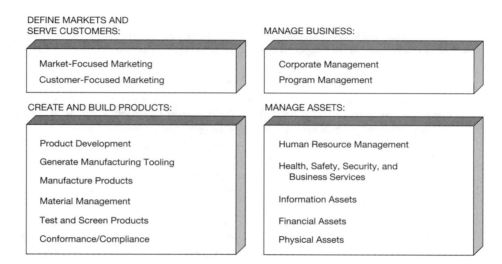

Figure 4-9   UTMC Enterprise and Business Segments

section of the UTMC employees and included all levels of management. Approximately 16 percent of UTMC employees served on the teams.

Constructing the Model

As part of the adapted Hoshin methodology, the MIS department held four separate meetings with each business segment team. At each meeting, MIS management continually stressed that current practices and organizational structure should not influence the model. The MIS group used creativity techniques during each meeting to solicit new ideas.

The First Meeting—Affinity from Chaos. During the first meeting, each business segment team identified target business activities and grouped them according to their natural relationships to each other. The grouping activity used the Hoshin planning affinity technique to develop an affinity diagram. The Hoshin planning affinity technique is an excellent tool for understanding complex issues, practitioners have found, and it is very effective at helping organizations overcome traditional ways of looking at situations. Both of these qualities were essential in this first step of the modeling process.

To develop an affinity diagram, team members first used the "blue slip creativity technique" to identify all business activities associated with their business segment. Each activity was written on a post-it note that was randomly placed on a large piece of blank paper. Then the participants silently grouped the post-it notes. This process allowed each member to participate equally. Finally, using a consensus approach, participants created business process headings for each group and business function superheadings for combined groups. The resulting affinity diagrams became the basis for a second meeting with the business segment team.

The Second Meeting—Refining and Organizing. During the second meeting, each team refined the business processes catalogued in the affinity diagram. The Hoshin planning tree diagram was used to organize the processes into a hierarchy. This involved a lively brainstorming session and required the participants to arrange the business activities into a tree diagram for each business function. This rational process complemented the creative affinity process by identifying missing or misplaced business activities. Next, the MIS group leaders modified each business segment's affinity diagram to reflect the tree diagrams.

Figure 4-10 shows the tree diagram for the "establish business direction" function of the corporate management business segment.

The Third Meeting—Defining Process Interrelationships. During the third meeting, each business segment team identified the information that flowed between its segment's varied business processes as well as the information that flowed to and from other business segments. The MIS leaders used the creative approach of extension to adapt the Hoshin planning interrelationship digraph to show this data flow.

The Fourth Meeting—Mapping Processes to Systems. During the fourth meeting, each business segment team used the Hoshin planning matrix to map the business processes to the systems that support them. Figure 4-11 shows the matrix for corporate management.

Defining the Target System Architecture

Next, the MIS team resolved disparities between the 15 business segment process interrelationship digraphs, where one group's digraph identified a relationship with another group, but the other group's digraph did not. Some of these omissions were oversights, but many highlighted existing business process problems. Exploration of these "disconnects" enabled the MIS team to identify opportunities to improve cross-functional awareness, cooperation, and integration.

With the business segment process interrelationship digraphs in agreement, the MIS team was ready to apply the knowledge gained during the 60 business segment team meetings. This resulted in a digraph for the entire organization. To complete the executive overview of the enterprise, the MIS team also developed an enterprisewide affinity diagram and tree diagrams for each of the four enterprise segments. These diagrams were derived directly from the completed process knowledge base.

The MIS team used the business segments' process-oriented interrelationship digraphs and their process/system matrices to develop interrela-

124

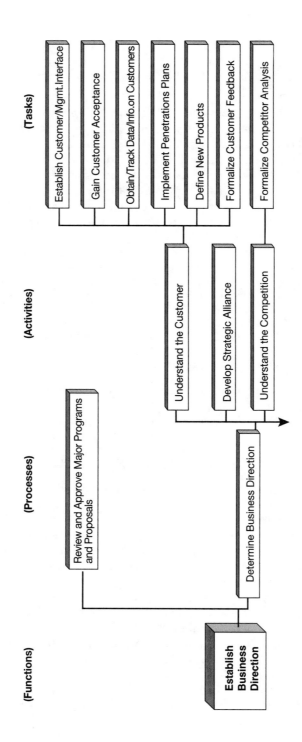

Figure 4-10 Tree Diagram—Corporate Management—Establish Business Directions

Systems	Business Processes	Allocate Resources	Management Process	Performance Mgmt.	Strategic Planning	Operational Plan	Business Model	Define Market	Review & Approve Major Programs & Proposals	Identify New Initiatives	Establish Leadership	Make Timely and Effective Decisions	Establish Community Involvement	Ensure Compliance	Develop HR Policies
	Business Model	x			x	x	x	x	x						
	Objective Tracking System		x		x										
	Decision Making Tool		x		x	x	x	x	x	x	x	x			
	EIS System		x	x									x		
	Hoshin Planning		x					x	x	x	x	x			
	Strategic Scheduling System												x		

"X" indicates that the system addresses the business process

Figure 4-11 Systems/Process Matrix—Corporate Management

tionship digraphs for information systems for each business segment. These represented the ideal systems architecture tailored to meet UTMC's business needs. The diagrams showed each system and identified target system interfaces to all other systems. This target system architecture enabled UTMC to evaluate its current system portfolio and clearly indicated the need for new systems, the need to enhance or restructure existing systems, and the need for new systems interfaces.

Initiating the Change Process

The enterprise model not only served as a road map for all future systems development, but it also identified many reengineering opportunities. This second result continues to be very important to UTMC's senior management because of its ongoing need to reengineer its business in today's competitive marketplace. Each of the 15 business segment teams reconvened to identify and set priorities for the business changes necessary to achieve the target model. The teams ranked each of their recommended changes as a high, medium, or low priority based on the following criteria:

- Company goals that will be met.
- Magnitude of problems that will be solved.
- Integration advantages.
- Logical sequence of changes.
- Benefits that will be received.

The ranking process identified 25 companywide high-priority changes. Many groups identified the same changes as high priorities, such as the need to improve engineering data collection and analysis.

Next, each business segment team elected a representative to participate in the final companywide ranking. These representatives presented their team's high-priority business changes to the other representatives, who then rated each change against the criteria supplied by UTMC's operating committee. The rating criteria included the seven Malcolm Baldrige award criteria:

- Improve leadership.
- Manage and analyze information.
- Improve quality planning.
- Develop and achieve human potential.
- Provide continuous quality improvement.
- Provide quality goods and services.
- Know and satisfy customers.

Additional criteria critical to UTMC's success included

- Make effective decisions.
- Improve utilization of employees.
- Free up time to sell products.
- Introduce new products in a timely manner.

This rating process produced a list of UTMC's greatest process improvement opportunities. The most important opportunities included

- Making significant changes to UTMC's work in progress and material planning process.
- Enhancing cost accounting to support improved management decision making.
- Creating a UTMC business model to evaluate the impact of business alternatives on the overall company.
- Enhance costing scheduling and reporting of UTMC programs.
- Increase customer focus.
- Improve management of executive information.
- More efficiently process changes to certify material vendors.

Enterprise Modeling Results

During the modeling process, UTMC experienced many unexpected positive results. Nearly all the 80 business segment team members initially had difficulty thinking in terms of business processes. They generally thought along organizational lines and focused on historical responsibilities without considering the business purpose for their actions. The model-building experience helped them to see relationships between groups that originally were not clear to them. Comments such as, "I always wondered how we did that" and "I never knew you did so much" were frequently made during the meetings.

The enhanced teamwork and understanding generated by the meetings supported UTMC's goal to develop a culture consistent with the Malcolm Baldrige National Quality Award. Identifying all the business processes in the company and encouraging UTMC employees to orient their thoughts toward processes have been important first steps toward this goal.

UTMC's CEO noted that these intangible results alone represented a respectable payback for the effort expended constructing the model. Impressed with the model, he requested that the MIS team that had worked with the 15 business segment teams document its observations. The team produced a list of 15 observations about UTMC's culture and nine general observations about UTMC business processes. These observations addressed such areas as

- Cultural inconsistencies throughout the company due largely to UTMC's short history. By addressing these issues, overall teamwork and cross-functional cooperation could be enhanced.
- The difficulty in looking beyond current ways of working to define the target enterprise. Companywide creativity training would improve UTMC's ability to adapt to a changing business environment.
- The difficulty employees experienced in balancing divergent activities, such as looking for better ways of doing their jobs, with the convergent activities of performing their every-day tasks. Arriving at the proper balance is a continuing management challenge for UTMC.
- The challenges management faces in clearly communicating future process changes and functional responsibilities. The enterprise model interrelationships digraphs should provide a companywide method for communicating such changes.

Because there was such broad employee involvement in developing the model, management considers the model to be a valuable company resource. They look to the model for insight when they assume new responsibilities or need to understand how another part of the company works.

While the rest of the company was gaining an increased cross-functional appreciation of UTMC, the MIS managers and analysts were gaining a valuable broad perspective of the company. When the MIS team began working with senior management on the corporate management model segment, they were able to demonstrate the knowledge they obtained from developing the other segments of the model. Previously, the senior managers saw a great need for a new UTMC business planning company, but they were unable to envision its structure. Aided by the incomplete model, the MIS team was able to present senior management with a proposal that eventually led to defining a single business planning system to support the companywide planning process.

Building for the Future

Implementation of the enterprise model at UTMC has dramatically changed the way the company plans for process and system changes. The model has provided a foundation for building long-range MIS plans and has facilitated alignment of the MIS department with UTMC's business needs. This focus will allow UTMC to maximize the return on its IT investment. And the enterprise model's integration blueprint is helping MIS management supply UTMC managers with concise, timely, and accurate information to support executive management decision making.

The enterprise model has also helped UTMC develop a culture that seemed unattainable just a few years ago. The cross-functional teams that designed the model's business segments improved teamwork, communications, and mutual understanding among UTMC departments. The enterprise model also helped tie together several major UTMC initiatives, including the Malcolm Baldrige Award, Hoshin planning, creativity, and product development's stage gate program.

According to UTMC's vice president of operations, Bob Cutter, "The enterprise modeling activity has assisted in focusing UTMC on a process culture. This will provide the foundation for significant improvements in future years. The improved cross-functional awareness and teamwork achieved during the initial phase of the project have already provided tangible payback. Understanding your own business processes and capability is the first step towards total customer satisfaction."

CONCLUSION

Based on the successes and failures of past information system planning efforts, we see two necessary ingredients to a good strategic planning effort. One is that the plans must look toward the future. This may seem obvious, but in these turbulent times, the future is not likely to be an extrapolation of the past. So a successful planning effort needs to support "peering into the future."

A second necessary ingredient is that information system plans must be linked to business plans. This may seem obvious, but, again, unless the planning methodology specifically requires such links, the systems plans may not be relevant because they do not support the corporate strategy. This is not so likely as it was a few years ago; business plans and system plans appear to be drawing closer together in more and more companies.

In this chapter, we have described a number of the most popular approaches to information system planning at the strategic level. No single method is best and no single one is the most widely used in business. In fact, many companies use a combination of these approaches because they deal with different aspects of planning.

QUESTIONS AND EXERCISES

REVIEW QUESTIONS

1. What are the primary differences between operational planning, tactical planning, and strategic planning?
2. Identify and describe several shifts in emphasis of systems from several years ago to now.
3. Identify and describe several reasons why strategic systems planning is so difficult.
4. What is the main contribution of the stages of growth theory to information systems planning?
5. What are critical success factors? How do they contribute to the systems planning process?
6. Explain how the investment strategy analysis approach can be used to formulate (or reveal) strategies in the use of information systems.
7. What are the advantages of the scenario approach to planning?
8. The text identifies the following areas that scenarios should include. Give a few considerations in each area that are relevant to systems planning.
   a. Business environment
   b. Government and society
   c. People changes
   d. Financial considerations
   e. Technology
9. What are the steps in the process of developing scenarios?
10. Briefly describe the goal of linkage analysis planning and the five steps in it.
11. What was EPRI's challenge and how did the institute solve it?
12. What is the creative problem-solving approach? List Couger's three variants to the classical CPS method. Why is this a valuable approach for information systems planning?
13. Draw a chart showing the steps in the enterprise modeling process used by UTMC. For each step, give the purpose and the name of the chart or diagram that represents the output from that step.

DISCUSSION QUESTIONS

1. Which of the frameworks for systems planning seems most useful to you? Why?
2. If you were in charge of systems planning for a small firm, what questions would you ask the company officers to determine which planning approach(s) would be most appropriate?
3. In Chapter 2, we state that strategies are out, visioning is in, because no one can plan in turbulent times. In this chapter we say that planning is crucial. How do you reconcile these two viewpoints?

EXERCISES

1. Survey the current literature on the subject of systems planning. Are there other approaches or frameworks not mentioned in this text? What automated products are available on the market to assist information systems executives in the planning process?

2. Visit the chief information officer of a local organization. What planning process does the organization use? What is the planning horizon? To what degree do the systems plans and the business plans relate to each other?

3. Create a simple information linkage analysis chart of your current personal relationships. Put yourself in the middle box, and each relationship in its own box around you, with a line from you to each box. Who has the "power" in each link? How might that power shift in the future? Which is the most important relationship to you? How could you make it more "win-win"?

4. Ask the CIO of a nearby company what electronic channels his or her firm has in place. Ask about the benefits both parties receive in each link.

REFERENCES

1. "THE END OF DELEGATION: INFORMATION TECHNOLOGY AND THE CEO," *Harvard Business Review,* September/October 1995, pp. 161–172.

2. NOLAN, R. L., and C. F. GIBSON, "Managing the Four Stages of EDP Growth," *Harvard Business Review*, January/February 1974, p. 76ff.

3. NOLAN, R. L. "Managing the Crisis in Data Processing," *Harvard Business Review*, March/April 1979.

4. BENBASAT, I., A. S. DEXTER, D. H. DRURY, and R. G. GOLDSTEIN, "A Critique of the Stage Hypothesis: Theory and empirical evidence," *Communications of the ACM,* ACM, May 1984, pp. 467–485.

5. CASH, J. I., F. W. McFARLAN, J. L. McKENNEY, and L. M. APPELGATE, *Corporate Information Systems Management: Text and Cores,* Richard D. Irwin, Inc., Homewood, IL, 1992, pp. 43–45.

6. ROCKART, J. "Chief Executives Define Their Own Data Needs," *Harvard Business Review*, March/April 1979, pp. 81–92.

7. *STAGE BY STAGE*, Nolan, Norton & Co., Boston, MA, vol. 4, no. 4, Winter 1985.

8. YANKELOVICH, SKELLY & WHITE, 575 Madison Ave., New York, NY 10022.

9. SCHOEMAKER, PAUL, "Scenario Planning: A Tool for Strategic Thinking," *Sloan Management Review*, Winter 1995, pp. 25–40.

10. PRIMOZIC, K. I., E. A. PRIMOZIC, and J. LEBEN, *Strategic Choices: Supremacy, Survival, or Sayanara,* McGraw-Hill, New York, 1991, 272 pages.

11. PORTER, M., *Competitive Strategy,* The Free Press, New York, 1980. Also see *Competitive Advantage*, 1985.

12. MANN, M. M., R. L. LUDMAN, T. A. JENCKES and B. C. McNURLIN, "EPRINET: Leveraging Knowledge in the Electric Utility Industry," *MIS Quarterly,* September 1991, pp. 403–421.

13. COUGER, J. D., *Creative Problem Solving (CPS) and Opportunity Finding*, Boyd and Fraser, Danvers, MA, 1995.

14. SIMON, H. A., *The New Science of Management,* Harper and Row, New York, 1960.

15. PARNES, S. J., R. B. NOLLER and A. M. BIONDI, (eds.), *Guide to Creative Action,* Scribner's Sons, New York, NY, 1977.

16. COUGER, J. D., *Creativity & Innovation in Information Systems Organizations*, Boyd and Fraser, Danvers, MA, 1996.

17. SNOW, T., "Designing a Target Enterprise: Business Modelling at United Technologies Microelectronics Center," presented at the Dooley Group 10th Annual Executive Conference, December 1991.

PART II

Managing the Essential Technologies

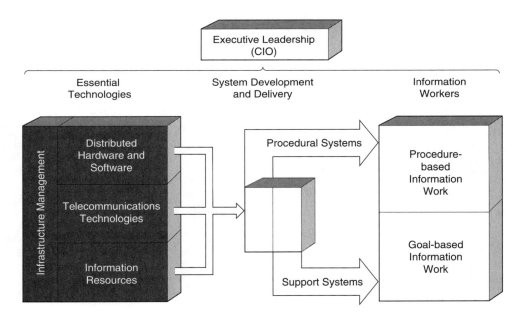

A Framework for IS Management

Part II—Chapters 5 through 8—focuses on infrastructure management, as shown in the figure above. The purpose of this part is to present the technological underpinnings of a corporate IT operation, and point out the major issues that must be addressed for it to be well managed.

Chapter 5 looks at various kinds of distributed system architectures, and also discusses the important concepts of IT architecture and infrastructure.

Chapter 6 discusses the links within a distributed system architecture. In this edition of the book, it can now realistically be said (in a growing number of cases) that "the network is the system"—as Sun Microsystems has been saying for many years. One focus of this chapter is, of course, the Internet.

While Chapters 5 and 6 deal with the structure of distributed systems (the overall environment), Chapter 7 deals with the content—the information resources. These resources have been referred to as data. But increasingly, this content has more context to it, which turns it into information, and also more intelligence and "actionability," which is knowledge. All three are discussed in Chapter 7.

Finally, Chapter 8 deals with operations, the day-to-day concerns of keeping elaborate, far-flung corporate distributed systems dependably up and running. Back in the old mainframe days, operations were pretty much taken for granted and housed in "the glass room." Today, even Internet users have operational concerns, such as security and privacy.

FIVE

INTRODUCTION

To begin Part II of this book, we discuss three subjects in this chapter: various kinds of distributed systems, one approach to describing an overall enterprisewide architecture, and different kinds of IT infrastructures.

The terms *architecture* and *infrastructure* are often mistakenly interchanged, which can be confusing. In this book, we adopt the following distinction. An IT architecture is a blueprint. It shows how the overall system, house, vehicle, or thing will look and how the parts interrelate.

An infrastructure, on the other hand, is the implementation of an architecture. A corporation's IT infrastructure is generally understood to be its information management capabilities that are intended to be shared. This includes the electronic links, the standards that ensure the information can be used effectively, and the skills for using IT and information [1] as well as the processors, system software, databases, phone systems, and computerized processes. Note that all of these components could be combined in any number of ways. A particular combination would be the architecture.

At the end of this chapter, we delve into both architecture and infrastructure in a bit more depth. But now, we discuss the topic of distributed systems, which is today's IT architecture of choice in the corporate world.

The architecture of old used mainframes performing batch and on-line processing communicating with "dumb" terminals—that is, they did not have their own processing capabilities. With the advent of minicomputers, computers moved into departments. And with micros, they moved onto desktops and into briefcases. Then processing was split between a client, which requests services, and a server, which provides those services. More recently, there is a move back to a central processing source model (with the Internet rather than a mainframe as that source) accessed by network computers (diskless computers that download applications from the source rather than house them themselves). It almost seems as if we have gone full circle, doesn't it?

Throughout this evolution, stand-alone processors (or processors with dedicated terminals) appeared first and then were gradually linked to other computers. As that happened, the notion of a distributed architecture developed. Today, the goal is a global network of distributed systems that can accommodate products from any vendor. This architecture would allow any device to access information from, do processing on, or communicate with any other device. Sounds like the Internet, doesn't it? Well, the Internet can be viewed as the center of such a worldwide distributed system. That is the revolution taking place today.

Four Attributes of Distributed Systems

The degree to which a system is distributed can be determined by answering four questions:

- Where is the processing done?
- How are the processors and other devices interconnected?
- Where is the information stored?
- What rules or standards are used?

Distributed processing is the ability for more than one interconnected processor to be operating at the same time. This usually means processing an application on more than one computer. The goal in distributed processing is to move the appropriate processing as close to the user as possible, and to allow other machines to handle the work that they do best (such as manage databases).

An advanced form of distributed processing permits interoperability, which is the capability for different machines using different operating systems on different networks to work together on tasks. They exchange information in standard ways without requiring changes in command languages or functionality and without physical intervention.

Charlie Bachman, a pioneer in the database and distributed system fields, pointed out to us that there are really two forms of interoperability. One is the transparent communication between *systems* using system protocols. In this form, the systems decide when to interoperate. Companies implementing the

International Standards Organization Open System Interconnection (OSI) reference model have developed protocols for standard file and job transfers to permit this form of interoperability, says Bachman. Internet fits into this category. (We discuss OSI in Chapter 6.)

The second form of interoperability is the interactive or two-way flow of messages between *user applications*. In this form, user applications can be activated by receiving messages; this, of course, is supported on the Internet and intranets. Both kinds of interoperability are important, according to Bachman.

Connectivity among processors means that each processor in a distributed system can send data and messages to any other processor through electronic communication linkages. A desirable structure for reliable distributed systems has at least two independent paths between any two nodes, in order to provide automatic alternate routing. Planned redundancy of this type is critical for reliable operation. Such redundancy has not been implemented in most LANs, which is one reason they have been so fragile. It is, however, a major feature of the Internet as well as most corporate wide area networks (WANs).

Distributed databases are being defined in at least two ways. One divides a database and distributes its portions throughout a system without duplicating the data. Any portion is accessible from any node, subject to access authorization. Users do not need to know where a piece of data is located to access it—the system knows where all data is stored.

The second definition sees a distributed database as one that contains distributed duplicate data. The same data is stored at several locations, with one site containing the master file. Synchronization of data is a *significant* problem in this approach, which is why it has not appeared in widespread use yet. In both approaches, common data definitions are important.

Systemwide rules mean that an operating discipline for the distributed system has been developed and is enforced at all times. These rules govern communication between nodes, security, data accessibility, program and file transfers, and common operating procedures.

In the 1990s, these systemwide rules have been increasingly based on the open system concept, which means that products from vendors that use open standards can be used in one system. The goal is to avoid being locked into the proprietary products of one vendor. Interestingly, the meaning of *open systems* has expanded as open systems have become a reality.

In the 1980s, open systems referred mainly to telecommunications and meant that a company intended to implement products that followed the OSI reference model, whenever they became available. At that time, OSI implementation was not a reality, just a target.

In 1990, the definition expanded to include operating systems, specifically UNIX, because it runs on many more platforms than any other operating system. At that time, UNIX was tentatively seen as appropriate for mainline business computing. Today, it has indeed gained a foothold in business computing, but it certainly has not displaced proprietary operating systems, such as Microsoft's DOS, Windows, or NT.

At the same time, in the data world, *open* meant SQL (Structured Query Language), the standard intermediary language for accessing relational databases. That definition continues today.

In 1992, the definition shifted again, this time to the interfaces between applications. Open meant standardized interfaces that would allow products to interoperate across multivendor networks, operating systems, and databases. Application program interfaces (APIs) came into being. They define the way data is presented to another component of a system—a machine, database, even an electronic mail system. APIs allow individual products to be innovative, yet connectable, and they make writing distributed systems far easier. Their importance continues today.

Today, the term *open* has come full circle. It again stresses the network. While the OSI reference model remains the definition of *open,* most people are far more familiar with its widest implementation, the network protocol used in the Internet, TCP/IP (Transmission Control Protocol/Internet Protocol). Corporate networks, both LANs and WANs, are increasingly migrating to TCP/IP to allow interconnection.

So the term *open systems* keeps expanding because it truly is the crux of distributed systems that allow products—hardware, software, data, and communications—from multiple vendors to work together.

Although some people see the main reason for distributing systems as improving the use of computer resources, that is just a technical reason. The real organizational impetus behind distributed systems is moving responsibility for computing resources to the business units that use them. With that in mind, we now briefly address the business reasons for distributing applications and the responsibilities that go with them.

When to Distribute Computing Responsibilities

Information systems management needs a corporate policy for deciding when the development, operation, and maintenance of an application should be distributed. Individual end users and departments should not be left on their own to make these decisions, especially where connectivity to the enterprisewide network is important. Although technical considerations are critical, they should not be the prime force behind a system architecture. Rather, the major reason for choosing a particular distributed system architecture hinges on: *Who should make the key management operating decisions?*

Decision-making responsibilities are being pushed down in organizations, with business managers and teams being given more autonomy and responsibility for the resources they use. One such resource is IT. People who make the decisions about how their portion of the business operates also should be making the decisions about how they use IT. Teamwork between IS management and business management is important in designing a distributed processing architecture that supports the business's goals.

Francis Wagner, a business data processing pioneer, once told us that he believes people perform best when they are responsible for their own mistakes. If they have no one to blame but themselves, then the quality of their performance increases. The result is a more effective use of corporate resources.

We therefore see a driving force behind distributed processing being the desire to give more people more control over their work. This autonomy can happen at any of six levels—company, division, site, department, team, or individual.

James Wetherbe, a professor at the University of Minnesota [2], suggests asking the following three *business questions* before distributing information systems functions and the responsibilities that go with them.

Are the Operations Interdependent? When it is important for one operation to know what another is doing, those operations are interdependent; therefore, their planning, software development, machine resources, and operations need to be centralized, says Wetherbe, in order to keep the operations synchronized. Two industries in which interdependency is important are manufacturing and airlines.

Are the Businesses Really Homogeneous? If the operations do not need to know what each other is doing, then many systems functions can be decentralized, *unless* the operations truly have a lot in common.

For example, in the fast-food business, each franchise has the same information processing needs; they are very homogeneous. But they do not need to know what each other is doing, so they are not interdependent. Under these circumstances, processing may be distributed, but planning, software development, and hardware selection should be centralized, says Wetherbe.

Deciding whether the information processing in two parts of a business is truly homogeneous is not always obvious, says Wetherbe. For instance, not all department stores are the same. One major retailer found that it needed to create two information systems for handling credit charges—one for its upscale stores and one for its discount stores. The needs of the two types of stores were so different that a single system would not suffice. But, says Wetherbe, its corporate IS department does control planning. This has given the retailer the ability to seize marketing opportunities quickly when it can reuse systems built by either operation. So centralized planning is important, whether processing is distributed or not, according to Wetherbe.

Does the Corporate Culture Support Decentralization? Even if the business units do quite different things and do not need to know what each other is doing, corporate culture might dictate that some functions be centralized.

Wetherbe cites the example of a large company with 60 widely diverse business units. Although it might appear logical for this company to distribute all functions, it has chosen to centralize finance, human resources, and systems planning to offer corporatewide career opportunities with as little retraining as possible. With the central staff doing systems planning and coordination, the company can more easily move people and reuse systems.

If none of these three criteria—interdependency, homogeneity, or corporate culture—forces centralization, Wetherbe suggests letting each business unit direct its own information systems activity, with the central organization coordinating the plans.

Two Guiding Frameworks

Now that we have briefly addressed the reasons to distribute systems, we look at how, via two guiding frameworks—one from an organizational perspective and the other from a technical perspective.

An Organizational Framework. One possible distributed system structure is to serve six organizational levels. Figure 5-1 illustrates the six levels.

1. Corporate
2. Region or country
3. Site (plants, warehouses, branch offices)
4. Department
5. Work group or team
6. Individuals

Not all these levels need to exist in a single organization, and increasingly, they can be interorganizational. For instance, a company might choose to share regional or country information with suppliers. Most of these levels are self-explanatory, except perhaps level five, which has become the "hot" organizational level of late: work groups and teams. We see two types at this level. One type of work group is a relatively small group of people (perhaps ranging from three to thirty) who do essentially the same work. Any one person in the group can substitute for any other, if necessary. In an accounting department, the entire

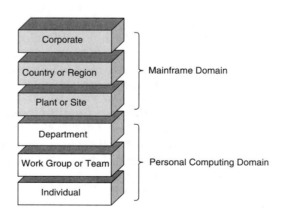

Figure 5-1   A Six-level Organizational Framework

accounts payable function might be handled by one work group. In a much larger organization, with a much larger accounting department, perhaps only the transportation accounts payable would be handled by one work group. Other groups would handle the other accounting functions.

The second type of group or team is the relatively new *self-managed work teams*. These are product and customer oriented and have moved into the service arena after cells proved successful in manufacturing. In a manufacturing cell, all the machines needed to manufacture one type of part are clustered together. In the service arena, self-managed work teams contain all the people who serve a particular set of customers or offer a particular product. These people represent all the necessary functions: legal, marketing, customer service, and so forth. The intent is to give them more autonomy and decision-making power to serve their customers better. By allowing them to manage themselves, it is hoped that they can offer more personalized and faster service.

A Technical Framework. In 1982, Einar Stefferud, David Farber, and Ralph Dement developed a conceptual framework for distributed systems [3]. It uses the acronym SUMURU, meaning "single user, multiple user, remote utility." Surprisingly, SUMURU is as appropriate today as it was in 1982—perhaps even more so because distributed systems are the focus of the computer field. Their framework includes four components—processors, networks, services, and standards. Figure 5-2 summarizes the SUMURU components and Figure 5-3 illustrates the architecture.

Processors. The authors see three levels of processors, usually with associated information storage. The name of their architecture, SUMURU, comes from these three levels of processors. *Single-user systems* (SUs) can operate in a stand-alone mode but also will be connected to local networks (LNs). Today, SUs are the clients in client/server computing. *Multiple-user systems* (MUs) serve local groups of users. Today, these are the servers. These MUs also provide (1) backup facilities for other MUs, (2) heavier-duty computation for SUs, (3) program libraries for themselves and SUs, and (4) database management for central files.

Figure 5-2   Components of the SUMURU Distributed System Architecture

Processors	**Services**
Single-user systems (SU)	Terminal access
Multiple-user systems (MU)	File Transfer
Remote utility systems (RU)	Computer mail
Networks	**Standards**
Local network (LN)	Operating systems
Remote networks (RN)	Communications protocols
	Database systems

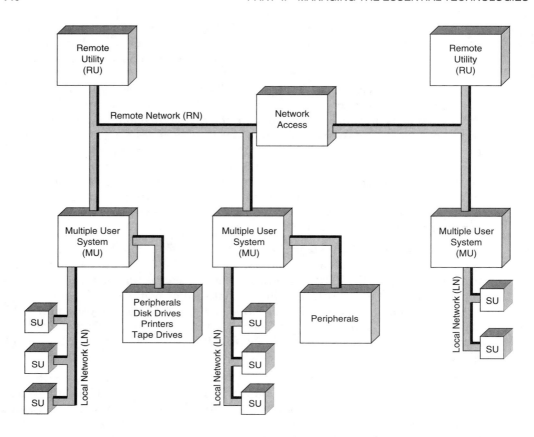

Figure 5-3   The SUMURU Architecture (from Stefferud, Farber, and Dement [3])

Ideally, according to the authors, the SUs will be scaled-down versions of the MUs—able to run the same software (to reduce software development and maintenance) but without all the features needed for shared operation on an MU.

Remote utility systems (RU) provide heavy-duty computing, corporate database management, remote batch processing, and backup for the MUs. For most organizations, RUs are the corporate mainframes as well as commercial value-added network services, such as on-line news wire services and commercial databases. Sites on the Internet can also be considered RUs.

Networks. The authors see a network architecture consisting of two levels. *Local networks* (LNs) will provide high-speed information transfer as well as close coupling between several SUs and a local MU. Today these are LANs. MUs may provide personal files, shared files, and program libraries for the SUs, and they can be the gateway between the LNs and remote networks. *Remote networks* (RNs) provide connections among MUs and connection to both in-house

and commercial RUs. RNs—which today include metropolita
(MANs), wide area networks (WANs), and the Internet—gen
transfer speeds than the LNs, but they still should have eno
provide file transfers within reasonable time limits.

Services. The authors see three main types of services ...
architecture will provide. One service is *access* to any SU, MU, or RU, subject
only to management constraints (not technical barriers). Users must also have
file transfer capabilities to send and receive entire files. To do this, a user must
have both read and write privileges at both ends of the transfer. Finally, the system must provide an *electronic mail* service. All three are essentially the services
now provided for the Net.

Standards. Corporate standards are needed in three areas: operating systems, communication protocols, and database management systems (DBMSs).
Corporate standards on operating systems are designed to minimize barriers to
transferring and using programs and data. Ideally, the selected operating systems should run on more than one vendor's equipment. Standard communication protocols are needed for terminal access, file transfers, and e-mail. In the
communication area, TCP/IP (which is used in the Internet) has become the de
facto standard. In the database arena, no distributed database management system has become a standard, although SQL has become the language of choice for
accessing different databases.

As mentioned, we believe this distributed system framework has stood the
test of time; it is still an appropriate design guide for distributed system architects. And although we have not seen it used these days, it provides a very clear
conceptual framework for understanding the various components of a distributed
system. Following are six system structures that have been called *distributed*.

SIX TYPES OF DISTRIBUTED SYSTEMS

As we noted earlier, the distributed system field has been continually evolving.
The following description of six forms of distributed systems basically follows
that evolution.

Host-Based Hierarchy

A hierarchy of processors was the first *data processing* distributed system
structure. It was favored by mainframe vendors because the large host computer
at the top of the hierarchy controlled the terminals at the lowest level. It was a
master-slave relationship. In between can be one or more levels of processors,
with the total workload shared among them. The important characteristic of this
structure is that the host computer is the central, and controlling, component.
The other important characteristic was that the processing was done on the computers; the terminals were simply access devices. See Figure 5-4.

It is not always clear just where the data is to be stored in such a system.
One view is to store all data at the top. Another is to have the master records at

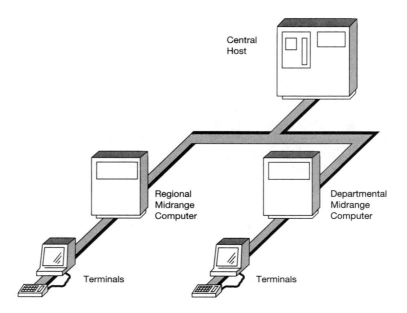

Figure 5-4   Host-based Hierarchy

the top but selected subsets at intermediate levels; the master records are then updated periodically and revised records are sent to the intermediate files. Still another view is to store master records where they are most used, and periodically provide updated records to the top for backup purposes. In any of these views, however, it is assumed that any processor in the hierarchy can access any data record within the system, as long as it is authorized to do so.

Network computers (NCs) are an intriguing flashback to this form of distributed computing. However, they have two important distinctions from the terminals of old. First, the central processing unit is the Internet, not a mainframe computer, and it is not in control of processing; the NCs are, by initiating requests. Second, the NCs handle processing; terminals do not. So there is not the same master-slave relationship as with mainframes and terminals.

Decentralized Stand-Alone Systems

Decentralized stand-alone systems do not really form a distributed system at all. (See Figure 5-5.) They are basically a holdover from the 1960s, when departments put in their own minicomputers, with no intention of connecting them to the corporate host or to other departmental systems. Hence, they are decentralized, not distributed. Over the years, many such "islands of computing" have been connected to allow a little data to flow, but this flow has been mostly upward to the corporate host. A major goal in reengineering has often been to

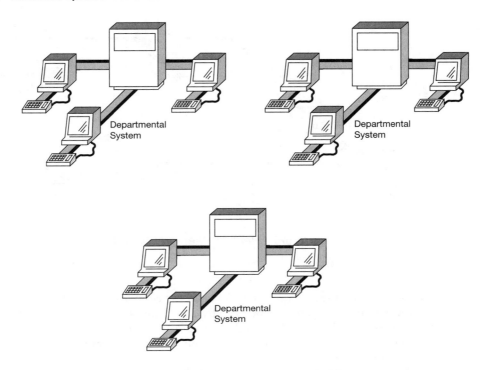

Figure 5-5   Decentralized Stand-alone System

connect these systems so that several of them could be accessed from a single desktop workstation.

Peer-to-Peer LAN-Based Systems

Systems based on a local area network (LAN) have become widely used as the basis for distributed systems. This approach began in the office system arena with LANs providing the links between PCs, print servers, and gateways to other networks. As shown in Figure 5-6 on the next page, this structure has no hierarchy. Like the telephone network, a LAN-based system allows peer-to-peer communications among components—rather than hierarchical communication through a central hub. This is the key characteristic of this structure: No computer is more superior than another.

Hybrid Enterprisewide Systems

The distributed system architecture that has become the default structure has essentially pulled together these three kinds of distributed systems using three kinds of networks—local area networks, wide area networks (WANs), and the Internet—as shown in Figure 5-7 on page 145. It combines the hierarchical

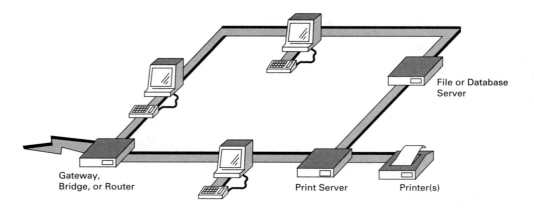

Figure 5-6   Peer-to-Peer LAN-based System

host-based processing approach favored for corporate computing, the departmental processing approach favored by departments such as manufacturing and engineering, and the LAN-based approach favored in offices. This structure is likely to be the structure of choice for many years, as companies link their various automation islands.

One important point is that this hybrid approach does not necessarily put all the machines under the aegis of the host mainframe computer. In fact, a number of companies have gotten rid of their mainframe(s) altogether, dispersing applications to departmental machines and servers. A host computer is shown in this diagram, but it is not the central control. For some applications, it could be the host; for others, it could be merely just another server.

A second important point is that this structure allows companies to begin to automate more of a business process, a process that can span several business functions within the organization, or even link to other organizations. We call this *cooperative processing* and it means that various components cooperate with each other to a perform task. As an example, to obtain, say, sporting event tickets, an order taker at a desktop machine accesses the corporate database over a WAN to see seat availability and reserve the seats. Once the seat selection is made, the order taker initiates payment authorization, with the system accessing a credit card authorization system. Once the cardholder's charge is approved, the system processes it and the clerk can send a request to the local printer, over the local LAN, to print the tickets. They are then handed to the customer, or put in the mail. Such cooperative processing allows companies to take advantage of the characteristics of individual machines, while at the same time extending the usefulness of their current IT investments. Following is an example of a mainstream application that uses these cooperative processing principles.

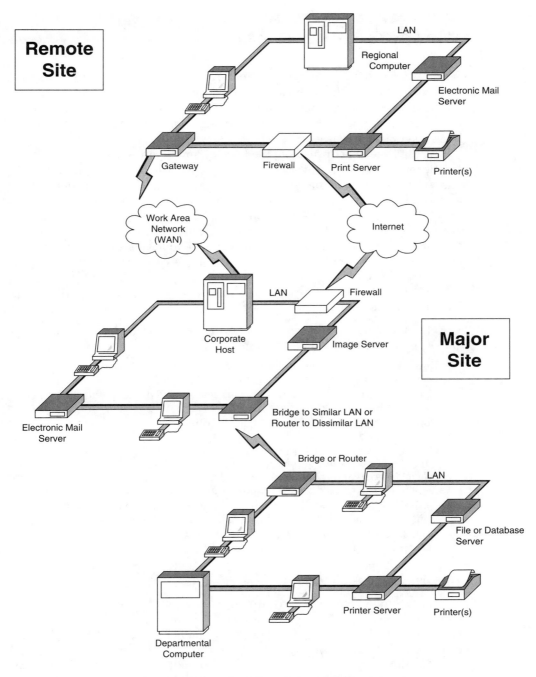

Figure 5-7 Hybrid Enterprisewide System

CASE EXAMPLE: Northwest Airlines

When Northwest Airlines, with headquarters in St. Paul, Minnesota, merged with Republic Airlines, it doubled its business and became a major national carrier. To compete as a world-class carrier, Northwest realized it had to revamp a number of its core systems. One of these systems calculates revenue from passengers.

At the time, Northwest sampled a very small percentage of its passenger tickets to estimate revenue. This approach was not yielding accurate passenger or revenue data. To improve accuracy, Northwest needed to audit all its redeemed tickets—something few major airlines do.

With the help of Andersen Consulting, Northwest built a system that uses a cooperative processing architecture and integrates products from 11 vendors and just about as many different technologies—including expert systems, imaging, relational databases, high-resolution workstations, servers, and LANs.

Management's Goals

Management established the following six major goals for the passenger revenue accounting (PRA) system:

- Enforce company pricing and commission rules to ensure that its services are properly priced and that travel agencies sell services at the correct fares.
- Calculate earned income for the corporation as well as track and reconcile air transport liability accounting.
- Cope with the volume explosion and the rapid pace of change caused by airline deregulation.
- Unhook volume growth from staff increases, so that the department could handle more work without equivalent increases in staff. The department had grown 700 percent—to 600 people. At that projected growth rate, the department would soon need its own building, unless it changed the way it worked.
- Gather, organize, and disseminate marketing information for making decisions on pricing, flight scheduling, and response to competitors' moves.
- Provide the flexibility to audit and report on special deals with travel agents and corporate purchasers.

The Distributed Architecture

Data communications are an integral part of this distributed system, which uses both LANs and a metropolitan area network among three buildings. The host IBM 3090 is linked to the backbone Ethernet LAN via an SNA-TCP/IP gateway.

The Ethernet backbone acts as a metropolitan area network, linking numerous Ethernet subnetworks. Ten of the subnetworks connect a Sun application server to about 40 diskless Sun workstations, which run UNIX. Northwest has minimized traffic across the backbone by designing the network to keep most client-to-server traffic on each subnet. In addition to the application servers, Northwest also has a FileNet image server for storing images of redeemed ticket coupons. They also have several special servers that perform the ticket auditing each night using expert system technology.

The workstations provide the passenger revenue accounting auditors with windows to the data stored on the various systems—the mainframe that stores the ticket database, external computer reservation systems, the application servers that store tickets with discrepancies, and the image database. The system accommodates large file transfers between these workstations and the mainframe because part of the processing is done on the IBM host and part is done on the workstations. For these file transfers, Northwest created a standard way for the COBOL applications (on the mainframe) to talk to the C applications (on the workstations). The workstations also draw on the host applications via 3270-terminal emulation on the Suns.

Image processing is also a key element. Each day, Northwest receives some 50,000 auditor coupons from travel agents and 100,000 lift coupons (redeemed ticket stubs) from passengers. Formerly, Northwest employed 20 to 40 people full-time just to retrieve these coupons from a huge storage basement. Now, Northwest scans both types of coupons, creating a photograph-like image and an index for each one. The images are stored on FileNet optical disks in jukeboxes.

The Revenue Accounting Process

Each day, Northwest receives data from three sources: (1) magnetic tapes of ticket sales taken from computer reservation systems and consolidated by regional clearinghouses, (2) audit coupons from travel agents, and (3) lift coupons redeemed from passengers as they board a plane.

The sales data is stored in a DB2 relational database and processed on the IBM mainframe. If all the information is not provided, the sales data is queued to an auditor, who adds the missing information by viewing the appropriate auditor coupon image that has been scanned into the system. Then the sales data for performing the nighttime audits is downloaded to Sun servers, and a C program retrieves all the travel agency rules that apply to each of these tickets.

At night, this sales data is run through expert systems, which apply the appropriate rules to recalculate the lowest fare, commission, and taxes. If the recalculation does not match the travel agency's auditor coupon data, the recalculation and corresponding coupon image are made available for review by an auditor.

The next morning, Northwest auditors view the various pieces of data in different windows on their workstations, and decide how to handle the discrepancies. Since all the coupon images are available electronically, handling one box of coupons takes two to three hours, rather than the former two to three days.

When a passenger's redeemed flight coupon is received by the department, the verified sales data is credited as earned income. Monthly books now close on the seventh of the month—one-half the time previously required. Thus, earned revenue can be recognized 50 percent faster.

Lessons Learned

Northwest learned the following four major lessons about developing complex distributed systems.

1. ***Benchmark and Prototype New Technologies to Verify Vendors' Claims.*** Do not let vendors run the benchmarks by themselves. In image processing, for instance, have the vendors scan most of the kinds of documents in the application, especially if different kinds of paper and different colors of ink are common.

2. ***An Open Architecture Works on Mission-Critical Applications.*** The passenger revenue accounting system had to integrate a variety of technologies. By using an open architecture, Northwest reduced the risk in building such a system. Risk was further controlled by creating an interface to these systems that shielded the developers from the technicalities of the new technologies. Finally, integration was demonstrated early through a small test project.

3. ***Large Distributed System Projects Need a Vendor Coordinator.*** Due to the complexity of PRA, there was no such thing as a clean design for creating a stable set of specifications for the vendors, so a big challenge was keeping the right people on the Northwest, Andersen, and vendor teams informed of current status. To fill this role, a full-time coordinator made sure that all the various projects stayed in close contact with each other. Otherwise, the end results would not work together.

4. ***Use of CASE Was Mandatory.*** Management believes that Northwest could not have done a project of this size without the tools and approaches of CASE. For one thing, CASE allowed more developers to work on different components of the system in parallel. And without CASE they could not have supported the team of up to 170 developers. Furthermore, it allowed users to play a larger role in development; even to the point of using the CASE design tool to document user procedures, design reports, and supply the text in the help system. Finally, CASE will allow them to use the data definitions from PRA in future systems, which will substantially shorten development time and improve system quality.

The huge system, which took 65,000 workdays to complete, has become a model for airline revenue accounting systems. Managers from over a dozen airlines around the world have visited Northwest to study it.

Client/Server Systems

The 1990s version of distributed systems has been client/server systems. Client/server computing has the distinguishing characteristic that it splits the computing workload between the *client*, which is a computer used by the user and can sit on the desktop or be carried around, and the *server,* which houses the sharable resources. At least that was the initial definition. As client/server computing has gotten more complex, both clients and servers make requests of one another. So at any point in time, either could be client or server. However, from the user's perspective, the client is the machine he or she is using, and the server contains the shared resources.

The trend in client/server is toward a three-tiered architecture, notes Roger Woolfe [4a], a British researcher at Wentworth Research. As Figure 5-8 shows, Tier 3 is the superserver, perhaps a mainframe. It is connected directly to the client/server system network via a server or two. This latter option allows companies to include their legacy applications in client/server systems. Short-lived and fast-changing data, as well as their corresponding integrity rules, are also stored at this superserver level so they can be shared by an enterprise. Tier 2 holds specialized servers, some of which are dedicated to housing databases or *middleware*—software that eases connection between client and server. Data specific to departments or workgroups is stored here also, as is data that does not change often yet needs rapid access. Tier 1 has the clients, either desktop or portable, connected via some sort of network.

The alternative architecture is two-tiered, consisting of only clients and servers or clients and mainframe. The three-tiered architecture reduces client

Tier 3
Superserver, often a mainframe,
connected to the network via one or more
servers, and sometimes directly as well

Tier 2
Multiple specialized servers, some
possibly dedicated to middleware

Local and wide area networks

Tier 1
Clients, some of which may be portable

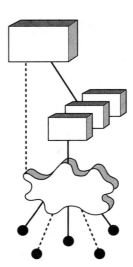

Figure 5-8   The Trend Is to Three-Tier Client/Server Arrangements
(from Wentworth Research [4a])

complexity by decreasing the number of interfaces that need to be accommodated by the client machines, notes Woolfe. The drawback is that clients are more complex and access to Tier 3 data is slower than to Tier 2.

The most famous depiction of client/server computing, however, comes from the Gartner Group [5], a highly regarded research group in Stamford, Connecticut, because it shows the possibilities for splitting work between the clients and servers; see Figure 5-9.

As shown in the figure, the network presents the all-important dividing line between what is housed on a client and what is housed on a server. The three components being split are the presentation software (what the user sees on the screen), the application software itself, and the data. Briefly, from left to right, the spectrum is as follows:

- *Distributed presentation* puts all the data, all of the applications, and some of the presentation on a remote server. This approach is one way to leave a mainframe-based legacy system in place while updating the user screen, making it graphical rather than character based.

- *Remote presentation* pulls all the presentation software onto the client machine, but leaves all the applications and data on the remote server. This approach also is a way to preserve a legacy system, and simply update the face it shows users.

- *Distributed function* places all the presentation software on the client, all the data on the server, and splits the application software between the client and server.

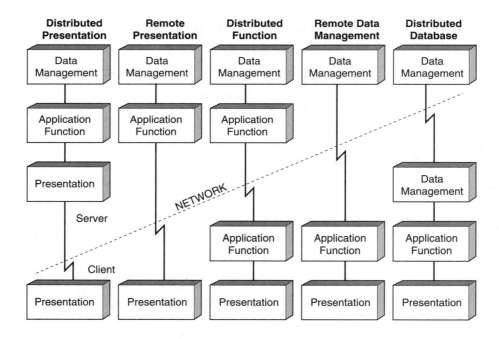

Figure 5-9   Client/Server Computing (from The Gartner Group [5])

This option is quite complex because splitting application processing between two machines requires coordination. However, it might be the most appropriate option for applications that run packaged software (such as spreadsheets or word processing) on a client in combination with corporate applications on a mainframe. It can also be good for small mobile computers that are being used to run major applications, such as order entry, inventory inquiry, and so on.

- *Remote data management* places all presentation and application software on the client, while leaving all data on the server. This option is popular because it keeps all the application software in one place (on a "fat" client), and takes advantage of the large processing capacity found on desktop computers these days.

- *Distributed database* places all the presentation and application software on the client as well as some of the data. The remaining data is on the server. This is a complex solution, especially if the numerous databases are intended to remain in sync. Distributed synchronous databases are just emerging. Even so, this is an important option for mobile computing, where the salesperson needs some data locally (probably the less dynamic data). The other up-to-the-second data can be stored on the master database and accessed only when needed. This option also leads to "fat" clients.

This description of client/server architecture has been used by many, many firms to describe their choices. In Woolfe's report, "Migrating to Enterprise Client-Server"[4a], he presents a case example of a company that plans to use two of these client/server approaches. Here's that company's story.

CASE EXAMPLE: An Aerospace Company

A corporate enterprise systems group develops systems for use across the company. The group's goal is to never again build monolithic applications. Instead, they intend to build systems—even million-dollar systems—from off-the-shelf hardware and software components.

The Software. All the client/server systems will use the same structure, with application code on the clients, data on the servers, and communication middleware software shared. The software will be written using object-oriented technology, and most of it will come from an object-oriented component library.

The Data. The heart of the architecture is a repository, which allows reuse of objects. The repository holds *meta data*—information about the data being used. This repository lets them build sets of common data under the auspices of an enterprise master database, so that data have common definitions. When in use, data is split between operational data in production systems and data warehouses, which are updated daily via replication software.

The Network. The network is an integral part of this client/server architecture. Each company site will have three components—desktop machines, servers, and one or more site hubs. Each of these components uses standard, plug-in equipment, so the architecture can be used anywhere in the world. To cope with the increased networking demands of client/server systems, the company is migrating from Ethernet to the higher-speed Asynchronous Transfer Mode (ATM) network. The conversion will take place at each site hub.

The applications will communicate to a site hub (a gateway), which will plug into the public telephone network, forming a ring structure of ATM switches. The speed of the ring will be 600M bit/s. (See Figure 5-10.)

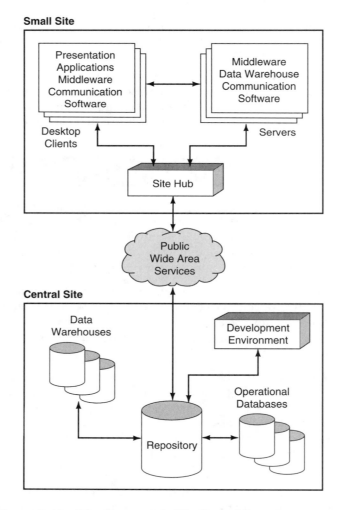

Figure 5-10   The Company's Distributed System Architecture

The Architecture. The client/server architecture is *remote data management,* to use the Gartner Group's terminology. Data resides on servers, and applications reside on clients. The company chose this approach because it discovered that only 5 to 6 percent of the average PC is utilized. The company plans to use the remaining 94 to 95 percent spare desktop capacity for application code.

The company will also use the distributed function approach, but only on a few complex systems because this approach requires more effort than remote data management.

The distributed presentation and remote presentation approaches do not take full advantage of this spare capacity, so they will not be used. The company also does not plan to use the distributed database approach, where databases are housed on client machines, because it is just too complex. The client machines must be polled to get the data, which is impractical except for highly structured work flow applications or conversation-oriented applications, such as Lotus Notes.

In short, the company will use the distributed function and remote data management configurations because they minimize total costs. The company's migration strategy for moving to object-oriented client/server systems has been first to build the architecture, then build the applications using as many reusable components as possible.

Benefits of Client/Server Computing. Client/server computing promised a number of benefits in the early 1990s. The following ones, we feel, have held true.

Better access to information. The primary benefit of client/server computing has been giving people access to the data or information they need when they need it—just-in-time data delivery. Mewes and Sobel-Feldman [6] note that a KPMG Peat Marwick survey found that 85 percent of the respondents said use of client/server computing improved customer service, 75 percent said it improved the ability to communicate customer needs to others in the organization, and 65 percent even said they could better anticipate customer needs. All were related to serving customers better.

Better access to information also allows companies to reduce cycle times. For instance, one manufacturer was able to reduce cycle time from receipt of an order to commencing production from 72 hours to 20 minutes.

Better access to information also helps companies compete better, for instance, with lower costs. Retail chains have used client/server systems to look into their stores to see what is selling, what is in inventory, and what is on order. This kind of precision lets them keep less stock on hand and replenish inventory on a more just-in-time basis. It also lets them react to changes in the market faster. And, perhaps most importantly, it can be used to better understand the underlying dynamics of their marketplace, according to Mewes and Sobel-Feldman, thereby identifying trends more quickly and capitalizing on them. So it has shifted the focus of computing from keeping track of the business to using information to fulfill its strategic objectives.

Empowered employees. Client/server computing has blended the autonomy of PCs with the systemwide rules and connectivity of traditional information systems. This combination has caused a major shift in the way corporatewide computing is viewed. In fact, it has turned traditional computing on its head, reversing the role of the host and the desktop. Whereas the host was previously the focus of attention, in client/server computing, the desktop is. This shifts the focus of computing to end users, and, as just noted, makes the main purpose of computing to put a wide variety of information and processing at people's fingertips. This has empowered employees, especially those who directly serve customers.

Increased organizational flexibility. One of the major drawbacks of traditional computing has been that it casts business processes in concrete—that is, in hard-to-change hardware and software. By modularizing systems into client and server portions, new technology and new software components can more easily be added, without affecting the rest of the system. Thus, it allows companies to be more responsive to change because their computer systems are less likely to impede organizational changes.

Client/server systems have also been used to streamline work flows between functional areas because they can allow authorized users to access information from anywhere, and communicate with others. Intecom, for instance, used client/server technology to tie order entry directly to pulling parts, manufacturing, order processing, and invoicing, note Mewes and Sobel-Feldman. As a result, Intecom can better track its business and analyze it. Even though volume increased by 30 percent, 20 percent fewer people are needed in order entry and 30 percent fewer in manufacturing.

These systems encourage people to work together via networks because they support work groups and teams—either colocated teams or those separated by great distances—giving them powerful local processing power, access to other people, and access to internal and external information.

And most powerfully of all, client/server computing supports new organizational structures via its connectivity. By providing a platform that supports individuals and groups who are geographically dispersed, it allows companies to experiment with new ways of working. In fact, you could say that experience with these technologies and their infrastructure is enabling companies to easily take advantage of the Internet. It is like a big client/server system.

Drawbacks. Other benefits touted in the early 1990s have not panned out. One was lower cost. Client/server systems are not lower cost than mainframe systems because they entail so much coordination. What initially looked like simple connections between clients and servers has turned into very large, often fragile, complex systems. So although they have made systems easier to use on the end user side, they have made systems far more complex for the systems department—making some wish for the good old all-in-one-box mainframe days. In fact, day-to-day management of the complex infrastructure—where servers can be in hundreds of locations—is the most costly part of a client/server implementation.

On the human side, they have led to organizational turmoil, as people deal with cross-boundary data flow, empowered employees, and cultural differences between people who are using the same data. So, as Mewes and Sobel-Feldman point out, the biggest challenges are not technical, they are organizational and cultural. And yet, companies believe that the benefits far outweigh the costs and headaches.

Network-Centric Systems

The advent of business use of the Internet has prompted a new form of distributed computing known as network-centric computing. This approach, at least in its idealized form, has either network computers or "thin" (and supposedly inexpensive) client machines that are used much like telephones. They are not intended to house applications as PCs do; they have no hard disk, just a browser, memory, keyboard, and a modem. Some may use a television screen. When they need to perform a function, they call into the Internet, download an operating system and then pull down the applications they need at the moment, often called *applets* (single-function applications). These applets may be written in Java, the first network-centric programming language.

This new type of computing can be depicted as simply a network computer and a network cloud (Figure 5-11). There is a great debate on where this new style of distributed computing will take hold. It seems logical for hand-held devices. It also appears to make sense for consumer applications.

To illustrate the potential power of a Web-centric system, Sun Microsystems presents the following hypothetical example at its Web site [7].

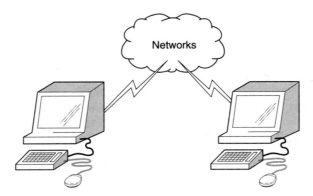

Figure 5-11   Network-Centric System

CASE EXAMPLE: "Bull Securities"

"Bull Securities" (a pseudonym), a global broker-dealer, serves its high net worth clients in 40 countries from its offices in New York City, London, and Tokyo. To improve its service to these clients, Bull has installed an intranet using Sun servers and firewalls, and given these clients access to a special "javatized" Web page. These clients have also received a Java desktop network computer equipped with a Web browser to access that home page from anywhere in the world.

To reach the special page, they simply turn on the NC and it automatically dials that page and brings up the screen. Clients can then click on, for example, "North American Market Update," which might download an audio applet with a recent update by Bull's chief economist. (Such audio updates are recorded on the Web site by Bull personnel using telephones anywhere in the world.) Clients might then choose to see an updated summary of their portfolio, with current prices and performance statistics, a graph of asset allocation, historical charts, and a money market balance. The summary is downloaded onto their NC in spreadsheet form along with a spreadsheet applet with which they can manipulate the data to test out different investment strategies. By double clicking on a stock's code, they can also automatically receive recent news about that stock along with historical charts. In addition, clients can ask to see pertinent research updates, which are downloaded to the NC along with an e-mail applet and perhaps some notes from their Bull financial advisor.

In essence, Bull has created an "extranet," in which they give external parties access to a portion of their intranet. In so doing, they are able to make information available to these high net worth customers continuously, rather than periodically, and with less (costly) human intervention. Furthermore, by offloading work to this extranet, the staff can concentrate on the 20 percent of these clients (and prospects) who appear most likely to generate the highest returns for the firm.

These, then, are the different kinds of distributed systems that have emerged. To conclude this chapter, we come back around to the beginning of the chapter and discuss the subjects of architecture and infrastructure.

DESCRIBING THE OVERALL ARCHITECTURE

For more than 20 years, John Zachman [8], an independent consultant, has been preaching the value of enterprise architecture and modeling data, processes, and networks. He has the most comprehensive view of this subject that we have seen, so we will briefly describe it here.

At a recent speech to the Southern California Client/Server User Group, Zachman noted that an architecture, with accompanying models, is absolutely necessary for client/server applications because it is too complex to comprehend otherwise—especially at the enterprise level. Furthermore, only models let people know where to make changes, if those models link to one another. He believes companies have disintegrated themselves with data, and the same is going to happen with networks. That is not good news.

Why Architecture Is Important

Tragically, the credibility of the IS community has deteriorated dramatically around the world for two reasons, he believes. First, the current inventory of legacy applications is hopelessly inadequate. Second, IS's ability to respond to current demands is hopelessly inadequate. The perception is that because past work has been inadequate, future work will be inadequate as well. If IS executives allow this problem to continue, says Zachman, their enterprise could do irrational things, such as (1) outsource IS, thereby taking away the organization's ability to assimilate change, (2) not do any development, just buy packages, which will only allow the organization to be average (based on the bell-shaped curve), or (3) not ask IS for help, just implement client/server themselves, which will disaggregate the organization by disaggregating the problem.

This is actually a terrible problem, yet few people are talking about it in public. There is an answer, but it is not magic. And it requires understanding the cause of the problem.

Architecture gives the context for describing the root cause. Think about the similarities between airframe manufacturing and information system implementation, says Zachman. The main difference between the two is that aircraft firms have figured out an architecture; IS has not. IS has been trying to build enterprise systems part by part, but the parts do not fit together. Airplanes can be maintained for 50 years in the face of a dynamically changing marketplace and technology; not so with IS. The solution, therefore, is to somehow transfer the conceptual knowledge behind building airframes into conceptual knowledge for building information systems. And that is what Zachman has been doing for 20 years.

An Enterprise Architecture Framework

The real world (an airplane, an enterprise, or a skyscraper) is so complicated that we cannot get our brain around it at one time, says Zachman, so we abstract out single variables. To completely describe an IS architecture, we need to look at the roles that people play and the components they deal with. Together, these create the rows and columns of a framework.

The Rows: Planner, Owner, Designer, Builder, Subcontractor, and Consumer or User. Over the years, Zachman has learned that there is no single architectural representation for an information system because six views must be taken into account when building complex products: planner, owner, designer, builder, subcontractor, and consumer or user. Six perspectives require six models. For instance, an airframe manufacturer needs a statement of the objectives for the planner, an architect's drawings for the owner, an architect's plans for the designer, a contractor's plans for the builder, and detailed representations for the subcontractors. The completed airplane is the consumer's view. The same is true in IS. We need a scope statement, a model of the enterprise, a model of the information system, a technology model, and a description of the components—all to produce the finished functioning system. These make up the rows in Zachman's enterprise architecture framework (Figure 5-12).

Each of these roles has its own constraints. For instance, the owner is constrained by the use of the end product. The designer is constrained by physical

A Framework			
	DATA **(What)**	**FUNCTION** **(How)**	**NETWORK** **(Where)**
Scope *Planner*			
Enterprise Model *Owner*			
Information System Model *Designer*			
Technology Model *Builder*			
Components *Subcontractor*			
Functioning System *Consumer or User*			

Figure 5-12   An Architectural Framework (from Zachman [8])

laws. And the builder is constrained by the state-of-the-art methods and technologies available. That is why we need six models, rather than one, and why these six representations need to be maintained in sync; that is called configuration management.

The Columns: Data, Function, Network. There is also no single graphical representation for the components of a complex system or for an information system. As in engineering, IS needs three components to worry about: data models (*what* it is made of), functional models (*how* it works), and network models (*where* the components are located). Zachman calls these the what, how, and where abstractions. They represent the physical manifestations of the system.

In addition, we need three more, he says, *who* (people), *when* (time), and *why* (motivation). These represent the soft side of systems. Once we have all six, we have defined a closed set. That is all we need to know to build a complex system, according to Zachman. So, the good news is that defining an enterprise architecture is not an infinite problem. The bad news is, no one has done it yet. But, a few are making progress, he notes. The entire enterprise architecture is shown in Figure 5-13 on the next page.

Use of the Framework. As can be seen, Zachman has populated the framework with a set of diagrammatic models. These, he says, can be used to describe any complex thing—an enterprise, an airplane, even a bicycle. All these models always exist, says Zachman; the question is whether or not you spend the time to make them explicit.

For instance, your organization has a data model, whether it is defined or not. And it is intended to work as your enterprise works. A problem occurs, however, when IS or users bring in a package that follows a different data model. If the rules in that model are inconsistent with the rules in your company, you will spend a lot fixing the package, says Zachman. That is one reason models are important—they allow you to properly evaluate packages. They also help builders align with what owners want. And they can help companies realize the changes that need to be made when they move to a new model, such as deciding to reorganize around customer sets rather than products.

To be an enterprise and not disintegrate as changes are made, you need to understand its architecture, says Zachman. That is the most important reason to make its architecture explicit.

Use for Knowledge Management. Of great interest to us is the final column, motivation, in which lies the key to knowledge management, suggests Zachman. Knowledge management is a topic that may well be finally receiving its due. We think it is important to note that Zachman gives IS departments a way to link this new area with the traditional data/function/network areas, rather than see them as completely isolated.

As a result of recent work on business rules, Barbara von Halle [9] has observed that the evolution of information in enterprises (Figure 5-14) follows the classic evolution of learning (Figure 5-15).

Figure 5-13 Enterprise Architecture—A Framework (from Zachman [8])

	Data (What)	Function (How)	Network (Where)	People (Who)	Time (When)	Motivation (Why)	
Objectives/ Scope (Contextual) / *Planner*	List of Things Important to the Business. Entity = Class of Business Thing	List of Processes the Business Performs. Function = Class of Business Process	List of Locations in Which the Business Operates. Node = Major Business Location	List of Organizations/Agents Important to the Business. Agent = Class of Agent	List of Events Significant to the Business. Time = Major Business Event	List of Business Goals/Strat. Ends/Means = Major Bus Goal/ Critical Success Factor	**Objectives/ Scope (Contextual)** / *Planner*
Enterprise Model (Conceptual) / *Owner*	e.g. Semantic Model. Ent = Business Entity, Reln = Business Relationship	e.g. Business Process Model. Proc = Business Process, I/O = Business Resources	e.g. Logistics Network. Node = Business Location, Link = Business Linkage	e.g. Organization Chart. Agent = Organization Unit, Work = Work Product	e.g. Master Schedule. Time = Business Event, Cycle = Business Cycle	e.g. Business Plan. End = Business Objective, Means = Business Strategy	**Enterprise Model (Conceptual)** / *Owner*
System Model (Logical) / *Designer*	e.g. "Data Model". Ent = Data Entity, Reln = Data Relationship	e.g. "Application Architecture". Proc = Application function, I/O = User Views	e.g. "Distributed System Architecture". Node = I/S Function (Processor, Storage, etc.), Link = Line Characteristics	e.g. Human Interface Architecture. Agent = Role, Work = Deliverable	e.g. Processing Structure. Time = Business Event, Cycle = Processing Cycle	e.g. Knowledge Architecture. Ends = Criterion, Means = Business Rules	**System Model (Logical)** / *Designer*
Technology Model (Physical) / *Builder*	e.g. Data Design. Ent = Segment/Row/etc, Reln = Pointer/Key/etc	e.g. "System Design". Proc = Computer Function, I/O = Screen/Device Formats	e.g. "System Architecture". Node = Hardware/System Software, Link = Line Specifications	e.g. Human/Technology Interface. Agent = User, Work = Job	e.g. Control Structure. Time = Execute, Cycle = Component Cycle	e.g. Knowledge Design. Ends = Condition, Means = Action	**Technology Model (Physical)** / *Builder*
Detailed Representations (out-of-context) / *Sub-Contractor*	e.g. Data Definition. Ent = Field, Reln = Address	e.g. "Program". Proc = Language Stmt, I/O = Control Block	e.g. "Network Architecture". Node = Addresses, Link = Protocols	e.g. Security Architecture. Agent = Identity, Work = "Transaction"	e.g. Timing Definition. Time = Interrupt, Cycle = Machine Cycle	e.g. Knowledge Definition. End = Sub-condition, Means = Step	**Detailed Representations (out-of-context)** / *Sub-Contractor*
Functioning System	e.g. Data	e.g. Function	e.g. Network	e.g. Organization	e.g. Schedule	e.g. Strategy	**Functioning System**

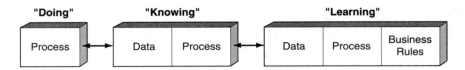

Figure 5-14   Evolution of Information (from von Halle [9])

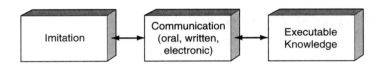

Figure 5-15   Evolution of Learning (from von Halle [9])

Zachman observes that this is entirely consistent with the classic understanding of the differentiation among data, information, and knowledge:

- *Data* consists of facts devoid of meaning or intent (where meaning and intent are supplied by a particular usage). On his architecture diagram, data is represented in column 2, the function models, which describe processes.
- *Information* is data in context, which means that the data has an explicit meaning within a specific context. On his architecture diagram, information is columns 1 and 2 taken together.
- *Knowledge* is information with direction, or intent, where intent is derived from strategies or objectives and is manifested in business rules (column 6, motivation, in his diagram). In his diagram, knowledge is represented by taking columns 1, 2, and 6 together.

As Zachman points out in Figure 5-16, it is the separation of meaning from usage that allows communication to take place, and the separation of intent from meaning and usage that allows learning to take place. When independent variables can be separated, each can be varied without affecting the others, and the overall impact can be observed. This is the basis for accumulating knowledge, that is, "learning."

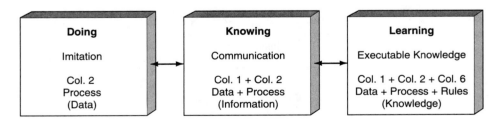

Figure 5-16   Representations of Data, Information, and Knowledge
(from Zachman [8])

THE IT INFRASTRUCTURE

In the arena of IT infrastructure, the best work we have seen has been led by Professor Peter Weill of the University of Melbourne [10]. Not only does Weill tackle the issue of defining an IT infrastructure, and distinguishing between different types, but he also addresses the very difficult question of how companies justify investing in IT infrastructure elements. They are a vital part of corporate information systems portfolios, yet they can be the most difficult to cost-justify beforehand and to measure benefits afterwards.

Four Types of IT Investments

Weill, Marianne Broadbent (also of Melbourne University), and Don St. Clair of IBM [10b, c] categorize IT investments into four types, as shown in Figure 5-17. All have different purposes and different measures of benefits.

Strategic investments aim to change the way a firm competes, the products or services it offers, or how it intends to increase revenues. These investments are generally longer term; thus, there is a long lead time before returns are produced. Also, their income stream is difficult to estimate; therefore, meaningful return on investment (ROI) calculations are not always possible. These investments are depicted at the top of the pyramid because they rely on and are supported by those underneath.

Informational investments provide a firm with the information employees need to manage and control the organization. These are systems such as executive information systems, support planning, accounting, management control, and communications, say Weill et al. These investments have a medium-term horizon, and like strategic investments depend on the firm's transactional and infrastructure investments. In fact, usually, the two lower levels must be in place before informational and strategic systems are feasible.

Transactional investments support operational management. They are usually intended to cut operating costs by substituting capital for labor so that higher volumes can be handled. They process repetitive transactions and support such operational activities as inventory control, order processing, receiv-

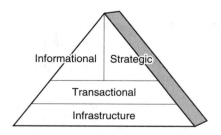

Figure 5-17   Types of IT Investments
(from Weill, Broadbent, and St. Clair [10b])

ables, payables, and so on. They generally have a short-term ROI. These systems feed summary data up the pyramid to the informational systems, and they are supported by the firm's infrastructure.

Infrastructure investments provide the base foundation of IT capability in a firm. Weill et al. distinguish this level from the other three saying that those three contain the applications aimed at running specific business functions or processes. The infrastructure does not run applications, it simply supports them.

What Is an IT Infrastructure?

Weill, Broadbent, and St. Clair define an IT infrastructure as

> the base foundation of IT capability budgeted for and (usually) provided by the information systems function in the form of reliable services and shared across multiple business units or functional areas. The IT capability includes both the technical and managerial expertise required to provide reliable services. [10b]

The shared characteristic differentiates an infrastructure from IT investments used by just one function. Elements in an IT infrastructure can include companywide networks, data warehouses, large-scale computing facilities, electronic data interchange capabilities, and even R&D aimed at identifying emerging technologies, say Weill, et al. (A comprehensive list of IT infrastructure services is found in Weill and Broadbent [10d].) On top of this infrastructure sit applications, which perform the business's processes. As such, infrastructure does not provide direct business performance benefits. Rather it enables other systems that do yield business benefits. That is what makes infrastructure so difficult to cost-justify.

Similar to Public Infrastructure. IT infrastructure is strikingly similar to public infrastructure—such as roads, hospitals, sewers, and schools—says Weill [10e].

1. Both are provided by a central agency and funded by some form of taxation.
2. Both are long term and require large investments.
3. A central agency provides an essential service that users are not motivated or able to provide.
4. Both enable business activity by users that would otherwise not be economically feasible.
5. Flexibility is valued in both because they must be in place before the precise business activity is known.
6. Both are difficult to cost-justify in advance as well as to show benefits in hindsight.
7. Both require a delicate investment balance—too little investment leads to duplication, incompatibility, and suboptimal use; while too much discourages user investment and involvement and may result in unused capacity.

The Value of an Infrastructure. Weill et al. believe there are generally two levels of IT infrastructure: (1) a firmwide infrastructure which provides the base for (2) infrastructure built by a firm's various business units. The value of these two kinds of infrastructures comes about in four ways. First, the firmwide infrastructure leverages and increases the return on IT investments made by the business units. Second, infrastructure built by each business unit can provide incremental benefits to that unit, such as flexibility, shorter time-to-market of its products and services, and reduced marginal cost of IT investments made by the business unit. Third, business units can reap operational benefits from more efficient business processes: higher capacity utilization, increased labor productivity, more on-time delivery, and lower defect rate. Finally, business units can receive effectiveness benefits: increased market share, higher return on assets, increased sales growth, and higher return on sales.

Three Views of Infrastructure

The benefits a firm actually realizes, however, depend on the firm's objectives for the infrastructure. Weill et al. see three possibilities. A firm might invest in infrastructure to provide (1) economies of scale (utility), (2) synergies between business units (dependent), or (3) flexibility to meet changes in the marketplace (enabling).

As a Utility. Companies that view their infrastructure as a utility see it as a necessary and unavoidable service that must be provided to the firm. Expected benefits are cost savings achieved through economies of scale. Normally, firms with this perspective treat infrastructure cost as an administrative expense, and they act to minimize this expense. They offer the fewest infrastructure services, say Weill and Broadbent [10], and, for instance, promote use of networks for messaging but not as part of inter- or intra-organizational business processes. This objective requires the lowest investment, but also only results in lowering costs (but not reengineering the business). Outsourcing may be viewed favorably because the IT infrastructure is not seen as strategic.

As Dependent. When a business ties its infrastructure investments to specific, known business programs, it takes the dependent view. Since investments are tied to business plans, the infrastructure is treated as a business expense, and its value is measured by short-term business benefits. Firms with this view include infrastructure planning in current business planning. They also see the network as very important. Furthermore, this view of infrastructure appears to smooth the way for simplifying business processes, noted Weill and Broadbent [10c]. In fact, they surmise that this view is a minimum requirement for successfully implementing business process reengineering.

As Enabling. This view is taken by firms that develop and continually modify their infrastructure in coalignment with their strategy—infrastructure influences strategy and vice versa. The primary benefit is long-term flexibility, so they do not limit infrastructure investments to current strategy. The infrastructure is intended to provide the foundation for changing direction in the future, if need be. Thus, infrastructure costs are seen as business investments. So, for example, they use networks extensively in businesses processes, both within the firm and with their customers and suppliers.

In a study of 11 Australian firms, Weill and Broadbent found that all that were implementing business process reengineering took either a dependent or enabling view of infrastructure. And those that took the enabling view had the capability to install completely new processes, not just simplify existing business processes.

Needless to say, the appropriate viewpoint is not a technical decision, it is a top-management decision. It is IS management's job to make this clear to senior management and show them the options. Again, as we pointed out in Chapter 2, teamwork among the various levels of management is absolutely necessary to align the technical investments with the business strategy.

No view is superior, however; different views are appropriate for different strategies. Moving from utility to dependent to enabling views increases the up-front investment and the number of IT infrastructure services provided.

To see how one organization has approached investing in infrastructure, consider the city of Sunnyvale, a case published along with Wentworth Research's IT Management Programme report on "Justifying Infrastructure Investment" [4b].

CASE EXAMPLE: City of Sunnyvale, California

The city of Sunnyvale, California, with 120,000 citizens and a budget of $120 million, is rated as one of the best-run cities in the United States. Its performance-based budgeting system, which has been honed over the past 20+ years, has fostered citywide fiscal soundness and day-to-day accountability by city administrators. This budgeting process, along with the city's 20-year planning horizon, is aiding the IT department in creating and financing the city's information infrastructure.

In early 1994, Sunnyvale hired Shawn Hernandez as the director of information technology to move the city into the future. He is concentrating on building the city's information infrastructure because the city sees infrastructure as its foundation for the future. The director, commented,

If the city of Sunnyvale is to succeed in leveraging technological resources to deal with increasing customer demands, as well as improve efficiency and customer service, the IT Department must first take responsibility for capturing accurate information and delivering that information in a timely manner. [4c, p. 1]

This statement is the driving force behind the city's IT department. The IT director believes the city needs to take a leadership position in technology and develop the appropriate infrastructure to leverage the use of technology and capitalize on technological opportunities. To accommodate future demands and to deal with the rapid technological changes in the IT field, the director also believes the infrastructure he installs must be capable of expanding.

The investment driver for the infrastructure is quality of service. To provide high-quality service to customers, the infrastructure users (city departments) must have timely and accurate information to do their jobs. For this to happen, the IT department must have the right pieces of information at the right place at the right time.

The infrastructure will provide connectivity between the city's traditional mainframes with attached terminals/PCs, and the numerous stand-alone LANs. It will be based on a fiber-optic backbone, client/server computing, and relational database technology. A three-level distributed architecture will be used, with enterprise servers, mid-tier servers, and desktop clients. The architecture will encompass more than traditional computing equipment, however. For example, the 40+ copiers throughout the city will someday be replaced by laser printers, so that employees can send a request for 50 copies of a report from their desktop rather than request a secretary or clerk to make the copies.

The information infrastructure is like the foundation for a home, says the director. It needs to withstand all the weight, all the noise, and all the things you want to plug into it. Since information technology is changing so rapidly, the city must think long term about its infrastructure to ensure that it can be easily expanded and upgraded, and will not hinder the city taking advantage of future technological opportunities. Unfortunately, the traditional fiber-optic vendors have not been able to support the required level of upgradability. As a result, the city laid a new type of fiber-optic conduit. From the end, it looks like a honeycomb with 19 cells, only two of which are used initially. New fiber bundles can easily be blown through the spare cells in the future using a special gas, thus making it easy to upgrade the fiber backbone to accommodate new services like video teleconferencing or heavy-duty video conferencing or combined voice and data transmission.

Infrastructure investments are paid for through chargeback. When the IT department places equipment on someone's desk, installs a software package on a computer, or hooks up a PC to a LAN, that equipment, software, or communication link immediately begins generating its own replacement funds. Sunnyvale charges back everything on rental rates because it knows everything will eventually need to be replaced.

Superrules guide technology investments. One such rule is that the city will standardize on products to make effective use of resources. Another unwritten superrule is that a person using a computer at, say, the Senior Center will have the same access and response time as someone working next to the mainframe. Another IT superrule is: All projects are subject to review by an executive body that represents all city departments. Thus, continuous buy-in, support, and fine tuning of demands form an improvement cycle. An outcome of this superrule is a more participative executive body—one that understands departmental priority and guides the city's IT goals as a high-performance team. A joint environment is established for a consistent framework from which all departments can benefit.

Is Infrastructure IS's Main Role?

At a recent UCLA Colloquium session, Lynne Markus of Claremont Graduate School [11] noted how the field has shifted its focus from a hardware/software dichotomy to an application/infrastructure dictotomy. Furthermore, she pointed out, more and more application development is leaving IS departments, as they buy purchased packages and as users get more involved. In the past, companies would rather custom develop applications than change the way they did business. Today, the opposite is true. If a package "almost" fits the way they work, they change their work processes to fit the package. This means that IS departments are really in the infrastructure business.

Furthermore, a number of CIOs recently told Markus that they are uncomfortable with the CIO title. They would prefer to be known as the chief technology officer (CTO) because they see their role more as implementing and managing the technical infrastructure.

These two trends raise a significant issue, she says, because, as Peter Keen has pointed out, infrastructure is totally cost. There is no intrinsic value in infrastructure, so no one wants to pay for this public good. Value comes from use of applications. The issue is that if CIOs focus mainly on infrastructure, they put themselves in charge of a cost center, not a center that delivers value. This is a recipe for obsolescence or extinction. Markus asked if this is what's really going on? Are CIOs retreating from managing a function that adds business value?

The ensuing stimulating discussion brought out a couple of points in this controversial area. Yes, perhaps this could be a recipe for extinction; however, this historical view of infrastructure may not continue. Some companies now make a case that infrastructure does have intrinsic value, especially when it is extended outside the organization. One company gives away Lotus Notes (an element of its infrastructure) to vendors so that they can link into its network. The company sees this as creating value in the relationship.

Yet another point was made that the assumption that IS departments will continue to concentrate on infrastructure may be incorrect. The trend may reverse itself. With the Internet, the companies may essentially outsource the infrastructure and take back application development. In this time of turmoil, there is no pat answer in the infrastructure arena.

CONCLUSION

Distributed systems dominate the computing development agenda in the 1990s, first in the form of client/server systems and now in network-centric computing. Information system departments had hardly gotten enough expertise and confidence in building client/server systems when the Internet crept up behind them and caused another significant mindshift. It has been a dizzying time.

Change is not likely to slow down, so companies need a way to fit the new technologies and developments into some sort of overall framework. One possibility is to create an enterprise architecture to cope with all this complexity. Although Zachman's framework and ideas have been around for 20 years, the situation may now have gotten so complex that companies will finally realize the importance of having this overall lay-of-the-land.

Furthermore, with the growth of distributed systems has come the importance of infrastructure (from the technical viewpoint) to provide the platform for allowing interconnection from anywhere to anywhere and (from the business viewpoint) to permit organizational flexibility. The viewpoint taken—as utility, dependent, or enabling—could well determine how a company unleashes the potential of distributing computing. And how much of a company's enterprise architecture it makes explicit (and up-to-date) may determine how well the company coordinates its organizational and distributed system efforts.

QUESTIONS AND EXERCISES

REVIEW QUESTIONS

1. What is the difference between an architecture and an infrastructure?
2. What are the four attributes of a distributed system?
3. How is an open system defined today?
4. List and briefly explain the questions that can be asked in deciding whether or not to distribute computing responsibilities.
5. What are the components of the guiding framework for distributed systems by Stefferud, Farber, and Dement?
6. Give six examples of system structures that can be called distributed.
7. What four lessons did Northwest learn about building their PRA systems?
8. What are the Gartner Group's five types of client/server systems? Which two did the manufacturer choose and why?
9. What are the main benefits of client/server computing?
10. According to Zachman, why is architecture important?
11. What are the six rows and six columns in Zachman's framework?
12. Describe four kinds of IT investments that companies make, according to Weill, et al.
13. What is an IT infrastructure?
14. What three ways can companies view an IT infrastructure?
15. Why does Lynne Markus say that focusing only on infrastructure is a recipe for obsolescence or extinction of the IS department?

DISCUSSION QUESTIONS

1. Which of the six types of distributed systems do you think is most likely to dominate in the future? Which is least likely? Explain your opinions.
2. Is network computing taking us back to the architecture of mainframes and dumb terminals? Are we coming full circle? Why or why not?
3. What do you think of the fact that some CIOs would rather be known as chief technology officers rather than chief information officers? How does this position relate to the responsibilities of the CIO described in Chapter 2?

EXERCISES

1. Find an article in the current literature that describes a distributed system.
   a. Describe it using the four attributes given in this chapter.
   b. Does it relate to the SUMURU architecture? How?
   c. What benefits are claimed for the system?
   d. Describe its infrastructure.
2. Identify a company in your local community that is using what it calls a distributed system. What was top management's or the business unit management's involvement in justifying the system? How do the system's characteristics compare with those given in this chapter? What challenges has the information systems department encountered building the system, and how has it dealt with these challenges?
3. Identify a company in your local community that has an information systems infrastructure. Does management see it as utility, dependent, or enabling? Explain management's rationale.
4. Find a description of an Internet-based network-centric application. Why was this approach taken? What benefits are expected?

REFERENCES

1. DAVENPORT, TOM and JANE LINDER, "Information Management Infrastructure: The New Competitive Weapon?" Ernst & Young Working Paper, Center for Business Innovation, One Walnut St., Boston, MA, October 1993.

2. WETHERBE J. C., "IS: To Centralize or to Decentralize," *SIM Network*, Society for Information Management, Chicago, IL, January 1987.

3. STEFFERUD, E., D. FARBER, and R. DEMENT, "SUMURU: A Network Configuration for the Future," *Mini-Micro Systems*, May 1982, pp. 311–312.

4. IT MANAGEMENT PROGRAMME, Wentworth Research, Egham, Surrey, England, http://www.wentworth.co.uk:

   a. WOOLFE, ROGER, "Managing the Move to Client-Server," January 1995.

   b. VARNEY, CORNELIA, "Justifying Infrastructure Investments," May 1995.

   c. VARNEY, CORNELIA, "Justifying Infrastructure Investments Sourcebook, City of Sunnyvale, California Case Example," May 1995.

5. THE GARTNER GROUP, 56 Top Gallant Road, Stamford, Connecticut 06904.

6. MEWES, KEN and KEN SOBEL-FELDMAN, "Client/Server Computing: Shaping Business Information Systems for the 21st Century," *Forbes*, May 20, 1996.

7. "SUN TECHNOLOGY APPLICATIONS FOR FINANCIAL SERVICES," (Chapter 6) Sun Microsystems, 2550 Garcia Ave., Mountain View, CA 94043, available at its corporate Web site: http://www.sun.com/javacomputing/finance/JavaPlatformIntro.html, November 1996.

8. ZACHMAN, JOHN, Zachman International, 2222 Foothill Blvd., Suite 337, La Cañada, CA 91011.

9. VON HALLE, BARBARA, 8 Calais Rd., Mendham, NJ 07945.

10. WEILL, PETER, PH.D., Director, Key Centre for Technology Management, Graduate School of Management, University of Melbourne, 200 Leicester St., Carlton 3053, Victoria, Australia.

    a. WEILL, PETER, MARIANNE BROADBENT, and DON ST. CLAIR, "Management by Maxim: The Formation of Information Technology Infrastructures," Melbourne Business School, Working Paper No. 8, November 1994, revised September 1996.

    b. WEILL, PETER, MARIANNE BROADBENT, and DON ST. CLAIR, "I/T Value and the Role of IT Infrastructure Investments," *Strategic Alignment*, Oxford University Press, 1996.

    c. WEILL, PETER and MARIANNE BROADBENT, "Infrastructure Goes Industry Specific," July 1994, pp. 35-39.

    d. WEILL, PETER and MARIANNE BROADBENT, "Infrastructure Mix and Match," *MIS*, October 1994 pp. 52-55.

    e. WEILL, PETER, "The Role and Value of Information Technology Infrastrucutre: Some Empirical Observations," *Strategic Information Technology Management: Perspectives on Organizational Growth and Competitive Advantage*, edited by R. Banker, R. Kauffman, and M. A. Mahmood, Idea Group Publishing, Middleton, PA, 1993.

11. MARKUS, M. LYNNE, "Thinking the Unthinkable—What Happens If the MIS Field As We Know It Goes Away?" Presentation at Professor E. Burton Swanson's UCLA Information Systems Colloquium, May 16, 1996.

SIX

INTRODUCTION

We treat telecommunications in this chapter in the broad sense—the sending of information in any form from one place to another electronically. In this sense, the telecommunications system is an "electronic highway system" for the flow of information among the corporate office, regional offices, sites, departments, work groups, individuals, between companies, and the outside world. Many IS departments are responsible for designing, building, and maintaining that information highway in the same way that governments are responsible for building and maintaining streets, roads, and freeways.

Once built, the system provides an infrastructure for the flow of information. That flow will be managed not by IS professionals but by users, just as users manage the flow of cars and trucks on the physical highway network. Government agencies provide standards and laws for the flow of highway traffic, enforced by the police and highway patrol. In the same way, IS departments develop and enforce the telecom standards for information traffic. This analogy could be pursued in more detail, but the point is clear. The telecom universe is becoming as important to the movement of information and communications as the highway system (the shipping lanes, the railroad right-of-ways, and the airspace) is to the movement of people and goods.

This analogy presents telecommunications as a technical linking mechanism, which it is. We need to mention, however, that the Internet has opened up a whole new way of viewing telecom: that of providing a *cyberspace*—a place where people can "exist" in a virtual world. Since this chapter discusses the technology view of telecom, we will limit our discussion to the linking paradigm. In Chapter 11, however, we discuss the cyberspace viewpoint because it relates to the use of telecommunication services.

THE EVOLVING TELECOMMUNICATIONS SCENE

Telecom is an exciting place, perhaps too exciting for some people. The changes are coming fast and furiously. To give an inkling of what is happening, we begin by talking about the evolving telecom scene.

The Status of Telecom Today

Nine "facts of life" relating to telecommunications lead to a better understanding of what is feasible and likely in the near future:

- Organizations have a multitude of networks.
- The reach of networks is expanding organizationally.
- Today's three primary telecom networks will be joined by new channels.
- "The last mile" is being opened up to competition.
- The telephone, PC, and TV are converging.
- Five technologies will underpin telecom advances.
- We are moving into an era of bandwidth abundance.
- The Internet has arrived (for business use).
- Intranets have become the next generation of computing.

Organizations Have a Multitude of Networks. Most organizations have served their telecom needs through separate, dedicated networks—a voice telephone network, the corporate telecom network and its links to the Internet, countless LANs, wireless manufacturing site networks, a video conferencing network, a corporate TV network, building security networks, and on and on. One aerospace company investigated its in-plant networks at one site. Instead of finding seven networks, as they had expected, they uncovered *nineteen*!

In most cases, each network has its own transmission medium (such as twisted pairs of wires or coaxial cable) because each was built at a different time and for a different need. There is little or no sharing of network capacity among them because each was designed just for its task. When a new need arises, it is generally given its own network. As a result, wiring ducts and conduits are stuffed, above-ceiling spaces are full, and these jammed sites are difficult to service—not to mention adding optic fiber.

The net result (sorry for the pun) is that these networks are "islands of automation." They cannot be monitored from a central site, they cannot share data, and they cannot take advantage of computing resources on other networks. It remains to be seen how quickly companies can actually connect these islands and permit them to interoperate.

The Reach of Networks Is Expanding Organizationally. Alan Kamman, of the Nolan, Norton & Co. consulting firm [1], suggests that wealth is created by organizations that can move information—replacing the movement of physical goods in importance. Companies will use connectivity in increasingly broader ways, he says, seeking competitive advantage. The following three types of networks demonstrate the ever-broadening scope.

Single-organization networks can span the globe. The Digital Equipment Corporation network, for example, has over 41,000 nodes in 26 countries. It allows the firm to operate in an elaborate matrix fashion, while maintaining central guidance.

Industry-specific value-added networks were the fastest growing types of networks in the 1980s, says Kamman. They link suppliers to one buyer in a specific marketplace. An example is J. C. Penney, whose network not only links its employees but also ties in manufacturers of apparel and fabric, such as J. P. Stevens and Du Pont. Penney electronically orders fabric and material and the manufacturers deliver orders directly to the apparel manufacturers in a just-in-time fashion.

Extended enterprise networks interconnect single-organization networks. They are not limited by industry, and they provide a type of electronic information consortium. The Mitsubishi Group represents an example, says Kamman. The group is comprised of 28 members, ranging from an oil company to a steel manufacturer to a bank. Each member has its own company network, but now these are interconnected. In addition, 100 other corporations—such as Nikon Camera and Kirin Beer—have financial links and electronic connections to these 28. No single firm dominates in networks with this arrangement. These networks are the infrastructure of the future, says Kamman.

Today's Three Primary Telecom Networks Will Be Joined by New Channels. In their premier report "Telecom: The New Agenda," Wentworth Research's Telecom Management Programme (TCMP) [2] in England points out that the public switched telephone network will continue to dominate. But wireless nets (based on cellular radio technology) and cable TV are gaining prominence in providing telephone service around the world—where regulation permits.

As shown in Figure 6-1, these three will be complemented by two newer technologies. Satellite networks will be used for wireless data transmission using very small aperture terminals (VSATs), also called satellite dishes. New digital terrestrial TV, when combined with the telephone network, can transmit large volumes of information on demand—including software, games, and video. And CD-ROM, while not a telecom technology, is a telecom alternative.

"The Last Mile" Is Being Opened Up to Competition. TCMP also reports that the bottleneck in telecom has often been "the last mile"—the link between a customer's premises and a telecom provider's local distribution point. Telephone companies have had a monopoly providing these local loop services.

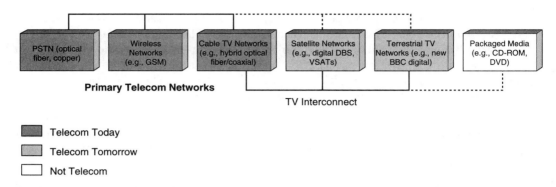

Figure 6-1   The Growing Diversity of Physical Networks
(from Wentworth Research and SRI [2])

But this market is now being deregulated around the world, and potential contenders include not only cable TV companies that are laying fiber and coaxial cable but also digital cellular radio providers and even gas, water, and electric utilities that might provide telecom services as well as read their meters remotely. Competition will transform the provision of the physical link market into a commodity by 2002, predicts the TCMP report, particularly in "the last mile."

The Telephone, PC, and TV Are Converging. There probably will not be a single, multipurpose information superhighway, states the TCMP report, but there will be a convergence of our three main communicating devices: the telephone, personal computer, and television, as shown in Figure 6-2. This trend leads TCMP to an intriguing observation:

> A most striking implication of convergence is that it will lead to the revolution of a single point of network access via broadband links, reducing the number of physical paths to any home or office building. [2, p.8]

That is why telephone companies and cable operators are in such fierce competition for that last mile to your home and office.

Five Technologies Will Underpin Telecom Advances. TCMP also points out that five raw technologies are setting the trends. One is *optical fiber* because it will give us unprecedented bandwidth. The second is *microelectronics*; its price/performance ratio still halves every 18 months, which will give us ever faster switching, computer power, and miniaturization. The third is *software*, especially object-oriented and new languages, such as Sun's Java, because it gives the intelligence to execute all kinds of tasks. The fourth pacing technology is *radio* because it allows large populations to communicate at costs lower than terrestrial networks. And the final technology is *digital*. Everything will be digital, leading to higher quality, better security, and growing convergence, predicts the Telecom Management Programme.

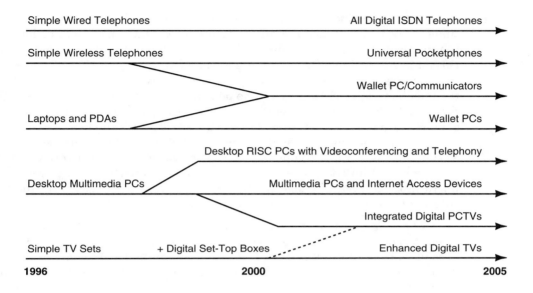

Simple Wired Telephones   All Digital ISDN Telephones

Simple Wireless Telephones   Universal Pocketphones

Wallet PC/Communicators

Laptops and PDAs   Wallet PCs

Desktop RISC PCs with Videoconferencing and Telephony

Desktop Multimedia PCs   Multimedia PCs and Internet Access Devices

Integrated Digital PCTVs

Simple TV Sets   + Digital Set-Top Boxes   Enhanced Digital TVs

1996   **2000**   **2005**

Figure 6-2   Relationships Between the Telephone, the PC, and the
TV Will Evolve (from Wentworth Research and SRI [2])

We Are Moving into an Era of Bandwidth Abundance. At a speech at the Aspen Institute, columnist and author George Gilder [3] noted that an era is defined by the plummeting price of the key factor of production. During the industrial era, that key factor was the plummeting price of horsepower, as defined in kilowatt-hours, which dropped from many dollars to 7.5 cents. For the past 30 years, the driving force of economic growth has been the plummeting price of transistors, translated into MIPS and bits of semiconductor memory. The latter has fallen 68 percent a year, from $7 some 35 years ago to a millionth of a cent today.

Today, however, we are approaching yet another "historic cliff of cost" in a new factor of production: bandwidth. "If you thought the price of computing dropped rapidly in the last decade, just wait until you see what happens with communications bandwidth," said Gilder [3], referencing a remark by Andy Grove, CEO of Intel. Up to this point, we have used MIPS and bits to compensate for the limited availability of bandwidth, said Gilder, but now we are moving into an era of bandwidth abundance.

Fiber optic technology is just as important as microchip technology. There are currently some 40 million miles laid in the world today. And in the United States, it is being laid at the rate of 4,000 miles a day. But half of it is dark—that is, it is not used. And the other half is used to just one-millionth of its potential because every 25 miles it must be converted to electronic pulses to amplify and regenerate the signal. The bandwidth of the optical fiber has been limited by the switching speed of transistors, 2.5 to 10 billion cycles per second.

But the intrinsic capacity of each thread is much more, said Gilder, ten times more is the capacity of all the frequencies commonly used in the air for communication, from AM radio to KU band satellite. But the capacity of each thread is 1,000 times the switching speed of transistors—25 terahertz. As a result, using all-optical amplifiers (just recently invented), we could send all of the telephone calls in America on the peak moment of Mother's Day on one fiber thread. And by putting thousands of fiber threads in a sheath, we create an era of bandwidth abundance that will dwarf the era of MIPS and bits.

Over the next decade, said Gilder, bandwidth will expand ten times as fast as computer power and completely transform the economy. Network computers will be based on the power of the network rather than the power of the microchip. The Java language and the Web computers are the start. In short, the Internet is the fastest growing force in the world economy.

The Internet Has Arrived for Business Use. The biggest telecom news to most people is the Internet, especially the surprisingly fast uptake for business uses, beginning around 1994. It caught many IS departments by surprise, not to mention the hardware and software vendors who serve the corporate IS community.

The Internet actually began in the 1960s when it was funded by the U.S. Department of Defense's Advanced Research Projects Agency and was called ARPANET. It was intended for electronic shipment of large scientific and research files. And it was built as a distributed network, without a controlling node, so that it could continue to function if some of its nodes got knocked out in a nuclear war. But, much to the surprise of its creators, it was mainly used for electronic mail among government contractors, academics, researchers, and scientists.

In 1993 it was still basically a worldwide underground network for researchers, scientists, academics, and individuals. But in 1994, that all changed when the World Wide Web was invented by Tim Berners-Lee at CERN in Geneva. This graphical, hyperlinked "layer" of the Net made it much more user friendly and its use by businesses skyrocketed. The Internet has done for telecom what the IBM PC did for computing: brought it "to the masses."

Intranets Have Become the Next Generation of Computing. The original culture of the Net was "all this information should be free," and in keeping with this philosophy, most information and software on the Net were free. Even when the Web arrived, its browser (first Mosaic and then Netscape's Navigator) were free. Once companies recognized the value of the Web, they decided to bring it in-house. The result has been intranets consisting of internal Web sites generally accessible only to employees.

Intranets are touted as the next generation of computing because they build on client/server concepts while adding some desirable features, such as a worldwide infrastructure that is already in place, easy-to-use standard access software (the browser), single points of information storage and maintenance at Web sites, access to information all around the world, and the ability to leverage years of investments by governments and academic institutions.

These, then, give an inkling of what is happening in the exciting world of telecommunications. Now just taking one piece of that world—the traditional telecom analogy of the highway system—we describe the single most important standards framework: the OSI Reference Model. With the use of this open systems model, the goal of globally interconnected electronic highways has become a reality, because products from different vendors can cooperate. Although discussions of standards can be ponderous and pretty boring, our intent is to make this description understandable and practical.

The All-Important OSI Reference Model

Complications in networking are often caused by incompatibilities, and incompatibilities can be reduced by using standards. In fact, standards should be the foundation of every firm's overall telecom architecture because they permit interconnection. Tailored solutions should be reserved for filling gaps where standards are not yet available. Fortunately, network standards—including de facto standards—are coming at us fast and furiously these days.

Closed versus Open Networks. The first concept that is important to understand is the difference between closed and open networks. A *closed network* is one that is offered by one supplier and to which only the products of that supplier can be attached. Mainframe and mini manufacturers used this approach for years to "lock in" their customers. Closed networks were originally adopted for the top three computing levels which we described in Chapter 5—corporate, regional, and site. Companies generally used the proprietary network offered by their mini or mainframe manufacturer. In the Internet world, the first commercial offerings (CompuServe, Prodigy, America On-Line, and Microsoft Network) all used proprietary software initially. But as direct connection to the Internet spread, these firms all finally embraced the Internet's open systems approach.

An *open network* is based on national or international standards so that the products of many manufacturers can be attached to it. Open networks have been favored by suppliers serving the lower three computing levels—departments, work groups, and individuals. Today, proprietary networks are out, open networks are in, because no company is large enough to serve all of a firm's telecom needs—to say nothing of connecting to other organizations and people.

We now live in an open systems world, and the most important architecture in this world is the Open Systems Interconnection (OSI) model.

Why It Is Called a Reference Model. The International Standards Organization (ISO), CCITT, and other standards bodies have adopted the seven-level OSI reference model for guiding the development of international standards for networks of computers. It is called a reference model because it only recommends the functions to be performed in each of the seven layers; it does not specify detailed standards for each layer. Those are left up to the standards bodies in the adopting countries.

Although we rarely hear about OSI these days, it provides the network architecture for all distributed systems. In particular, its description of the types of communication protocols that need to exist at each layer is used by the biggest distributed network of all, the Internet. Furthermore, OSI is used by all suppliers to make their products interconnectable. So, understanding the OSI reference model is a first step toward understanding telecom.

An Analogy: Mailing a Letter. In the model's layered architecture, control information is used to route messages to their destination. The following is a four-level analogy of one executive mailing a letter to another executive (Figure 6-3). Notice that control information—the address and type of delivery—is on

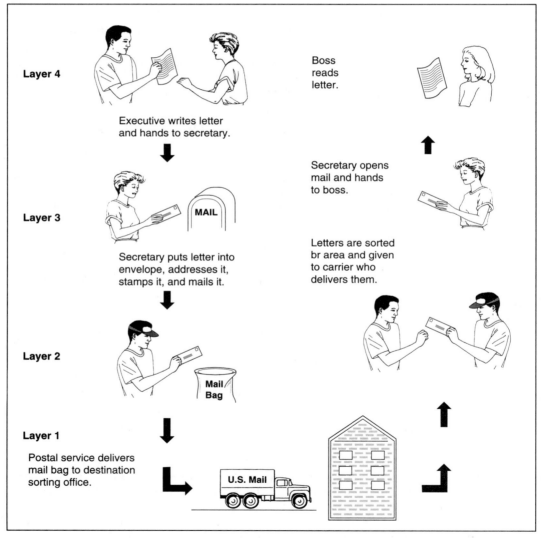

Layer 4

Executive writes letter
and hands to secretary.

Boss
reads
letter.

Secretary opens
mail and hands
to boss.

Layer 3

MAIL

Secretary puts letter into
envelope, addresses it,
stamps it, and mails it.

Letters are sorted
br area and given
to carrier who
delivers them.

Layer 2

Mail
Bag

Layer 1

Postal service delivers
mail bag to destination
sorting office.

U.S. Mail

Figure 6-3   How Control Information Is Used to Route Messages

the envelope or mailbag. This control information determir
provided by the next lower layer, and it contains addressi
corresponding layer on the receiving end. It defines the
layers as well as the dialog within a layer.

- At layer 4, the business executive writes a letter and gives it to
- At layer 3, the secretary puts the letter into an envelope, addresses
  puts the return address on the envelope, stamps it, and then mails it.
- At layer 2, the mail carrier takes the letter to the post office sorting office, whe.
  all mail for the same postal district is put into one bag with the destination postal
  office name on it. Mail of different types—express mail, first-class mail, third-
  class mail—have their own bags.
- At layer 1, the postal service delivers the mail bag to the destination sorting
  office.
- At layer 2, the sorting office checks that the bag has been delivered to the right
  office. Then the letters are sorted by area and passed on to the individual carriers,
  who deliver them.
- At layer 3, the recipient's secretary rejects any mail delivered to the wrong
  address, opens the letter, and passes it on to the recipient, saying, "Here's a letter
  from . . ."
- At layer 4, the recipient takes the letter and reads it.

When a layer receives a "message" from the next higher layer, it performs
the requested services and then "wraps" that message in its own layer of control
information for use by the corresponding layer at the receiving end. It then passes this "bundle" to the layer directly below it. On the receiving end, a layer
receiving a bundle from a lower layer unwraps the outermost layer of control
information, interprets that information, and acts on it. Then it discards that
layer of wrapping and passes the bundle to the next higher layer.

The Model's Seven Layers

In a similar way, the OSI reference model describes the types of control
data produced by each layer. Smalheiser and Florence [4] give a good description
of the main function of the seven OSI layers, and Network General [5] has published a large wall chart that shows many protocols at each level. We combine
the two in the following description and in Figure 6-4.

Starting at the top of the model, that is, the layer closest to us users, here
are the layers and what they basically do.

Layer 7 Is the Application Layer. In this layer are the telecommunications protocols that are embedded in the applications we use. One familiar protocol at this level is HTTP (HyperText Transfer Protocol), which anyone who has
surfed the Web has used in addressing a Web site. Other familiar TCP/IP protocols at this level are File Transfer Protocol (FTP) for transferring files on the
Internet, and Telnet for logging onto and using a remote computer on the Net.

OSI also has defined some somewhat familiar protocols at this level that
permit worldwide communication in various ways. For instance, ISO's X.500
Directory Services protocol is for creating distinct Internet (or other) mailing

Figure 6-4   The OSI Reference Model

Layer	Name	Job	Protocol Examples
7	Application Layer	Interface to application	HTTP, X.500, X.400, ODA, PC LAN Manager, Postscript
6	Presentation Layer	Translates data to and from language in Layer 7	NetBIOS
5	Session Layer	Controls dialog, acts as moderator for a session	SSL (Secure Sockets Layer)
4	Transport Layer	Controls flow, ensures reliable packet delivery	TCP
3	Network Layer	Addresses and routes packets	IP, X.25, Packet level Protocol
2	Logical Link Layer	Makes sure no data is lost or garbled	Ethernet, Token Ring, FDDI, ISDN, ATM, Frame Relay
1	Physical Layer	Defines physical connection to network	Ethernet 50 ohm coaxial cable, 10 Base-T, twisted pair, fiber optic cable

addresses. OSI's X.400 Mail Handling Service is for permitting dissimilar electronic mail systems to handle e-mail created and sent from other (dissimilar) systems. And ODA (Office Document Architecture) works in the document arena.

For users of text formatting programs, such as PageMaker, the printing protocol, Postscript, is also found in this seventh layer. In the IBM networking world, PC LAN Manager is in this layer. So this layer probably contains the most familiar telecom protocols because it is the layer closest to the users.

Layer 6 Is the Presentation Layer. The telecom protocols in this layer translate data to and from the language and format used in Layer 7. This layer does not have very many familiar protocols. For people in the IBM world, the protocol that might be familiar is NetBIOS, which is used to communicate among peripherals, such as the monitor, printer, and so on.

Layer 5 Is the Session Layer. Telecom protocols in this layer control the dialog for each application and act as moderator, seeing that messages are sent as directed and can be interrupted, if necessary. A very important protocol in this layer is Secure Sockets Layer (SSL), introduced by Netscape in 1994 to provide Internet security (just above the TCP layer). It uses a combination of public key and cryptography to provide confidentiality, data integrity, and authentication of servers (optionally clients), notes Bhimani, of Lucent Technologies [6a]. SSL has gained widespread support and use because it initially did not provide client authentication. That would have required distributing public-key certificates to every Netscape user on the Net—obviously impractical. It is much more practical to give servers the capabilities to handle digital signatures and key management. However, there is now growth in client authentication.

Layer 4 Is the Transport Layer. Protocols in this layer handle flow control and ensure the integrity of each message, resequencing portions, if necessary. Analog voice calls create a continuous circuit, which means that the telephone circuit is tied up between those two points. It is a very inefficient way to use the lines. To be more efficient, most data communication is handled by packets (little chunks of data with an address) because packets from lots of sources to lots of other sources can be intermixed. This layer ensures reliable packet delivery. So, one of the main protocols at this level is TCP (Transmission Control Protocol), which is the TCP found in TCP/IP, the underlying protocol of the Internet. This TCP portion manages the connections made by IP (Internet Protocol) in the next lower layer, Layer 3.

Layer 3 Is the Network Layer. Protocols in this layer address and route packets to their destination. Here resides the all-important (IP), the portion of Internet's TCP/IP that allows packets to traverse an *internet*—that is, a network of network. So IP, and other routing services, such as X.25 Packet Level Protocol (used in most corporate data networks), work at this level.

Layer 2 Is the Logical Link Layer. As Smalheiser and Florence note, protocols at this layer mainly do error correction. They make sure no data is lost or garbled. Next to the protocols in Layer 7, those in this layer are the second most familiar because LAN protocols work here. So Ethernet, Token Ring, and FDDI (Fiber Distributed Data Interface), to name just three, work at this level. These technologies deserve a little additional description.

Ethernet is a local area network protocol that operates at 10 mbps in a broadcast mode. Computers broadcast their messages all at once. If there is a collision, the sending machine does not receive an acknowledgment from the receiver and realizes it needs to retransmit. *Token Ring* is a bit slower and packets are transmitted if they have a token, sort of like a seat in a train.

FDDI is an Ethernet-like protocol that operates at 100 mbps. A traditional 10-mbps Ethernet can get overloaded if it is attached to PCs that run at 85 to 100 MIPS and make large file transfers to and from a server. In fact, just a few of these PCs can totally swamp an Ethernet LAN, note the people at Network Peripherals [7]. They say that handling such large chunks of bursty traffic on a traditional LAN is like trying to inhale olives through a straw. An option is to install a high-speed LAN that uses FDDI.

FDDI has also been discussed as appropriate for metropolitan area networks (MANs). The city and county governments in Tallahassee, Florida, are using FDDI in this manner, says MaryFran Johnson [8]. When their local telephone company, Centel's Central Telephone Company of Florida, heard that they were planning to install their own FDDI network, it built them an FDDI MAN. These government offices need FDDI to move images and data in a geographic information system among three government buildings—the city hall, the county courthouse, and the city electrical department. A 10-mbps LAN would have been swamped by that volume of data. So rather than install their own network, the governments are outsourcing their network to Centel.

The WAN world also has some important (and perhaps increasingly familiar) protocols at this Layer 2. One is *ISDN* (Integrated Services Digital Network), which operates at speeds starting at two 64-kbps channels up to 1.92 mbps. It has been around for years and now appears to be finding a niche for linking remote offices (and offices in the home) to the Internet or to corporate networks because it is the next step up in speed from most modems, which operate at 14.4 kbps and 28.8 kbps.

Two other important technologies whose protocols reside at this level are called fast packet switching technologies. The term *fast packet switching,* as defined by the people at Vertical Systems Group [in 9], is a communication architecture that supports both voice and data at T1 speeds and above (that's 1.544 mbps). The term refers to two packet switching technologies: frame relay and ATM (Asynchronous Transfer Mode).

Frame relay uses variable-length packets and is slated to replace the workhorse of today's data networks, X.25 (which only operates at 56 kbps, twice as fast as common Internet access modems). It is for bursty communications, which occur between LANs, or terminal and host, and over the Internet. It envelopes each packet in a frame that contains its destination information (hence its name, frame relay). In addition, frame relay provides bandwidth-on-demand because it creates virtual circuits. That is, it does not require a dedicated connection the way a voice telephone call does. It is therefore appropriate for transmitting images, still-frame video, and bulk files.

ATM (Asynchronous Transfer Mode) is a very important high-speed telecom protocol that transmits fixed-length packets. That makes it suitable for transmitting voice and video, both of which require fixed intervals between packets to produce natural-sounding speech. If the packets arrived at varying intervals, voices could vacillate between sounding like Donald Duck to sounding like Goofy. Thus, cell relay is being touted as the transmission medium for multimedia communications.

Layer 1 Is the Physical Layer. Protocols at this level are responsible for defining the physical connection of devices to a network. This is the most basic level and it actually defines the electrical and mechanical characteristics of connections. So, these protocols describe modem standards as well as the characteristics of transmission wires, such as Ethernet 50-ohm coaxial cable, 10 Base-T twisted pair wire, fiber-optic cable, DS1 and DS3 (which support speeds of 1.544 and 44.736 mbps respectively), and so on.

That, in a nutshell, is the OSI model, today's most important map of telecom protocols. It provides the standards which allow companies to implement a cohesive telecom architecture.

Now we turn to a specific telecom technology, one that will play an increasingly important role in computing, and has yet to reach its potential: wireless communications.

WIRELESS COMMUNICATIONS

Wireless will be the leading access technology because people are mobile, said George Gilder in his Aspen Institute speech [3]. The most common "PC" of the next era will be a digital, cellular phone—"as mobile as your watch, as personal as your wallet." It will recognize speech and navigate streets in your car using geopositional satellites. It will collect your mail, keep track of your paycheck, and perform a wide range of functions that we scarcely imagine today.

Wireless communications are already with us, of course, in the form of cellular car phones, portable phones, very small aperture terminals (VSATs), pagers, building-to-building microwave links, and infrared networks. With people becoming increasingly mobile—in their work and their personal lives—wireless communication options will grow. Here are three growth areas: wireless LANs, wireless WANs, and wide area personal communication services.

Wireless LANs

Wireless local area networks (LANs), which are currently more expensive than wired LANs, have the advantage in certain settings, says Peter Clegg in *LAN Times* [10]. Local area networks extend within a building or a set of buildings. Examples include hazardous environments, historic buildings where wiring ducts are full, and disaster recovery situations. Furthermore, there are many instances where temporary communications are needed, says Clegg, such as for audits, special projects, seasonal businesses, and so forth. Even in permanent locations, about one-half of the respondents to a *LAN Times* survey said that they relocate nodes on their LANs about six times a year. Wireless LANs are much easier to reconfigure than their wired counterparts.

Wireless LAN Technologies. Robert Rosenbaum [11] expands on Clegg's discussion with a good description of the technologies used in the wireless LAN marketplace. He notes that wireless LANs use either light (in the form of infrared) or radio (in the form of narrowband or spread spectrum) technologies to transmit signals.

Infrared light LANs transmit at frequencies just below red light—the lowest frequency in the light spectrum visible to humans. Like other forms of light, infrared light cannot penetrate solids, such as walls, ceilings, dust, and rain. Therefore, all the transmitters and receivers must be in line-of-sight with each other, or be reflected off a surface. But infrared has the advantage that it has a wide bandwidth (say, for FDDI, which transmits at 100 mbps). No government bodies control light frequencies; therefore, infrared can be used unlicensed anywhere.

Narrowband RF (radio frequency) LANs transmit on a center frequency, which can cause "ghosts" (to use television terminology) that pollute the signal, as signals are deflected off objects. Use of smart antennae can overcome this problem, but RF transmitters must be licensed because governments regulate the use of radio signals.

Spread spectrum LANs use RF bands that have already been allocated to wireless nets in the United States by the Federal Communications Commission. So that transmissions do not interfere with one another on the same frequency, the signal is "spread" by transmitting a "chip pattern" rather than the actual bits. Each network has its own "chipping code," so that each receiver only accepts signals that it can decode. Spread spectrum technology provides highly reliable communications in RF-noisy environments, such as factory floors.

Wireless LAN Topologies. Regardless of the technology used, wireless LANs have two basic topologies, says Rosenbaum [11]. One is *peer-level systems*, which allow each unit to communicate with every other unit. This is the lowest-cost alternative because no master control units are needed. But this topology generally breaks down as traffic grows because more and more collisions occur, unless a token ring protocol is used. Furthermore, when nearby units and far-away units transmit simultaneously, the bandwidth is not used efficiently. Peer-level systems also make security and diagnosis more difficult.

The second topology is wireless *LANs with central controllers*. In these systems, a central controller is linked to a wired LAN and communicates with user units that connect with, say, eight workstations. The control unit handles all communications (to near and far workstations) and has centralized network management and access control (see Figure 6-5). Wireless LAN technology is new, and its use is likely to grow as prices drop.

Wireless WAN Services

Wireless wide area networks (WANs) are a crucial component of mobile computing. WANs cover greater distances than LANs, generally beyond cities. David Hayden, who presents a concise overview of the wireless WAN arena [12], says there are three choices: cellular data communications, one-way electronic mail, and two-way mobile data communications.

Cellular Data Communications. The most common form of wireless communications is the cellular telephone. In addition to serving voice calls, these networks can also handle data and Fax. In fact, they are the least expensive and most accessible means of wireless data communications, but they also are the most problematic.

People can easily attach their portable computer to their cellular phone; however, the networks can be noisy, they have relatively slow transmission speeds, the signals fade in and out, and data can be lost when the call is handed off from one cell to another. These problems have been tolerated for voice calls but can be too disruptive for data communications, which require continuous, error-free transmission. Vendors are tackling these problems, says Hayden. For example, today's cellular systems, which are analog, will be supplemented by digital cellular systems. Digital cellular is static-free, has no fading, and provides full privacy.

One-Way Wireless Systems. A one-way wireless system is essentially a "souped up" paging system that allows people to link their hand-held or note-

Peer Level System

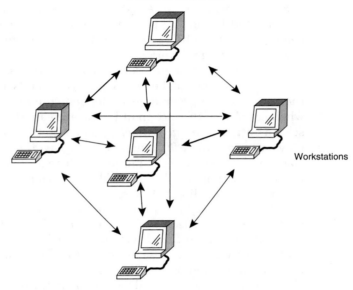

Workstations

Centrally Controlled System

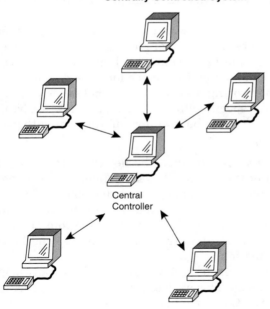

Central
Controller

Figure 6-5 Wireless LAN Configurations

book computer to a paging receiver and receive electronic mail. This mail can be text messages, faxes, spreadsheet updates, as well as news, weather, and stock reports. Jeff Ubois [13] notes that paging systems are far more versatile than beepers. They are being transformed from a simple local service to a complex global messaging network.

Four types of paging services are offered, says Ubois. *Tone-only,* which is the most basic and least expensive service, sends a tone to the beeper unit telling the user to call a prearranged telephone number. This service is most effective when coupled with voice mail because it can alert users of new messages. The second option, *numerical display,* has been the most popular because it can display a message up to 20 digits. *Voice paging,* the third option, sends the beeper a voice message six to eight minutes in length. This service is expensive and has not been very popular. But it could stage a comeback with new voice compression techniques, according to Ubois.

The fourth option, *alphanumeric paging,* delivers full text messages, and allows the user to decide what action to take on the spot. Most nationwide services are moving in this direction, says Ubois, and it may become popular now that software to send these message is becoming available. Paging is increasingly being integrated with other messaging technologies, says Ubois, as a way to alert people of newly arrived voice mail, faxes, or electronic mail. The pager/voice mail connection is currently the most widely used. All major voice mail services offer paging.

Hand-held computers are also being used with pagers, where a paging service is used as a store-and-forward network to deliver messages, either in cheaper nighttime hours or within minutes of being sent. The high-end pager, says Ubois, will have a computer and communicating device for receiving wireless electronic mail or information monitoring alerts, such as messages from an alerting service that the price of a specific stock has fallen below a certain threshold. Ubois expects paging systems to be used for information gathering and monitoring as well as messaging.

Two-Way Mobile Data Communications. The newest wireless WAN option is packet-switched communication networks, says Hayden. These networks, which use packet radio technology, require special radio modems for communication. These modems can be internal or external to the computer. Some specially designed computers—called "wireless PCs" or "portable communicating PCs"—contain both a radio modem for data transmission and a traditional cellular modem for facsimile transmission.

The packet radio networks transmit data faster than cellular networks, they do not involve handing off transmissions as does cellular, and they include encoding for security and error correction for reliability. Hayden believes that wireless networks will be used by corporations to support both mobile employees and consumers. For example, the Hoboken, New Jersey, fire department links its firefighters to fire stations via a wireless network to transmit important information, such as the location and pressure of fire hydrants, possible chemical hazards in the area, and the location of children and handicapped residents in buildings.

These three wireless technologies, along with future satellite networks, will vastly expand data communication options, says Hayden.

Personal Communication Services

The vision of the future is person-to-person rather than station-to-station communications. That is, each person will have his or her own personal telephone number, associated with a lightweight telephone that he or she carries around. The benefit will be that people can communicate from anywhere to anywhere.

Personal communication services (PCS) will spring up around PCS networks, permitting people to not only transmit telephone conversations but also computer-based information, voice mail, electronic messages, call screening, and other personal services.

The Regional Bell Operating Companies are interested in offering PCS. Many other companies, such as cable television companies which already have fiber links to homes, might want to carry these signals, perhaps in combination with cellular links.

PCS will unlock levels of freedom we do not now know, and they will become important in special events, such as political conventions and sporting events, as well as for emergencies, such as those caused by natural disasters. But before these systems become a reality, complex technological and public policy questions need to be addressed.

A fundamental issue has been the overcrowded RF spectrum. In the United States, the government uses about one-half the radio spectrum for marine navigation, air traffic control, military communications, and space exploration. Television, AM/FM radio, and civil services (such as police and fire) use a large part of the nongovernment spectrum. The remaining bands are taken up by taxi dispatchers and ham radio operators.

In the United States, the other bandwidths have been auctioned off by the government for personal communication services; however, no one really knows how much bandwidth PCS will need. In addition, if countries assign different frequencies, cross-country communications will be difficult. Furthermore, if the frequencies assigned have trouble penetrating buildings, then costs will be higher because vendors will need to build more powerful systems. Frequency allocation is a complex international issue.

Wireless technologies have been developing gradually. But one technology that has exploded onto the scene is the Internet.

THE INTERNET

As masters of ceremonies say when they introduce a famous person, "So-and-so needs no introduction," we feel the same way about the Internet. If you don't know about the Net, you don't have a computer, you don't read business magazines, you're not a sports fan, you don't work, and you don't have teenagers. It really needs no introduction, so here's just a short one.

Its Past and Present

Briefly, the Internet is a worldwide telecommunications network that is fully distributed; it has no controlling nodes. Until it received its graphical interface—the World Wide Web—in 1994, it was all text based. In this text-only cyberspace, people used mainly four different kinds of programs to do four different things. They had e-mail programs, of course, to send messages, maintain their mailing lists, and interact with newsgroups. They used Telnet to log onto distant computers and use their facilities. They used Gopher services to search and download files from electronic databases. And they used FTP (File Transfer Protocol) to download files and software.

Today, the fastest growing part of the Net is the World Wide Web, whose graphical user interface contains hyperlinks, permitting users to jump from one Web site to another by clicking on a highlighted word that contains the hyperlink to that other site. In a white paper on its home page, Netscape [14] notes that the Web's explosive growth as been due to seven key enablers:

- Proliferation of PCs, LANs, and modems, giving people the tools to access the Net.
- Open standards, such as TCP/IP (for networking), HTTP (for universal addressing of Web sites), and HTML (HyperText Markup Language, for defining multimedia Web pages).
- Cross-platform support.
- Multimedia support and ease of use via the Web.
- Support for secure transactions.
- Standardized, easy-to-use browsers to access Web sites.
- Low-cost alternative to proprietary systems (the driving force for businesses to create intranet Web sites).

A summary of the facilities needed to provide access to the Internet and the Web is shown in Figure 6-6.

In 1981, when the IBM PC was introduced, its architecture was open—all the design specifications were published. This openness led to thousands of peripheral manufacturers, component makers, and clone makers producing compatible products. A whole industry developed around this open architecture. The same has happened with the Internet because it provides the same kind of openness, this time, in the telecom arena. Thus, vendors have a standard set of protocols to work with, and products can be compatible with each other. So companies do not need to commit to a proprietary architecture. And, like the PC, this openness yields the most powerful solutions and the most competitive prices.

As Netscape [14] points out, the Internet has two attributes that are very important to corporations: reliability and scalability. As we noted earlier, ARPANET was designed to survive computer crashes by allowing alternate routing. This makes it very reliable. People might not be able to access a particular downed node, but that does not keep them from accessing all other nodes that are operating. The Internet has also been able to sustain incredible growth since its beginning as the ARPANET in the 1960s. And specific Web sites can handle tremendous amounts of traffic. In one day, for example, Netscape recorded *40 million* "hits" (the number of user accesses of a site). Now that's scalability!

Figure 6-6 Components for Providing Internet Access
(from Catanzano and Henderson [15])

Catanzano and Henderson [15] of Shiva (a company that provides Internet connection devices and remote access servers) note that there are nine components needed to provide access to the Internet within a corporate setting. These are:

Ubiquitous TCP/IP Deployment

Internet communications are primarily built on the TCP/IP (Transmission Control Protocol/Internet Protocol) communication protocol. Therefore, corporate LANs must include an IP application, and it must be installed on every desktop and remote computer that is to have network access.

Web Browser

This is the front-end product that allows users to access the Web. Browsers are graphical, user friendly, and are so standard (in that they all operate in such similar manners) that they require little or no training. They, too, need to be installed on every desktop and remote computer.

Web Server

A Web server contains the applications, databases, security software, and communication software for answering a user query or passing the query on to another machine.

Remote Access Server

A remote access server links remote users to corporate resources, intranet applications, and the Internet. It needs to handle multiple communication protocols and needs to have an array of communication ports to handle the projected volume of calls.

Client Dial-In Software

Remote PCs need remote dial-in client software. The client software initiates the call, negotiates the connection, and terminates the connection when the remote session is over. Obviously, this remote access client software needs to be available for all the different operating systems on remote user workstations.

Internet Connection Device

A router is necessary to connect a corporate site to an Internet Service Provider (ISP). This Internet connection device typically provides IP protocol support and packet-level filtering.

Leased Line Connection

Most often, corporations connect to the Internet via a leased line provided by the Internet Service Provider. They can range from fractional T1 to full T1 (1.544 Mbps). The choice depends on the amount of activity between the corporation and the provider.

CSU/DSU

A CSU/DSU connects to the leased line router and determines the speed and type of connection.

Firewall

A firewall allows a company to protect its corporate IP addresses from being accessed by outsiders. Filtering criteria, called proxy daemons, are used to scrutinize all incoming requests for connection. But, note Catanzano and Henderson, firewalls do not provide total security. Companies really need tiers of security.

The Issue of Growth

In the *Communications for the ACM,* the official magazine of the largest computer association, the Association for Computing Machinery, Robert Hinden [6b] writes about the thinking behind the design of the Internet Protocol next generation (IPng). The two issues he raises should be of interest to all executives who will increasingly need to support Internet use in their enterprises.

The first issue raised by Hinden is growth. He notes that IPng must be able to handle addressing and routing to support reasonable scenarios of future growth. He notes that the past growth of the Internet has been driven by the computer market because the focus has been to connect computers together. And it has been growing exponentially. The number of networks on the Internet was estimated to be about 80,000, as of January 1996, and is doubling every 12 months. The end points of these networks have ranged from PCs to supercomputers; however, most have not been mobile.

Hinden speculates that the next phase of growth will not be driven by the computer market but by new markets that are extremely large and have different requirements. One certain market, says Hinden, is nomadic personal computing devices, which will replace today's cellular phones, pagers, and personal digital assistants. All of these will be networked, and unlike today's PCs, they will communicate via different types of network attachments. When disconnected, they will use radio-frequency wireless nets. When used in a networked facility, they will communicate via an infrared attachment. And when docked, says Hinden, they will hook to a wired network. They will obviously need a common internetworking protocol, and that protocol must support large-scale routing, addressing, and autoconfiguration, as well as built-in authentication and confidentiality because they are mobile.

A second consumer market is networked entertainment for video-on-demand and networked video games. In this market, every TV could be an Internet host, speculates Hinden, especially with high-definition TV (HDTV).

A third possible market is using IPng as a control device to control all kinds of everyday devices, such as equipment, motors and machines controlled today by analog switches. Networking the control of these devices could yield huge cost savings. This could be an enormous market, notes Hinden, but it requires a protocol that is simple, robust, easy to use, and very low cost.

These markets will all appear, with or without the Internet, says Hinden. If the IPng is a good fit, it will be used. If not, each will develop its own protocol, and most likely, these would not interoperate.

The Issue of Transition

Between 1999 and 2006, the Internet will need a new version of the Internet protocol because the routing based on the 32-bit addresses of the current version is becoming strained. It will eventually run out of network numbers. The goal is to implement the new version before this happens. And it cannot be the typical controlled rollout that corporate IS departments have used to completely replace an old version of a widely used application with a new one. The Internet is just too large for this approach to succeed. Instead, the new version will need to coexist and interoperate with the old version, for as long as ten years or perhaps even for the life of the new version. Thus, it will have to be deployed piecemeal and not require specific local changes. Thus, as with many computer products, backward compatibility will be important.

Hinden concludes his article by describing IPv6, the name for the next generation Internet Protocol and says that it is in the works and is meant to support both issues he discussed—growth and transitioning.

THE IS DEPARTMENT'S ROLE

As we see it, the IS department has two main technical roles in the telecom world:

- Create an overall architecture.
- Achieve connectivity.

Create an Overall Architecture

While a network architecture can contain a set of diagrams, as Zachman pointed out in Chapter 5, it also needs to contain a set of company policies and rules which, when followed, are expected to lead to the desired network environment. International standards—such as OSI—have become crucial in architecture planning. In fact, they have become mandatory for successfully creating the links—the highway system.

What do we *not* mean by a network architecture? An overall network architecture does not imply one telecom network for all uses. Nor does it imply or require that the offerings of only one vendor be used in an attempt to achieve connectivity. It also does not imply the need to standardize on one type of technology for providing local connectivity. Nor is the architecture one design for a multilevel network of computers that all units of an organization must use. In short, an overall network architecture is not one utopian solution for all network problems. It is a set of policies, principles, and guidelines that will lead to more widespread connectivity.

Factors to Consider. Some of the factors that will influence an organization's overall architecture are the following.

The desired levels of computing. At what levels—ranging from corporate headquarters to individual office employees—is it desired to provide computing power and data storage? As we noted in Chapter 5, we see computing power needed at six levels: (1) corporate, (2) region, country, or division, (3) site, (4) department, (5) work group or team, and (6) individual.

Level 2 —region, country, division—is where there can be substantial differences from company to company. But it is also the level at which companies may choose to share data to jointly market new products and services.

Company organization. The company's policies on centralization versus decentralization of management and operations play a key role in the overall architecture. The virtual organization has made telecom architectural planning a must.

Current computing environment. This factor includes the existing computers, which usually come from different manufacturers. No one has hardware from only one manufacturer, operating systems from only one vendor, DBMSs from only one company, and telecom services from only one carrier. Each additional variable increases connectivity problems.

Company policies on the use of standards. How important does the company consider the use of IS standards? The more that standards can be employed, the cleaner the overall architecture can be made. In the absence of standards, tailored solutions must be used for each communication interface. Although the use of TCP/IP has become the standard in data networking, companies that plan to offer consumer services over cable TV may need to deal with other standards.

How will IT serve the business? Peter Keen addresses telecom planning and architectures in his book, *Competing in Time* [16]. His theme is that telecom planning must follow from business planning. He cites many examples of how companies have successfully used telecom to improve their competitive positions. To add flavor, he also includes some examples of failures—and draws some "do and don't" conclusions for increasing the chances of success.

The 1990s is the decade of integrated technologies, including computers, telecom, laser memories (such as CD-ROM), artificial intelligence and expert systems, computer-aided design and manufacturing, voice mail, electronic mail, various forms of conferencing (video, audio, computer), and others.

The driving force will have to be managers who see how these technologies can best be used to serve the business. However, overall management of the use of these technologies must be coupled with crucial technical skills. A range of technologists will be required, and it will be no simple matter to obtain those skills. In short, says Keen, telecom planning needs to begin with business needs, and where the business wants to go, not with the technology. Furthermore, this planning has three main steps, says Keen:

- Vision—"What is happening in our industry? Where do we want to go?"
- Policies—The bridge between a vision and the architecture of systems to support the vision.
- Architecture—The high-level design of the systems and infrastructure to accomplish the vision—that is, the systems, people, and procedures.

The role of the overall architecture, then, is to recognize these diverse factors and then specify the desired computing environment for the future as well as the policies to bring it about.

Achieve Connectivity

The key challenge in network design is connectivity, said Howard Frank[17] at a TeleCommunications Association conference. The goal is not a single, coherent network, but rather finding a means to interface many dissimilar networks. With this in mind, he offered the following advice:

- Build systems that are coherent at the interfaces. Let the users *think* they have one network.
- Be realistic about time frames. Every big advance in the past 20 years was not predicted; they were only understood after they were in existence.
- Remember that progress takes longer than advertisers would have you believe. Practically nothing can be started today that will have strategic significance for at least five years. Mission-critical information systems and their supporting networks take that long to develop and install.

More and more organizations are seeing the need to tie together their islands of automation, seeking what the worldwide telephone system already provides: the ability for any telephone user to be connected with any other user. Connectivity means allowing users to communicate up, down, across, and out of an organization. Many companies have therefore standardized on a few vendors to permit easier connectivity.

Two important aspects of connectivity are providing higher bandwidth within work groups and aiming for interoperability.

Within Work Groups. Not all networks or networks of networks need to provide equal connectivity. Einar Stefferud [18], a communications consultant, believes the highest speed networks are needed for tightly coupled work groups—engineering design teams, product development groups, customer service teams, and other work groups whose ability to share information and ideas quickly and easily is critical to their work. These groups need high reliability and fast response; that is why work group computing has taken on such importance in the 1990s.

The network connections *between* different work groups do not need to bear the same amounts or kinds of traffic, but they do need to be interconnected. Stefferud cites the situation at a research center where the network that connected work groups and laboratories had a maximum speed of 10 mbps, while the gateway to the outside world ran at only 28.8 kbps. This speed discrepancy was not a problem as long as most of the traffic at the center was internal. However, when the need arose to routinely access outside databases and to form tightly coupled work groups that extended beyond company boundaries, the center had to increase their gateway speeds.

Aim for Interoperability. The concept that best describes the promise of linking client machines to server machines via networks is *interoperability*. It means the capability for different machines, using different operating systems, on different networks to work together on tasks—exchanging information in standard ways without any changes in the command language or in functionality and without physical intervention.

According to William Darden of Northrop Corporation, a truly interoperable network would allow PCs and workstations to interoperate with servers running UNIX and NT and mainframes running MVS. Interoperability is a responsibility of processors, not networks, says Darden. Achieving true interoperability can have a large impact on the utilization of corporate IT resources.

CONCLUSION

The telecom world is big, and getting bigger by the day. Some see it as a global electronic highway system where the goal is to establish links and interoperability. Others see it as a cyberspace, where people can form new kinds of communities, or take on different identities. From whatever view, it is clear that telecom will play an increasing role in the life of enterprises, and could well be the hub of future enterprises. Therefore, the IS department needs to provide the underlying architecture and strive for connectivity.

QUESTIONS AND EXERCISES

REVIEW QUESTIONS

1. What are the nine "facts of life" in the telecom industry?
2. What is an open network?
3. In principle, how does a layer work?
4. Briefly describe each layer of the OSI reference model.
5. What is ATM?
6. Where are wireless LANs likely to be the best alternative? Describe the two kinds of technologies that these LANs use.
7. What are the three types of wireless WAN services?
8. What are personal communication networks? Why is there a potential market for them?
9. According to Netscape, what two attributes of the Net are important to corporations?
10. According to Hinden, what types of new markets may appear for the Net?
11. What are the two technical roles of the IS department?
12. Define interoperability.

DISCUSSION QUESTIONS

1. The chapter implies on the one hand that a company should stay at the forefront of telecommunications technology lest it fall seriously behind. On the other hand, it might be better to let others go first, and then learn from their mistakes. Which approach is better? Why?
2. The Internet can provide all the network infrastructure a company needs. That will put the IS department out of the infrastructure business. Discuss.

EXERCISES

1. Read five articles on telecom. What developments not discussed in this chapter are seen as important, and why? Present a short briefing on these to the class.
2. Contact the information systems manager at a company in your community. What is the company's telecommunications architecture? What telecommunications stan

Chapter 6 Managing Telecommunications

dards are they using? How are they using the Internet? What are th future? How many Web sites do they have? Describe a few of them

3. Find one article that discusses top management's or line managen com or the use of the Internet. What role does management play? A ship with IS? Briefly discuss in class.

4. View the Web version of this chapter at http://www.earthlink.net/~bmchann... r ... three Web sites to link to the chapter and explain in a short paragraph why each link should be incorporated into the Web version. Submit it to your professor, who may submit the three best link recommendations from the class to the authors, along with the names of the people (or class) who should be given credit for the suggestions.

REFERENCES

1. KAMMAN, A., "Global networks," *Stage by Stage*, Nolan, Norton & Co., Lexington, MA, Vol. 9, no. 6, 1990, pp. 1–6.

2. "TELECOM: THE NEW AGENDA," The Telecom Management Programme, Wentworth Research, Park House, Wick Road, Egham, England TW20 OHW, http://www.wentworth.co.uk, premier issue, February 1996. Authored by SRI.

3. GILDER, GEORGE, columnist and author of *Life After Television*, spoke at the Aspen Institute on July 18, 1996; his speech was broadcast on C-SPAN in August 1996.

4. SMALHEISER, K. and D. FLORENCE, "An OSI Tutorial," *Business Week,* McGraw-Hill, Inc., New York, June 1, 1987, pp. 131–136.

5. "NETWORK GENERAL GUIDE TO COMMUNICATION PROTOCOLS," Network General , 4200 Bohannon Dr., Menlo Park, CA 94025, http://www.ngc.com, 1995.

6. *COMMUNICATIONS OF THE ACM,* 1515 Broadway, New York, NY 10036, http://www.acm.org, June 1996:

   a. BHIMANI, ANISH, "Securing the Commercial Internet," pp. 29–35.

   b. HINDEN, ROBERT, "IP Next Generation Overview," pp. 61–71.

7. "FDDI FOR WORKGROUP COMPUTING," Network Peripherals, 2890 Zanker Rd., San Jose, CA 95134, October 1990, 10 pages.

8. JOHNSON, MARYFRAN, "An Offer They Couldn't Refuse," COMPUTERWORLD, April 15, 1991, p. 56.

9. WEXLER, J., "Frame Relay Showing Its Stuff," *Computerworld,* November 12, 1990, pp. 67–76.

10. CLEGG, P., "LAN Times Lab Tests Wireless LANs," *LAN Times* (7050 Union Park Center, Suite 240, Midvale, Utah 84047), July 8, 1991, p. 79.

11. ROSENBAUM, R., "The Technology Behind Wireless LANs," *LAN Times*, July 8, 1991, pp. 84–87.

12. HAYDEN, DAVID, "The New Age of Wireless," *Mobile Office*, May 1992, pp. 34–44.

13. UBOIS, JEFF, "Paging: The Whole Story," *Mobile Office*, November, 1991, pp. 36–40.

14. "INTERNET WEBS AS CORPORATE INFORMATION SYSTEMS," White Paper on Netscape Web site: http://www.netscape.com. Netscape, 501 E. Middlefield Rd., Mountain View, CA 94043, March 1996.

15. CATANZANO, STEPHEN and KIRSTEN HENDERSON, "The Fully Connected Corporation," a Shiva technology brief, available on the Web at either http://www.netscape.com or http://www.shiva.com. Shiva, 28 Crosby Dr., Bedford, MA 01730, March 1996.

16. KEEN, P., *Competing in Time: Using Tele-Communications for Competitive Advantage*, Ballinger Publishing Co.,Cambridge, MA 02138, 1986; 235 pages.

17. FRANK, HOWARD, Network Management, Inc., 11242 Waples Mill Road, Fairfax, VA 22030.

18. STEFFERUD, EINAR, Network Management Associates, 17301 Drey Lane, Huntington Beach, CA 92647.

SEVEN

Managing
Information
Resources

INTRODUCTION

Data, information, knowledge. Three often confused words. In this chapter (and in this book) we distinguish between the three by drawing on John Zachman's [1] view of the classical distinction as we noted in Chapter 5: Data is comprised of facts. Information is data in context—its meaning depends on the surrounding circumstances or usage. And knowledge is information with direction or intent—it facilitates a decision or an action.

The amount of internal and external data and information available to organizations is increasing by leaps and bounds. Internally, the intranet has caused a revolution because it allows companies to bring internal data and information together from far-flung files and databases and makes them available companywide, giving many employees far more corporate data and information than they ever had before. The ability to handle and transmit multimedia—voice, video, and image—is increasing the variety of information formats and content as well. At the same time, the availability of external data, both hard facts and "soft" intelligence information, has exploded with the Internet.

Yet, in the midst of this growing richness of data and information, companies are still struggling to get their internal alphanumeric data under control. The installation of companywide software packages such as SAP, enterprise data warehouses, and intranets has once again brought to the fore the problems of "dirty data"—data from different databases that do not match, have different names, use different time frames, and so on. Add to this data problem the issue of managing information, specifically, being able to present information with the all-important contextual information that surrounds it. Then, just recently, corporate managements began to truly worry about their companies' greatest asset: The knowledge embedded in their employees' heads, their software and patents, their culture, and their organizational processes.

In this chapter we explore these three information resources. We will discuss data warehouses in Chapter 13, because it is used for decision support. Briefly, a data warehouse is a database that contains data from many sources, including operational sources. It is updated periodically, and it comes with a repository of metadata that describes precisely what each type of data means—in terms that marketing folks, the sales force, management, and others can understand. A major driving force behind data warehouses is more finely targeted marketing—the desire to gather customer data in one place, segment it into customer groups such as profitable and unprofitable customers, see the buying patterns in these customer groupings, and then develop new products and services targeted at these different customer groups.

GETTING CORPORATE DATA INTO SHAPE

Attempts to get corporate data under control began in the late 1960s and early 1970s with the use of database management systems (DBMS)—that is, systems to manage databases. Not long after that, the database administrator appeared to manage DBMS and their use. Then, in the 1970s, the broader role of data administration was created to manage all the computerized data resources of an organization. Today, these two functions have become even more important as companies attempt to once again round up their data and make it consistent companywide.

The Problem: Inconsistent Data Definitions

In a nutshell, the problem has been incompatible data definitions from application to application, department to department, site to site, and division to division. How has this happened? John Zachman [1] blames expediency. To get application systems up and running quickly, system designers have sought the necessary data either from the cheapest source or a politically expedient source, he says. Generally, this has meant using data from existing files and adding other new data. In effect, data has been "dribbled" from application to application. The result has been data showing up in different files, with different names for the same data, the same name for different data items, and the same data in different files with different update cycles.

The use of such data may be acceptable for routine information processing, but it is far from acceptable for management uses, says Zachman. Management cannot get consistent views across the enterprise under such conditions. Also, changes in data and programs are hard to make because a change can affect files anywhere in the organization. Furthermore, such inconsistency makes it difficult to vary tracking and reporting of the organization's products, markets, control structure, and so on, to meet changing business conditions.

If a major role of the IS department is *managing data*—instead of getting applications running as quickly as possible—then quite a different scenario would occur. All the types of data in which the organization is interested would first be identified. Then the single source of each data type would be identified, along with the business function that creates that data. Finally, a transaction system would be built to collect and store that data, after which all authorized users and applications would have access to it.

This data-driven approach does not result in one huge database to serve the whole organization, but it does require administrative control over the data, as well as designing the databases to support end users from the outset. So, recommends Zachman, start out by describing the data the enterprise needs. Then select the approach for providing the data that gives a good balance between short-term, application-oriented goals and long-term, data-oriented goals.

The Role of Data Administration

The use of DBMS reduced, to some extent, the problems of inconsistent and redundant data in organizations. It is clear, however, that merely installing a DBMS is not sufficient to manage data as a corporate resource. Therefore, two additional thrusts have moved organizations in this direction: broader definition of the data administration role and effective use of data dictionaries.

Database administration concentrates on administering databases and the software that manages them. Data administration is broader. One of its main purposes is determining what data is being used outside the organizational unit that creates it. Whenever data crosses organizational boundaries, its definition and format need to be standardized under the data administration function.

The data dictionary is the main tool by which data administrators control standard data definitions. All definitions are entered into the dictionary, and data administrators monitor all new definitions and all requests for changes in definitions to make sure that corporate policy is being followed.

To bring order to the data mess that *still* exists, data administration has four main functions:

- Clean up data definitions
- Control shared data
- Manage data distribution
- Maintain data quality

Clean Up Data Definitions. Data administration needs to have the responsibility and authority to ensure data compatibility throughout an organization by getting rid of redundancies and inconsistencies among definitions. For instance, two or more names should not exist for the same data item, nor should the same name be used for two or more different data items. In most companies, sorting out existing data synonyms and then reconciling them is a monumental job. More and more companies are finally tackling this job seriously in the late

1990s to support a data warehouse effort, to install a companywide package, such as SAP, or, in some instances, to consolidate country-based corporate databases into an intranet where everyone in the company worldwide draws from the same data pool.

In this role of cleaning up data definitions, data administrators design standard data definitions, the data dictionary, and the databases to reconcile conflicting user needs. They also design the data integrity process to flag suspected data and guard against inaccurate, invalid, or missing data polluting the pool of correct data. Finally, data administrators train users on the meanings and proper use of the data. Unless users understand the data definitions, the clean data will not stay that way for long.

Control Shared Data. While data used solely by one organizational unit might be considered local and under the control of that unit, data used by two or more units should be considered shared data. The data administration function must control the definitions, and some of the processing, of all shared data.

There is a controversy in this area. One side says that essentially *all* the data in the organization should be under the control of data administration. Just because some data is currently not being used across organizational boundaries is no reason to suppose that it will not be in the future. The other view is that each organizational unit can do whatever it wishes with *its* data; only data that must flow to other units needs to be standardized. It is impractical to try to standardize everything, and it would impose unreasonable rigidities, say these people. Data administrators have to confront this issue and decide how broadly or narrowly to define shared data.

The data administration function must also analyze the impact of proposed changes to programs that use shared data. All programs that would require changes need to be identified before approving the change. A data dictionary is a tremendous help here because it provides one place to look for all uses of the data. Finally, approval to proceed with the change might be held up until all affected programs have been changed in order to keep those applications from aborting. Changes also require informing users of changes in meanings of data, if this occurs. Otherwise, users may base decisions on incorrect assumptions about the data they are using.

Manage Data Distribution. Shared data, as defined here, crosses organizational boundaries. Distributed data, on the other hand, is geographically dispersed data. Managing data in a distributed dimension, with probably several levels of detail, presents significant challenges to data administrators, challenges that have, to date, caused companies to stick with the single master file concept and only distribute copies that do not need to be kept in sync.

Maintain Data Quality. Cleaning up data definitions and the other important functions of data administration can become useless unless policies and procedures are developed to maintain data quality. A dominant guideline has been to decentralize or distribute this function—put the owners of the data in charge of editing and verifying data accuracy and quality. But this requires resolving the question of who owns the data.

Maintaining data quality also requires putting processes in place that ensure that correct data is being input into databases. People do not enter incorrect data on purpose, but many times the inputting process permits errors, rather than catching them at the source where they can easily be corrected. The two elements of maintaining quality are to clean up the current data in databases (the data pool) and then ensure that the data stream is not polluting that pool with bad data.

The Importance of Data Dictionaries

In the previous section, we referred to a data dictionary as the primary tool to manage data definitions. Data dictionaries are systems and procedures—either manual or automated—for storing and handling an organization's data definitions. Data definitions are often called "metadata" these days. A data dictionary does not, in itself, generally produce data for an organization. Instead, its purpose is to eliminate errors of understanding, ambiguities, and difficulties in interpreting data.

Ideally, a data dictionary should be considered at least as soon as a database management system is considered. An ideal sequence is to (1) set up the data administration function, (2) develop data standards, (3) purchase and install a DBMS, and (4) install a data dictionary as the first database application. Unfortunately, the most prevalent situation has been to bring in a data dictionary after the DBMS has been used as an access method rather than as a true DBMS. In this case, many database applications have been run with little integration among them and little or no documentation of data definitions, so they are redundant and inconsistent. This is the huge clean-up mess many organizations are facing head on today.

To illustrate one company's success in getting its corporate data in shape, consider the work of Monsanto, a case study that accompanies the Wentworth Research report, "Managing the Integrity of Distributed Systems" [2].

CASE EXAMPLE: Monsanto

Monsanto, based in St. Louis, Missouri, is a $9 billion provider of agricultural products, pharmaceuticals, food ingredients, and chemicals. It is heavily international—with some 50 percent of revenues outside the United States—and it has always had a tradition of being decentralized. Recently, the CEO described a new vision that included five global themes: being responsive and efficient in meeting customer needs, thinking and acting from a global perspective, taking some risks to enter new markets, treating the earth as a closed system where consumption and contamination of finite resources cannot be sustained, and creating an environment of trust, honesty, openness, and initiative where people can thrive.

To accomplish these (and other) goals, Monsanto has three large enterprisewide IT projects underway. One is to redevelop operational and financial transaction systems using SAP software. The second is to develop a knowledge-management architecture, including data warehousing. The third is to link transaction and decision support systems via common master data, known as Enterprise Reference Data (ERD), as shown in Figure 7-1. Monsanto wants to be "small but connected," to benefit from both global integration and local flexibility. ERD is a key to achieving both simultaneously. The Center of Technical Expertise is implementing all three initiatives.

Transaction Systems. The worldwide operations and finance project is dominated by SAP software. SAP, a German firm, sells an extensive integrated software product that covers all core business transactions, including finance, order processing, inventory management, product planning, and manufacturing resource planning. SAP is international and handles multiple languages and multiple currencies.

Monsanto is too large and complex to operate SAP as a single installation. Hence, it has created a distributed SAP architecture, with separate instances of SAP for reference data, finance, and operations in each business unit. The master reference data integrate these distributed components.

Knowledge Management. To convert SAP data to knowledge, Monsanto uses data warehouses, which are targeted at mid- to upper-level management. These warehouses focus on the big picture of the company and contain data from internal and external sources that can be "sliced and diced" with drill-down capability from summary data to supporting details. Again, the reference data allows the warehouses to compare and leverage information across Monsanto.

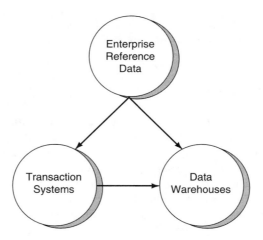

Figure 7-1   The Role of Enterprise Reference Data (from Monsanto)

Enterprise Reference Data. ERD, a separate use of SAP, is the repository for most master table information in the company. The information includes vendors, customers, suppliers, people, materials, finance, and control tables. Each table has multiple views. For instance, materials has separate views for purchasing, engineering, accounting, safety, and so on. The beauty of using a system such as SAP is that it can ensure referential integrity (adhering to complex relationship rules) of the data.

The sole source of master data is ERD, but the data can be distributed wherever it is needed, in transactional SAP systems as well as in the data warehouses. However, as comprehensive as SAP is, it still does not contain all the reference data. Monsanto stores external data, such as crop statistics and economic trends, outside SAP.

The purpose of ERD is to enable integration. Vertical integration enables closer coordination with suppliers, which will reduce Monsanto's working capital and improve customer service. Horizontal integration across Monsanto's business units enables team marketing, leveraged purchasing, and interplant manufacturing. For example, common vendor and material tables enable Monsanto to leverage purchasing across the company. With total purchases of about $5.5 billion a year, even a few percentage points of leverage can yield significant savings. Without ERD, Monsanto had to rely on limited polls of many purchasing functions—a process that could not be sustained.

Getting the Data in Shape

Turning data into a corporate resource is not an easy task for a large company with a history of decentralization. To accomplish this, Monsanto has had to change its entire data management process. To start, Monsanto created a formal department known as ERD Stewardship. This department is independent of MIS or any other function and its job is to set data standards and enforce quality—hence, its nickname, "the data police."

Another new function in ERD management is entity specialists. These are the key managers with the greatest stake in the quality of the data. For example, the specialist for vendor data is the vice president of purchasing. In cases where there has been no obvious specialists, a steward has been appointed.

The third part of ERD management are the analysts who manage the data. In many cases, they are the same people who maintain systems, but they must now adhere to the new ERD rules. This has led to a large cultural change because these folks formerly only maintained local data. Now they maintain a global resource that the entire company uses. The idea of "tweaking" a system to fix a local discrepancy—which was formerly a common occurrence—can now cause a major disruption in operations or a bad decision based on faulty data.

etting the data right in the first place is a very large undertaking, one
an easily take several work-years per table to extract the data, put it
ommon format, eliminate the duplicates, add missing data, and load
he ERD. Even with tools, this is a very labor-intensive process. Where
possible, Monsanto is using "standard" external codes, such as Dun &
Bradstreet numbers, Universal Product Codes, or European Article Numbers so that the company's trading partners can recognize the reference
data for electronic commerce purposes. Unfortunately, none of these number schemes is truly universal, so the need to build, maintain, and cross-
reference reference data appears to be unavoidable. Monsanto is working
through this process and is already reaping bottom-line benefits from better integration (horizontally and vertically) and greater flexibility.

MANAGING DATA

Database management systems are the main tool for managing computerized
corporate data. They have been around since the 1960s, and are based on two
major principles: a three-level conceptual model and several alternative data
models for organizing the data.

The Three-Level Database Model

One of the easiest to understand discussions of database technology is by
James Bradley [3] in his description of the three-level database model, which
was the result of work done by the Standards, Planning and Requirements Committee of the American National Standards Institute (ANSI/SPARC) in the mid-
1970s. The concept is still an underpinning of the DBMS field. The following discussion is taken from Bradley, Martin [4], and Atre [5]. It begins with the level
that the application developer sees.

- *Level 1* is called the external, conceptual, or local level. As Figure 7-2 illustrates,
  this level contains the various user views of the corporate data used by application programs—each has its own view. At this level, there is no concern for how
  the data will be physically stored or what data is used by other applications.
- *Level 2* is called the logical or enterprise-data level. It encompasses all an organization's relevant data, under the control of the data administrators. Data and
  relationships are represented at this level by one or more DBMS. This level contains the same data as level 3, but with the implementation data removed.
- *Level 3* is called the physical or storage level. It specifies the way the data is physically stored. A data record consists of its data fields plus some implementation
  data, generally pointers and flag fields. The end user, of course, need not be concerned with these pointers and flags; they are for use by the DBMS only.

The advantage of this three-level model is that the logical data (the data
administrators' view) can be separated from the physical storage method, so that
different physical devices can be used without changing the application pro-

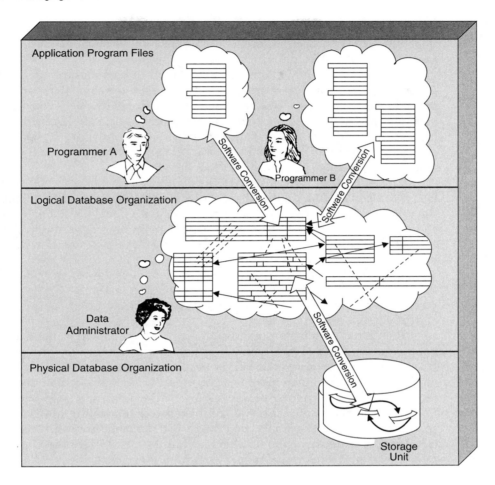

Figure 7-2   The Three-Level Database (from Martin [4])

grams. The logical data relationships can also vary for different programs that use the data, without requiring data redundancy. In addition, applications can use a subset of the database and organize it, again without redundancy, in the best manner for the application.

Three Traditional Data Models

The second major concept in database management is alternate ways to define relationships among data. These so-called data models are methods by which data is structured to represent the real world and the way that data is accessed. There are a number of data models in use today, but three have been the most widely used since the 1970s: hierarchical, network, and relational.

The *hierarchical model* structures data so that each element is subordinate to another in a strict hierarchical manner, like the boxes in an organization chart. This model uses the terminology *parent* and *child* to represent these relationships. This approach, where a data item can have only one parent, is represented by IBM's IMS database management system.

The *network model* allows each data item to have more than one parent. Assembly parts lists illustrate this structure, where the same part can be used in more than one assembly. This approach is represented by the Codasyl-type database management systems, such as Computer Associates' IDMS. In both the hierarchical and network models, the data relationships are stated explicitly, generally by pointers stored with the data. These pointers provide the means by which programs access the desired data records.

The *relational database management system* was proposed in 1970 by Edgar F. Codd of IBM [6]. It is the most recent of the three traditional models. In the relational model, the relationships among data items are not expressly stated by pointers. Instead, it is up to the DBMS to find the related items, based on the values of specified data fields. Thus, all employees of a certain department are found by searching for the department number in each employee record.

Relational databases store data in tables. Each row of the table, called a tuple, represents an individual entity (person, part, account). Each column represents an attribute of the entities. Eight relational operations can be performed on this data, as shown in Figure 7-3.

Relational systems are not as efficient as hierarchical or networked database systems, where the navigational maps through the data are predefined. But because relational systems allow people to create relationships among data on the fly, they are much more flexible. Hence, they have become the database technology of choice in today's systems.

The relational model has caught the attention of the industry because computer scientists see it as a good theory of data structure, while users find its tabular representation comfortable and familiar. Database management systems based on the relational model were first used primarily to handle end user queries; they are now widely used in high-volume transaction systems with huge files.

Figure 7-3 Relational Operations

- SELECT chooses particular columns.
- PROJECT chooses particular rows.
- JOIN concatenates rows from two or more tables, matching column values.
- PRODUCT concatenates rows from two or more tables but does not match column values.
- INTERSECTION selects rows whose value(s) exist in both tables.
- DIFFERENCE selects rows whose value(s) exist in one table but not in the other.
- UNION merges two tables that have similar data, eliminating duplicates.
- DIVISION also merges two tables, but with more complicated selection capabilities. For a simple example, suppose there is a table that contains all the products you buy and a table that contains all your suppliers and the products they sell. Relational division can be used to find all suppliers that can supply all the products you buy.

Much of the current interest in relational systems comes from their capability to enable on-the-spot concatenation of data from several sources. This is precisely the capability end users want because they do not know the format of many of their ad hoc queries ahead of time. This capability also increases the flexibility of large mainline systems.

Next-Generation Database Management Systems

Next-generation database systems, according to a special issue of *Communications of the ACM* [7], are object-oriented or extended relational DBMS. As Cattell [7a] of Sun Microsystems notes, these DBMS are designed to widen the use of databases to new kinds of applications—CASE, CAD, medical applications, office automation, and knowledge representation for artificial intelligence.

These systems draw on data management techniques from the past, but they include two other major concepts as well. One is object management—the management of complex kinds of data, such as multimedia and procedures. The other concept is knowledge management—the management of large numbers of complex rules for reasoning and maintaining integrity constraints between data. Together, these three techniques—data, object, and knowledge management—describe the underpinnings of the next-generation database management systems.

The new data models in these DBMS, which have already been built and tested in research labs, have two important architectural features, says Cattell. First, they are designed for high performance on objects. Second, they are closely integrated with programming languages. Some even combine the programming language and data manipulation language. Yet all these systems retain traditional DBMS features, including end user tools, high-level query languages, concurrency control, recovery, and the ability to efficiently handle huge amounts of data.

For data modeling, these systems combine the best features of relational DBMS and object-oriented programming languages, says Cattell. In fact, there are two main categories of next-generation DBMS, depending on their heritage. Some are extensions of object-oriented programming languages, which add database capabilities. Others extend relational DBMS with object-oriented language capabilities.

Object-Oriented Database Systems. There is growing use of object-oriented technologies in several areas of IT. One of those areas is database management. The newest data model is object oriented. The object-oriented approach expands the view of data by storing and managing "objects," each of which consists of

1. A piece of data
2. "Methods"—procedures that can perform work on that data
3. Attributes describing the data
4. Relationships between this object and others

Objects are important because they can be any type of data—a traditional name or address, an entire spreadsheet, a clip of video, a voice annotation, a photograph, a segment of music, and so on. A collection of objects is called an *object-base*, although such terms as *object database*, or *object-oriented database* are used by some vendors to signify the relationship between objectbases and database management.

Although these new database models may not replace the traditional three (hierarchical, network, and relational), they will *significantly* expand the kinds of data stored in databases.

Stonebraker and Kemnitz [7b] provide an example of an application that requires object management as well as data management and knowledge management. It is a newspaper application that needs to store text and graphics and be integrated with subscription and classified ad data. In this application, the customer billing requires traditional data management, while storage of text, pictures, and the newspaper's banner require object management. Finally, it needs the rules that control the newspaper's layout. One rule might be, "Ads for competing department stores cannot be on facing pages."

Stonebraker and Kemnitz believe that *most* data management problems in the future will require all three dimensions: data, object, and rule (or knowledge) management.

A Look to the Future. Silberschatz, Stonebraker, and Ullman [7c] report on a workshop that looked at the driving forces for future database technology and the corresponding research needed to meet these needs. The workshop participants drew three main conclusions:

1. Twenty-first century technologies will require radically new database technologies.
2. Next-generation database applications will involve much more data, multimedia support, complex objects, rules processing, and archival storage.
3. Cooperation among organizational units will require heterogeneous distributed databases.

The authors give five examples of future database applications that cannot be handled well, or at all, with today's database products or technologies.

- NASA estimates that it needs to store 10^{16} bytes of satellite images from just a few years worth of space exploration in the 1990s. How can it store and search such a massive database, which is enough to fill 10,000 optical disk jukeboxes?
- CAD data for a skyscraper must maintain and integrate information from the viewpoints of hundreds of subcontractors. For example, when an electrician drills a hole in a beam to run an electrical wire, the system should, ideally, recalculate the stresses on the beam to ensure that its load-bearing capabilities have not been compromised.
- The U.S. National Institutes of Health and the U.S. Department of Energy have a joint project for constructing the DNA sequence of the human genome, which is several billion elements long. Matching patients' medical problems to differences in genetic makeup is a staggering problem requiring new data representation and search technologies.
- Large retail chains record every product code scanning action of every cashier in every store. Corporate buyers explore this data using ad hoc queries to uncover buying patterns. This procedure, called data mining, is sure to grow, not only in retailing, but in medicine, science, and many other fields.

- Databases of insurance policies are going multimedia—storing photographs of damaged property, handwritten claim forms, audio transcripts of appraisals, images of insured objects, and even video walk-throughs of houses. Such image data is so large that these databases will be enormous. This application also pushes the limits of available technology.

Tomorrow's databases will store all kinds of data, such as protein structures, program standards, and images. And they will be able to "chunk" large objects into manageable pieces for applications to process. Future databases will also permit rules processing. For example, a design database should notify the designer when one of his or her system designs is affected by a modification made by another designer. These systems could encompass elaborate sets of triggers to track important actions. Separate rule-based systems, common today, probably are not efficient enough to handle these large, complex situations.

We also need new data models, say Silberschatz, Stonebraker, and Ullman, to handle spatial data, time, and uncertainty. Finding the closest neighbor to a data element in three-dimensional space requires new multidimensional access methods. Exploring the state of a database at a point in time, or retrieving the time listing of a data value, will be functions requested by engineers, retailers, and physicists. Unfortunately, time is not supported in today's commercial databases.

Just as there is essentially one worldwide telephone system and one worldwide computer network, some believe we will eventually have a single worldwide file system. To achieve this requires collaboration among nations, which is actually happening in some areas. The human genome project is one example.

Defense contractors want a single project database that spans all subcontractors and all portions of a project. An auto company wants to give its suppliers access to new car designs, under certain circumstances. Both of these needs require intercompany databases. Future database systems will accommodate distributed heterogeneous databases. The challenge is making these databases behave as though they are part of a single database. This is interoperability—the main challenge of distributed systems, as we noted in Chapter 5.

Yet another challenge for future DBMS is providing easy-to-use, uniform browsing tools that work across heterogeneous databases. These query systems must be able to explain to a user where an inconsistency occurred, or where a database was missing; otherwise, these systems cannot be trusted to perform complete searches.

Silberschatz, Stonebraker, and Ullman suggest that mediators will be built to coordinate users' requests with heterogeneous databases. These special programs would know how to handle very specific kinds of queries, so they will be able to detect and report missing data and inconsistencies.

Finally, security is a major failing in today's DBMS, and distributed, heterogeneous, Internet-linked databases exacerbate the problem. Companies may want to permit access to some portions of their databases while restricting other parts. This will require reliably authenticating inquirers. Unless security and integrity are strictly enforced, users will not be able to trust the systems.

To date, the database industry has shown remarkable success in transforming scientific ideas into products, say Silberschatz, Stonebraker, and Ullman. Further advanced research is needed to tackle these challenges for the future.

Distributing Data

Cattell notes that the second main challenge facing the data management field—beside developing next-generation DBMS—is distributing data. At the moment, this may sound a bit unusual because everyone is placing so much emphasis on creating intranets that consolidate data. But, in truth, intranets and even electronic commerce will foster more coordination among distributed databases.

"True" Distributed Databases. Chris Date [8], of Codd and Date Consulting Group, formulated 12 rules for a distributed database. These rules, listed in Figure 7-4, have become *the* fairly technical definition of a true distributed

Figure 7-4   Twelve Rules for Distributed Databases (from C.J. Date [8])

1. Local autonomy. Local data is owned and managed locally, with local accountability and security. No site depends on another for successful functioning.

2. No reliance on a central site. All sites are equal, and none relies on a master site for processing or communications.

3. Continuous operation. Installations at one site do not affect operations at another. There should never be a need for a planned shutdown. Adding or deleting installations should not affect existing programs or activities. Likewise, portions of databases should be able to be created and destroyed without stopping any component.

4. Location independence (transparency). Users do not have to know where data is physically stored. They act as if all data is stored locally.

5. Fragmentation independence (transparency). Relations between data elements can be fragmented for physical storage, but users are able to act as if data was not fragmented.

6. Replication independence. Relations and fragments can be represented at the physical level by multiple, distinct, stored copies or replicas at distinct sites, transparent to the user.

7. Distributed query processing. Local computer and input/output activity occurs at multiple sites, with data communications between the sites. Both local and global optimization of query processing are supported. That is, the system finds the cheapest way to answer a query that involves accessing several databases.

8. Distributed transaction management. Single transactions are able to execute code at multiple sites, causing updates at multiple sites.

9. Hardware independence. Distributed database systems are able to run on different kinds of hardware with all machines participating as equal partners where appropriate.

10. Operating system independence. Distributed database systems are able to run under different operating systems.

11. Network independence. Distributed database systems are able to work with different communications networks.

12. Database independence. Distributed database systems are able to be built with different kinds of databases, provided they have the same interfaces.

database. Although it is not stated, these operating principles depend on the underlying databases being relational.

A Standard Query Language. There is a myriad of technical challenges facing designers of distributed systems. Fortunately, SQL is currently the standard language for accessing relational databases. It is not a full-application development language nor an end user query tool. Rather, it is an English-like language for manipulating data and performing queries against relational tables. It has three components.

1. A *data definition language* for creating relational tables, creating indexes to data, and defining fields of data.
2. A *data manipulation language* for entering information into a database and accessing and formatting the data.
3. A *data control language* for handling security functions.

The use of SQL provides a number of benefits. It can be embedded in procedural languages, such as C or COBOL, and it can be incorporated in packages, such as spreadsheets that run on PCs and workstations. It can act as an intermediary between production applications and databases, between client requests and server responses in client/server systems, and between browser-based applications and databases. It thus insulates applications from changes in physical and logical database structures. Furthermore, it provides the foundation for standard communications among heterogeneous databases via application programming interfaces (APIs) for databases.

Alternatives to True Distributed Databases

Many databases do not have to be true distributed databases, as defined by Date. Many alternatives have sufficed quite well. Following are five alternatives:

- Downloaded data files
- Copies of data stored at nodes
- Not fully synchronized databases
- Client/server databases
- Federated databases

Downloaded Data Files. Sending data from mainframes and minis to PCs is very common, and sending them to a data warehouse is the goal of many IS shops. In fact, it is the most popular method for distributing data. In some cases, report files are distributed in place of printed reports. When delivered in this manner, the report formats can be changed to meet local needs. And, of course, users see the data much earlier than when the printed reports are physically distributed.

End users can also request downloads of selected files. Some companies do not allow such files to be updated on a PC and then uploaded directly to the production files for fear that the integrity of the data will be compromised. Many do not even allow direct downloading of data from production files to PCs. Instead, data is extracted from the production files and put into a data warehouse.

Copies of Data Stored at Nodes. A second approach to distributing data is to locate working copies of data at nodes. These data files are accessible to remote users for query and sometimes to post updates and changes. This so-called memo posting provides fast answers to queries and helps process customer activity during the workday. The master files reside at one or more data centers, and the "official" updating of the files is done at these centers, usually at night. Then, during early morning hours, only the new and changed records are downloaded to the nodes for use during that workday.

Not Fully Synchronized Databases. Einar Stefferud [9] points out that it may not always be necessary to have distributed databases that are synchronized at every point in time—as long as the errors can always be caught quickly and fixed easily. This is the case with the distributed name service on networks. This service stores the names and addresses of files on the network. Each service node has one authoritative copy and one secondary copy of these names and addresses.

The secondary copy is kept in cache (fast memory) and is responsible for refreshing itself from the primary copy. But it does not worry about synchronization because if it gives out a wrong address, the requesting message quickly discovers the error, returns, and asks the primary copy for the correct address. Where this alternative is possible, it is a simple and robust solution, says Stefferud.

Client/Server Databases. George Schussel [10], who has hosted a number of database conferences, believes there are significant differences between true distributed databases and client/server databases. He says the difference is in the concept of location transparency. In a true distributed database, each node has a copy of the DBMS and the dictionary; therefore, the application need not know the location of the data because the node can determine the access strategy. In client/server systems, on the other hand, only a limited number of nodes run the DBMS, so the applications must know where the data is located. Therefore, they do not support location transparency. Nevertheless, they are very appropriate for higher-performance transaction processing, he believes.

Federated Databases. At a workshop on the future of DBMS [mentioned in 7c], the researchers stated that companies are likely to have federated databases rather than distributed databases. This means that existing databases will retain their autonomy, their data will continue to be defined independently, and each local DBMS will essentially take care of itself, while retaining rules for others to access its data.

We have seen this approach work when incompatible databases—such as those that contain text, alphanumeric, and image—are needed in a single application. These databases are left intact on their own machine, and their data is pulled together at the workstation. The application software on the client machine calls on the various databases, and displays data from each one in a different window, in whatever format it has been programmed to use. For handling multidimensional data, this is the approach we expect companies to take. A good example of this approach is the Northwest Airlines System, discussed in Chapter 5. This is also the approach being used in intranet-based applications and data-warehouse-based applications.

MANAGING INFORMATION

"Information is power." "We are in the information age." These and similar statements would lead you to believe that managing information is a key corporate activity. In fact, some believe that information management rather than technology management is the main job of the IS department. We believe they are both important. The technology can be viewed as the infrastructure with the information as the asset that runs on that infrastructure. Yet, information is just an intermediary—an intermediary for action. In this important intermediary position, the management of information is important and raises a number of management issues. We discuss several here, followed by four types of information.

Information Management Issues

If information is to be viewed as an asset (as many companies now view it), it must be treated differently from the traditional assets of labor and capital because it is different from them, says Thomas Davenport, at the University of Texas at Austin [11]. For one thing, it is not divisible. Nor is it scarce. In addition, ownership cannot be clearly defined. Davenport discusses three categories of issues in managing information:

- Value issues
- Usage issues
- Sharing issues

Value Issues. Information's value depends on the recipient and the context. It is contextual. In fact, most people cannot put a value on a piece of information until they have seen it. Despite these drawbacks, people do, indeed, place values on information. Look at all the information services that people buy. Information marketplaces do exist, inside and outside companies. The only practical way to establish the value of information, says Davenport, is to establish a price for it and see if anyone buys. Pricing possibilities include charging for the information itself rather than for the technology or the provider, charging by the document rather than a smaller unit, charging by length or time or number of users, and charging by value rather than cost.

A number of tools are being used at companies to increase the value of information, states Davenport. Four are

- *Information Maps.* These can be textual charts or perhaps even diagrammatic maps that point to the location of information—whether in written material, experts' minds, and so forth. IBM, for example, created a guide to market information so that managers can find out where to get quick answers to their ad hoc questions. The result has been less money spent on duplicate information and increased understanding of the kinds of questions people typically ask.

- *Information Guides*. Guides are people who know where desired information can be found. Librarians have traditionally played this role. Hallmark Cards, for instance, created a guide job in its business units to help employees find computer-based information on available jobs. These guides have substantially reduced the time needed to find information.

- *Business Documents.* Business documents are yet another tool for sharing information. They provide organization and context. One fruitful way to embark on information management is to uncover what documents an organization needs. This can be easier and more useful than defining common terms, notes Davenport. Dean Witter, for instance, discovered that its brokers all used the same documents, over and over. Some 90 percent of these documents could be put on one CD-ROM, kept on local servers, and updated monthly, greatly facilitating information use.

- *Groupware*. Groupware is a tool for getting greater value out of less structured information. It allows people to share information across distances in a more structured manner than electronic mail. Lotus Notes is such a product. Groupware can ease discussions and aid distribution of information, but its success depends upon the culture. For one thing, better access to information increases (not decreases) people's appetite for more information. However, employees using sophisticated groupware products need education to learn how the technology can be used to improve work habits and profits, neither of which flow naturally from the technology.

To have value, the databases need to be managed—even pruned and restructured. Knowledgeable people are needed to manage the information resource and its use. This is true of intranet and Web sites as well.

Usage Issues. Information management is a management problem, states Davenport in an article in *Harvard Business Review* [11], because it deals with how people use information, not how they use machines. He makes the following three points with regard to managing information use.

First, information's complexity needs to be preserved. Information should not be simplified to be made to fit into a computer because this truncates sharing and conversations. Information does not conform to common definitions. It is messy. It naturally has different perspectives, which are important and need to be preserved. There will be tension between the desire for one common global meaning and numerous familiar local meanings; therefore, companies that want to settle on common corporate terms must do so with line people, not technical people, because line people will use the end results. The IS organization can facilitate these discussions, but the businesspeople should determine the meanings.

Second, people do not easily share information, even though its value grows as it is shared. Culture often blocks sharing, especially in highly competitive organizational cultures.

Third, technology does not change culture. Just building an information system does not mean that people will use it. This is a false assumption that too many IS people make, notes Davenport. To change the information culture of a company requires changing basic behaviors, values, attitudes, and management expectations.

Sharing Issues. If information sharing is the goal, a number of contentious problems must first be resolved. One is that a sharing culture must be in place or the existing disincentives will thwart use of a sharing system such as Notes.

Technical solutions do not address the sharing issue. For example, there has been much talk about information architectures, where the definitions of stable types of corporate data—such as customers, products, and business transactions—can be specified ahead of time and used consistently across the firm. This approach has yet to fulfill its promise, states Davenport. The enterprise models are difficult to understand, they take years to populate, and they are probably outdated before they are usable. But even more importantly, information architectures have failed because they do not take into account how people use the information. Managers get two-thirds of their information from conversations and one-third from documents—almost none from computer systems. So a common information architecture is not likely to solve the information management problem.

An issue in sharing is: Who determines who has legitimate need of the information? The "owning" department? Top management? And who identifies the owner? The development of the principles for managing information—how it is defined and distributed—is more important than the final principles, states Davenport, because the touchy subject of information sharing is brought out into the open. In short, working out information issues requires addressing entrenched attitudes about organizational control.

Is sharing good? Not in all cases. Forcing employees to share information with others above them can lead to intrusive management. Some executive support systems limit "drill down" for just this reason. This is the type of issue managers must think about in information management.

Unlimited information sharing does not work, notes Davenport. There need to be limits. On the one hand, the sharing of corporate performance figures is beneficial, even when corporate performance is poor, because it usually increases morale; uninformed employees usually guess the worst. On the other hand, the sharing of rumors (noninformation) generally demoralizes people. Separating information from noninformation is an information management issue. Allowing employees to send messages to large distribution lists exacerbates the information management problem. Managements have awoken to the fact that they need to address this issue. Vendors are developing filters and agents to be used with electronic mail systems. These will only help resolve corporate information management issues if the correct underlying policies are put in place.

Even hiring practices play a role in information management. If promotions are based on circulation and publication of new ideas, a sharing environment exists. If these activities are not rewarded, sharing may be an anathema to the culture.

In all, getting value out of information requires more than technology. It is inherently hard to control. It is ever expanding and unpredictable. Only when executives view it in this light will they manage information for the most effective use.

ur Types of Information

To characterize the full scope of information management, and to explore me of its ramifications, we consider four types of information. First, there are /o types of information generated and managed internally in the organization:

1. Information based on data records, such as those found in databases.
2. Document-based information, such as reports, opinions, e-mail, and proposals.

The first type of internal information pertains primarily to entities, such as individual employees, customers, parts, or transactions. Well-structured data records are used to hold a set of attributes that describe each entity. The second category pertains primarily to *concepts*—ideas, thoughts, and opinions. Less structured documents or messages, with a wide variety of information forms, are used to describe these.

The same two types of information are also generated externally to the organization. There is external record-based information, such as government data on economic and financial conditions, stock price quotations, and airline schedules. There is also external document-based information, such as printed reports, newsletters, economic forecasts, Web-based documents, and so on. Figure 7-5 shows these four types of information in a simple matrix, along with the information management activity that has characterized each in the past.

Internal record-based information has been the focus of attention of information systems because that is the type of information computer-based application systems generate and manage easily. External record-based information can now be accessed over the Internet, or through other electronic means, via public databases. End users themselves have generally handled the procurement of this kind of data by subscribing to database services. Generally, IS executives have paid little attention to document-based information, either internal or external. Intranets have changed that. Documents are now an integral part of the kinds of information these sites house. Even in companies where the administrative vice president or the corporate library has felt this continues to be their

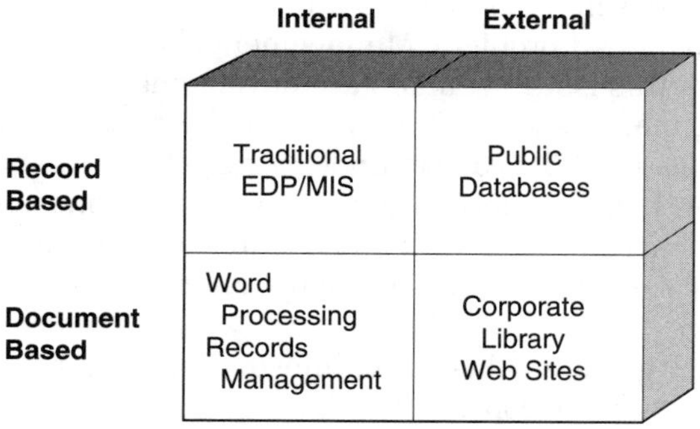

Figure 7-5 Four Types of Information

realm, after a short time, they gladly turn responsibility for the technical issues over to IS. We now look at ways companies are managing and utilizing these four types of information.

Internal Record-Based Information. Thus far, this chapter has dealt with the internal record-based cell of the matrix in Figure 7-5. As we have seen, the three-level database is the conceptual model for organizing internal record-based data. Database management systems manage data using data models that define the relationships among entities and attributes of the data. The three dominant data models are the hierarchical, network, and relational model, with object-oriented data management promising to play a strong role in the future.

Monsanto represents the recent resurgence of effort in getting record-based information into shape. Monsanto and others have discovered that it requires a two-pronged approach. One is to get the pool of data cleaned up. The second is to ensure that the data streams that feed that pool input clean data. Dealing with data inputting processes requires tracking those processes through the company to uncover any sources of errors, perhaps using a quality management approach. As Cornelia Varney notes in her Wentworth Research report, "Managing the Integrity of Distributed Systems" [2], one company routed orders that contained errors into an "error bucket." The data quality group then followed these data errors "upstream" to find the root cause. From there, they and the users who input the data decided how to change the process to eliminate the errors. Often, all that was required was to explain the use of the data—something those users had never been told.

Internal Document-Based Information. The management of internal document-based information generally resides with the vice president of administration, who oversees records management (document records, not data records). However, document management has been identified as a crucial issue facing CIOs [12]. For our purposes, a document is a semiformal package of information with some organizational impact that is filed, transmitted, and consequently maintained. Traditional database management of alphanumeric records deals with facts that are driven by an entity (such as an account number) and their attributes. In documents, a fact is replaced with a concept, an entity with an idea, and attributes with information that illuminates the idea.

Electronic document management, which we discuss in Chapter 16, includes a variety of technologies, such as document and image processing, text retrieval, hypertext and hypermedia, EDI, and desktop publishing. In addition, electronic document management includes the technologies that have been used for years in traditional records management areas—micrographics (film and fiche), computer output microfilm (COM), and automated records center applications. The documents handled by this enlarged set of technologies might be letters, blueprints, sales notes, voice mail messages, images, or multimedia documents. Increasingly, they include documents from external sources, such as news items, the Internet, government or industry reports, and even incoming correspondence.

Data management and document management together encompass the total information resource of the firm. The information systems manager should plan to unify these two resources. However, this unification involves understanding the true importance of document management. For example, studies show that 95 percent of the information in most organizations required to conduct business is in document form; only 5 percent is in computerized files and records. Despite over 40 years of progress in computerizing information processes, many organizations still have a huge, crucial amount of "paperwork" required to do business. Despite 15 to 20 years of developing management information systems, decision support systems, and executive information systems with data, we have just begun to include the valuable information contained in documents, particularly those from external sources.

External Record-Based Information. It has generally been users, not the IS department, who have managed the acquisition of information from external databases. Strategic planning departments, financial planners, and other user departments have sought out services that provide this type of information. Yet, with the increasingly turbulent business environment, companies will want to coordinate their use of such external services, as well as combine internal and external information to better understand consumers. As an example of an external source of record-based information, consider Isuzu's use of geographic information system data.

CASE EXAMPLE: American Isuzu Motors

American Isuzu Motors recently became a bigger user of external information, the director of strategic planning told a meeting of the Southern California Chapter of the Society for Information Management. At the time, Isuzu noted that a global shift was underway from mass marketing to one-to-one personal marketing. Furthermore, power was shifting from the manufacturers to the retailers; Isuzu dealers controlled the shelf space, as they do today. With real-time point-of-sale data and credit card data, Isuzu and other companies could know what specific consumers liked. So there was a change in focus from completing transactions to building relationships.

Realizing that it costs five times more to get a new customer than to retain an old one, Isuzu shifted its focus from share of the market to share of a customer's wallet. The goal was to integrate IT with marketing to bring customers in to find out where Isuzu could offer value.

Isuzu's marketing intelligence system allows it to get closer to its customers and get feedback directly from them. With current technology, it is possible for Isuzu to house every customer record on one database. Furthermore, it is possible to amend these records with information gathered by conversations with customers who call on the toll-free number. To complete the customer profile, Isuzu is appending these records with information it buys from external sources. This external data comes in many forms, including lifestyle data, geographic data that pinpoints where consumers with each type of lifestyle live, automobile registration data, purchasing behavior data, economic data, and forecasting data. In many cases, Isuzu obtains this data over the Internet.

Isuzu's use of these external geographic information systems has changed how it does business. To be a better marketer, it has learned that it must know who its customers are and the message that entices them to buy Isuzu products. To do this, Isuzu initially hired a market research firm to identify customers by lifestyle. It then created profiles of customers and ran these profiles through a geographic information system to find where consumers with those same profiles live. To validate these owner profiles, it has used several segmentation techniques such as cluster coding. In one case, cluster coding segments lifestyles into 50 different clusters, from most affluent to least affluent.

One of the most dramatic uses of this external data was to test the market launch of the *new* Isuzu Trooper four-wheel drive vehicle. Formerly, the Trooper was boxy, practical, and cost $13,000. The new Trooper was luxurious, state-of-the-art, and cost $25,000. Via lifestyle clustering, Isuzu found that the buyers for one model of Trooper are generally established professional singles and young families. They often live in state capitols. They are often snow skiers, avid book readers, wine connoisseurs, and gourmet cooks. Income is the biggest differentiator (near $75,000), age is the next (the younger the better), and home ownership is the third.

To perform the market test, Isuzu used the Trooper owner lifestyle profile to find 600 prospects in a 32-square-mile test area in Washington state. Each was sent a video tape about the Trooper, invited to test drive it, and was also told that after the test drive they could be "product managers for a day" and critique the Trooper, telling Isuzu what they wanted in a $25,000 sport vehicle. For their effort, they would receive a gift.

Isuzu learned a lot from those consumers. They expected to love a $25,000 vehicle, not just like it. They wanted cup holders. They loved the sun roof. And on and on. Isuzu listened and made the changes. The results were dramatic. Sales of Trooper in the two Isuzu dealerships in the test area increased by 300 percent and 450 percent respectively.

Since that time, Isuzu has tracked the profile of Trooper buyers and has found that the profile has not changed. Isuzu continues to use cluster maps from external geographic information services to see where households with this profile live to best target its advertising.

Isuzu now believes that to expand its relationships with its customers, it must have more knowledge, not just from internal systems but from external databases as well. It now sees the power of having this information.

External Document-Based Information. Many IS executives have considered external document-based information as the least manageable form of information. It has been the responsibility of corporate librarians in most companies. Yet, as the amount of such external information grows, and as more and more of it becomes computerized, it will become increasingly important for inclusion in IS executives' jurisdiction. Just witness what is happening with the Web and its plethora of external documents.

One area is environmental scanning—searching the world of external information in areas relevant to an organization. Environmental scanning services have been available for many years. They review publications, clip out pertinent articles or create abstracts of these articles, and then pass them along to the client. A newer development is the delivery of this information to a company's internal computer, perhaps even a PC, where it can be searched, browsed, and interpreted by managers. Yet a newer development is the Web, with its plethora of information.

It is not surprising that there is an extremely rapid growth of computer-based document and reference services. Jane Fedorowicz [13] describes this growth and the technology advances that have enabled it. She cites a study by Information Market Indicators, Inc. that shows U.S. businesses increased their on-line database expenditures by 117 percent in three years. Companies are retrieving more and more information from text databases, such as Dow Jones News Retrieval. The increased reliance on external market indicators and improved sources of information have dramatically boosted the demand for on-line text database services.

Typically, users of these systems are trained librarians who provide a service within their company, or PC users who access general-purpose databases. Most of the time, the results of the search are hard copy reports of bibliographic, financial, or other stored information; although, increasingly, they can be files downloaded from the Internet. Some decision support and executive information system products provide links to external databases and display the results of prespecified searches on the screen. The use of an on-line search service at California State University, Los Angeles illustrates the extent of external document-based information.

CASE EXAMPLE: California State University, Los Angeles

The librarian at California State University, Los Angeles explained at a meeting of the Southern California chapter of the Society of Information Management that he trains the faculty and some 5,000 students each year how to use the Internet and on-line databases, such as Nexis Lexis. Students get eight hours of instruction in the class, and most of them can learn Nexis Lexis commands in an hour, says the librarian. Then they can be considered power users.

Lexis contains 300 million legal citations, while Nexis contains 300 million business citations, from 1977 to present. They contain full text databases of biographical reports of company filings, SEC filings, bankruptcy filings, and the like. Subdatabases contain financial information of companies worldwide.The students can see the text of corporate filings on-line 24 hours after they have been filed with U.S. Securities and Exchange Commission. Thus, market research people can find out what their competition is doing, what companies say about themselves in a 10K filing, and so on.

Some 1,400 computers on campus can access Lexis Nexis. The freshmen love the news file, which contains the text of all major magazines and newspapers as well as transcripts of some evening news programs. They can search on a person's name and date, and get information that is up to 24 hours old.

In summary, IS executives need to take a broader view of information management if they plan to manage it as a corporate resource. As a way of representing the breadth of this topic, Figure 7-6 lists the four categories of information and shows the typical corporate authority, sources of information, and examples of technologies used in managing each.

Figure 7-6   The Scope of Information Management

	Typical Corporate Authority	Information Sources	Technologies Used
Internal record-based information	Information systems department	Transaction processing Organizational units	DBMS Data dictionaries Enterprise data analysis techniques
Internal document-based information	Administrative vice president Word processing center Records management	Corporate memos, letters reports, forms	Word processing Micrographics Reprographics Text retrieval products
External record-based information	End users Corporate planning Financial analysis Marketing	Public databases	Time-sharing services Public networks Analysis packages
External document-based information	Corporate library	Public literature News services Catalogs and indexes Subscriptions Purchased reports	Bibliographic services Environmental scanning Public networks

TOWARD MANAGING KNOWLEDGE

The IS world seems to be moving from data management to information management to knowledge management. This third arena, often referred to as "managing intellectual assets," is just beginning to be explored.

We recently attended a conference on knowledge management, The Knowledge Imperative, hosted by the American Productivity and Quality Center and Arthur Andersen [14]. To summarize briefly, here are the main themes we heard at that conference.

Those who distinguish between information and knowledge appear to believe that knowledge is what is in someone's head, while information is in databases. The most important message at the conference was that the term *knowledge management* creates the wrong impression. The term *management* often brings forth the "we can control it" mindset. Knowledge cannot be controlled or engineered, so the mechanical metaphor is wrong.

It can only be leveraged through processes and culture. The biological or ecological metaphor is much better, numerous speakers at the conference said. The more people are connected, and the more they exchange ideas, the more their knowledge spreads and can thus be leveraged.

The process is the key. The main area of discussion at the conference was learning how to transfer tacit knowledge—knowledge in someone's head that they cannot easily explain to others. In this regard, IT is seen as one enabler, but not the main enabler. The key seems to be getting people together face-to-face about how they do things. Once people sit down and talk about what they do and why, barriers fall, knowledge flows, and sharing increases. Unfortunately, people are not given the time nor the space these days to do this; "free time" to share is not seen as important.

So, unlike information, knowledge "management" is more akin to knowledge "gardening." It needs to be nurtured, the correct environment and sharing norms need to be in place, and only then will the sharing take place. To better understand the tack that can be taken to change processes and increase sharing, consider what one large pharmaceutical company is doing.

CASE EXAMPLE: A Pharmaceutical Company

A project at a major pharmaceutical company was aimed at improving the process of developing new drugs and getting them approved by the U.S. Food and Drug Administration (FDA), a process that takes five to ten years, costs $250 million, and can yield revenues of $1 million a day per drug, once it reaches the market.

This project, described at the Knowledge Imperative Conference [14a], revolved around creating a knowledge infrastructure—one that manages information, enables understanding, and supports learning. The crux of the matter was to understand the customer's needs. In this case, the FDA is the primary customer; however, insurance companies, doctors, and consumers are also customers. The company sells all of them knowledge about disease, treatment, and how a drug will work in particular scenarios. When the employees understand the type of knowledge they need to create a product for these customers, and their role in its creation, then they figure out better ways to work.

The project began by studying and codifying 60,000 pages of documents filed with the FDA to discern how the teams developing drugs and filing their results were sharing knowledge. These regulatory files explain to the FDA what the company knows about a drug, how it learned those things, and what conclusions it has reached.

The knowledge infrastructure project team found the files lacking. Each should have four parts: purpose, content, logic, and context. Only one of the files had a statement of purpose (which stated the problem to be solved). A file without a statement of purpose shows that the author does not know the reason for the document. Many files had contradictions, which told the team that the authors had not talked to each other. For instance, they disagreed on whether the drug should be taken once or twice a day.

To rectify the situation, the study team created a generic knowledge tree of the questions the FDA asks when deciding whether or not to approve a drug. The top of the tree has their three main questions: Is it safe? Does it work? Does it have sufficient quality? The tree lays out the supporting questions for these three issues, in layers, which showed the teams which questions they needed to answer to the FDA's satisfaction. It also showed people why others needed specific information, thus giving them a context (beyond trust) for sharing.

In a pilot project, the knowledge infrastructure team also used a different process with one team: writing as a tool for thinking. They got the team to write up its ten-year drug study before the team did it, so team members were clear about the data they needed to gather and present to the FDA. Furthermore, they wrote this report template publicly as a team. To do it, they wrote critical points that had to be in the report on Post-It notes. Next, they prioritized them on huge sheets on the meeting room wall. Then they designed studies to prove the points that had to be proven. In creating this virtual prototype of the knowledge to be presented to the FDA, publicly, on the wall, they could physically see what knowledge was needed. They created a common mental model of the results. It was a powerful technique.

Since the work of this team is not completed, the results of this new process are not in. However, they have seen tangible progress in filling in the report sections on content, logic, context, and purpose. In another case, where an existing drug was to be registered for use with a new disease, the team had not made much progress in two years' time. After they were shown the knowledge tree over a two-day period, they were able to submit the file to the FDA in three months (they had previously estimated 18 months), and the FDA approved it in 18 months (the team had estimated three years).

CONCLUSION

As can be seen by the wide-ranging discussion in this chapter, the job of IS departments is widening significantly. Not only must they get corporate data in shape, they also need to create and build an infrastructure for managing the full range of information types. Finally, they play a role in helping their firm leverage the knowledge that its employees carry around in their heads. Companies that address all three areas, and start implementing IT-based programs in all three, will have a significant edge over their competitors because they will be able to leverage their intellectual assets.

QUESTIONS AND EXERCISES

REVIEW QUESTIONS

1. What is the difference between data, information, and knowledge?
2. What is the main problem in managing data?
3. What are the four roles of data administrators?
4. What three ERD management components has Monsanto put in place?
5. Define the three-level database concept. What are its advantages?
6. What are three traditional database models?
7. What is the next-generation DBMS?
8. Give one example of an application that will require these new DBMS.
9. What are the 12 guiding principles that describe true distributed databases?
10. What are five alternatives to true distributed databases?
11. According to Davenport, what are three management issues in managing information? Briefly describe each.
12. What are the four kinds of information that define the scope of information management? Describe each briefly.
13. How has American Isuzu Motors used external geographical information?
14. What is a better paradigm than knowledge management?
15. What did the pharmaceutical company do to create a knowledge infrastructure?

DISCUSSION QUESTIONS

1. In this chapter the assertion is made that IS departments should concentrate on getting data right rather than getting systems up and running quickly. Discuss the pros and cons of this argument.

2. Information is in databases; knowledge is in people's heads. Argue for or against whether or not we can store knowledge in computers.

3. Technology does not change culture. Agree or disagree? Explain your point of view.

4. An ethical question regarding electronic mail is whether the contents belong to the sender or the corporation. What is your opinion? Explain your reasoning.

EXERCISES

1. Find two articles on data management. Present any new ideas in these articles to the class.

2. Find an example of each of the four kinds of information presented in Figure 7-5. They may be from company documents, the Web, or public publications. What new ideas on (1) corporate authority, (2) technologies used, and (3) information sources did you gain from where you found these items? Did you find any evidence of a merging (or a diverging) of the management of these different types of information?

3. Find two articles on knowledge management. What new ideas did it contain? Present them to the class.

4. Visit a local company with a data administration function. Talk to the data administrator and find out:

(a) What kinds of data does the department control or not control?

(b) What types of data problems is the group trying to solve?

(c) What progress is the group having in bringing data under control?

5. Visit a local company and talk to either the corporate librarian or the manager of records management and find out:

(a) What information technologies are used to store, catalog, and retrieve documents, literature, and citations?

(b) What kinds of information sources are used?

(c) What various kinds of searching capabilities are available?

(d) What kinds of information technology are used to disseminate information?

6. Visit a local company and ask the CIO what kinds of projects have been conducted to nurture knowledge sharing.

REFERENCES

1. JOHN ZACHMAN, Zachman International, 2222 Foothill Blvd., Suite 337, La Cañada, CA 91011.

   a. ZACHMAN, JOHN, "A Framework for Information Systems Architecture," *IBM Systems Journal*, vol. 26, no. 3, 1987, pp. 276–292.

   b. ZACHMAN, JOHN and JOHN SOWA, "Extending and Formalizing the Framework for Information Systems Architecture," *IBM Systems Journal*, vol. 31, no. 3, 1992, pp. 590–616.

   c. ZACHMAN, JOHN, "Enterprise Architecture: The Issue of the Century," *Database Programming and Design*, February 1997.

2. VARNEY, CORNELIA, "Managing the Integrity of Distributed Systems," IT Management Programme report, Wentworth Research, Park House, Wick Road, Egham, England TW20 OHW, January 1996, http://www.wentworth.co.uk.

3. BRADLEY, JAMES, "The Elusive Relation," *Computerworld* (Box 880, Framingham, Mass. 01701), March 8, 1982, pp. In Depth 1–16. (This material was based largely on the author's book *File and Data Base Techniques*, Holt, Rinehart & Winston, 1982.)

4. MARTIN, JAMES, *Principles of Data–Base Management* (Englewood Cliffs, NJ: Prentice Hall, 1976).

5. ATRE, SHAKU, *Data Base: Structured Techniques for Design, Performance, and Management* (New York: John Wiley & Sons, 1980).

6. CODD, E. F., "Relational Database: A Practical Foundation for Productivity," *Communications of the ACM*, Association for Computing Machinery (1515 Broadway, New York, NY 10036), February 1982, pp. 109–117.

7. "SPECIAL SECTIONS: NEXT-GENERATION DATABASE SYSTEMS," *Communications of the ACM*, October 1991; pp. 31-131.

   a. CATTELL, R.G.G., guest editor, pp. 31-33.

   b. STONEBRAKER, M. and G. KEMNITZ, "The Postgres Multi-Generation Database Management System," pp. 78-92.

   c. SILBERSCHATZ, A., M. STONEBRAKER and J. ULLMAN (editors), "Database Systems: Achievements and Opportunities," pp. 110-120.

8. DATE, CHRIS, *An Introduction to Database Systems*, Vols. I and II, 4th ed. (Reading, MA: Addison-Wesley, 1987).

9. EINAR STEFFERUD, Network Management Associates, 17301 Drey Lane, Huntington Beach, CA 92647.

10. SCHUSSEL, GEORGE, "In Depth: Distributed DBMS Decisions," *Computerworld*, May 6, 1991, pp. 81-83.

11. DAVENPORT, TOM, "Saving IT's Soul: Human-Centered Information Management," *Harvard Business Review*, March/April 1994, pp. 119-131.

12. "CRICITICAL ISSUES IN INFORMATION SYSTEMS MANAGEMENT, 1991-1995", *IS Analyzer*, January 1991, pp. 9-10.

13. FEDOROWICZ, JANE, "A Technology Infrastructure for Document-Based Decision Support Systems" in Sprague, R., and H. Watson, *Decision Support Systems: Putting Theory Into Practice*, 3rd ed. (Englewood Cliffs, NJ: Prentice Hall, 1993).

14. THE KNOWLEDGE IMPERATIVE SYMPOSIUM, Arthur Andersen and The American Productivity & Quality Center (123 North Post Oak Lane, Houston, TX 77024), September 1995.

   a. SEEMANN, PATRICIA, "Building Knowledge Infrastructure: Creating Change Capabilities," tape cassette #B13, AVW Audio Visual, 3620 Willowbend, #1118, Houston, TX 77010.

EIGHT

Managing Operations

INTRODUCTION

A discussion of managing the essential information technologies is not complete without describing operational issues facing information system executives. Since the late 1980s, due to mergers, corporate downsizings, the changing economics of IT, and the Internet, the subject of computer operations has received a lot of attention. Systems operations are important because, if they are not professionally run, a company could suffer a computer or network breakdown that could essentially shut it down for some period of time. It is not a trivial area. Furthermore, poorly run IS shops cause IS executives to lose credibility, causing them to end up fighting fires instead of setting policy, or find themselves looking for a new job, or having their operations outsourced.

We begin this chapter by presenting one former IS executive's views on the breadth of the operations job and how it needs to be managed. Then we discuss four major operational issues:

- Improving data center operations
- Outsourcing information systems functions

- Managing today's complex networks
- Providing disaster recovery for distributed systems

WHAT ARE OPERATIONS?

In a lecture at the University of California at Los Angeles (UCLA), William Congleton described the important operational issues he faced in the IS department he ran.

Why Talk About Operations?

Keeping the shop running is getting increasingly difficult, he said. The reasons become apparent at budget time. His total annual IS department budget had the following split:

- 33 percent for systems and programming—of which 70 percent was for maintenance and 30 percent was for new development.
- 10 percent for department administration and training.
- 57 percent for operations.

So, one reason operations are important is because they involve more money than any other part of the department.

At his company, operations included computer hardware at 64 locations, including 12 seaports, 12 parts warehouses, and 12 sales offices. Hardware included computers, disk drives, tape drives, printers, and terminals. Operations also included communication lines and equipment, and software, such as operating systems, compilers, and networking software. In addition, the budget included data center personnel, such as systems consulting for programmers, operators who scheduled and ran production jobs, mounted tapes, delivered reports, and monitored the machines and network. And operations included disaster recovery planning and security.

"Putting all these things together sometimes gave me more excitement than I could stand," quipped Congleton, "plus they were more expensive than I wanted. Therefore, achieving a 10 percent reduction in operations had a far greater effect than a 10 percent reduction in any other area. That is why operations are important."

Solving Operational Problems

Systems operations problems are obvious to the entire company—on-line response times are slow, networks are down, data is not available, or data is wrong. What can be done to improve operations? There are three strategies, said Congleton. One is to buy more equipment. As equipment costs drop, this solution might appear the most cost-effective—unless you run out of room for the equipment. The second approach is to continuously fight fires and rearrange priorities—getting people to solve the problem at hand. This solution really only moves the problem of poor management from one hot spot to another. The third solution is to continually document and measure what you are doing, to find out the *real* problems, not just the apparent ones. Then set standards. This is the solution Congleton preferred. It is needed no matter who runs operations, the in-house staff or an outsourcer.

Operational Measures

Operational measures are both external and internal. *External measures* are what customers see: system and network uptime (or downtime), response time, turnaround time, and program failures. These directly relate to customer satisfaction. *Internal measures* are of interest to IS people: computer usage as a percentage of capacity, availability of mainline systems, disk storage utilized, job queue length, number of jobs run, number of jobs rerun due to problems, age of applications, and number of unresolved problems.

Problems reported by the external measures can generally be explained by deviations in the internal measures. To help uncover the problems related to equipment capacity, quality of applications, or improper use of systems by users, numerous venders sell monitoring software and devices. Other measurement systems log performance of the various kinds of computer and telecom equipment, said Congleton. Storage management systems manage space more efficiently. Schedulers, which have been available for the past 25 years, schedule jobs. And library management systems keep track of versions and backups of files and programs. So there are plenty of tools to help IS departments measure how efficiently their equipment is being used.

The Importance of Good Management

Tools are useless, however, unless IS management has created a corporate culture that recognizes and values good operations, said Congleton. It is hard to find good computer operations managers because the absence of prestige (and sometimes pay) does not attract individuals with the proper combination of skills and training. This is unfortunate, he said, because in a good environment, an operations job can be very rewarding—both financially and professionally.

The skills required of an operations manager are similar to those needed in a factory or oil refinery. The factory manager must schedule work to meet promised delivery dates, monitor performance as work flows through the key pieces of equipment, and respond quickly to production breakdowns. In a well-run factory, the manager can usually recover from one or two individual problems. In a poorly run factory, there are so many little problems that the manager does not know where to start to fix the problems. The same is true in computer and telecom centers where the "factory equipment" is the disk drives, database machines, host computers, servers, network gateways, routers, and bridges, and the like.

The vice president of IS must take an active interest in good operations, and strike a proper balance between development (building for tomorrow) and operations (keeping things running today). In most cases, only the vice president can effectively influence the developers to take the time and effort to design and program good operational characteristics into their applications. Poorly designed or poorly written programs can create operational problems that make

Figure 8-1   Trends in Operations (from Bill Congleton)

1. Hardware costs continue to drop. If this decrease lulls management into not taking an aggressive interest in this area, poor operations and inefficient programs will waste computer resources faster than falling hardware costs can compensate.

2. Lights-out computer rooms or unattended operations will be the norm. Companies are replacing computer operators and other data center personnel with software and hardware, so that the centers can run without people.

3. The increasing use of PCs and workstations has spread operational problems to LANs.

4. The number of automated tools to run computers and networks is increasing. But as systems become more powerful, they also become more complex.

5. Expert system technology is being used to automate computer operations.

even a good operations manager look bad. However, if operations are well managed, the operations manager can spot problem programs and ask that they be rewritten to improve performance.

In conclusion, the vice president of IS needs to be concerned about operations, said Congleton, but should emphasize putting the proper operations environment in place. (See Figure 8-1.) The key to managing operations is the same as in any management job, he concluded, set standards and then manage to those standards by finding an outstanding operations manager.

IMPROVING DATA CENTER OPERATIONS

Companies are taking two internal approaches and one external approach to improving data center operations. First, they are increasing efficiency. We discuss that subject by looking at the results of a study that compared efficient and not-so-efficient centers. Second, they are automating data centers, so they run in unattended mode. And third, as the external approach, they are outsourcing operations.

Running Efficient Data Centers

At a conference [1], Christopher Disher of Nolan, Norton and Co. [2] described a study conducted by NNC to find out why some data centers were more efficient than others. Data from 160 data centers was collected on expenditures, number of staff, staff mix, and machine resources. Not surprisingly, larger data centers achieved economies of scale. But there were wide variations in expenditures among similar-sized centers—some centers were spending millions of dollars more a year to achieve the same results as other centers.

NNC found no correlation between expenditures and the industry in which a firm operated. However, they did find a correlation between data center efficiency and the following four characteristics of the quality of applications:

1. *Functional quality of the applications*, measured by how well they met user needs
2. *Technical quality of the applications*, measured by how easy they were to maintain and how efficiently they ran

3. *Application age*
4. *Portfolio coverage,* measured by how much work that could be automated had been automated.

The least efficient centers—that is, those that spent more money than similar centers doing the same amount of work—had older applications; their average system age was 8.7 years as compared to 4.2 years for the most efficient centers. The technical quality of their applications was poorer, and they did not support as much of the business—24 percent of the business as compared to 40 percent in the more efficient centers.

It was not by accident that the most efficient centers had younger and higher-quality applications. Many of those IS shops had purposely redesigned, rewritten, or replaced old applications—to run more efficiently and to use fewer machine room staff.

The NNC study found the efficient and inefficient centers also had a different mix of staff. The inefficient centers had more employees, and some 50 percent of them were "hands-on people"—tape mounters, console operators, print distributors, and so on. The efficient centers had fewer data center employees, and some 65 percent of these people were "knowledge workers"—technical service, management, planning, and operations support people.

Application quality turned out to be the main factor that distinguished efficient centers from inefficient data centers, said Disher. Applications written ten years ago are likely to be more expensive to operate than most people realize, he concluded.

One of the companies that has worked with NNC to improve its data center's efficiency is Mutual of Omaha.

CASE EXAMPLE: Mutual of Omaha

Mutual of Omaha is an insurance company with headquarters in Omaha, Nebraska. About 75 percent of its business is in health and accident insurance, but it also handles mutual funds and provides property, casualty, and life insurance. Mutual of Omaha was interested in the data center work done by Nolan, Norton and Co., and asked NNC to help improve data center operations. David Pepple described their experiences at a conference [1].

About 30 percent of the systems staff works in operations, said Pepple, and about 50 percent of the systems budget is spent on operations—hardware planning, technical support, the computer service center, and voice and data communications. The company has one data center with seven processors: three for production work, two for development and testing, and two for end users. They also have minicomputers, micros, terminals, and hand-held computers throughout the company.

The goal at Mutual of Omaha was to provide data center services at the least cost. The company's main question concerned future direction: Should it decentralize the center or not? The NNC study postulated that the company would gain economies of scale by remaining with one data center. Mutual of Omaha wanted to know if that would be true.

In comparison with the NNC database, Mutual of Omaha found that its application portfolio was quite old. The average application was a high-volume, batch application about 11 years old. The company had the average number of people in its data center compared to other centers its size, but it spent much less money than others. Although this apparent efficiency looked good on the surface, two reasons were discovered for the lower expenditures.

First, for the past ten years the company had kept technology costs low due to careful planning. That was good. But second, it had a larger percentage of hands-on people in its center, and these people had lower salary levels. That was not so good. Mutual of Omaha did not have the mix of people that NNC said reflected an efficient data center operation.

After some study, Mutual of Omaha believed it could reduce data center staff by 30 percent with a resulting cost reduction of 25 percent. But to reduce staff, it would need to change data center operations—significantly. It would need to reduce the amount of hands-on work by moving files from 60,000 tapes to disk and by reducing the amount of printing done at the center. As the applications were recoded or replaced to achieve this, the job mix at the data center changed to include more knowledge workers and fewer direct operations people. The company needed to retrain people, create new operations career paths, and hire new types of staff. Mutual of Omaha decided to remain with one data center to achieve the economies of scale.

Toward Unattended Computer Centers

Howard Miller [3] defines a data center as a computer processing center without regard to computer size or vendor. He defines unattended operations as the totally automated operation of all data center functions; it is a dark-room environment in which computers run without human intervention. Unattended operations, he believes, should eliminate console monitoring, input/output control, manual media distribution, data center librarians, and production coordinators. (See Figure 8-2.)

How Close Are We? Rosemary LaChance [4] has been pushing for unattended data center operations for more than 13 years. Her business card carries the slogan, "It's better with the lights out." She and her partner, Arnold Farber, were running a data center at a bank in 1984 when they saw the need to automate operations.

The question no longer is, "Do we need to automate our data centers?" says LaChance. The question has become, "How soon?" Outsourcing has forced sys-

Figure 8-2   Steps to Implementing Unattended Operations (from Miller [3])

1. Define the areas of human intervention and divide them into two categories: (1) procedures that are easy to eliminate, and (2) those that are difficult to eliminate. Further divide the difficult procedures into those that can be resolved with installed software and those that require new software.

2. Define the instructions that could be added to application software to eliminate the procedures identified in Step One.

3. Agree on a method for incorporating the new instructions into new applications and into all changes made to existing applications.

4. Isolate the instructions that are easy to implement, organize them into projects, and do them.

5. When unattended operation appears easy to achieve, organize a project to do it.

tems management to study how well its centers are run. Even executive management has turned some attention to data center operations because it now realizes that computing is the heartbeat of the company. It is not a technical luxury, so it must operate effectively and efficiently. If the in-house staff cannot do it, they are willing to hand the responsibility over to an outsourcer.

But IS departments can underbid outsourcers, says LaChance, if they are doing a good job. Outsourcing is fine for the short term to allow the in-house staff to move to a new computing platform. Some applications, such as payroll, are also appropriate for outsourcing. But for the long term, LaChance believes companies will be better off automating their computer operations rather than outsourcing them.

Computer operators are going the way of telephone operators: being available for complex work but not for handling routine day-to-day work. The operators in today's lights-out data centers work behind the scenes installing new software releases, fixing breaks, installing new equipment, and planning how to keep the center running. These centers look like the DASD (disk drive) floor—no people. Today's operators can work a normal 8:00 a.m. to 5:00 p.m. workday, leaving the center to operate unattended at night and on weekends.

Companies that have moved to unattended operations have found ways to prevent computer programs from nighttime *abending*—encountering an *abend* (abnormal end). They have programmed their computers to fix themselves, restart automatically from remote instructions, and even automatically transmit backups to remote mass stores or cartridge tape drives. The systems alert the fire department, not a remote operator, when a fire alarm goes off. PCs rather than operators are used to monitor operations because PCs can respond faster and more consistently and accurately. On-line reports have replaced printouts. And tape drives have been replaced with tape cartridges run by robotic arms. These systems can assure on-line access to historical data within three to four minutes, so not as much data needs to be kept on disk drives.

But automation is not necessarily cheaper, says LaChance. Saving money cannot be the driving force. Improving quality of service is the true benefit.

Unattended operation is not only changing the work of operators, it is changing the job of data center management. These managers no longer need to be technical managers. They need to be business managers, says LaChance, because their job is providing good service. They need to understand the business needs and fulfill them. And they need to be planners rather than reactors. One leading-edge firm recently promoted a line manager to data center manager because line managers understand this need.

Companies that are moving the fastest toward unattended operations are those that are fighting for survival, are facing outsourcing, or have executives who allow creativity in the data center. Running a data center without automation is like trying to solve today's problems with yesterday's tools, says LaChance. Lights-out data centers are possible today; a few firms have done it.

A Product Wish List. In a Gartner Group report [5a], Schulman divides the market for unattended operations products into two sectors. The first is companies that require industrial-strength products for two reasons: (1) Their systems are large and complex, or (2) they recognize the strategic importance of managing operations more efficiently and effectively. Industrial-strength products provide companies with a way to manage their operations in a more integrated fashion. The second type of product is for companies that only want to handle message management. They are seeking immediate relief from operator console overload. To have a true industrial strength product, the Gartner Group says the following four components are necessary.

An Automated Operator. This system monitors messages from the operating system, subsystems, and applications. It initiates actions by matching elements of message text to if. . . then rules. The actions an automated operator might take include suppressing messages, rerouting them, replying to them, or initiating a series of preprogrammed commands. An automated operator also can initiate messages and then examine the results. One goal of using an automated operator is to manage the data center by preventing or predicting events—rather than reacting to them after they have happened. Thus, an automated operator also must be capable of calling for help—either by sending messages to an on-site computer operator through a terminal or by beeping an off-site person.

An Enhanced Console Facility. This system is a companion to an automated operator. While an automated operator monitors messages, an enhanced console facility can consolidate complex or frequently used commands, such as start up a system, shut one down, or reconfigure a system. In addition, an enhanced console can give end users a means for submitting jobs, manipulating them, and inquiring about their status or their output from an on-line terminal.

An Operations Automation Language. This language is used to write commands and procedures to automate data center policies and procedures. When well implemented, it allows both systems programmers and operators to create procedures for automating operations.

A Timed-Events Automation Facility. Automating timed events is t
final element in the Gartner Group's list of essential features. This capability is
needed, they say, because precise execution of events at prescribed times or
intervals is essential to the operations job.

CASE EXAMPLE: U S West

U S West, with headquarters in Denver, Colorado, is one of the regional
telephone companies created following the break-up of AT&T. The corporate information services department is responsible for providing information services to all of U S West's subsidiaries including U S West Communications, which provides local telephone service to 14 western states.

U S West operates ten data centers in seven western states. Consolidating
these centers as much as possible is a mission of the information services
department. Initially, the company maximized efficiency at each center
and then it reduced the number of centers and managed the remaining
ones with as few people as possible. Systems managers believe data centers
can be managed better and more efficiently through software rather than
people.

Initially, two systems programmers studied data center operations and
created a long-range strategy for improving efficiency and, where possible,
automating operations. Since that time, the two-person team has grown to
a department of seven people. Each of the staff members specializes in a
different aspect of system automation—systems programming, systems
operation products, involving the local systems department, and database
and administrative control. In addition, other teams have been established
at the other U S West data centers, and a manager is assigned to coordinate the efforts of all the teams.

The First Step: Message Management. The team first analyzed system message traffic. The messages studied were those displayed on the
control consoles in the Bellevue, Washington computer center. These messages appeared on operators' console screens at the rate of 10 to 15 per
minute.

Few of the messages were critical, but all had to be read by the operators. Most were status report messages. The team categorized the messages into two groups—those that always required the same response and
those that could have a variety of responses. They found that one-half of
the messages always needed the same response. To relieve the operators
from looking at these messages, the staff wrote a program to trigger the
appropriate responses without human intervention.

The team's next step was to add some decision-making capabilities to
take care of the messages that had several responses. All possible courses

on were encoded in command lists—lists of what normally would be
ex commands. Using these, a system could trigger the appropriate
se when a message occurred. The automation team has found that it
to continually update these lists because the workloads at the cen-
e constantly changing.

More than 80 percent of the messages that previously flashed on the
operations console screens are no longer seen by the operators. This
automation resulted in an immediate productivity payback. One operator
can easily handle a set of consoles that formerly required several operators.
And that operator can be more efficient and just concentrate on those messages that do appear. The center is staffed by one person and its atmos-
phere is one of relaxed efficiency. Before the automation project was started, there was much more tension and chaos in the center.

More recently, the automation group consolidated message traffic from
multiple systems into one PC. The team is also displaying more of the traffic data in graphical form to help the operators more quickly and easily
understand the messages. Staff members use Netview, IBM's network
management system, as their network management tool, and are using it
to control remote processors. And they are investigating having all the data
centers operate in an unattended mode by being monitored and controlled
from a single location.

Recommendations to Others. The automation team recommends
involving as many of the people who will be affected by the automation project as possible. Team members encountered some fear of change as they
implemented their automation steps, but those fears disappeared as soon
as the operations staff realized that automation would increase the quality
and amount of work they could perform. The automation project staff also
found the ideas of the two dozen staff were essential to the success of the
project because they were the operations experts.

OUTSOURCING INFORMATION SYSTEMS FUNCTIONS

The new phenomenon that appeared in the information systems field in the late
1980s was outsourcing, which means turning over a firm's computer operations,
network operations, or other information systems functions to a vendor for a
specified time—generally, at least for five years. Outsourcing has become an
option that all CIOs must consider to satisfy management that their operation is
being run efficiently and effectively.

At a meeting of the Chicago Chapter of the Society for Information Management, Mel Bergstein of TSC [6] talked about outsourcing. His main message
was that outsourcing is another step in the evolution of the information systems
field. He believes both system integration and outsourcing will be central to
managing information systems throughout the 1990s.

The Driving Forces Behind Outsourcing

Outsourcing descended on IS departments as a follow-on to the merger and acquisition activities in the 1980s, said Bergstein. In the 1960s, only 10 percent of the U.S. economy had global competition. In the 1970s, that rose to 70 percent. In response, companies had to *focus on core businesses* in the 1980s, which led to the huge amount of merger and acquisition activity. This activity was also driven by a new market for corporate control. High-yield bonds allowed a few people to buy a company, leveraging it with debt. Companies were "priced" based on their *shareholder value*, that is, their discounted cash flow.

These two drivers—focus and value—are still leading companies to restructure and focus on core businesses by asking themselves, "Where do we really add value?" As examples, some apparel companies no longer cut, sew, manufacturer, or distribute goods, said Bergstein, because they see their core businesses as design and marketing. Likewise, some publishers no longer manufacture books. They manage and finance projects—and outsource everything else.

So outsourcing is part of the drive for focus and value, and it is not solely an information systems issue, said Bergstein; it is a business issue. Since top management must stress value, it must consider outsourcing in all its nonstrategic functions.

The Expanding Scope of Vendor Options

Outsourcers perform the same activities for a company that its IS department performs in-house. But, over time, the amount of work done by outsiders has increased, said Bergstein, as the following expansion in vendor-customer relationships illustrates.

Traditionally, IS departments have *bought professional services*, such as planning (or consulting), building or maintaining applications, building or maintaining networks, and training. They have also *bought products*, which may or may not include training. And they have *bought transactions*, such as payroll checks from a service bureau or credit reports from a credit-rating service. This third type of relationship is good for buyers because their costs become variable, and hence more controllable. It is also good for the sellers because in taking the risks, they can have higher margins.

With the increasing use of packages and the need to integrate components to create client/server systems, companies have contracted with *a systems integrator*, who generally handles the entire life cycle—planning, development, maintenance, and training—for major systems projects. Finally, the most bundled approach to contracting for IS services is *outsourcing*, where the outsourcer contracts to handle all or most of certain information system activities. The main difference between the latter two options is that system integration is project based while outsourcing is time based.

This five-option continuum, shown in Figure 8-3 on the next page, demonstrates how the IT field is moving, said Bergstein. As you move from the more traditional professional services category (on the left) to the newer outsourcing (on the right), four changes occur in the vendor-customer relationship:

Relationships

Activities	Professional Services	Product	Transactions	Systems Integration	Outsourcing
• Planning/consulting	X			▓	▓
• Building/maintaining applications	X		▓	▓	▓
• Building/maintaining networks	X			▓	▓
• Training users/clients	X	X	X	X	X
• Operating platforms		▓	▓	▓	▓
• Performing administrative functions		▓		▓	▓
• Building/using product		▓		▓	▓

Figure 8-3   Customer-Vendor Relationships (from Mel Bergstein, TSC [6])

1. Information systems management loses an increasing amount of control because more of the activities are turned over to outsiders.
2. The vendors take more risk as they offer options on the right.
3. The vendors' margins improve as they offer services on the right.
4. The importance of choosing the right vendor becomes more important to the right because there is more at risk in using an outside source.

Trends in IT Outsourcing

Major changes are occurring in the outsourcing field, said Rita Terdiman, vice president and research director at the Gartner Group [5b]. She spoke at a meeting of the Sourcing Interests Group [7], a group founded by Barry Wiegler, that discusses various sourcing issues, especially IT outsourcing. One change has been in attitudes, said Terdiman. Outsourcing is not only an accepted practice, it is now seen as a way for companies to improve their competitive positions, often as part of major restructuring activities. This is the strategic view of outsourcing, and it often results in megadeals and full-service outsourcing.

But a second change has been the huge increase in selective outsourcing, where only parts of the IS department are outsourced—just the data center, or the PCs and the help desk, or the network. These deals are shorter term (two to five years) as opposed to strategic deals (five to ten years). And companies are outsourcing more and more specific areas, said Terdiman. The driving force is lack of skills and the desire to offload non-core-competency areas to providers.

A third kind of outsourcing is transformational outsourcing, where companies ask for assistance in bridging the gap between their in-place systems and

infrastructure (mainframe based) and their desired fut
(client/server based). Outsourcers are either asked to maintai.
and phase them out as the new systems come on-line or they are a.
op the new systems because the client does not have the client/server,
ented, or system integration skills.

Another change has been companies' willingness to admit failure. The ﹍
cess of the deals is linked to how realistic the client's expectations are. Anﹶ
although most deals seem to have been fairly successful, said Terdiman, 12 percent recently reported failures. Furthermore, because the business environment
is changing so rapidly, Gartner Group believes there is a good chance that 75
percent of the users will restructure their existing deals by the year 2000, and
another 5 percent will switch to another provider.

One of the latest changes has been outsourcing applications. Previously,
companies felt that their applications were their competitive edge, so they would
not outsource them. Now, however, they have decided it is wiser to get the apps
built fast and in use.

In the near term, Terdiman believes that companies will use a "one-stop
shopping" approach to outsourcing when they outsource infrastructure functions (LAN operation, desktop, mainframes) and a "best of breed" approach
when they outsource applications. In the longer term, she believes that companies will use "best of breed" partnering, with one vendor acting as the prime
contractor. In such cases, the client and prime contractor will strive more for a
partnering relationship rather than a simple customer/supplier relationship.
Figure 8-4 shows the difference between traditional outsourcing and partner-

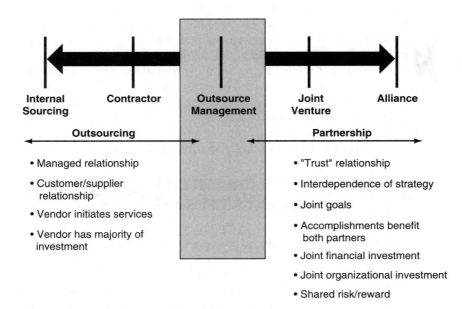

Figure 8-4 The Outsourcing Management Spectrum (from Gartner Group [5b])

ships, where trust, joint goals, joint financial investment, and perhaps some risk and rewards are shared.

Recommendations to Management

Outsourcing is like a marriage, said Bergstein [6], so the decision is not trivial. According to Bergstein, the decision to outsource data center operations, PC support, application development, network management, help desks, application maintenance, or other systems activities should hinge on the answers to the following four questions:

- *Which information system activities are strategic to our company's business*? Those should not be candidates for outsourcing.
- *Will outsourcing save us at least 15 percent*? If not, outsourcing is not a good choice. Outsourcers should be able to generate larger savings by taking advantage of economies of scale, enforcing standards, and using better price/performance equipment.
- *Does our firm have access to the needed technology and expertise*? If not, outsourcing may be the answer to acquiring these resources.
- *Does outsourcing increase our firm's flexibility*? Outsourcing shifts capital budgets to operating expenses, which can give a firm more financial flexibility. Furthermore, outsourcing may free up personnel to work on new systems, while the outsourcer maintains the existing ones. Also, it can increase the firm's flexibility for acquiring new technologies sooner.

There are four activities that management should not outsource, warns Bergstein. These are their strategy, the architecture of the system (including the network), the decisions about when to introduce IT into the organization, and managing the vendor. Although management can outsource the development and operation of information technologies, it should never outsource its policy role. When the systems department is well managed, and where IT is a core competency, outsourcing should not be an option.

To illustrate how one company is managing outsourcing, we look at Eastman Kodak Company, the first company with a healthy IS department that outsourced to improve its competitiveness back in 1989. That started the outsourcing avalanche. The following description comes from research reports published by the Sourcing Interests Group [7a and b] over the past several years; it focuses on the alliance between Kodak and ISSC (IBM's outsourcing subsidiary).

CASE EXAMPLE: Eastman Kodak Company

Eastman Kodak Company, with headquarters in Rochester, New York, is an international manufacturer of imaging and chemical products with worldwide sales of nearly $15 billion. In 1989, the company rocked the information systems world by announcing strategic relationships with four suppliers to manage significant portions of its IS organization. Until that time, outsourcing had been viewed by those in the industry as a desperation move to improve poorly run IS departments. Since Kodak's unit was well run, and benchmarked accordingly, its pioneering stance caused many IS executives—and a few CEOs and CFOs as well—to seriously reconsider outsourcing.

Kodak announced that IBM (now ISSC) would operate its data centers and SNA networks, Digital Equipment Corporation would manage its telecommunications, BusinessLand (now Entex) would handle PC support, and Tigon (now Octel Network Services) would manage voice messaging. Initially the agreement with ISSC was U.S.-based; it was later expanded to include Canadian operations, other U.S. divisions, and eventually six international sites. Kodak encourages ISSC to leverage its data center for both Kodak and other companies' work for improved efficiencies. Due to efforts on both sides, the Kodak/ISSC relationship is working well. They have mutually developed good trust and good processes. As a result, there are few problems, and when issues do arise, the relationship has effective processes to deal with them.

Outsourcing Management Structure

Kodak views its outsourcing management role as exercising leadership, staying in control, and managing the high value-added functions for flexibility. This means that Kodak sets the tone for its key IT relationships. The major themes of the ISSC relationship have been collaborative (not adversarial), long-term mutual benefits (not short term), and making systemic improvements on a global basis (not local). The management structure has six elements: a management board, an advisory council, a supplier and alliance management group, a relationship manager for each relationship, ad hoc working groups, and client surveys.

The management board, which meets twice a year, includes senior management from both companies. It focuses on strategic issues, in addition to any policies or practices on either side that are getting in the way of mutual success. It has dealt with international strategies, IT architecture, telecom directions, disaster recovery plans, and so forth.

The advisory council, which meets monthly and has 15 members, handles technical and operational issues by focusing on *what* Kodak wants, not *how* the services are or will be delivered. Gradually Kodak's trust in ISSC has grown, so it now leaves more of the *how* details up to this service provider. The advisory council reviews service levels, usage measurements and forecasts, tactical plans, migration objectives, business recovery plans, and the like.

The supplier and alliance management group manages the longer-term outsourcing relationships as well as other contracts with large IT suppliers. It works very closely with IS management. This group of ten people includes a manager, the relationship manager for each of the primary alliances, plus support staff and supplier management for other IT sourcing. Initially, this group managed only the alliances. Contracts with major vendors were handled in other groups. But in 1994, all these functions were brought together to increase their focus, leverage global agreements, and align the management of alliances and suppliers. About one-half these people have IS backgrounds; the other half come from purchasing.

The relationship manager is a key ingredient in the success of a strategic relationship, Kodak believes, because this person is the focal point between itself and its service provider. The job of each of Kodak's four relationship managers is to ensure that Kodak receives more than just delivery on the contract. Thus, they manage value creation, not just adherence to the contract. The relationship managers negotiate, coordinate, and manage agreements and ensure that the service-level agreements (SLAs) are established. They also assist in pricing and billing strategies.

Working groups, which were not part of Kodak's original outsourcing management structure, were added to deal with specific technology areas. They are chartered by the advisory council. Their goals are to facilitate changes in processes, promulgate standards, achieve business recovery in case of disruption, and promote effective use of IS services. They have proven to be effective vehicles for talking about important issues, such as agreeing on the timing and appropriateness of upgrading to new releases of software. The groups are represented mainly by operational people. For example, database administrators from the major sites are in one working group.

Client surveys are sent out twice a year to nearly 5,000 internal users of the services being provided. Feedback on quality, cycle time, and product and service leadership are assessed and shared with the service providers. Improvement plans are mutually developed to close any perceived gaps in performance.

Since Kodak's outsourcing has such a large scope, draws on four main suppliers, and covers a large geographic area, the company has discovered that it needs all these forms of coordination for effective supplier management.

MANAGING TODAY'S COMPLEX NETWORKS

Network management—generally thought of as the day-to-day management of network operations—is a crucial job of the systems department, whether it is handled by the in-house staff, outsourced to a vendor, or performed by a common carrier. Networks have played a role in systems ever since terminals were connected to mainframes. But links in those single-vendor, terminal-to-host systems were relatively simple and were managed by the mainframe's communication front-end processor. Today, with multivendor distributed systems, managing the network is orders of magnitude more complex. And since processing is performed around the enterprise network, and on the Internet as well, when one or more networks go down, the entire system could be down unless there is alternate routing. In a growing number of firms, the network is the system. Keeping it up and running is therefore akin to keeping the company operational.

The Index Foundation issued a report to its members on network management [8], which noted that the definition of network management is generally taken for granted, yet rarely defined. They define network management as "the set of activities required to plan, install, monitor, and maintain all network components in order to achieve specified service levels reliably, at an acceptable, and agreed, cost." This definition includes the following five activities:

- *Fault handling.* Identifying, diagnosing, and repairing faults that occur to network components or finding alternate service.
- *Performance monitoring.* Tracking usage to identify the need for additional capacity; regularly analyzing performance of networks, services, and suppliers; and measuring service levels to users.
- *Change management.* Installing and controlling additions, moves, and changes of users, hardware, software, and circuits, as well as controlling the network configuration and maintaining the network inventory.
- *Tactical planning.* Ensuring that the networks can accommodate future growth or new services in the near future.
- *Cost control.* Monitoring operating costs and reconciling invoices.

In addition, the network management group shares responsibility with other groups in the systems department to bill users for services, provide end user support via help desks and training, negotiate contracts, and provide network security, according to the Index Foundation report.

Trends in Network Management

We gleaned the following four trends from our research on network management:

- Integrated network management has become a major goal.
- Management of distributed applications is coming.
- Automation of network operations will increase.
- Outsourcing of network management will increase.

Integrated Network Management Has Become a Major Goal. The term *integration* has several meanings in the world of network management. One obvious meaning is being able to manage an enterprisewide network, from LANs through WANs. Another meaning is the ability of network management products from different vendors to work together and appear as a single system to a network manager. Today, it is possible to monitor various parts of networks from one workstation, but it is not always possible to see these parts in the same window or with as much detail as the network manager would like.

One of the roadblocks of integration among products has been that each one has designed its software to be the "manager of managers," so all other vendors are supposed to send their network alerts to this vendor's product. In essence, there have been too many "bosses" and not enough "workers." For a truly integrated multivendor network management *system*, the vendors must allow their products to be workers to others' products.

A third and more sophisticated meaning of integration combines network management with system management. It means being able to correlate network alarms and traffic flow with database and computer use, says Elisabeth Horwitt [9], because poor network performance could result from the network, a computer, or the network operation system. A fourth form of integration is between voice and data networks. And a fifth form adds management of distributed applications to other management duties, as we discuss next.

Management of Distributed Applications Is Coming. A new view of network management is cropping up: allowing network managers to also manage distributed client/server applications. Lotus, for example, has embedded network management software in its work group product Notes, so that servers running Notes can send network management information to a network management system. A network manager can use these statistics and alarms to monitor how well Notes is performing across a network, to see whether any of the Notes servers are running out of disk space, and so forth, notes Stanley Gibson [10].

Automation of Network Operations Will Increase. Steve Miller, network manager of AutoSource, a retailer in Indianapolis, Indiana [cited in 11], believes that network management software should be proactive, where the tools listen to the network's wire conditions and send an alarm when a threshold has been exceeded. Miller would much prefer these triggers to identify the problem, launch the fix, and then notify him of the solution. The system should try to find him through fax, electronic mail, or paging only if the network cannot be automatically fixed. This would be a more proactive and automated system.

Outsourcing of Network Management Will Increase. Due to the crucial role of networks in today's businesses and the increasing complexity of these networks, more companies will outsource network management. We expect them to not only outsource day-to-day oversight of network operations but also ownership of the communication nodes and some of the links. This appears especially true of multicountry and intercontinental networks, which are so complex and expensive to build and operate. Finding telecommunications talent in many countries is a difficult task in itself, a task that might best be left to an international telecommunications provider.

These then are four trends we see in the network management world. Let us now turn to network security, an increasingly important topic, especially in the Internet world.

Security and the Internet

No one can talk about networks and network management these days without talking about the Internet and security. The problem is that the Internet was originally designed for researchers, not business transactions. So its protocol (TCP/IP) does not have fundamental security services. Anish Bhimani [12] of Lucent Technologies explains that one inherent flaw is that Layers 1 and 2 (such as Ethernet) broadcast messages; therefore, it is possible for any machine on a LAN to "eavesdrop," either on messages for other computers on a LAN or on messages sent between two Internet Service Providers.

A second flaw is that none of the TCP/IP protocols authenticates the communicating parties; therefore, it is virtually impossible to verify that they are who they say they are. Systems can easily impersonate another system and the Net doesn't know the difference. Furthermore, contents of packets are not authenticated; therefore, contents can be modified en route. Finally, some implementations of TCP have sequence numbers that are easy to guess; therefore, when combined with the lack of authentication, it is easy to establish fraudulent connections without raising any alarms, says Bhimani.

In this section we will actually deal with two aspects of this security problem. One is providing secure access to the Internet so that companies can operate as they choose (allowing suppliers, contractors, and customers into their files) without jeopardizing the confidentiality in the systems they wish to keep from prying eyes. The other is ensuring end-to-end transaction security over the Net.

Providing Secure Internet Access. The key to successfully increasing productivity (while decreasing costs) is to provide access to up-to-date sources of information on-line without exposing the corporate network to security risks, according to Stephen Catanzano and Kirsten Henderson of Shiva (a company that provides Internet connection devices and remote access servers) [13]. There are three options for providing such access, they say:

- *Remote access* is needed to serve traveling workers and telecommuters, and the best approach is to implement a remote node to provide access to a corporate LAN. This requires special software on the remote client PCs and a remote access server, which supports the different LAN communication protocols and client operating system software. Another less flexible solution is a dedicated PC on the LAN, which allows remote control by a remote PC.
- *Internet access* is needed by employees who need to access information outside the firm: Competitive research information, industry news, interorganizational groups, and so forth. On the other side of the coin, your firm may want to make company information available to the on-line world at large. Home pages are the most common way to promote one's products and services on-line. Both of these Internet options do open the company to security problems, so those need to be addressed.
- *Intranet access* involves establishing company-only Web sites on the corporate LANs, for use by employees, partners, and other parties to whom access is given. A Web server can receive e-mail, compile data and feedback, and encrypt messages, depending on the level of security it supports.

The best approach to Internet security is to use a layered approach, say Catanzano and Henderson, beginning at the Internet connection device (such as a router), which connects the corporate site to the Internet Service Provider. A screening router, for example, can be used to verify the source and destination of every packet sent to the corporate network by packet filtering. The router uses the filtering criteria set by the network manager. Based on that criteria, each packet is either permitted or denied access to the network. Screening routers can filter outgoing as well as incoming traffic, using separate filters.

A second layer of security can be applied to the application and presentation layers (Layers 6 and 7) of the OSI model, through the use of a firewall, note Catanzano and Henderson, with preset authorization rules based on time and type of access requested. Firewalls that monitor the top three OSI layers (application, presentation, and network) are even stronger.

To protect against security breaches via remote access, remote access servers often have several levels of security, such as passwords, authorized user names, dial back, and perhaps even compatibility with a third-party security device (such as a security keypad).

Catanzano and Henderson present the following five scenarios to demonstrate how companies in different situations can provide secure Internet access.

CASE EXAMPLE: Five Interconnect Scenarios

Internet technology is connecting local and remote employees, partners, and customers, resulting in higher-performance extended organizations. Catanzano and Henderson [13] provide the following five scenarios on how companies can present the interconnections that make such extended organizations a reality and ensure security at the same time.

Scenario 1: A corporate site with about 90 employees (including telecommuters) needs to connect to the Internet to access industry news, market data, and competitive information.

Solution: Since this site has over 90 users, a dedicated leased line is the best solution. This requires an Internet connection device and a CSU/DSU to choose the connection speed and type; see Figure 6-6 on page 189.

Scenario 2: A global organization wants to provide remote and Internet access to traveling workers and a significant telecommuting population. In addition, employees need to be given anytime-anywhere access to the corporate LANs, not only for data but to use the on-line electronic processes—while maintaining the security of this corporate data.

Solution: The company can configure a Web server on a LAN (intranet) to house employee information and install a Web browser on remote PCs (for remote access). Employees will then be able to dial in and connect to the network with their dial-in client, becoming a node on the network and thus being able to access the resources as if they were on-site—including the private Web server and the Internet. The remote access server's firewall prevents unwanted users from gaining access to the corporate network.

Scenario 3. A corporation has an extensive network of resellers, suppliers, and customers. Communicating with these partners has become very expensive. The firm therefore wants to provide current information to them as well as facilitate communication with them. In so doing, it can extend the reach of its products, services, and corporate message.

Solution. The company can install a dedicated remote access server and Web server to provide these partners with dial-in software for their remote PCs along with a Web browser. The dedicated servers ensure that only these partners can access the information. In addition, the company can install a firewall behind the partners' remote access server to restrict partners from accessing other information on the corporate network.

Scenario 4: A company realizes it is at a competitive disadvantage because it does not have a public Web site to announce and advertise products, provide end user product support, post bulletins, and generally enhance its image.

Solution: The company can install a Web server on the corporate LAN in front of its firewall to provide an avenue for the public to not only learn about the company but even download software and provide comments via e-mail. Catanzano and Henderson recommend two levels of security to prevent the public from entering the corporate network. One is a router to filter users based on their IP address. The second line of defense is the firewall, which provides security at the application layer of the OSI by examining the actual IP address of all visitors.

Scenario 5: A company has some customers and vendors that would like access to the company's Web site but also need access to the demonstration programs or other public information on the LAN that might involve other protocols. It also has some users that do not have Internet access.

Solution. The company can place a screening router on a public LAN in front of the firewall and give out the phone number for the router and dial-in client software to customers or partners who do not have Internet service. This solution allows the company to give selective Internet access to these parties as well as to employees. The firewall prevents accessing the corporate LAN, and the screening router ensures that only authorized users can dial in to the public LAN.

Ensuring End-to-End Transaction Security on the Net. Bhimani of
Lucent Technologies [12] points out that securing a network involves protecting
against five kinds of attack: eavesdropping, password "sniffing," data modification, spoofing, and repudiation.

Eavesdropping is easy on the Net, as noted earlier, and can lead to theft of
credit card numbers, account balances, billing information, and other account
information that people want to keep to themselves. It can also lead to theft of
services, and it can invade privacy. Simply knowing about transactions between
two parties can alert competitors to potential future events.

Password sniffing can be used to find out passwords to gain access to a system. As stronger cryptographic algorithms are used to encode passwords and
messages, there will be a shift toward trying to retrieve the cleartext (not
encrypted) versions of these passwords and messages in poorly protected systems, says Bhimani.

Data modification involves changing the wording in a transaction, such as
changing the payee on an electronic payment or modifying an order transmitted
over the Net.

Spoofing involves masquerading as another party, says Bhimani. For
example, a criminal might set up a storefront and collect thousands (or millions)
of credit card numbers and other information from naive consumers. Even
worse, the criminal could pose as a financial clearinghouse or credit card company and collect payments from customers and fees from merchants.

Finally, *repudiation* involves refusing a transaction. If, for example, one
party reneges on an agreement after the fact, the other party may be left paying
for the transaction processing even though the transaction was nullified. For
instance, a bank might bounce a check, not for insufficient funds (which is normal) but because the bank could not verify the check's authenticity.

So what is happening to make the Internet safe from these kinds of
attacks? Firewalls provide access security, says Bhimani, but they do not ensure
end-to-end transaction security. That is achieved only by ensuring

- *Confidentiality.* Restricting all communications between parties to only those
  parties, which is usually achieved through encryption.
- *Authentication.* Ensuring that the parties know who they are *really* communicating with, which is usually achieved through digital signatures and public key certificates.
- *Data integrity.* Data cannot be modified in transit or in storage, which is usually
  achieved through digital signatures and public key certificates.
- *Nonrepudiation.* Neither party can deny having participated in a transaction
  after the fact, which is usually achieved through digital signatures and public key
  certificates.
- *Selective application of services.* Allowing some parts of transactions to be hidden
  (such as credit card numbers), which are not handled by traditional security measures.

A number of cryptographic protocols are being used to provide these services on the Net, says Bhimani, but there is no agreement on where these facilities should be placed in the OSI hierarchy. Numerous efforts attempt to incorpo-

rate security into the Internet itself, says Bhimani. For example, in the Network Layer (Layer 4), IP now contains authentication headers and provisions for confidentiality using the Data Encryption Standard (DES) algorithm. In Layer 5 (the Session Layer), as we noted in Chapter 5, Netscape's Secure Sockets Layer (SSL) protocol provides confidentiality, data integrity, and authentication of a server. Another route is to secure the data in individual transactions and not worry about securing the Net. This route is being taken by Visa and Mastercard, and their alliance partners. The result has been Secure Electronic Transactions (SET).

Bhimani concludes by noting that security is the leading barrier to widespread commerce on the Internet. Since standards for the Internet take so long to develop, he expects to see immediate use of SSL and SET, until the next-generation Internet protocol is rolled out.

DISASTER RECOVERY FOR DISTRIBUTED SYSTEMS

Although information systems are just one part of a company operation, they have become a crucial part. Thus, disaster recovery for information systems is imperative. Disaster recovery practitioners we talked with were unanimous in their views that: (1) Contingency planning needs to be an integral part of doing business, and (2) commitment of resources to disaster recovery processes must be based on an assessment by top management of cost versus risk. Companies essentially have two options for disaster recovery—use internal or external resources.

Using Internal Resources

Organizations that rely on internal resources for disaster recovery generally see this planning as a normal part of system planning and development. They cost-justify backup processing and telecommunications based on company needs during foreseeable emergencies. We found companies using the following four approaches to backing up their computer systems, data, and communication links with company resources:

- Multiple data centers
- Distributed processing
- Backup telecommunications facilities
- Local area networks

Multiple Data Centers. Organizations with large IT budgets have had multiple computer centers, although less so now with downsizing and outsourcing. These centers can provide at least some emergency backup for critical applications. Organizations that do not have multiple data centers have backup telecom equipment and links to outside disaster recovery centers and service bureaus from their various operating sites.

For backing up data, companies create protected disk storage facilities—sometimes called "DASD (direct access data storage) farms." These farms are regularly refreshed with current operating data to speed recovery at an alternate data center. They are normally company-owned, unattended sites, and remote from the primary data center. They house disk controllers and disk drives that can be accessed either on-line or in batch mode.

Distributed Processing. Other organizations are using distributed processing to deal with disaster recovery. They perform critical processing locally rather than at the data center so that operations can continue uninterrupted for several days when a disaster hits a data center. Companies that use this approach standardize hardware and applications at remote locations, so that each local processing site can back up the others.

Distributed processing solutions to disaster recovery can be quite costly when data redundancy between the central and remote sites is required. Therefore, this alternative is most commonly used for applications that must continue to operate, such as order entry and financial transaction systems. Until true distributed database technology becomes available, files cannot be distributed cost effectively.

Backup Telecom Facilities. Companies appear to be handling telecom backup in two ways: (1) by building duplicate communications facilities, and (2) by using alternate technologies that they redeploy in case of an emergency.

Depository Trust Company (DTC) of New York City is a cooperative owned by financial industry clients. It serves as a clearinghouse for the settlement of securities trades, and it provides services to the banking and brokerage industry. The company uses Sungard Disaster Recovery Services [14] facilities for processing backup. DTC operates a large telecom network, linking its users at remote sites to its data center in New York City through leased and dial-up lines. DTC is expanding its network with a complete duplicate backup communication center at an alternate location in New York City. This center includes duplicate lines, telecommunication switches, modems, and multiplexors that can be quickly linked to disaster recovery facilities at Sungard to keep the remote sites on-line if the corporate computer center becomes inoperable.

Other companies turned to alternate communication technology when their communication links fails, such as when the infamous Hinsdale fire destroyed the Hinsdale Illinois Bell Telephone Company central office switching station. The station handled 118,000 long-distance lines, 30,000 data lines, and 35,000 local voice lines, reported Jeff Bozman [15]. It served as a hub for some 30 local exchanges in northeastern Illinois. The fire disrupted telephone service to the area for up to four weeks. Local companies used at least two alternative technologies to handle their telecommunications needs in this emergency.

Crockett [16] reported that MONY Financial Services in Syracuse, New York, switched a satellite link from its smaller San Juan, Puerto Rico, office to its large Hinsdale office by installing a very small aperture terminal (VSAT) dish on the roof. It was used to communicate via satellite to a communication hub in New York City, and from there via land lines to Syracuse. The San Juan office then instituted its own communication backup plan using terrestrial lines to communicate to Syracuse.

Zurich Insurance Company, in Schaumburg, Illinois, used a different alternative, reported Crockett. It established a line-of-site microwave link between its headquarters office and an AT&T switching office located about two miles away. A number of companies turned to microwave to bypass the Hinsdale center. Crockett reports that 38 temporary microwave links were established either by AT&T or MCI in the Chicago area.

One way to avoid being dependent on one telephone company switching office is to have communication links to two local switching centers. This option appeared unnecessary and too expensive for many companies, until the Hinsdale fire. More recent outages, especially in New York City, have made most top executives aware of the danger of depending on one common carrier.

Local Area Networks. Servers on one LAN can be used to back up servers for other networks. As with mainframe DASD farms, data servers used for such backup need to be refreshed on a regular basis to keep their data up-to-date. This is accomplished by linking the networks through shared cabling. Network master control programs permit designating alternate devices when primary ones fail.

Using External Resources

In many cases, a cost-versus-risk analysis may not justify committing permanent resources to contingencies; therefore, companies use the services of a disaster recovery firm. These services include

- Integrated disaster recovery services
- Specialized disaster recovery services
- On-line and off-line data storage facilities
- Service bureaus, consortia, and informal cooperative arrangements

Integrated Disaster Recovery Services. In North America, major suppliers of disaster recovery services offer multiple recovery sites interconnected by high-speed telecom lines. Services at these locations include fully operational processing facilities that are available on less than 24 hours' notice. These suppliers often have environmentally suitable storage facilities for housing special equipment for their clients.

Subscription fees for access to fully operational facilities are charged on a monthly basis, notes Weill of the Gartner Group. Actual use of the center is charged on a daily basis. In addition, a fee is often charged each time a disaster is declared. Mobile facilities—where a mobile trailer containing computer equipment can be moved to a client site—are available at costs similar to fully operational facilities. And empty warehouse space can be rented as well.

Recognizing the importance of telecom links, major disaster recovery suppliers have expanded their offerings to include smaller sites that contain specialized telecom equipment. These sites allow users to maintain telecom services when disaster recovery facilities are in use. They house control equipment and software needed to support communication lines connecting recovery sites with client sites.

Specialized Disaster Recovery Services. Some suppliers of backup services can accommodate mainframe clients who also need to back up midrange machines. In addition, a growing number of backup services are designed solely for midrange systems. Some will even deliver a trailer with compatible hardware and software to a client location.

Telecommunications backup has become an important consideration in many companies. In the United States, some of the regional Bell operating companies offer a type of recovery service—a network reconfiguration service. For example, Pacific Bell offers a service that allows users to reconfigure individual channels within T-1 lines. Users can reroute circuits using either PCs or terminals that are linked directly to Pacific Bell network computers. Thus, telecom people at user sites can reroute their circuits around lines with communication problems.

Other specialized telecom backup services are beginning to appear. For example, Hughes Network Systems, in Germantown, Maryland [17], helped a company that had 49 of its pharmacies affected by the Hinsdale telephone switching station fire. Within 72 hours, Hughes installed a temporary network of VSATs at 12 sites. The 37 remaining sites had small satellite dishes installed within two weeks. Other firms offer data communications backup programs, where they will store specific data communications equipment for a customer and deliver that equipment by air to the customer's recovery site when needed.

On-line and Off-line Data Storage. Alternate locations for storage of tapes and other records have long been a part of disaster planning. Services generally consist of fire-resistant vaults with suitable temperature and humidity controls. Several suppliers offer electronic vaulting for organizations that need to have current data off-site at the time a disaster occurs. These suppliers use two methods to obtain current data from their clients. One method uses computer-to-computer transmission of data on a scheduled basis. The other uses dedicated equipment to capture and store data at a remote location as it is created on the client's computer. This latter method ensures uninterrupted access to data from an operationally ready disaster recovery facility selected by the client.

Service Bureaus, Consortia, and Agreements. Service bureaus can offer limited but economical emergency processing support. Their primary business is serving the normal operating needs of their clients, but they can be used for backup purposes. However, unless special capacity provisions have been made to assure priority for disaster recovery, they cannot handle large emergency workloads for several weeks of backup use.

Consortia with other user organizations are another backup option, but they have had limited success. They are most effective when a third party administers the arrangements. And each member needs to be sure that their hardware and software remain fully compatible.

Moberg [18] describes how four firms in Minneapolis, Minnesota, formed an alliance to provide voice communication backup for each other and to share the lease of a spare PBX. They each use the same type of PBX, they are in the same industry, and they have agreed to provide remote communication facilities to each other in case of emergency. The agreement was drawn up by a consultant, and a local telecommunications company performs backup installation when needed. After testing the arrangement twice, these four companies found that they can establish communications for 300 telephone lines in about eight hours.

Summary

Disaster recovery needs have not always shaped the architecture of computer systems, so the cost of reconfiguring these systems to provide the needed redundancy and backup can be prohibitive. In these cases, external backup alternatives may be a more cost-effective form of insurance. But companies planning major network and system enhancements today appear to be including disaster recovery as an integral part of their system design. For example, they are connecting their external recovery sites into their corporate networks. We anticipate companies will use both internal and external resources, rather than relying on just one or the other.

To illustrate the use of disaster recovery facilities, consider the case of Household International.

CASE EXAMPLE: Household International

Household International, with headquarters in Prospect Heights, Illinois, is a major provider of consumer lending, banking, insurance, and commercial financial services in the United States. The company also provides similar services in the United Kingdom, Canada, and Australia through subsidiaries.

The core of its consumer finance business is serviced by some 700 consumer lending branches and 60 bank branches throughout the United States. Household is also a large credit card issuer in the United States and operates a major credit card service center in Salinas, California. Household's major data center is in its corporate offices. The center is linked to the branch network via leased lines, with regional connections to over 10,000 remote devices and terminals.

Typical of large financial services institutions, Household justified its disaster recovery planning based upon legal and regulatory requirements and the need to maintain uninterrupted customer service. The centralized design of its data network simplified recovery planning but made the headquarters data center critical to recovery.

The company established a full-time staff to prepare, maintain, and exercise (test out) disaster recovery plans. After exploring several alternatives, including adding reserve processing capacity to its network, Household decided to rely on Comdisco Disaster Recovery Services [19]. Comdisco is a major supplier of alternate site data processing services in North America.

Services provided by Comdisco include use of facilities at one or more of its several recovery centers throughout North America, and hot-site equipment and software to provide immediate operational support on request. In addition, Comdisco provides technical assistance in disaster planning, testing, and the use of recovery centers. Household viewed the monthly cost of these services as its most economical recovery alternative.

After six months, all critical banking applications had been tested at the alternate site and contingency procedures had been developed for the bank branches. Household had also begun developing contingency plans for the consumer lending operation and testing application programs at the alternate site. In addition, it had begun developing business recovery priorities and operating procedures for end users.

In the midst of this effort, nature intervened. At 9:00 a.m. on a Friday, after meeting with key personnel, Household declared a disaster. More than nine inches of rain had fallen on the Chicago area in 12 hours. Widespread flooding had closed major highways, leaving thousands of homes and businesses without power or telephone service. A retention pond at corporate headquarters had overflowed, causing an overnight runoff into the basement of the headquarters building where the data center was located. By 10:30 a.m. the water had risen to 31 inches—nine inches above the 22-inch false floor—and it rose further before the disaster ended.

With telephone lines down in the area and the company PBX out of service, the recovery coordinator relied on plans made earlier in the year. Computer operations were transferred to the Comdisco alternate site in Wood Dale, Illinois, which was 20 miles away. Fortunately, he made his call to Comdisco early; other clients who called later were relocated to sites as far away as New Jersey—some 800 miles (1,300 kilometers) away. Since five Chicago area businesses declared disasters, Comdisco's hot-site resources in Illinois were quickly saturated.

At the backup site, work began on restoring vital bank and check processing systems. Critical processing for most bank branches resumed within 24 hours. Teller systems at branches used local computers, so they operated without interruption. However, on-line information on the current status of customer accounts was not available until the following Monday.

After pumping out the flooded data center, the data processing staff found extensive damage to disk drive motors and circuit boards below the high-water mark. However, they were able to quickly restore the communication control units. They were then able to use these units as the links for all communications between the backup site computers and the remote terminals installed in the branches. Their local telephone company used a central switch to establish a link between the disaster recovery alternate site and the Household home office.

By the third day, all the important work that had been moved to key Household locations was up and running, and communication links among these locations were working. Communication links to all offices were available by the sixth day.

A few days after the disaster, over 220 analysts and programmers were assigned to work at the alternate site on a 24-hour schedule. The disaster recovery coordinator arranged for special food service, dressing facilities, and rest areas at the alternate site. Workstations were created using rented furniture and equipment.

Special meetings were held with senior management to establish recovery priorities for the consumer lending operation. Daily meetings, chaired by the executive vice president of information systems, were attended by nearly all managers and vendors affected by the disaster—some 40 to 50 people in all. These meetings became the day-to-day means for reporting status, handling special problems, and developing recovery schedules. The meetings turned out to be the best means for communicating quickly and making decisions using the existing organization. The meetings lasted several hours each day and covered a wide range of topics. Thus, no special organizational structure was used for managing the disaster; however, the disaster recovery manager played a key role in coordinating the recovery.

The company left the backup site on the fifteenth day. Eighteen days after the disaster, normal operations had been fully restored.

Lessons Learned

They learned six lessons from this disaster, which they offer as recommendations to others.

1. Consider the risks of a natural disaster in selecting a data center location. Areas with high exposure to flooding, heavy rainfall, fire hazards, or earthquakes will be more costly to protect against these risks.

2. Create a plan to return to the primary site after the disaster. This plan is just as important as a plan to move to an alternate site.

3. Do not expect damaged equipment, disks, and tapes to always be replaced in kind or restored to original condition. Therefore, make plans for new configurations, and regularly monitor sources of equipment and supplies to ensure early delivery of replacements.

4. Test hot-site resources under *full workload conditions* to ensure that sufficient computer capacity is available to meet high-priority needs.

5. Plan for alternate telecommunications routing for multiple-site operations during a disaster. Household's original telecommunications disaster recovery plan called for key sites around the country to handle the headquarters processing load in case of a home office disaster. But the quick recovery of the communication control units at the headquarters data center allowed Household to use an alternate plan: to rely mainly on processing at the nearby disaster recovery site. Thus, for 16 days Household operated with both the headquarters center and the disaster recovery center. The other key Household centers handled mainly their normal work, but their computers were available if needed.

6. Maintain critical data at the alternate site or at another nearby location for fast system recovery.

Household has used its experience to refine and complete the plans it started before the rain storm. In addition, Comdisco services have been extended to other subsidiaries under a corporatewide contract. In retrospect, key participants believe that the early restoration of the headquarters computer center, the existence of computer and telecommunications backup procedures, staff who were familiar with the backup plans, and use of normal management channels were all important in their rapid recovery.

CONCLUSION

Interestingly, the subject of managing computer operations seems to ebb and flow. There was a lot of attention in the early 1990s, as outsourcing and corporate downsizing took hold. Now things are relatively quiet, except for all the excitement created by the Internet and its security issues. The move to client/server systems and interconnections with the Net have presented challenging operational issues because these far-flung operations open companies up to more security threats. Clearly, operations is one of the essential technologies that needs to be well managed to keep a business humming.

QUESTIONS AND EXERCISES

REVIEW QUESTIONS

1. What does the operations budget at Congleton's company include?
2. What are three solutions to operations problems, according to Congleton?
3. What are six trends in data center operations, according to Congleton?
4. Companies that run efficient data centers also have applications with what four characteristics, according to Disher?
5. What is Mutual of Omaha doing to make its data center more efficient?
6. What are five steps toward automating data center operations, according to Miller?
7. How close are we to fully unattended operations, according to LaChance?
8. What are the driving forces of outsourcing, according to Bergstein?
9. What are the five customer-vendor relationships?
10. What changes are taking place in IS outsourcing, according to Terdiman?
11. What four questions should management ask when investigating outsourcing?
12. What six management elements has Kodak put in place to manage its outsourcing relationships?
13. According to the Index Foundation, what are the five main activities of network management?
14. What are four trends in network management?

15. What is the best approach to Internet security, according to Catanzano and Henderson?
16. Describe five interconnect scenarios.
17. According to Bhimani, how can one ensure end-to-end transaction security on the Internet?
18. What internal disaster recovery alternatives are used by companies?
19. What external disaster recovery services are available to companies?
20. What six lessons did Household International learn from its disaster?

DISCUSSION QUESTIONS

1. Outsourcing offloads a burdensome technical responsibility and allows management to focus on its core business. Outsourcing strips a company of an important core competence—IT know-how. Which statement do you agree with and why?
2. Distributed systems will eventually mitigate the need for companies to contract for outside disaster recovery services because companies will have multiple sites to do their own internal backup. Do you agree or disagree? Why?

EXERCISES

1. Read several articles on Internet security issues. Present new information to your class.
2. Read a few articles about outsourcing. What did you learn about outsourcing that is not mentioned in this chapter? Relay this to the class.
3. Read a few articles about network management. What new ideas did you learn that are not presented in this chapter? Present them to the class.
4. Visit a company in your local community. Learn about its disaster recovery plans. Which threats are plans aimed at? Which threats are not dealt with? What is the company doing about Internet security?

REFERENCES

1. "Transforming the Data Center in an Information Utility," AFIPS National Computer Conference.

2. Disher,Christopher, Nolan, Norton and Co., 150 N. Michigan Ave., Chicago, IL 60601.

3. Miller, H. W., "Planning for unattended data center operation," *Mainframe Journal* (8533 Ferndale Rd., Suite 202, Dallas, TX 75238), January/February 1988, p. 10.

4. Farber/LaChance Inc., P.O. Box 26611, Richmond, VA 23261.

5. The Gartner Group, 56 Top Gallant Road, Stamford, CT 06904.

   a. Schulman, J., "Industrial-strength ASO product features: Part I and II," "ISV ASO products: Part I and II," and, "OPS/MVS: The ASO pacesetter," *Software Management Strategies Service*, April 8, 1988.

   b. Terdiman, Rita, speech at Sourcing Leaders '96, Sourcing Interests Group Semi-Annual Conference, June 1996.

c. WEILL, J., "Disaster recovery alternatives," a one-page document from its *Industry Service Report,* No. SPA-150-530.1.

6. BERGSTEIN, MEL, TSC, 205 N. Michigan Ave., Chicago, IL 60601.

7. SOURCING INTERESTS GROUP, 30 Hackamore Lane, Suite 12, Bell Canyon, CA 91307.

    a. MCNURLIN, BARBARA, "Eastman Kodak Company's PC Outsourcing Strategic Alliance," Fall 1992.

    b. MCNURLIN, BARBARA, "Managing Outsourcing Results," Fall 1995.

8. *NETWORK MANAGEMENT,* Index Foundation (CSC Index, 5 Cambridge Center, Cambridge, MA 02142), Research Report No. 65, August 1988, 58 pages.

9. HORWITT, E., "Distributed Management Tools Coming," *Computerworld*, November 25, 1991, pp. 1, 92.

10. GIBSON, S., "Lotus Notes to Get SNMP Support," *Communications Week* (600 Community Dr., Manhasset, NY 11030), March 16, 1992, pp. 1, 59.

11. HENDERSON T., "A Tub Full of Network Management Software," *LAN Times* (7050 Union Park Center, Suite 240, Midvale, Utah 84047), April 6, 1992, p. 26.

12. BHIMANI, ANISH, "Securing the Commercial Internet," *Communications of the ACM,* June 1996, pp. 29–35.

13. CATANZO, STEPHEN and KIRSTEN HENDERSON, "The Fully Connected Corporation," a Shiva technology brief, is available from Shiva's Web site, http://www.shiva.com or Netscape's Web site: http://home.netscape.com. Shiva, 28 Crosby Dr., Bedford, MA 01730.

14. SUNGARD RECOVERY SERVICES, 1285 Drummers Lane, Wayne, PA 19087.

15. BOZMAN, J. "Illinois Phone Effort Puts Data Links Last," *Computerworld*, May 23, 1988, p. 101.

16. CROCKETT, B., "Users Turned to Satellite, Microwave Links After Fire," *Network World* (Box 9171, Framingham, MA 01701), June 27, 1988, pp. 31-32.

17. HUGHES NETWORK SYSTEMS, 11717 Exploration Lane, Germantown, MD 20874.

18. MOBERG, K., "MAP: A Plan for Disaster Recovery," *TE&M* (Telephone Engineer & Management, 124 S. First St., Geneva, IL 60134), May 15, 1988, pp. 113-114.

19. COMDISCO DISASTER RECOVERY SERVICES, 6400 Shafer Court, Rosemont, IL 60018.

PART III

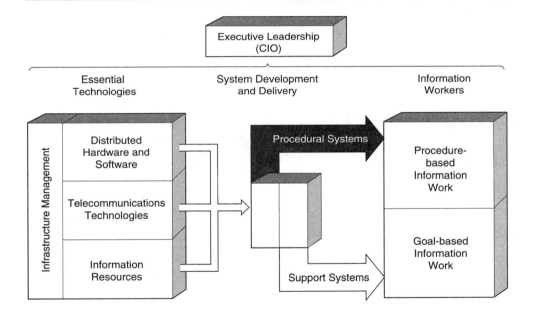

A Framework for IS Management

Part III of this book consists of two chapters that deal with developing procedural systems—traditional system development. As noted in the accompanying figure, system development has traditionally been aimed at procedure-based work. Procedure-based activities are large-volume transactions where each transaction has a relatively low cost or value. The activities, which consist mainly of handling data, are well defined and the principle measure for gauging their performance is efficiency. Information systems were, in most cases, first built to automate this kind of work, beginning initially with accounting, and then progressing into manufacturing, administration, sales and marketing, and so on. Development of these procedural systems has been handled by IS professionals.

In Chapter 9 we concentrate on the system development technologies and methodologies that have risen to prominence since the 1970s, concluding the chapter with a discussion of the development of Web-centric applications.

In Chapter 10 we discuss a number of management issues that surround traditional system development.

NINE

Technologies for Developing Systems

INTRODUCTION

One of the toughest jobs in information systems management is developing new systems. It seems to be an area in which Murphy's Law—if anything can go wrong, it will—reigns supreme. As a result, there has been a significant amount of work since the 1960s devoted to strengthening the tools and methodologies for system development.

In spite of the complexity of system development, the information systems field has made significant progress in improving the process of building systems. The traditional approach, with variations, of course, appears in many textbooks and professional books. Two of the first books to describe a life cycle approach for developing systems were published in 1956 and 1957, both written by Richard Canning [1].

During the 1970s, a relatively well-defined process, called the "system development life cycle," emerged. This life cycle improved the development process significantly. However, continued backlogs, cost overruns, and performance shortfalls underscored the difficulty and complexity of the system development process.

The 1980s saw progress in more friendly languages and automation of portions of development, such as code generation. Yet, maintenance continued to eat up 70 to 80 percent of the system development resources in most companies. The 1990s began with the promise of significantly increasing developer productivity and reducing maintenance by relying more on packages, and by building systems by linking together components. And then, all of a sudden, in the mid-1990s, Web technology appeared, and promised yet another easing of the development problem—again promising to offload some of it to the users. Well, this may all be well and good, but there's still a lot of systems work to be done in-house or outsourced. And, as yet, there are still no "silver bullets" on the horizon. In this chapter, we review the evolution of system development to provide an understanding of the underlying principles.

THE 1970s

In the early years, system development was considered a "craft," subject mostly to the whim and creativity of systems analysts. In the 1970s, structured system development emerged to make the process more standard and efficient than before. It was characterized by

- Hand coding in a third generation language (such as COBOL)
- A structured programming development methodology
- An automated project management system
- A database management system
- A mix of on-line and batch applications in the same system
- Development of mostly mainframe applications
- Programming by professional programmers only
- Various automated (but not well-integrated) software tools
- A well-defined sign-off process for system delivery
- User participation mainly in requirements definition and installation phases

This development approach supposedly followed the famous "waterfall" approach, shown in Figure 9-1 [2a]. Norman Enger [3] describes these phases in

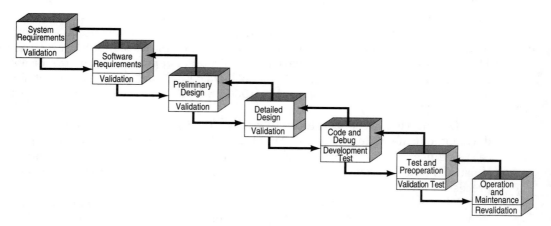

Figure 9-1   The "Waterfall" Development Life Cycle (from Boehm [2a])

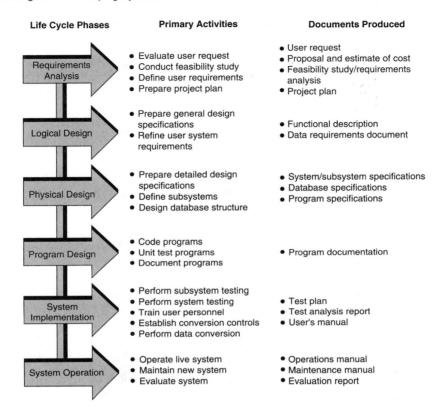

Life Cycle Phases	Primary Activities	Documents Produced
Requirements Analysis	• Evaluate user request • Conduct feasibility study • Define user requirements • Prepare project plan	• User request • Proposal and estimate of cost • Feasibility study/requirements analysis • Project plan
Logical Design	• Prepare general design specifications • Refine user system requirements	• Functional description • Data requirements document
Physical Design	• Prepare detailed design specifications • Define subsystems • Design database structure	• System/subsystem specifications • Database specifications • Program specifications
Program Design	• Code programs • Unit test programs • Document programs	• Program documentation
System Implementation	• Perform subsystem testing • Perform system testing • Train user personnel • Establish conversion controls • Perform data conversion	• Test plan • Test analysis report • User's manual
System Operation	• Operate live system • Maintain new system • Evaluate system	• Operations manual • Maintenance manual • Evaluation report

Figure 9-2   Development Life Cycle Phases and Products
(from Enger [3])

Figure 9-2, and uses somewhat different terms, to illustrate the activities and resulting documents in each phase. In truth, says Bob Glass [4], a well-known author in software development, this unidirectional waterfall was much touted but rarely used. Development did not proceed in a straight line from requirements through operation; a lot of backtracking and iteration occurred. Instead, says Glass, developers really always followed the spiral approach, also generally attributed to Barry Boehm [2b]and shown in Figure 9-3 on the next page.

The Goals of Structured Development

Structured development methodologies accompanied this system development life cycle and were meant to handle the complexities of system design and development by fostering more discipline, higher reliability and fewer errors, and more efficient use of the resources.

More Discipline. By establishing standards for processes and documentation, the structured methodologies attempted to eliminate personal variations.

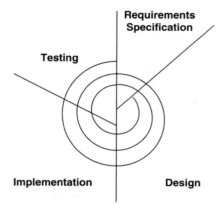

Figure 9-3   The Spiral Model of System Development
(from Boehm [2b])

At first they seemed to threaten programmers' creativity, but their discipline did increase productivity and permit developers to deal with greater complexity. The complexity was handled through successive decomposition of system components, coupled with preferred practices for conducting analysis, design, and construction. The result was a more disciplined system development process.

Higher Reliability and Fewer Errors. The structured methodologies recognized that mistakes of both omission and commission were likely at all stages of system building. One of the main tools for coping with this tendency was (and still is) inspections, performed at every development stage and at every level of system decomposition. The goal has been to catch errors as early as possible. The methodologies also recognized that iteration would be required to redo parts of the system as mistakes were uncovered.

More Efficient Use of Resources. The project management approaches usually included in the structured methodologies contributed to cost savings, increased productivity, and better allocation of human resources. By imposing a time and cost control system, the classic approach decreased (but did not eliminate) the tendency for system development efforts to incur cost and time overruns.

Emphasis on the Early Phases

In the late 1970s, developers began concentrating on the early phases of development because the longer an error persists, the more costly it is to correct. Boehm [2a] notes that if correcting an error in the requirements stage costs $1, the cost will be $5 to correct the error if not caught until the design stage, $10 to correct in the programming stage, and a whopping $100 if it is not found and corrected until the operational stage. For this reason, system developers want to catch serious errors in the requirements and design stages.

This emphasis on doing the early phases right was evident in two system development approaches that emerged in the 1970s. One was data-driven development, where emphasis was placed on defining a program's data first, because it is more stable, and then defining the processes to manipulate that data. A number of data-driven methodologies appeared in the late 1970s.

The second approach was the use of group design sessions to more quickly solidify requirements and design of a new system. The various approaches, the most common of which was JAD (joint application design), forced developers and users to specify an entire application in just a few days' time, down to detailing the screen layouts, by participating in day-long design sessions. JAD and the other group design techniques followed specific steps to ensure that the design process was completed in those few days and accomplished its goal. These sessions significantly accelerated design because they brought together all the decision makers at one time and one place.

THE EARLY 1980s

In the early 1980s, two major developments occurred. One was the availability of fourth generation languages (4GLs). Previously, developers only had third generation languages, such as COBOL and PL/1. The advent of 4GLs allowed end users to develop some programs, or allowed programmers to use a different development method: prototyping.

Prototyping was an alternative to the traditional system development life cycle. Formerly, system requirements were fully defined before design and construction began. With prototyping, development was iterative: Specify as much as possible, prototype it, try using the prototype, refine the prototype based on this experience, and so on until the specs were fully defined via the prototype.

As we note later, both 4GLs and prototyping have proven to be important underpinnings for today's application development world.

Fourth Generation Languages

Fourth generation languages are really more than computer languages; they are programming environments. The major components or characteristics of 4GLs are listed in Figure 9-4.

The heart of a 4GL is its database management system (DBMS) for storing formatted data records as well as unformatted text, graphics, voice, and perhaps even video. Almost as important is the data dictionary, which stores the *definitions* of the various kinds of data. The language that the programmers and users use is nonprocedural, which means that the commands can occur in any order, rather than the sequence required by the computer. The commands can be used interactively to retrieve ad hoc information from files or a database or to print a report. This facility is provided by a report generator. The screen painter allows the user or programmer to design a screen by simply typing in the various data input field names and the locations where they are to appear, or by choosing graphics off of a menu. Some 4GLs include statistical packages for calculating time series, averages, standard deviations, correlation coefficients, and so on.

Figure 9-4   Features and Functions of Fourth Generation Languages

---

- Database management system
- Data dictionary
- Nonprocedural language
- Interactive query facilities
- Report generator
- Selection and sorting
- Screen formatter
- Word processor and text editor
- Graphics
- Data analysis and modeling tools
- Library of macros
- Programming interface
- Reusable code
- Software development library
- Backup and recovery
- Security and privacy safeguards
- Links to other DBMS

Suggestions on Using a Fourth Generation Language. Mary Rich [5], an independent contractor who has worked with 4GLs since the mid-1970s, has some suggestions on their use. Her suggestions are still applicable today, especially to end users who want to rush into creating, say, a Web site to replace an application, without thinking through their needs.

Applications especially suitable for 4GL are those subject to rapid changes, or where the need for ad hoc reporting is high, as in human resources or budgeting systems. She also recommends that 4GL programmers spend time doing system analysis work before they begin coding. It is true that 4GLs, when coupled with a prototyping methodology, do not require the same exhaustive systems analysis as the classic approach with hand coding in COBOL. However, inexperienced 4GL programmers can get themselves into problems if they forgo analysis, thinking that prototyping makes this unnecessary. Prototyping does allow developers to experiment with different ways of doing things, such as changing the database structure.

However, since 4GLs permit easily creating and manipulating data, their improper use can lead to a proliferation of "little databases." This is a management problem, says Rich, not a technical one. Systems management should establish and enforce policies for database maintenance by the end users. Users will think twice about creating little databases if this policy is enforced. (Interestingly, client/server computing has led to similar disparate databases. Intranets with Web sites devoted to providing one type of information for the

entire enterprise are promised as a solution to this problem. It ma
der if we will ever stop running around in this decentralize/central

Another potential problem is "private programs." If a user w
program over to the information systems department to maintair
mends that management require a minimum level of documentation—a user
guide, plus comments in the program that describe the overall flow and the complex algorithms.

Due to their ease of use, fourth generation languages led to a new programming practice in the early 1980s—prototyping.

Software Prototyping

According to *Webster's Twentieth-Century Dictionary*, the term *prototype*
has three possible meanings: (1) It is an original or model after which anything
is formed, (2) it is the first thing or being of its kind, and (3) it is a pattern, an
exemplar, or an archetype.

J. David Naumann and A. Milton Jenkins [6] believe the second definition
best fits the prototypes used in data processing because such prototypes are a
first attempt at a design that generally is later extended and enhanced. Franz
Edelman, a pioneer in the use of software prototyping, described the process of
software prototyping as "a quick and inexpensive process of developing and testing a trial balloon."

A software prototype is a *live, working system*; it is not just an idea on
paper. Therefore, it can be evaluated by the designer and/or the eventual end
users through its use in an operational mode. It performs actual work; it does not
just simulate that work. *It may become the actual production system*, or it may be
replaced by a conventionally coded production system. Its purpose is *to test out
assumptions* about users' requirements, or about the design of the application or
perhaps even about the logic of a program.

A prototype is a software system that *is created quickly*—often within
hours, days, or weeks—rather than months or years. With only conventional
programming languages, such as COBOL, it was much too expensive to create
both a prototype and a production version. So only production systems were
developed. With end user tools, people can get prototypes up and running quickly. The prototype *is relatively inexpensive* to build because the language creates
much of the code.

Prototyping *is an iterative process*. It begins with a simple prototype that
performs only a few of the basic functions. Through use of the prototype, system
designers or end users discover new requirements and refinements to incorporate in each succeeding version. Each version performs more of the desired functions and in an increasingly efficient manner.

To demonstrate a dramatic use of both a 4GL and prototyping, we describe
work at Santa Fe Railroad in the early 1980s when the use of a 4GL was unique
because it took the opposite approach of just about everyone else. Most companies used 4GLs for management reports and end user applications, that is, as a
sidelight for their operational systems. Santa Fe, on the other hand, used the

4GL for its operational system and left the management reporting in COBOL. This approach, using today's tools, would be just as unique in the late 1990s. The reasons for the railroad's unusual decision are made clear in the case example.

CASE EXAMPLE: Santa Fe Railroad

The Atchison, Topeka and Santa Fe Railway Company, with headquarters in Topeka, Kansas, had 12,000 miles of railroad track, running from Chicago, Illinois, to California. It had 2,000 locomotives, 52,000 freight cars, and 9,000 truck trailers.

In the early 1980s, many of its trains were reaching their destinations without the accompanying paperwork. This was against Interstate Commerce Commission rules, so the railroad began receiving heavy fines for the missing paperwork. The railroad had to write a new waybill system in a hurry, but the systems department could not do the job using the traditional development methods. And no other railroad's application system was appropriate for Santa Fe because much of its business was in piggybacking—loading two truck trailers on a flat car and shipping them to their destination. Then Santa Fe heard about Mapper, a fourth generation language from Unisys. Since it appeared to be the only alternative, a freight scheduler and several clerical supervisors were taught Mapper and given the assignment of automating the paperwork for the huge Corwith piggybacking yard in Chicago.

In adopting Mapper, Santa Fe Railway made three significant programming decisions:

- Create an operational system in a 4GL using prototyping.
- Teach operational railroad employees to program, rather than teach programmers the intricacies of railroad operations.
- Create generic databases that would remain stable and be used throughout the company.

The group started by creating the generic databases with standard data definitions, formats, and functions. The basic waybill system for the Corwith yard was created in several months' time, followed by a yard inventory system, and then a full-blown trailer-on-flat-car system. The complete operations expediter system (OX), which consisted of these three interrelated systems, was put into operation in 18 months. The system handled the day-to-day railroad operations and sent subsets of data to the corporate database for corporate marketing, accounting, and operating summary purposes. Later, as the system expanded, with the addition of more switching yards, new databases were created for each yard. Each database used the same generic data definitions, formats, and functions. The Mapper database grew large but was composed of many small databases, identical for each yard. Mapper could handle this structure; in all it processed 1.7 million transactions daily.

With the adoption of Mapper, Santa Fe divided its information systems into two parts—the operational part and the corporate database part. The operational part was converted to Mapper, while the corporate database was kept in COBOL because the railroad had a large investment in IBM programs that it did not want to replace. Interestingly, the two parts had quite different characteristics. The IBM shop had 116 application programmers, 44 systems support people, and 80 people in operations for a total of 240. The Unisys center, which ran the railroad operations using Mapper, had only 35 application programmers, 11 systems support people, and 32 people in operations for a total of 78.

Although the two shops performed an equivalent amount of work, the Unisys shop was more cost-effective because it only needed one-third the people. The vice president of IS attributed the difference to Mapper. It required less support, but it required about twice as much hardware. In total, the overall costs for the use of Mapper were one-half those of COBOL applications.

Santa Fe also felt that the Mapper programmers were four to eight times more productive than the COBOL programmers. Furthermore, system problems could often be handled by the operational people. They controlled the system, so there were essentially no operational complaints to the IS department.

In retrospect, the vice president of IS believed that a 4GL can have a *significant* impact on a company, but only if it was used to automate daily operations—not merely as a tool for generating reports. The operational world was the most volatile part of the railroad, so that was where Santa Fe wanted the fastest and most versatile programming.

So what has become of 4GLs and prototyping? Well, 4GLs appear to be on at least their fourth iteration (or generation) and, hence, they are no longer called 4GLs. Generally, they are just called "tools" or even "languages." These end user languages began as mainframe alternatives to COBOL, as noted. When PCs appeared, their second iteration occurred. And with client/server their third iteration occurred. It now appears that their fourth iteration is for Web-based (or network-centric) development. As for prototyping, it has become standard practice for programmers and end users.

THE LATE 1980s

In the late 1980s, two more developments built on the past: computer-aided software development (CASE) and object-oriented development. They, too, have contributed much to the development environment of the late 1990s.

Computer-Aided Software Engineering

While the structured programming and analysis techniques of the 1970s brought more discipline to the process of developing large and complex software applications, they required *tedious* attention to detail and lots of paperwork. CASE aimed to automate structured techniques and reduce this tediousness.

Definitions. At a CASE Symposium, sponsored by Digital Consulting, Inc. [7], Carma McClure [8], a CASE pioneer, defined CASE as any automated tool that assists in the creation, maintenance, or management of software systems. In general, a CASE environment includes:

- An information repository
- Front-end tools for planning through design
- Back-end tools for generating code
- A development workstation

Often not included—*but implied and necessary*—are a software development methodology and a project management methodology.

An information repository forms the heart of a CASE system and is its most important element, said McClure. It stores and organizes all information needed to create, modify, and develop a software system. This information includes, for example, data structures, processing logic, business rules, source code, and project management data. Ideally, this information repository should also link to the active data dictionary used during execution so that changes in one are reflected in the other.

Front-end tools are used in the phases that lead up to coding. One of the key requirements for these tools is good graphics for drawing diagrams of program structures, data entities and their relationships to each other, data flows, screen layouts, and so on. Rather than store pictorial representations, front-end tools generally store the meaning of items depicted in the diagrams. This allows a change made in one diagram to be reflected automatically in related diagrams. Another important aspect of front-end design tools is automatic design analysis, for checking the consistency and completeness of a design, often in accordance with a specific design technique.

Back-end tools generally mean code generators, for automatically generating source code. A few CASE tools used a 4GL. Successful front-end CASE tools provided interfaces to not just one, but several, code generators.

A development workstation is the final component of a CASE system, and the more powerful it is the better to handle all the graphical manipulations needed in CASE-developed systems.

One of the most intriguing CASE products and approaches we encountered was the "Timebox," which was a technique that used CASE to guarantee delivery of a system within 120 days. While CASE proponents would have argued that such an approach would not work with very large, very complex systems (and that is where CASE proved to be the only alternative), IS departments now (in the late 1990s) honor speed over complexity, which is why many are turning to a development technique known as Rapid Application Development (RAD). This story illustrates a RAD technique, so it is applicable in the late 1990s.

CASE EXAMPLE: Du Pont Cable Management Services

Du Pont Cable Management Services was formed in the late 1980s to manage the telephone and data wiring in Du Pont's office buildings in Wilmington, Delaware. AT&T had owned and managed the wiring for Du Pont's voice networks, but in 1984, responsibility passed to Du Pont's corporate telecommunications group. At Du Pont's Wilmington headquarters campus, cabling is complex and wiring changes are continual. The average telephone is moved one and one-half times a year. Much of the telephone moving cost is labor to find the correct cables and circuit paths.

When the cable management services group was formed, the manager realized he needed a system to maintain an inventory of every wire, telephone, modem, workstation, wiring closet connection, and other piece of telephone equipment. Technicians could then quickly locate the appropriate equipment and make the change. Although several cable management software packages were available, none could handle the scale or workload required by Du Pont. The only option was a custom-built system.

The system had to be flexible because the company's telecommunications facilities were expanding—from voice to data and video. So it needed to handle new kinds of equipment. Furthermore, since the need for cable management services was new and not unique to Du Pont, the manager believed he could sell cable management services to other large companies. Therefore, the system needed to be tailorable.

Since the manager did not want to hire programmers, he decided to use Du Pont Information Engineering Associates [9], another Du Pont business service unit.

Du Pont Information Engineering Associates (IEA) began selling system development services to others in the late 1980s. It was spawned in the mid-1980s by some Du Pont system developers who were using CASE. These developers used Application Factory, a code generator for DEC VAX systems marketed by Cortex Corporation. These developers believed they could significantly speed up development if they combined the code generator with software prototyping and project management. The resulting methodology, which was used by IEA, was called RIPP (rapid iterative production prototyping).

Using RIPP, a development project could take as few as 120 days to complete; it had four phases.

- *Phase 1: Go-Ahead.* Day 1 is the go-ahead day. IEA accepts a project and the customer agrees to participate heavily in development.
- *Phase Two: System Definition.* Days 2 through 30 are spent defining the components of the system and its acceptance criteria. At the end of this phase, IEA presents the customer with a system definition and a fixed price for creating the application.
- *Phase Three: The Timebox.* The following 90 days are called a "Timebox," during which the IEA/customer team creates design specifications, prototypes the system, and then refines the prototype and its specifications. The final prototype becomes the production system.
- *Phase 4: Installation.* On Day 120, the system is installed. The customer has three months to verify that the system does what it is supposed to do. If it doesn't, IEA will refund the customer's money and remove the system.

Cable Management's Use of IEA. The cable management group contracted with IEA to develop the cable-tracking system. After spending the first 30 days defining the scope of the project, IEA estimated that the system would require two Timeboxes to complete—about 210 days.

During the first Timebox, IEA developed those portions that the cable management group could concisely define. During those 90 days, one cable management engineer worked full-time on the project, another worked part-time, and IEA had a project leader and two developers. The system they developed included display screens, the relational database, basic system processes, and reports.

At the end of the 90 days, IEA delivered a basic functional system, which Du Pont began using. The second Timebox added features uncovered during this use. Both parties agreed this phase was ambiguous, which might affect the 90-day limitation. So they extended the project to 110 days. By that time, the development team had entered Du Pont's complete wiring inventory, enhanced the basic system, and delivered a production version.

In all, the system took about nine months to develop. The department manager realized that was fast, but he did not realize how fast until he talked to other telecommunications executives who told him their firms had spent between two and three years developing cable management systems.

The cable management group is very pleased with its system. It was initially used only to manage voice wiring but has since been extended to handle data communications wiring.

Object-Oriented Development

Just as 4GLs were a revolutionary change in the 1970s, object-oriented development was a revolutionary change in the late 1980s. Object-oriented programming languages had been used in computer science research labs since the 1960s. In the 1980s, object-oriented development languages and tools moved into PC system development where they became the mainstay, especially for developing graphical user interfaces. By the late 1980s, object orientation was beginning to be noticed for business system development. That trickle became a tidal wave when client/server systems appeared in the early 1990s, as developers attempted to simplify the extreme complexity of client/server systems by reusing objects. In the early 1990s, object-oriented system analysis and design techniques began to appear to be used in conjunction with the object-oriented languages, such as C++ and Smalltalk.

Object-oriented development differs from traditional development in several ways. These are listed in Figure 9-5.

What Is an Object? Brad Cox [10], one of the pioneers in the field, points out that object-oriented programming is not so much a coding technique as a code-packaging technique. It packages functions with data so that the two can be reused. These reusable components are called "classes." At run time, each class can produce instances called "objects." Objects hold all the code and data in an object-oriented system, says Cox.

Objects. As shown in Figure 9-6, each object is some private data and a set of operations (called "methods") that can access that data. When an object receives a requesting message, it responds by first choosing the operation that implements the request, then executing this operation, and finally returning the results to the requester. An object's data is private; it cannot be manipulated by other objects.

Combining data and procedures in an object—*encapsulation*—is the foundation of object orientation. It restricts the effects of changes by placing a wall of code around each piece of data. All accesses to the data are through messages that only specify *what* should be done—the object chooses *how* its operations are performed. A change in one part of the system need not affect the rest of the system but can be dealt with inside the part directly affected. Thus,

Figure 9-5 The Ways Object-Oriented Development Differs from Traditional Development

- Object-oriented development creates a new type of system: a model of the business. When an object-oriented system runs, it simulates that business. This is conceptually different from the traditional view of separate data and processes.

- Developers and users communicate with one another using business terms—such as accounts, customers, statements, and so forth—rather than using technical terms.

- Object orientation does not separate code and data as in conventional systems; both are bundled together in objects.

- The data is active, not passive, in that the data (in objects) knows how to perform work on itself. In traditional programs, the program is active and the data is passive.

- The inherent characteristics of object-oriented languages practically mandate reusing existing components, unlike conventional development where reuse is optional.

- New development is just like maintenance; both reuse existing components to create new functions.

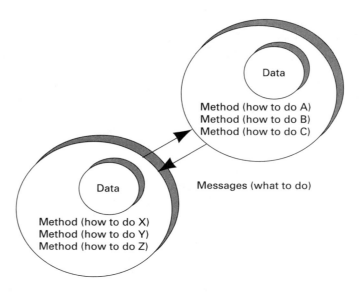

Figure 9-6   An Object

encapsulation helps produce software that is far more tolerant of change. Furthermore, the objects are much more likely to be reusable because there is a separation between the "what to do" (in the messages) and the "how to do it" (in the methods).

Classes. Objects are organized into classes and instances. The concepts of class and instance will be familiar, says Cox. "Betsy is a cow" is just a short way of saying "Betsy is an *instance* of the *class* cow." Betsy is a cow, but Betsy is also Betsy, the individual. She is like other cows in most ways, yet different in the ways that set her apart from the herd. Classes are arranged in hierarchies shaped like trees, says Cox. Specific classes, such as Holstein, are at the branches; intermediate classes, such as cow or mammal, are at the trunk; and generic classes, like vertebrate or animal, are near the root. Such hierarchies allow a wealth of information to be derived about any given instance. By knowing that Betsy is a cow, one can immediately conclude that she eats grass, is warm-blooded, feeds her young on milk, and so on. This class hierarchy, a simple technique for organizing facts used in object-oriented programming, permits inheritance.

Allowing classes of objects to inherit characteristics from other classes of objects—*inheritance*—is an innovative aspect of object-oriented systems not provided by conventional languages. Inheritance allows automatically broadcasting traits, attributes, and code. Programmers do not start each module with a blank page, but instead reuse classes already in a library, modifying them by describing how the new class differs from the one in the library.

Inheritance permits defining new software in the same way we introduce a concept to a newcomer—by comparing it with something that is already familiar. Inheritance links concepts into a related whole, so that as a higher-level concept changes, the change is automatically applied throughout. It provides enormous simplification because it reduces the number of things that must be specified and remembered.

The appeal of these ideas is the possibility that the software industry might obtain some of the benefits that the silicon chip brought to the hardware industry: Namely, the ability of a supplier to deliver a tightly encapsulated unit of functionality to be specialized for its intended function, yet independent of any particular application.

Object-oriented development is most important in three types of applications:

- *Graphical applications*—because inheritance provides consistent behavior among objects, which is important in providing easy-to-remember user interfaces.
- *Multimedia applications*—because no other database management technique can handle a variety of data, such as voice, data, images, text.
- *Complex systems*—because objects manage complexity better by reducing the dependencies among functions.

Object-oriented development is the reigning standard in the PC and workstation world because it significantly eases development of the graphical user interfaces. Developers just point and click at generic items—menus, dialog boxes, radio buttons, and other components of graphical displays—and then rearrange them to create a screen. This form of programming is coming to be known as "visual programming."

Although object-oriented development promises significant benefits, there are also costs, especially at the outset. Initial object-oriented projects can frustrate project managers and users because the developers spend much time defining and redefining classes and class hierarchies. The initial projects also require more effort than if done conventionally. But thereafter, projects can take less effort, if the classes are reused.

Object-oriented development is primarily entering the business world by way of client/server systems; it has rarely been used in mainframe development. The most "famous" use was at Brooklyn Union Gas, which contracted with Andersen Consulting [11] to build the utility's mainline customer information system using object-oriented techniques.

CASE EXAMPLE: Brooklyn Union Gas

Brooklyn Union Gas provides natural gas for some 1.1 million customers in the New York City area. In 1986, their 13-year-old crucial customer information system had become so inflexible that it was inhibiting the company from adding new kinds of marketing-driven services, and from meeting new regulatory requirements. The straw that broke the system's back was a mandate to generate plain-language, graphic customer bills. The system could not be extended to print those bills. In short, this heart-of-the-business system was preventing the utility from responding to change.

Management Issues

Management considered various approaches to updating the system. Replacing individual functional components was deemed too prohibitively expensive and risky; therefore, the company had to replace the entire system. In directing its IS division to proceed, management made it clear that the utility should never be placed in that untenable situation again, where it would have to replace the entire mainline system all at once. The new system had to allow piecemeal upgrades.

After weighing the alternatives, IS management chose object-oriented development, believing this state-of-the-art technology would provide the most stable, yet flexible, base for gracefully absorbing significant technical and business changes over the next 20 years. This stability and flexibility would come from the use of objects, which are based on data and are, therefore, inherently more stable than processes. The utility would always have customers, meters, and bills, even though the processes surrounding these items might change. Furthermore, the objects would be discrete pieces that could be changed without affecting each other.

The new system was to perform 70 to 80 percent of the same functions as the former customer information system. To cost-justify the investment, Brooklyn Union treated it as an asset—one that could be depreciated just as the company depreciates its 4,000 miles of pipe. On average over the 1980s, the utility replaced 12 miles of pipe each year at an annual cost of $18 million. In the same way, the new system will require regular "parts replacements" to accommodate the technological changes expected through the year 2010.

The project was truly pioneering. No other organization in the world had created a mainframe-based object-oriented system of this size—10,000 program modules, 400 on-line programs, 118 batch programs, 150 on-line dialogs, and 1,000 business functions. The system was to handle 10 messages a second during peak hours, and generate 40,000 bills, 80,000 credit activities, and 250 reports each night. The system, which was used by 80 percent of Brooklyn Union's employees, had to work. To reduce the risk of the undertaking, the utility froze many of the other variables. It stayed with its familiar language, PL/1, extending it with object-oriented concepts. It also stayed with the mainframe platform because of its stability and its well-understood performance characteristics. Eventually, the utility intends to move the system to a workstation environment.

Construction

The project, which began in 1986 and culminated in January 1990, was a joint effort between Brooklyn Union Gas and Andersen Consulting. Development of a data model was the first step because the objects would be based on the data definitions for customer, billing account, meter, and so forth. At the outset, IS management also spent three months exploring object orientation, including creating a sample program to demonstrate the technology. Developers were gradually introduced to the new concepts by initially concentrating on using functional decomposition to define "function managers"—programs that coordinate the work of objects. Then the developers moved on to defining objects to perform those functions.

To package the objects to achieve long life, the system is divided into three layers, as shown in Figure 9-7. The user interface layer connects the system to the outside world. This layer is the most subject to change because as new technologies arrive, such as workstations and hand-held devices, they will be added via this layer. In fact, these new technologies will be able to draw on the same code in the other two layers. The second layer is the function layer, which defines business functions, such as "apply

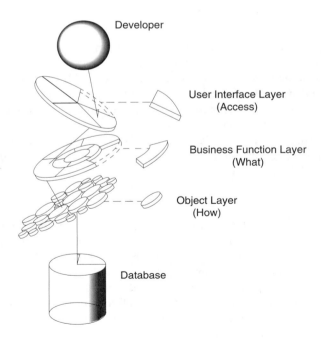

Figure 9-7   The Three Layers of Brooklyn Union Gas's
Object-Oriented System (from Andersen Consulting [10])

a payment." The 10 to 20 business steps performed in each function are coordinated by the function manager. Once invoked, a function manager delegates its work to objects by sending them messages in the proper sequence. The third layer is the object layer, which contains both business function objects and data objects.

Benefits

The new system is smaller, even though it handles more functions. The old system had 1.5 million lines of code; the new one is 40 percent smaller with 900,000 lines because the batch and on-line programs use the same code, eliminating redundancy. The system is also easier to maintain. Since going into production, a number of enhancements have been made, with a dramatic reduction in the amount of new code that has had to be rewritten. One example involved developing a new on-line dialog to correct service order discrepancies. The change required 2,000 new lines of code, but, in reality, the function draws on 40,000 lines of code—a 20-to-1 gain over traditional maintenance. Maintenance is also easier because it is just like new development; both reuse objects to create new functions. The result is that creating a new function in the system now takes no longer than resolving the business problem—a significant advance for the utility.

So what has happened to the two major late 1980s developments, CASE and object orientation? Well, both have become the underpinnings of today's development environments. The tenets of CASE, such as the repository and automation of the recordkeeping, are used in numerous toolsets. But as the field has moved to packages and smaller systems, there has not been as much need for large CASE systems. Object orientation, on the other hand, has moved into the mainstream in packages and client/server development. However, Brooklyn Union Gas's example has not been followed; everyone is too busy moving applications off the mainframe.

THE 1990s

To recap system development to this point, the field achieved discipline through structured system development in the 1960s and 1970s. In the late 1970s, the field turned toward ease of use, with the advent of 4GLs and prototyping. These two approaches made development of smaller systems cost-justifiable. In the late 1980s, CASE and object-oriented techniques aimed to simplify development, both of huge corporate systems as well as small personal systems. In the 1990s, two developments have been the major news: Client/server systems and Web-based (or network-centric) development.

Underlying these two trends is the increasing use of packages and system integration. As much as possible these days, companies prefer to buy a package rather than to build the application in-house. To develop large applications, companies integrate hardware and software components. For example, they buy a ready-made Web browser to become the standard access software for Web-based applications rather than write their own front-end client software. So, in both realms, the major construction method is system integration or component-based development.

Client/Server Computing

Client/server systems generated a lot of excitement in the early 1990s because they promised far more flexibility than mainframe-based systems. The desktop and laptop clients could handle graphics, animation, and video, while the servers could handle production updating. It was a very clever way to meld the pizzazz of the PC world with the necessary back-end production strengths of the mainframe world, even though mainframes were not always in the picture. The following is a typical example of the allure of client/server computing, and how one company—MGM—developed its first client/server system. It is based on a case that accompanied a Wentworth Research ITMP report by Roger Woolfe [12].

CASE EXAMPLE: MGM

Metro-Goldwyn-Mayer (MGM), the movie studio in Hollywood, has an extremely valuable asset: Its library of TV shows and movies. The studio's first client/server application was built at the urging of end users to leverage this asset. The vice president of IS knew that the only way to meet the users' expectations for a multimedia, laptop-based system with a graphical interface was to employ client/server technology.

Previously, more than 26 disparate systems on PCs, Prime minicomputers, and the corporate mainframe were used to maintain rights to show MGM's films. As a result, it was not possible to get a consolidated, worldwide picture of which films were being leased. The client/server system—the largest IS project in Hollywood at the time—collected and consolidated all data on the film library, so that MGM would know what films it has rights to license to whom.

Client/server technology was chosen because it could empower MGM's 20 worldwide film rights salespeople. They can now visit the head of a cable TV network anywhere in the world with an SQL database on their laptop and built-in CD-ROM capabilities to play 20- to 30-second clips of their films. They can browse the laptop's inventory database to verify availability of films, and then print the licensing deal memo on the spot. Details of the deal are then transmitted to headquarters when convenient. Only a client/server system would provide this flexibility.

The System's Three-Level Architecture

The system's architecture has three layers. At the core is an AS/400, which acts as the central processor for the database that contains descriptions of 1,700 TV shows and movies, an index, their availability in different regions, license time periods, status of bills, and so forth. MGM deliberately chose a tried and tested traditional transaction-based AS/400-based rights licensing software package to manage the database. It provides the needed processing, but it does not support user-friendly graphical interfaces, laptops, or decision support . So MGM surrounded the package with the most tested technology possible for the client/server components. In fact, wherever possible, MGM minimized technical risk by using proven products—PowerBuilder, Sybase, Micro Decision's gateway to the AS/400, Microsoft Office, and Lotus's cc:Mail.

The second layer is an H-P 9000 server, which contains data and processing, but no presentation software. The Hewlett-Packard–based Unix front-end was built using PowerBuilder. In one hour with PowerBuilder, developers can do eight to ten hours of COBOL-equivalent work.

The third layer is the client machines, either desktop or laptop. They contain local processing, local databases, and presentation software. The laptops contain a Watcom database, which puts an SQL database at the salespeople's fingertips. They will upload information from their laptops to the AS/400 via dial-up lines every few days. The premier skill required in this environment was systems integration, where developers must have both hardware and software expertise, encompassing Unix and NT, Power-Builder and SQL Windows.

The Development Environment

While partnering was always possible in the mainframe era, it is mandatory with client/server computing. With tools like PowerBuilder and a development life cycle that relies on prototyping, developers must constantly interact with users. They cannot seclude themselves for months. Moreover, there is no boss on client/server teams. The users and developers are equal; neither tells the other what to do.

So the role of IS at MGM has changed from system development and delivery to one of cooperating and partnering. This has required a huge cultural shift in the roles and attitudes of IS staff. Developers who formerly buried themselves in code must now conduct meetings and work side by side with users. In short, they have to learn people (interpersonal) skills and the business. Interestingly, the CIO felt that women have an edge because, generally speaking, they have better interpersonal skills.

With client/server systems, the hardware is cheaper, development is faster, and software support is cheaper—all by orders of magnitude. But operating costs are not as inexpensive as MGM had originally thought; they could even be more expensive than mainframe operational costs, but only by a small percentage. PCs are more expensive to operate when they are used to emulate terminals, and version control of client/server software is costly.

Service and systems management are also causes for concern because they require more manual intervention.

Middleware. As it turns out, this new world is far more complex than the all-in-one-box mainframe world. Many new kinds of products have been created to reduce this complexity, but even so, they remain complex systems. One class of development products is middleware, which, as its name implies, works between the client and server portions of the systems. As Woolfe [12] points out, middleware simplifies development by acting as the glue that binds the components together, allowing them to work together. There is a plethora of kinds of middleware, as Figure 9-8 illustrates. Some are for communication among applications, others are for managing transactions across platforms, and still others provide general services, such as security, synchronized timing, or software distribution.

The preferred approach to building complex client/server systems is to take a component-building approach by first choosing the standard building blocks

Figure 9-8   Types of Middleware Used In Client/Server Applications
(from Wentworth Research [12])

Interapplication communications facilities: link components
- Application programming interfaces (APIs): provide a standard way of interfacing
- Remote procedure call (RPCs): enable a dialogue between two geographically dispersed applications
- Object request brokers (ORBs): allow applications or utilities to interwork in standard ways
- Message-oriented middleware (MOM): uses asynchronous message passing for interapplication communications

Transaction managers: handle transactions across multiple platforms
- Standard query languages (SQLs): stadardize the way in which databases are accessed
- TP monitors (CICS, for example): monitor on-line transaction processing with a database
- Two-phase commit: a protective mechanism for transactions that fail to complete successfully

Utilities: provide general services
- Directory services: resource allocation
- Time services: timing
- Security services: encryption, and so on
- Software distribution: including configuration control

and then using them to piece together the systems. To illustrate the development steps involved in this component-building approach, we draw from another case study that accompanies Woolfe's report.

CASE EXAMPLE: An Aerospace Company

An aerospace company has chosen to build all future systems following a client/server architecture using a component-building approach. It decided it wanted to use not only object-oriented techniques but also create a visual programming environment. So it has standardized on ParcPlace's Visual-Works for writing programs for the client machines, the Smalltalk object-oriented language for programming for the servers, and Sybase's Open Client/Server for middleware. VisualWorks was chosen because it was the most productive for developing a graphical user interface, and because it can also be used on servers. Sybase was chosen because it had a relational design, a good combination of middleware, allows access to other databases, and supports applications distributed across multivendor networks.

The Main Goal: Object Reuse

A central code repository is a critical element of the infrastructure because it facilitates the reuse of objects. It provides browsing facilities and configuration management (which allows several versions of an object to exist at one time). So developers can assemble applications on the fly and build editions of methods and classes. They divide objects into three types:

- Domain objects, which hold business rules and data
- View objects, which are used to build user views
- Controller objects, which manage the relationship between a domain object and a view object

Developers started with a simple approach to fostering reuse: a software junkyard. After agreeing on requirements for applications, developers would browse the Smalltalk class library and update the models. Then they would use the ParcPlace library, update the models again, and increase the number of lines reused. Finally, they put the methods and classes back into the library.

The company believes this low-cost approach to sharing initially yielded two-thirds of the possible reuse. Substantial cost reductions resulted just from on-line browsing. But the 700 classes and 15,000 methods became too large to browse quickly. A configuration management system was needed. So the company asked ParcPlace Systems to add descriptions of the objects—when and how they could be used. In addition, the company created a template for objects, and assigned one person to manage reuse. Interestingly, this new approach did not increase the amount of reuse. This experience supports the assertion that it is not possible to go much beyond 60 percent reuse—even though some experts say otherwise.

The Four-Phase Development Approach

The company was unable to find a complete set of integrated object-oriented development tools, so it adopted a mixture of techniques and tools, centered around Barry Boehm's spiral development approach.

Phase 1 (5 percent of the effort). The objectives are determined and the alternatives for achieving them are identified. The alternatives are evaluated and the requirements are developed.

Phase 2 (25 percent of the effort). The development plan and budget are prepared and a prototype of the graphical user interface is produced. This prototype has no functionality but it is used by the users to test the application's usability. In effect, it is used to confirm the requirements because people cannot explain all their requirements in advance. The company has discovered that the final user interface is often quite different from the initial one. In fact, sometimes it is completely rebuilt. During this phase, a model of the objects and data is also built.

Phase 3 (35 percent of the effort). The acceptance criteria and test plan are agreed upon and functional prototypes are built to test the feasibility of building the high-risk components. Network modeling tools are used to assess the impact of the application's design on the network, and coordination between the server and client components is also tested. Finally, the design model is built, and objects that have not been built before are prototyped.

Phase 4 (35 percent of the effort). The test plan is completed, an operational prototype is created, and the final system is built. This phase finalizes the design of the objects, the tests to be run, and the documentation. The company tried to document applications during prototyping, but the applications changed too much. So now documentation is created at the end of the project.

Benefits of This Approach

Development productivity has improved considerably. The four-phase methodology has reduced the time to build a function point from 12 hours to 5 hours. The main productivity improvement comes from the 60 percent reuse of code. However, the approach does require more user involvement because more time is spent ensuring the requirements are correct. The development group does try to complete projects in no more than 12 months, and often they only last six months. Team size varies from two or three to twenty or more.

There is also a steep learning curve. It takes several months to become fully proficient in the methodology and in VisualWorks, which has 15,000 methods. With hundreds of developers, this is a huge cost. Outside trainers and consultants are used to get the developers up to speed. Once formal training is completed, mentors are used. Each project has one experienced person, much like a chief programmer, who is paid out of the overhead budget to spend 40 percent of his time mentoring. (The other 60 percent is spent on writing the difficult bits.) In practice, the mentors become component builders, but this is not formalized.

The company has implemented 16 general business client/server applications using this object-oriented methodology. Although this is a tiny proportion of the 30,000 applications in the company, the company believes that any of its business systems could be implemented in the same way. All components are stored in a library and, as a result, an application becomes a logical concept. Once the design is complete, the final stage consists mainly of plugging components together.

Web-Based Intranet Applications

The most recent development in application development has been the phenomenal growth of Web-based intranet applications. As Netscape [13] points out, the former programming paradigm was to develop specialized applications, each with a different front-end access program. The new paradigm is to use Web browsers as the standard means of access to corporate, departmental, individual, and even cross-organizational applications. Once someone knows how to use the browser, he or she knows how to access all applications that use this front-end. Therefore, the former islands of automation become accessible because the browsers can access any application, no matter which databases, operating systems, or programming languages are used. Even legacy systems can be linked to Web sites. Furthermore, Web-based applications are touted as costing less to develop because they not only eliminate the need to write customer front-ends, but they also use the Internet's communication protocols as the common linking mechanism.

In general, people are developing three kinds of Web applications, according to Netscape: one-to-many publishing applications, two-way transaction applications, and many-to-many community applications.

One-to-Many Publishing Applications. These are basically broadcast uses of a Web site where teams, departments, and even corporations post information for widespread access, generally to reduce paper reports, procedure manuals, newsletters, company circulars, and such. The immediate paybacks are reductions in all paper processing costs (printing, distribution, updating, etc.). The result is more efficient corporate operations, faster, more widespread communication, lower costs, and better informed employees.

As Netscape points out in yet another White Paper on its Web site [13], electronically published price lists and product descriptions allow worldwide sales forces to get product information from headquarters much faster, which speeds up the sales cycle and lowers sales costs.

Examples of the types of information published at intranet Web sites include job openings, telephone directories, corporate policies, the annual report, comparisons of benefit plans, upcoming training programs, product schedules, news releases, and so on.

Two-Way Transaction Applications. These are interactive applications, where employees can access a Web site to change their benefits program, submit an expense report, fill out a project time card, submit a sales order from a customer, or register for a company training course. These uses often replace paper forms and phone calls. Again, the result is more efficient corporate operations through faster processing and, often, more accurate information.

For instance, the Netscape White Paper notes that sales reps at one pharmaceutical company can fill out a form requesting that a letter be sent to a doctor explaining the risks associated with using one of its products during pregnancy. This saves the salesperson time and handles the doctor's request much faster.

Yet another example from the White Paper is the use of an internal "cybermall" of approved products to simplify purchasing of, say, supplies and software, perhaps even office equipment. Employees can browse the "mall," select the products they need, and the rest is done electronically. The order is sent to the appropriate supplier, perhaps with next-day delivery, and payment is also handled electronically.

Many-to-Many Community Applications. These include internal forums, chat groups, and newsgroups, where people exchange information, teamwide, groupwide, divisionwide, or companywide. For instance, some sales organizations maintain Web sites for salespeople to exchange information on competitors, pass along personnel changes at client firms, give out promising sales leads, provide analyses of contract wins and losses, and give tips on how to compete against specific competitors or specific competitive products. As Netscape points out, others use them to let product teams share product plans, design documents, and product schedules throughout development of a product, which results in faster time to market and lower development costs.

In short, intranets are an important addition to a company's IT toolkit. In fact, they are becoming the next major mainstream platform for computing. As a result, vendors are building better application development tools, system management tools to better manage Web applications, and middleware tools to connect legacy systems to Web sites. Some tools are aimed at Web site creation. These overlay the Hypertext Markup Language (HTML) so that users (and programmers) can more easily create "live" multimedia documents. These are based on the Java language, along with such multimedia formats as Adobe's Acrobat and Macromedia's Director.

More sophisticated application development tools are aimed at programmers and make it easier for them to build production-quality applications on top of Web platforms. These applications will conduct complex transactions against databases, legacy systems, and other corporate information sources. System management tools help system managers of internal Web sites manage links, expiration dates, and ownership. As the number of internal Web sites grow, these site and document management tools will become increasingly important.

These kinds of applications require developers with expertise in distributed computing, Unix, TCP/IP, HTML, as well as graphics design and page layout, says Philip Gill [14], a writer. This expertise is in short supply in most IS departments. We have heard this lament before. IS departments seem to be almost continually "behind the curve" in having the skills to develop new applications. That is the reason why packages have become so popular, in fact, mandatory to keep up with the quickening pace of change in system development.

As an example of the development of Web-based intranet applications, consider the following two case examples, one of a groupware application and one of a corporate intranet/electronic commerce strategy.

CASE EXAMPLE: Developing a Web-Based Groupware Application

In a paper at an Association for Information Systems (AIS) conference, Alan Dennis and Sridar K. Pootheri of the University of Georgia [15] describe a first-generation Web-based groupware system. They believe the Web represents a revolution in system development and will become the preferred development environment for network applications, so that they can run on Macintosh, Windows, and UNIX simultaneously.

To test their belief, they developed a groupware system using a different approach from past groupware systems. Lotus Notes, for example, is data centered, which limits the types of group processes it supports (e.g., voting requires writing a special procedure). Conferencing room tools, such as GroupSystems, are process oriented, but integrating data into processes is difficult because each process is supported by a separate tool and, hence, treats its data separately.

Dennis and Pootheri decided to take an object approach, with common data and processes in each, where an object is a project (and, of course, there is a hierarchy of subprojects), and projects have sets of topics. Initially, in selecting a browser, they used the "lowest common denominator" strategy, so that the system could work with any browser. However, halfway through the project they realized that the browsers worked so differently that they had to select one. They chose Netscape 1.1—one step behind the leading edge, at that time.

They chose a fast DBMS that handled a subset of SQL and up to 75 clients concurrently, MiniSQL. They wrote the programs in C to work on the SQL database to generate HTML forms, each of which captures user commands and presents information in response. Each form contains the information needed to process the current request, know who the user is, and what application he or she is using. The forms are read by the browser and displayed.

Lessons Learned

Dennis and Pootheri learned a number of lessons from this development project. First, they learned they could develop a major application using the Web. In fact, the browser had many advantages over traditional development due to its built-in functions. Generally, the user interface is 80 percent of the application. But Dennis and Pootheri found that interface coding was reduced to 40 percent because all they needed to do was specify which browser functions to use. This saved a significant amount of programming time, they state, even though they were limited to the capabilities of the browser.

Second, they learned to deal with user expectations. Those users who viewed it as a Web application saw it as novel and appreciated it. But those who saw it as a desktop application expected drag-and-drop capabilities, pull-down menus, and multiple windows. They were disappointed. They would have to wait for the next generation of browsers.

Third, they learned that they needed to test the system on a wide variety of computers because the browser produces slightly different displays among UNIX, Macintosh, and Windows machines. And each version of the browser has its own bugs.

Based on their experience, Dennis and Pootheri believe in their premise that the Web will become the development environment of choice, and that those who use it first and push its limits will learn its intricacies and reap a competitive advantage.

CASE EXAMPLE: Snap-On, Inc

Snap-On, Inc. makes high-quality automotive tools and sells them through 3,400 franchisees, who visit 200,000 businesses and 1 million automotive technicians each week.

As the CIO, Lawrence Panatera, wrote in the Society for Information Management's quarterly publication, *Network* [16], business success in the next century will depend on electronic commerce because companies will conduct a significant amount of their external and internal business over networks. He has two main reasons for this view. First, downsizing has cast off noncore businesses, but these businesses will need to stay in just-in-time contact with the parent company. Electronic commerce will allow this. Second, companies are becoming increasingly dependent on suppliers. Again, the two must stay in continual communication with each other. Electronic commerce will be the means.

Due to these views, Snap-On has developed an electronic commerce strategy called Store Without Walls. Part of this strategy is an intranet that Snap-On can use to keep its 3,400 franchisees informed about the latest products, promotions, sales figures, marketing tips, and other company information. Franchisees also need a way to keep in touch with each other, to share sales leads, insights, and so on, notes Panatera.

Snap-On's secure Web site gives franchisees access to a central database as well as other franchisees. They chose the intranet option because they needed to permit access from a wide geographic area, they wanted a low-cost system, and they wanted to be able to quickly "publish" their current documents in electronic form. Use of HTML has allowed this.

Development Strategy

Snap-On divided its intranet into areas that correspond to corporate functions—sales, marketing, credit, technology, and so on. In addition, each area has a formal editor, who is responsible for the information in that area. Snap-On believes that this formalized job responsibility ensures that the content is monitored and kept up-to-date—a very important aspect to the company.

The top level of the site gives franchisees five options—product/service information, managing a franchise (on-line "training classes"), sales/marketing program updates, franchisee forums, and news. The franchisees used the forums to share their experiences with each other and to record best practices. Each forum has an editor to keep it running smoothly. The news section contains news especially relevant to Snap-On. For instance, Snap-On sponsors many car races and other activities. This section not only keeps franchisees abreast of these events, but also allows them to send e-mail to some race car drivers and crews. The news section also includes Deal of the Month awards, stock prices, growth strategies, and so on.

Snap-On has found that the intranet improves its communications with its employees and permits global problem solving. But it sees this as more than an adjunct to the Internet. The company sees it as a move toward electronic commerce.

CONCLUSION

The traditional approach to system development from the 1960s evolved to give the process more discipline, control, and efficiency. It was valuable in moving programming and system analysis from pure free-form "art" to a better defined "craft." Problems remained, however, with long development times, difficult user involvement, and lack of flexibility in the resulting systems.

In the late 1970s, data-driven development and group design sessions stressed improving the early phases in development to catch problems early. Then, in the early 1980s, 4GLs and software prototyping permitted more rapid development, and even experimental development, and were thus seen as revolutionary techniques by conventional developers.

In the late 1980s, two more important trends influenced system development—CASE and object-oriented development. The first one represented the evolutionary viewpoint of automating the tried-and-true structured development techniques. The second one was revolutionary, yet built on traditional system design tenets, such as hiding information from others to localize the effect of system changes.

The 1990s has seen two more advancements of the application development field—client/server computing and Web-based development. Both emphasize flexibility, speedier development, reuse, and "chunking" of applications. But, due to their complexity, both stress integration of components and packages. It appears as if we have indeed entered a new era of application development with our entry into network-centric computing, and in so doing, again have expanded the universe of applications toward intercompany and customer-interactive applications.

QUESTIONS AND EXERCISES

REVIEW QUESTIONS

1. What are the goals of the traditional system development life cycle approach?
2. Refer to the list of features and functions of 4GLs in Figure 9-3. Briefly explain each.
3. What are the problems of little databases and personal programs? How do 4GLs help or hinder in dealing with these problems?
4. What are the main characteristics of the prototyping approach?
5. Describe the main points of Santa Fe Railroad's use of Mapper.
6. Define the components of a computer-aided software engineering system.
7. What is unique about Du Pont Cable Management Service's use of CASE?
8. How does object-oriented development differ from traditional development?
9. Describe an object.
10. Why did Brooklyn Union Gas choose object-oriented development?
11. Describe MGM's three-layer client/server architecture.
12. Describe the aerospace company's four-phase system development life cycle.
13. According to Netscape, what are the three types of Web-based applications being developed?
14. What lessons did Dennis and Pootheri learn from their development experience?
15. Why does the CIO of Snap-On believe electronic commerce is the future of business?

DISCUSSION QUESTIONS

1. IS departments will no longer need to develop a proprietary infrastructure because they can just rely on the Internet. Therefore, they will again focus mainly on developing applications. Discuss.
2. The field is moving too fast for companies to keep developers abreast of the state of the art. To keep up, they should outsource application development. Discuss.

EXERCISES

1. Find a detailed description of a Web-based application. What features does it have? Why did the company choose the Web?
2. Visit a company in your community that has an information systems department with at least five professionals. Prepare a short case description to summarize the company's current approach to developing systems. Does it have one standard approach or a combination of several? Is it building client/server systems or Web-based systems? If so, describe one or two.
3. Find four articles on object-oriented systems. What's the state-of-the-art in this approach, according to these articles?
4. Present a scenario of what you think system development will be like in leading-edge firms in five years. What will change? What will not change?

REFERENCES

1. CANNING, R. G., *Electronic Data Processing for Business and Industry*, 1956, and *Installing Electronic Data Processing Systems*, 1957, John Wiley & Sons, New York.

2. BOEHM, BARRY:

   a. *SOFTWARE ENGINEERING ECONOMICS* (Englewood Cliffs, N J: Prentice Hall, 1981).

   b. "THE SPIRAL MODEL OF SOFTWARE DEVELOPMENT," *IEEE Computer*, May 1988.

3. ENGER, N. L., "Classical and Structured Systems Life Cycle Phases and Documentation," in *System Analysis and Design: A Foundation for the 1980s*, edited by Cotterman, W. M., J. D. Couger, N. L. Enger, and F. Harold, Elsevier North Holland, Inc., 1981, pp. 1-24.

4. GLASS, ROBERT, *Building Quality Software* (Englewood Cliffs, NJ: Prentice Hall, 1992).

5. RICH, M., PFS Inc., 731 Bayonne St., El Segundo, CA 90245.

6. NAUMANN, J. D., and A. M. JENKINS, "Prototyping: The New Paradigm for Systems Development," *MIS Quarterly*, September 1982, pp. 29-44.

7. DIGITAL CONSULTING, Inc., 6 Windsor St., Andover, MA.

8. MCCLURE, CARMA, Extended Intelligence, Inc., 25 E. Washington Blvd., Chicago, IL.

9. DU PONT INFORMATION ENGINEERING ASSOCIATES, Nemours Building, 9th Floor, Wilmington, DE 19898.

10. COX, B., *Object Oriented Programming: An Evolutionary Approach* (Reading, MA: Addison Wesley Publishers, 1987).

11. *CLOSE-UP: BROOKLYN UNION GAS* AND *TRENDS IN INFORMATION TECHNOLOGY,* Andersen Consulting, 69 W. Washington Blvd., Chicago, IL 60601, 1991.

12. WOOLFE, ROGER, "Managing the Move to Client-Server," IT Management Programme, Wentworth Research, Egham, England, January 1995, http://www.wentworth.co.uk.

13. "INTERNAL WEBS AS CORPORATE INFORMATION SYSTEMS," White Paper on Netscape's Home page: http://home.netscape.com.

14. GILL, PHILIP, "Web Development Sets a Breakneck Pace," *LAN Times*, June 17, 1996, pp. 41-44.

15. DENNIS, ALAN and SRIDAR POOTHERI, "Developing Groupware for the Web," *Proceedings of the Americas Conference on Information Systems*, Phoenix, Arizona, August 1996. The authors can be contacted at adennis@uga.cc.uga.edu and sridar@math.uga.edu.

16. PANATERA, LAWRENCE, "Intranet Strategies," *SIM Network*, Society for Information Management, 401 N. Michigan Ave., Chicago, IL 60611, http://www.sim.org.

TEN

Management Issues In System Development

INTRODUCTION

Chapter 9 reviewed the tools, techniques, and approaches for developing systems that have evolved over the first 35 years of the computer revolution. During that time, the process of managing the development of systems has increased in importance and complexity. In this chapter, we deal with the management issues of system development by addressing four critical questions:

1. What applications should be deployed?
2. How can system benefits be measured?
3. How can higher-quality systems be developed?
4. How can legacy systems be improved?

System development has been, and continues to be, one of the largest information systems jobs in organizations, whether it is performed by the centralized IS department, an outsourcing vendor, or a functional unit. As the spectrum of tools, development methodologies, languages, and staff have broadened, so too have the kinds of applications developed. This broadening of application types raises a significant management question: What applications should be deployed?

Although many companies may profess to take a portfolio approach to managing their storehouse of applications, we wonder how many proactively choose their applications based on gaps in the portfolio. This issue should not be answered by IS management alone. Rather, it should be answered together with executive and line management. We therefore begin this chapter on application development management issues by discussing this overarching question. Then we delve into three others. One is the age-old issue of estimating the benefits of systems, which is a particularly thorny question when strategic systems are being envisioned. Another question has also been around for a long time: How can companies develop higher-quality systems? Finally, we end the chapter discussing the question most IS executives would prefer to ignore: What do we do about our legacy systems? These ten-to twenty-year-old systems could someday cause a real disaster. In this section we address the very real example of that impending disaster—the most urgent system development question of the late 1990s—how to make systems Year 2000-compliant by January 1, 2000.

WHAT APPLICATIONS SHOULD BE DEPLOYED?

One of the important questions IS management and corporate management need to answer is: What sorts of applications should we deploy? In many cases, the answer has been left to line management, based on their needs. But as Bob Benson of Washington University in St. Louis and Marilyn Parker of IBM [1] pointed out years ago, there is a synergistic relationship between the business and IT. We discussed their model in Chapter 2, shown in Figure 2-2 on page 37. That model shows that the IT architecture needs to align with current strategy, and that IT opportunities influence or even change business strategy. Therefore, IS management has a responsibility to point out those opportunities to top management and line management to best help the enterprise. They cannot just sit and wait for users to figure out what they need.

Besides keeping alert to new opportunities, IS management also needs to take a portfolio view of applications, and manage that portfolio to ensure that no serious gaps creep in. What sort of framework should management use to evaluate the application portfolio? Interestingly, we found an answer in two different places.

Take a Portfolio Approach

As we noted in Chapter 9, the people at Netscape [2] point out that intranets are being used for three purposes: to publish up-to-date information, to enable transactions, and to facilitate communications among people. David Flint, a researcher at Wentworth Research [3], proposes a similar framework in his 1994 ITMP report "Application Delivery in the 1990s." Flint believes that applications must support all aspects of work, and he says that means supporting three human activities: knowledge, transactions, and discussion, as shown in Figure 10-1 on the next page. Every job has aspects of all three components, although in very different proportions. These three therefore form the portfolio framework for assessing future applications, he believes.

Traditionally, companies have *automated* mechanistic work via transaction processing systems, says Flint, but they have not been so attentive to the

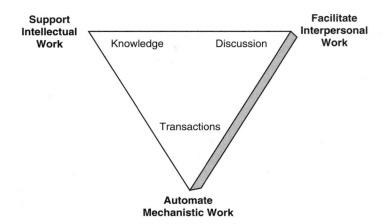

Figure 10-1   Three Kinds of Application Needs (from Wentworth Research [3a])

other two aspects of work—intellectual work and interpersonal work. Effectively supporting intellectual work requires mastering the management of knowledge, notes Flint. And supporting interpersonal work requires mastering discussion management.

Furthermore, says Flint, all three need to be integrated at the desktop, creating a "user toolkit" as it were. So, a user screen might provide, for example, e-mail for discussing matters with others, an electronic catalog for purchasing supplies, and a library of job-related information. Providing this breadth requires developers who can concentrate on all three aspects of work (not just automate functions or processes), and developers who really understand the work being supported, so they can design the user interface properly, says Flint. This, in turn, probably argues for prototyping, so that users are involved in the interface design and rapid application development (like the Du Pont case cited in Chapter 9).

Since transaction systems are familiar, and since we will talk about discussion management in our chapter on groupware, here is an example of the third type of system, from the Sourcebook that accompanies Flint's report [3a]. It is a knowledge management system being developed by a computer company. We expect to hear more about this type of system in the future. It is an electronic performance support system (EPSS) intended to provide information support to employees as they do their jobs.

CASE EXAMPLE: A Computer Company

A major computer supplier has recognized a problem with the training of its service and support staff, which are dispersed around the world. In the past, the staff learned about every model of computer in depth. But now, its computers have fewer parts and are much more reliable. So staff do not need this depth of knowledge. The company is therefore developing a new approach to getting the appropriate information to its staff.

The original intent was to build an expert system. However, the development team concluded that the rules in the knowledge base would be too difficult to maintain. Therefore, the company is building an EPSS instead to provide employees with all the information they need, including company policies and procedures, not just information on how to fix a fault or repair a machine.

In building the EPSS, the developers first had to learn how to create models of users' knowledge, so they could understand how the users view their knowledge, especially the concepts they use. The developers expressed these concepts as a semantic network, a network whose nodes are concepts and whose links are the relationships between the concepts. This process is similar to developing an expert system; however, it does not require such detailed information to answer users' questions. Rather, the system only needs to provide them with the knowledge they need to answer the question. Whereas IS has been good at converting data to information, an EPSS is aimed at converting information into productivity—an entirely different ballgame.

The prototype version of the system was developed on Sun workstations using Servio Corporation's Gemstone DBMS, an object-oriented system. Deployment started in the company's Worldwide Support Center because it handles a wide range of problems. From this experience, the company has decided to go into the business of building EPSSs for customers. Its service will include the knowledge management database, tools, and consulting help because populating the database is not intuitively obvious, the company found.

We believe that Flint's three-part portfolio approach to applications is an appropriate framework for IS management to use with executive and line management in discussing the coverage of current and in-development applications. It will help uncover the gaps and allow planning a more balanced portfolio of applications. However, balancing the portfolio across the three categories must include an assessment of the benefits of new applications.

HOW CAN SYSTEM BENEFITS BE MEASURED?

Cost justification of information systems has been increasingly on the minds of executives as costs of systems have increased and results have fallen quite short of expectations. Initially, companies measured efficiency—doing something right. But the largest payoffs from IT lie in improving effectiveness—doing the right thing. However, this is a much tougher measurement problem, so the real benefits have gone unmeasured.

Office systems and desktop systems cause measurement problems. So do decision support systems—which include executive information systems, management support systems, and expert systems, because they intend to change such "unmeasurable" actions as improved decisions, better identification of opportunities, more thorough analysis, and enhanced communication among people. Strategic systems, which aim to improve a firm's competitive edge or protect its market share, also elude measurement. It makes no sense to determine their return on investment (ROI) in terms of hours saved when their intent is to increase revenue or enter a new market. Finally, infrastructure investments, upon which future applications of all kinds will be built, cannot be justified on ROI because they have none. Only the subsequent applications will show a return on investment. This has been the measurement conundrum.

In their research for the special report *Uncovering the Information Technology Payoffs* [4], Walter Carlson and Barbara McNurlin uncovered the following three suggestions, as well as numerous others, on how to deal with these measurement dilemmas:

- Distinguish between the different roles of systems.
- Measure what is important to management.
- Assess investments across organizational levels.

Distinguish Between the Different Roles of Systems

Paul Berger [5], a management consultant, believes that companies can measure the value of IT investments by using many of the management measures now in place. Some of his ideas are found in *Measuring Business Value of Information Technologies* [6]. Information systems can play three roles in a company, Berger told Carlson and McNurlin. They can *help other departments do their job better*. Berger calls these "support systems." Their goal is to increase organizational efficiency.

Second, information systems can *carry out a business strategy*. Examples are CAD systems that customers and suppliers can use together to design custom products. Other examples are EDI and automated teller machines. These strategic systems are measured differently from support systems because they are used directly by customers, suppliers, and clients, says Berger; support systems are not.

Third, systems can be sold as *a product or service or as the basis for a product or service*. For example, offering a cash management account that combines a checking account, a cash management account, and an investment account would not be possible without the underlying information system. Another example is testing or design software that a company sells to another firm, says Berger.

Measuring the benefits of these three kinds of systems differs.

Measuring Organizational Performance. Organizational performance has to do with meeting deadlines and milestones, operating within budget, and doing quality work. Performance measures *efficiency* of operations, says Berger.

A number of years ago, Berger worked on developing a large human resources system with decision support capabilities, and then tracking its benefits. To measure the value of the system, the development team compared the productivity of people who used it to the productivity of people who did not. Data was collected on the cost of operating the system and the total costs of running the human resources departments.

Operating costs did not rise as fast in the human resources departments where the system was used, the team found. In the base year, two departments had costs of $82 per work unit. "Cost of a work unit" was the annual cost to process one employee, including hiring, salary administration, benefits, counseling, overhead loading, and so on. At the end of that year, the system was installed in one of the departments. In the second year, the unit cost in the department using the system rose to $87; the cost in the nonusing department rose to $103. By the fifth year, the using department had a cost of $103 per work unit while the nonusing department's cost was $128 per work unit. Following the fifth year, all human resources departments used the system, so no further comparisons could be made. But during those five years, the unit costs in the departments using the system rose about 25 percent; the nonusing department's costs rose over 56 percent.

Measuring Business Value. While measuring business unit *performance* deals with internal operational goals, measuring business *value* deals with marketplace goals. Systems that are part of a business plan can be measured on their contribution to the success or failure of that plan. But, in order for systems to be measured on their business value, they must have a *direct* impact on the company's relationships with its customers, clients, or suppliers, says Berger.

The system cited earlier was measured on departmental performance. It could not be measured on business value because its effect on the corporate bottom line was indirect. No direct link to increased revenue could be identified. This distinction is important in measuring the value of IT investments.

In another firm, several information systems were developed to help its direct-marketing people analyze their customer base—both current and potential customers. The goal was to improve the quality of their customer base so that sales per customer would increase, while, at the same time, sales and promotion costs would decrease.

After implementing the systems, advertising and customer service costs decreased. The company also experienced higher customer retention and lower direct sales costs compared to industry standards. Since they were able to equate the particular information system expenditures to marketing, they could identify a direct correlation between system costs and sales revenue. They could measure business value. The information systems affected their sales directly through marketing decisions the system supported, so the value of the investment could be stated in business terms.

Measuring a Product or Service. An information system can be offered as a product or service, or it can contribute to a product or service that is intended to produce revenue. In these cases, its value is measured as any other business venture—by its performance in the market. The measures are typical business profitability measures, such as return on investment, return on assets, and return on equity.

Measure What Is Important to Management

Charles Gold, of the Ernst & Young Center for Business Innovation [7], recommends measuring what management thinks is important. Information systems support can only be linked to corporate effectiveness by finding all the indicators they use besides the traditional financial ones. Relating proposed benefits to these indicators can make it easier to "sell" a system, at both the individual and aggregate levels.

Try to assess benefits in terms such as customer relations, employee morale, and "cycle time," that is, how long it takes to accomplish a complete assignment, Gold suggests. Each is a measure that goes beyond monetary terms, but which few executives deny are vital to a company's success. He gave Carlson and McNurlin two examples.

As a measure of customer satisfaction, one power company kept a log of how many complaint letters customers sent to the Public Utilities Commission each month; this commission regulates the utility companies within its state. The power company installed a computer system for its customer service representatives, giving them on-line access to the information they needed to answer customers' questions. When the system was in operation, the number of complaint letters decreased; when the system was down, the number of letters increased. So, one aspect of the effectiveness of this system was measurable in terms of public opinion.

A second possible measure is cycle time. Faster cycle time can mean much more than saving hours. It can mean higher-quality products, beating competitors to a market, winning a bid, and so on. The benefit may have nothing to do with *saving* money. Rather, it may focus on *making* money.

So, says Gold, concentrating only on cost and monetary measures may be short-sighted. Other measures can be even more important to management.

Assess Investments Across Organizational Levels

Kathleen Curley, now at Lotus Institute, and John Henderson, of Boston University [8], recommend measuring benefits at several organizational levels. They have developed the Value Assessment Framework for assessing the value of an IT investment across corporate levels.

The Value Assessment Framework. Since the potential benefits of IT investments differ at various organizational levels, Curley and Henderson believe companies need a systematic way to separate these benefits by organizational level. They see three organizational levels, or *sources of value*, in particular, that benefit

- The individual
- The division
- The corporation

With the current emphasis on business reengineering and redesigning business processes, Curley and Henderson also see the *impact focus* of an IT investment extending beyond business performance measures to encompass three dimensions:

- Economic performance payoffs—market measures of performance
- Organizational processes impacts—measures of process change
- Technology impacts—impacts on key functionality

Combining the two views forms a 3 x 3 matrix for systematically assessing the impact of a potential IT investment in nine areas. This framework was used by a trucking company, and its use uncovered benefits that otherwise would not have been measured.

CASE EXAMPLE: A Trucking Company

This small trucking company in the refrigerated carrier business has been around since the 1920s. When the Motor Carrier Act of 1980 deregulated trucking companies and competition increased, small firms like this one were hit the hardest. By 1984, even though it had been one of the top five refrigerator trucking firms, its share of shipped tons fell to less than one-half the 1977 level because national and regional carriers had taken away its business. In response to the crisis, management made two decisions:

- Manage the company by information—transforming company procedures and tracking success via a large suite of measures
- Use information technology to differentiate itself from other refrigeration trucking firms—initially with a whopping $10 million investment in a state-of-the-art satellite system and a computer in every truck cab, so that its drivers could be in constant voice and data communication with the company and customers.

The results were remarkable. Tons shipped increased from 300,000 tons in 1986 to 1,100,000 tons in 1991, and the trucker became an industry leader in the innovative manipulation of information. It introduced ground-breaking information services that provided superior levels of customer service.

The Measurement Program

On the measurement front, the company developed world-class goals for each of its three mission statement objectives:

Our mission is to exceed the expectations of our customers. Earn a return on investment that is the best in the industry. Provide our employees an opportunity to attain fulfillment through participation.

Overall performance is measured in three ways:

- Customer satisfaction determined by "moment of truth" questionnaires filled out by customers to rate the company's service performance
- Return on investment measured by an operating ratio

- Employee satisfaction determined from questionnaires that capture employee sentiments and chart them on an index.

The company created interim performance improvement goals that are to be achieved by specific dates. These interim measures are used to see how fast and how well the company is progressing toward its world-class goals. There are not only companywide goals but also world-class goals for each department. These include the overall company performance goals as well as specific departmental goals, all of which are raised as performance improves. In this way, performance improvement is built into the measurement system.

After studying the company's measurement and tracking processes, Kathleen Curley said, "They have one of the most detailed sets of measures I have ever seen."

Measuring the Value of the Satellite System

Following IBM Consulting's recommendation, the trucker used the Curley/Henderson Value Management Framework to evaluate the satellite investment after the fact—with eye-opening results. It began by identifying the specific process improvements made possible by the system, entering them into the framework along with an outcome and outcome measure for each one. For example, at the individual level, the company estimated that improved communications from the truck cab would increase driver production time by one-half hour a day. The result was a savings of $59.60 a month per driver. At the work group level, it was estimated that improved load truck matching would save 1 percent deadhead time, which translated into a $49.68 savings per month per truck. At the business unit level, it was estimated that improved customer service would increase market share, but a dollar amount could not be pinned down for this increase. Once these figures were calculated, a manager was assigned to achieve these savings targets, so that the company could assess whether or not it was realistically leveraging the investment. It intended to manage the value it was receiving from its investment, not just make the investment and hope it paid off.

The most interesting piece of the Value Management Framework analysis, Curley said, was not the identifiable cost savings but the large, unexpected revenue benefits. Due to the analysis, management discovered that customers were willing to pay a premium price for the ability to call a truck driver directly from the customer's warehouse. Constant communication with drivers was worth a lot—a lot more than management thought. This discovery gave the company even more confidence in its decision to bet on technology, and in its ability to sell information-based services. Due to its sophisticated and ingrained measurement system, the company is even able to see the effect of its pricing on market share. So, indeed, it is managing by information.

HOW CAN HIGHER QUALITY SYSTEMS BE DEVELOPED?

One of the most vexing issues in software development arises after the system is installed. The maintenance/upgrade phase of the life cycle typically requires at least as much cost and effort as were expended to develop a system in the first place. In other words, when the system is installed, the job is less than half done! Over the years, it has become clear that maintainability can be significantly improved by building in quality.

Traditionally, however, applications have experienced gradual "hardening of the arteries." That is, their initial clean system design deteriorates due to the uncoordinated way in which changes and add-ons are made. As a result, changes in one module unexplainably affect others. When this happens, the applications actually become dangerous to the healthy functioning of the organization because they become less and less able to accept change without crashing. In this situation, software maintenance—to fix bugs, add user-requested enhancements, and improve performance—becomes a necessary evil. It does not improve these systems, it simply keeps them up and running. In short, traditional ad hoc maintenance practices have caused the quality of many applications to deteriorate over time. These practices, however, can be changed to maintain system quality.

A quality system has a number of attributes, as shown in Figure 10-2. Following are three tactics for maintaining system quality:

- Focus on the "right" work.
- Manage the data and its quality.
- Develop a maintenance strategy.

Focus on the "Right" Work

One way to improve quality when building a system in-house is to devote systems staff time to the tougher modules and less time to the easier ones. Unfortunately, that is not usually what happens, said Denis Meredith [9], at a Los Angeles chapter meeting of the Association for Computing Machinery. Meredith is an independent consultant who specializes in software testing and risk assessment.

Figure 10-2   The Attributes of a Quality System

- It meets users' needs.
- It withstands the test of time, continually meeting the users' needs. That is, it changes gracefully as the users' needs change.
- It contains no bugs. It only does the work it was designed to do, and it does that work properly.
- Its inherent structure stays intact over time, so it remains maintainable.
- It is simple for the users to understand.
- It simplifies the user's life; that is, it was designed with the user in mind.
- It is easy to use.

Generally, project managers assign the easiest modules first, said Meredith, to get them out of the way. But that is the wrong strategy for developing quality software because, as a general rule, *modules that are written first are tested the most*. To develop quality software, the first modules written and tested should be the most difficult and the most risky.

How can project managers estimate riskiness when only the design specifications exist? Meredith suggests rating each module on two kinds of risk—failure impact and fault likelihood.

- *Failure impact* is the cost or damage that could occur from a failure. Estimates are based on such things as frequency of use and the value of the results to end users.
- *Fault likelihood* estimates the chances that a system fault will occur. System fault can mean several things: failure to run to completion, failure to comply with government regulations, economic loss through improper payment or billing, inappropriate business decisions based on incorrect or improperly presented information, or loss of data. Estimates of fault likelihood risk are based on such things as module complexity and the technologies to be used.

Meredith suggests that project managers evaluate module risk using a one-page questionnaire [10]. Then rank the modules based on their scores for these two risks. Finally, assign project resources to modules based on their riskiness. The 17 questions on the questionnaire can be completed in five to fifteen minutes for each module. "It has to be brief, easy to fill in, and useful," says Meredith, "or people will not use it." As an example, one question is: "Kind of module: inquiry, report writer, data extract, algorithmic data manipulation, file or database access, edit, or conversion." Each of these seven possibilities has an associated score—the more complex the type of module, the higher the score. That score is multiplied by a weight for failure impact or likelihood of fault. These weights were estimated by the project manager based on the question's contribution to risk.

The scores for the two types of risk are added separately for each module, and each module is ranked on the two scales. Obviously, the most risky modules have a high score for both failure impact and likelihood of fault; these modules should be developed and tested first, says Meredith. The next most risky are those with a high impact score and low likelihood score. The third most risky have a high likelihood score but a low impact score. The least risky modules score low on both—these modules should be developed and tested last.

The project managers who used this technique at one company told Meredith that it helped them focus their attention on the aspects that were likely to cause problems. So it was doing its job. But Meredith warns that the numbers are only estimates; they should only be used to judge the approximate relative risk of modules. The difference between two modules with scores of 60 and 70 means little. But the difference between modules with scores of 50 and 90 probably indicates significant risk difference between the two. In addition, the actual numbers may not be important, says Meredith. In one case, two project managers evaluated the same project and arrived at quite different numerical totals, but their overall ranking of the modules was the same.

System development strategy should focus on quality, says Meredith. One way to do that is to direct attention to risky modules so that project teams concentrate on the "right" work.

Manage the Data and Its Quality

Data is finally being recognized as a valuable company asset. John Zachman [11], a pioneer in the field of data management, believes that improving data consistency is imperative to the future well-being of organizations. As managers begin to rely more and more on computerized data, they must be able to obtain consistent views of the enterprise. The spread of desktop systems is hastening management's use of such data.

One traditional approach for obtaining data for a new application is to use data from an existing application. Data is "dribbled" from one application to another. This practice leads to different names for the same data, the same name for different data items, and the same data in different files but with different update cycles. Under these circumstances, getting a consistent view of the organization is difficult, if not impossible.

It is also hard to make changes to data that is scattered among different applications, says Zachman. Even more difficult is maintaining an application that receives dribbled data from other systems and dribbles some of its own data on to other systems. These practices make it difficult to change an organization's infrastructure—its products, markets, organizational structure, and so on—because changing the supporting information systems is expensive.

If information systems management sees one of its major functions as managing data, then improving data consistency will improve system quality. The Monsanto case in Chapter 7 describes leading-edge data quality work in the mid-1990s.

The Importance of Data Context. Zachman and Monsanto address the issue of data *content*, and point out the importance of getting the data process correct—an aspect of the total "system" that surrounds use of a computer system. But content is not the only aspect of data that needs attention. Cornelia Varney, author of the Wentworth Research ITMP report on managing integrity in distributed systems [3b], makes the very interesting point that data *context* also needs to be managed. And the problems are really quite different. By context, she means "the business context" in which the data is used. A warehouse manager needs stock-on-hand data, while an accountant wants to know the inventory's total value. These different needs lead to divergent approaches to data and information, notes Varney, and problems arise when data collected for one purpose is used for another. Common symptoms of context integrity problems include conflicting terms and definitions as well as lack of awareness of similar data created by other departments. National and cultural differences can cause obvious problems, which management must increasingly handle as companies operate across borders.

The key to reducing context problems, says Varney, is to improve communication because context differences only become problems when information is transferred between people who work in different contexts. The problems can be reduced if people take account of their contextual differences (presuming they know them). This, in turn, requires appropriate communication channels and, perhaps, a common language.

As illustrated in Figure 10-3, businesses need to choose the communication channel that is most likely to reduce the data context problem, depending on the two dimensions of the problem: the amount of difference between the business contexts of the communicating parties and the amount of information interdependence between the two parties.

For instance, where contextual differences are small, simple communication channels that rely on routine or automated procedures will suffice. But if contextual differences are large—such as between IS and marketing—much richer communication channels are needed. One example is a face-to-face meeting, which can explore the differences and create understanding through drawings, words, and body language—all of which may be necessary to communicate meaning between the two.

Furthermore, the amount of information that needs to be exchanged determines the appropriate communication channel. If the two parties are highly dependent on each other's information, then it may take time to uncover and

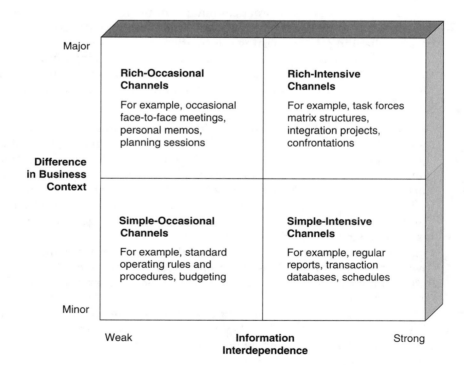

Figure 10-3   Choosing an Appropriate Communication Channel to Reduce Data Context Problems (from Wentworth Research [3b])

resolve political undertones and status issues. Thus, facilitators or task forces, which last as long as the issue exists, may be necessary.

Although the issue of system quality has generally been discussed in terms of the "correctness" of the data within the system, we think this broader view, which includes the business context in which the data is used, is also important and is a system development management issue.

Develop a Maintenance Strategy

Ken Orr [12], a well-known system development consultant, likens application systems to the telephone system. He believes that IS departments could benefit from taking the view that telephone companies take toward maintaining their telephone service. Telephone companies try to maintain their systems without interrupting service, and they attempt to make the service appear consistent to users by not changing operating procedures. In essence, they try to insulate telephone users from internal system changes. Orr believes this is a goal for information systems as well, and that a good software maintenance program would do just that. It would include

- Continual repair to fix errors
- Continual enhancement to make user-requested changes
- Continual revisions to upgrade systems technologically while protecting user views of each system

Orr asserts that organizations should follow the lead of software companies that manage the entire life cycle of their products. His premise is that maintenance can be managed because most maintenance is redesign, and redesign can be managed using the proper tools. Changes should not be simply added on but should be designed into programs and systems, says Orr. By using the structure chart of a program to determine how to incorporate the change into the design, the program's design will retain its robustness and hence its quality. This requires using a design methodology during maintenance, which many companies do not do.

To manage the maintenance process, Orr suggests using change reports for four levels of change. The problem is first identified in a change *report*, and it is given as high a *change* priority as practical. When a correction is made, a system update is distributed, if necessary. This is the lowest level of change to a system. Then, at regular intervals, a group of updates is combined and released as a *system temporary update*. The documentation as well as the code are updated for this second level of change.

On a longer time frame, a series of system temporary updates is combined into a *system release*. At this time, the changes are retested, documentation is updated, and the changes are integrated. At the most significant fourth level, a *new version* of the system is created. Versions represent major changes to systems, such as major new functions, a restructured database, a new platform, and so on.

As more and more end users begin using computers directly, "backbone" systems will become increasingly important, says Orr, because they will feed the other smaller (perhaps user-developed) systems. Maintaining the quality of these mainline systems so that they are adaptable will become increasingly important. He feels that a managed maintenance strategy is necessary to accomplish these ends.

In summary, these three strategies for improving system quality are

1. Concentrate on the hardest modules first so they are the most fully tested.
2. Improve the data used in the system.
3. Manage the entire life cycle of a system rather than leave it to chance.

These are things that can be done to improve new systems. But what about existing applications?

HOW CAN LEGACY SYSTEMS BE IMPROVED?

Most information systems executives feel trapped by the past. They have thousands—even tens of thousands—of old legacy programs and data files that they would love to replace. But with the onslaught of client/server computing and now Web-based intranet applications, they see no way of finding the resources to replace these legacy systems. But replacement is not the only option, and in many cases, it may not be the wisest option.

To Replace or Not to Replace?

To replace or not to replace? That is the question. In 1995, the Boston Consulting Group (BCG) [13] studied 18 manufacturing companies, service firms, and government organizations in North America, Europe, and Japan that had either just replaced or upgraded legacy systems or were in the process of replacing or upgrading. Of the 21 projects, 12 were successful in that they worked and had a bottom-line impact. But the other nine were either unsuccessful or did not deliver the anticipated results.

From these findings, the BCG concluded that upgrading (rather than replacement) made more sense in most cases, even if it was difficult and not seen as exciting as a totally new system. They noted that people get seduced by a new technology and want to rush out and replace old systems with it. But BCG found that most of the replacement projects that failed could have been upgrade projects. In fact, in some cases, the company then reverted to upgrading the old system anyway.

When a system's technology is so obsolete that it does not exist in many places, then replacement is probably the only choice. But otherwise, BCG recommends that companies perform three analyses. First, do a rigorous analysis of the costs and benefits of the new system. Most companies underestimate the cost of replacing a system and overestimate the achievable business value—even on the successful projects. Furthermore, they do not factor in the risk of failure. Second, determine how specialized the new system really is, advises BCG. Sometimes, companies think they need a made-to-order system when a purchased solution would do just fine. Their requirements are not as unique as they think.

And third, assess the IS staff's capabilities honestly. Several of the
the study failed to develop replacement systems because manageme
rated the staff's skills. In conclusion, BCG recommends that the bur
needs to lie with those who advocate replacement of a legacy system r
those who advocate an upgrade—especially for strategic systems.

Options for Improving a Legacy System

With this very interesting and recent study as our backdrop, we now discuss six choices companies have for dealing creatively with legacy systems, from
(ideally) least to most amount of change. Many of these options, shown in Figure
10-4, have taken on increased importance in the face of the Year 2000 problem
(which we discuss shortly).

Any of these options can be performed in-house or sourced to an outside
firm. But in moving to a totally new platform, generally from a mainframe-based
application to a client/server one, companies are taking one of two strategies in
using outsourcing firms.

The traditional approach has been to keep the legacy maintenance work in-
house and hire a consulting firm to build the new client/server system—and then
phase out the legacy maintenance work. But some companies have opted for
what is called "transitional outsourcing." This means that they have outsourced
the legacy systems to an outsourcer to maintain so that the in-house staff can
focus on developing replacement client/server systems. As these new systems
come on-line, the outsourcer turns off the old legacy systems, hence, the name
transitional outsourcing. Companies take this approach when they feel they
have (or can get) the in-house expertise required by the new platform. Skill levels, as the Boston Consulting Group found in its 1995 survey, are a major issue
in determining whether or not such an approach is even feasible.

Here then is the spectrum of options for improving legacy systems.

Restructure the System. If an application program is basically doing its
job, but it runs inefficiently or is "fragile" or unmaintainable, then it may simply
need to be *restructured*. For years, vendors have offered software products to aid
in this process. The most popular ones use automated tools, restructuring
engines, to turn running "spaghetti code" into more structured code. The process
involves the following seven steps:

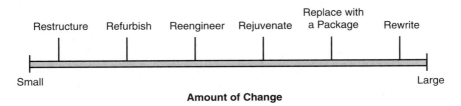

Figure 10-4   Options for Improving a Legacy System

1. Evaluate the amount of structure in the current system—number of layers of nesting, degree of complexity, and so forth. Use the tools to present a trace of the program's control logic. Subjectively evaluating the code is also necessary to determine whether restructuring is warranted at all, or if more extensive change is required; this can only be performed by people.

2. Compile the program to be sure it is in working order. A code restructuring tool will not make a nonoperative program run.

3. Clean up and restructure the code using structured programming concepts by running the program through a structuring engine. This automated process does not change the logic of the program; it simply replaces poor coding conventions with structured coding conventions, such as reducing the number of GOTOs, removing dead code and alter statements, highlighting looping conditions, and grouping and standardizing input/output statements. It uncovers the structure hidden inside the convoluted code.

4. Reformat the listing, making it easier to understand, by using a formatting package.

5. Ensure that the old and new versions produce the same output by using a file-to-file comparator.

6. Minimize overhead introduced by restructuring by using an object code optimizer package. After optimization, restructured programs generally require between 5 percent less and 10 percent more run time than the unstructured versions.

7. "Rationalize" the data by giving all uses of the same data one data name. This step is optional.

These seven steps can be used to restructure a functional system or to get it in shape to be reengineered.

Reengineer the System. A step beyond restructuring is reengineering, which means extracting the data elements from an existing file and the business logic from an existing program and moving them to new hardware platforms. This use of the term *reengineering* should not be confused with the term *business reengineering,* which was used in Chapter 3. This term *system or application reengineering* is much narrower and refers only to software. The other term refers to redesigning business processes. Like code restructuring, reengineering requires automated tools because the process is too complex to be cost-justifiably done manually. Database reengineering tools began appearing on the market in the late 1980s.

Charles Bachman [14], a pioneer in the database field, introduced the first widely accepted set of database reengineering tools. He believes that the major problem in the computer field has been the way applications have been developed and maintained. Rather than consider existing systems as liabilities that have to be maintained—and thus take resources away from developing new and exciting applications—management needs to see existing systems as assets from which to move forward.

If developers can reverse engineer a system that is, extract the underlying business logic, then they can forward engineer that business logic to a new system platform, such as a new database management system. With this approach, existing systems become assets. Developers can extract the intelligence in them, rather than starting over from scratch as they do today.

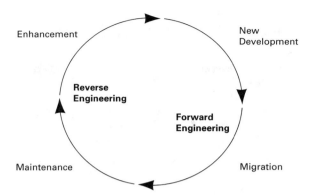

Figure 10-5   The Reengineering System Development Life Cycle
(from Bachman [14])

Bachman sees a new system development life cycle emerging, using automated products to help perform the reverse engineering. It encompasses all
four basic development activities—maintenance, enhancement, new development, and migration. This life cycle is circular rather than linear, as shown in
Figure 10-5.

- *Reverse engineering.* Existing programs, along with their file and database
  descriptions, are converted from their implementation-level descriptions—
  records, databases, code, and so on—into their equivalent design level components—entities, attributes, processes, messages, and so on.
- *Forward engineering.* This goes in the opposite direction—from requirements-
  level components to operational systems. Design items created by reverse engineering are used to create new applications via forward engineering.

The cycle continues because as new applications go into operation, they
become candidates for reverse engineering whenever they need to be changed.
Neither people nor automated tools can use this new life cycle by themselves,
says Bachman, but together, it becomes feasible. GTE Directories is an example
of a company that used Bachman's reengineering tools.

CASE EXAMPLE: GTE Directories

GTE Directories is a leading telephone directory publishing company with
headquarters in Dallas, Texas. It produces, markets, and distributes over
1,500 different telephone directories in some 14 countries. To accelerate its
response to changing markets, GTE Directories began automating its telephone directory publishing business.

The directory publishing system has four main databases. The largest
supports all the administrative functions for creating and selling Yellow

Page advertising—from sales to photo composition. The second is used by representatives who sell Yellow Page advertising for non-GTE directories. The third database handles billing. And the fourth database provides order entry for independent telephone companies, for whom GTE produces telephone books.

The databases were originally designed application by application. The result was that records contained data elements that had no business relationship to each other, making them very difficult to reuse, enhance, and change. The data administration group acquired the reverse engineering tools from Bachman Information Systems to help it maintain and improve these databases.

How to Use the Reengineering Tools

To reverse engineer the database, a designer used the Bachman/Database Administrator to display the existing database definitions on a graphical workstation. The design was reversed engineered into the Bachman/Data Analyst, where the designer made changes by manipulating the graphical icons. The Data Analyst helped draw complete and consistent entity-relationship diagrams because it had the intelligence to identify inconsistencies and incomplete structures.

Once the new database design had been created, the designer forward engineered the database design back to Bachman/Database Administrator and ran the physical implementation design rules. This product made recommendations to improve the design. When the design was satisfactory, the Database Administrator was used to automatically generate database statements.

Here are two examples of projects where GTE Directories used the Bachman tools for database maintenance.

The Blueprint Project

Since the largest database was not properly designed, the data administration group used the toolset to create a blueprint of what the database should look like. It reverse engineered the existing database from its physical to its data model from which they created a new, properly designed data model using entity-relationship modeling techniques. By experimenting with this model, the groups created a design that was more adaptable to change. It became the blueprint for the future and was used to guide maintenance work. As the database administrators maintained the database, they made changes to bring it closer into line with this blueprint. Without the reengineering tools, they would not have even attempted this project because they could not have done the what if modeling necessary to create the blueprint.

A Reuse Project

The database administrators reused some of the data elements in the largest database for a new production scheduling system. The company had scheduled production of its 1,500 directories among its three printing plants using a 15-year-old system. Some scheduling data was in the system, some was in the new administrative system.

GTE Directories created a new scheduling system, drawing some scheduling-related data from the administrative database. Again, the data administrators used Bachman tools to create the design models for the new scheduling databases. From these models, they used a Bachman tool to generate the necessary database statements. With the new system, salespeople no longer had to interrogate both the 15-year-old publishing system and the administrative system, which had different sets of data, to see directory publishing schedules.

Since maintenance was the bulk of the work of the database administration group, the Bachman tools became invaluable in helping the group redesign old databases, design new databases using portions of existing ones, and create its blueprint for the future.

Refurbish the System. If the old system is maintainable and is causing no major problems, it may be worthwhile adding some extensions. Potential extensions would supply input in a new manner, or make new uses of the output, or allow the programs to deal more comprehensively with data.

Refurbishment is actually occurring quite a bit these days because of the World Wide Web. Companies are leaving existing systems in place but adding a Web front-end and accompanying query translation software, so the system can be accessed directly by employees, suppliers, or even customers. Witness FedEx's Web site, which allows customers to directly access the company's tracking database. In such cases, companies generally follow a "surround" strategy, where they treat the old system as an untouchable "black box" and surround it with new facilities. This has been a very popular way to upgrade legacy systems, even before the Web's appearance. Unfortunately, such front-ends are exacerbating the Year 2000 conversion problem because their date fields are more difficult to find and change than the date fields in the underlying legacy systems.

Rejuvenate the System. Rejuvenating an old system is a step beyond refurbishing the system because it adds enough new functions to a system to make it much more valuable to the firm. The first step is to recognize a system's potential. The second is to clean up the system, perhaps using the restructuring tools mentioned earlier. The third step is to make the system more efficient, perhaps using the reengineering approach just mentioned and then porting the system to a new operating environment and database structure. The fourth step is to give the system a more strategic role, such as allowing it to feed a data warehouse so that people in field offices can access data far more quickly. Another possibility, as mentioned earlier, is to give it a role in a company's electronic commerce strategy by using it as a back-end system accessible via the Web.

Replace with a Purchased Package. Many, many old systems have been replaced by purchased packages. One reason for choosing this option is to replace numerous old and disjointed applications with a corporatewide system, as companies are doing with SAP. The other popular option is to move applications from the centralized mainframe environment to a distributed client/server one. Yet another strategy is to distribute an application's workload among a host computer, some servers, and many PCs and laptops. There are an increasing number of commercial packages that permit such three-tiered processing. These packages not only support communication between the three types of machines but they also split the processing job and facilitate downloading and uploading of files.

Another reason to consider replacing an old system with a commercial package is that these products are becoming more versatile. Many offer selectable features that allow purchasers to tailor the package to their work style. The options can be turned on or off using control files, so no programming is necessary. Even end users can specify some of the operating instructions. Even so, replacing one or more applications with a package is not a trivial task. Just ask the people who are installing SAP.

Rewrite the System. In some cases, a legacy system is too far gone to rescue. If the code is convoluted and patched, if the technology is antiquated, and if the design is poor, it may be necessary to start from scratch. Generally, rewriting a system today means system integration, that is, finding packages that do pieces of the work, then using client/server tools to write the underlying logic that ties them together. The difference from buying a single package is that the user company, or a system integration firm, becomes the integrator.

The Year 2000 Problem

Just like the Internet, the Year 2000 problem should need no introduction because it has become a global deadline for just about every computer system. The problem, in a nutshell, is that in order to save money on storage and processing, the year date fields in almost all computer applications have been truncated to just two digits. So 1965 became 65. The 19 was assumed. This practice started long ago, when management presumed the systems would be replaced before the year 2000. But they have not been. As a result, when applications encounter 00, which is meant to represent the year 2000, they think it means 1900. This throws calculations into havoc. That is the crux of the problem.

January 1, 2000 is definitely the worst deadline most IS departments have ever faced.

The Issues. One of the main issues is cost. The magnitude of fixing the problem is staggering. The Gartner Group initially put the cost of compliance at $300 to $600 billion dollars, but the number keeps going up. Estimates started at

$.40 per line of code. It was then upgraded to $1.10, then $1.50, and it could likely go higher—and this is just to keep a company in business. In actuality, the true cost can vary from $.20 to $10.00 per line of code, depending on many factors, such as age of the application, existence of documentation (or not), language used, programmer availability, tool availability, and so on.

A second major issue is the magnitude of the problem. At a recent conference of the Sourcing Interests Group [15], Mitch Mayo of ALLTEL Information Services [16] described the magnitude of the problem. Most companies have hundreds of programs, said Mayo, which translates into tens of thousands of applications and tens of millions of lines of code. Generally, 80 percent of that code is in COBOL, another 10 percent is in assembler, and the remaining 10 percent is in other languages. It appears that one-half the Year 2000 conversion work will be spent fixing the 80 percent in COBOL code, said Mayo. The other half will be spent on the other two areas because they are too specialized for automated conversion.

A third issue is time. The longer a company waits to begin tackling the problem, the less time it has to act. Mayo presented three scenarios for three different size portfolios—25,000 programs to fix, 50,000 programs, and 75,000 programs to fix, assuming that all the code must be fixed by November 1998, so that it can run a full year (to uncover any glitches) before the bewitching January 1, 2000. Figure 10-6 shows how many programs must be copied out of production, repaired, tested, and put back into production *per week*, depending on four start dates: January 1997, April 1997, July 1997, and October 1997. The numbers are staggering, as can be seen in the figure.

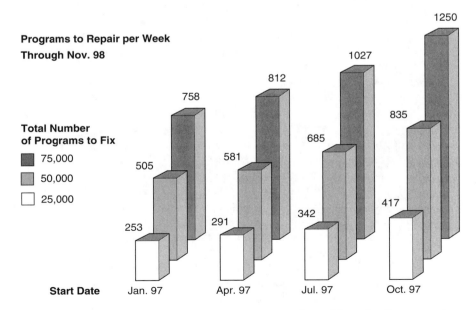

Figure 10-6   Weekly Repair Rate (from Mayo [16])

A fourth issue is approach. There are essentially three approaches. One is to expand the year date field to the full four digits. This is the cleanest approach, but it is also the most time consuming, and it requires dealing with programs, files, and job control language. A second approach is interpretation, also known as windowing, where the application is made to work within, say, a 100-year window, such as 1950 to 2050. If the two-digit date is larger than 50, such as 89, then the date must be in the twentieth century—1989. If it is less than 50, such as 32, then it is in the twenty-first century—2032. The third approach is encapsulation, where a routine captures the two-digit date, rolls it back 28 years, the calculations are performed, then the date is rolled ahead 28 years. The 28 is appropriate because 1972 is exactly the same as the year 2000, 1973 is exactly like 2001, and so on.

This brief discussion gives only a hint of the complexity and magnitude of the issues facing IS departments around the world. As an example of how one company is approaching the Year 2000 issue, consider what Merrill Lynch is doing, as described at the recent Sourcing Interests Group conference.

CASE EXAMPLE: Merrill Lynch

Merrill Lynch is the largest brokerage firm in the United States. In late 1995, six people from the production maintenance group embarked on the company's Year 2000 initiative. They brought in a specialist, whose maintenance methodology they had been using to maintain some of their systems. For two weeks, they and the specialist worked on devising a strategy for making all Merrill systems Year 2000-compliant by the end of 1998.

Merrill faces a number of challenges. For one thing, since it is moderately decentralized, some of the business units build and operate their own information systems. Until the Year 2000 initiative, the central IS departments had no need to know the details of all the applications. These various businesses have different development cultures, which further complicates the task. The Corporate and Institutional Client Group (capital markets group), for instance, builds systems iteratively so that new products can be brought to market quickly. The Private Cients Group, on the other hand, aims for stability in serving private clientele.

In addition, as if the internal challenges are not enough, the Year 2000 team knew it had to make sure that Merrill systems will interface with the systems of the stock exchanges, agencies, and other brokerages. Just solving its own systems problems is not enough.

Once the group decided on a strategy, it began looking for best-of-breed partners. To the dismay of all in the group, they found none. They then realized they had to lead. After interviewing software companies and running pilots, the group selected two vendors as strategic partners. One partner, which has an inventory tool for mainframe applications, is working with Merrill to build a "factory" for separating mainframe data from applications in preparation for converting the mainframe code. Merrill has decided to expand all year date fields to four digits (except in reports and user screens). This strategy requires separating applications and data. The second partner is developing a "factory" for converting the mainframe code once it has been separated.

The group also decided that despite Merrill's heritage of allowing some business units to handle their own systems work, in this case, a single resource center would be established. This group is focusing solely on the Year 2000 and is using a purchasing and supplier management operating model to contract for all the additional resources Merrill needs for the Year 2000 work. In turn, project teams obtain all the additional manpower they need from this group when an application is ready to be converted. The project teams are responsible for the conversion; the central group simply provides the resources and the conversion know-how. For instance, they give each team the script to follow in making the conversion. The central group also monitors Merrill's progress and reports to three management committees that are overseeing the effort.

To obtain the manpower needed, the group contracted with five firms to provide a pool of consultants to do the work for a three-year period. The group assigns the appropriate consultants to a conversion project, and when the project is done, the consultants return to the pool to be reassigned. They also report back what they have learned on the assignment, so that the entire pool establishes and learns best practices as rapidly as possible. Merrill believes that this strategy will allow it to best leverage the talent of these people as well as relieve project teams from having to search out resources, as they have in the past.

In late 1996, the Year 2000 group had 40 employees and 100 consultants at work. The group has until late 1998 to convert 1,200 systems. Merrill believes that although the conversion is a huge job, some 60 percent of the effort will be testing, both internally and with others in the brokerage industry.

SUMMARY

As the variety of computer applications has broadened and as companies have become more dependent on IT, the management issues surrounding application development have proliferated. The question of creating a portfolio that supports all three aspects of work—transactions, discussions, and knowledge—is increasingly important for competition's sake. The relatively new question of measuring the benefits of IT is being asked more often, even in the business press. Meanwhile, IS management is grappling with how to create higher-quality, more flexible systems—both for new applications and for upgraded legacy systems. Finally, IS departments around the world are faced with the hair-raising specter of severe business disruption if they do not make their systems Year-2000 compliant. In all, system development continues to be a challenge.

QUESTIONS AND EXERCISES

REVIEW QUESTIONS

1. Describe Flint's three types of application needs.
2. What are the three roles of information systems, according to Berger?
3. Explain the six elements of Curley and Henderson's Value Assessment Framework.
4. According to Meredith, what is the "right" work?
5. What is data context and why is it important?
6. Which does the Boston Consulting Group recommend, replacing or upgrading a legacy system?
7. List the six ways to improve legacy systems.
8. List the steps in restructuring a system.
9. Why did GTE Directories turn to reengineering?
10. Explain the Year 2000 problem.
11. How is Merrill Lynch organizing to make its systems Year-2000 compliant?

DISCUSSION QUESTIONS

1. Creating systems that encompass all three application needs—transactions, discussion, and knowledge—will be too expensive and ponderous. They are impractical. Different systems handle different needs. Discuss.
2. There is no way to estimate the benefit of a system that is intended to generate new revenue. Management must build the system on faith, not estimates. Do you agree or disagree? Discuss.
3. The strategy of minimum maintenance until a system must be completely redone is still best for challenging and developing the programmer/analyst staff. The few people that like nitty-gritty maintenance activities can take care of the programs that need it, while the majority of the development staff can be challenged by the creativity of new development. The six options in this chapter turn most developers into maintenance programmers. Do you agree or disagree? Discuss.
4. The Year 2000 problem is going to wreak havoc throughout the business world on Monday, January 3, 2000. Do you agree or disagree? Discuss.

EXERCISES

1. Make a table showing the advantages and disadvantages of each of the six options for improving legacy systems. Derive from the table a list of characteristics of a legacy system that can serve as a management guideline for deciding which options are best in a given situation.
2. Find a company in your community that has over ten years of experience using computer systems. Develop a descriptive case study for that company showing how it deals with its legacy systems. Include an inventory of major systems and the company's strategies for maintenance and modernization. Indicate which of Flint's three types of work each system handles. How does the company decide which applications to upgrade and which approaches to use? Explain how top management and

line management get involved in application portfolio decisions. If they don't, why not? Describe the company's approach to making its systems Year-2000 compliant.

3. Read three articles or find five Web sites that discuss the Year 2000 problem. What new information did you learn? Present it to the class.

REFERENCES

1. BENSON, ROBERT and MARILYN PARKER, "Information Economics: An Introduction," EWiM Working Paper, 1987, Center for the Study of Information Management, Washington University, St. Louis, MO 63130.

2. "INTERNAL WEBS AS CORPORATE INFORMATION SYSTEMS," White Paper on Netscape's Home page: http://home.netscape.com, March 1996.

3. IT MANAGEMENT PROGRAMME REPORT, Wentworth Research, Park House, Wick Road, Egham, England TW20 OHW, http://www.wentworth.co.uk

   a. FLINT, DAVID, "Applications Delivery in the 1990s," March 1994.

   b. VARNEY, CORNELIA, "Managing the Integrity of Distributed Systems," January 1996.

4. CARLSON, WALTER, and BARBARA McNURLIN, *Uncovering the Information Technology Payoffs*, a special report published by *I/S Analyzer* (11300 Rockville Pike, Suite 1100, Rockville, MD 20852), Fall 1992.

5. BERGER, PAUL, Paul Berger Consulting, Inc., P.O. Box 6813, Lawrenceville, NJ 08648.

6. *MEASURING BUSINESS VALUE OF INFORMATION TECHNOLOGIES*, International Center for Information Technology (ICIT), 1000 Thomas Jefferson St. N.W., Suite 501, Washington, D.C. 20007, 1988.

7. GOLD, CHARLES, Ernst & Young Center for Business Integration, One Walnut St., Boston, MA 02108.

8. CURLEY, KATHLEEN and JOHN HENDERSON, "Assessing the Value of a Corporate-wide Human Resource Information System: A Case Study," Special Issue, *Journal of Management Systems*, Maxmillian Press, 1992.

9. MEREDITH, DENIS, 2042 Kathy Way, Torrance, CA 90501.

10. MEREDITH, DENIS, "A Risk-Driven Approach to Program Development Strategy," *Proceedings of Pacific Northwest Software Quality Conference, 1986*, Lawrence & Craig (P.O. Box 40244, Portland, OR 97240).

11. ZACHMAN, JOHN, Zachman International, 2222 Foothill Blvd., Suite 337, La Cañada, CA 91011.

12. ORR, KEN, Ken Orr and Associates, 1725 Gage Blvd., Topeka, KA 66604.

13. KIELY, THOMAS, "Computer Legacy Systems: What Works When They Don't?" *Harvard Business Review*, July-August 1996, pp. 10-12.

14. BACHMAN, CHARLES, Bachman Information Systems, 4 Cambridge Center, Cambridge, MA 02142.

15. SOURCING INTERESTS GROUP, 30 Hackamore Lane, Suite 12, Bell Canyon, CA 91307. This group is headed by Barry Wiegler and holds two conferences a year on the subjects of outsourcing, insourcing, and sourcing.

16. MAYO, MITCH, ALLTEL Information Services, 4001 Rodney Parham Rd., Little Rock, AR 72212.

PART IV

Managing the Expanding Universe of Computing

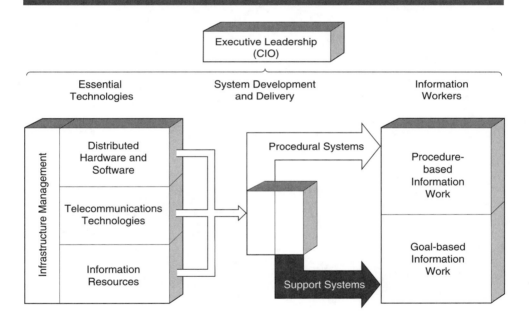

A Framework for IS Management

Part IV of this book consists of two chapters that deal with developing user-oriented systems. These are systems to support the performance of individual users.

Part III dealt with managing traditional system development—the development of procedural systems. But there is a second type of system development taking place, and that is in the realm of end user development. The toolset is not the same as in traditional development nor are the development approaches the same. Nonetheless, individuals—be they acting as employees, customers, suppliers, or consumers—are using recent developments in information technology to construct new ways of working and interacting with others to accomplish their goal-based work.

This part explores this new universe. Chapter 11 deals with the underlying technological developments that now allow individuals to construct new work environments. Chapter 12 deals with the issues facing IS management in supporting this new universe of computing.

ELEVEN

The Expanding Universe of Computing

INTRODUCTION

In the 1970s and 1980s, the use of computers by individuals was called end user computing (EUC). End users almost exclusively used computers in their role as employees. IS departments established end user computing support groups, often called information centers, to support the use of PCs as well as fourth generation languages on mainframes. The history of Mead Corporation's information resources department, presented in Chapter 1, is typical of this evolution—from developing applications in the 1970s, to encouraging end users to access computers directly on their own in the 1980s, to integrating end user computing into enterprisewide computing in the early 1990s.

In the 1990s, there has been no widely accepted term for the use of computers by individuals because today this use is no longer just a small category of computing; it is the future of computing. Computing does not emanate from a data center as it formerly did; now it is everywhere.

We see the universe of users of corporate computing also expanding. As shown in Figure 11-1, the users of corporate information services through the 1970s and mid-1980s were mainly employees at their work sites. In the mid-1980s, organizations opened up access to their computer systems to some supplier and customer organizations. In the late 1980s, with the advent of portable computers, IS departments began to support their mobile employees, giving them direct access to corporate computers wherever they were located. Today,

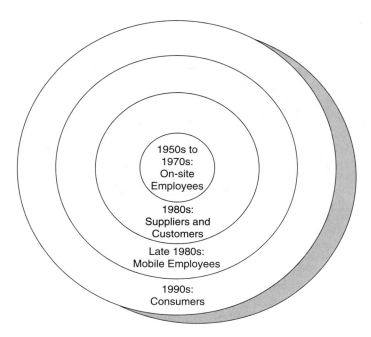

Figure 11-1   The Expanding Universe of Users
of Corporate Computing Services

with the explosion of the Internet, and especially the World Wide Web, this universe of users is expanding further still to include consumers. Serving them directly is the next frontier for corporate IS departments.

At the same time, the technology world seems to be growing by the minute, with more kinds of computing devices, new telecommunication options, and many new, potential uses announced monthly. In traditional enterprise computing systems, applications were developed mainly by programmers using such things as programming languages, databases, object libraries, middleware, and the like, as we discussed in the past two chapters. But if we take a look at the end users point of view, they use quite a different toolset to create their own work environment. They draw on the technological developments of mobile computing, e-mail, and multimedia, and, of course, the Internet.

In this chapter, we look at some technological developments that form the infrastructure for the new ways of working. In the next chapter, we discuss the issues that IS management faces in supporting this vastly expanded universe of computer users.

Six Technologies Underlying the New Work Environment

In a speech at the UCLA Associates annual symposium [1], Roy Weber of AT&T Business Communications Services described six technologies that AT&T believes will underlie the new work environment. Here is what he had to say.

Multimedia Workstations with Real-time Video Conferencing. Video conferencing systems used to cost $100,000. Today they are on a single PC board and cost $500. This is a major technological breakthrough that will significantly support distance collaboration. It allows people to see who they are talking to and visually share with them in real time. They can bring up a document on their screen, share it with their collaborator, and even share control of it. Even more promising is the potential multipoint capability, where each person can see several others, each in a different video window on the screen. This leads to a whole new way of working, said Weber. Furthermore, the entire "meeting" can be saved and replayed by others. Or, at the next meeting, the last three minutes can be replayed to remind everyone where the prior meeting left off. The technology can also be used to leave multimedia messages and provide training.

A few major banks have experimented with this technology in dealing with consumers. When someone walks into a branch and wants to know about a tax law change, the tellers do not have the answer. But with a multimedia kiosk equipped with a video conferencing link, one of the bank's tax experts can talk directly to the customer. It is not quite as simple as making a phone call, but it will be, said Weber.

Electronic Documents. Document technologies have an important role. One insurance company scans every piece of paper that enters the company and stores these documents on optical jukeboxes for displaying on PCs. Others store photographs of car accidents and attach them to claim files. And Xerox is trying to change the world's mindset from print-and-distribute to distribute-and-print with its Docutech machine that can produce bound documents remotely. This will change industries, such as the textbook industry. Instead of the typical sequence—print, store in warehouse, then truck to bookstores—the new model could be: capture the book electronically, store it, communicate it electronically to the bookstore, print, and bind on demand.

Speech Recognition. This is a technology that has been unsuccessfully used for 20 years. Now it is coming of age due to processing and algorithm power. Today, when we call a customer service line, we encounter a menu that we navigate with a push-button phone. It is possible, however, to speak the number 1, 2, 3, 4, and so on with 90 to 99 percent recognition accuracy. This is known as word spotting. It searches for specific words; when it encounters one, it performs an action.

The step beyond word spotting is language modeling, where the computer has a template of a typical phrase, such as, "I'd like to speak to an operator." When it hears the phrase, it responds with a natural language response. A current test has 3,000 people making airline reservations with such a system, with the system asking such things as, "Where would you like to go?" The system transfers the call to a live attendant if it cannot understand one answer. The success rate has been 80 percent in the trial. Voice recognition that really works is coming, said Weber.

Advanced Information Services. There will be public data services, such as global directories, that will sit on networks and the Internet; many will permit secure communications. While companies are putting storefronts out on the Web, they are loath to actually conduct work in the unsecured Internet space outside their firewalls. But advanced secure services are coming. One example is Network Notes that will not only allow people to put information (including video clips) in folders, but will allow those folders to be replicated across companies securely. For instance, one test of the system allowed a company to issue specifications for a new product into a folder. Suppliers with access could look at the specs, knowing they had seen the latest version. In addition, the issuing company knew which suppliers had accessed the file.

Global Personal Calling. In the future, we will place calls to people, said Weber, not to devices (telephones, pagers, etc.). Today's personal toll-free numbers are a move in this direction. Weber has a personal 800 number, as does his wife and his secretary. They can reach each other without having to know where the other person is. A trial currently taking place with 200 people allows people to dial a personal number and input their own personal identification number, so the recipient knows who is calling. The caller is put on hold while the call goes to a nationwide satellite paging system, which connects to the phone where the person is located, and that appropriate telephone rings. If the phone is not answered, the system can switch to voice mail or fax. One way to use the system in a family is to have a single number for the family and then a menu for each family member.

Multimedia Broadband Services. Multimedia broadband services are the driver for this world of desktop collaboration, where images and video clips flow through networks and people talk "face-to-face" to several others at one time over great distances. These services will be based on ATM technology, said Weber.

Eventually, the connections will be seamless. For example, a trucker may stop off for lunch, and at his table will be a computer that he can use to check for future jobs. He may learn that another company is searching for a specific-size truck to pick up a load at a city near him the next day by 7:00 a.m. and deliver it by 2:00 p.m. While eating his lunch, he can bid on that job, sign his name electronically, and later, if he wins the bid, he receives the confirmation of the job on his truck cab computer, with a map of the exact pickup location. Or a banker can attend meetings being held across the country from her desk, using video conferencing.

The "killer app" of this new work environment is time compression, said Weber, coupled with global reach. With these two capabilities at their fingertips, people will gain competitive advantage.

In the remainder of this chapter, we look at three of these underlying technological developments that are allowing companies to recreate their way of working.

- Mobile computing
- Multimedia
- Internet

MOBILE COMPUTING

There is no doubt that people are becoming increasingly mobile, not only in *where* they live and work but in *how* they live and work. Portability has become one of the strongest selling points in today's market, from travel-size cosmetics to pocket-size video games and CD players to, of course, pagers, mobile phones, and laptop computers.

Three of the driving forces behind mobile computing are the incredible shrinking computer, the widespread use of electronic mail, and wireless WAN communications. We discussed the latter in Chapter 6; we discuss the other two here.

The Incredible Shrinking Computer

Dick Tracy, here we come. The real world is driving toward the comic-book world at blinding speed, and providing more truly personal computing power than comic book artists dreamed possible. Massive computing power is being stuffed into smaller and smaller packages. We are in the age of the incredible shrinking computer.

First there were desktop computers. Then there were "luggables," which felt like bowling balls. Next came true portables—seven-pound PCs that fit inside a briefcase. Then came pen-based clipboard computers, which have had only limited reception. Then came hand-held computers and personal digital assistants—electronic organizers and special function computers that you carry in your pocket.

Hand-held Computers and Personal Digital Assistants. The hand-held computer has been exemplified by the Sharp Wizard, first introduced in 1988. The Wizard was originally intended to be a hand-held electronic organizer small enough to fit inside a coat pocket; but it has been continually enhanced to be much more. At the end of 1996, Sharp introduced the Zaurus, an offshoot of the Wizard family. Its features are shown in Figure 11-2.

The Zaurus can be used to send and receive e-mail via the Internet. Or a pager card can be plugged in so that the office (or the kids) can send messages.

Figure 11-2   Features of the Sharp Zaurus

- 2 megs of memory plus PC card slot to add more memory or a fax/modem card
- Backlit color 5-inch touch screen with 320 x 240 pixels
- Infrared communication
- Serial port to connect a fax modem or transfer data to a PC (the optional fax modem fits on the left side of the keyboard and is often used to hold the Zaurus)
- Requires 2 AA batteries
- Weighs 13.6 ounces and is 6.7" x 3.9" x 1.0"
- Built-in browser, pen-based interface, slide-show software, video and voice capture

---

With the fax modem, documents can be faxed over a cellular phone. The Zaurus can also be connected to a desktop PC, laptop, or other peripherals via infrared or cable for uploading and downloading data. It even has a capability to "grab" information from a remote PC over a communication link, and it has a pen that can be used to create spreadsheets, tables, graphs, or sign a proposal. Plus it has a feature for linking letters or appointments to client records.

Another class of devices in the hand-held family is specialized computers, such as Sony's Data Discman. The size of a paperback book, it can play three-inch CD-ROMs, each of which can hold 100,000 pages of text. It is the world's first hand-held electronic book player. It has a small screen that can display text and simple graphics, plus a keyboard. Although people might not use it to read novels, they will use it to reference catalogs, parts lists, and other reference works.

What is interesting about the hand-held field is that these small multipurpose computers are merging with a class of hand-helds called personal digital assistants (PDAs). These unique portables hit the marketplace in 1993 with the introduction of Apple's Newton. Although the first generation of PDAs did not have the thundering reception that was expected, this class of consumer devices is far from dead.

PDAs are meant to be intelligent assistants, able to store and recall names and addresses, fax notes, and even recognize handprinted letters, pen strokes, and simple shapes. The uniqueness of these machines is represented by their intelligence. Rather than simply performing tasks requested by the user, these devices will be able to perform series of commands and anticipate actions before they are requested. For example, it can format a note into a business letter, supplying the full name and address, salutation, and formatting—perhaps even dial the telephone number to fax it. In short, these little systems are meant to apply their tremendous power to the user interface, making them handy, carry-around digital assistants.

PDAs are likely to come in numerous flavors, some for handling handprinting, maybe even handwriting, and some for performing speech recognition. They will also probably be equipped with card slots for storage or special-purpose programs.

The Widespread Use of Electronic Mail

Although electronic mail has been around since the first computer conferencing in the 1970s, it has only recently become an important element in the corporate information technology infrastructure. IDC [2] claimed it is the corporate backbone for providing a host of enhanced communications services. Specifically, e-mail systems provide the platform for

- integrated voice mail, fax, and person-to-person messaging systems
- work flow and work group applications
- people-to-application communications
- continual communications between mobile employees and their home office
- "mail-enabled applications" via messaging application program interfaces (APIs)

- intercompany transmissions via electronic data interchange (EDI)
- worldwide people-to-people communication via the Internet

Until recently, electronic mail networks were seen simply as the means to distribute text messages among users. Now, however, electronic mail is seen as a main infrastructure component—the piece by which people and computer applications can interact with each other—either through private networks or through the Internet. Although the main use is still people-to-people communication, it can become the middleware for many people-to-application and application-to-application communications as well. The term *mail-enabled applications* refers to the use of application programming interfaces (APIs) for electronic mail systems. These allow applications to interact with each other using popular electronic mail systems as the go-between. The APIs provide standard interfaces between applications and mail systems.

In the 1980s, electronic mail was a primary feature of centralized office automation systems, such as Digital's All-in-1 and IBM's PROFS. These systems allowed internal electronic communications but no links to the outside world. Today, LAN-based e-mail systems have replaced the proprietary ones, and they are used not only for person-to-person messaging but also for automated routing of work. Most recently, e-mail systems have been embedded in Web browsers, making them even more ubiquitous. They have indeed come to be one of the building blocks of the office of the future—wherever that office may reside.

Field Force Automation

The growth of mobile information technologies has thrown open the possibilities of who can use computers and when. Increasingly, the answer is anyone from anywhere at anytime. Companies are taking advantage of portable computers, e-mail, fax, and wireless networks to unleash their field employees from offices. Field force automation is in full swing because traveling employees can maintain the all-important link to their offices from wherever they are located—in their car, a customer's office, an airport, a hotel room, or at home.

To illustrate how two companies are taking advantage of mobile computing to decentralize their business, consider Nissan Motor Corporation/USA and Kraft Foodservice.

CASE EXAMPLE: Nissan Motor Corporation/USA

Nissan Motor Corporation/USA, with headquarters in Carson, California, is decentralizing operations and broadening decision making in its field force by drawing on notebook technology and cellular communications.

As Michael Roney [3] notes, for automobile manufacturers to successfully address niche markets, they must stay in much closer communication with their dealers. It no longer suffices for regional offices to allocate cars to dealers without fully understanding the dealers' current demands and preferences. The way to really understand a market is to live in it, not ask about it from afar.

To achieve this up-close understanding, Nissan decided to move its district managers out of regional offices into the communities they serve. The concept was pilot tested in the Dallas region, where the district managers were equipped with notebook computers with internal modems, Motorola cellular telephones, and hand-held scanners.

Along with a new location and a computer system, the district managers received broader responsibilities in such areas as dealer profitability, sales results, warranty status, and customer satisfaction, reports Roney. Formerly, these responsibilities were handled by different people. By consolidating them, the district managers have more complete relationships with their dealers.

To achieve closer coordination in the other direction—with the region and headquarters—required giving the district managers a way to manage information in more timely, concise, and convenient ways. The new system addresses this need. It allows the district managers to access regional and corporate data to help dealers better forecast monthly sales, more accurately report expenses, and receive better allocations of cars.

The driving goal behind Nissan's field force automation work is moving decision making as close as possible to the point of customer contact. The new system moves them to the dealer showroom, and allows their district managers to stay in continual close contact with the dealers in those showrooms.

CASE EXAMPLE: Kraft Foodservice

Kraft Foodservice, with headquarters in Deerfield, Illinois, provides fresh and frozen food products to restaurants, hospitals, schools, and other institutions. It equipped one-fourth of its sales representatives with notebook computers, reports Roney [3], to improve ordering and delivery of Kraft products. The system covers eight markets and will eventually encompass the full sales force and 45 markets across the United States.

Each night, these sales reps turn on their notebook computers and leave them running. While they sleep, the computer downloads inventory data, sales information, software upgrades, and order status. In the morning, the rep runs the "Good Morning" program, which describes the downloaded items as well as the status of the orders placed the previous day.

The software, which was written by the IS department, provides data on product availability, delivery information, pricing, account status, and purchasing history, says Roney.

One of the major goals of the system was to help the sales reps surmount one of the most frustrating aspects of the business: receiving accurate, up-to-date inventory information for their customers. Those customers want to know exactly how much of their order will be delivered the following day. Using the laptop, the representatives can access the catalog of 8,000 Kraft items whose status has been updated the night before. Based on this daily update, they can confirm customer orders on the spot and ensure an accurate order and prompt delivery.

One of the main challenges in implementing the system is synchronizing training with the technology. Due to the rapid changes in the mobile technology field, Kraft is continually upgrading both the software and hardware in the system. To keep the sales reps apprised of the new features of their systems, Kraft has installed a 24-hour, toll-free hot line to field questions.

MULTIMEDIA

Information delivery is becoming an important responsibility of IS departments, to present information in the most natural ways. Multimedia plays a major role as a front-end to a growing number of systems, and it will be the technology of choice for public access systems.

What is multimedia? A number of definitions are floating around the field. The one we like best came from Christine Hughes [4], who defined it as the combination of time-based media, such as voice, animation, and video, and space-based media, such as text, graphics, and images. Others believe that multimedia means full-motion video. This appears to be the original definition, but that definition has broadened. Most real-life business uses of multimedia do not yet employ full-motion video because it is so expensive. In the long run, as the computing world becomes multimedia, perhaps Nick Arnett's definition will have the most meaning [5]. He says that multimedia computing is not about combining media; it is about choosing the right medium for the message.

In the early 1990s, multimedia became *the* buzzword for selling PC products. The number of multimedia products, such as video capture boards, multimedia authoring tools, CD-ROM products, audio and music production and editing packages, and multimedia clip art, ballooned. Until that time, the multimedia folks had been in a world of their own, creating corporate presentations, movies, television, graphics art, and corporate training.

With the advent of the Web, multimedia has taken yet another step forward; although with slow modems, video from the Web can be splashy but only after it has taken several minutes to download. As the Web demonstrates, the underlying technology for running multimedia applications is hypermedia—the means to navigate through Web sites or other multimedia databases via links.

People used to ask how all the power in a PC would be used. The answer is now clear: to make the interface far more natural and intuitive. These enhanced interfaces, in turn, cause people to want more kinds of information in electronic form.

Developers generally create a multimedia piece using an authoring tool, such as Director, to synchronize sound clips, graphics elements, and still images along a timeline, which Director calls a "score." The fill-in-the-blank score has separate timelines for specifying tempo, color palette, transitions between elements, and graphics, image, sound, and video elements. For adding animation, Director provides over 50 special transition effects, each selectable by clicking on a menu item. It also has selectable options for animating graphics and words—such as bringing words on-screen from any position off-screen, fading in, and so forth—at any speed and following any path the developer wishes.

Using such a tool, a developer can specify a photograph or single frame of video as the background, and overlay it with a voice or music while animated graphics and words appear. So developing multimedia applications is more like making a movie than writing a software program. In fact, most multimedia developers use TV, film, and publishing terminology; multimedia is bringing about the convergence of the publishing, broadcasting, and computer fields.

Two Future Multimedia Interfaces

Multimedia is changing how people interact with computers—not just by presenting data in more natural forms but by permitting new concepts for interacting with computers. To demonstrate such new concepts, two possible future user interfaces that incorporate multimedia are agents and rooms.

Agents. Alan Kay, now an Apple Fellow, was one of the developers of the predecessors of today's graphical user interfaces. In recent speeches, conversations, and articles, he talks about agents becoming a major interface of the future. An agent is an electronic entity that performs tasks, either on its own or at the request of a person or a computer. Agents are often characterized as talking heads on screens; you talk to them, they talk to you. That scenario is a bit futuristic, but it epitomizes how people and agents might work together in a natural, conversational manner.

Rather than manipulate icons, people will manage agents, says Kay. People will have agents that sort their electronic mail and search out items of interest to them from databases and news wires. They may have agents who keep their calendar or format their memos.

When network computing finally arrives, says Kay, the complexity of keeping abreast of all the information available on the networks, and all the people communicating over the networks, will be mind-boggling. People can only handle so many icons on a screen; therefore, this form of user interface becomes totally inadequate in the network environment. People will need agents to act on their behalf, scanning the electronic links for the information they need and filtering the deluge of information they will receive. For more of Kay's ideas on interfaces, see [6].

In an issue of ACM's *Communications of the ACM*, Pattie Maes of MIT's Media Lab [7a] discusses different approaches to building agents. One is to create an end user interface program that consists of a collection of rules for processing information related to a specific task. Once programmed, the agent can run on its own, perhaps filtering news wires for information on specific topics.

A second approach is to endow the interface agent with some domain-specific knowledge. One example is an agent that knows, say, the kinds of entertainment a person likes and can then recommend shows, books, and music the user will like.

A third approach is to allow the agent to learn from a user's use of a system and then program itself to assist the user. In such a system, the agent would acquire its competence from four sources, says Maes. The first is by watching and recording the user's actions and then uncovering recurring patterns or trends. For instance, if the user always stores specific e-mail messages in certain folders, the agent can volunteer to perform that task automatically after each message has been read. Second, the agent can learn from direct or indirect feedback from the user, such as when the user accepts or ignores the agent's suggestion and takes the recommended action or a different action. Third, the agent can learn from examples provided by the user, such as which kinds of news items to retrieve and not retrieve on a specific topic—positive and negative examples. The fourth way the agent can learn is to ask advice from other agents that perform the same task for other users. When the agent is unsure of the action to take in a situation, it can solicit recommendations from others. Once the agent has received initial knowledge for making choices, it can continue to learn from the positive and negative feedback it receives on its choices from the user.

In coordinating the collection of articles in *CACM* on intelligent agents, Doug Riechen of Bell Labs (now Lucent) [7b], notes that there are many important questions that need to be addressed in intelligent agent development work. These include: How should agents and people communicate with each other? How will people trust their agents and instruct them if they make a mistake? Should agents be humanlike or just computer programs? Should agents have emotions? If not, how should they measure their performance relative to human feedback? And can agents improve the performance of humans or groups?

Rooms. The researchers at Xerox PARC, a leading U.S. research lab, talk about their work in an issue of *Benchmark* [8], the quarterly Xerox magazine. They believe future user interfaces will help people visualize information via three-dimensional, animated "rooms" of information. Their "Rooms" research project is based on the idea that people often use time, location, color, or size to find items in their office. The rooms in this futuristic Xerox interface draw on these notions by having items floating in space, with shadows and other visual cues to help people use their perceptual abilities.

The researchers have created a number of kinds of rooms; each holds information in a different way. For example, their "cam room" organizes the top 600 nodes of the Xerox organization chart, and fits it onto one screen. Formerly, this organization chart required 80 pages. The tiered structure contains carousels of names, with reporting relationships shown as translucent cones. Click on a name and the entire structure rotates to bring that name to the forefront. The animation allows the user to continually see the relationships as a new name is brought to the fore. Underneath each name in a hidden layer that can be seen by clicking on a name is the biography and photograph of the job holder.

Another room contains a "time wall," where all the information is organized on a timeline. Click on a month and the wall visually slides by you, bringing the selected month front and center, yet still connected to the other months. This month can be stretched to spread out its files, which appear as though they are floating in space along a timeline.

The goal of the Rooms project is to augment the human intellect, say the researchers, by (1) allowing people to deal with large amounts of interrelated information through visualization, and (2) giving people ways to quickly and easily manipulate the information or structures. These capabilities will allow people to work on larger intellectual problems, they believe. Users of business applications are the intended audience of this PARC research. Eventually, these researchers would like to make the barriers between the paper world and the electronic world disappear altogether.

To demonstrate one use of multimedia for visualizing different forms of data, consider a product that American Airlines offers travel agents; it is called SABREvision.

CASE EXAMPLE: SABREvision

The SABRE Information Network, a division of American Airlines, introduced to travel agents a multimedia adjunct to their text-only SABRE computer reservation system. The system, called SABREvision, presents hotel information via text, color photographs, and maps displayed on a PC.

In 1987, American installed its first PCs in travel agencies. Today, over half of the SABRE terminals are PCs on LANs. SABREvision takes advantage of this PC base.

The purposes of SABREvision are to improve travel agent productivity and profitability while increasing the number of hotel bookings made through SABRE. Prior to SABREvision, agents relied mainly on hotel and travel books because on-line information was insufficient or hard to find. By teaming up with Reed Travel Group, Reed's electronic Jaguar Hotel Directory could be used in conjunction with SABRE. The directory contains textual information on 50,000 hotels, with over 6,600 electronic "pages" with color images and a worldwide mapping system, all stored on one CD-ROM (compact disk, read-only memory) disk. The CD-ROM drive is connected to the file server on each agency's LAN.

An agent can use SABREvision in different ways. One way is to enter a city name and create a list of qualifiers from over 100 provided by the system. For example, a client may want a nonsmoking room in a downtown hotel that provides room service, has a pool and exercise room, offers facsimile service, and costs less than $125 a night. From these qualifiers, the system builds a list of hotels that meet the criteria. Current rates and availability obtained from SABRE are integrated with the local CD-ROM data displayed on the agent's screen. Hotels with images on the system are shown in boldface.

Agents can also call up a map of the area, with the locations of major landmarks and the boldfaced hotels noted. The maps have several levels of magnification and agents can move north, south, east, and west from the on-screen map. Maps, as well as text, can also be printed for clients.

By selecting a hotel listed in boldface, the agent can see color photographs of various aspects of the hotel—a meeting room, a restaurant, a room, the hotel exterior, and an aerial view—along with information about the hotel. Agents can tailor the system by highlighting hotels that their agency prefers and adding comments about individual hotels—to document their experiences or experiences of clients.

Since SABRE and SABREvision are integrated, agents can book a hotel room without leaving SABREvision.

The system, which was developed by North Communications [9], uses three major databases: the map database, the CD-ROM database, and the SABRE host database. The map database is included on the CD that Reed updates each quarter and ships to American, which then distributes the disks to the subscribing agencies.

Testing the friendliness of the user interface as well as the speed of the database searches was done in American's usability lab. The system was tested three times—after each of two prototypes and for the final product. One at a time, specially selected agents spent several hours in the lab performing specific tasks. As they used SABREvision, their actions were videotaped, their thinking-out-loud comments were tape recorded, and analysts watching from another room noted areas that needed revision.

THE INTERNET

No discussion of technological developments would be complete without a discussion of the Internet. In Chapter 6 we discussed the technological side, comparing it to a highway system. Here, we take an end user view. Specifically, we deal with two aspects of the Internet. One is the mindset that exists on the Internet. The other is the important culture of communities that has developed on the Internet.

The Internet Mindset

Just as PCs turned the mainframe data processing mindset upside down, this new world of communications, with its multidimensions and interactivity, wreak havoc with businesses unless they understand and embrace the mindset of the global on-line world. The four components of this mindset are described by Barbara McNurlin and Elizabeth Ghaffari [10], an IS consultant in Los Angeles:

- Communication is personal, not mass market.
- Customer contact is interactive, not broadcast.
- The customer service timeframe is theirs, not yours.
- The culture is bottom up, not top down.

Communication Is Personal, Not Mass Market. The World Wide Web makes a significant break with the past. Its communication is "up close and personal," not top-down mass marketing.

Personalized home pages differ substantively from those of major corporations. Many are personal vanity plates, resembling family photo albums where individuals tell their life story. These pages are alive, interesting, entertaining, humorous, personalized, and constantly changing. Their message to traditional marketing departments is, "Your ad copy is boring, dead."

Other Web pages are owned by frustrated writers who publish their own electronic magazines, called "e-zines." Their message to the publishing industry is, "Your editorial filters are too tight. If you won't pay us to publish our work, we will pay to publish it ourselves." The Web demands that customers be viewed outside the traditional publishing frame of reference. Who is the customer of a magazine, really? Is it the reader? Or might it be the writer? What are people willing to pay for?

Some corporate Web pages are stuck in the traditional advertising model, merely duplicating the printed page but in the new graphical, dynamic, and global medium. Large brand-name companies have littered the on-line world with digital equivalents of paper-based coupons. They're using the wrong mindset: mass market rather than personal.

Customer Contact Is Interactive, Not Broadcast. The single most important point of view to take toward the Internet is to view it as interactive, not broadcast: incoming, not outgoing. It is a get-the-message, listen-to-the-customer, capture-the-feedback milieu. In essence, the Internet is a customer's window to companies. And it is substantially different from TV because customers can initiate communications with a firm rather than merely react to its ads. They can express satisfaction or dissatisfaction with products. And they can suggest improvements they would like to see in products. Today's consumers are more self-sufficient and intelligent than their parents. They want to define what custom-made means to them.

The best example of on-line consumer-initiated communications is in the area of medical self-help information. Every major Internet service provider now has forums or conference areas where individuals can peruse medical information, outside the parameters of the American Medical Association. While the medical establishment bemoans "snake oil salesmen," the Internet gives consumers a way to search for the information they want on their own terms. Departments or groups that use the Internet for such interaction will succeed because they will tap this huge, latent resevoir of customer needs, current thinking, and goodwill.

Customer-initiated dialog supported by the Internet will significantly challenge marketing departments, customer support groups, and fulfillment folks. The eight-week turnaround from postcards in once-a-month magazines, for example, will pale in comparison with just-in-time delivery of information requested by customers.

The Customer Service Timeframe Is Theirs, Not Yours. Through the Internet, customers are closer than most companies have ever experienced. In fact, they are closer than most companies can handle. For example, how can a company that serves customers one at a time and answers its phones, "All of our agents are busy . . .", ever hope to handle tens of thousands of "hits" (customer inquiries) from on-line requests for the latest product and pricing data?

Being "put on hold" will increasingly irk customers. Companies that stay with this level of disservice use the wrong mindset. Today's consumers are busy folks. They have little patience with waiting. In the Internet world, they can do two or more things at once, performing several tasks using multiple windows and fast comparison shopping. As with TV remote controls, customers that do not get immediate satisfaction will switch to the competition with a point and a click.

This more intimate customer environment means that companies can hear directly, "I couldn't find your product in three stores today. Where do I get it?" without the protective layers of intermediaries or other buffers. Firms that have the organization in place to listen and respond to these closer voices of customers will hold on to those customers. Others could lose them.

Thus, before an IS department can assist other departments in exploring the Internet world, it needs to assess its proposed Internet business solutions using a new metric: "Will our firm's Internet strategy truly help all our customers communicate with us?"

The Culture Is Bottom Up, Not Top Down. The Internet is not the expert's world, where the few impart their knowledge to the many. In this information-intense world, "netizens" know that "together, we know more than any one of us alone."

This lesson even holds true for government officials who think they know what's best for their constituents. Recently, in Spokane, local officials tried to levy a 6 percent tax on Internet providers. Netizens revolted and inundated city fathers with e-mail and phone calls. So a Web site was established to gather their thoughts on the proposal.

The message is as clear for IS departments. IS cannot work in the top-down, broadcast mode, "I'm IS and I'm the expert, so here's your solution, customer." More than ever, IS must get input from its customers to determine the services they want, when they want them, and where they want them.

The traditional hierarchical expert model, where IS designed solutions, followed by tests, migration, acceptance, and maintenance, will no longer work. The customers of IS, too, can go elsewhere to find the expertise they need. They can "browse" the Internet to review Hewlett-Packard's lower-cost and lower-maintenance servers, view EDS's recommended best business practices posted on-line, or download MCI's modeling software to compare alternative network costs in their market.

Furthermore, IS departments that are studying the feasibility of putting up a corporate home page to hold the parts catalog, or are talking to marketing about designing on-line ads, are using the outdated broadcast, top-down, mass market mindset. Departmental customers are one step ahead of that. They are sending e-mail asking when the latest release of Java will be available because they want to develop applets so that suppliers can perform their own keyword searches on the parts inventory.

Rather than merely dump traditional corporate copy onto the Internet, the IS department needs to create channels for its departmental customers to continually communicate with other parts of the firm and alliance firms. Furthermore, it needs to help its company view customers through a finer, more timely mesh than ever before.

To hear from customers directly, without intermediaries, is both a gold mine and a massive challenge to those with a broadcast mindset. To truly take advantage of this gold mine requires viewing the Internet as an interactive medium and redesigning the corporate listening mechanisms to hear and understand all that feedback—straight from the customer.

Internet Communities

The Internet can be seen as a network that provides new kinds of "spaces": a world of on-line communities, of virtual chat rooms, of three-dimensional virtual worlds. This cyberspace paradigm is very different from the highway one. In essence, it is a virtual universe that exists in parallel to our physical universe. People can join a deeply personal community (at 2 a.m., for instance) and talk about the things that really terrify them, such as what it's like to live with a spouse with Alzheimer's disease. Or they can (if they wish) adopt many personae (creating avatars or virtual beings) that are far different from what they are in real life. They can have adventures unencumbered by physical laws and physical reality.

We believe that any talk of telecom needs to encompass both the highway view and the cyberspace view. The job of corporate executives, IS staff, and even company employees is to leverage both views for the good of the enterprise. Therefore, we now spend a bit of time talking about Internet communities.

In the *Harvard Business Review*, Arthur Armstrong and John Hagel III [11], both of McKinsey & Company, point out that the notion of community has been at the heart of the Internet since its inception, with scientists and academics forming on-line research communities. More recently, on-line users have joined scores of different kinds of communities on Prodigy and America Online.

And yet, say Armstrong and Hagel, commercial enterprises have been slow to understand the community-building capabilities of the Net or make use of them. If they did, they could build customer loyalty that far surpasses what is possible off-line, say the authors.

Armstrong and Hagel believe that electronic communities meet four needs. *Communities for transaction* mainly facilitate buying and selling. Most of these have not been communities in the classical sense, but they could be. For example, people wanting to buy a used car might want to chat with others on-line. *Communities of interest* bring together people to talk about particular subjects—gardening, investments, wrestling, the Grateful Dead, and on and on. One of the most interesting has been the Motley Fool on AOL. David and Tom Gardner host this personal investment community where people comment on the Gardners' stock portfolio. The result is both information and entertainment, note Armstrong and Hagel. *Communities of relationship*, which have developed around life experiences, can be quite intense because people talk about troubling personal experiences, such as addictions, traumas, and life-threatening illnesses—as they are living through them. People can be unusually candid about their feelings, and as a result, people within these communities can form deep personal bonds. *Communities of fantasy* are the fourth kind of on-line community. This is where people take on different personae and act out all kinds of fantasies.

Fantasy On-Line

For some, the *real cyberspace* is this fantasy world—or, more accurately, an infinite number of virtual fantasy worlds—that exists without our physical limitations or even societal norms. In this cyberspace, there are chat rooms, Multi-User Dungeons (MUDs)—social virtual-reality places—and more recently, animated and verbal three-dimensional virtual worlds where people choose an avatar (an identity) and cruise around talking to others.

The foremost researcher of this world is Sherry Turkle, of MIT [12], whose book, *Life on the Screen: Identity in the Age of the Internet*, is the first serious book on the multiple personalities that people live through in cyberspace, says Pamela McCorduck in her profile of Turkle in *Wired* magazine [13]. Turkle says that we are moving away from a computer culture of calculations and rules to a computer culture of simulation, navigation, and interaction. For example, *Sim-Life* is a simulation game where the goal is to interrelate creatures and habitat to create a sustainable world. It is about making choices, getting feedback, and giving the creatures a kind of aliveness.

The new spaces in which millions of people congregate on the Net are changing how they think and the way they form communities. In this culture of simulation, she says, people play out their fantasies and perhaps use that life that they create in the MUDs to become comfortable with new ways of thinking about evolution, relationships, sexuality, politics, and identity. For anyone interested in the postmodern world, her writings are a must. She believes that cyberspace is a true postmodern world.

Turkle talks about "windows," which she says allow people to be in several contexts at one time—e-mail, word processing, and a chat room. This distributed self gets people to think of themselves as existing in many worlds, playing many roles, all at one time. And real life can be just one of those windows.

MUDs are a new form of community, says Turkle. They take place in a facsimile of a physical space—a church, a courtyard, a closet—and they have been text based. As a result, they have created a new form of collaborative literature, where the MUD players are both authors and consumers. But, says Turkle, the players actually become authors of themselves, constructing a new self—one that exists only in that MUD—as they converse with other characters. The players are anonymous, so they can express unexplored aspects of themselves, try on new identities, become the opposite sex, become a different species, and perhaps switch among several MUD personae at one time. Some people have even told Turkle that they feel more like "themselves" when "MUDding" because they don't feel as limited as in physical space.

It's a new and far freer form of self expression. Some people can get lost in these virtual idealized worlds, far preferring them to their physical world. Therefore, says Turkle, we cannot think of life in cyberspace as insignificant. We must understand the dynamics of these virtual experiences to foresee who might put them to best (and worst) use. Some will use their experiences to enrich their physical lives; others may not. Her important message is that this computer culture foreshadows what will be important in the larger culture in the future, so it needs to be taken seriously.

The idea of businesses purposely encouraging on-line communities is a new world worth pondering. Some could conceivably encourage, or sponsor, fantasy worlds. Others could host communities of interest or communities of relationship. We think this new world is one that IS and line managers need to ponder.

CONCLUSION

In the first three editions of this book, much of the excitement in computing related to PCs and end user computing. That excitement continues, unabated, but in the now-expanded universe of mobile computing, reaching out to consumers, and the Internet. The opportunities for IS departments to serve new audiences grows as computers shrink, as communications become untethered from wires and strands of glass, and as the Internet provides a whole new world of possibilities. That has been the subject of this chapter: the exciting new technological developments that have expanded the computing horizon. The challenge becomes putting those technologies to good use. We address this challenge in the next chapter, by discussing how information system management can support the use of these new developments.

REVIEW QUESTIONS

1. Describe how the universe of corporate computing has expanded.
2. According to Weber, what are the six technologies underlying the new work environment?
3. What is a personal digital assistant? What makes it unique from the other portables?
4. What are seven potential uses of electronic mail networks?
5. Why is Kraft Foodservice using portable computers?
6. What is multimedia?
7. What are agents? What will they do?
8. According to Maes, what are four ways a learning agent can learn?
9. Describe Xerox PARC's Rooms interface.
10. What is SABREvision? Why is it an improvement for travel agents?
11. What are the four mindsets of the Internet?
12. What are four types of communities?
13. According to Turkle, we are moving away from computer cultures of calculations and rules to what kind of cultures?

DISCUSSION QUESTIONS

1. Doug Riecken asks a number of intriguing questions relating to agents. Two are "Should intelligent agents have emotions?" "How will people trust their agents and instruct them if they make a mistake?" State your opinion on one of these questions. Discuss.
2. The original Internet culture, described by Ghaffari and McNurlin as four mindsets, is not going to last. It is going to revert to the mass communication mindset of TV and Madison Avenue. Do you agree or disagree? Discuss.
3. All that cyberspace stuff about communities, MUDs, and avatars has nothing whatsoever to do with "real" business. We can ignore all that. Discuss.

EXERCISES

1. Talk to three people who use a hand-held or PDA computer. What do they like about it? What would they change? How can it be improved? Share their ideas with the class.
2. Read three articles about intelligent agents. What new information did you learn that is not in the text? Share that with the class.
3. Visit a local information systems department and find out how it is using portable computers, electronic mail, multimedia, and the Internet. Summarize your visit for the class.
4. Experience an on-line community and report your impressions to the class.

REFERENCES

1. UCLA I/S ASSOCIATES PROGRAM, headed by Dr. Lewis Leeburg, The Anderson School at UCLA, June 1996.

2. "ELECTRONIC MAIL: THE NEW CORPORATE BACKBONE," IDC White Paper inserted into *Computerworld*, June 22, 1992.

3. RONEY, M. "Special Report: Corporate Computing," *Mobile Office*, December 1991, pp. 35-42.

4. HUGHES,CHRISTINE, The Myriad Group, P.O. Box 142075, Coral Gables, FL 33114.

5. ARNETT, NICK, Multimedia Computing Corporation, 3501 Ryder St., Santa Clara, CA 95051.

6. KAY, A., "User Interface: A Personal View," in *The Art of Human-Computer Interface Design*, Brenda Laurel, ed. (Reading, MA: Addison-Wesley, 1990).

7. *COMMUNICATIONS OF THE ACM*, ACM, 1515 Broadway, New York, NY 10036, July 1994.

   a. MAES, PATTIE, "Agents That Reduce Work and Information Overload," pp. 31-40.

   b. RIECKEN, DOUG, "Intelligent Agents," pp. 18-21.

8. "ROOMS WITH A VIEW," *Benchmark*, (Xerox Corporation, 101 Continental Blvd., El Segundo, CA 90245), Summer 1990, pp. 10-12; free to Xerox customers.

9. NORTH COMMUNICATIONS, 3030 Pennsylvania Ave., Santa Monica, CA 90404.

10. GHAFFARI, ELIZABETH and BARBARA MCNURLIN, "The Internet Mindset," unpublished paper. Elizabeth Ghaffari, President, Technology Place, 2807 Highland Ave., Suite 5, Santa Monica, CA 90405, techplace@earthlink.net.

11. ARMSTRONG, ARTHUR and JOHN HAGEL III, "The Real Value of On-Line Communities," *Harvard Business Review*, May–June 1996, pp. 134-141.

12. TURKEL, SHERRY, "Who Am We?" *Wired*, January 1996, pp. 149-152+; excerpts from her book *Life on the Screen: Identity in the Age of the Internet,* Simon and Schuster, 1995.

13. MCCORDUCK, PAMELA "Sex, Lies, and Avatars," *Wired*, 520 3rd St., 4th floor, San Francisco, CA 94107, http://www.hotwired.com, April 1996, pp. 106-110+.

TWELVE

Supporting the Expanding Universe of Computing

INTRODUCTION

In this chapter we address ways in which information systems management can respond to the expanding universe of users and the expanding universe of information technologies. We begin with an intriguing assessment of the predisposition of individuals, groups, departments, and even companies toward new technologies. This discussion sets the groundwork for exploring how IS departments can support specific new technological developments.

THE TECHNOLOGY CAMEL

Individuals, work groups, departments, even business units have different levels of eagerness concerning any new technology. Therefore, if the IS department is truly going to help them use a new technology, such as the Internet, IS needs to understand their comfort level. Elizabeth Ghaffari and Barbara McNurlin [1] present the following guidelines on how to do this. They cite the Yankee Group and Find/SVP, two market research firms, as distinguishing levels of comfort with technology using five clusters. The Yankee Group uses these clusters to describe the 100 million U.S. households and how they view contemporary technology:

- 1/2 million are innovators, constantly sniffing out new technologies
- 5 million are early adopters of new technologies
- 30–35 million are early majority households
- 40–50 million are late majority households
- 10–15 million are technically averse

The Technology Camel. When graphed on a chart, these clusters look a lot like a two-humped camel, note Ghaffari and McNurlin. It is lying on its stomach with its nose inside a tent—say, the Internet technology tent. The first cluster is his nose as he nudges the flaps of the tent. The second is his slowly rising neck. The third and fourth are his two big humps. And the fifth cluster is his rump. See Figure 12-1.

In marketing parlance, these five groups represent the spectrum from chomping-at-the-bit innovators (the camel's nose) to those who prefer to leave new technologies well enough alone (his rump). These concepts hold equally well for business users, departments, companies, and industries as for U.S. households.

For greatest success, IS departments would do well to first benchmark their customers, employees, and business units against these groupings, then introduce the new technology, such as the Net, in a manner that reflects each cluster's willingness and ability to assimilate this new technology. Here are the different possible strategies for assisting each group to utilize the Internet at its comfort level.

Eager Beavers: The Innovators and Pioneers

The smallest group is the noisiest: the zealots, proselytizers, salespeople, writers, and Internet server owners. They are ecstatic about the Internet. Everything about it, by definition, is pretty wonderful.

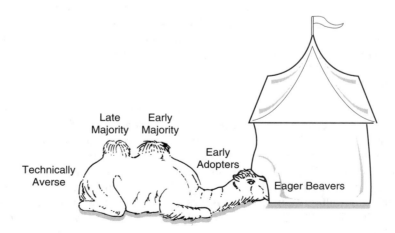

Figure 12-1   The Technology Camel (from Ghaffari and McNurlin [1])

In 1996, this group was talking about Java (the language that runs single-function applications that can include motion, interactivity, and, soon, three-dimensional virtual reality) and HotJava (the enhanced browser to view all that Java promises). They are now excited about electronic commerce over the Net. They rave about telephoning and teleconferencing via the Net. These pioneers are so far out ahead of mainstream technology that most people just shake their heads and think to themselves, "Talk to me in a year; that stuff's not relevant to me now."

Most of these people are in software and hardware companies, where their enthusiasm and vision might be an asset. Some large IS departments have an advanced technology group charged with tracking new technologies and determining when and how to begin testing and implementation. In the average corporation, however, they can be a money drain, if they are given the reins to lead the company into new technologies too early. If, for instance, innovators had convinced management to jump on the Web in 1995 with the then-latest version of Mosaic, by early 1996, IS would have had to retool to migrate to either Netscape Navigator or to one of the product strategies introduced as the Microsoft Network. And then retool again in early 1997 with the integrated browser suites. That company would have spent a lot of money just to say they were part of the leading edge.

The recommended IS approach to the eager beavers is to support them with some funding and to learn from them. Perhaps 1 to 3 percent of the IS budget is enough for R&D, provided there are some business objectives being supported. But let the market shake out the hype before investing much more in their ideas. If, on the other hand, being at the leading edge of technology is a company's business, these folks need to be supported with more money. In other cases, companies take a big risk following these zealots.

Early Adopters: The First Consumers

In 1996, companies could barely constrain early adopters of Internet technology. They were the disciples' apostles, not too far behind the innovators. They were pushing to get corporate data on the World Wide Web. They probably even had their own home pages.

IS can recognize early adopters by their glassy stare over the top of their PC magazines and their "Gee whiz, I've gotta get me one" mentality. They are the ones who stood in line for hours to get Windows 95 at midnight August 23, 1995. They also bought a lot of BetaMaxs, 8-reel tapes, and CB radios. They have a lot of discretionary income and tend to think the corporation does too.

In the Internet world, an early adopter company was Time/Warner with its Pathfinder home page: a glossy, flashy, gee-whiz kind of page. Or HotWired's new, dynamic, MTV kind of place. Neither made money, but "hey, they were hot stuff." Early adopters' personalized home pages were vanity sites with individual photographs, their collected writings in an electronic magazine (their own "e-zine" discussing the future of the Internet) among other digital clippings in that great time capsule called the Web.

Companies could miss a market by ignoring these folks. But they need to be managed. They need IS's help and encouragement, but they should not be allowed to overwhelm their department or the company. Use them to generate showpieces, a few early successes, but do not let them run the company's Internet presence because they will blow any budget and may not want to listen to the customer feedback which their success might generate. Monitor their performance like a hawk. And make sure they invest their own money in their experiments.

Early Majority: The First Big Wave

The first of two big consumption waves include the folks, departments, and companies that say they are willing to use new technologies, but they need some help to make it happen. They are not the self-sufficient pioneers nor the risktakers. In the Internet world, they want to put up Web sites because they see the on-line world as a way of offloading the escalating burdens they face due to outsourcing, downsizing, and reengineering. They have hit information overload, but they think home pages are positive, interesting, and challenging. However, they are confused by the terminology, the proliferation of products and services, and the multitude of options for creating a site—and they have no time to learn a lot about this new stuff. It looks like chaos to them. "Is it worth my time, money, and support costs to do this?" they ask.

These early majority folks tend to be in relatively important positions in the organization, so they can make or break the introduction of a new technology, even more so than top management. The real business impact of a new technology depends on what these early majority folks do with that technology. So IS management needs to understand how they view the company, customers, and competition. Then help them choose a strategy to expand their familiarity with, say, the Internet at a self-paced rate that can be incorporated into the way their group does business. If the Internet does not help them work better, it is not worth IS's time or money.

Early majority folks want to be informed. They want to understand, not just swallow the hype of the innovators and early adopters. They want to feel secure enough to say, "Yes, our customer feedback form is producing results. Now, we're ready to expand the service." IS has to be ready to listen, on the other hand, when they say, "No, I don't like this new groupware package because it takes too long to access while a customer is waiting."

So IS management must become adept at creating options that can be tested for acceptance or rejected if they do not match needs. At the same time, IS will be doing a lot of training and explaining to these folks. Do they want to set up Web home pages? Hold work group dialogs? Do on-line business research? Investments with this group are well placed. Before approaching these folks, however, IS needs to understand the nontechnical products and services that consume these folks' time and attention. Learn about their business.

Web pages are not the only option that could benefit the business. IS can deliver other Internet capabilities to early majority folks, including aggressive use of electronic mail or groupware scheduling tools to help them become more productive within the organization.

Work groups in different locations can communicate and share project information securely using on-line resources. Educated use of the Internet can empower them to reach outside of their own group to tap the research resources of the work, whether in California, New York, Hawaii, or Finland and Australia. IS's challenge is to educate these folks on how to share information electronically in a manner that supports and serves the corporation's business goals and objectives.

Late Majority: The Technology Skeptics

Late majority people, departments, and companies are not afraid of a technology, but they do have serious concerns about risks and costs. They are concerned about wasting time and money searching for information on the technologies, and the kinds of investments needed to make solid, informed decisions about what it will do for them. Technology skeptics also ask questions about whether the company's clients really will benefit from the technology or whether early users are just a bunch of lookie-loos out for a free ride.

On the Internet scene, late majority folks are waiting for some of the key issues to be resolved: security, compatibility, standards, bandwidth, simplicity. In fact, they would prefer to wait until the major telecommunications firms make the Web as simple to use as the telephone or TV. "Call me when it's ready," they say. They own a lot of the information content that would do well on the Internet. But they are hesitant, arguing that, "We can't put the corporate catalog on the Internet until we can guarantee that hackers won't change our prices."

Schools traditionally have dominated the late majority sector because they have faced such severe budget pressures. They bought Apples in the mid-1980s and still have most of them in their classrooms. Today, however, schools are becoming much better negotiators for bottom-dollar deals. The corporate late majority will likewise have to come out of its fiduciary shell very soon.

For these late majority folks, IS management needs to be as prepared to address risks and costs as they are to address technology opportunities. IS needs to show an appreciation of bottom-line concerns and address security questions at the level that late majority people can appreciate. It is not necessary for corporations to put their storefront in its entirety on the Web. IS can point to examples, such as Lands End and Eddie Bauer, where on-line information is an adjunct to traditional information delivery methods. Web sites can be a sales sampling resource, isolated and independent of the private, internal corporate network. As a complementary source of advertising, the Internet can also be used to broaden exposure to new potential buyers in the on-line community without sacrificing the reputation and the relationship with established clientele.

Technically Averse: "Not on My Time You Don't"

The people, departments, and companies who resist technology are not currently considering doing anything on the Internet. In many cases, their concerns about loss of privacy, security, control, and possible exposure to competition override any perceivable benefits.

Two industries that have traditionally been technology averse are real estate and publishing. Real estate has a sunk cost and protected monopoly position over multiple-listing books. Publishing has a sunk cost and a protected monopoly position over local media and advertisements. It is rare, but there are some breakthrough cases in these two industries—generally by companies capturing niches by going outside the system. In real estate, for instance, a few have set up Web pages to advertise directly to customers—bypassing the realty infrastructure. And traditional publishing media have been the source of the strongest criticism of the Internet and its problems. In part, they simply don't know how to take advantage of it, yet.

To guide them, IS first needs to understand their concerns. They have justifiable business fears, which need to be identified and addressed before there can be any thought of using a new technology for business purposes. The challenge here is education, not applications. These people need the greatest amount of time to assimilate all the change taking place in their lives. Only then can IS help them explore the potential.

The message, then, is for the IS department to recognize and acknowledge each cluster's concerns about new technology, and then develop a multitiered approach to respond to the diverse concerns.

SUPPORTING END USERS

End user computing (EUC) began as the way to introduce employees to computers in the 1970s and 1980s. During the 1980s, EUC gradually merged with mainline computing rather than being treated as a separate entity, as it originally started. The work of training end users, and then supporting their computing needs, became centralized in IS organizational units called information centers. Information centers were yesterday's response to the need to bring end user computing into firms, mainly via personal computers. The watchword of information centers was "support." Support and train every interested employee on every type of product. The centers focused on conducting training classes, staffing help desks, and doing troubleshooting consulting. Their main goal was to help employees become self-sufficient in using computers and creating their own applications.

Generally, information centers did not grow very large, no matter what the size of the firm. In one case, 35 staff members were serving 10,000 employees. The staff members became experts in specific products and specialized in either mainframe or PC products. To bring some control to the rapidly proliferating number of PCs, information center managers initiated hardware and software standards.

Top management believed that once employees were given PCs and a few hours of training, they would become self-sufficient. Therefore, after the first few years of dramatic growth, information centers were not given more resources. In fact, top management expected them to go away, believing they were no longer needed. Interestingly, the lack of funding gave rise to a problem that few information system executives knew about: "the PC guru," people who became so enamored with a PC product or application that they promoted its use wherever they could. They became the bane of information centers because they often promoted nonstandard products. The cost of undoing problems caused by PC gurus may have been high, but it was only seen by information center managers. Many line and systems managers thought these gurus were doing the firm a favor by devoting some of their time to helping others with computing. This would be true, *if* they were following company policies and standards.

Supporting Today's End Users

Yesterday's information center performed its job in helping employees learn about computing, but that is not today's environment. So the information center solution, as originally conceived, is no longer the answer in most large firms, but the lessons are still valuable.

Today's end user computing environment differs markedly from the 1980s' environment. Everyone who could be called a "power user"—that is, someone who takes the initiative to learn how to use computer applications in their work—now has a computer. And employees who use PCs generally know quite a bit about the computer products they use. Therefore, when they run into a problem, their requests and questions are complex, difficult, and time-consuming to answer. Furthermore, end user computing has evolved into a demand-pull environment, where users may want new products faster than the support staff can provide them.

As a result, today's response to end user support has become the help desk and its multiple tiers of assistance. The following case study of a computer company's response to this changing end user support environment is based on a presentation given at an Ernst & Young IS Leadership Forum [2]. It demonstrates how the company reduced its dependence on technical help-line specialists, moved support into the business units, decreased support costs, and increased the computing knowledge level in the firm.

CASE EXAMPLE: A Computer Company

When the company faced the computing industry's price wars a few years back, the IS department, like the other departments, had to cut back significantly. To handle the situation, the department created a war room in order to develop a plan and implement it within one month's time. The eight heads of IS from across the company met for two weeks to craft their plans and strategies. Every aspect of the department's work was challenged. The eight decided to reengineer IS based on four major objectives: (1) be a leader in supporting end users, (2) facilitate cross-functional decision making, (3) encourage the flow of information across the decentralized business units, and (4) target the bulk of all new investments to new applications, thus minimizing investments in operations and support. Since new development was not to be cut, most of the cuts would come from support. Head count was to be cut by one-fourth.

Reengineering the Help Desk

One area that absorbed its share of cuts was help-line support. Upon investigation, management found six specialized help centers, each focusing on particular applications. Furthermore, there were three tiers of support for the desktop (local assistance, help-line, and on-site technicians); therefore, problems were not always solved quickly and there was too much infrastructure. Many of the experts who staffed the help desks sat waiting for the phone to ring. This did not add value.

The group was chartered to take a companywide view of employee support, which consisted of three main support components: help line, product distribution and services, and repair/troubleshooting. The central support function was redesigned into a virtual center to be located in several places, to serve the entire company, and to provide training as well as support for the desktop. The main center was relocated to a less expensive region of the United States, and the company recruited local community college computer science majors as interns to staff the help lines. The students wanted to work part-time off hours for as long as they were in school. The company had similar goals—a lower-cost, technical work force willing to work off hours.

In restructuring, head count dropped from 98 to 63. These 63 provide hardware and software upgrade support, work the help line, provide tools training and desktop repair, and handle network repairs. Overseas hardware/network repair work was handled by other support people. The help-line staff supported all 40 major applications—manufacturing, human resources, finance, sales, and so forth—for employees around the world.

The help-line staff performs problem tracking, escalation, and resolution. This data showed that 85 percent of all calls were handled on the first phone call.

Getting Software Closer to Users

In addition, the company decided that it was important to get the right software into the hands of the users. The company does not dictate software standards, but it does recommend certain hardware and software products by supplying and supporting only those products.

To make supported technologies easy to obtain, the company expanded its program that delivers supported computing products—both hardware and software—once a week to 70 locations. Employees can therefore get supported products in about five minutes. Formerly, this program served only 20 percent of company locations. Following the reorganization, it was expanded to serve all sites. Each quarter, the center also distributes CDs containing site-licensed software to technical coordinators. This has become the most valued software within the company. Both distribution methods have received high marks from the field. Given a choice, most employees will opt to use a supported product rather than order a special, unsupported product, for two reasons. First, the supported product is available immediately, and second, the local technical coordinator will help install it or help with a problem. Employees also prefer the hand delivery mode over electronic mail because they receive the user manual as well as the software, and they do not need to tie up their machine for the 30-minute electronic download.

Increasing the Importance of Technical Coordinators

Concurrently, the company wanted to increase the number and role of its technical coordinators. These are volunteer users who spend 5 percent of their time making sure the work group near them has the latest software and a functioning network. They are considered part of the virtual support center and are the first line of support for all employees with computer problems.

Rather than add extra work for technical employees, the IS department consciously targeted administrative staff for this role to elevate their skills. But technical coordinators do not become IS employees. They remain in their job function. Five people in the help center support the technical coordinator program and there is currently one technical coordinator to every 15 employees. Interestingly, the technical coordinators' locations correspond to the worldwide population of the company.

The technical coordinator program grew by grass roots. Most often they were administrative staff, and they seem to be self-selecting highly motivated employees. They are trained and certified as system experts. They mainly use self-paced training, often during off hours. But, in addition, they attend brown bag lunches, billed as "a feast for your brain." At some, suppliers give training and product reviews. At others, they see video presentations. They also have an annual conference, funded by the IS department. It is both a reward and a training experience. One year it was held at Disneyland. At this week-long training, hundreds of workstations are networked and run simulated hardware and software problems. The technical coordinators receive hands-on training.

The technical coordinators are given a lot of recognition. They receive a banner in their cube with a designation of their skill level—apprentice, certified technical coordinator, or champion. An apprentice has not yet taken all the courses. A certified technical coordinator has taken the minimum number of courses, used the self-paced learning, and passed a competency test. And an information champion—a name they chose for themselves—has completed all the training and passed a competency test. The banner has been powerful; it is widely respected throughout the company.

Twice a year, the IS department meets with the managers of technical coordinators, encouraging them to recruit additional technical coordinators so that no one is overburdened. Managers now realize how productive their groups become with a technical coordinator in their midst. Most managers actively encourage people to volunteer.

In all, the technical coordinator program has saved the company large amounts of money in computer support, it has provided valuable services to work groups via local employees, and it has increased the level of computing know-how in the company.

The new organization surpassed expectations. The new virtual support center exceeded its work force reduction goal and even delivered more with less. Call volume increased 300 percent, yet due to a new call-tracking system, wait time was reduced from 10 minutes to 30 seconds. The center receives about two kudos a day. Some employees even send flowers. There has been much positive reinforcement, especially from new managers who sincerely appreciate the staff's assistance in helping them do their job. So the center is seen as adding value and decreasing the amount of time needed to get systems up and working.

ENCOURAGING THE USE OF MULTIMEDIA

As we noted in Chapter 11, the driving force behind the use of multimedia, in proprietary systems as well as on the Web, is to make the use of computers more natural by broadening the ways computers and people communicate with one another. We see multimedia to be important in two areas:

- To help people cope with a more complex environment
- To create more knowledgeable users

Multimedia will become increasingly important because it is a vastly better—that is, more understandable and more usable—way to present electronic information.

To Cope with Complexity

The business world is becoming more complex. Companies are analyzing more product characteristics in order to target their goods and services to more finely defined consumer groups. Businesses are speeding up their business processes. To become more dynamic, they are keeping track of more variables in a more timely manner. Firms are offering better and faster customer service by keeping more records at their representatives' fingertips. And firms are attracting employees by offering more flexible, and more complex, employment terms.

Two uses of multimedia have emerged to help people deal with such complexity. One helps people grasp complex information and concepts more easily. This is the area of interactive multimedia Web sites. The second helps people cope with large amounts of data; this is data visualization.

Interactive Web Sites. Multimedia is becoming the front-end of choice on intranets in the form of corporate Web pages to house all manner of corporate information in accessible, easy-to-use form. One example is corporate Web pages to help employees tailor the company's benefit plan to their needs. Flexible benefits plans have become very, very complex because they offer a myriad of options in dental plans, vacation time, sick pay, stock purchases, giving, and so forth. Since few human resources employees know the details of all the options, many companies are turning to multimedia Web pages to help their employees select the options that best fit their lifestyle. These systems can contain video clips of experts explaining the options in such areas as dental insurance, child care, health insurance, vacation time, and so forth. The various segments in the system can be controlled by an expert system, which answers an employee's question by showing the appropriate segment. The system is interactive in that it lets employees actually select the options they want on-line. Or they can send an e-mail message to the HR department if they have a question.

Data Visualization Systems. The possibility of seeing the unseeable through computer simulations is opening up to more and more potential users as the price of computer power drops. Thomas DeFanti and Daniel Sandin established the Electronic Visualization Laboratory at the University of Illinois at Chicago in the late 1970s [3]. They and their staff and students have been concentrating on visualization in scientific computing, which is the interactive use of computer graphics animation to study scientific problems. At its best, it combines the number-crunching power of the computer with the pattern recognition capabilities of people interactively.

More recently, the staff members turned their attention to the financial services industry. They held a week-long workshop where seven financial experts each worked with a graduate student to see how interactive graphics could help them visualize financial data.

One of the two-person teams worked on the traveling salesman problem— that is, finding the shortest route through a number of points scattered over a geographic area. The team found that by letting a person first create a rough path among the many points, and then giving that approximation to the computer to refine, that the problem got solved very fast—in a few seconds of elapsed time. People are good at seeing large gaps among points and avoiding them. Had the computer been given this problem to do on its own, it would have taken hours, if not days, to solve. This example illustrates the power of a person and a computer working interactively on a problem using graphical data.

Another team wanted to see if they could predict interest rate changes for the upcoming six months by matching the current partial patterns with past completed patterns. Once the user selected a section of the trend line, the computer searched the remaining data for a similar pattern, and highlighted the best matches it found. Then the financial analysts studied those to find the best match.

Such visualization work in the business realm is new, but DeFanti, Sandin, and their staff believe that some of the lessons they are learning about scientific visualization can be applied to business problems as well.

At a MacWorld conference, we saw an interesting demonstration along these same lines. The product, MacSpin, from Abacus Concepts [4], allows statistical data to be plotted in a simulated three-dimensional space. The demonstration plotted automobile data, where each point represented one make of car in one year, with three variables: miles per gallon, weight, and price. The plot could be rotated to show the clusters of points from different angles. Groups of points could also be highlighted to compare American, Japanese, and European cars. For example, the points could even be animated to show changes in miles per gallon over time. The differences between car makes and trends in their characteristics became very clear once shown in these various ways.

Those professionals who need to study reams of data to uncover patterns will find data visualization a boon to their work. They include market researchers studying buying trends, corporate executives determining locations for new plants and offices, and analysts studying trends in products.

For More Knowledgeable Users

Another great promise of multimedia is training. Companies are in dire need of better and more cost-effective ways to train and educate their people, and perhaps even train consumers on the use of their products and services. Multimedia can addresses these needs.

On-Demand Training. The main trend in this area is just-in-time training, sometimes called on-demand training—where people can access training whenever they need it via their workstation. Systems with embedded training are being called performance systems because they contribute to increasing job performance. One example is an automobile diagnostic system to help mechanics diagnose and repair today's increasingly electronics-laden cars. It contains an expert system that suggests tests the mechanic can run to isolate the problem. The context-sensitive help assists the mechanic in performing these tests, via graphics, schematics, and printed instructions. The system also helps the mechanic fix the problem.

Training via Simulation. In other cases, training is stand-alone, not embedded in an application. Using multimedia, simulation becomes feasible. The major difference from the past is that this computer-based training (CBT) is not meant to be an adjunct to traditional stand-up classroom instruction; it is meant to replace it. As an example of multimedia CBT, consider what the people at Codex have done.

CASE EXAMPLE: A Training Course from Codex

Codex, in Mansfield, Massachusetts, is an information networking company. They have an educational arm that provides CBT to their own people as well as to customers. Their courses can be obtained through Codex Express [5].

Codex decided to experiment with multimedia training by creating a "Basics of Digital Voice Technology" course. The four-hour course demonstrated that using simulation to teach technical material cut training time in half, and the "students" had a lot of fun using it. The three developers at Codex gained so much experience building that multimedia CBT course that they embarked on creating a second course, "Basics of ISDN (Integrated Services Digital Network)," without outside help.

This four-hour course is taken at a Macintosh or a PC. The first screen presents "your office." It shows a line drawing of the office of the communications manager of "Heart International," a fictitious global publishing company that has an advertising agency, lumber mill, lumber supply store, paper mill, printer, and direct-mail house. Your task, as this manager, is to recommend to your boss which ISDN applications Heart should investigate, in some detail and with your reasons.

To begin the course, you can click on any item in your office—your in-box, telephone, diskette file, electronic mail, and so forth. It is recommended that you start with the memo from your boss, which explains your assignment. The final memo that you send to your boss to complete the course is a fill-in-the-blank form describing the ISDN applications you recommend. To gather the information to write this memo, you can talk to a colleague over lunch, visit a trade show, ask your mentor for guidance on where to find certain information, view a library of "videos," and attend a seminar, in whichever order you choose, all simulated by the system.

The course contains animation so that when you click on the diskette file, it opens. When you talk to someone, you see a digitized image of that person talking. Codex created its own lip-sync program to make the mouths of these photographed people appear to speak as their voice is played. The course also contains humor; when you call on your communication analysts, they march across your screen, saying, "Hey, boss," and then provide you with information.

The people who have taken the digital voice technology and ISDN courses say the difference between these courses and traditional CBT is like night and day. CBT seems like electronic page turning, they say; multimedia training feels as if you are having an experience where you are in control of what you do.

Codex management says CBT is cost-effective because training time is shorter (by at least one-half), it can be given when it is needed (reducing retraining), and it does not involve traveling to a training site. However, development is more costly than classroom training due to the up-front design costs. The four-hour ISDN course took one work-year of effort, including the outside graphic art help and the instructional design and programming done in-house.

The Codex development manager's recommendations for companies embarking on writing multimedia training are threefold:

1. Use a knowledgeable consulting firm the first time to learn the tricks of the trade.
2. Use an authoring language the first time to obtain guidance.
3. Invest in quality graphics artists and designers.

People have high expectations of computers and multimedia from their experiences with PCs and television. If you do not live up to these expectations, your credibility will be hurt.

REACHING OUT TO CONSUMERS

Some information systems departments have been directly serving consumers for a number of years. Some obvious examples are automated teller machines, voice response systems for checking on the status of a bank account, and self-serve airline reservation systems. But these services have been quite limited. We expect systems departments in the 1990s to significantly expand their reach to consumers, if not via the Web then by other means.

Convenience is today's driving force. Consumers want convenience to ease the numerous demands on their time. Information technology supplies convenience, not only by making corporate information available around the clock, but by making it available from many more locations. Information technology also enables fast response to consumer questions. Again, this increases the convenience of doing business with these organizations. By supporting convenience, information technology can give organizations an advantage over their competitors.

As an example of a corporation using its information technology resources and peoples' comfort with the telephone to directly serve consumers, consider The Huntington National Bank's alliance with AT&T.

CASE EXAMPLE: The Huntington National Bank

Huntington Bankshares, Inc., with headquarters in Columbus, Ohio, is a $13 billion regional bank holding company with 271 banking offices in seven states. Its mortgage, trust, investment banking, and automobile finance subsidiaries operate 51 offices in 16 states. The Huntington became the first organization to offer a new in-home banking, bill payment, and information service using AT&T's Smart Phone.

The New Service. The AT&T Smart Phone is a telephone, a modem, and a display, all in one; AT&T bills it as the next-generation telephone. The phone has a handset along with a 4-inch by 6-inch liquid crystal touch screen display. There are no actual buttons on the phone; all interaction is done via pictures of the buttons on the screen. The screen changes depending on its current use. For example, the standard screen shows a keypad plus additional telephone buttons, such as speaker, redial, and program. The display also has a volume bar and numerous user-created buttons, such as family, friends, emergency, repairs, and so forth. Pressing one of these buttons brings up a second-level menu with a list of the appropriate names and phone numbers.

The telephone is versatile, allowing the customer to choose either the standard typewriter keyboard or an alphabetic keyboard for text entry. It includes standard telephone features as well as enhanced telephone functions, such as caller ID. Caller ID displays the caller's telephone number as the telephone rings, or displays the caller's name if it is stored in the phone's memory.

The Huntington's customers can use this phone for banking, bill paying, and other transactions. By dialing a special, bank-provided phone number, the Smart Phone is connected to the bank's computer system. After entering a personal identification code and a secret password, the phone displays a list of buttons, such as banking, bill payment, shopping, travel, and so on. Pressing the "bill payment" button, for instance, displays the customer's personal bill-paying screen, which displays the list of organizations the customer has previously paid through the phone, such as the gas company, cable TV, department stores, and the like. To pay a bill, the customer touches the appropriate button and enters the amount to be paid. Or a new payee can be added.

The Huntington is providing access to other services as well, such as shopping by catalog, making travel arrangements, and ordering gifts and flowers. Under development are still more services, such as local restaurant menus, entertainment listings, stock quotes, and local weather and traffic reports.

The system has also been designed to provide service on behalf of other financial institutions, thereby allowing The Huntington to provide Smart Phone services to its customers as well as to those of other banks across the United States. Thus, The Huntington can become a service provider to other financial institutions.

The Behind-the-Scenes System. The Huntington designed its system to work with the special AT&T telephone. The system, called SmarTel, includes software and hardware for accessing the bank's mainframe, pre-

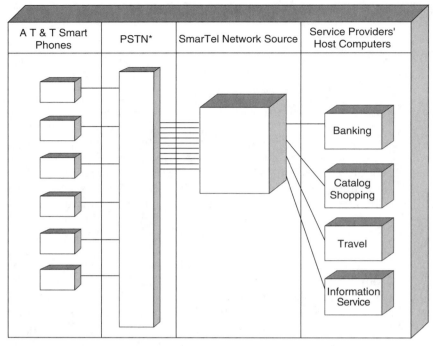

A T & T Smart Phones	PSTN*	SmarTel Network Source	Service Providers' Host Computers

Banking

Catalog Shopping

Travel

Information Service

* Public Switched Telephone Network

Figure 12-2   The SmarTel System

senting information to the caller's telephone screen, and providing access to third-party information providers.

As shown in Figure 12-2, the entire system contains four components: the AT&T Smart Phones, the public switched telephone network, the SmarTel network service (which acts as the hub of the service), and service providers' host computers.

So The Huntington is using its access to its customers, as well as customers' familiarity with touch-tone telephones, to become an information provider—not only of its own banking services but of services from other providers. Since this is a telephone-based service, the customer has the option of interacting with the service provider either by computer, by touching the appropriate button on the phone, or by voice.

IMPLICATIONS FOR IS MANAGEMENT

What does this expanding world of portable computers, mobile communications, multimedia, and the Internet mean to IS executives? As we see it, there are several implications

First, these new technological developments are causing computer use to take another great leap forward, as it did with PCs. With the explosion of types of portable computers, multimedia, and telecom options, computing is becoming a major tool in more employees' lives. Information systems executives can take advantage of this more versatile computing environment in ways not envisioned before. Thus, we suggest forming teams to study ways to take advantage of mobile computing, e-mail, multimedia, and the Internet. The more pilot projects are initiated, the more technology transfer is likely to occur.

Second, use of these technologies should not go unguided. IS management needs to be out in front, not ignore or disregard these technologies as many did with the PC. Otherwise, they will end up playing catch-up. In fact, they may already be in this position. All these technologies that directly touch employees and customers should be viewed as new windows to organizational computing—windows that are sure to spur the new work environment and the new marketplace environment. IS managers should play a large role in creating these environments.

Third, these technologies can be used to record corporate memory. Portables, for instance, are not just smaller PCs, although they can be used that way. They have characteristics not generally associated with PCs. For instance, their portability makes them actually feel personal, convenient, and informal. They can be used on the spur of the moment, for a quick task, something people rarely do with a PC. Therefore, they lend themselves to people entering or retrieving small pieces of data and information. For example, if entering information is quick and easy and provides a benefit to the user, corporations will finally have a way to tap into the corporate knowledge that is going unrecorded. Coupled with wireless communication technology and the Net (and the sharing forums it encourages), these valuable entries by mobile employees can more easily be shared.

Finally, these technologies may need some new corporate guidelines. If portables and the Internet, for instance, are to play a role in creating "corporate memory," some issues need to be resolved. Privacy is one. The reason many people prefer to tell others sensitive information, rather than record it, is to maintain some control over its dissemination. Once recorded—say, as a digitized voice note or electronic mail message—however, its privacy is essentially lost because it can be so easily rerouted via distribution lists to many people. Corporations need policies about which information should not be recorded and routed electronically. Searching electronic information is far easier than paper files, so the deterrent of effort is significantly reduced. Encryption may become an important weapon in safeguarding sensitive electronic information, but that has not happened yet.

Moving Toward Doug Engelbart's Vision

We conclude this chapter by looking both backward and forward at the same time, by describing ones man's ideas about a good user interface. Several of the most popular features on PCs these days (and a few on the Internet as well) originated at one source: a research team at Stanford Research Institute headed by Douglas Engelbart [6]. Between 1957 and 1977, Engelbart's team conceived and implemented a computer system for knowledge workers called NLS that used a mouse for cursor control, detachable keyboards, split screen displays, and more. Believe it or not, all of his ideas have still not been widely implemented, so we present them here as a target for the future.

Engelbart believes that the main role of computers is to augment peoples' intellectual work; therefore, an electronic workplace should be relatively easy to learn but not simple-minded. He prefers a powerful system, even though it increases the learning difficulty, because it has the greatest potential for leveraging the effectiveness of knowledge workers. Following are six technical capabilities he believes such systems should have:

1. An open-ended vocabulary
2. Fast, concurrent control
3. Writing and structuring
4. Naming and addressing
5. Remote jumps and manipulations
6. Views, filters, and windows

Open-Ended Vocabulary. The system should allow users to receive customizable services, such as the commands they use, the amount of feedback they receive from the system each time a command is issued, the subsystems automatically available at log-on, the time zone the user wants to work in, the number of versions of documents to be kept, and the types of peripherals to be used. The system can achieve this flexibility with a user interface module to define these attributes for each user. Users can modify these attributes, even creating a new command by defining it in terms of other commands. The interface module can act as a translator for all applications, no matter where the applications programs are located.

Fast, Concurrent Control. When people think, they use "little windows in their minds," says Engelbart, and they jump effortlessly from one subject to another, and from one view to another. Information in a computer should be manipulated similarly, he says, and with less than 0.25-second response time. To permit fast, concurrent manipulation, in the mid-1960s Engelbart designed two devices, the mouse and the chording keyset. The mouse needs no description; it is familiar to most readers by now. The keyset has five parallel keys (somewhat like a piano) that can be used individually or in combinations (chords) to select codes representing letters of the alphabet. It is used with one hand, for command designation and short entries, while the other hand manipulates the mouse, for cursor control and selecting. Experienced users can work as fast as they can think, because they can be moving the cursor while they are defining the operation they want to perform next.

Writing and Structuring. Engelbart believes that electronic tools can loosen some of the limitations imposed by paper and pencil, assisting writers in doing their jobs better. His hierarchical file structure has allowed intermixing all types of communications—text, data, graphics, voice, and image. Users can define relationships between items in many ways, such as organizing a document hierarchically and then displaying only section headings to get an overview, or printing only the first two lines of each bibliographic citation, and so on. Users can store items at different levels and quickly move up and down among the levels.

Naming and Addressing. Users should also be able to assign a name or address to any electronic item so that it can be uniquely identified in other documents, messages, and so on. In his system, Engelbart allowed names and addresses to be assigned to single words, lines, paragraphs, sections, graphs, documents, or collections of documents—anything a user chose. A permanent library of addressed items—from one-line messages to book-size documents— was available for retrieval at any time.

Remote Jumps and Manipulations. Once items can be addressed, users should also be able to jump directly to an address, pull an addressed item onto the screen, print a series of addressed items, and so on. Where this is possible, users can easily move through huge amounts of on-line documents by just pointing to links embedded in the text (as they now can on the Web).

Views, Filters, and Windows. Users should be able to select how they format and view information. For instance, they may want to place two or more items side by side to compare them; to facilitate this, Engelbart's project used split screens. In addition, users should be able to retrieve information based on text strings, or look at all items that were recently changed by a specific person. Views and filters are short programs or query commands that allow users to display or print only the information they want. With these capabilities, users can create and store elaborate processes for manipulating documents, filing electronic mail, printing documents, and so on.

Engelbart's conceptual framework for systems includes not only the tool system just described but also "the human system"—the methods of work, skills, knowledge, language, training, roles, and organization. The real challenge facing organizations, he believes, is to give balanced support to the coevolution of both, in a guided manner, so that knowledge work can be truly augmented.

SUMMARY

Support for end users in the 1980s centered around creating information centers and staffing them with people who liked to help people, rather than write computer programs. That approach was feasible when PCs were new. But now, IS departments must be more sophisticated. A promising approach is to assist individuals, groups, departments, and even consumers use a new technology, such as the Internet, at their level of acceptance of technology—be they eager beavers, late majority, or technology averse. Companies can also encourage the use of multimedia because it is a more natural way for people and computers to communicate with each other. In addition, IS management can emphasize more natural, more powerful uses of computers by considering Doug Engelbart's vision for user interfaces. In conclusion, supporting the expanded universe of computing involves assessing the proclivity of people to adopt a technology, assisting them at that level, and making computer use as natural as possible.

QUESTIONS AND EXERCISES

REVIEW QUESTIONS

1. Briefly describe the five clusters that represent one's willingness to assimilate a new technology. How many U.S. households are approximately in each cluster, according to the Yankee Group?
2. What was an information center? What was its job in the 1980s?
3. How is today's environment different from the early 1980s?
4. At the computer company, who are the technical coordinators, what do they do, and how does the company recognize their importance?
5. What are two uses of multimedia that help people deal with complexity? Give an example of each.
6. What are on-demand training and training by simulation?
7. How is The Huntington National Bank serving consumers using information technology?
8. What are four implications for IS management of this expanding world of computing?
9. According to Douglas Engelbart, what six technical capabilities should every system provide for knowledge workers?

DISCUSSION QUESTIONS

1. IS departments should only address clusters of employees and customers who are receptive to new information technology. They should forget about the late majority and technology adverse because it is not worth the effort. Do you agree or disagree? Discuss.
2. The only technology IS departments should promote in dealing with consumers is the Internet, specifically the Web. Do you agree or disagree? Discuss.
3. Yes, consumers may want convenience, but they also want the human touch. By putting information technology between employees and customers, organizations run the risk of alienating consumers rather than serving them better. Do you agree or disagree? Why?

EXERCISES

1. Visit a local company and find out how the IS department is now handling end user computing. How has this changed from five years ago? What are its biggest concerns with supporting computing today? Does it have any multimedia applications? If so, briefly describe them. Does it have any computer systems used directly by consumers? If so, briefly describe them.
2. Read four articles about computer systems used directly by consumers. Describe them to the class. Or visit ten consumer-based Internet Web sites. What approaches are these taking to entice consumers to buy their products?
3. Read several articles about or visit several Web sites that deal with data visualization. What sorts of data is being turned into graphs, animation, and so on? What are the most interesting aspects of this work, in your opinion? Present your findings and opinions to the class.

REFERENCES

1. GHAFFARI, ELIZABETH, and BARBARA MCNURLIN, "The Technology Camel," unpublished paper. Elizabeth Ghaffari, President, Technology Place, 2807 Highland Ave., Suite 5, Santa Monica, CA 90405, http://techplace@earthlink.net.

2. IS LEADERSHIP FORUM, Ernst & Young, Center for Business Innovation, One Walnut St., Boston, MA, January 1993.

3. THE ELECTRONIC VISUALIZATION LABORATORY, University of Illinois at Chicago, P.O. Box 4348, M/C 154, Chicago, IL 60680. For DeFanti's original, ground-breaking discussion, see "Visualization in Scientific Computing," a special issue of *Computer Graphics*, from ACM's Special Interest Group on Computer Graphics (ACM, 1515 Broadway, New York, NY 10036), July 1987.

4. ABACUS CONCEPTS, 1984 Bonita Ave., Berkeley, CA 94704.

5. CODEX EXPRESS, 20 Cabot Blvd., Mansfield, MA 02048.

6. ENGELBART, DOUGLAS, Bootstrap Institute, Palo Alto, CA.

PART V

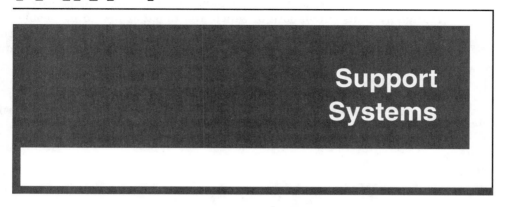

Support Systems

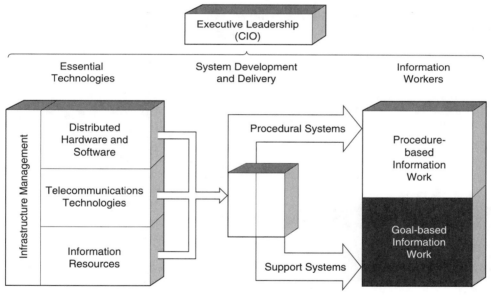

A Framework for IS Management

Part V of this book consists of four chapters that deal with support systems. As shown in the book's accompanying framework diagram, we distinguish between procedure-based and goal-based information-handling activities. The two previous chapters, in Part IV, dealt with the technical and managerial environment within which people are using IT in goal-based activities. The four chapters in this part discuss four sets of applications and systems that deal with goal-based activities—support systems. These are *systems* that *support* people in performing information-handling activities to ascertain goals, pursue objectives, and solve problems.

Chapter 13 discusses decision support systems (DSS) and executive information systems (EIS), both of which are aimed at providing people with the kinds of computer-based information that help them make better decisions.

Chapter 14 deals with group systems, which support the communication and interaction among people as they work in teams or groups.

Chapter 15 discusses expert systems, which support decision making in situations that can be structured according to sets of complex rules.

And Chapter 16 focuses on electronic document management, which is emerging as an important means for moving information around, in, and among businesses.

THIRTEEN

Decision Support Systems and Executive Information Systems

INTRODUCTION

Decision support systems (DSS) can be viewed as a third generation of computer-based applications [1]. First, mainframe computers were used mostly for transactions processing. Then there was a growing realization that computers and information technology could be used for purposes other than automating paperwork, for example, for management reporting, so the field of management information systems (MIS) took hold. Meanwhile, assistance for decision making was the domain of management scientists and operations researchers who created structured models, for which computers served primarily as computation engines.

This environment was fertile soil for the paper by Gorry and Scott Morton [2], which explored the concept of structure in decision making. They developed a now-famous matrix, which showed the interaction between a level of management and the amount of decision-making structure at that level. As the level of management increases from operating management to executive levels, the decision-making process moves from semistructured to unstructured. The thrust of their argument was that management science models were effective for structured decision making, but decision makers needed tools and technology to assist them in dealing with semistructured or unstructured problems. This rationale set the stage for Scott Morton's thesis on what he called management decision systems [3].

During the 1970s and 1980s, the concept of DSS grew and evolved into a full field of research, development, and practice. DSS was both an evolution and a departure from previous types of computer support for decision making. Management information systems provided (1) scheduled reports for well-defined information needs, (2) demand reports for ad hoc information requests, and (3) the ability to query a database for specific data. Operations research/management science (OR/MS) employed mathematical models to better analyze and understand specific problems. Both MIS and OR/MS lacked some attributes needed to support decision making—attributes such as focus, development methodology, handling of managerial data, use of analytic aids, and dialog between user and system.

Initially, there were different conceptualizations about what decision support systems were. Not only did academicians give different definitions, but vendors, quick to adopt anything to help sell their products, also applied the DSS label very loosely. When the characteristics of DSS were described to a vendor, he said, "That's it! That's the name we need for our new product." The term *decision support system* had such an instant intuitive appeal that it quickly became a buzzword.

DSS and Other Systems

As the DSS field evolved, there were continued questions about how it related to, or differed from, MIS and management science. The structured-versus-unstructured decision-making framework was helpful, but did not adequately explain the variety of activities that seemed to go beyond decision making. It became clear from conference discussions and academic papers that the focus of DSS should be higher than a single decision event. Decision making is a process, one that involves a variety of activities, most of which deal with the handling of information.

To illustrate these concepts, consider a scenario of a problem-solving task and the technology that might be used to assist decision makers in handling it in the mid-1990s.

CASE EXAMPLE: Problem-Solving Scenario

1. The vice president of marketing discovers a sales shortfall in a region. He notices this from using an executive information system to compare budget to actual sales.
2. He uses the capability of the EIS to "drill down" into the components of the summarized data. No apparent causes for a shortfall are revealed so he must look further.

3. He sends an e-mail message to the district sales manager requesting an explanation. The sales manager's response and a follow-up phone call reveal that there is no obvious single cause, so they must look deeper.

4. The vice president investigates several possible causes:

   a. Economic conditions. Through the EIS, he has access to wire services, bank economic newsletters, current business and economic publications, and the company's internal economic report on the region in question. These sources reveal no serious downturn in the economic conditions of the region.

   b. Competitive analysis. Through the same sources, he investigates whether competitors have introduced a new product, launched an effective ad campaign, or whether there are new competitors entering the market.

   c. Written sales reports. He then browses through the written reports of individual sales representatives to detect possible problems. A concept-based text retrieval system allows quick searches of topics, such as poor quality, inadequate product functionality, or obsolescence.

   d. A data mining analysis. He asks for an analysis of the sales data to reveal any previously unknown relationships buried in the customer database and relevant demographic data.

5. The vice president then accesses the marketing DSS, which includes a set of models to analyze sales patterns by product, by sales representative, and by major customer. Again, no clear problems are revealed.

6. He decides to hold a meeting with the regional sales managers and several of the key salespeople. They meet in an electronic meeting room supported by GDSS software such as GroupSystems by Ventana Corporation or TeamFocus from IBM. During this meeting, they:

   a. Examine the results of all the previous analyses using the information access and presentation technologies in the room.

   b. Brainstorm to identify possible solutions.

   c. Develop an action plan.

7. Because no discernible singular cause has led to the shortfall in sales, the group decides that the best solution is to launch a new multimedia sales campaign that sales representatives can show on their laptop computer when they visit customers.

8. A revised estimate of the sales volume, with the new sales promotion plan, is entered into the financial planning model and distributed to the sales force in the region.

9. A sales meeting is held in the GDSS room, and by video conference, to launch the campaign and train sales personnel in the use of the multimedia presentation.

This scenario illustrates the wide variety of activities involved in dealing with a decision-making and problem-solving task. Where does the decision making start and stop? Which are the crucial decisions? It does not really matter because all the activities are part of the overall process of solving the problem. The scenario also illustrates the wide variety of technologies that can be used to assist decision makers and problem solvers. Which of the technology-based systems are DSS? In the broad sense, all of them are, because they all improve the effectiveness or efficiency of the decision-making or problem-solving process.

The definition of DSS, which has evolved since the 1970s and prevails today, was articulated in *Building Effective Decision Support Systems*, by Ralph Sprague and Eric Carlson [4]. It defines DSS as

- computer-based systems
- that help decision makers
- confront ill-structured problems
- through direct interaction
- with data and analysis models

The last two items have become the basis of the technology for DSS, which Sprague and Carlson call the DDM paradigm—dialog, data, and modeling. In this conceptualization, there is the *dialog* (D) between the user and the system, the *data* (D) that supports the system, and the *models* (M) that provide the analysis capabilities. While the components differ somewhat from application to application, they always exist in some form. Sprague and Carlson make the point that a good DSS should have balance among the three capabilities. It should be *easy to use*, to support the interaction with non-technical users, it should have access to a *wide variety of data*, and it should provide *analysis and modeling* in numerous ways. Many systems claim to be DSS when they are strong in only one area and weak in the others.

THE ARCHITECTURE FOR DSS

Figure 13-1 shows the relationships between the three components of the DDM model. The software system in the middle of the figure consists of the database management system (DBMS), the model base management system (MBMS), and the dialog generation and management system (DGMS).

Because the DDM model defines the architecture for DSS, let us look at each of the components more closely.

The Dialog Component

The set of attributes that comprises the dialog component can be called a "dialog style." For example, one dialog style results from a system that requires users to keep a reference card and to remember which commands to enter with a keyboard in order to obtain a printed report. Quite another dialog style results from using a mouse to access pull-down menus and move icons on a color screen to get a graphical presentation of analysis results. The latter dialog style, popularized by the Apple Macintosh, revolutionized the dialog component in the 1980s. The explosive growth of Microsoft's Windows for the PC, X-Windows for UNIX, and the Macintosh interface have made this dialog style the dominant standard for end user computing.

The DSS

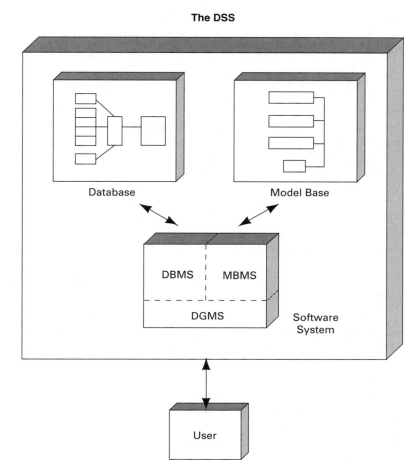

Figure 13-1   Components of a DSS

The Data Component

Data plays an important role in a DSS. Data is either accessed directly by the user or is an input to the models for processing.

Data Sources. As the importance of DSS has grown, it is becoming increasingly critical for the DSS to use all the important data sources within the organization, and from external sources also. Indeed, the concept of data sources must be expanded to *information sources*—moving beyond only accessing database records to accessing documents containing concepts, ideas, and opinions that are so important to decision making.

To characterize the full scope of information sources relevant to DSS, it is helpful to recall the four types of information discussed in Chapter 7. Figure 7-6 on page 221 shows the four kinds of information that result from considering external and internal information, which contains either (1) information based on data records such as is found in data files, or (2) document-based information such as reports, opinions, memos, and estimates.

Few DSS need data at the transaction level. Summarized data is more typical and can be obtained in several ways. One way is to have the DBMS for the transaction processing system extract the transaction data, summarize it, and make the data available to the DSS. Another option is to extract the data but have the processing done externally to the DBMS. While this is ideally a computerized process, some DSS rely on manual processing. This may be appropriate when the processing requires little effort or when the DSS is needed quickly and a more elegant solution cannot be implemented in a timely manner.

Some organizations give end users only access to *extract files*. These are files maintained externally to the DBMS and are created specifically to meet the data needs of end users. Extract files are used for security, ease of access, and data integrity reasons. In organizations with extract files, the DSS obtains data from these files. This suggests that the database for a DSS may be separate from the transaction processing database, and, for several reasons, this indeed is the case in most organizations.

Data Warehouses, OLAP, and Software Agents. Separate databases for decision support applications are also being developed through the creation of data warehouses. These are special databases that are designed to allow decision makers to perform their own analyses. They are also sometimes referred to as information databases. Typically, data is first extracted from mainframe and other databases. Prior to being placed in the data warehouse, the data is processed (i.e., "cleansed") to make it more usable for decision support. Several vendors provide software specifically for this purpose. The data is then maintained on a file server, and special-purpose software is used to better support DSS activities.

Managers and professionals doing decision support analyses (without help from intermediaries or information systems professionals) is commonly referred to as on-line analytical processing (OLAP). The term contrasts with on-line transaction processing (OLTP). OLAP is driven by (1) the need for information; (2) the emergence of software that supports the building, maintenance, and use of data warehouses; and (3) more computer proficient end users who are able and willing to do their own decision support.

Even though decision makers are better equipped to analyze the vast quantities of data stored by organizations, manual searching is inadequate because important developments may go undetected if no one is looking for them. In response to this problem, vendors now offer software agents (also known as intelligent agents) which continually send queries to databases in order to find exceptional conditions. When one is found, it is automatically sent to the appropriate person, often through e-mail. Software agents provide a "detect and alert" capability. They reflect an exciting integration of artificial intelligence and decision support.

The Model Component

Models provide the analysis capabilities for a DSS. Using a mathematical representation of the problem, algorithmic processes are employed to generate information to support decision making. There are many different types of models and various ways to categorize them. The models in a DSS can be thought of as a *model base*. A variety of models can be included: strategic, tactical, and operational, as well as model-building blocks and subroutines. Each type of model has unique characteristics.

Problems with Traditional Modeling. From a historical perspective, organizations' experiences with models are mixed. While there are many successes, there are often many failures. With hindsight, it is possible to identify the problems that lead to failure:

- Difficulties in obtaining input data for the models.
- Difficulties in understanding how to apply the output from models.
- Difficulties in keeping the models up-to-date.
- Lack of confidence in the models by users; therefore, the models are not trusted.
- Little integration among models.
- Poor interaction between the models and users.
- Difficulty for users to create their own models.
- Little explanation for a model's output.

The DSS approach to modeling attempts to minimize the traditional modeling problems by emphasizing that a *system* (e.g., dialog, data, and models working together) to support decision making is required. In other words, the models in a DSS are likely to be more useful because they are adequately supported by the data and dialog components.

Summary

The dialog, data, and models paradigm provides a powerful conceptual model for understanding the components and relationships in a DSS. Each is critical if a DSS is to live up to its decision support potential. Let us now assess the current status of DSS and look at a few examples.

THE CURRENT STATUS OF DSS

It seems that new topics in information systems are introduced with grandiose promise, only to fall back to a limited and somewhat mundane role. Academics and visionaries develop a theoretical definition; practitioners understand only pragmatic solutions. If an idea survives the overpromise and underdelivery backlash, it can usually make a valuable contribution to the field.

Management information systems originally promised to be the "electronic nervous system" for organizations; they actually became well-structured reporting systems. Office automation promised the paperless office; it actually became first word processing, and later, personal computers. In a similar way, the

promise of DSS was described earlier. For a while, however, DSS to most practitioners meant a computer-based financial planning system. Fortunately, the
promise of DSS is still understood and interest is still growing. Here are a few
examples of DSS.

Typical Examples

The size and complexity of DSS range from simple ad hoc analyses that
might be called end user computing tasks to large complex systems that have
many of the attributes of a major application in the system portfolio. We will call
these "quick-hit DSS" and "institutional DSS," respectively.

Institutional DSS. Institutional DSS are generally systems built by professionals, often decision support groups. These systems are intended for organizational support on a continuing basis, and they are generally written using a
decision support language. In the past, most have run on mainframes, but an
increasing number are being designed to run on client/server systems. The following two case examples illustrate institutional DSS.

CASE EXAMPLE: Ore-Ida Foods

Ore-Ida Foods, Inc. is the frozen food division of H. J. Heinz and has a 50
percent share of the retail frozen potato market. Marketing DSS must support three main tasks in the decision-making process. The first is data
retrieval, which helps managers find answers to the question, "What has
happened?" The second is market analysis, which addresses the question,
"Why did it happen?" The third is modeling, which helps managers get
answers to, "What will happen if . . . ?"

For data retrieval, a large amount of internal and external market data
is available at Ore-Ida. Much of the latter, such as economic indexes and
forecasts, is purchased. However, the company makes very limited use of
simple data retrieval. Only about 15 to 30 pages of predefined reports are
prepared each sales period.

Market analysis is the bulk (some 70 percent) of Ore-Ida's use of DSS—
for analyzing "Why did such and such happen?" Data from several sources
is combined and relationships are sought. The analysis addresses such
questions as, "What was the relationship between our prices and our share
of the market, for this brand in these markets?"

Modeling, for projection purposes, offers the greatest potential value to
marketing management. The company has found that, for successful use,
line managers must take over the ownership of the models and be responsible for keeping them up-to-date. The models must also be frequently updated, as market conditions change and new relationships are perceived.

CASE EXAMPLE: Sara Lee

Sara Lee, in Deerfield, Illinois, uses a DSS for sales forecasting. Formerly, when all sales forecasts came from the sales force, the forecasts were too optimistic so inventories became excessive. When time series analysis of historical data was used to give sales estimates, the analyses did not handle the impact of sales promotions well. So the company began using multiple regression models to inject explanatory variables into the analyses. An explanatory variable is an additional variable, such as a sales promotion program or the consumer price index of food, that helps explain the performance of the main variable being forecasted. With some 200 stock-keeping units (such as flavors of a given product), it was hard to keep these models up to date with all the product promotion plans and other such activities.

More recently, a policy decision that all products within a product line would have the same promotion plans cut the number of models from 200 to 36. Sara Lee uses the ADDATA sales forecasting system from Temple, Barker & Sloane, Inc., of Lexington, Massachusetts. This method uses a bottom-up approach, performing time series analysis of historical data at the SKU level. The trend line or pattern is then projected into the future to forecast the SKU sales for the next several periods. These SKU forecasts are then combined to forecast product sales, which in turn are summed to get product line sales, and so on. The percentage that each SKU's sales represents to total product sales is developed.

Then a top-down approach is used. A multiple regression is used to analyze past total product sales data, including one or more explanatory variables. The sales pattern is used to forecast total sales for the product. At this point, management reviews the model's total sales forecast and can override the model's figures to give the final forecast figures. These final total sales are then distributed back to the individual SKUs by way of the percentages that were developed. Forecast errors in the order of 15 to 20 percent at the SKU level generally are reduced to 1 to 2 percent at the product level. Also, errors in weekly forecasts generally smooth out by the end of the forecast period.

Forecasts are prepared twice a month and transmitted to the company's mainframe for entry into the production planning process. This sales forecasting method has reduced inventories, while at the same time increasing the service level (sufficient stock in inventory to meet the demand) to greater than the industry average of 97 percent.

As these two case examples illustrate, institutional DSS tend to be fairly well defined, they are based on predefined data sources (heavily internal, perhaps with some external data), and they use well-established models in a prescheduled way. Variations and flexible testing of alternative what-if situations are available, but seldom done during interaction with the ultimate decision maker.

"Quick-Hit" DSS. While there is no commonly used name, the term *quick-hit* DSS means a system that is quite limited in scope, is developed and put into use quickly, and helps a manager come to a decision—a decision that the manager might have to make on a recurring basis or one that is strictly one-time-only. The term *ad hoc* has also been used to distinguish from institutional DSS, although some quick-hit systems become used regularly.

A quick-hit DSS can be useful for (a) getting managers started in using DSS, (b) providing decision support for certain types of management decisions on either an ad hoc or a recurring basis, (c) providing a basis for deciding whether or not to build a full DSS, and (d) supporting decision situations where the executives cannot wait for a full DSS to be built. A quick-hit DSS can be every bit as useful for small companies as for large ones. Three typical types of quick-hit DSS include

- Reporting DSS
- Short analysis programs
- Those built with a DSS generator

Reporting DSS. These quick-hit DSS are used to select, summarize, and list data from existing data files to meet managers' specific information needs. Other than summarizing the data, a few arithmetic operations may be performed. If computer graphics are used, however, then trends, variances, and so on can be shown. It is likely that reporting DSS is, and will continue to be, the most widely used form of computerized decision support. In fact, reporting DSS were the forerunners to executive information systems, which emphasize reporting with fast response, flexibility, and high-quality presentation. EIS are discussed later in this chapter.

Short Analysis Programs. These programs analyze data as well as print or display the data; they can be surprisingly powerful. Managers can write these short programs themselves, and they generally use only a small amount of data, which may be entered manually.

A major services company with offices throughout the United States and Europe provides a good example.

CASE EXAMPLE: A Major Services Company

The vice chairman of the board at a major services firm was considering a new employee benefit program, an employee stock ownership plan (ESOP). He wanted a study made to determine the possible impact of the ESOP on the company, by answering such questions as: How many shares of company stock will be needed in 10, 20, and 30 years to support the ESOP? What level of growth will be needed to meet these stock requirements?

He described what he wanted—the assumptions that should be used, and the rules that should be followed for issuing ESOP stock—to the manager of the information services department. The information systems manager himself then wrote a program of about 40 lines that performed the calculations that the vice chairman wanted, then printed out the results. These results showed the impact of the ESOP over a period of 30 years, and those results contained some surprises.

The vice chairman presented the results to the executive committee and, partially based on this information, the ESOP was adopted. Some of the other executives became excited about the results of this analysis and asked if the computer program could be used to project their individual employee stock holdings for 10, 20, and 30 years. This was done, and it aroused even more attention. At this point, it was decided to implement the system in a more formal fashion. The company treasurer became so interested that he took ownership of the system and gradually expanded it to cover the planning, monitoring, and control of the various employee benefit programs.

This example shows that simple programs of 100 lines of code are indeed practical and can be used to support real-life decisions. In this case, a 40-line program was adequate for the initial evaluation of the ESOP. Eventually, of course, the programs for this system became much larger, but the 40-line program started everything. This example also illustrates the concept of iterative development (a form of prototyping), which is a key concept of DSS.

Decision Support System Generators. These products provide a third approach to developing quick, high-payoff DSS. Vendors sell products that are more than specific DSS packages or general DSS languages. These products include languages, interfaces, and other facilities that aid in setting up specific DSS. Sprague and Carlson point out that a DSS generator can be useful for building a number of specific DSS within a class of decision support applications.

The Role of Computer Graphics

For almost two decades, supporters of computer graphics systems have been urging their use for business management purposes. The military pioneered the use of computer graphics in command and control. Computer graphics systems have also been put to effective use in such areas as computer-aided design and manufacturing, real-time simulation, animation, and video games. At long last, computer graphics systems for business management have become the norm. Graphics are especially important for business problem solving and decision making because they help managers visualize data, relationships, and summaries. They are also important in goal-based information activities because they provide good representations of concepts with which managers must deal.

Types of Graphics. A wide variety of graphics forms is in use today. All forms can be generated by PCs.

- *Text* plays a critical role in graphics—for listing points that the speaker is discussing, for showing subject titles, for identifying components and values of a chart, and so on. Text must be easily readable.
- *Time series charts* are perhaps the most widely used form of graphics, showing the value of one or more variables versus time. The value scale can be linear or logarithmic.
- *Bar and pie charts* can be used to show total values (by the size of the bar or pie), as well as component values, such as breakdowns of, say, "sources of money received" and "where the money was spent."
- *Scatter diagrams* show the (imperfect) relationship between two variables, such as the number of air travelers that fly on Mondays, on Tuesdays, and so on.
- *Maps* can be two or three dimensional. Two-dimensional maps are useful for showing spatial relationships, for example, the locations of customers and the locations of a company's customer service facilities. Three-dimensional maps show surface contours with a three-dimensional effect. With black and white rendition, they can show the relationship among three variables; with color, four or even more variables can be related. These "maps" are not limited to geographic information but can show relationships among any three variables, such as the number of employees by age and by years of service with the company.
- *Layouts* of rooms, buildings, or shopping centers convey much information in relatively simple diagrams.
- *Hierarchy charts,* such as organization charts and module charts, are widely used.
- *Sequence charts*, such as flow charts, show the necessary sequence of events, and which activities can be done in parallel.
- *Motion graphics,* such as animation, motion pictures, and television, have an exciting future when, through the use of computers, they are used in combination with the graphics techniques listed previously.

In addition to these traditional graphic forms, new developments are continually increasing the value and capability of computer-generated graphics. Silicon Graphics, Inc. has based its entire product line on powerful graphical capabilities for data visualization, usually in scientific areas. The company is now moving to explore the competitive advantage of data visualization in business areas. The Xerox project that developed the "Rooms" interface, described in Chapter 11, has been expanded into the "information visualizer" project [5] to explore new ways to use graphics and animation to visualize and understand complex information. Apple Computer's QuickTime makes possible the use of videoclips as part of reports and electronic documents.

In summary, computer-based graphics increases the effectiveness of decision making and problem solving by providing a way to visualize data relationships. As an example of a decision support system where graphics played an important role, consider the experience of Marine Terminals Corporation.

CASE EXAMPLE: Marine Terminals Corporation

Marine Terminals Corporation operates marine terminals and provides stevedoring services at ports in California and Alaska. Headquarters is in San Francisco, California, and the firm has a second major office in Long Beach. Marine Terminals used a DSS on a proposed project for building a new supply base terminal for the offshore oil industry near Santa Barbara, California.

The project made use of a PC to perform decision support analysis. By testing alternative ways to structure and finance the terminal, management and investors were better able to decide whether or not to go ahead with the project. Most of the decision support models were created by the vice president of marketing. He developed a financial projection model to show the financial effects of using different financing methods (borrowing, sale of stock, and so on) and following different operating policies.

One important aspect was the financial effects of different configurations of the terminal. A given number of ships could be loaded or unloaded using one number of berths and working only during daylight hours, or using a smaller number of berths and working around the clock, with consequent higher labor costs. Because each berth costs about $2 million, this analysis was important to both management and potential investors.

The vice president made color slides of the numerous analyses, including net present value of fixed costs, income, operating costs, net income after taxes, and investment tax credits.

Since the proposed terminal was to be built at a very scenic part of the California coast, the effect on the environment was carefully studied. Different approaches for minimizing the visual and environmental impacts of the terminal were considered. The model showed the firm the financial implications of these approaches. The results of these analyses were also displayed by the computer color graphics form. These graphics could be shown to small groups, such as a management meeting, directly on the computer display. Changes could be suggested and entered, with the display changing immediately. For larger audiences, such as for a conference presentation, color slides were created directly from the graphics file.

The terminal project was approved and the terminal was built. The vice president gives a lot of credit to this "corporate DSS on a micro," where graphics played an important part in the decision making and implementation.

CURRENT DEVELOPMENTS AND TRENDS

Advances in recent years in several IT areas have combined to impact the field of DSS. Each of these trends had a significant effect on the growth and development of DSS; taken together their effect has proven to be dramatic. They include

1. The PC revolution; the hardware, the software, and the emphasis on ease of use through common interfaces such as Windows, and common representations such as spreadsheets
2. The increasing capability and decreasing cost of telecommunications, both for wide area networks and local area networks
3. The Internet and its vast source of external data
4. The growth of artificial intelligence techniques such as expert systems and natural language processing
5. The rapid increase in end user computing and the increasing knowledge and computer literacy of end users
6. The increasing availability of large color screens and color graphics software
7. The increasing availability of mobile computing and communication

Important Developments in DSS

The intersection of the continued progress in DSS and the trends just cited resulted in some important developments in DSS. We have seen the trends:

1. Personal computer-based DSS has continued to grow. Spreadsheets took on more and more functions, eventually encompassing some of the functions previously performed by DSS generators. Newer packages for creativity support became more popular as extensions of analysis and decision making. These developments further strengthened the use of PCs for these applications, especially for personal support for independent thinking and decision making rather than for institutional DSS, such as budgeting and financial planning.
2. For the popular institutional DSS that support sequential, interdependent decision making, the trend is toward distributed DSS—close linkages between mainframe DSS languages and generators and PC-based facilities. Vendors of both mainframe and PC products now offer versions that run on, and link with, the other.
3. For interdependent decision support, group DSS (GDSS) have become much more prevalent in the past few years due to the growing availability of local area networks and group communication services, such as electronic mail.
4. Decision support system products are incorporating tools and techniques from artificial intelligence. The self-contained, stand-alone products in artificial intelligence have proven to be like the stand-alone statistical and management science models of a decade ago—they increasingly are embedded in DSS, which serve as a "delivery system" that facilitates their use. DSS will provide the mechanism for the assimilation of expert systems, knowledge representation, natural language query, voice and pattern recognition, and so on. The emerging result is intelligent DSS that can "suggest," "learn," and "understand" in dealing with managerial tasks and problems.
5. Continued efforts to leverage the usefulness of DSS to gain benefit and value have resulted in focused versions targeted at specific sets of users or applications. The first strong thrust in this direction was executive information systems (EIS) aimed at top managers, primarily for flexible reporting and status monitoring. EIS use enhanced graphics and other user-friendly capabilities, less modeling and analysis capability, and more support from systems professionals to cus-

tomize the system to a specific executive. Another popular specialization of DSS is the group DSS mentioned previously.

6. DSS groups have become less like special project "commando teams" and more a part of the support team for a variety of other types of end user support.

7. Cutting across all the trends given earlier is the continued development of user-friendly capabilities. This, more than any other feature, is what enabled early DSS. The development of dialog support hardware, such as the mouse, touch screens, and high-resolution graphics, will be further advanced by speech recognition, handwriting recognition, and voice synthesis. Dialog support software such as menus, windows, and help functions is continuing to advance. The "virtual desktop" dialog pioneered by Xerox, and currently used by Apple Macintosh computers and Microsoft Windows, embodies many user-friendly features and has nearly become a de facto standard.

Summary

DSS have taken their place in the portfolio of applications and tools to support problem solving, decision making, and other goal-based information activities. The DSS label was first used to describe a large general class of applications, and the DSS movement of academics and developers defined the concepts, principles, and products to implement the systems. As the field grew, specialized views of DSS emerged for groups, for executives, and for office work. The DSS label now refers mostly to systems for analysis of complex situations, having absorbed most of the work of management science and operations research in business organizations. In later chapters we discuss other types of support systems. In the remainder of this chapter we devote our attention to DSS for executives—EIS.

EXECUTIVE INFORMATION SYSTEMS

Executive information systems (EIS) and a somewhat more general variant called executive support systems appear to be experiencing renewed interest, after a few years of quiet progress. Originally, some authors argued that CEOs would not use computers directly, and quoted CEOs who agreed with them. But the tone of such claims does not seem as confident now because of the experiences of the past several years. In this section we discuss the nature of EIS, the critical factors that determine whether an EIS will be successful or not, what it should do, and what the future might hold.

Executives Do Use Computers!

Lou Wallis [6] reported on three executives from major U.S. corporations who sponsored the development of an EIS and then "wondered how their companies ever did without it." Strong positive testimonials came from Paul A. Allaire, president of Xerox, William D. Smithburg, chairman and chief executive officer of the Quaker Oats Company, and Finn M. W. Caspersen, chairman and chief executive officer of Beneficial Corporation. Each used an executive support system for some time for the following, noted Wallis:

1. Company performance data—sales, production, earnings, budgets, and forecasts
2. Internal communications—personal correspondence, reports, and meetings

3. Environmental scanning—for news on government regulations, competition, financial and economic developments, and scientific subjects

With this set of functions, these systems qualify for the broader term of *executive support systems (ESS)*. The label *EIS* (executive *information* systems) is generally used to refer only to the set of functions recorded in company performance data. In fact, using the DDM paradigm described earlier, EIS can be viewed as a DSS that (a) provides access to (mostly) summary performance data, (b) using graphics to display and visualize the data in a very easy to use fashion (frequently with a touch screen interface), and (c) with a minimum of analysis for modeling beyond the capability to drill down in summary data to examine components. ESS (executive *support* systems) add functions to support the other major responsibilities and activities of top executives such as communications and environmental scanning/alerting.

The experience at Xerox is a good example of the successful development and use of ESS. Paul Allaire became the executive sponsor of Xerox's ESS project while he was corporate chief of staff. Although he felt that an ESS would be valuable to the executive team, he insisted that it earn its usefulness, not that it be "crammed down their throat." In fact, the system began small and evolved to the point where even skeptical users became avid supporters.

A key to success, says Wallace, is that Allaire did not just throw money at a vague sense of problems or grandiose dreams. Improving communication and the planning processes were clear objectives from the start. For example, Allaire describes the problem of getting the briefing information to executives in preparation for regular executive meetings. Due to the time required to prepare the materials, and mailing delays to Xerox international offices, many executives ended up reading a hundred pages or more the night before the meetings without access to related information or time for discussions with staff. Now it is all on ESS. The result is that the executives rarely have a meeting in which they do not have enough information or preparation to make the necessary decisions.

The other job that got executives involved in using the ESS was strategic planning. ESS helped make this crucial work more efficient and resulted in better plans, especially across divisions. Instead of each division preparing plans that were simply combined, the ESS allowed the executives to explore interrelationships between plans and activities at several divisions. So the ESS is playing an important role at Xerox, and the executives do indeed use computers.

Stories such as this one are appearing frequently in the public and trade press. The implication is that computers are finally being used by executives to help them perform their management jobs better. The underlying message is that the use of computers for executive support is just a matter of using popular software packages, and that the only reason more executives are not using computers is their timidity.

We do not think the situation is that simple. Successful support of executive work with computers is fraught with subtle pitfalls and problems. Consider the following case study of a failure.

Doing It Wrong

Watson [7] describes the experience of a (hypothetical) company and its well-intentioned effort to develop and install an EIS. The IS director at Genericorp had heard of successful EIS experiences, such as Lockheed-Georgia (the case example later in this chapter). He thought such a system would be valuable to his company, so he arranged for a presentation by a DSS vendor; it was very well received by the executive team. After some discussion, the executives decided to purchase the product from the vendor and develop an EIS. The allocated budget was $250,000.

They assembled a qualified team of IS professionals, which interviewed executives concerning their information needs (whenever the executives could find the time), and developed an initial version of the system consisting of 50 screens to be used by five executives. The response from these executive was quite good and, in some cases, enthusiastic. Several of them seemed proud to finally be able to use a computer, says Watson.

With the system delivered, the development team turned it over to a maintenance team and moved on to other new projects. The maintenance team was to add new screens and new users—in short, to evolve the system. Nine months later, very little had happened, apparently because other systems maintenance projects had been more urgent. About this time, there was a downturn in revenue that generated cost-cutting pressures on nonessential systems; the EIS was discontinued.

What went wrong? Watson identifies five problem areas that serve as a guide to the hidden pitfalls that should be avoided in developing a successful EIS.

1. *Lack of Executive Support.* Although this has been listed as a potential problem area in system development for years, there are special reasons why it is crucial for EIS. Executives must provide the funding, but they are also the principal users so they need to supply the necessary continuity.

2. *Undefined System Objectives.* The technology, the convenience, and the power of EIS are impressive, maybe even seductive. But the underlying objectives and business values of an EIS must be carefully thought out.

3. *Poorly Defined Information Requirements.* Once the objectives of the system are defined, the required information can be identified. This process is complicated because EIS typically need nontraditional information sources—judgments, opinions, external text-based documents—in additional to traditional financial and operating data.

4. *Inadequate Support Staff.* The support staff must have technical competence, of course, but perhaps more important is the understanding of the business and the ability to relate to the varied responsibilities and work patterns of executives. A permanent team must manage the evolution of the system.

5. *Poorly Planned Evolution.* Highly competent systems professionals using the wrong development process will fail with EIS. EIS are not developed, delivered, and then maintained. They need to evolve over time under the leadership of a team that includes the executive sponsor, the operating sponsor, executive users, the EIS support staff manager, and I/S technical staff.

Although EIS development is difficult, many organizations are reporting that it is worth the effort. Avoiding the pitfalls identified by Watson improves the probability of a successful EIS.

Critical Success Factors for EIS

Quite a bit of research on executive, managerial, and office use of computers has been done at the Center for Information Systems Research, in the Sloan School of Management at MIT [8]. As reported by David DeLong and John Rockart [8a], in a survey of 45 randomly selected *Fortune* 500 companies, 30 had at least one executive with a PC on the desk.

The authors then made in-depth studies of the 30 companies and found a variety of experiences, to the point where they could select eight critical success factors (CSFs) for what they call an "expert support system" (ESS). The top three are: (a) a committed and informed executive sponsor, (b) an operating sponsor, and (c) a clear link between the ESS and the business objectives.

A Committed and Informed Executive Sponsor. The desire for an ESS must come from top management, say the authors. Such a system is hardly ever used by executives if initiated solely by the information systems department. One executive must be the sponsor, and must put in the time and energy to see that the system is "right." The sponsor's expectations must be realistic about what the ESS can and cannot do. Furthermore, the sponsor should understand the basics of the implementation process itself—what human and financial resources will be needed, what the organizational impact of the new system is likely to be, and where resistance may appear.

An Operating Sponsor. The development of an ESS is often delegated to a trusted senior executive, say the authors, someone who can communicate both with the other executives and the development staff. This operating sponsor, who needs to be the primary and most enthusiastic user, is the most critical in shaping, refining, and extending the system's capabilities.

A Clear Link to Business Objectives. Often an executive wants an ESS on such short notice that the step of defining the system's business objectives is overlooked, report the authors. The developers assume that the executive is too impatient for this process to be done properly. As identified by Watson earlier, however, this is one of the major pitfalls in EIS development. Business value objectives must be the primary driver.

The full list of critical success factors identified by DeLong and Rockart is

1. A committed and informed executive sponsor
2. An operating sponsor
3. A clear link to business objectives
4. The use of appropriate resources from the information systems function
5. The use of appropriate technology
6. Recognizing the existence of data problems (inconsistencies, etc.) and managing the solution of those problems

7. Managing organizational resistance
8. Managing the spread and evolution of the system

In summary, it is clear that executive use of computers is not a straightforward matter. It involves much more than putting a PC on an executive's desk and providing a few popular software packages—because those software packages usually do not address the needs of the executives.

ACHIEVING SUCCESSFUL EIS

There are many questions to be answered when considering an EIS. Some of the answers are specific to the organization—who it will serve, where and when it will be developed—so it would serve no purpose to discuss them. However, the other questions—why, what, and how—can have more general answers.

Why Install an EIS?

There is a range of possible motivations, on the part of the project's executive sponsor, for installing an EIS.

Attack a critical business need. EIS can be viewed as an aid to dealing with important needs that involve the future health of the organization. In this situation, almost everyone in the organization can clearly see the reason for developing an EIS.

A strong personal desire by the executive. The executive sponsoring the project may want to get information faster than he or she is now getting it, or have quicker access to a broader range of information, or have the ability to select and display only desired information and to probe for supporting detail, or to see information presented in graphical form. A related motivation occurs within divisions, where corporate management is using an EIS and divisional management feels at a disadvantage without one.

"The thing to do." An EIS, in this instance, is seen as something that modern management must have in order to be current in management practices. The rationale given is that the EIS will increase executive performance and reduce time wasted looking for information.

These motivations are listed in the sequence of strongest to weakest, as far as probable project success is concerned. A strong motivation, such as meeting a critical business need, is more likely to assure top-management interest in, and support of, the project. At the other extreme, a weak motivation can lead to poor executive sponsorship of the project, which can result in trouble. Thus, motivation for the EIS is fundamental to its success because it helps to determine the degree of commitment by the senior executives.

What Should It Do?

What the EIS should do is second only to motivation, in our opinion, as a critical success factor. It determines to what extent the executives will actually make hands-on use of the system.

We will present two viewpoints on what an EIS should do, each of which makes valid points. Perhaps these two viewpoints are more complementary than conflicting, but they are not synonymous. It is important that all the people associated with the project have the same understanding of just what the new system is expected to do—how it will provide executive support. These two viewpoints illustrate the types of points that should be settled at the outset of the project.

A Status Access System. At its heart, an EIS should filter, extract, and compress a broad range of up-to-date internal and external information. It should call attention to variances from plan and also monitor and highlight the critical success factors of the individual executive user.

This view sees an EIS as a structured reporting system for executive management—providing an executive with the data and information of his or her choice, and in the desired form. It is primarily a status access system, for monitoring what is going on in the company and in the outside world. With this information at hand, the executive can then work to resolve any problems that he or she has uncovered.

EIS can start small and quickly with this data-and-information approach, but still accomplish something useful. For example, EIS developers asked the company president of one large insurance company what were the ten things he would look at first after returning from vacation. He gave them this list. Two weeks later, they gave him an EIS terminal with those ten items listed on the main menu, as the first iteration of the EIS. The president was delighted, and was soon asking for more!

This data-and-information approach is based on information with which executives are already familiar. Executives already get, or would like to get, most of the information that the EIS provides—but the EIS provides it faster, in more convenient form, pulling things together that previously had to be viewed separately, and using graphics to aid comprehension.

Human Communications Support. Much of the work that executives (and other office workers) perform is based on person-to-person communications. The steps in getting results via such communications are the following:

1. Make requests and receive promises for action.
2. Discuss and negotiate to clarify an assignment and the responsibility for results.
3. Follow up on progress toward, and barriers in the way of, obtaining the desired results.
4. Redirect the assignment when necessary and renew commitments, or acknowledge failure of the assignment.
5. Receive (or deliver) results.
6. Acknowledge completion of the assignment.

This viewpoint sees an EIS in terms of the human communications support that it provides. Data and information can help managers discover what is missing, but human communications are needed to bring the missing work into being. The manager makes up his or her mind about some future action and then calls on a "network of help." This network consists of personal relationships with peers, subordinates, clients, customers, suppliers, and others. The manager makes requests, gives instructions, and asks questions to selected members of this network in order to get people going on the desired action. The manager acts through communications, and a critical role for many EIS is to support these communications.

Which Is More Important? Both of these viewpoints are valid, and they appear to be more complementary than conflicting. But the question remains: When initiating an EIS project, should it aim at performing mainly data and information handling or the communications that are needed for action? Some systems on the market accommodate both. Obviously, the choice will depend on the needs of an organization and its executives, but the choice should be consciously made. Ambiguity—or, even worse, vacillation—in what the system should do almost surely will lead to eventual lack of acceptance.

What Data Sources?

Generally the EIS should *not* try to give executives direct access to production data files, even through friendly front-end software. There is just too much detailed knowledge needed to access, interpret, and use such data. Instead, desired information should be extracted from the production databases, formatted, and put into the EIS database. In fact, data and information from many sources should be put into the EIS database. External information and predictive data generally are not found in production databases, and will have to be supplied from other sources. The information should be organized in hierarchical fashion, so that highlights are in the top layer. The most important data must be the easiest to find. When a user wants to see supporting detail, it should be available.

Many production data files carry mostly current information, with little historical detail. To spot trends, however, the EIS database needs to carry relevant historical data, such as time series data. Furthermore, the user needs to be able to track the external environment and to spot significant deviations from assumptions.

In general, the information on which EIS would draw includes all four of the sources we identified in Chapter 7—data records and documents from both internal and external sources. Perhaps the fastest growing information source, with the development of text retrieval software and high-speed communication lines, is the external document-based information. EIS that tap this information source will give executives greatly enhanced ability to assess environmental and competitive conditions.

To summarize our discussion of EIS, consider how an EIS was developed and has evolved at Lockheed-Georgia over the past several years.

CASE EXAMPLE: Lockheed-Georgia

Lockheed-Georgia, a subsidiary of Lockheed Corporation, has its head-quarters in Marietta, Georgia, where it employs some 19,000 people in the production of C-5B and Hercules transport aircraft and other programs. Lockheed-Georgia was one of the earliest users of computers for manufacturing and accounting functions—and it is one of the early users of executive information systems.

As described by Houdelshel and Watson [9], the initial interest was expressed by Robert Ormsby in 1975, when he was president of Lockheed-Georgia. The existing information systems had not been designed to provide information for management needs, Ormsby felt. The result was that managers found it hard to locate desired information. Also, the printed reports often were not sufficiently current, and data inconsistencies (for reasons such as timing differences) led to management misunderstandings.

The Initial Project

In late 1978, work began on the management information and decision support system (MIDS), with Ormsby as the executive sponsor and key initial user. A project team of five was formed, with a manager (who reported to the vice president of finance), two people from finance, and two from information services.

The project got underway with the team's study of the information requirements of Ormsby and his staff. The project team gathered this information, say the authors, by interviewing these executives and their secretaries to find out what information they actually received. The executives' use of existing reports was also studied.

Then the team searched for the best sources of the desired information. They wanted adequate detail behind the information presented to the executives to support any probing. The team also wanted to avoid information that had been distorted by the perspective of the organizational units where the data originated.

Design Criteria

Several design criteria played an important role in the eventual success of the project, Houdelshel and Watson report. One important design principle was to make training largely unnecessary by making the system simple to use. This goal was accomplished by providing a hierarchy of menus; training of a new user is done in one 15-minute training session without the need for written instructions.

Another design criterion was that information be organized in a top-down fashion, with a summary paragraph at the beginning, followed by supporting graphs, tables, and text. Explanatory comments would be provided as necessary to indicate, for instance, that an apparent variance from schedule had almost been corrected.

Other design criteria included fast response times, only a few terminal keystrokes needed to call up any display screen, and features to help executives locate desired information. Furthermore, each user was to have a MIDS terminal (based on a PC) on his or her desk. Color graphics capabilities would help in the presentation of graphic data.

There were no commercial systems of this type on the market at the time, so Lockheed-Georgia developed MIDS in-house. The initial version was working in just six months' time. Ormsby was the key user, and when the system was first installed, he could access 31 screens of information. The initial MIDS programs and data were on a PC.

How MIDS Has Evolved

Eight years later, in 1986, the MIDS system consisted of over 700 displays, with a user population of 30 top executives and 40 operating managers. As the number of users increased, the system was moved to DEC minicomputers and then to an IBM 3081, the authors report. To minimize the use of hard copy, the system did not support printers attached to the PCs. The only printers were in the MIDS office.

A "double" security system was installed to control access to the information. Each user was given a password. In addition, access by a user can be limited to only certain terminals. For example, an executive might be able to access certain sensitive information from the terminal in his or her office but not from a terminal in a conference room.

The MIDS staff grew from the original five people to a staff of nine—the manager, six information analysts, and two computer analysts. Each information analyst was responsible for maintaining about 100 of the displays—and about 170 displays were updated daily to meet changing conditions! It has been essential, said the company, that the information analysts understand the information for which they are responsible. Most of these analysts have worked in, or have been trained in, the functional areas they serve, and they are encouraged to take additional appropriate courses.

The Benefits

Lockheed-Georgia feels that MIDS has improved information flow for the executive users, report Houdelshel and Watson. The system provides more timely, accurate, and relevant information based on the needs of the individual executives. The system highlights problem areas and items requiring management attention and includes pertinent comments along with these highlights.

MIDS has also improved management communications because it operates within the IBM PROFS electronic mail system. Also, two or more executives are able to view the same information simultaneously on their screens, while talking on the telephone. This feature helps avoid disagreements that arise from inconsistent information.

User acceptance has been good. The number of users has grown from 1 to over 70, and the frequency of use (number of screens viewed per user per day) has also grown. Middle managers began asking for a version of MIDS. MIDS-II (described later) promises to make that feasible.

During the design phase, no attempt was made to formally cost-justify the system; instead, the project was approached as research and development. Authorization to continue enhancing the system depended at each stage upon the usefulness of the previous stage.

While justification by cost displacement was not a criterion, there have been some cost savings, primarily associated with the reduction in printed reports. In fact, some of the printed reports that MIDS executives no longer receive are ones that were prepared manually (the information is now in MIDS) and ones prepared on other systems (summaries of which are now in MIDS).

Houdelshel and Watson point out several factors that contributed to the success of MIDS. Foremost was a committed senior executive sponsor—President Robert Ormsby. Then came careful design of system and information requirements, along with a team approach to design. The evolutionary development approach was crucial because no one could (or can) visualize at the outset what the eventual system will be like. Hardware and software were also selected carefully. Now the success of MIDS and advances in technology have led to the next major phase in the evolution—MIDS II. Watson recently described this upgrade.

MIDS II: The Ongoing Story

In 1990, after 12 years of successful MIDS operations, it became necessary to update the hardware technology. This change was required because the Intelligent Systems Company (ISC) graphics computers that were used by the MIDS support staff to design and update the screens were no longer in production and replacement parts had become difficult to find. The MIDS staff faced the real possibility of not being able to maintain the system due to lack of hardware. Therefore, the company undertook a comprehensive review of the hardware *and* software options available for MIDS.

The company decided it was more economical to purchase commercial EIS software than to develop another system in-house, so several commercial products were evaluated; Comshare's Commander EIS was chosen. It offers a large number of capabilities that facilitate the development and maintenance of an EIS, including

- Support for multiple user interfaces
- On-line, context-dependent help screens
- Command files
- Multiple methods for locating information
- Access to external databases (e.g., Dow Jones News Retrieval)
- Interfaces to other software (e.g., PROFS, Lotus 1-2-3)
- Integrated decision support (e.g., System W, IFPS)
- Screen design templates
- Application shells
- Data extraction from existing organizational databases
- Graphical, tabular, and textual information on the same screen
- Integration of data from different sources
- Security for data, screens, and systems
- Support for rapid prototyping
- Support for multiple computing platforms
- Support for hard copy output (e.g., paper, overhead transparencies, 35mm slides)

Two important changes to the Comshare software were requested, however, before a contract was signed. The changes retained capabilities that were in MIDS but not in Commander EIS. The changes needed to be made to the basic Comshare product and not to just a special version for Lockheed to ensure compatibility with later releases of Commander.

The two changes permitted users to operate the system through a keyboard (in addition to a mouse or touch screen) and provided for monitoring the use of the system. Lockheed executives had enjoyed the MIDS system advantage of going from any screen to any other screen without retracing a path or returning to a predetermined point. This capability was retained by allowing executives to enter the number of the desired screen. Monitoring of system usage had always been performed by the MIDS system management and it had become invaluable in keeping the MIDS system up-to-date. With these changes, Commander EIS became the development environment for MIDS II.

Even though commercial EIS software was selected for MIDS II, the original screen designs were retained. In fact, when Lockheed asked vendors to prepare demonstration prototypes, they requested screens that looked like those currently in use. Considerable thought and experimentation had gone into screen design over the years, Lockheed's executives were familiar with them, and MIDS II was to continue the look and feel of the original system.

In addition to new software, hardware improvements were made to take advantage of state-of-the-art technology and to position MIDS II in Lockheed's long-range computing plans. The Comshare software helped make this possible through its ability to run on a mixed platform of IBM

PS/2s and Apple Macintoshes. A Novell LAN was installed to improve the system's response time and reliability.

MIDS II was developed and rolled out to users in 1992 and was expected to provide a variety of benefits over the original system: faster response time, easier navigation (through "drill down" to more detailed information), better links to other resources (internal and external databases), reduced maintenance costs (automatic update of some screens), shared EIS techniques with other Commander EIS users, and a state-of-the-art technology platform that permits future improvements and growth within information systems long-range planes. The original MIDS system has served Lockheed very well since 1978, and MIDS II has been designed to carry this tradition into the future.

FUTURE OF DSS

Recalling our earlier discussion in Chapter 1 of the ultimate mission of information systems, the vision for DSS should be the application of a variety of technologies to improve the performance of information workers in organizations especially as they deal with ill-structured problems. Goal-based information-handling activities exist in a wide variety of forms, and systems to support them are equally varied.

Challenges

Several challenges will have to be met if this vision of DSS is to be realized. We must pursue the connectivity necessary to link all the people who work together in decision making and problem solving, and we must develop richer data sources and more intelligence in the model bases.

Integrated Architecture. The workstation on the desktop of the information worker is becoming the "window" into the world of information. A common dialog interface will allow access to all the information resources, and previously separate systems can be called and run from this common interface. The graphic user interface represented by Windows, Mac, and others, is becoming common enough to be a de facto standard for this purpose, but the applications and data must be compatible enough to be accessible from this window.

Connectivity. The workstations of information workers will be connected whenever people must cooperate or communicate. Communication is recognized as an increasingly important function to be supported by technology, so it will be an integrated part of the information systems delivered through the workstation. Connectivity means, first, the actual ability to connect workstations through local area networks and among LANs through the Internet. It also requires a bandwidth or data transfer rate to accommodate the interchange of large files, graphics and figures, digital images, photographs, and video. Rich communication in the process of decision making and problem solving will require rich media and, therefore, high-capacity communication channels.

Document Data. The well-structured data in databases has long been valuable for decision support. Even more important may be the concepts and ideas contained in less well-structured documents. Technologies are emerging that will allow access to, and management of, documents in addition to data records. This vastly increased set of information resources will have a major impact on the strength and effectiveness of DSS. These expanded information resources are made even more valuable with new search and structuring technologies such as concept retrieval, hypertext, and multimedia. Chapter 16 discusses the growing importance of document resources in DSS.

More Intelligence. As expert systems began to develop and be used, some thought that they would replace DSS. DSS builders realized, however, that expert systems are enhanced forms of models, but if used only on a stand-alone basis, they suffer from the same limitations as stand-alone management science models. Thus, they were added to the model base and the DSS was used as a delivery system for the expert systems.

More recently, components of expert systems and other AI approaches have been integrated into DSS. The knowledge base becomes a form of combined data/model base, the inference engine can be viewed as a knowledge-based management system (similar to the data base management system and dialog management system), and the language system is a part of the dialog. The future will bring much more integration and extension of the intelligence capability in DSS.

CONCLUSION

The concept and technology of DSS have received much attention during the past decade. The theoretical ideal of university researchers became primarily financial planning systems at first. But DSS technology and its application are continuing to grow in strength and value. The current status can be characterized by a predominance of institutional systems, increasing instances of personal DSS, and a growing interest in group DSS. Two other developments include the increased use of computer graphics and the popularity of spreadsheets. We see continued growth of PC-based DSS, distributed DSS that link PCs to mainframes, growing use of group DSS, and the addition of expert systems.

Of these trends, we considered EIS in some detail. Potentially, executive information systems that are within today's state of the art can

1. Provide status information on how things are going both within and outside of the organization.
2. Help executives communicate with others to identify and define needed actions.
3. Help make those needed actions happen.

However, EIS cannot be imposed upon executives, they must individually be receptive to it. Furthermore, an EIS must present information in a manner desired by each individual executive, although some standards can be employed on designing the screen displays, for example, the use of colors, size and placement of text, and so on.

Success of an EIS depends, we think, on having a strong motivation for installing it in the first place, a committed and informed senior executive sponsor, an appropriate operating sponsor and project organization, a definition of what the EIS is expected to do (and not do) at the outset, and being easy to use, even for infrequent users.

QUESTIONS AND EXERCISES

REVIEW QUESTIONS

1. According to evolved discussions, what is the definition of a decision support system?
2. What is the DDM paradigm for DSS suggested by Sprague and Carlson? How is it useful? Summarize the most important attributes of each component.
3. What is an institutional DSS? Give a example.
4. What is a quick-hit DSS? When is it useful? Define three types.
5. What are DSS generators?
6. When are graphics useful in decision making?
7. What are the major trends in DSS?
8. What are the three main kinds of support derived from EIS by Xerox, Quaker Oats, and Beneficial Life? Use this list to distinguish between EIS and ESS.
9. What are the two main benefits Xerox derived from the ESS?
10. What are the pitfalls in ESS development identified by Watson?
11. What are the three major CSFs for successful EIS, identified by DeLong and Rockart?
12. What is a strong reason for installing EIS? A weak reason?
13. Give two opinions on the main role of EIS.
14. What were the design criteria that have contributed to the success of MIDS at Lockheed-Georgia?
15. What are the four future challenges for DSS?

DISCUSSION QUESTIONS

1. Graphics are crucial to DSS and EIS. Without good graphics, such a system is doomed. Do you agree or disagree? Why?
2. From the case examples and discussions in the chapter, which of the attributes of a DSS or EIS do you think are most important? Why?

EXERCISES

1. If you have ever used a spreadsheet package, describe one of your uses and the decisions the package helped you to make.
2. Find one or more current articles on DSS or EIS. What characteristics or attributes are described? How do they compare with the ones in the text?
3. Visit a local company and talk to a user or a developer of decision support systems. What types of DSS are being used or developed? What tools are being used? Briefly describe one or two applications.

REFERENCES

1. SPRAGUE, RALPH H. and HUGH WATSON, *Decision Support for Management*, Englewood Cliffs, NJ, Prentice Hall, 1996.

2. GORRY, MICHAEL and MICHAEL SCOTT MORTON, "A Framework for Management Information Systems," *Sloan Management Review*, Fall 1971, pp. 55–70.

3. SCOTT MORTON, MICHAEL, *Management Decision Systems: Computer Support for Decision Making*. Cambridge, MA, Harvard University Press, 1971.

4. SPRAGUE, RALPH H. and ERIC CARLSON, *Building Effective Decision Support Systems*, Englewood Cliffs, NJ, Prentice Hall, 1982.

5. CARD, S., G. ROBERTSON, and J. MACKINLAY, "The Information Visualizer: An Information Workspace," Xerox Palo Alto Research Center, Palo Alto, CA.

6. WALLIS, LOU, "Power Computing at the Top," *Across the Board*, January/February 1989.

7. WATSON, HUGH, "Avoiding Hidden EIS Pitfalls," *Computerworld*, June 25, 1990.

8. Reports of the Center for Information Systems Research, Sloan School, Massachusetts Institute of Technology, E40-193, 77 Massachusetts Avenue, Cambridge, MA 02139.

   a) DELONG, DAVID and JOHN ROCKART, "Identifying Attributes of Successful Executive Support System Implementation," CISR WP 132, January 1986.

   b) BULLEN, CHRISTINE, and JOHN BENNETT, "Office Workstation Use by Administrative Managers and Professionals," CISR WP 102, April 1983.

   c) ROCKART, JOHN, and DAVID DELONG, "Executive Support Systems and the Nature of Executive Work," CISR WP 135, April 1986.

9. HOUDELSHEL, GEORGE, and HUGH WATSON, "The Management Information and Decision Support (MIDS) System at Lockheed-Georgia," *MIS Quarterly* (MIS Research Center, University of Minnesota, 269 19th Avenue South, Minneapolis, MN 55455), March 1987.

FOURTEEN

INTRODUCTION

In this chapter, we focus on groups, rather than individuals, and the systems and technologies that support the communication and interaction among people as they work in groups. As in all the chapters in this support systems section of the book, we emphasize goal-based systems, which are those systems that support work activities that do not follow the same or similar process every time and also deal with information (and knowledge) that cannot be easily encapsulated.

One way to "chunk" the activities of groups is to say that they perform two generic activities. One is *communication and interaction*, that is, communication is the transmission of information from one person to another (or to several others); interaction is repetitive (usually back and forth) communication over time. The other major activity is *decision making or problem solving*, where members of a group reach a decision or form a consensus. It could be argued that communication is a necessary part of group decision making, so it is encompassed by the latter function. It seems, however, that communication is a valuable function in its own right, to aid in coordinating activities in an organization, whether or not a decision or consensus is reached.

Much of the current activity in group support systems has originated from one or the other of these two major functions. Office systems, and in particular electronic mail, are oriented toward supporting people-to-people communication. Researchers in the area of "computer supported cooperative work" [1] generally emphasize technology to aid communication, such as enhanced computer conferencing and systems to assist two or more people to work on the same project. On the other hand, group DSS work, evolving from the DSS community, focuses on reaching a conclusion, decision, or consensus, even though it includes technology to support communication.

A second way to "chunk" the work of groups is the way Gerardine DeSanctis, of Duke University, and Brent Gallupe, of the University of Minnesota, did in one of the early frameworks [2]. Their matrix, shown in Figure 14-1, has *proximity* of group members on one dimension (together/dispersed) and *duration* of interaction on the other (limited/ongoing). The figure gives one technology example per cell. Note that this matrix is relevant for both communication and decision

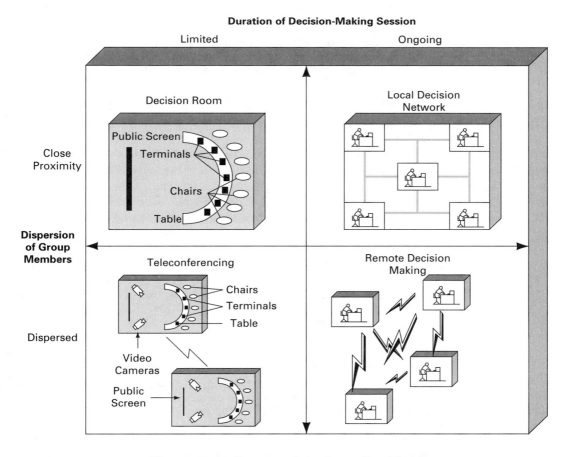

Figure 14-1   Framework for Group Decision Support
(from DeSanctis and Gallupe [2])

making. For example, decision making has been the intent of decision rooms, while LANs are usually perceived mainly as communication support tools.

Yet a third way to "chunk" the work of groups is to use a variation of the DeSanctis/Gallupe matrix, by having *time* on one dimension (same time/different time) and *place* on the other (same place/different place). It appears that this third characterization has come to be the predominant one, so we will present it later in the chapter when we discuss the different kinds of group support systems. But first, we discuss the characteristics and types of groups.

Characteristics of Groups

Not all groups are the same. And there are different types. Some of the characteristics that differentiate groups are the following.

Membership. Groups can be open, where almost anyone can join. Or they can be closed, where membership is restricted. Actually, there is a "gray scale" between open and closed, based on the degree of difficulty to gain membership.

Interaction. The group can be loosely coupled, where the activity of each member is relatively independent of the other members. Salespeople who have their own sales territories often fall in this category. Or the group can be tightly coupled, such as a project team where the work of each member is tied closely to the work of the other members. As in the case of gaining group membership, there is a range of group couplings, from loose to tight.

Hierarchy. A group can be just one part of a chain of command. Large public events, such at the Olympics or the Rose Parade, for instance, are planned and conducted by a hierarchy of committees. At the top is an ongoing committee that sets the general plans for years in advance and selects the site and the top people for putting on each event. The top committee for the event then oversees the work of the various detail committees. In addition, each of the detail committees may have subcommittees working on specific portions of their responsibility.

We cite these characteristics to illustrate that providing computer-based support for groups is not straightforward because there are so many variations. Initially, support was for intracompany groups, but the Internet has led to worldwide support, as we demonstrate later. The main issues are what types of groups need support and why.

Types of Groups

Furthermore, there are all kinds of groups. Here is a list of just a few:

- *Authority groups* involve formal authority (and often hierarchy), such as boss and subordinates, team leader and team members, and so on. Membership is closed and coupling is tight. In matrix management, people may have two bosses, one technical, one administrative.
- *Intradepartmental groups* can have members all doing essentially the same work, often under the same boss. Membership is closed, seniority generally exists, and interaction can range from tight (only do one job, each on his or her own) to loose coupling (work with neighbors). LANs and departmental computers have been installed for these groups.

- *Project teams* generally have members who work full-time to accomplish a goal by a specific time. Generally, membership is closed, coupling is tight, and a hierarchy can exist.
- *Interdepartmental work groups* pass work from department to department (purchasing, receiving, accounts payable) in a chain, forming a supergroup. Membership is closed, coupling is tight, and hierarchy tends not to be present.
- *Committees and task forces* are formed to deal with a subject area or issue. Generally, neither requires full-time participation. Committees are usually ongoing; task forces just deal with the issue and disband. Membership may not be quite as closed as a project team, and interaction might not be as tightly coupled as among committee members.
- *"Communities of practice."* The people at the Institute for Research on Learning [3] have coined this term to mean a group of people who work or play together for so long that they have developed an identifiable way of doing things. Such communities arise naturally at school, work, volunteer organizations, sports clubs, and elsewhere.
- *Business relationship groups* are relationships with customers, groups of customers, suppliers, and so on. Membership often is closed in that a new organization may have to "earn" real acceptance. Interaction is loosely coupled. A hierarchy is not too likely, but favored customers and suppliers can have dominating influences.
- *Peer groups* meet to exchange ideas and opinions. Examples are fraternal organizations, secretaries who call on each other for help, and prospects called together for a sales presentation. Membership can range from relatively open to closed and the interaction tends to be loosely coupled. Hierarchy usually is not much in evidence.
- *Networks* are groups of people who socialize, exchange information, and expand their personal network of acquaintances.
- *Electronic groups* such as chat rooms, multiuser domains, user groups, and virtual worlds are all types of groups that have formed on the Internet to socialize, find information, entertain themselves, gain comfort, or just experiment with the new on-line world. Membership is generally wide open, interaction is loosely coupled, and there is no hierarchy.

WHY ARE GROUP SYSTEMS IMPORTANT?

Why should information system executives be interested in supporting groups? Robert Johansen [4], of the Institute for the Future and an author of two books on group working, notes that group support systems are important because most people spend 60 to 80 percent of their time working with others. Yet, from informal polls he has taken, people seem to feel they are most productive when they are working alone. Thus, they are not happy about how they work with others. This shows there is a need for systems that support groups.

However, groupware—electronic tools that support teams of collaborators—represents a fundamental change in the way people think about using computers, says Johansen. The things people need to work with others are different from the things they need to work alone. So groupware is different from past software.

In the future, groupware that takes full advantage of information technology will be just another part of corporate information systems, says Johansen. The products most likely will be built on existing platforms—electronic mail systems, LANs, departmental systems, and public network services, such as the telephone. Yet use of these technologies will advance beyond the "horseless carriage" stage and lead to new organizational structures, he believes.

Specifically, we see group computing being important for three reasons:

- Teams may be the basis for future organizations.
- Coordination theory may guide organizational design.
- Companies want to "manage" knowledge.

Teams: The Basis of Future Organizations?

Peter Drucker's article, in the *Harvard Business Review*, "The Coming of the New Organization," became the most reprinted *HBR* article in its first year [5]. Apparently it struck a responsive chord. In it, Drucker states that he believes organizations will become information based, and that they will be organized not like today's manufacturing organizations but more like a symphony orchestra, a hospital, or a university. That is, the organization will be composed mainly of specialists who direct their own performance through feedback from others—colleagues, customers, and headquarters.

This move is being driven by three factors, says Drucker. First, knowledge workers are becoming the dominant portion of labor, and they resist the command-and-control form of organization. Second, all companies—even the largest ones—need to find ways to be more innovative and entrepreneurial. And third, information technology is forcing a shift. Once companies use information technology to handle information, not just data, their decision processes, management structure, and work patterns change.

For example, spreadsheets allow people to perform capital investment analysis in a few hours. The calculations are so complex that, before this technology was available, these investment analyses generally had to be based on opinion. With computing, the calculations become manageable, and more importantly, the assumptions underlying the calculations can be given weight. In so doing, the investment analysis changes from being a budget question to being a policy question, says Drucker, because the assumptions supporting the business strategy can more easily be discussed.

Information technology also changes organizational structure when a firm shifts its focus from processing data to producing information, he says. Turning data into information requires knowledge, and knowledge is specialized. The information-based organization will need far more specialists than middle managers who relay information.

Thus, organizations will be flatter with fewer headquarters staff and many specialists out in operating units. Even departments will have different functions, says Drucker. They will set standards, provide training, and assign specialists. The work will be done mainly in task-focused teams, where specialists from the various functions work together as a team for the duration of a project.

Team-based organizations will work like hospitals or orchestras, says Drucker. Hospitals have specialty units, each with its own knowledge, training, and language. Most are headed by a working specialist—not a full-time manager—and that specialist reports to the top of the hospital; there is little middle management. Work in the units is done by ad hoc teams, assembled to treat a patient'. Symphony orchestras are similar. They have one conductor, many high-grade specialists, and other support people.

Drucker believes we are at the beginning of the third stage of the evolution in the structure of organizations. The first, which took place around 1900, separated business ownership from management. The second, in the 1920s, created the command-and-control corporation. The third, happening now, is the organization of knowledge specialists.

As an example of this move toward teams, consider the redesign work at NYNEX. The following description is based on an article in *Communications of the ACM* by Patricia Sachs [6], when she was technical director of the Works Systems Design group, and a Sourcebook case example from Roger Woolfe of Wentworth Research [7a].

CASE EXAMPLE: NYNEX

NYNEX, the New York-based telecommunications company, is in the midst of a huge upheaval as the entire U.S. telecom industry reinvents itself. In the early 1990s, NYNEX targeted 12 major processes for redesign in a companywide business process redesign initiative. Eleven used the traditional Rummler-Brache approach: looking at lines and boxes, "as is" and "should be" in a three-day off-site redesign effort.

The twelfth group used participative design and involved the Work Systems Design group along with eight employees from the process to be redesigned, the T1 provisioning process. The team spent one year from analysis to implementation, with everyone full-time. This project was the only one of the 12 implemented, and it yielded very good results. (The other processes were addressed again in an intensive, large-scale process reengineering effort.)

The Work Systems Design group, whose charter is to create productive workplaces, is an interdisciplinary group with expertise in computer science, telephony, anthropology, and graphic art. It takes a sociotechnical view toward the analysis of work, which is fairly unusual in the industry (the sociotechnical approach is described in Chapter 18). In the quality movement, companies aim to correct processes to eliminate errors. The sociotechnical view, on the other hand, equips people to handle problems, believing that all errors cannot be eliminated. Rather than operate under the common assumption that work can be automated (and thus people can be downskilled), the group wants to upskill employees.

Work is accomplished by people in working communities who possess all kinds of expertise nurtured by that community. The Work Systems Design group, therefore, looks at "communities of practice" and their worlds of expertise. Redesigning processes requires looking at an entire working community, its set of practices, its knowledge, and its expertise. To remain durable, these networks need to be nurtured, supported, and even made formal as teams or as communities of practice—a notion they got from working with the people at the Institute for Research on Learning [3].

In the T1 provisioning redesign project, the goal was to redesign how NYNEX provides high-speed T1 communication service to businesses. The team looked at how work was actually done, created an implementable design, and then disbanded. The operational members returned to their original T1 provisioning work using the new process. That process is unique in NYNEX. Rather than pass a T1 customer among specialized groups, all the people in the process work together, in one area, as a multifunctional team. Thus, engineers work alongside salespeople.

Since this multifunctional team structure is counter to NYNEX's culture and predominant work organization, it has caused problems. When new managers have taken over, they have not understood this way of working. They want the group to return to the familiar structure with all the engineers in one group. So the group's new, more productive structure is weakening. A major difficulty with an innovative new process, NYNEX has learned, is underrating how difficult it is to keep it going when it is counter-cultural.

Coordination Theory May Guide Organizational Design

Thomas Malone, of the Massachusetts Institute of Technology [8], believes that lessons learned about how large groups coordinate their work can be applied to coordinating large groups of computing resources, or even hybrid groups that include both people and computers. Such an understanding is paramount in the emerging field of electronic commerce.

Malone believes that a multidisciplinary study of coordination theories will advance the computer field. For example, using ideas from economic theory, Malone and others at MIT are studying how to allocate processing resources in a distributed computing environment using prices and competitive bidding. They have found that in networks of workstations, where the machines "contract" to process a task, several configurations are possible. These are analogous to human organizations, he says. For instance, the machines could coordinate their own work, as in a decentralized market. Or some machines could be brokers, as in a centralized market. Or these broker machines could be specialized—printer brokers, high-speed processing brokers, and such—as in a functional hierarchy. Or each processor might have its own peripherals, as in a product hierarchy.

These various forms of coordination all have associated costs. Yet, says Malone, it is likely that IT can be used to reduce these costs in human organizations. Look at what has happened as technology has been used to reduce transportation costs, says Malone: (1) People substituted train travel for horse-drawn carriage travel, which (2) increased the amount of traveling people did, since travel was cheaper and more convenient, which, in turn, (3) allowed people to move to the suburbs and go to shopping malls. These represent first-, second-, and third-order effects of cheap, convenient transportation.

The use of IT to reduce costs of coordination could have similar effects: (1) IT replaces some forms of human coordination, such as middle management, which (2) may increase the overall amount of coordination, which (3) may encourage a shift toward more coordination-intensive organizational structures, such as highly networked, decentralized organizations. Uncovering desirable coordination structures and the effects they may have on organizations are two of the goals of Malone's coordination work.

Companies Want to "Manage" Knowledge

One of the hottest subjects in the IT field these days is knowledge management. Top corporate executives realize that their greatest corporate assets walk out the door every evening, taking with them another crucial asset, knowledge. There have been attempts, and continue to be attempts, to capture knowledge in computer systems. The next chapter, on intelligent systems, discusses just that. But for some experts and researchers in the field, knowledge is not something that can be captured in a machine; it only exists inside a person. Information can be captured in computers, knowledge cannot. This view, of course, is in hot debate, and it has raised the question, "OK, if we cannot disembody knowledge, how do we better manage the knowledge within people to leverage this asset?"

Tony Brewer [7b], of Wentworth Research, has researched this topic and notes that as we move from a service economy to a knowledge economy, companies are moving toward managing their intellectual capital in a more formal and deliberate way. He notes that knowledge exists in two states, tacit and explicit. Tacit knowledge exists within a person's mind, and is private and unique to each person. Explicit knowledge has been articulated, codified, and made public. Western management practices have concentrated on managing explicit knowledge, but cultivating and leveraging tacit knowledge are just as important. Effective knowledge management requires transferring knowledge between these two states.

So how is that done? Well, says Brewer, since knowledge is not a physical asset, we should not think of it in terms of manufacturing analogies, such as storing it in inventory. Rather we need to think in ecological terms, such as nurturing it, cultivating it, and harvesting it. Furthermore, we need to find ways to transfer knowledge back and forth between its tacit and explicit states, which generally means encouraging the free flow of ideas and information, something that many of today's organizational norms, departmental boundaries, and national differences inhibit.

"The Rudy Problem." Just discovering who has what knowledge is a step in the right direction. Yet having knowledge is not always rewarded by management, as the following story illustrates.

In September 1995, Arthur Andersen and The American Productivity and Quality Center convened The Knowledge Imperative Symposium [9] at which speakers from around the world described how their companies were managing knowledge—and 1,500 people attended!

One of the many insightful speakers was Patricia Seemann [9a], who, at the time, was working for a large pharmaceutical company. She told the story of Serge and Rudy (whose names had hopefully been changed). Serge, she said, was a "real" manager. He had a three-window office, a big desk, and a title. And if you asked him what he did the past year, he would say, "I registered 600 products in 30 countries." Rudy, on the other hand, is a headache, his manager says, because he does not work. He just stands around and talks all day. Whenever you see him, he is talking to someone. And when you ask him what he did the past year, he says, "I sort of helped out."

The company downsized and guess who got laid off? Rudy. And then what happened? His department fell apart because there was no one to help, to provide guidance. When they fired Rudy, they fired their organizational memory, said Seemann. He was a crucial, yet unrecognized asset, because he was willing to share his knowledge.

While at this company, Seemann and her team created a yellow pages of company knowledge brokers. Guess who was in the book and who was not? Rudy, of course, was in the book. Serge was not, and neither was top management. How can companies fix what she calls "the Rudy problem"? One way is to create a technical career track and promote knowledge brokers. Giving Rudy a title would have made an enormous difference, Seemann said, because it would have sent a signal that knowledge sharing was recognized in the company. Companies cannot appoint knowledge brokers. They just emerge. And when they do emerge, give them support, she recommends.

As another example of what a company can do to promote knowledge sharing (that is, group support), even on a global basis, consider the approach that Buckman Laboratories has taken. This description is based on the Sourcebook that accompanies Brewer's ITMP report "Managing Knowledge," from Wentworth Research [7b].

CASE EXAMPLE: Buckman Laboratories

Buckman Laboratories, an industrial chemical company based in Memphis, Tennessee, has over 1,200 employees around the world. The concept of sharing knowledge and best practices has been around in Buckman for over ten years. In fact, the company's code of ethics reinforces the sharing culture. Buckman believes that successfully transferring knowledge depends 90 percent on having the right culture and 10 percent on technology.

To bring the knowledge of *all* Buckman's employees to bear on a customer problem anywhere in the world—whether in Europe, South Africa, Australia, New Zealand, or Japan—Buckman established a knowledge transfer system called K'Netix, the Buckman Knowledge Network. The goal of K'Netix is to get people who have not met each other, but belong to the same business, to communicate with each other and develop trust in each other—trust that the other person is interested in your success, trust that what you receive from them is valid and sincere, and enough trust in the culture to help someone else.

Ten years ago sharing was accomplished mainly by people traveling all over the world to see each other. There were lots of face-to-face conversations and meetings. Today, such meetings still occur, but the technology helps people stay in touch between these meetings, making communications more continuous.

When employees need information or help, they just ask via forums, which are Buckman-only on-line forums (originally provided by CompuServe). In all, there are seven forums. TechForum is organized by industry and is open to all employees.

One particularly influential conversation—which set the tone for companywide sharing—took place over TechForum and concerned Buckman's global sales awards. A large cash award was split among the top three salespeople worldwide; the top 20 got plaques. It was based on a formula that took many factors into account. The salespeople, however, were unhappy with the formula. When this discussion appeared on the companywide forum, then-CEO Bob Buckman jumped into the fray and decided that the entire company should iron out the problems in front of all employees. Hundreds of messages were recorded, and the entire award structure was restructured on-line in front of everyone. This was a rare opportunity to allow everyone to share in an important, yet sensitive, company subject. Moreover, top management did not dictate the results. This conversation reinforced the sharing culture.

The conversations are the basis for transferring knowledge around the company. So the important ones are captured. Volunteer experts identify the ones that contain valuable information and, more importantly, valuable streams of reasoning. These are then edited to remove extraneous material, given key words, and stored in the forum library. In essence, Buckman is capturing the artifacts of its virtual teams in action. In so doing, it is creating a self-building knowledge base, which can be used for what-if analyses and can be mined to create new knowledge.

The prime benefit is timely, high-quality responses to customer needs. For example, a new employee in Brazil was scheduled to visit a customer with a particular problem. He posted the problem and his suggested solution in a forum and sought advice from anyone with more experience. He quickly got a response: "I've faced this and your pH is too high, it will cause odors and ruin the paper. Bring the pH down by two points. That won't hurt the process, and it will clear up the problem." As a result, this new employee—who had only modest experience—was able to present a proposal with the experience of a 25-year veteran. He made the sale.

TYPES OF GROUP SUPPORT SYSTEMS

As we noted earlier, Bob Johansen [4], of the Institute for the Future, is a leader in the field of groupware. He and his colleagues at IFTF extended the DeSanctis/Gallupe matrix shown at the beginning of the chapter. Their time/place framework, shown in Figure 14-2, appears to be the dominant one used to discuss where a particular groupware technology of product fits.

The two values on each dimension—same/different—designate whether the group members are communicating and interacting over time and/or distance. The "same time/same place" cell in the upper right, for example, includes electronic meeting support systems. The "different time/different place" cell in the lower right incorporates the communication-oriented systems such as e-mail, computer conferencing, and use of Lotus Notes.

To date, the greatest amount of research and number of products have taken place in these two cells. Therefore, in the discussion that follows, we spend more time on them. Interestingly, there has been little integration among the systems in these two cells, or with the other two cells, even though it is clear to researchers and developers that true group support systems must aim to support "anytime, anyplace" group work.

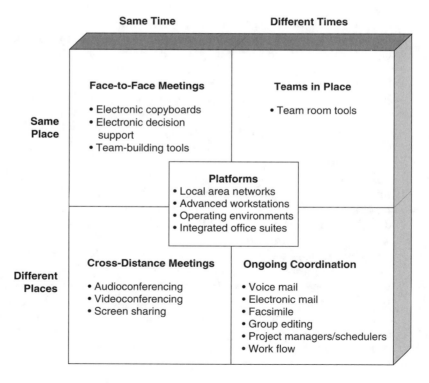

Figure 14-2   Groupware Options (from Johansen [4])

Now, on to discussing progress in the four cells, beginning with same time/same place.

Same Time/Same Place Group Support

Supporting same time/same place groups has generally meant supporting meetings. And there has been a lot of work in this area. Robert Half, the international recruiting firm, with headquarters in New York City, commissioned a study that found that the average executive in a U.S. company spends over 800 hours a year in meetings. Not only is this a large portion of total work hours (on the order of 30 percent) but, even worse, the executives reported that they considered about 240 of those hours to have been wasted in useless meetings.

The Problem with Meetings. From the many meetings we have attended, many shortcomings have been evident. There is no agenda, or only a superficial one. No problems are clearly spelled out in advance, and no specific action items are proposed to address the problems. If actions (or motions) are proposed, alternatives are not fully considered. If documentation about the issues has been provided before the meeting, some members choose not to study it; they expect to be "briefed" at the meeting. The chairperson may do little or no follow-up between meetings to see that the members carry out their assignments.

Some meetings are doomed from the start. Key people arrive late, or do not attend at all. Necessary information does not arrive. Some group members have forgotten to fulfill their assignments. Then the meeting chairperson may do a poor job of managing the meeting time. Discussion may be allowed to wander from the subject. Time may be spent on briefing attendees or on routine matters such as reviewing and correcting minutes of prior meetings, getting committee progress reports, and so on. Such meetings tend to run over their allotted time, with important items receiving poor consideration. Often, too, a few people dominate the discussion; not infrequently, these people are very repetitious, saying the same things over and over. Conversely, some people do not speak up and contribute their ideas. Finally, many meetings are wasteful from a cost standpoint. A meeting involving even a few managers and professionals costs hundreds of dollars per hour in salaries alone; large meetings can easily cost thousands of dollars per hour. If travel is required, costs are even higher. Add to this the fact that the participants are unavailable for other activities while tied up in the meetings.

Information Technology Can Help. The goals of group support systems for improving meetings are to: (a) eliminate some meetings, (b) encourage better planning and better preparation for those meetings that must be held, and (c) improve the effectiveness as they are held.

Eliminate some meetings. The most likely candidates for elimination, it seems to us, are the meetings that do not call for a group decision or group action—they are just for group updating. Progress report meetings are an example, particularly if progress (actual progress versus planned progress) can be reported frequently by means of computerized information systems. Meetings where key people cannot attend, or where needed information is not yet available, can be canceled at the last moment. Electronic and voice mail systems allow the word to be spread rapidly. In short, some of the work done in meetings can be shifted from the "same time, same place" cell to the "different time, different place" cell in the time/place matrix.

Better preparation for meetings. Computer conferencing can play a significant role in improving preparation for meetings. A computer conferencing system is actually a form of enhanced electronic mail. Participants can log on at their convenience, read all entries made by others since they last logged on, and make their contributions. In the planning stage of a meeting, such a system can be used to obtain reactions to the proposed agenda, and those reactions might spur debate and alternatives. Furthermore, routine matters might well be taken care of before the meeting, such as review and approval of minutes, receiving committee progress reports, voting on routine action items, and so on. Group members can give attention to these matters at their convenience, saving valuable face-to-face meeting time for more important business. The chairperson can also use the conferencing system for follow-up activities. Finally, the system can provide a written record of pre- and postmeeting communications.

Improve the effectiveness and efficiency of meetings. One of the major benefits of meeting support systems is improved meeting efficiency and effectiveness. Meetings are more effective when the ideas generated by the group are more creative and the groups commitment to its activities is great. Meetings are more effective when this happens more quickly. Following is a case in point.

CASE EXAMPLE: Burr-Brown Corporation

Burr-Brown Corporation, with headquarters in Tucson, Arizona, manufactures and sells electronics parts to other electronic manufacturers. It has about 1,500 employees and $180 million in annual sales.

When the University of Arizona, also in Tucson, created a decision room in their IS department, the chief executive officer of Burr-Brown decided to use it for his three-day annual strategic planning meeting. He was so pleased with the results that the firm used it again the following year for the same purpose.

The Decision Room

The room has 24 IBM PS/2s, arranged in a semicircle on two tiers. Up to 48 people can use the room, two persons per workstation. A PS/2 in an adjacent control room is the file server, and at the front of the room is a facilitator's control station, as well as a rear projection screen for video, slides, and movies, and a white board. The room uses an IBM token ring network with Novell network software.

The University of Arizona has developed some 20 decision room software tools, and over 100 groups have used this decision room. That software is now marketed by Ventana Corporation [10] under the name Group-Systems. IBM also markets it under the name TeamFocus.

The Electronic Brainstorming System is the most popular of the tools; it is used by more than 70 percent of the groups. Like most of the tools, it allows participants to simultaneously and anonymously key in ideas on a specific question. After an idea is entered and sent to the file server, the participant can see the ideas entered by others.

After the brainstorming portion of a meeting, many groups use the Issue Analyzer to organize the ideas. There is also a voting tool to rank ideas and a topic commenter to attach comments to ideas already in the system. Finally, the groups can use the policy formation software to study alternatives. So most group "discussions" using these tools are done via keyboards rather than by talking. Some other tools do encourage face-to-face discussions.

Burr-Brown's Use of the Room

Burr Brown's annual strategic planning meetings had always been held off-site, with some nine to ten executives attending. When they used the decision room, 31 executives attended. The IS department at the university provided a meeting facilitator to help plan the meeting and then facilitate it. During the meeting, the facilitator explained each tool before it was to be used. He also kept participants on track, and was the neutral leader of the meeting, so that Burr-Brown's CEO could attend as a participant. In addition, an assistant facilitator and three assistants were present. They helped the participants use the hardware and software, make copies of the documents generated by the system, and so on.

Before the meeting, several planning meetings were held to settle on the meeting agenda. Each of the 11 divisions was asked to prepare a document to describe its one-year action plan and rolling five-year plan—including objectives and projected budgets. Participants received these plans before the meeting.

The agenda for the three-day meeting was

- Day 1: Long-term strategy planning
- Day 2: Short-range action planning
- Day 3: Wrap-up in both areas

The meeting began with the group using the workstations to generate ideas about expected corporate performance in the coming years. Participants then organized these ideas to create the framework for discussing each division's plans.

For the next day and one-half, they entered comments on the five-year strategic plans and one-year action plans of each division, one division at a time.

Participants also spent some time brainstorming on ways to accomplish the year's objectives, and then ranking the ideas. The group settled on specific actions it would take on the top seven issues.

On the last afternoon, participants divided into four groups to discuss important topics face-to-face. The planning meeting ended with the four groups presenting their recommendations.

Executives' Reactions

After the three-day session, the participants were asked to summarize their reactions to the room. They reported the following.

It Increased Involvement. One senior vice president commented that the decision room allowed them to do in three days what would have otherwise taken months. The CEO noted that the past sessions could not include more than ten people to be manageable; and in those sessions, only two or three people really spoke up. With the decision room, 31 people were able to attend without hampering deliberations, and the group's comments were much more open than in the past, he noted.

During one of the one-hour electronic brainstorming sessions, 404 comments were made. There were two people at some workstations, with the fewest number of comments from any of the 24 workstations being four and highest being 27; seven workstations contributed more than 20. So contributions were relatively evenly distributed across the group.

The group had mixed reactions about the efficiency of the system. In a postsession questionnaire that 26 participants answered, 11 stated that it was more efficient than past meetings, nine said it was not, and six were neutral. However, the majority agreed that the facilitator was important in helping them use the room.

The Planning Process Was More Effective. Several executives mentioned two aspects of the session that enhanced its effectiveness. The main one was anonymity. Due to anonymity, more people asked more questions and made more suggestions than they did in the former meeting methods—where all discussion was done verbally, which identified the contributor.

Second, the planning process itself was extremely educational, said the CEO. "People walked in with narrow perceptions of the company and walked out with a CEO's perception. This is the view that is sought in strategic planning, but is usually not achieved," he commented three months after the session. This type of education had not happened at previous planning sessions.

One Year Later. One year later, 25 executives participated in a two-day session. About 16 of them had attended the year before. This year, the intent of the meeting was different. It was to critique plans, so that their impact on others and the support they needed from others were more explicit.

After the CEO described the firm's objectives and the economic climate, the planning session began with the group critiquing the previous year's results companywide. The two-day session ended with each business unit manager commenting on the ideas he had received about his unit and how those ideas might affect his unit's action plan.

From the previous year's session, they learned that brainstorming is effective if the groups are structured properly. A large group can consider a few issues, such as corporate objectives, and present participants' ideas on those topics. But a large group cannot "converse" because there are too many ideas to consider.

For "dialogs," Burr-Brown found it is best to form several small groups, with each group addressing a few issues. One person puts in a statement, another person comments on it, then someone else comments, and so on. In the second year, they conducted small-group dialogs and found them effective.

The company also learned that the room is not a substitute for a planning process. It is excellent for generating many ideas in a short time. But since there is less face-to-face interaction, people are less likely to make commitments and agree on courses of action than in a face-to-face setting. So Burr-Brown does not use the room to reach consensus; it uses it to critique plans rather than to create them.

The communications manager recommends that others who are planning to use such a room tell the participants about the room beforehand. Just send them a memo that describes the room and include a photograph, he suggested. Also, explain to participants how their comments will be used, he told us, because the use probably will affect how they answer questions.

In all, Burr-Brown participants were pleased with the candor and objectivity the decision room elicited. They believe that its use has enhanced their annual planning meetings.

Different Time/Different Place Group Support

One of the most promising uses of groupware is for ongoing coordination by groups that work at different times and in different places. With the increasing marketplace emphasis on cycle time reduction, companies can use the globe and its three main regions (Europe, Asia, and the Americas) to extend their workday to round-the-clock, by passing work from groups in one region to the next at the end of each one's workday.

Author Barbara McNurlin says

I had that experience for the first time not long ago.

On one of my first projects for Wentworth Research, the author of the report, who works in England, e-mailed me his thoughts and questions on the topic at the end of his workday. During my workday, while he was sleeping, I did some thinking and research on the topic, and then e-mailed my thoughts and findings back to him. And when I slept, he worked. He and I worked this way, swapped long e-mail messages, for about one week. But we got at least two week's worth of work done. It was tremendously exhilarating and productive—without either of us having to work long hours.

There has been much talk about using the Internet and intranets as groupware tools. There is no doubt this will happen as more and more companies explore the benefits of global working. That brings up the question, "How does groupware change an organization?" This is the question studied by Ojelanki Ngwenyama, of the University of Michigan [11]. He presented the following preliminary findings at a UCLA colloquium hosted by Professor Burt Swanson [12].

CASE EXAMPLE: International Consulting Firm

A manufacturing software development group in an international consulting firm builds software for mid-size manufacturing firms. Its product has a whopping 3 billion lines of RPG/400 code in 30 modules because it must handle global currencies, specifications, accounting practices, EDI capabilities, and so on. The group's practice has been to release a new version of the manufacturing software every 12 to 14 months; for each release, some 1 to 2 million lines of code are changed. Development takes place via distributed teams. The 45 U.S. designers and programmers handle design and some programming, the 10 to 20 Asians do the programming, and the 15 Europeans handle documentation and interfaces for six European languages.

Requirements take one month, product design two to three months (in the United States), programming four to six months (Asia does the "U.S. night shift," taking over where the U.S. day shift leaves off), and testing takes one to two months. Documentation takes four to six months, in parallel with design and programming.

The group had just successfully implemented Lotus Notes for its sales and customer services group when it decided to use Notes to manage its own distributed system development environment. Notes can be viewed as a combination of document creator and indexer, database generator and manager, and messaging system. It is like e-mail and computer conferencing all in one. And users can put unstructured text documents into databases, with fields that can be searched and indexed. Then these documents can be shared, modified, and searched by anyone with access to one of the replicated databases. One of the reasons Notes is popular is because of this ability to handle documents (rather than just messages) in electronic form. We will discuss other advances in electronic documents and their management in Chapter 16.

Effect of Groupware Use

Ngwenyama studied how the development group's use of Notes changed its development processes in five areas: (1) communication, (2) problem solving, (3) organization structure, (4) system integration, and (5) social integration.

Communication. By using Notes to coordinate group work, defects are driven out much earlier because the on-line discussions uncover possible defects sooner, so they are fixed sooner. Team size has been reduced, even though the coordination of using Notes costs them more work. Ngwenyama conjectures that "social visibility" has caused some people's nonwork to be exposed because now everyone knows what others are doing. People are not able to hide because they pick up their work at the beginning of the day from Notes, and then post their work at the end of the day on Notes for the other regional team to pick up.

Furthermore, the developers now know who to go to with a question. Before, the Asian developers asked a question of their manager who asked the manager in the United States. Now they talk directly to the person they believe can answer their question. This has made the organization more like a network rather than a distributed hierarchy.

Before Notes, the Americans did not know the Asian programmers' names, nor did they have any relationship with them. There was no rapport, so they had problems communicating. Initially, communications were awkward. Messages between the two were long and rambling. And from Asia, they were very formal, "Dear Sir. It is a pleasure to inform you that we have completed. ..." But as the developers got to know each other on-line (and how to pronounce each other's names), there was less alienation. Communications became more relational. Informality increased. And messages got shorter and more cryptic. They understood each other much better. Asian staff would now ask, "How was your weekend? Would you send me a T-shirt from your city's baseball team because my son is interested in them?" In all, the teams constructed a life world. Formerly, it had just been file transfers.

Furthermore, as time went on, fewer iterations were needed to settle issues. The number of messages tapered off, length decreased, and they began thinking more alike across the ocean, "Yes, I was thinking about that." "I was just about to take care of it."

Problem Solving. Before Notes, the Asian programmers were told what to do; they had no involvement in problem solving. But after Notes, the Americans discovered that the Asians were good at more than programming. As a result, the two groups have become more of a team; they discuss design issues. The problem-solving process has become more collaborative, and the Americans now ask the Asians how they suggest fixing a problem rather than simply demand that it be fixed.

Organizational Structure. Notes is restructuring the group work situation. Formerly, the Americans made file transfers to Asia by going up to the office head, then across the Pacific to their office head, and then down to the developers. Now they are more of a team with daily lateral transfers of information. These changes are permeating the structure of the organization.

Equally interesting, in developing their Notes support system, the developers discovered that they (like their users) could not articulate their full requirements at the outset. So they took an iterative development approach, first determining the core set of work activities to be handled by the software and then the it-would-be-nice-to-have features. They planned to build the core and then add the others a year later, just as they did with their manufacturing software. But one month into the project, they discovered they had completely forgotten several crucial items. Rather than wait a year (as they had required of their manufacturing software users), they immediately added the missing functions. This experience made them realize that they had not been very customer oriented when responding to changes in each release of their manufacturing software. Since they would not make changes for a year, users had to devise work-arounds for that year. Having not been users of their own software before, they had not realized the problems they were causing users.

System Integration. People who are peripheral to the team, such as suppliers, now also get involved in problem solving and design.

Social Integration. The communications and working relationships have become more relational. And there appears to be a bidirectional drift between the organization and the groupware applications, said Ngwenyama in his UCLA presentation. Norms are becoming embedded in Notes, as rules and by accident. Conversely, certain Notes routines have drifted into the organizational realm. The review cycle, for example, takes a much different approach due to Notes. Reviews are faster, and there are more of them. So review policies have changed—on how often they should be done, on what portions of the code, who should be involved, and who has the final word.

Now that we have elaborated on two of the cells in Johansen's groupware framework, we turn to lessons learned on support group work with IT. These are framed in the form of guidelines.

GUIDELINES FOR GROUP SUPPORT

With a field as important and as fast moving as this, studies and research on what works and what does not work are very important. We found some interesting studies on supporting work groups with information technology. In this section, we present the findings of some CSCW researchers. Based on their work, we offer the following guidelines for supporting work groups with information technology:

1. Build on electronic mail.
2. Support frequent communication.
3. Expect changes in group work.
4. Realize the importance of mediators to guide use.
5. Be sure the system fits the culture.

Build on Electronic Mail

One of the most logical and common platforms for providing tools for work groups is electronic mail. Here is the experience of one organization that illustrates the value of e-mail for group support, and a report on some research on extending or enhancing e-mail.

At a Services Firm. Lynne Markus [13], of Claremont Graduate School, studied the use of an electronic mail system at a services firm with headquarters in Los Angeles, California. The firm employs some 7,500 people, 825 of whom are managers—from first-level supervisors through corporate officers. Markus wanted to know how managers and executives would use electronic mail.

She studied a regional vice president in charge of three districts and 400 employees. He is located at headquarters, two of his districts are in the central United States (two time zones east of him) and one district is in the Eastern time zone (three hours ahead of him). He supervises the executive director of each region and he is the liaison between his districts and the corporate departments—such as pricing, processing, and customer and supplier relations.

He uses electronic mail extensively, leaving his computer on whenever he is in the office, so that he can hear the beep that signals the arrival of a new message. He told Markus that the mail system is his primary communication tool. He believes he could not handle his volume of work without the system.

On the day Markus visited him, he handled 110 electronic mail messages—44 he composed himself and 66 he received from others. Only four of the received messages were via electronic distribution lists, and only three others were replacements for paper. The remaining 59 were sent directly to him.

Markus saw that the availability of the "forward" command, in particular, supported the regional vice president in his work in groups. Of the 66 messages he received, 34 were "mosaic messages"—that is, they contained from one to six additional messages attached to them.

A mosaic message is created by using the "forward" command rather than the "reply" command when composing a response. The intent of the forward command is to transfer a message to a party other than the original sender or receiver. It is used to append one message to the bottom of another. In fact, messages can be forwarded repeatedly, thus building up a transcript of the discussion of a problem or issue, as the mosaic messages are passed from person to person around the organization.

Markus witnessed the regional vice president using the forward command a number of times the day she visited. In one case, as the intermediary between headquarters people and a regional manager, he coordinated the resolution of a payment question, using electronic mail only. Within 11 minutes, communications between line and staff traversed 2,000 miles and four levels of management to resolve this urgent issue. The firm was able to rush payment to the irate supplier that day.

In another case, over a five-hour time period, a headquarters vice president, the regional vice president, and one of his executive directors held a sometimes two-way, sometimes three-way electronic mail conversation about a state law in one of the districts. At the end of the mail conversation, the executive director forwarded the entire mosaic message to one of her subordinates for follow-up. In both of these cases, temporary groups "met" over the electronic mail system, compiled a trail of comments and discussion, reached a decision, and then disbanded.

Markus found the executives at the company preferred to use electronic mail to explain complex or ambiguous issues. They felt such issues were more clearly and quickly explained in writing than in speech. In addition, the mail system provided a record that could be forwarded to others, if appropriate.

Support Frequent Communication

When people are not located near each other, IT can be used to support cheap, frequent, spontaneous communication because informal and unplanned interaction is crucial for good teamwork.

An experiment conducted at Xerox Palo Alto Research Center (PARC) supports this viewpoint. When PARC created an audio/video link between two Xerox research sites that are 400 miles apart, they found that 70 percent of the uses of that link were casual, drop-in style conversations that lasted less than five minutes. The researchers surmise that those communications would not have occurred without the video link. These results suggest that companies should pay more attention to using IT to support informal communication, in addition to formal meetings.

Video conferencing has been used this way at two other companies. At Boeing, the engineers building the 757 jetliner who had tight schedules to meet needed frequent and informal communication among three sites 30 miles apart—the airfield, an engineering site, and a manufacturing facility. They did not have time to travel among the sites, so they rigged up a two-way television system with cameras and TV screens at each site. They found that this video conferencing arrangement was, and still is, the only way they can meet tight schedules.

J. C. Penney also uses video conferencing, not to replace existing meetings but to include junior people in video discussions because these employees do not have the travel budgets to travel between Penney's headquarters sites in New York City and Dallas, Texas. Penney also uses its video conferencing links to broadcast fashion shows from its Dallas studio to its senior buyers around the

United States. Prior to the conferencing links, these buyers relied on merchandising specialists at their previous New York headquarters to select the merchandise their stores would sell. Now the local buyers make their own selections, tailoring their merchandise to their store's customers.

As video technology has become more affordable, a range of video conferencing options has opened up—from large, formal video conferencing rooms to smaller systems that accommodate remote working sessions of three to four people, to personal "glance" windows on a PC that allow team members to see where their teammates are located at the moment [1a]. Unplanned encounters where people exchange little bits of information are important. Information technology should be used to support this kind of group work also.

Expect Changes in Group Work

At a large southern California utility, a task force of volunteers—one-half retired and one-half still employed at the utility—agreed to work together for a year to develop a set of recommendations about preretirement planning for employees about to retire. One group was to use computers and electronic mail, the other group was not. The two groups were similar in size and participant characteristics. Several differences in the work of the groups evolved because of the difference in technology support. Tora Bikson and J.D. Eveland [1c] report on the results.

The Group Structures Differed. Initially, both groups subdivided themselves into six committees. Each committee was to work on one issue, such as finances, health, family and social adjustment, and so on.

The conventional group participants spent quite a bit of time organizing themselves—balancing the size and make-up of the committees, considering the interests of the members, and so on. Each member joined one committee. The electronic group, on the other hand, spent little time organizing itself. Each member selected the committees he or she wanted to join; each of them joined two or more committees.

These committee structures lasted for the entire year. However, during the year, the electronic group also formed six procedure-based committees to coordinate the work between the issue-based committees. So the electronic group formed a matrix organization of committees; the conventional group did not.

Leadership Differed in Two Ways. The degree of centralization differed between the groups. Centralization is the extent to which communications are concentrated among a few group members. The conventional group was the more centralized of the two; it relied on a few individuals to carry out the work. The electronic group became less centralized with individuals' participation evenly spread among the group members.

Leadership stability also differed. The conventional group experienced greater stability in leadership roles—the same people tended to play key roles throughout the project. Meanwhile, leadership shifted over time among members of the electronic group—both among the retired and the employed members.

Perceptions of Effectiveness Were About the Same. The groups were asked several times during the project how effective they felt they were. The electronic group was more positive about its effectiveness, although both groups rated their effectiveness high.

Interestingly, the retirees in the electronic group and the employees in the conventional group gave higher marks to the medium—electronic or not—that they were using. The employees felt conventional communications were all they needed; the retirees said the mail system helped them communicate even though they were geographically dispersed.

The employees in the electronic group and the retirees in the conventional group gave lower marks; the retirees even noted that they were at a disadvantage because they could not easily communicate with each other since they were so geographically dispersed.

The Final Reports Differed. Perhaps most intriguing is the difference in the reports that the two groups produced. The conventional group's report was 15 pages long and contained mainly anecdotal advice about preparing for retirement that the group had gathered from conversations.

The electronic group's report was 75 pages long and was composed mainly of tables describing the results of an opinion survey they had designed and analyzed on-line. They had mailed a 33-question survey to 1,325 retired and working people. Some 441 surveys were returned and analyzed.

It is clear that the work tools significantly affected how these groups approached their task—how they structured themselves, what they chose to do, how they handled leadership, and what their end product contained.

Realize the Importance of Mediators to Guide Use

In a study of the introduction of a groupware system in Japan, researchers Kazuo Okamura (Matsushita Electric Industrial Co.), Masayo Fujimoto (Sumitomo Research Institute), and Wanda Orlikowski and JoAnne Yates (both of MIT) [1b], discovered that a small group of users had shaped others' adoption and use of the system. They call these people "technology-use mediators," and they believe they play an important role in (1) adapting the new technology to the company context, (2) modifying the organizational context to accommodate the new technology, (3) and supporting ongoing changes to both—as happened in this case.

They studied the introduction of a "news-system" in the R&D laboratory of a large Japanese manufacturing company. The news-system consisted of various topic areas (from "official" to recreational) that users could use to post and read messages, in bulletin-board fashion. It was to support some 175 members on six teams, all of which were developing an innovative computer product. The project was to last 17 months.

A year before the project began, a group of young software engineers ported a news-system to the R&D lab for their own use. When they were assigned to the new project, they decided to set up a similar system for it. Once they realized that such a large project would require technical and communication infrastructure support to foster information sharing and collaboration, they volunteered to play this role. Management accepted their proposal and formally authorized them to form a group responsible for administering the network and establishing and promoting the news-system. The group has nine members.

The researchers discovered that the group's activities fell into two phases. The first was to define the role of the news-system and promote its use. The second focused on changing the definition and use of specific news-groups and the overall structure and nature of the news-system.

To Define the System's Role and Promote Its Use. A first task was to decide the system's role. Should it be used for official communication? The researchers asked this question via e-mail, thus prompting a discussion and, in effect, guiding this policymaking process by building support rather than dictating policy. After achieving consensus, the use-mediation group positioned the new medium in relation to other communication media used in the project—such as lunch-time meetings, routing slips, and e-mail. The use-mediation group wanted most of the information to be exchanged via the news-system, so it added several news-groups (and defined the purpose of each) to better accommodate the breadth of communications on the project.

From there use-mediators promoted the system's use by getting managers to require their team members to use the system every day. This made the system the official communication medium. They also created a local news-group for each team, to not only replace team members' former use of e-mail but also to provide an easy way for beginners to start using the system and give a feeling of intimacy to each team. This tactic seemed to work because about one-half of the early messages were on the local news-groups. To encourage information sharing across teams, the local news-groups were not restricted; they were open to everyone, and everyone was encouraged to read and contribute to them. This tactic also seemed to work. About one-third of the messages on the local news-groups were from "outsiders." In all, their actions dramatically increased use of the system.

To Support Ongoing Evolution. Two types of changes were needed: modifications and reconfigurations. The use-mediators modified definitions and usage rules in response to user feedback, say Okamura et al., for example, when users improperly posted messages or when they asked questions of the use-mediators. When a modification did not suffice, they reconfigured the system, changing the system's schema or creating a new news-group (such as "headlines" to announce the acquisition of a new book or magazine subscription).

For example, the group promoted proper use of each type of news-group and proper formulation of each message (i.e., embedding only the relevant portion of prior messages in its responding message). Furthermore, the group redefined, in particular, the two news-groups ("general" and "announce") that were required reading for all project members, so that they were only used for messages of critical importance to the entire project. When this tactic did not work fully, the group combined the two and gave it a new name—"official".

The changes were in response to users' wanting to use the system in new ways (such as archiving old messages so they could be easily searched or referred to in new messages) or to speed up access time (by deleting rarely used newsgroups). The user-mediators felt they needed to keep the system in sync with its changing use.

Although they researched only one site, Okamura et al. believe that an organizationally sanctioned group of mediators may help an organization overcome the significant hurdles in successfully introducing a group support system. Design extends into use and mediators, therefore, must not only manage the technical issues but contextual and usage issues as well.

Be Sure the System Fits the Culture

The largest obstacle to successfully installing and using a groupware product is corporate culture. If the two conflict, either the product will fall into disuse or employees will be forced to work as the product requires. Wanda Orlikowski [1d], at MIT, uncovered two main determinants of success in the use of groupware. One is culture; the other is people's perception of a product.

When the unwritten rules of behavior, the reward structure, and tenets of getting ahead in the firm (its culture) do not support cooperation, the effective use of groupware is diluted, Orlikowski says. Furthermore, when the perception of a product's usefulness varies among different groups of people (such as managers, users, and technologists), then the technologists might not implement systems that users view as useful.

Orlikowski studied the use of a groupware product in a large firm where the corporate culture is up-or-out—perform to expectations or leave. In this highly competitive environment, employees quickly realize that they are promoted based on their individual worth. Their goal is to personally stand out, so they see information as power. Cooperation and sharing, while perhaps verbally promoted, are not seen as true success factors. Therefore, the groupware product has found limited use in the firm because it conflicts with the individualistic, competitive culture.

Unfortunately, said Orlikowski, neither the technologists nor the senior executives noticed this mismatch when they made the investment decision. The IS executives who promoted the product honestly saw it as a revolutionary way to move expertise around the firm. Furthermore, since the product is easy to use, they also presumed employees would have no trouble visualizing numerous uses for it.

Upon study, however, Orlikowski discovered that the users had a completely different view of the product. They saw it as only an incremental improvement, like a "database in the sky." While it might help them communicate better and work at home more, it would not help eliminate faxes or telephone calls. In fact, they only saw a few uses for it. In addition, they had great concern for the confidentiality, security, and quality of sensitive information—concerns apparently not shared by the IS executives. The users wanted to personally control the information they shared. Putting it into the system would dilute their personal control, so there was quite a bit of fear about putting important information into the system.

Furthermore, the employees were not given time to use the product. They were expected to bill 100 percent of their time, and spend their own time entering information into the system and perusing its contents. So the informal messages they received—using the system did not support career advancement— conflicted with the formal "use it" messages broadcast throughout the firm.

Interestingly, the employees who have become the greatest fans of the product and use it extensively are the information systems staff. They are not on the up-or-out career track. They share information extensively, so the product matches their culture.

Orlikowski's study not only points out the importance of culture but also of understanding the various viewpoints in implementing groupware, or any new information technology. She believes that three viewpoints—manager, user, and system designer—are significantly different; therefore, they define success very differently. For example, while managers might define success as "the system supports business strategy," systems professionals would define success as "the system meets the specifications." Users would take an entirely different view, saying success is when "the system helps me with my job."

Unless these various viewpoints surface and are explored, use of a technology can fail miserably, with everyone blaming the product rather than the true culprits: the corporate culture or the various groups' conflicting perceptions.

Groupware alone will not create sharing in a competitive culture, as Orlikowski's preliminary findings show. The culture must reward teamwork and sharing over individual contributions—a difficult cultural change to make. This is the main message of groupware— it requires the appropriate culture to be effectively used. When that match exists, the benefits can be dramatic.

THE FUTURE

In a white paper on their Web page, entitled "The New Way to Share Groupware Information," Netscape [14] states that it sees intranets as a form of groupware that uses Web technology. It also notes that companywide information—the first type of information to be put on most intranets—is just the tip of the iceberg in Web-based groupware because most information in firms is specific either to a department or work group. Netscape sees Web publishing moving downward in companies to department and group levels—not to mention the personal sites already populating the Web. As Web sites expand to include new types of applications for collaboration and group sharing, Netscape foresees even greater company benefits through increased team and group productivity.

Until the explosion of the Web, most groups depended on desktop software, access to file servers, and e-mail to collaborate electronically. Lotus Notes has been used, but not widely. So most teams have depended on tools that were not designed for easy sharing and collaboration. For instance, file servers do not help people find information. E-mail is for sharing, but mainly on a one-on-one basis, or groups of people whose interest in a subject is known to the e-mail sender.

These messages miss others who might benefit, or benefit the sender with their feedback. There is no central storage site. And these messages load up networks and hard drives because they send copies to each recipient. In essence, they follow the old print, copy, and distribute paradigm. Companies that use groupware have also needed to deal with proprietary software, which has been expensive to buy and keep current. Even public folders, such as offered in Microsoft Exchange, are fairly tedious to use (double clicking on folder icons).

The Web will move downward organizationally, due to the personal Web-page authoring tools that make it as easy to publish information on an intranet as save it in a word processing document. Each document can have access control, and can be accessed by local or remote users. So it can be used by distributed work groups. And by providing links to the new document, others can be made aware of its existence. The Web facilities of full-text searching and cataloging (to see documents by subject) are automatically available. Web authoring systems, such as Netscape's Navigator, will increasingly include software agents that monitor new documents added to the Web site. When one is added, it informs the catalog server so that the document can be cataloged.

In short, the Web will increasingly be used to support groups, teams, departments, and even interenterprise groups and communities.

QUESTIONS AND EXERCISES

REVIEW QUESTIONS

1. What are the three ways to "chunk" the work of groups?
2. What are the three characteristics of groups?
3. Name several types of groups and describe each briefly.
4. What are three reasons for the importance of group support systems?
5. Describe the new organizational structure of the T1 provisioning group.
6. According to Brewer, what are tacit knowledge and explicit knowledge?
7. What is "the Rudy problem" and how did the pharmaceutical company attempt to deal with it?
8. Describe Buckman Laboratories' solution to sharing knowledge worldwide.
9. Describe the four cells of the time/place matrix, and give an example of a technology used in each.
10. What are some of the ways IT can help improve meetings?
11. What benefits did Burr-Brown get from its use of a group decision room?
12. In what five ways did the international consulting firm benefit from using Notes to coordinate application development, according to Ngwenyama?
13. What roles do technology-use mediators play?
14. How does Netscape see the Web relating to group work?

DISCUSSION QUESTIONS

1. Support for communication and coordination is quite different from support for group decision making. The technologies should be different. Do you agree or disagree? Explain your reasoning.

2. Knowledge can be transferred onto computers. Do you agree or disagree? Explain your reasoning.

3. The Web is being touted as the solution to all computing needs, including group support. But it really will not truly help group work as much as, say, Notes, which is specifically designed as a groupware tool. Do you agree or disagree? Explain your reasoning.

EXERCISES

1. Find an article that describes a group support system of some kind. What is its major purpose? What technology is used?

2. Conduct a survey of products available in the marketplace for group support (by using a directory of software or contacting several vendors). What kind of support do the systems provide? How do they compare with the systems described in this chapter?

3. Visit a local company that is using technology to support group work. Map its activities into the time/place matrix. What infrastructures has it they developed?

REFERENCES

1. COMPUTER SUPPORTED COOPERATIVE WORK is a series of bi-annual conferences sponsored by ACM, which publishes the *CSCW Proceedings* (P.O. Box 12114, Church St. Station, New York City, NY 10257).

   a. TANG, JOHN, ELLEN ISAACS, and MONICA RUA, "Supporting Distributed Groups with a Montage of Lightweight Interactions," *CSCW 1994 Proceedings*, pp. 23-34.

   b. OKAMURA, KAZUO, MASAYO FUJIMOTI, WANDA ORLIKOWSKI, and JOANNE YATES, "Helping CSCW Applications Succeed: The Role of Mediators in the Context of Use," *CSCW 1994 Proceedings*, pp. 55-66.

   c. EVELAND, J.D. and T. BIKSON, "Work Group Structures and Computer Support: A Field Experiment," *CSCW 1988 Proceedings*, pp. 324-343.

   d. ORLIKOWSKI, WANDA, "Learning from Notes: Organizational Issues in Groupware Implementation," *CSCW 1992 Proceedings*, pp. 362-369.

2. DESANCTIS, G. and B. GALLUPE, "Group Decision Support Systems: A New Frontier," *Data Base*, ACM, Winter 1985.

3. INSTITUTE FOR RESEARCH ON LEARNING, 66 Willow Place, Menlo Park, CA 94025.

4. JOHANSEN, ROBERT, Institute for the Future, 2740 Sand Hill Road, Menlo Park, CA 94025.

   a. JOHANSEN, R. ET AL. *Leading Business Teams*, Addison-Wesley Publishing Co., 1991.

   b. O'HARA-DEVEREAU, MARY, and ROBERT JOHANSEN, *Global Work: Bridging Distance, Culture, and Time*, Jossey-Bass, 1994.

5. DRUCKER, P.F., "The Coming of the New Organization," *Harvard Business Review*, Harvard Business School, Boston, MA 02163, January-February 1988, pp. 45-53.

6. SACHS, PATRICIA, "Transforming Work: Collaboration, Learning, and Design," *Communications of the ACM*, September 1995, pp. 36-44.

7. IT MANAGEMENT PROGRAMME REPORT, Wentworth Research, Park House, Wick Road, Egham, England OHW TW20; http://www.wentworth.co.uk.

   a. WOOLFE, ROGER, "The Business of Innovation," May 1996.

   b. BREWER, TONY, "Managing Knowledge," November 1995.

8. MALONE, T. and K. CRANSTON, "Toward an Interdisciplinary Theory of Coordination," CCS #120, Center for Coordination Science, MIT Sloan School of Industrial Management, April 1991.

9. The Knowledge Imperative Symposium, Arthur Andersen and The American Productivity & Quality Center (123 North Post Oak Lane, Houston, TX 77024), September 1995.

   a. SEEMAN, PATRICIA, "Building Knowledge Infrastructure: Creating Change Capabilities," tape cassette #B13, AVW Audio Visual, 3620 Willowbend, #1118, Houston, TX 77010.

10. VENTANA CORPORATION, 1430 E. Fort Powell Road, Tucson, AZ 85719.

11. NGWENYAMA, OJELANKI, "Organizational Context, Social Action, and Technological Interventions: A Case Study on the Development and Use of a Groupware Application," speech at UCLA IS Colloquium, February 16, 1995. Ngwenyama can be reached at the University of Michigan at okn@umich.edu.

12. SWANSON, E. BURTON, IS Colloquium, various Thursday afternoons, Anderson School at UCLA.

13. MARKUS, M. LYNNE, "Electronic Mail as the Medium of Managerial Choice," working paper, MIS Research Program, Anderson Graduate School of Management, UCLA, November 1988.

14. "THE NEW WAY TO SHARE GROUPWARE INFORMATION," Netscape Home Page: http://www.netscape.com, September 1996.

FIFTEEN

Expert Systems

INTRODUCTION

Expert systems and *intelligent systems* are two terms for real-world uses of artificial intelligence (AI)—the group of technologies that attempts to mimic our senses or emulate certain aspects of human behavior, such as reasoning and communicating, says Harvey Newquist [1], a well-known consultant and columnist in the field. AI technologies include expert systems, neural networks, fuzzy logic, machine translation, speech recognition, and natural language.

AI has been a promising technology for many years. In the early 1990s, that promise finally began to unfold, quietly. In particular, expert systems, also called knowledge-based systems, became one of several system development alternatives. Many large companies used it, along with other technologies, such as imaging and object-oriented development, where it best suited the needs.

In this chapter we concentrate on expert systems because they are the most prolific application of intelligent systems. The automobile industry uses them to troubleshoot robots and check cars for noise and vibration. Communications firms use them to diagnose switching circuits. The financial services industry uses them to choose financial planning and tax planning alternatives. Manufacturers use them to plan raw material usage, evaluate designs, control and monitor automated material-handling equipment, and identify and track equipment failures at customer sites. Corporate education and training departments even use expert systems as tutors. And the list goes on and on.

WHAT IS AN EXPERT SYSTEM?

An expert system is a type of analysis or problem-solving model, almost always implemented on a computer, that deals with a problem the way an "expert" does. The solution process involves consulting a base of knowledge or expertise to reason out an answer based on characteristics of the problem.

Clyde Holsapple and Andrew Whinston [2] define an expert system as "a computer-based system composed of a user interface, an inference engine, and stored expertise—that is, a rule set, a knowledge base, or an entire knowledge system. Its purpose is to offer advice or solutions for problems in a particular area. The advice is comparable to that which would be offered by a human expert in that problem area." An expert system should be able to solve a problem, explain to some extent how it solved that problem, and provide a reliable means of solving similar problems.

Expert systems are not new. The first was the Logic Theorist, developed in 1956 by Allen Newell and Herbert Simon, of Carnegie-Mellon University, together with J. C. Shaw of the Rand Corporation. Another early expert system was DENDRAL, a program that interprets data produced by a mass spectrometer to determine molecular structures; it dates back to the mid-1960s. However, the means for creating expert systems changed with the introduction of AI languages such as LISP and Prolog, as well as other new artificial intelligence software development tools. These tools brought expert systems out of the research laboratories and universities and into businesses. The field changed again with the introduction of PC-based development tools, called shells, that used conventional languages, such as C. Today, a wide spectrum of expert system building tools is available, ranging from tools for for novice end users to tools for experienced knowledge engineers in a systems department.

One of the first commercially successful expert systems was built at American Express. It is still in use today and is actually a fundamental part of the company's everyday credit operation. Here's that story, based on the Sourcebook case history from Wentworth Research's "Managing Knowledge" report [3].

CASE EXAMPLE: American Express

In 1988, American Express implemented the Authorizer's Assistant, an expert system that approves credit at the point of sale. It started as an R&D project, took two years to develop, and was put into production with 800 rules. Today, it has over 2,600 rules and supports all AmEx card products around the world. Its purpose is to minimize credit losses and catch frauds. It saves the company millions of dollars a year and has been a phenomenal success.

Whenever a American Express card is run through a point-of-sale device, the transaction goes into AmEx's credit authorization system (CAS)—a very important system for AmEx, which, in essence, gives away money. CAS is implemented worldwide and operates seven days a week, 24 hours a day. It is such a significant system that the company president is notified if it is down for 45 minutes.

Coprocessor systems, such as the Authorizer's Assistant, have been added to CAS. The Authorizer's Assistant authorizes credit by looking at whether cardholders are credit-worthy, whether they have been paying their bills, and whether a particular purchase is within their normal spending patterns. It also assesses whether the request for credit could be a potential fraud. Before development of the Authorizer's Assistant, transactions that were not automatically approved by CAS were referred to a person for analysis and decision. The most difficult credit-authorization decisions are still referred to people, but the Authorizer's Assistant has automated judgment to raise the quality of authorization decisions.

Authorization decisions are driven by the type of credit charge—store, restaurant, and so on. They are also influenced by whether cardholders are in their home city or are on vacation or traveling—a hotel bill or charges in a city other than where they reside would point to the latter. To detect fraud while someone is on vacation, the credit authorizer looks at the number of charges per day. So an appropriate question to ask would be: "Is the cardholder's spending velocity 'in pattern' (following his or her typical spending pattern)?" Customer servicing issues and credit policies are also taken into account in the authorization decision. For example, a restaurant charge needs to be handled differently from a camera store charge because the restaurant charge happens after the service has been rendered and the purchase, unlike a camera, cannot be resold. AmEx does not want to embarrass the cardholder in the social setting of a restaurant, so authorization of this type of charge is handled differently from purchases of resalable items.

Development of the System

The Authorizer's Assistant is a rule-based expert system, and in creating the rules, AmEx had to refine its company policies. One example was the commonly used phrase "sound credit judgment." Before the system was built, this phrase was often used but never defined. Developing the system forced the company to define the phrase in "quantifiable" rules.

A rule might be framed in terms of the question, "Does this person shop at this store or often buy this kind of merchandise (electronic equipment, say)?" If the answer is "yes," the charge would be "in pattern." If the amount is high, another rule might ask, "Does the cardholder pay his or her bill on time and is his or her 12-month credit history good?"

The rules were generated by interviewing authorizers with various levels of expertise. Five were assigned to work with the developers. Some were the top experts (who made correct decisions at least 90 percent of the time); others had a track record of being right only 80 to 89 percent of the time.

Both types of experts were used so that the developers could compare good and not so good decisions.

To codify the experts' knowledge, the developers studied individual charge histories in detail, decomposed the decision process into its components, and focused on each one to refine it. Sometimes they proposed cases to the experts and recorded the information they asked for to make a decision.

Two kinds of knowledge are captured in the Authorizer's Assistant: policy knowledge and judgment knowledge. Policy knowledge is like textbook knowledge. Judgment knowledge is applied to bend the rules set down in the policy to benefit the cardholder (and keep his or her business). This type of knowledge is very important because it enhances customer service in the eyes of the cardholder. Thus, the rules in the system both protect the company against loss and protect the cardholder from embarrassment.

The seven developers also spent several weeks working in the credit-authorization environment so they could understood what the experts were talking about. The system was designed to mimic how people made credit-authorization decisions. The knowledge engineers, therefore, had to develop expertise in credit and fraud as well as in the analysis of cardholder charge patterns. In essence, they acted as credit authorizers for a short time, talking to real cardholders and making authorization decisions on the telephone on the fly. This experience helped them to realize how time sensitive authorization decisions must be. The cardholder may be waiting at an airline counter to get the charge approved; a delay could cause the card holder to miss the flight. The system had to be designed to deal with this type of customer-sensitive situation—AmEx does not want to embarrass a cardholder by bringing him or her to a telephone unnecessarily.

The vice president of risk management states that the system can be adapted quickly to meet changing business requirements. For example, if a large manufacturing company falls on hard times, AmEx can change the rules that apply to the cities where that company is a major employer, so that it can respond compassionately and quickly to the credit issues that inevitably will arise. In all, management reaction to the Authorizer's Assistant has been very positive.

Components of Expert Systems

There are three components in an expert system:

1. A user interface
2. An inference engine
3. A knowledge base

The *user interface* is the interface between the expert system and the outside world. That outside world could be another computer application or a person. If the system is being used directly by a user, the user interface contains the means by which the user states the problem and interacts with the system. Traditionally, the user interface has been a simple menu, or ordinary word processing, database, or spreadsheet screens on a workstation. But some new systems are using multimedia, as we discuss later in the case of Tulare County. When the expert system is interacting with another application, the interface is the program that presents the facts to the expert system. For example, the Northwest Airlines system described in Chapter 5 contains a program that gathers the data about each airline ticket from the ticket database and presents those facts to the expert systems.

The *inference engine* is that portion of the software that contains the reasoning methods used to search the knowledge base and solve the problem. The expert system generally asks questions of the user to get the information it needs. Then the inference engine, using the knowledge base, searches for the sought-after knowledge and returns a decision or recommendation to the user. Unlike conventional systems, expert systems can deal with uncertainty. Users can enter "Don't know" to questions in some systems, or answer "Yes (0.7)"—meaning "The answer probably is yes, but I'm only 70 percent certain." In these cases, the system produces several possible answers, ranking the most likely one the highest.

A *knowledge base* contains facts and data relevant to a specific application. The inference engine uses this information to reason out the problem. Here are some ways knowledge can be represented in a knowledge base.

Knowledge Representation

Knowledge is being represented in expert systems in an ever-widening spectrum. In this section we discuss that spectrum, beginning with the most familiar representation—rules—and concluding with two very new options—case-based reasoning and fuzzy logic. As these new options appear, the definition of an expert system can likewise expand.

Rules. The most common way to represent knowledge in expert systems is through rules. The rules, also called *heuristics*, are obtained from experts; therefore, they can draw upon experience, common sense, ways of doing business, and even rules and regulations. Rules generally present this knowledge in the form of if-then statements. The number of rules determines the complexity of the system. Small systems have perhaps 50 to 100 rules; large systems have several thousand rules. Rules are most appropriate when knowledge can be generalized into specific statements. When this is not possible, the following alternatives may be more appropriate.

Semantic Networks. Semantic networks represent knowledge in nodes. Semantics is the study of meaning, and seeks to define what objects and symbols stand for. In the case of an expert system semantic network, the nodes may contain physical or conceptual objects or symbols, and descriptors for those entities. Two nodes are linked by an *arc* whose name denotes the meaning of the relationship it represents. A semantic net is shown in Figure 15-1, from Ralph Sprague

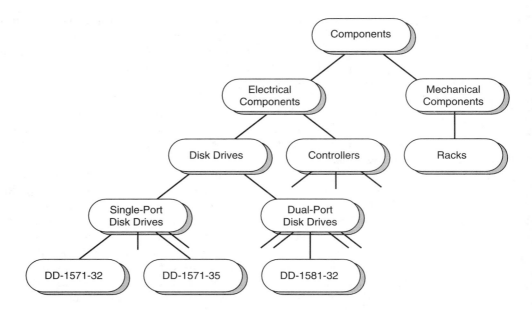

Figure 15-1   A Semantic Network (from Sprague and Watson [4a])

and Hugh Watson (University of Georgia) in their newest book, *Decision Support for Management* [4a].

Frames. Frames put knowledge into containers that have slots with information, values, rules, and procedural code that can redirect the query until the correct answers or solutions are found. Frames are fairly similar to objects in object-oriented systems because the slots can contain code. Frames can be used to represent a salesperson's annual performance because they can hold his or her name and the products sold, along with quarterly sales, quotas, gross margins, and so on. Even if most knowledge is represented in the frames, rules are still needed to perform the inferencing. Sprague and Watson present a frame in Figure 15-2.

Electrical Component	
Part No.	
Length	
Width	
Height	
Volume	

Figure 15-2   A Frame (from Sprague and Watson [4a])

Blackboard. The blackboard approach connects complementary expert systems to share information in a common data structure called a blackboard. A "manager" controls the various systems and helps the combined systems arrive at a solution. For example, a blackboard expert system could conceivably be used to solve the problem of sudden surges in automobiles. One expert system could analyze the fuel system, while another analyzes the automatic transmission, another the brakes, and another the pedal controls. Using them in concert, the "manager" could see how several elements in combination cause the surges.

Software Agents. In his recent book, *Being Digital*, Nicholas Negroponte, director of MIT's Media Lab [5], notes that the next generation of computer interfaces will be "agent-based interfaces" so that we can delegate tasks rather than have to perform them ourselves, as we now do with our "point and click" interfaces. Delegation will be necessary in order to cope with the vast amount of information in digital form, as on the Internet. As David King of Comshare [4b] points out, agents are software programs that focus on a single task and operate in the background. They automate repetitive tasks, and they support conditional processing, so they generally use rules and pattern matching to make decisions.

Software agents are called "intelligent" if they have the capacity to learn, notes King, but very few currently have that capability. "Learning" for an agent means that it changes its behavior as it observes a user's habits, interests, and behaviors. Although there is much talk about intelligent agents, there are many applications for agents that simply work on rules and pattern matching. In general, notes King, the focus in this technology is on monitoring, filtering, summarizing large or frequently changing files, and distributing the results to the users—sometimes in the form of personalized electronic newspapers.

Case-Based Reasoning. Case-based reasoning (CBR) is a recently popular form of knowledge representation in expert systems, arriving on the market in 1991. These systems draw inferences by comparing a current problem (or case) with hundreds or thousands of similar past cases. Case-based reasoning is best used when the situation involves too many nuances and variations to be generalized into rules.

Evan Schwartz and James Treece [6] provide an excellent example of a CBR system—the Apache III system used by the intensive care unit at St. Joseph Mercy Hospital in Ypsilanti, Michigan. When Sharon, 35, entered the hospital with a potentially fatal respiratory disease, the physicians and nurses in intensive care entered her vital statistics and medical history into a workstation running Apache III. The system drew on the records of 17,448 previous intensive care patients to predict whether Sharon would live or die. Its first prediction was that she had a 15 percent change of dying.

As the statistics were entered daily, the system compared her progress to the base of previous cases. Two weeks later, the prediction of death soared to 90 percent, alerting the physicians and nurses to take immediate corrective action. Then, literally overnight, her chance of dying dropped to 60 percent, and 12 days later to 40 percent. She did recover.

The intensive care unit's director credits the system with catching the increased likelihood of death days before his staff would have seen it. So the system is helping the unit respond faster and control costs better.

Esther Dyson [7] points out that CBR permits reusing knowledge because it allows retrieving all kinds of information associated with cases in a case base, such as instructions, diagrams, active links to hypertext documents, multimedia sequences, and even an automatic phone dialer that calls a help desk. CBRs can present a single recommendation or a set of possibilities, says Dyson, and there are innumerable uses, including

- Answering questions at a help desk
- Matching job requisitions to job candidates
- Selecting form letters to reply to incoming letters
- Finding legal precedents
- Identifying code modules for reuse

A CBR system contains a case base that has been indexed for one of three kinds of retrieval, says Dyson. *Hierarchical* retrieval uses a hierarchy to search for related cases; this approach is the most efficient but it requires indexing the cases. *Template matching* uses the input case as a straight query against the database to find matches; it uses traditional database indexing techniques. The nearest-neighbor approach uses common text retrieval techniques to scan the text and calculate the relative closeness of the new case to those in the case base; this technique takes the most processing time.

Dyson believes CBR is likely to become just another retrieval technique used in mainstream applications, just as rule-based expert systems have become reasoning modules in traditional applications.

Fuzzy Logic. Fuzzy logic is an AI technology that allows computers to precisely handle concepts and fuzzy notions, such as tall, warm, cool, good, near, far, and so forth. It therefore allows computer systems to more closely work the way people talk and think. Fuzzy logic was created in 1965 using set theory by Lotfi Zadeh at the University of Berkeley. It represents yet another way to represent knowledge or information.

Traditional programs require a specific definition for a characteristic, such as 68°F is hot while 67°F is cold. Such sharp boundaries cause abrupt changes in the output of conventional control systems, notes Kevin Self [8]. Fuzzy logic, on the other hand, allows characteristics to be classified by their degree of membership in a class, which softens the traditional hard delineations. Fuzzy logic permits precisely dealing with imprecision.

Larry Armstrong [9] explains fuzzy logic by describing how a heater's thermostat works. If the thermostat is set at 68°F, the heater would generally kick on at 66° and kick off at 70° if it were controlled by a traditional program that controls an on-off switch on the heater fan. Therefore, the room alternates between too cool and too warm. Fuzzy logic, however, can keep the room at a more constant temperature because it performs more complex calculations. Each temperature setting is a member of two classes from a set of four—cold, cool, warm, or hot. The 68° setting, for example, might have a 50 percent membership in the cool class and a 15 percent membership in the warm class. Simple if . . . then . . . rules in the system translate these membership percentages into heater fan speed. For instance, a fan speed setting of 50 percent medium and 15 percent low might correspond to 44 rpm fan speed. When the temperature changes, the system recalculates the fan speed to maintain the desired 68°.

Fuzzy logic simplifies complexity; therefore, it is very useful for controlling very complex systems or situations that cannot be easily represented by if . . . then . . . rules. Furthermore, fuzzy logic can be combined with an expert system to handle previously unsolvable problems. The fuzzy logic portion processes the large number of variables into a small number of membership sets that can then be very quickly handled by a small expert system.

Fuzzy logic is being widely used in Japan in consumer products—auto focus cameras, elevators, washing machines, subway trains, and so forth—because it allows smoother operation of machines and appliances. Fuzzy logic can also be used to control networks, processing plants, and other operational information systems; therefore, we see it eventually playing a role in systems built by systems departments.

Earl Cox and Martin Goetz [10] believe that fuzzy logic will become important in information retrieval because it allows people to think in general terms, such as "Find all companies whose revenue is growing rapidly and whose profit-to-earnings is very low." In such a search, the system not only responds with the citations but also indicates where they sit in the fuzzy set—near the defined goal of "growing rapidly" or above or below it. Cox and Goetz also believe fuzzy logic will be used to enable experts to state their expert system rules less precisely. For example, a doctor could have a rule, "If the patient is very old, do not recommend strenuous exercises." They also believe fuzzy logic will reduce software maintenance, by reducing the number of rules needed in applications, and by separating the variables used by the rules.

By allowing computers to work more like people, fuzzy logic opens up a new range of computer applications and permits existing applications to be able to handle imprecision and changing situations.

Neural Networks. Neural networks are still another type of intelligent system. Although they are not expert systems, they are another way of representing knowledge; therefore, we discuss them here.

Neural networks are organized like the human brain. The brain is a network of neurons—nerve cells—which fire a signal when they are simulated by smell, sound, sight, and so forth. As Brian O'Reilly [11] explains, scientists believe that our brains learn by strengthening or weakening these signals, gradually creating patterns. A neural network contains links (called synapses) and nodes that also fire signals between each other. Neural networks are more intelligent than the other forms of knowledge representation discussed because they can learn.

O'Reilly presents a good description of how a neural network learns by describing how a simple one might evaluate credit applications. As shown in Figure 15-3, the first layer of this neural net has six "neurons" that represent the criteria for distinguishing good credit risks from bad credit risks. The six criteria are high salary, medium salary, owns a home, less than three years on the current job, prior bankruptcy, and has a dog. (The dog probably does not have an effect, but who knows?) Each of the six is connected to the two neurons in the second layer: profitable customer and deadbeat.

To train the system to distinguish between these two, the network is fed the example of an applicant with a high salary who owns a house and has a dog. Each of these three neurons sends a signal of equal strength to both the profitable and deadbeat neurons because it has not been trained. The network is trained by telling the two second-level neurons the outcome of this previous loan: It was paid back. So the profitable neuron sends a signal back to the three saying, in effect, "You are right, send a stronger signal next time." The deadbeat neuron, on the other hand, replies with, "You are wrong, send a weaker signal next time." The network is then given many more examples so that it learns the predictors of profitable customers and deadbeats, readjusting its signal strengths with each new case.

Once the network is trained, the high-salary neuron might send a signal worth ten points to the profitable neuron, while the homeowner neuron might send only two points. And the less-than-three-years-on-the-job neuron may send two points to the deadbeat neuron and a minus two points to the profitable one. Since owning a dog is irrelevant, it will send zero points to both. New applications will be evaluated based on these learned patterns.

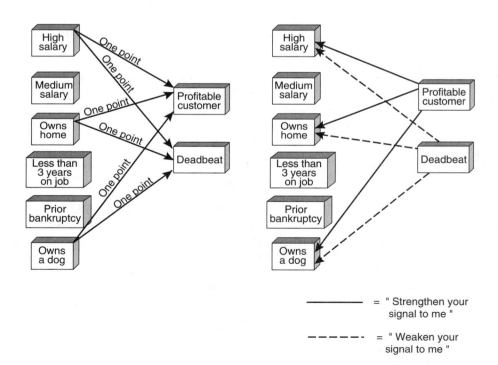

Figure 15-3   Training a Neural Network (Based on O'Reilly [11])

Neural networks have been used by an automaker to detect defective motors, by oil drillers to describe the progress of underground rock cracking based on sensor data, by a manufacturer to track manufacturing variations to determine the optimum manufacturing conditions, and by computer manufacturers to recognize handprinting. As with expert systems, the extravagant claims made about neural networks in the late 1980s have faded and their true uses are gradually being uncovered. Also like expert systems, they will increasingly be used to complement other reasoning techniques.

Now that we have explained the basics of expert systems and various ways to represent knowledge, we present an example of a rule-based expert system with a multimedia front-end, built intentionally for use by the general public—a fairly new use of the technology.

CASE EXAMPLE: Tulare Country, California

Tulare County, with 300,000 residents, is located in central California. As an agricultural county, Tulare has many people on government assistance. As described in *I/S Analyzer* [12], from 25 to 31 percent of Tulare's residents (some 90,000) are on welfare and another 10 percent are unemployed. About 40 percent of the residents are Hispanic and over 7,000 are immigrants from Southeast Asia.

The eligibility workers in the Department of Public Social Service qualify residents to receive government aid, but the department has had a tough time retaining these workers because their job is tedious and not highly paid. They must memorize a stack of state and federal welfare regulations six and one-half feet tall; and that stack grows at the rate of one page a day.

Many social service agencies around the world have given their workers computer-based tools to ease their workload. Tulare decided to go further by building a system that residents can use on their own. Many people believed this could not be done, considering the low educational level of these people and the language translation problems inherent in working with Hispanic and Asian residents. But the system is in and its success has exceeded all expectations.

The system, called The Tulare Touch, allows welfare applicants to conduct their own interview to qualify themselves to receive funds from the Aid to Families with Dependent Children and food stamp programs. The applicant uses a touch screen (no keyboard) as the system presents the information in one of six languages—English, Spanish, or one of four Southeast Asian languages. A host or hostess, speaking in one of the languages, appears in videos and as the behind-the-scenes voice. This guide introduces them to the system, asks them questions, and presents them with the possible options.

The real driver of The Tulare Touch is an expert system, which runs on the department's IBM 9000 series mainframe. It not only selects the next question and sequence of visuals to show, but it also calculates the applicant's benefits at the end of the interview. The system has a total of 1,049 questions; but because of the expert system, no applicant ever needs to answer all of them.

The system shortens the interview process by handling the thousands of complex rules and regulations better than the eligibility workers. It is also reducing errors and catching more fraud because it applies the rules more consistently. And department management has found that many applicants prefer dealing with a computer rather than a person because they believe they get fairer treatment. Economically, this $3 million system is also a hit; it is saving the county $20 million a year, $15 million of which is through reductions in erroneous overpayments—even though their 3 percent error rate is below the national average.

Use of the System

When applicants enter one of the county social services offices, they first talk to a receptionist eligibility worker who determines the reason for their visit and then enters their name into the system. The system checks the mainframe database for other information on the applicant and then initiates a transaction record. If the resident is a first-time applicant, or returning for a six-month recertification, the receptionist directs the applicant to a booth with the system that speaks his or her language. The receptionist also transfers the applicant's records to that system.

The applicant is then interviewed by the system. Animated graphics, combined with the host's "voice over," make the multiple choice questions easy to answer. For example, when the host says "January," the word *January* flashes on the screen. In some cases, the multiple choices are created on the fly, such as listing family members. Even applicants who cannot read any language can use the system successfully because it is so visual and combines audio and visual cues.

At the end of the interview, the system prints out a completed application form, which an eligibility worker then reviews with the applicant to verify the facts, look at any pertinent employment documents, and explain the results. Therefore, rather than filling in forms, the eligibility workers now concentrate on applicants' needs. Their interviews are now of higher quality.

Developing the Tulare Touch

The main problem Tulare encountered in developing the expert system was its design—figuring out the order of the questions. The county used decision trees to diagram the logic, which has made maintenance easy, even with the continual stream of new regulations. Whenever a change is made, the system indicates which other rules are affected.

The major challenge in designing the multimedia front-end was deciding how to avoid having to recut the laser disk master often, yet keep the system up-to-date. The mastering process costs $2,000; copies cost $15. To keep remastering down to twice a year, the system only uses video clips of the host or hostess for the introduction and the generic instructions, such as help. Only their voices are used everywhere else. Most of the voice portions are stored in analog form on the laser disk; however, new voice and text portions are stored digitally on hard disk, until a new master is cut.

Due to the uniqueness of the system, Tulare is being visited by government agencies from around the world.

Degrees of Expertise

The degree of expertise in an expert system can be characterized by the kind of assistance it might provide to a person. It might function as

1. An assistant
2. A colleague
3. A true expert

While many popular discussions of expert systems view them in terms of the third, or most expert, level, many expert systems are of the assistant or colleague levels.

In the least expert of these, an expert system is viewed as an *assistant* to help do routine analysis and point out those portions of the work where the expertise of the human is required. Dipmeter Advisor developed by Schlumberger Ltd. falls into this category. It reads charts produced by instruments that have been lowered into an oil well that is being drilled. Reading such charts, looking for a small amount of significant data, is a tedious job for humans. The expert system reads the charts and indicates those portions where the human experts should concentrate their attention.

A second level of expertness is that of a *colleague*. With an expert system of this type, the user "talks over" the problem with the system until a "joint decision" is reached. In this type of use, the user may employ the "why" and "how" features to understand the system's train of logic. When the system seems to be going down the wrong track, the user puts in more information to get it back on track. The resultant decision is thus a joint effort.

The third level of expertise is the *true expert,* where the user accepts the system's advice without question. This means the expert system performs as well as the top 10 percent to 20 percent of the experts in the field. Psychologists posit that it takes approximately ten years to acquire 50,000 discrete pieces of expert information, and that an expert possesses between 50,000 to 100,000 different pieces of expert information. So, such a system may employ the expertise of more than one person in a particular field.

Choosing Appropriate Applications

When is expert system technology most appropriate? We answer that question with the following suggested criteria for locating situations where the technology can have the greatest usefulness.

Locate experts under pressure. Find a subject area where the few experts are under severe job pressure. They may be doing a lot of traveling, receiving urgent phone calls at night or on weekends, and so on. Such experts generally will welcome a system that removes some of this pressure.

Look for complex jobs. Find a job that has become sufficiently complex that the people are having a hard time doing it accurately. Examples might be job shop production scheduling, dispatching, or equipment configuration checking. American Express, Tulare County, and Merced County (later in this chapter) are prime examples of fulfilling this need.

Handle important but infrequent decisions. Another possibility is to find a decision area that is very important but not performed frequently enough for people to develop (and retain) expertise. Examples are what to consider when shopping for a home mortgage or how to repair a complex machine.

Consider life safety areas. Where life safety is important, and decisions must be made in a hurry, expert systems may help the people who are responsible to make faster, better decisions. Network and systems management systems, for example, are gradually incorporating expert systems.

Focus on the decisions of another organization. An expert system that has captured the decisions of some other organization—such as a government regulatory agency—is not only useful but likely to be accepted by the employees.

Selecting areas such as these for building intelligent systems should improve operational efficiency and effectiveness by reducing employee resistance, thereby promoting acceptance of the systems.

USES OF EXPERT SYSTEMS

Although expert systems play an increasing role in company operations, we concentrate on two specific uses: to assist knowledge workers and to augment conventional systems.

To Assist Knowledge Workers

As alluded to earlier, knowledge workers need all the help they can get in dealing with the flood of information now available to them and increasing exponentially over the Internet. Paul Saffo, a director at the Institute for the Future (in 4b), notes that network computing has brought us "half the information revolution—access and volume." What remains is the "other half of the revolution—reducing the flood (of informatin) to a meaningful trickle." This is where intelligent systems can help:

- Approve routine requests
- Manage information
- Perform a task
- Diagnose a problem
- Supply input for decisions

Approve Routine Requests. Companies can build, for example, a purchase approval system. These days, more and more companies are downsizing the number of suppliers and putting in place long-term contracts with the few remaining suppliers. Generally, these contracts spell out the price of each item. When an item is ordered against this contract, an expert system could authorize the purchase, after validating the necessary purchasing guidelines.

Manage Information. Managing information involves looking for questions, problems, or anomalies, or locating information that may be needed in the future. As we noted earlier, this is a job that can be handled by software agents. As an example, one hotel has created a system (an agent) that surveys future reservations each night, comparing them to expected reservation patterns. In some cases, management wants to know about discrepancies. In other cases, the executives have defined the actions they want the expert system to take when specific conditions arise. The system prints out its findings and actions taken for hotel management to use the following morning.

Alan Kay, a fellow at Apple Computer, believes that in five years time, we will no longer directly manipulate things via computer; instead, we will "manage" the agents who do the direct manipulating. These agents could have so much intelligence and autonomy, said Kay, that people will need to manage what they do because some agents could become too eager in their work.

Perform a Task. In her book, *Electronic Performance Support Systems*, Gloria Gery [13] explains that EPSS provide support for a user in achieving a performance objective by applying knowledge, a process or procedure, or a rule to a situation. Many different kinds of software can be used in an EPSS. One important type is an expert system—to structure a problem, provide information for a decision, analyze data, or even diagnose a situation—because the task being supported can be complex and difficult to perform. They may act simply as an advisor, as in the case of one that can be used by sales reps to "qualify a lead" to decide whether or not the lead appears to be a potential future customer and should be called. In equipment troubleshooting, a technician might call on an expert system to diagnose the problem. The system might even recommend an action and coach the technician through a complex repair task, notes Gery.

Diagnose a Problem. Creativity involves relating remote bits of information; the further apart the bits, the more creativity is needed to relate them. Expert systems that learn from examples (inductive learning systems) are most helpful when people do not know everything about a process; the system helps them gain new knowledge from the data. For example, consider one particular diagnostic system for a tubing process described at a conference [14]. Although that manufacturing process was fairly well understood due to years of experience, some unexplainable fluctuations in tubing quality continued to sporadically appear. The engineers created an inductive learning system to uncover the cause of the anomalies. They fed it data from actual tubing processing and it generated the rules represented by the data. Unexpectedly, the system uncovered a relationship the engineers had not seen. It found a new rule—temperature fluctuations of the lubricants had to be controlled around the *original* lubricant temperature, not around the temperature of the machine. Such insights are dramatic, but they are not common.

Supply Input for Decisions. Knowledge-based systems can eliminate frustrations and allow people to do the work they want to do by giving them the information they need to make a decision—rather than making the decision for them. For example, one hotel asks that its registration clerks follow management's daily goals when registering guests. Rather than just "following the rules," the clerks can thus use their discretion when assigning rooms and rates to attain these goals. The clerks like the system because it helps them deal with guests more equally and consistently—and leaves the decision in their hands.

Improving the processes that knowledge workers use is of strategic importance to organizations. Helping them at important decision points is especially crucial. A case in point is the system built at Merced County, California, to help its eligibility workers evaluate welfare applications. This work is described in two publications by Andersen Consulting [15].

CASE EXAMPLE: Merced County, California

Merced County, California, has some 178,000 residents to whom the county government provides traditional public services. The Human Services Agency determines residents' eligibility for welfare and other government programs. Due to the variety of programs administered, each eligibility worker previously dealt with nearly 750 different forms and was responsible for distributing some $2 million a year in benefits to recipients. Due to the importance of accuracy, these clerks spent 75 percent of their time checking and rechecking eligibility criteria after completing an interview with an applicant. The jobs were complex and not well-paying; therefore, worker turnover was 35 percent a year. Furthermore, the agency's case load was rising 15 percent a year, which was straining the agency's budgets and resources.

To rectify the situation, agency management decided to entirely revamp the way services were delivered based on attaining three objectives:

- *Focus on families* by having each eligibility worker manage households eligible for multiple programs, rather than only serve individuals.
- *Make a computer system responsible* for applying regulations, making accurate calculations, determining benefits, and managing tickler files. This would free the eligibility workers to concentrate on the applicants' needs.

- *Significantly reduce administrative costs* with an eye toward decreasing staff size without sacrificing service.

With the help of Andersen Consulting, the agency built a system that standardizes the all-important interviewing process. It guides the eligibility worker through the interview process by presenting each question to ask the applicant, with the exact wording to use. Based on the applicant's answer selected from the multiple choice options presented on the screen, the system decides what further questions to ask. Therefore, each interview is tailored to the applicant's specific situation.

The heart of this system is a 4,500-rule expert system, which resides on each of 200 Hewlett-Packard workstations. The system not only guides the interview but also performs all the calculations and determines who in the household is eligible for programs and what benefits the applicant is qualified to receive. During the interview there are no longer any paper forms, system codes, regulation books, or calculators. The system operates in a client/server environment with 70 percent of the on-line activity handled by the workstations. The remaining processing is handled by a departmental server and a central host.

The system was meant to do more than simply automate the agency's existing manual operations; it was intended to improve them. Therefore, management involved many staff members in the project. During design, the project team uncovered hundreds of agency policies and procedures that required changing if the organization was to be streamlined. To involve the supervisors in initiating change, a two-day working conference was held. Teams of supervisors and managers tackled groups of procedures and policies, rewriting 85 percent of them in those two days. One team alone rewrote 70 policies. Agency management also enlisted the help of professionals in the community who work with the same disadvantaged people during system design.

The system was successfully installed and the agency is receiving numerous benefits. Clients are receiving better, faster, and more consistent services. The quality of work life in the agency has improved because the system interprets the detailed eligibility rules and performs the complex calculations; therefore, turnover has dropped. And regulatory changes are incorporated faster. Finally, follow-up work and reminders are not forgotten because they are performed by the system. All these benefits allow the eligibility workers to handle more applicants and handle them in a more humane manner.

To Augment Conventional Systems

Expert systems have quietly slipped into business systems to complement traditional processing. Tim Mikkelsen [16] sees three ways of combining expert systems with conventional systems:

1. The expert system is the main controlling program.
2. The expert system is embedded within an existing application.
3. A conventional language is used to do symbolic, rather than numeric, processing.

When *the expert system is the main controlling program*, it needs information, so it calls the appropriate program or subroutine, which may be written in another language. This approach is easy to accomplish, says Mikkelsen, because expert system tools have facilities for calling other programs or accessing databases or spreadsheets.

When *the expert system is embedded within an existing application*, says Mikkelsen, the expert system modules and conventionally coded modules can call each other; neither one is necessarily the controlling module. This approach can be taken only when the development environment allows writing applications in a combination of languages, such as C, Pascal, Fortran, LISP, and Prolog.

Mikkelsen's third approach is to *use conventional languages to do symbolic processing*. Expert systems can be written in any language, but the effort is much greater in conventional languages. To overcome this hurdle, Mikkelsen recommends prototyping the expert system portion of an application with expert system tools, to test the concept and explore the possibilities.

Expert system development has become another form of programming—a new approach to dealing with previously unprogrammable applications. As an example of a company that combined a conventional system and an expert system, consider Northern Telecom.

CASE EXAMPLE: Northern Telecom

Northern Telecom, a telecommunications company, manufactures private branch exchanges, telephone systems of all sizes, satellite repeaters, electronic switching systems, and other telecommunications equipment. Northern Telecom has built a system that combines an expert system with a traditional information system.

The Application

The company's product administration system contains information on all Northern Telecom products, including how they are designed and manufactured. It runs on IBM computers at the firm's 22 manufacturing plants and uses a distributed relational database accessed using SQL. The 22 sites save the daily changes and update the master database at night. Then the master database sends revised records to all 22 sites.

The systems department wanted to enhance the system by adding procedures for processing engineering changes to reduce the engineering changes approval cycle—from several weeks down to days or even hours. At the time, all but one of the plants used paper-based engineering change

Chapter 15 Expert Systems

441

procedures. Of course, moving from paper to electronic form speeds things up. But the system could also reduce the amount of information needed by people in an approval chain, if it only asked questions relevant to that particular type of change. This capability would reduce the time a change request spends at each step.

The 22 manufacturing plants also used different procedures; therefore, the developers could not create one common procedure that all the plants would use. They therefore decided to create a system that lets each plant manager create customized engineering change procedures for that plant.

Choosing an Approach

After reviewing the specifications for the new system, an outside programming firm concluded that it was an expert system application, for the following reasons:

- It needed to include knowledge about when to authorize or not authorize a proposed engineering change, so it needed a database of decision rules.
- The engineering change process is complex; links between authorization steps can be quite involved, especially when exceptions or new requirements occur. Thus, Northern Telecom needed a modular system to reduce the complexity.
- The engineering change process was not well understood. People had a hard time explaining when they would not approve an engineering change. Therefore, the firm needed a system that could be updated easily as new change procedures were uncovered.
- The system needed to be maintained by end users; only a system with an English-like user interface would permit user maintenance.

After studying several expert system development products, the company chose ADS from Aion Corporation [17]. Using ADS, expert systems can be developed and run on either an IBM mainframe or a PC. These expert systems can call conventional applications or be embedded within them, and they can access SQL relational databases. These capabilities were just what Northern Telecom needed.

To test the concept, two programmers spent two months building a fully functional prototype. It contained 113 screens, ten menus, and accessed the engineering database. Coding was surprisingly fast, we were told. ADS appeared to increase programming productivity by 30 percent to 50 percent over a conventional language. The objectives of the prototype were to learn about ADS, to test the feasibility of the application, and to see whether or not an expert system could be embedded in the existing system. After the prototype was used on a test basis for one month, the team received approval to create the production system using ADS.

Programming the Application

The developers used ADS to create *menus* for initiating change requests, processing changes, inquiring about change status, and so on.

The system first leads the user through the appropriate dialog to uncover what is needed. If a change is to be initiated, the system assembles a customized "script" of the steps needed to obtain approval of the change based on the questions initially answered by the user. The system routes the request to each person specified in the script, and even helps each person reach a decision.

The developers also defined *decision rules* for the various authorization steps. Once the system is given the pertinent facts by an engineer, designer, or purchasing agent, it uses these rules to recommend a decision.

The team also created *escape hatches*, so that users can leave the expert system if it has no built-in procedure for handling a step. A main concern of the programmers was that users would revert to their old, paper-based procedures whenever they encountered something lacking in the system. The escape hatches are meant to help users handle such situations.

The programmers also wrote *interfaces* between the expert system, the relational database, and existing Pascal, C, and Fortran routines. The programmers used whichever language was best for a particular task. For example, they often chose to create reports using one of the conventional languages.

The team also created a *set of tools* to help plant managers build scripts defining engineering change procedures used at their site. Each script describes who is to handle each step under each circumstance, how exceptions are to be processed, and so on.

Due to the complexity of the application, the programmers believed it would take at least two years of use before all the decision rules used at the various plants had been uncovered and encoded in the system. To make the system useful during that time, they were able to add rules on-line without interrupting the production system.

In all, Northern Telecom was very pleased with its use of expert system technology; it believes the application would not have been practical using conventional programming technologies.

MANAGING EXPERT SYSTEM DEVELOPMENT

As we noted earlier, expert systems can range from a few rules to thousands of rules. These systems are being developed by end users, information systems professionals, and third-party developers. Based on our research, we offer the following three guidelines for managing the development of expert systems:

- Quantify the development effort.
- Take a balanced approach.
- Draw on PC support lessons.

Quantify the Development Effort

Mark Meyer of Northeastern University and Kathleen Curley [18] of Lotus Institue, developed a four-part framework for categorizing expert systems. They then studied 50 expert systems to determine whether particular approaches were used to develop the four kinds of systems. They classify expert systems on the two dimensions of knowledge complexity and technical complexity. Knowledge complexity relates to the depth and specialization of the knowledge of the experts as well as to the scope of the processing and level of expertise required in the application. Technical complexity relates to the depth and scope of the development effort, the user environment, and other technical considerations. Combining these two dimensions yields the matrix shown in Figure 15-4.

Quadrant 1: Low Knowledge, Low Technology. These personal productivity systems contain the least knowledge and technical complexity. They are often developed by end users and generally work on stand-alone PCs or without significant database or communication links. An example of this type of expert system, write Meyer and Curley, is a system called TAX that is used by a European airline to monitor the travel of employees stationed abroad for longer than one year. The company pays the country taxes during this time, if required. The purpose of the system is to help these employees plan elective business and personal travel to reduce the company's tax liability. TAX has a small knowledge domain. It runs on one PC. And it was developed in three months' time using a PC expert system shell. Development cost was $15,000.

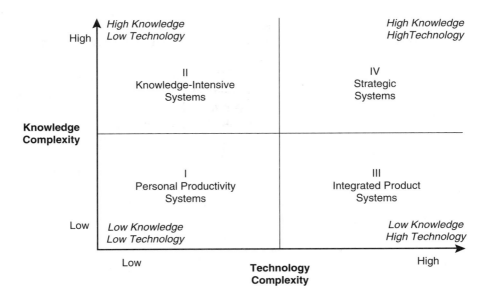

Figure 15-4   An Expert System Framework (from Meyer and Curley [18])

Quadrant 2: High Knowledge, Low Technology. The knowledge-intensive systems include expert systems with "deep" knowledge, that is, requiring elaborate reasoning in a highly specialized field. These systems may also span several domains; however, they are technically fairly simple and operate on a single hardware platform with small databases. One example given by Meyer and Curley is the Coal Advisor, developed by an American engineering service company to assist coal buyers in making purchasing decisions. The system takes into consideration over 100 characteristics of coal and includes multiple domains in depth, yet it runs on a stand-alone PC with a graphical user interface. It took three years and $2 million to build.

Quadrant 3: Low Knowledge, High Technology. These integrated product systems have fairly simple knowledge bases but significant technical attributes, so they require formal project management and testing, similar to major systems projects. One such system is Extel, developed in Europe by a computer firm and a telephone company. It assists customers in selecting the best telephone service, based on their calling patterns. The knowledge base is straightforward; however, implementation is not because the system is dispersed throughout hundreds of branch offices and requires accessing central databases. This system took three years to develop and cost between $1 and $2 million.

Quadrant 4: High Knowledge, High Technology. These strategic systems require large-scale knowledge engineering (that is, creating rules from expertise) and complex technology, such as integration with other systems. An example is a life underwriting system that operates on both a PC and a mainframe. It combines medical, actuarial, and underwriting knowledge to screen and rate insurance applications. It also requires working with client mainframe systems and external databases. The different data models in these various systems significantly complicated development. The system took over three years to build for a cost of more than $5 million.

Development Lessons Learned. Meyer and Curley uncovered several development lessons from using this framework to categorize the 50 systems. Although the final systems had different overall development times, building a prototype of the system—which was always done—took about six months for all but the very complex systems in Quadrant 4. The complexity of the system design for these systems lengthened the prototyping stage.

The systems were mainly user driven—68 percent of the 50 systems were conceived by users and only 14 percent originated with a systems person. The remainder were inspired by customers, consultants, and vendors. Likewise, the development projects were often user managed. Some 62 percent of the projects were controlled by the business departments. And in several cases where the system was a large-scale strategic system, a new business unit was formed to control development. It was staffed with line and systems people. Logically, the IS department managed the more technically complex projects, while the business units managed the knowledge complex ones.

This framework provides IS management with guidelines for planning a development strategy, depending on the characteristics of the system, say Meyer and Curley. For instance, technically complex systems will benefit from early involvement by systems people while knowledge-intensive systems need at least close linkage with the business staff, if not control by them. The framework also can be used to evaluate the evolution of existing expert systems, whether they are becoming more technically or knowledge complex, and the implications of this evolution on project requirements.

Take a Balanced Approach

Taking a balanced approach means building both large and small systems. Tom Schwartz [19], a consultant in the field, says that companies should be able to develop one large expert system and many small ones in three years' time. He believes companies should aim to achieve such a mix.

Encourage Many Small Systems. Many experts recommend using PC-based shells to develop small rule-based systems. The definition of *small* is not clear, but it probably means a system with 50 to 100 rules. But that does not mean it is trivial. Schwartz gave us his guidelines for determining which applications are appropriate for a 50-rule system. He calls it his "telephone test:"

1. It has fewer than 20 outcomes.
2. The procedure can be taught to someone in three hours to three days time.
3. A full discussion of the problem between the programmer and the user can occur over the telephone, using no diagrams, in less than one-half hour.

A 50-rule system can still be complex and important. Robert Anderson of the Rand Corporation [20] described a 50-rule system that he wrote to determine which missile to fire at a target from a jet fighter plane—based on the distance to the target, the number of targets approaching, their location, their speed, and so on. The possible outcomes are to fire one of three kinds of missiles, or fire nothing at all, based on about one dozen characteristics of the target and the quality of the radar signals. In all, 40 attributes needed to be considered. This is appropriate for a 50-rule system, he said. Although this is a stand-alone system, it is not a trivial one. A 50-rule system that accesses an external database can be a much more powerful system.

Some applications are "growable" in that they can be divided into chunks that can then be linked together. These chunks can be different functions, or the same functions performed on subsets of data. By starting small, the investments are less risky, says Schwartz, and the company can experiment with different ways of measuring economic impact. If the initial prototype does not cost justify itself, and if it is expandable, it could be the basis for a system that does provide economic payback, says Schwartz. Encourage lots of small applications, he suggests, but be cautious on building large ones.

Develop Large Systems Cautiously. Edward Feigenbaum, an AI pioneer, provided his guidelines for developing large expert systems at a Texas Instruments Satellite Symposium on AI [14]. He suggested choosing only problems that will earn or save several million dollars a year because large expert systems are expensive to build and can take from one to ten work-years. The crucial phase is formulation, said Feigenbaum. Determining the scope of the project is crucial. It is equivalent to a Ph.D. student choosing a thesis theme. One-half the work is picking the right scope of the project. Therefore, you should spend money on getting help in guiding the selection process. Next, calculate the value of the system in advance, while you are determining its scope, he suggested. Whether that value represents earnings or savings, keep that number in mind. Be specific about the system's inputs and outputs, and do not change the scope of the system in midstream.

Others advise picking projects where the knowledge is so well defined that the output is clear. This implies that the knowledge is known by practitioners, that experts on the subject can agree on the knowledge needed to solve the problem, and that the knowledge base can be made relatively stable.

And most experts recommend building a prototype to determine whether or not the problem is solvable. One airline estimated that it could increase revenues by $12 million a year by obtaining just one more passenger on each flight. But to achieve that goal, it needed to quickly see its rate structure per flight. The company built a prototype and demonstrated that this was possible, so it continued the project. The wise advise is to proceed cautiously when developing large expert systems.

Draw on PC Support Lessons

As Meador and Mahler point out [4c], some companies choose to centralize expert system development by creating a group that specializes in this area. American Express has done this, following the successful development of Authorizer's Assistant. Other companies take a dispersed approach, where they encourage widespread use of PC-based expert system shells. Du Pont, to be discussed shortly, takes this approach. Companies in this latter category are wise to reuse the lessons learned in supporting PC computing in the 1980s. Here are three of those lessons.

Establish a Support Organization. An important lesson from widespread PC use is the need to establish a support organization to guide use. This group establishes the strategy, chooses the products, coordinates the training, provides consulting help, and markets the technology within the company.

Standardize on a Few Tools. It is wiser to offer users a few tools than to give them the freedom to choose whatever they want; otherwise, support becomes a nightmare. At Du Pont, they chose four tools that ran on many of their installed machines.

Ed Mahler, program manager of the Du Pont group, notes that the ideal expert system tool for end users has five characteristics. First, it *supplies a structure*. All the user needs to do is enter the knowledge. If the resulting answer is wrong, it is due to wrong knowledge, not a problem with the tool. Spreadsheets provide this capability; they supply the wherewithal to process what is put into the cells.

Second, the tool has *type-over menus*. That is, it presents a menu with predefined default values, but the user can enter new values. In essence, the system provides a skeleton from which to work, just as graphics packages do. Users can use the default values to quickly see a graph or they can change the defaults to customize the graph.

Third, the tool has *image capture and display capabilities* because it is often important to include a picture or diagram—such as a diagram of the position of switches on a machine. It is especially nice if the user can change the images, said Mahler.

Fourth, the system would provide *automatic database interaction* to popular PC packages because users often download mainframe data to their PCs.

Fifth, an ideal tool has *powerful behind-the-screen facilities*, providing, say, the ability to customize screens or create specialized links to other applications.

Stress User Self-Sufficiency. One of the goals of PC support has been to make users self-sufficient. Du Pont is taking the same approach with expert systems by helping users to get started using a tool, but users are expected to complete and maintain their own work. Knowledge-based systems are never finished; they can always be expanded. So user self-sufficiency is important to avoid creating an expert system backlog in the IS department. With this preamble, here is Du Pont's approach. It is by far the most well-known example of a company that has encouraged widespread development of small expert systems.

CASE EXAMPLE: E.I. duPont de Nemours & Co.

E.I. duPont de Nemours & Co. is a large diversified chemical, energy, and specialty products company with headquarters in Wilmington, Delaware. Its business units are involved in energy, manufacturing textile fibers, polymer products, and agricultural and biomedical chemicals.

Although Du Pont is a large organization, the program manager for AI sees it as many small businesses. Thus, he believes the company will get greater benefits from AI technology by creating many small expert systems rather than a few large ones. An AI group was formed and has become the catalyst for widespread expert system development within Du Pont.

Management believed that getting users to use expert systems would be a bigger issue than building the systems. Since users are more likely to use a system they create themselves, the company decided to take an end user computing approach to building expert systems.

Helping Users Develop Their Own Expert Systems

The AI group's goal is to make expert system development just another computing tool—like word processing, spreadsheets, desktop publishing, and electronic mail. The group selects the tools, provides the training, offers consulting help, serves at the help desk, and sometimes does initial development with users to get them started. In addition to the core group, the company has site coordinators who know about specific expert system tools. The core group trains these site coordinators to handle users' questions. So the company has a two-tier support structure to help users develop expert systems.

Due to this approach, users have developed hundreds of expert systems; the average size is 150 to 300 rules each. Most of the systems provide a seven-to-one to eight-to-one payoff on the full investment—equipment, software, training, and work-hours to develop the system.

Some systems assist the salespeople, such as recommending the best Du Pont film to replace a competitor's product. Some assist mechanics in diagnosing problems in process control computers. Others provide engineering expertise around-the-clock to equipment operators. Still others are value-added services, such as advising volunteer firefighters how to handle chemical spills at the scene of an emergency.

Educating Managers As Well As Users

The AI group created three training courses on expert systems within Du Pont. A two-hour management awareness seminar explained expert systems, where they are most useful, how they are developed, and why they are important. A four-hour introductory course for users and supervisors discussed both managerial and technical issues. One management issue is deciding when a system is complete. Users often want to add "just one more function." Management needs to decide when enough is enough.

A third course provides two-day training on how to select the proper tool and then develop a system. During these two days, attendees learn to use three tools. Following this course, users can get consulting help from the staff. In some cases, consultants do help create the first prototype. But they never finish it—they want the user to do that.

Resolving "Ownership" and Payback Issues

The success of any systems project depends on getting users to "own" the system—to feel that it belongs to them. When a knowledge engineer develops a system for employees, the users are less likely to feel that they "own" it than if they developed it themselves. To foster experimentation by the end users, the core group members used both the formal and informal company structures. Initially, they depended on the informal network of people they knew to attain early successes. Then the formal structure provided the impetus to get systems developed.

Although payback is important, Du Pont does not spend much time analyzing it for the small expert systems. Any task that takes an expert more than a few minutes or less than a few hours to complete is worth prototyping. So the company is aiming for the small applications because there are lots of them, and they tend to grow and become very useful.

FUTURE DIRECTIONS

Based on his attendance at a major conference on artificial intelligence, Lance Eliot [21], a consultant, made these observations (among others) about the future of AI in business. Case-based reasoning is a hot commercial AI topic, with much of the research being put into products. There is a fair amount of research discussing distributed AI, that is, intelligent agents interacting and cooperating to solve problems. This research will move closer to commercial use in the late 1990s, believes Eliot. Researchers are also interested in "constraint reasoning"— that is, how AI systems can track the correctness of their knowledge and actions. The commercial world will not realize the importance of constraint reasoning until some expert systems fail, surmises Eliot.

Most commercial systems use the simplest forms of logic and handle only straighforward techniques of knowledge representation. Future ones will use different forms of logic and ways of incorporating probabilities and uncertainty, he believes. Similarly, commercial products do a poor job of explaining what they have done. We need more explanation techniques, he felt. In addition, few commercial expert systems handle planning; they try to accomplish their goals without planning. As they become more sophisticated, this act-first plan-later approach will no longer be appropriate, says Eliot.

And learning is still an emerging area. Most AI systems do not learn; they must be updated by hand. The neural network approach is a viable learning technique, one that is being explored for other types of systems. Another leading-edge area in research is physical systems reasoning, which means diagnosing faults in physical systems by matching a system's expected behavior with its actual behavior.

Many of the papers at the conference were coauthored by industry research and development personnel, which indicates that the two are attempting to link up with each other.

CONCLUSION

The field of expert systems is no longer limited to laboratories and experiments. Many expert systems have been put in production, either through major expert system projects or by encouraging end users to write smaller knowledge-based systems. Since both types yield significant payoffs, we believe IS management should follow a balanced approach to building these systems—encourage many small systems and carefully develop large systems. Expert systems, once viewed as an arcane use of IT, has become just another tool in the IS toolkit.

QUESTIONS AND EXERCISES

REVIEW QUESTIONS

1. What is an expert system?
2. What does the Authorizer's Assistant do and how does it do it?
3. What are the three components of an expert system?

4. Explain the different ways of representing knowledge.
5. Explain two uses of expert systems.
6. What five things did the Northern Telecom programmers create with ADS?
7. Describe the four categories of expert systems uncovered by Meyer and Curley.
8. What is a balanced approach to developing expert systems?
9. What are three lessons learned from PC support?
10. What are the main components of Du Pont's approach to managing expert system development?

DISCUSSION QUESTIONS

1. Expert system technology is too complex for end users. It should be left for professional IS developers to create "real" expert systems. Argue for and against this claim.
2. Expert systems are dangerous. People are likely to depend on them rather than think for themselves. If the system contains some bad logic, bad decisions will be made and lawsuits will result. Argue for and against this claim.
3. The Tulare County and Merced County systems use very different approaches to essentially do the same job—qualify welfare recipients. Which approach is better? Why?

EXERCISES

1. Visit a company in your area that has developed some expert systems. What are the systems used for? Are they assistant, colleague, or true expert systems? Who has developed these systems and how?
2. Read three articles about expert systems. What new facts did you learn that were not in this chapter? Share these ideas with the class.
3. If you know of an expert system, explain what it does, how it is used, how it was developed, who it is meant to help, its benefits, and its shortcomings.
4. Find three companies or articles that discuss expert systems on the Internet. Present your findings to the class. What did you find the most intriguing about these discussions?

REFERENCES

1. NEWQUIST, H., "Nearly Everything You Want to Know About AI," *Computerworld* (375 Cochituate Road, Framingham, MA 01701), July 29, 1991, pp. 64.
2. HOLSAPPLE, C. W. and A. B. WHINSTON, *Business Expert Systems*, Richard D. Irwin, Homewood, IL, 1987, ISBN 0-256-05544-0.
3. BREWER, TONY, "Managing Knowledge," IT Management Programme report, Wentworth Research, Egham, England, http:www.wentworth.co.uk, November 1995.
4. SPRAGUE, RALPH and HUGH WATSON, *Decision Support for Management,* Prentice Hall, Englewood Cliffs, NJ, 1996.
   a. "EXPERT SYSTEMS: THE NEXT CHALLENGE FOR MANAGERS," pp. 373-389, a reprint of Fred Luconi, Thomas Malone, and Michael Scott Morton, "Expert Systems: The Next Challenge for Managers," *Sloan Management Review*, Summer 1986, pp. 3-14.
   b. KING, DAVID, "Intelligent Support Systems," pp. 182-205.

c. "CHOOSING AN EXPERT SYSTEMS GAME PLAN," pp. 414-423, a reprint of Lawrence Meador and Ed Mahler, "Choosing an Expert System Game Plan," *Datamation*, August 1, 1990, pp. 64-70.

5. NEGROPONTE, NICHOLAS, *Being Digital*, Alfred Knopf, New York, 1995.

6. SCHWARTZ, E. and J. TREECE, "Smart Programs Go to Work," *Business Week* (1221 Avenue of the Americas, New York, NY 10020), March 2, 1992, pp. 97-105.

7. DYSON, E., "Case-Based Reasoning: A Familiar Story," *Release 1.0* (EDventure Holdings, 375 Park Ave., New York, NY 10152), January 31, 1992, pp. 1-15.

8. SELF, K., "Designing with Fuzzy Logic," *IEEE Spectrum*, (IEEE, Box 1331, Piscataway, NJ 08855), November 1990, pp. 42-44, 105.

9. ARMSTRONG, L., "Software That Can Dethrone 'Computer Tyranny,'" *Business Week*, (1221 Avenue of the Americas, New York, NY 10020), April 6, 1992, pp. 90-91.

10. COX, E. and M. GOETZ, "Fuzzy Logic Clarified," *Computerworld* (375 Cochituate Road, Framingham, MA 01701), March 11, 1991, pp. 69-71.

11. O'REILLY, B., "Computers That Think Like People," *Fortune* (Time-Life Building, Rockefeller Center, New York, NY 10020), February 27, 1989, pp. 90-93.

12. MCNURLIN, BARBARA, "The Emerging World of Multimedia," *I/S Analyzer*, (11300 Rockville Pike, Suite 1100, Rockville, MD 20852), March 1991.

13. GERY, GLORIA, *Electronic Performance Support Systems*, Ziff Institute, Cambridge, MA 02141, 1991.

14. ARTIFICIAL INTELLIGENCE SATELLITE SYMPOSIUM, sponsored by Texas Instruments. Three were held in the 1980s.

15. *CLOSE-UP: HUMAN SERVICES AGENCY MERCED COUNTY, CALIFORNIA AND TRENDS IN INFORMATION TECHNOLOGY*, Andersen Consulting (Chicago, IL 60602), 1991.

16. MIKKELSEN, M., "Mixing AI and Conventional Techniques," *A Review of Products, Services, and Research*, July 1987, pp. 58-59.

17. AION CORPORATION, 101 University Ave., Palo Alto, CA 94301).

18. MEYER, MARK and KATHLEEN CURLEY, "An Applied Framework for Classifying the Complexity of Knowledge-Based Systems," *MIS Quarterly* (MIS Research Center, Carlson School of Management, University of Minnesota, 271 19th Ave., S., Minneapolis, MN 55455), December 1991, pp. 454-472.

19. SCHWARTZ, TOM, 801 W. El Camino Real, Suite 150, Mountain View, CA 94040.

20. ANDERSON, ROBERT, Rand Corporation, 1300 Main St., Santa Monica, CA 90403.

21. ELIOT, LANCE "Where Theory Meets Practice," *AI Expert* (500 Howard St., San Francisco, CA 94105), October 1991, pp. 9-11.

SIXTEEN

Electronic Document Management

INTRODUCTION

Harnessing information technology to manage documents is one of the most important challenges facing IS managers in this decade because most of the valuable information in organizations is in the form of documents, such as business forms, reports, letters, memos, policy statements, contracts, agreements, and so on. Moreover, most of the important business processes in organizations are based on, or driven by, document flows.

Electronic document management (EDM) promises major productivity and performance increases by applying new technology to documents and document processing. EDM is the application of new technology to save paper, speed up communications, and increase the productivity of business processes. From a broader perspective, EDM is a major expansion in the domain of information management and a concomitant increase in the responsibilities of IS managers and executives.

In this final chapter of Part V on support systems, we focus on a set of systems and technologies for handling documents [1]. The pervasiveness and importance of documents are not going to change anytime soon, but the form that documents take is changing radically.

Computer systems have mostly handled facts organized into data records. Far more valuable and important to organizations are the concepts and ideas contained in documents. Reports drawn from computerized databases fill important roles in status assessment and control, but frequently they must be accompanied by a memo or text report which explains and interprets the computer report. Indeed, in one study [2], CEOs rated computer reports least valuable for decision making from among a set of communication mechanisms. Meetings, phone conversations, news items, written memos, and noncomputerized reports were rated much more highly. Technology applied to the handling of documents promises to improve these forms of communication.

Until recently, technology for document processing has been limited mostly to better and faster ways to generate, print, and transport text documents. Now, several trends and developments suggest that we are on the verge of a major advance in computer-based information management. Technology developments enabling these advances include digital image processing, large-capacity storage, hypertext, multimedia documents, high-bandwidth communication channels, electronic printing, electronic mail, facsimile, and improved techniques for retrieval of concepts, information, and data. Many of these technologies are proving valuable for replacing paper, managing work flow, training and education, records management, and internal reporting.

In this chapter we will first consider the definition and scope of EDM. Then we identify a taxonomy of application areas that is generating business value from the use of document technologies. Those technologies are then summarized in a layered architecture. Finally, we consider what IS managers should do to prepare for document management.

DEFINITION AND SCOPE

A document can be described as a unit of "recorded information structured for human consumption" [3]. It is recorded and stored, so a speech or conversation for which no transcript is prepared is not a document. This definition accommodates "documents" dating back to cuneiform inscriptions on clay tablets; what has changed lately are the ways the information is represented, and the ways the documents are processed. Information previously represented primarily by text is now also represented by graphical symbols, images, photographs, audio, video, and animation. Documents previously created and stored on paper are now digitally created, stored, transported, and displayed.

This definition also accommodates a wide variety of documents used in organizations. Examples include

- Contracts and agreements
- Drawings, blueprints, and photographs
- Reports
- E-mail and voice mail messages
- Manuals and handbooks
- Video clips
- Business forms

- Scripts and visuals from presentations
- Correspondence
- Computer printouts
- Memos
- Transcripts from meetings
- News items and articles

The application of technology for processing even the more traditional documents in this list is making a major change in what documents are and can accomplish in organizations. A definition more oriented to technology comes from *Byte* magazine [4].

A document is a snapshot of some set of information that can

- incorporate many complex information types;
- exist in multiple places across a network;
- depend on other documents for information;
- change on the fly (as subordinate documents are updated);
- have an intricate structure, or complex data types such as full-motion video and voice annotations; and
- be accessed and modified by many people simultaneously (if they have permission to do so).

Another perspective suggests that a document is the unit record of conceptual information. A data record contains the attributes of an entity such as an employee in a personnel system or a part number in an inventory system; a document contains the information necessary to represent a concept or idea. Although most documents currently contain a cluster or set of these concept nodes, future documents may be composed of a network or web of linked conceptual unit records. These chunks or bundles of information will have attributes that make them more useful and human than traditional data records. Context, tone, richness of representation media, and flexibility of structure will make the information in documents more consumable and accessible to humans. This perspective strengthens the understanding that document management is an expanded form of information management.

In spite of these broad definitions, the dominant connotation of a document is that it is relatively structured and formal information, primarily text, printed on paper. Therefore, EDM must handle paper documents or their electronic equivalent. Older technologies for document handling include micrographics, computer output microfilm (COM), and automated records center applications. A newer technology is digital image processing, which represents a page of a paper document with a digital image of that page.

Increasingly, however, EDM emphasizes *electronic documents* and their management. An electronic document uses a variety of symbols and media to represent a set of ideas and concepts. In addition to traditional letters and numbers (text), an electronic document may contain graphical symbols, photographs and other images, voice, video clips, and animation. This clustered set of symbols can be stored, retrieved, and presented electronically as a compound document. For example, an internal report on a product improvement may present, on a

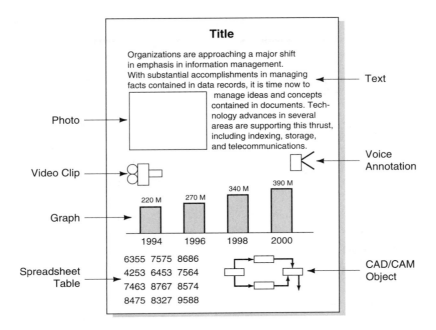

Figure 16-1   Structure of a Compound Document

computer screen, the text explaining the feature, a photograph, an engineering diagram, a voice notation from the product designer, and a video clip of the product in use. Figure 16-1 shows the conceptual structure of a such a compound document. A Web page is a popular example of a compound document. This is a richer, enhanced definition of what we have traditionally called a document, so EDM requires us to expand our connotation of this old and comfortable word.

The Roles Documents Play

It is hard to think of anything more pervasive and fundamental to an organization than documents. Figure 16-2 shows several examples of the roles documents play, with an example of each.

Taken together, these roles lead to the conclusion that documents are the stored memory for the organization, its groups and its individuals, as well as being the primary mechanism for conducting business.

The overall impact of applying a set of emerging technologies to document management is potentially significant. Since documents contain concepts and ideas, EDM promises to advance the management of conceptual information in organizations. Because most of the work of information workers at managerial and professional levels deals with concepts and ideas, EDM promises improved levels of support and productivity. And since documents are the primary vehicle for business processes, EDM promises to make a major contribution to business process redesign and quality improvement efforts.

Figure 16-2   Roles Documents Play

ROLES	EXAMPLES
To record or to "document" contracts and agreements	Employment contracts, maintenance agreements, consulting contracts, purchase agreements, leases, mortgages, loans,etc.
To record policies, standards, and procedures	Procedure manuals, standards specifications, instruction handbooks, executive memos and letters that state corporate policy, etc.
To represent a view of reality at a point in time (reports and plans)	Status reports, problem analyses, operational, reports, staff recomendations, budgets, strategic plans, etc.
To create an image or impression	Annual reports, marketing brochures, TV or radio commercials, etc.
To generate revenue as a product	A book for sale by a publisher, a report by a consulting firm to be sold to its client, a news item from a wire service, a reference from a bibliographic service, etc.
To support revenue by adding value to a product	A user's manual for a car or appliance or a software product, a warranty form, a catalog, a discount coupon for the next purchase, etc.
To act as a mechanism for communication	Memos, letters, presentations, email, messages, and interacton among people and groups minutes of meetings, etc.
To act as a vehicle for organizational process	Orders, invoices, approval letters, most business forms, etc.
To provide a discipline for capture and articulation of concepts and ideas	Nearly all the kinds af documents that carry concepts and ideas.

ELECTRONIC DOCUMENT MANAGEMENT APPLICATIONS

This section describes some of the application areas that are particularly susceptible to EDM. They are generic functions in organizations that:

- Depend on the document as the primary mechanism for getting the work done,
- Are susceptible to emerging document technologies, and
- Have proven business value resulting from the application of EDM technologies and approaches.

As technology and organizational processes evolve, EDM applications will be developed in several areas, and for several purposes. To illustrate the areas in which EDM can be applied, consider the case of a medium-sized manufacturing firm that discovered several EDM applications evolving in separate areas. These application areas, and the departments in which they evolved, are summarized in Figure 16-3.

Figure 16-3   EDM Applications in a Medium-Sized Manufacturing Firm

Department	Application
Records Management	An imaging system for archival storage and access to legal and tax documents. Replaced an aging microfilm system. Implemented on a network to eliminate physical shipment of paper documents among several offices in different cities.
Manufacturing	An extended version of a CAD/CAM system to use imaging to manage the blueprints and engineering diagrams.
Human Resources Management	An imaging system to support the hiring process. Candidates' resumes are scanned into the system when they apply and then are circulated in image form among the many people involved in the hiring process.
Systems and Procedures	A plan to improve the process of printing and distributing the procedure manuals to secretaries and administrative assistants.
	Currently—manuals printed centrally and mailed to all users; revised yearly with interim modification sheets.
	Phase I—Print manuals over the network on high-speed remote printers at each major site (distributed printing).
	Phase II—Allow secretaries and administrative assistants to print sections of the manual on their local printer as needed (reprint on demand).
	Phase III—Add retrieval and reference capabilities so that users can access relevant parts of the manual on-line as needed.
Customer Service	A new system for publishing and distributing owner's manuals, repair manuals, product descriptions, and product specifications. In the past these have always been printed on paper and mailed to customers, distributors, and sales personnel. Recently they have begun to be distributed on CD-ROM.
Administrative Services	Development of work flow system utilizing electronic forms for such tasks as office supply orders from stores, check requisitions, internal office equipment orders, telephone change requests, etc. A new version of the system will include such features as authorization, encryption, and signature verification that will permit the use of electronic forms for larger and more important processes also.
Training and Education	A plan to evolve the process of teaching administrative assistants and secretaries.
	Currently—a classroom course, based heavily on the procedures manual, which uses multimedia presentation materials to explain the steps in these procedures and show the forms that must be used.
	Phase I—Convert the multimedia course to a computer-based training course for use on a workstation instead of in the classroom.
	Phase II—Structure the software so that each procedure module can be accessed as needed rather than as part of an entire course.
	Phase III—Use real forms instead of sample forms as part of the source material. These forms can be filled in on the workstation and sent over e-mail so that the system becomes a real work flow system that actually performs the tasks. Access to reference material and training/education are additional built-in features.

Figure 16-3 illustrates that EDM turn up in several application areas. Generally, the departments that install EDM are not aware of the developments in the other areas. These early EDM applications generate business value by improving customer service, revising business processes, speeding the distribution of documents, reducing storage costs, or improving access to documents. They are different enough in structure, purpose, and users that they are separately developed, but they use similar technologies and approaches. Imaging, for example, is a technology used in several of the applications. A document server with multimedia storage and a strong search engine is needed for several. And the concept of "just in time" (printing, learning, forms processing) pervades the design philosophy in all areas. Without some planning in the development of these applications and their extensions, however, incompatibilities will limit the effectiveness of the applications in all areas.

EDM applications that generate value can be organized into the following seven generic categories:

1. To improve the publishing process
2. To support organizational processes
3. To support communication among people and groups
4. To improve access to external information
5. To create and maintain documentation
6. To maintain corporate records
7. To promote training and education

Before we look at these categories in more detail, here is an example of a company with document systems in several of the preceding categories. Through better forms management and electronic printing, the company made major improvements in these applications, while enhancing the corporate image at the same time.

CASE EXAMPLE: Tapiola Insurance Group

Tapiola is a group of three insurance companies with headquarters in Espoo, Finland, a suburb of Helsinki. By Finnish law, an insurance company can sell only one type of insurance; therefore, each of the three companies in Tapiola sells either life, nonlife, or pension insurance. They call themselves "an insurance department store."

Some 90 percent of insurance in Finland is sold by five insurance "groups"; Tapiola is the fourth largest group. They have 14 percent of the market, with 1.5 million customers and 3 million policies. Each year Tapiola's mail room sends out 4 million letters, so printing is an important and expensive part of its operation. We talked to the people in Tapiola Data— the wholly-owned information systems subsidiary of Tapiola—about their electronic document and printing activities.

In the mid-1980s, the Tapiola group offered 150 kinds of insurance policies, and it had 300 different insurance policy forms—half in Swedish and half in Finnish because both are official languages in Finland. The policy forms were all preprinted by an outside print shop, generally on sprocket-fed computer paper. Then the forms were filled in by printers connected to IBM mainframes.

This mode of operation presented several problems. If a change was made to a form, the inventory of old forms had to be discarded. Reprinting new forms often took weeks. That time represented possible lost revenue. Also, the computer printers could print on only one side of each sheet of paper. Finally, for more complex policies, large-size computer paper had to be used, which was often unwieldy to handle and mail.

Document Processing Goals. The production manager and the insurance applications development manager looked around for an alternate way to print policies and statements. They had several goals. One was, of course, to reduce costs. A second goal was to stop using preprinted forms. Their third goal was to give Tapiola marketing people new ways to advertise insurance products by making computer-generated letters to customers more flexible. The fourth and most important goal was to make Tapiola "the most personal insurance company in Finland." Thus, these two systems managers wanted their computer-generated correspondence to prospective and current policyholders to appear more "human"—as if a Tapiola employee had used a typewriter to write a personal reply to an inquiry or request for information.

Centralized Solution. To overcome the computer-generated appearance of their output, they switched to plain paper printers from Rank Xerox, the European subsidiary of Xerox Corporation. Xerox is best known for its photocopiers, but it is increasingly creating products for electronic document processing—where a document can include text, data, image, and graphics. Conversion of the output equipment at Tapiola took 15 months, during which time Tapiola reduced its 300 preprinted forms to four.

Four New "Forms." Tapiola's four "forms" are actually four types of standard European A4 cut paper. (In the United States, the equivalent would be the 8 1/2 x 11 sheet of paper.) The first form is a plain white A4 sheet of paper. It is used for internal communications within Tapiola.

The second form is the same blank white paper with four holes punched along the left-hand side, to fit in the standard European four-ring binder. (In the United States, the standard is generally a three-ring binder.) This form is also mainly for internal use.

The third form has the Tapiola logo preprinted in green in the upper left-hand corner and both sides of the paper have the word *Tapiola* printed in *tiny*, faint green letters over most of the page. This form is their standard company stationery, and it has become one of their standard computer printout forms for communicating with the outside world.

The fourth form is the same as the third except that it has a 4 x 6 inch (10 x 15 cm) perforated area in the lower right-hand corner. This form is used for all insurance policy bills. The tear-off portion can be paid at any bank; the money and information about the payment go directly from the bank to Tapiola.

Programming and Conversion. Reprogramming the IBM applications was extremely easy, we were told, because only the output routines needed to be changed. That programming took two work-years of application programmer time. In addition, one systems programmer spent six months working with Xerox on the IBM-to-Xerox system software interfaces. One forms designer spent 15 months redesigning all 300 preprinted forms into 240 printing formats for the application programmers. About 60 forms disappeared altogether because they were found to be unnecessary; the remaining 240 forms are not all different because one-half of them are in Swedish and the other half are in Finnish.

The forms designer used the Xerox forms description language for IBM mainframes, HFDL, after spending ten days learning HFDL. It is a character-based language, not a graphics-based language, so the forms designs were done on an installed IBM character-based terminal. The only new equipment purchased was a Xerox 8700 printer—one of the first installed in Europe—and a Xerox 9700 printer. Tapiola upgraded both to the higher-speed Xerox 9790 and bought a third Xerox 9790 printer at the same time.

The conversion was done in two stages. First, customer policy statements were printed in a formlike manner, on two sides of the new size paper. These looked somewhat like the old forms so that policyholders could understand the changeover. Then, the terse, tablelike data was replaced with text to make the statements look more like personal letters.

Envelope Stuffing. Interestingly, these redesigns of customer documents were the easy part of the conversion. The more difficult—and sensitive—part was making sure that each envelope contained the correct pieces of paper. Since Tapiola was now using smaller sheets of paper, employees often needed to include several sheets in each envelope, and, of course, they did not want to put a cover letter for one policy holder into the same envelope as a statement for another policyholder.

To solve this problem, they found an envelope-insertion machine made by PMB Vector, in Stockholm, Sweden. This machine contains a microprocessor that can read an eight-dot code printed at the top of each sheet of paper. Thus, the Xerox printer not only prints the correspondence but, at the same time, it prints a code at the top of each sheet of paper—one code for all pages to go in one envelope. The Vector inserter machine makes sure that each envelope only contains pages with the same code.

Decentralized Expansion. This document processing conversion was just one part of the company's effort to improve and humanize its customer correspondence. In the midst of the document redesign, Tapiola also decided to move some printing of customer correspondence to its 62 branch offices. Thus, Tapiola became the first European user of the smaller Xerox 4045 printers. Tapiola now has some 100 such printers around Finland to print customer letters. These printers are connected to the computers and databases at the Espoo data center via leased lines and the Finnish public data network.

To illustrate how a remote printer is used, consider the case of a female policyholder who has received medical care. She can mail the medical bills to Tapiola or visit her local office in person. If she visits the local office and presents her bills to a Tapiola employee, that employee uses an IBM terminal to access the policyholder's data from the central database. If she has brought all the proper documents needed for reimbursement, the employee can initiate a *direct electronic payment* from a Tapiola bank account to the policyholder's personal bank account—no matter which bank they both use.

Once a day, Tapiola transmits all such electronic transactions to its bank and those transactions are cleared that same day. (The five major Finnish banks have collaborated and created a sophisticated and fast banking system. A large number of individuals and companies in Finland use debit cards and other forms of electronic banking rather than checks or cash.) The employee then gives the policyholder a letter verifying the transaction. That letter is generated by the central IBM computer but is printed on the local Xerox printer. If the policyholder is missing some information, the employee can create a personalized letter explaining what is missing by assembling phrases stored in the central database, and then printing the letter on-site.

The people at Tapiola Data recommend that other information system departments become involved in electronic document management by first looking at the output their computers are generating. It is easy to mix traditional mainframe technology with document processing technology, they told us.

A recent poll of Finnish citizens showed that Tapiola is seen as a dynamic company, and it has the best reputation among young people of all the insurance groups. The people at Tapiola Data believe their use of document processing technology is helping to build and reinforce this image.

As the Tapiola case illustrates, major benefits are available from developing EDM applications in several areas. Here is a short discussion on each of the seven areas in our taxonomy.

Improving the Publication Process

Technology is enabling a major restructuring of the process of publishing and distributing paper documents. For those organizations that produce documents as a product or as support for a product, this change is reengineering their document production processes. The stages of the traditional process, designed primarily for high-volume and high-quality documents, are shown in Figure 16-4. The document is created, generally with the use of electronic tools, and a photographic plate is made for an offset printing press. The offset press requires long print runs to amortize the extensive set-up costs. Thus, a large quantity of documents is produced and stored in a warehouse, then shipped to their destination when they are required.

This process has several inefficiencies. The offset presses are large, expensive, and use toxic chemicals. The infrequent long print runs require storage of documents, which become obsolete between runs. And transportation is an inordinately large part of the total cost of the process. In fact, R.R. Donnelly, the largest U.S. publisher, estimates that 60 percent of the total cost of delivering these documents is in storage and transportation.

Figure 16-5 shows the steps in the revised publishing/distribution process using newer technologies. Documents are stored electronically, shipped over a network, and printed when and where they are needed. The major benefits result from the reduction of obsolescence (revisions are made frequently to the electronically stored version), elimination of warehouse costs, and reduction or elimination of delivery time.

Supporting Organizational Processes

Documents are the vehicle or mechanism through which most processes in organizations are accomplished. Typical examples include processing a claim in an insurance company, hiring a new employee, or making a large expenditure. The documents are primarily forms, which flow through the organization carrying information, and accumulating input and approval from a sequence of people. These work flow systems are still heavily based on the physical circulation of paper forms in most organizations.

The use of technology to support these processes generates significant value in reduced physical space for the handling of forms, faster routing of forms (especially over geographical distances) and managing/tracking of forms flow and overall workload. Two trends in organizations have increased the importance of work flow systems: quality improvement processes and business process reengineering. Both tend to depend heavily on documents.

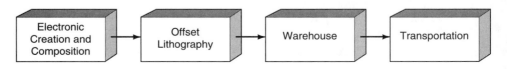

Figure 16-4   Traditional Publishing Process

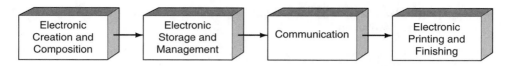

Figure 16-5   Reengineered Publishing Process

In addition to transaction-oriented business processes, which can be improved with EDM, many organizations are finding that documents are important to the management processes of reporting, control, decision making, and problem solving. Several executive information systems now supply documents to supplement the more traditional data-based reports. Organizations with a custom developed EIS are also adding so-called "soft" information, in the form of documents [5].

Supporting Communication Among People and Groups

The purpose of applications in this area is to facilitate communication among people, and groups of people, in organizations. In the broadest sense, all EDM applications support this function, but included here are specific systems to support the transfer of information among people across time and space. Communication *can* take place without documents, of course. The conversation in the hall, a phone call, a video conference, a presentation—all are communication events that do not necessarily require a document. However, if the concepts, ideas, and information are to be communicated over time, they must be captured in a document. If they are to be communicated over distance, without voice or video connection, they must be captured in a document. Even when communication takes place between people at the same time and in the same place, a document might be used to improve the articulation or formation of the concepts. The primary value of EDM applications in this category derives from the richer communication offered by multimedia or compound documents, and the reduced time needed for the electronic distribution of documents. An additional value results from the simultaneous sharing of documents among a group of people, coupled with the rapid feedback and interaction that ensue. The popularity of Lotus Notes and the Internet to support a variety of organizational communication illustrates this set of benefits.

Improving Access to External Information

The purpose of applications in this area is to provide better access to external information resources. Two general kinds of external resources are time-critical information (news) and reference material. The documents include news wire items, newspapers, periodicals, magazines, electronic bulletin board items, books, video tapes, research reports, proceedings of conferences, and so on. Traditionally performed by a library, these applications are increasingly computer based with on-line card catalogs, direct user access to on-line text databases (e.g., DIALOG, NEXUS, World Wide Web), circulation of full-text research papers, and so on.

Creating and Maintaining Documentation

Another cluster of applications in EDM involves the creation, maintenance, and distribution of documentation. The purpose of these applications is to maintain documents that contain policies, procedures, reference material, product descriptions, and so on. They differ from records management applications, which capture and store documents for archival purposes, and infrequent access based on a request from an internal user. Documentation applications, on the other hand, maintain the current version of documents; therefore, they must be updated and accessed frequently by a wide variety of requesters. Documents tend to be reports, manuals, drawings, and reference material; they have been mostly text in the past but are increasingly using multimedia. Examples include:

- Internal standards and procedures manuals.
- Engineering blueprints and diagrams, possibly created with a CAD/CAM system.
- Systems documentation and operating manuals.
- Product documentation manuals and other product information, both for internal users and customers.

Access to documentation can be provided in several ways. For internal users, on-line access through a workstation is most common, perhaps using the company's intranet. For external users, access to documentation improves customer service by providing answers to customer queries or solving problems with the right reference material.

The benefits of EDM for these applications are (1) quicker access to the documents, (2) more efficiency in the search process, (3) simultaneous access by several people to the most current version of the document, and (4) reduced cost of printing and distributing documents.

Maintaining Corporate Records

Organizations must maintain official documents and records concerning their obligations, agreements, and financial performance, primarily to satisfy legal requirements. Traditionally the responsibility of the records management department, this application area involves storage and retrieval of contracts, financial records, internal reports, and other important corporate documents. These are documents in the traditional sense, mostly text, mostly on paper. The role of EDM applications in this area is to manage this set of official corporate records by providing archival storage and occasional retrieval. The methodologies, approaches, and technologies have evolved from a tradition of library operations, from an earlier emphasis on automated records center applications, micrographics (film and fiche), and computer output microfilm (COM), to an emphasis today on digital image processing.

For large records management applications, the savings from image processing in storage space and ease of retrieval alone are impressive. Other sources of value from the application of technology to records management include:

- Reduced misfiling of important documents
- Quicker and more accurate retrieval
- Better access and sharing over geographic distances
- Better version control
- Improved retention management

For records management and documentation applications, a government initiative is becoming important. CALS (computer-aided acquisition and logistic support) has been defined as a requirement for documentation by the U.S. government. Starting with the Defense Department, it has been adopted by many other government agencies. Eventually, it is likely that any organization with government business will need to be CALS compliant.

CASE EXAMPLE: CALS: A U.S. Government Initiative Worthy of Attention

An important event affecting the future of technical document management is the CALS initiative; however, its importance in industry is not yet widely recognized. CALS stands for computer-aided acquisition and logistics support. It is a program initiated by industry and the U.S. Department of Defense (DoD) to facilitate electronic interchange of *technical data*. The program is being coordinated with other government agencies, such as NASA and the U.S. Departments of Energy, Transportation, and Commerce.

Although government information processing standards often have had little direct impact on the business world as a whole, the CALS initiative is strongly influencing the technologies and business practices of all American manufacturing.

First, it directly affects all major U.S. defense contractors. The DoD now requires all technical documentation related to major weapons systems to be submitted in electronic form using the CALS standards. These deliverables include engineering drawings, product definition data, technical manuals, definitions of support equipment, and logistics support analyses. Subcontractors are also feeling the effects of CALS. And most vendors that supply the industry with hardware and software recognize the importance of CALS. If they do not offer CALS-compliant products, their market share could erode.

Ultimately, CALS will affect the entire discrete manufacturing industry—those in heavy machinery and equipment, aerospace, electronics, automotive, machine tools, and medical and precision equipment. They face problems similar to those in the defense industry—increasingly complex products and growing use of trading partnerships with suppliers and buyers. The CALS initiative is equally relevant to their problems.

CALS currently has two defined phases. Phase One was the digital data exchange phase, where contractors and government agencies exchanged technical data electronically. The intent of this phase was to eliminate paper.

Phase Two—from 1991 through 2000—is the integrated database access phase. The focus is on creating databases within private industry that are accessible by all trading partners and the government. The goal is to create source data once, and reuse it and transfer it many times, rather than replicate it.

There are numerous standards adopted in CALS; more are being considered. For the interchange of raster-based images—such as those created by office scanners—CALS has specified the use of the CCITT Group 4 compression standard. For telecommunications, they specify GOSIP, which is a U.S. government implementation of the OSI network protocol.

For the interchange of vector-based graphics—such as engineering drawings—they have adopted IGES (Initial Graphics Exchange Specification). This is the major existing standard in this area. It is not the best one because it is not truly neutral; however, it is the only one available right now. It is used as an intermediary translator of graphical data between dissimilar CAD systems.

For technical illustrations—such as those found in maintenance and operating manuals—CALS has adopted CGM (Computer Graphics Metafile). CGM is the preferred exchange standard for two-dimensional or three-dimensional graphics and illustrations. It is also used for printing and displaying these graphics.

For text, CALS has specified SGML (Standard Generalized Markup Language). SGML is used by publishers to designate the parts of a document and how the text is to be formatted. It consists of codes and declarations that are added to text to designate subject matter and position of text. When SGML codes have been added to text, an entire document can be sent as an ASCII file. Once in SGML format, the text can be output to a printer, magnetic tape, typesetting machine, or even CD-ROM. Tools have emerged that provide SGML capabilities for word processing packages.

These existing standards emphasize the exchange of data *between* systems. But the real goal of CALS is the common development and sharing of databases. These databases are expected to be logically integrated but physically distributed and heterogeneous. In Phase Two, when management of the large common databases will be necessary, SQL is targeted as the standard database access language.

One of the key components of the shared databases is common product definitions. The goal is to make these definitions contain sufficient information to be directly interpreted by advanced CAD/CAM application programs. This is the aim of PDES (Project Data Exchange Specification)—to be able to communicate complete and unambiguous product models between organizations. Thus, PDES will handle geometric data, including representations of solid shapes. In addition, PDES will support a wide range of other kinds of product-related data and relationships, such as manufacturing processes, material properties, surface finishes, and support requirements.

In summary, the emphasis of the CALS initiative is on motivating industry to adopt existing standards for databases and electronic interchange. Its use will spread beyond U.S. government contractors because it is being heavily pushed by industry to help reduce documentation costs. For further discussion of the CALS initiative, see the special government report [6].

Promoting Training and Education

The purpose of the applications in this area is to teach or train people in an organization. The documents are curricular training materials or reference materials, and the use of multi-media documents, perhaps with hyperstructure, is proving to be extremely effective. A primary characteristic of these applications is the continuous, sequential interaction between the user and the information through the learning process over time, rather than a specific search and retrieval event to obtain a document.

Training and education applications are good early examples of the use of multimedia documents and hypertext. As mentioned earlier, hypertext is the most promising approach to structuring conceptual information. The body of knowledge to be learned or understood consists of concept nodes, which are linked or cross-referenced to form a web of ideas and concepts.

Converging Application Areas

These categories of applications illustrate the benefit and value of EDM. The good news is that there are many opportunities in many different areas. But these applications use many common approaches and technologies, and, as the earlier case example illustrates, it will be desirable for them to converge eventually. If they have been developed separately, without a plan to integrate them, it will be very difficult to reap the potential benefits.

TECHNOLOGIES FOR DOCUMENT MANAGEMENT

Underlying Infrastructure

The rapid developments in EDM are partly the result of advances in basic technology infrastructure. These underlying, enabling technologies improve the handling of information in any form, but several have attributes that support document processing and management. These enabling technologies can be organized in five major categories.

Stronger Desktop Workstations. Powerful desktop computers based on RISC technology are equipped with large, high-resolution color screens. These workstations permit the display of documents, a full page or two at a time, delivering (and capturing) nontext media such as voice, video, and animation.

Storage Media. High-capacity storage media hold the large volume of bits required for multimedia documents. The capacity of magnetic media (hard disks and diskettes) in workstations and file servers has been increasing rapidly, but it is still barely adequate. Optical storage media such as CD-ROMs and laserdisks, perhaps in clusters called jukeboxes, provide orders of magnitude increases in storage capacity. Holographic storage devices increase the amount of readily available storage capacity by several more orders of magnitude.

Networks. Networks will interconnect the workstations of most, if not all, information workers, within and between organizations. These connections have increasingly high bandwidth to transmit the large volume of data contained in electronic documents and forms. Relevant technologies were discussed in Chapter 6.

User-Friendly Software. The continued growth of graphic user interfaces is enabling the multitude of people who handle paper documents, many of whom are not yet computer literate, to deal more easily with documents on computers. Even for experienced computer users, however, interface software must continue to advance so that users can move beyond managing hundreds of files to managing thousands of documents on the desktop workstation.

Operating Systems. Client/server operating systems and network management systems are increasingly document oriented. In fact, new operating systems shift focus from the application to the document. They are also object oriented. This approach, or paradigm, is gaining popularity for improved software design and for the design of operating systems.

Document Management Technologies

In addition to the underlying technology infrastructure, there is a set of technologies aimed directly at handling documents. Often called document *middleware*, these technologies provide the functionality for the processing and management of documents, both electronic and paper. There are actually two sublayers in document middleware: functions for document processing and functions for document management. Summarized next is the set of document *processing* technologies (organized by the major steps in a document life cycle), and the document *management* functions; together they form the document technology infrastructure.

Capture and Creation. These are basically technologies to digitize information. For documents already on paper, hardware and software digitize an image of a page, and then electronically handle that image. Scanners capture the image while algorithms convert it to digital form, frequently with compression to save storage space. After a document page is scanned and digitized, it can be further analyzed to recognize the characters. Current software can capture full text in editable form in a variety of fonts, sizes, and formats. Extensions of these pattern recognition techniques can recognize voice, some images, and patterns in graphics, animation, and video.

Storage and Organization. Several technologies determine how documents are stored and organized. The primary developments are the compound document architecture, distributed storage management software, the integration of documents and databases, and hypertext.

Compound Document Architecture. Such an architecture is required for the different objects that make up a compound document to be handled together. In several implementations, the compound document consists of objects (e.g., a text object, a graphics object, a spreadsheet object, a digital photograph object), which may be stored on different devices, brought together logically through the use of pointers.

Distributed Storage. Documents are stored on local PC hard drives, servers (including large-capacity document servers), mainframes, and large repositories. A recent survey by the Gartner Group [7] found that 80 percent of the documents stored in a PC networked environment are stored on the local hard drives, not on the server. This underscores the importance of distributed document management software to provide organization and access to this valuable resource.

Integrating Documents and Databases. Making documents an integral part of the information resources of an organization requires integration of document collections and databases. So far, most approaches have been to extend the database to accommodate documents, or vice versa. Organizing, cataloging, and retrieving concepts in documents are likely to require an entirely different architectural approach than those which have been used for facts in data records.

Hypertext. Software which implements a hypertext structure enables nonlinear access to the logical structure of text within a document, and multiple cross-references between documents. *Hypermedia* technology provides the same functionality with multimedia or compound documents.

Retrieval and Synthesis. *Information retrieval* selects documents from a collection according to the presence or absence of key words assigned by an indexer. *Text retrieval* uses algorithms that eliminate the need for an assigned index. All content-bearing words are indexed. A further enhancement called *concept retrieval* uses thesauri and word co-occurrence analysis to select documents that use similar but different words to represent a concept [8]. Queries can result in a list of selected documents ranked in order of likely relevance. An extension of this approach allows automatic synthesis or summarization of documents.

Transmission and Routing. E-mail systems are moving beyond simple text messaging to become the primary transport mechanism for electronic documents and forms. Object independence allows transmission of compound documents consisting of a variety of objects (text, graphic, image, audio, video). Other functionality required for business transport of electronic documents includes

1. Authorization—ensuring that the correct user is accessing the workstation and documents.
2. Authentication—ensuring that the digital signature of the user is valid.
3. Encryption—coding and decoding documents for security.
4. Filtering—automatically routing messages or documents according to their content.

Print and Display. Most documents will be printed at some time in their life cycle, so an important technology is the wide variety of digital printers and copiers on the network. These printers, along with text-handling software, page layout languages, and WYSIWYG displays (what you see is what you get) put high-quality printed output within reach of nearly everyone. Laser printers significantly reduce the need for preprinted forms. Desktop printers permit distributed printing of richly formatted documents. Xerox's DocuTech production publisher operates on a network, accepts Postscript files, allows printed tab inserts, and offers a variety of covers and binding. The result is a new form of distributed printing and print-on-demand services that can print small or large runs of complex documents at remote sites under the direction of a workstation.

Document Management Functions

The second sublayer of the document technology infrastructure consists of document management functions that cut across the phases of document processing. This set of functions is what enables managing documents as an information resource rather than as a collection of files. These document management functions include

- Status reporting—Who has a document? What is its recent activity?
- Access control—Who "owns" it? Who can read it? Change it?
- Version control—What is the current version? What previous versions are still needed?
- Retention management—What are the legal retention requirements? Corporate policy requirements? How do we destroy paper and electronic versions?
- Disaster recovery—How and where are backup copies kept? What are the recovery procedures?

This technology section can be summarized with the conceptual layered architectural diagram shown in Figure 16-6. The lower level is the basic infrastructure and the middle layer (with two sublayers) is the document infrastructure that is required for EDM. The top layer is the application layer, which shows four main areas of business value.

GUIDELINES FOR IS MANAGERS

As usual, the technology engineering is not as difficult or important as the organizational engineering required to implement EDM. In this final section of the

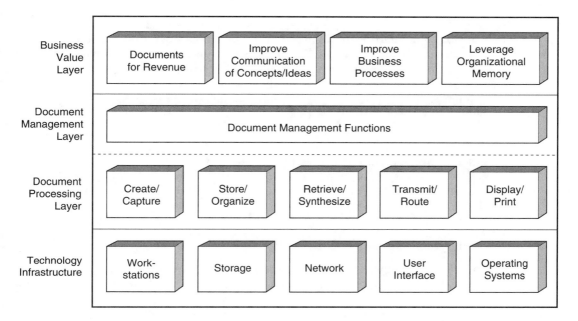

Figure 16-6   Technology Architecture for EDM

chapter, we look at some key issues IS managers must face in developing EDM. First, here is a case study that illustrates some of the organizational aspects of an EDM infrastructure.

CASE EXAMPLE: Saab-Scania Group

The Saab-Scania Group, with headquarters in Linkoping, Sweden, near Stockholm, manufactures automotive vehicles. The Saab division builds Saab cars; the Scania division builds trucks, buses, and components for Saab cars. Saab also has an aircraft division and Scania does research in military electronics and robotics. Saab-Scania employs some 50,000 employees; about one-half of them are in Sweden.

Saab-Scania designs its vehicles for easy customization. For example, a customer for a fleet of trucks can choose from a selection of engines, gears, axles, driver cabs, and so on, from which Saab-Scania can create customized vehicles using standard parts.

In the 1980s, an office automation group was formed to manage any piece of office equipment that is electronically linked to other equipment. In addition, this group coordinates the use of all unstructured information throughout Saab-Scania, such as text, graphics, images, and video. This ten-person group also creates interfaces for information retrieval from public databases. The group handles all products used on PCs, and it coordinates all teleconferencing facilities, message handling systems, and electronic document management systems—including electronic printing and publishing.

Group members see their role as providing employees with easy access to various PC tools that deal with unstructured data. Their electronic document management work has three components:

1. A document system infrastructure
2. A system architecture strategy
3. Experimenting with willing user groups

Document Systems Infrastructure

The information systems department uses computers from a number of manufacturers. For administrative information systems and computer-aided design, the department uses IBM. For manufacturing and engineering, it uses DEC. Its PBX (private branch exchange) is from Northern Telecom. Terminals and PCs linked to their mainframes are from Ericsson. And document workstations and publishing systems are from Rank Xerox.

These various systems are located in a six-building complex with 10 mbps fiber-optic links between the buildings. Within the buildings, Saab-Scania has five Ethernet LANs that also operate at 10 mbps. One Ethernet has become the hub network for document processing. Through it, users can access laser printers or high-volume Xerox document printers.

Systems Architecture Strategy

The IS department's long-term interconnection goal is to use OSI—the open systems interconnection standards from the International Standards Organization. As OSI standards have become available, IS has migrated to them. For example, X.400 is the OSI electronic mail standard that handles messages in a store-and-forward mode. Saab-Scania has adopted X.400 as the means for allowing its three electronic mail systems to "talk" to each other. A message created and sent on its IBM, DEC, or Xerox mail system is translated into the X.400 protocol. Then it is routed to its destination and retranslated into the recipient's mail system protocol. Using standards to perform this translation is much easier than writing specific vendor-to-vendor interfaces, they told us.

IS is also working on extending the X.400 capability to electronic mail systems offered by the Swedish PTT (Postal, Telephone, and Telegraph authority) and to U.S. and U.K. systems.

Experimenting with User Groups

In document processing, end users generally want much more than is currently technically economical or feasible, we were told. For example, users would like to use their graphical workstations to, say, create service manuals that contain text, line drawings, photographs, and color. And they want to print those manuals in high volumes.

Currently, in-house high-volume electronic printing of such complex documents is not feasible because (1) the company does not have many document scanners for digitizing images, (2) its scanners only record at 300 dots per inch (DPI) resolution, and (3) color separation is not economical. But the goal of the office automation group is to allow such multimedia documents to be fully composed and printed electronically in-house—in high volume, if need be. These high-volume documents would include vehicle service manuals, parts catalogs, some advertising brochures, and so on.

The office automation manager has some ambitious goals in the document management and printing area. For example, he believes the company should be able to print a vehicle owner's manual that exactly matches the vehicle that the purchaser buys. Therefore, each owner's manual would be unique. This is not only desirable but achievable, he believes. The cost of producing such tailored manuals is becoming almost as low as the cost of mass-producing standardized manuals.

The office automation group is starting with the most economical and feasible uses of new document processing technologies. For example, currently, electronic storage of images is not economically feasible because each image requires so much storage space. Therefore, the automation group is starting by electronically storing only those images that are needed for a short time, such as images of visual aids for speeches. As optical storage becomes more economical, the group will increasingly store longer-term images.

Interestingly, although storage of images presents an economic problem, transmission of images within Saab-Scania does not. The 10 mbps Ethernet LANs have enough bandwidth to last for a long time. The company currently uses only 20 percent of their capacity. And since images are most likely to be transmitted from a file server in a store-and-forward mode—and then manipulated interactively at the workstation—the networks will not become overburdened as more and more images are sent over the network. Putting the processing-intensive manipulation part of the image processing job at the workstation reduces the bandwidth required on the networks.

Thus, Saab-Scania is experimenting with new document processing products with willing departments. Once a system is running in a production mode, the office automation group turns over full operational responsibility to the user group. And the office automation group is promoting standards to create a companywide document processing infrastructure to enable people to use whatever equipment is best suited for their job, without worrying whether the technology is old or new, or whether the machines will work together.

Roles and Responsibilities

One major management issue will be structuring the roles and responsibilities of the departments and functions for which documents are strategic. Here are some of the organizational groups and departments that must play a major role in EDM.

- *The IS department.* The technology is now advanced enough and pervasive enough that the IS function will be responsible for evolving the technical infrastructure. However, the fundamental structure and processing of the conceptual information in documents is quite different from the facts in data records. Moreover, the principles and techniques of document storage, classification, indexing, retrieval, and retention are foreign to most IS professions.
- *Records management.* With its traditional role of managing the corporate records, and with its foundations in library science, the records management department has valuable experience in document management practices. But it tends to view technology in terms of its ability to meet specific short-term needs. The records management tradition also emphasizes paper documents and their electronic equivalent—the narrower view of EDM.
- *Office management.* Much office work has been computerized to some extent, but internal and external correspondence and reports still generate large amounts of redundant and hard-to-access paper files. In the future, these files will need to be cross referenced among departments and linked with IS databases.
- *Library.* External sources of information are increasingly available in electronic form, with search and retrieval capability from large document collections.
- *Print shop.* Computer-based technology is becoming dominant. The new DocuTech line of high-speed printers and copiers from Xerox is digital (not light-lens) and contains more computer power than many mainframes.
- *Training and education.* Increasingly based on multimedia technology and computer-based courseware, education and training can be delivered through EDM technologies and approaches.

Coordinating the role and responsibilities of these and other departments is important because the applications and the suite of technologies required to realize the promise of EDM are evolving rapidly.

An Action Plan

The IS department has the opportunity to play a leadership role in coordinating the efforts of these user departments and document support departments in order to evolve the infrastructure and applications needed to support EDM. Playing this leadership role may be more difficult than it has been in the past. In this era of distributed systems and distributed responsibility for systems initiative, IS managers will need to educate a variety of user departments and document-handling departments, convincing them to cooperate in the development of an EDM strategy and technology infrastructure. Here are some steps that IS managers can take now to prepare for these developments.

Form a Document Council. Form a council consisting of representatives from each of the document support departments identified previously which have been charged with managing some part of the document processing cycle in the past. The council's first assignment would be to identify mission-critical documents and work back to applications and departments that depend on them. An initial set of applications will undoubtedly evolve from the members of the group. They have probably been responsible for producing and managing these documents in the past.

There will also be important applications which have been developed directly by the user departments, so the group should develop a way to find important applications of which it is not aware. Mechanisms for doing this include examining the areas and examples mentioned earlier in this article, finding examples in journals and trade publications, distributing surveys and questionnaires in the organization, and so on. The work of this group and the technology tracking group described next should proceed in parallel, with periodic joint meetings for coordination and status reporting.

Form a Document Technology Group. Assign the task of tracking and forecasting the emerging document technologies to a small group with technical proficiency in several areas. If there is an advanced technology group, this assignment would probably fit into its charter. The assignment should cover both the infrastructure technologies as well as document technologies.

Prioritize Applications. The application group, perhaps in consultation with people who have been using the documents, should then prioritize the applications by business value and technical feasibility. There might be a difference in long-and short-range perspectives, so both should be considered. The prioritization should also include consideration of fit or linkage between applications, especially when two or more applications can use the same technology or approach.

Develop an EDM Plan. As a result of their regular joint meetings, the document council and the document technology group can jointly develop a plan for adding the necessary technology to the infrastructure and developing the applications. These applications might not be developed by the IS department, or even by the departments represented in the group, but their development and approximate time schedule should be included in the plan. As it is refined and developed over time, this plan becomes an integrated EDM architecture and a plan for implementing it.

Revise Responsibilities. By this time, it may become clear that some of the roles and responsibilities of some departments may need to be revised. The council can develop recommendations to management concerning these changes.

By performing this step last, any shifts in responsibilities will result from discussions based on the evolution of the applications and technologies, measured by business value. This will reduce the probability of a "turf war" that could result from the changes in the way documents are managed.

The benefits of EDM will evolve as the technology and our ability to use it evolve over the next several years. It is not too early, however, for IS managers to begin the planning processes to build the technology infrastructure for document management, and to harness these new technologies to improve the performance of their organizations.

SUMMARY

Electronic document management is becoming prevalent because of a suite of new technologies that makes it possible to computerize information in documents. These technologies include digital imaging processing, large-capacity storage devices, high-bandwidth communication channels, multimedia devices for handling image, voice, video, and animation, hypertext/hypermedia, and improved methods for retrieval of information and text.

The impact of these developments is significant. Generally, EDM will allow the electronic handling of concepts and ideas in documents, as well as facts in data records. Since managers and executives deal heavily with concepts and ideas, EDM will improve the performance of these high-level employees. Finally, since many important business processes depend on document-based information flows, EDM will support the improvement of these processes.

The challenge for IS executives is to manage this evolution during the next decade. New technologies should be adopted and used as they emerge because the benefits are substantial. But over time, they must be integrated to avoid separate, incompatible systems. This will require a strategic plan for EDM that identifies what applications should be developed (and in what order), what roles the many interested parties should play, and what technologies are required. It is clear that EDM will be a significant area of applications in the 1990s.

QUESTIONS AND EXERCISES

REVIEW QUESTIONS

1. Give three definitions and several examples of a document.
2. What are the roles that documents play in organizations? Give an example of each.
3. What are the seven categories of EDM applications? Describe how each can improve an organization.
4. Give two of the major benefits realized by Tapiola Insurance from its EDM project.
5. What is the importance of CALS?
6. What are the three layers of technology architecture for EDM? Identify the elements in each layer.
7. List the departments in an organization that would be involved in EDM.
8. What is the importance of an action plan for EDM? What are the steps?

DISCUSSION QUESTIONS

1. Do you agree that the IS department should take the lead in developing EDM? Why or why not?
2. If your answer to question one was "yes," how will IS motivate all the other departments? If "no," who will coordinate the development of the systems and how?

EXERCISES

1. Consult the current literature to compile a list of technologies that are important for EDM. For each technology, describe it briefly, and indicate its role in EDM.
2. Visit a local organization that is developing applications in at least two of the areas in EDM—perhaps image processing and desktop publishing. Who is leading the development effort? What benefits are being realized? What are the plans for the future?

REFERENCES

1. SPRAGUE, RALPH H., JR., "Electronic Document Management: Challenges and Opportunities for Information Systems Managers," *MIS Quarterly*, March 1995, pp. 29-49.

2. McLEOD, RAYMOND, JR., and JACK WILLIAM JONES, "A Framework for Office Automation," *MIS Quarterly*, March 1987, pp. 87-104.

3. LEVIEN, ROGER E., *The Civilizing Currency: Documents and Their Revolutionary Technologies.* Rochester, NY: Xerox Corporation, 1989.

4. MICHALSKI, G. P. "The World of Documents," *Byte,* April 1991, pp. 159-170.

5. WATSON, HUGH, CANDICE HARP, GIGI KELLY, and MARGARET O'HARA, *Soft Information in Executive Information Systems: Conceptualizations, Findings, and Propositions.* College of Business, University of Georgia, 1993.

6. CALS REPORT TO THE COMMITTEE ON APPROPRIATIONS OF THE U.S. HOUSE OF REPRESENTATIVES, July 31, 1988. Available from the National Institute of Standards and Technology, CALS Office, Sound/B106, Gaithersburg, MD 20899.

7. POPKIN, J. and A. CUSHMAN, *Integrated Document Management—Controlling a Rising Tide.* Gartner Group, Stamford, CT, 1993.

8. CHEN, H., K. J. LYNCH, K. BASU, and T. NG, "Generation, Integration, and Activation of Thesauri for Concept-Based Document Retrieval." *IEEE Expert*, 1993.

PART VI

People and Information Technology

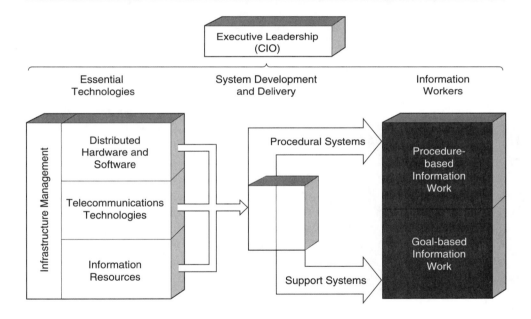

A Framework for IS Management

In this final part, we discuss the impact of IT on information workers and organizational structure; see the book's accompanying framework figure.

Chapter 17 deals with increasing information workers' comfort level with information technology. What do executives need to know about IT and what is their role in guiding its use in their organization? Moving downward in the organization, what is the role of middle managers and supervisors in helping people become comfortable with technology? The thesis is that IT is changing faster than organizations, so that organizational change has become the "gating" factor that determines how fast IT is put to use. We contend that successfully managing IT-based change is an important part of line management's job. Finally, IT professionals need to be reskilled to keep up with the changing technology landscape.

Chapter 18 deals with creating the new work environment by presenting a number of important and complementary concepts that describe the emergence of new ways of working. The chapter also discusses ways to implement job redesign. This final chapter of the book is meant to stimulate thinking about how IT is providing the underpinnings for the new work environment.

SEVENTEEN

Helping People Become Comfortable With Information Technology

INTRODUCTION

With corporate success increasingly reliant on leading-edge uses of IT, corporate executives need to know enough about the issues underlying deployment of the new and emerging information technologies to make wise decisions about putting them to competitive use. Other line and staff managers, on the other hand, need to know enough about the potentials of these technologies to see how they can be leveraged in their businesses, functions, or processes function. Furthermore, they must manage the changes required to operate in our computer-abundant world because they generally are the key to ensuring successful use of IT. End users, too, need to be self-assured enough to use and experiment with IT. Finally, information systems staff need to be technologically current to support the increasingly ambitious IT plans of the business units. In essence, all four groups—top executives, other senior managers, end users, and systems staff—need to be comfortable with IT. That is the subject of this chapter.

Being comfortable with IT is even more important today than in the past because of the increasing pace of change in IT. In his speech at the Aspen Institute, which we cited previously, author George Gilder [1] explained why the pace of IT change is increasing, and even more importantly, why it will increase ever faster from now on. He noted that the technologies of sand (silicon chips), glass (fiber optics), and air (wireless telecom) are governed by exponential rules. Mead's law, named after Carver Mead of California Institute of Technology, says that N transistors on a sliver of silicon yield N^2 performance and value. This is the rule of semiconductors, which is why this technology has been so powerful. But now this law of semiconductors is joined by the law of the "telecosm"—networking N computers yields N^2 performance and value. Combining the two laws leads to the compounding force of exponentials that we see sweeping through the world economy today, said Gilder.

To get a sense of the power of exponents and why it is inexorable, consider the story of the emperor of China and the inventor of chess, said Gilder. The emperor was so exultant with the invention of chess that he told the inventor he could have anything he wanted in his kingdom. The inventor thought for a moment, and then said, "Just one grain of rice, your majesty, on the first square, two on the second, four grains of rice on the third, and so on through the 64 squares of the chess board."

There are two possible outcomes to this story, said Gilder. One is that the emperor goes bankrupt, because 2^{64} = 18 million trillion grains of rice, which is 10 grains per square inch, which would cover the entire surface of the earth with rice fields two times over, oceans included. The other possibility, which is even more alarming, is that the inventor loses his head. Confronted with exponential technologies, emperors often decapitate. So one rule of this story is "Keep an eye on the emperors," said Gilder, because they can suppress the spread of technology very effectively. The governments of Europe have done just that in stifling IT through their PTTs.

It is also worth noticing, said Gilder, that after the first half of the chessboard (at 32 squares), the emperor only needs to give 2^{32} grains of rice (4 billion), which he could easily do from his rice fields. So nothing much happens during the first 32 squares. But after that, look out.

To relate this story to the present day, Gilder presented the following astounding facts: In 1995, there had been exactly 32 doublings of computer power since the invention of the digital computer after World War II. So since 1995, we have been on "the second half of the chess board." This is why a whole stream of profound developments (in 1995 and 1996 alone) have epitomized the power of these technologies, he said. E-mail outnumbered postal mail for the first time in 1995—95 billion units of external e-mail to 85 billion units of postal mail. The number of PC sales overtook the number of TV sales for the first time in late 1995. The network computer emerged much more rapidly than anyone expected. And on and on. Such changes will only accelerate, he predicts. This is why we believe everyone in business must become comfortable with IT to cope with this brand-new world of ever-increasing technological change.

Increasing Technological Maturity

We define a technologically mature organization as one that realizes the business value of information and IT, and manages the assimilation of IT into its business. Its people are comfortable managing, using, and experimenting with new information technology. A mature organization that continually experiments with new uses of computers and telecommunications can more quickly use them in its business. This ability to move quickly is especially important when computers are used for competitive purposes. To maintain a competitive edge, a business must continually enhance its operations, services, and products, and understand how IT fits into such enhancements.

Drawing on groundbreaking work of Chuck Gibson and Dick Nolan on stages of growth [2], McFarlan and McKenney [3] note that IT grows in an organization in four phases: (1) identification and investment, (2) experimentation, learning, and adaptation, (3) control, and (4) widespread use. At any point in time, organizations will be at different phases with different technologies. IS departments play an important role in moving their organizations through these phases in the following four ways:

- Educating executives on information technology
- Helping line managers manage information technology
- Training end users on the technology
- Reskilling systems staff for the future

EDUCATING EXECUTIVES ON INFORMATION TECHNOLOGY

Since the early 1990s, there has been a significant change on the question of educating executives, says Chuck Gibson [4], a long-time top-level consultant who has kept us abreast of the IT executive education market since the late 1980s. Many of the ideas and concepts in this section resulted from an extensive conversation with Gibson. The change has two main drivers. One is the astounding extent to which IT has become a critical part of industry and business strategy. All the statements about the strategic importance of IT taught in executive education courses in the late 1980s have come true. At that time, most executive audiences had to be convinced. Today, most do not. They understand that mastery of IT is critical to strategic success. IT's importance extends beyond the back office and operations, where it influences cost, service, and support. It is now important in the front office, in product design, in product delivery, and in the enhancement of products and services with information. IT allows companies to be responsive, flexible, and innovative in the marketplace.

The other factor contributing to the sea change is the increasing number of executives who use PCs and are on-line with e-mail. In leading companies, executive use of PCs is between 60 and 90 percent. However, this high level of personal use is a two-edged sword, at least with regard to knowing how to manage information and the IT function.

On the one hand, these executives are computer literate and somewhat familiar with desktop systems. On the other hand, few executives have the depth of background in IS that they have with other functions, such as marketing or finance. As a result, most still do not understand the issues that drive the IS function, such as the need to invest in infrastructure. Most still think primarily only of applications and IS as a cost.

This superficial awareness is exacerbated by the current hype and potential of the Internet and e-commerce—both of which sound relatively easy to do because the infrastructure is invisible. For example, one IS department was wrestling with migrating to a single companywide e-mail system (from the six to eight currently in use). During the discussion, one computer-literate executive vice president—an avid PC user—recommended using the e-mail system in a commercial on-line service. He did not understand the underlying issue that e-mail is a base on which to build other enterprise systems, such as groupware that would not be possible on a commercial service.

As a result, there is still a big gap between what executives *believe* is important about IT versus what they *really* need to know about managing information and creating the client/server architecture to exchange information among separate platforms.

Why Educate Executives?

In the September/October 1995 issue, the *Harvard Business Review* [5] points out that the rules of the IT game have shifted so significantly that it now requires general management leadership. Top management can no longer delegate IT to the CIO. IT now plays a role in just about everything a company does. Therefore, the CEO and the other top corporate executives need to know much more about this resource, so that it can be deployed to develop new products, support sales and service, provide market intelligence, supply tools for decision analysis, and allow information from multiple systems to be accessible throughout the company, and even to customers and suppliers. Here is a sample of three opinions from that *HBR* article about CEOs' responsibility toward IT.

IT risks and business risks have become intermingled, says Bob Martin, CEO of Wal-Mart, and it's up to the CEO to distinguish between the two. Technology decisions have associated risks, which must be managed, and they impact the business and the corporate culture. CEOs cannot delegate decisions with these kinds of impact. IT investments are no longer just financial decisions, Martin notes.

To manage IT effectively, says Gene Batchelder, CFO of GPM Gas Corporation, CEOs must address the age-old frustrations head-on. These include, on the one hand, IT professionals' frustrations in delivering their services in a "strategic vacuum" where the focus is only on cost reduction, and on the other hand, the frustrations of line managers on IT's increasing costs and seeming inability to focus on business needs. These two views need strong general management leadership, notes Batchelder. Business considerations, not technical considerations, now drive IT investments. The CEO must drive the cultural change to putting IT management under the aegis of line managers, just as the bottom line and human resources have become part of their general management responsibilities.

CEOs need to understand how IT is changing their businesses, says Jonathan Newcomb, CEO of Simon & Schuster, and in some industries, such as publishing, IT is literally transforming the products they make and the core economics of the business. CEOs do not need to know the latest technologies, such as video compression, but they do need to understand the opportunities this technology, or another, may offer the company. For instance, Newcomb knows he must understand the impact of technologies on Simon & Schuster's live interactive classroom television broadcasts.

Summing up these and other comments, we believe senior executives need education to carry out the following executive roles.The rationale in each case comes from our conversation with Gibson.

Set the Tone of the Organization Toward Technology. This is one of the most important jobs of top management because management sends a message through its actions. The importance of IT and information must be modeled by top executives through their personal use of the technology and their IT knowledge. They may need education in performing this role well.

Use IT to Promote Business Change. Although the hype over business process reengineering has faded, it may actually be coming into its own these days, because companies are adapting the ideas in major change programs. For example, three out of four of Gibson's recent consulting clients were implementing a major software package, such as SAP. Management in these companies has used that implementation to reengineer processes and create an integrated platform for data and transactions. The education needed here is that implementation of a powerful package, such as SAP, cannot bring about major business change on its own, but it can be a powerful catalyst and tool for top management.

Guide Technology Introductions. The IS department cannot be the driver of the change. Top management must be. This issue goes back many years, yet it is still with us. A growing number of executives are aware of this, so they are holding line management responsible for business change. If line management does not lead the change, it will not stick. Preparing managers for this is a key educational challenge.

Envision How IT Can Serve Business Strategy. Top management must foresee how key business strategies can be enabled by IT. The educational component here is a sense of technology trends and alternative scenarios of technological opportunities for business use.

Align IT with Business Objectives. There is no question that this alignment is crucial to business success. Most executives now know this. However, some still believe that the IS function is a machine room, the CIO is a technician, and the IS function can stay a step behind business planning. Where these attitudes persist, there is a problem aligning the IS department with the business importance of IT and information, Gibson has found. Education on the role of the CIO and how to effectively integrate planning are both part of the remedy.

Assess Costs and Benefits. This subject continues to be relevant because there is continuing tension between strategic objectives and the need to invest in IT infrastructure before people realize they need it. Companies must now be ahead of the requests for applications and have data resources available for unanticipated user needs. Education in this centers around the appropriate use of cost/benefit criteria, and the need to invest in nonquantifiable IT infrastructure.

Use Systems with Comfort. Now, more than ever, executives need to be computer literate, which means being able to use a PC. But even more than that, they need to be information literate. Jerry Kanter of Babson College distinguishes the two by saying that information literacy means being aware of the underlying issues in using information as a resource. Such issues include infrastructure and application development. Executives need to be comfortable discussing the technology at this level, not just at the PC use level.

Types of Executive Education Programs

It has become clear that most companies no longer can afford to "stop the business" and take their senior executives away to an IT seminar for even a few days, says Gibson. But the necessity for education is as great as ever, even while the audience is busier and more demanding of "learning relevance." Therefore, the rule these days is to present IT education integral to, or in conjunction with, discussions or meetings that are focusing on another topic, such as acquiring a business, reengineering processes, or strategic planning.

In such meetings, the business topic is in the foreground, and discussions about new technology opportunities or how IT fits into the business's strategy are in the background. Half the discussion is about the business, half is about IT—but only IT topics that are relevant to the business discussion. The outcomes of such discussions are decisions on how IT affects the business issue, down to such specifics as desktops, integrated systems, packaged software, outsourcing, and so on.

Such learning can also occur through the more direct executive exercise of the development of an IT strategy, says Gibson. Here, the business issue is *about* IT, its integration, position, and investments in the context of business strategy. Educational sessions on IT topics are easily viewed as relevant to this task.

The real challenge for CIOs and educators is that such focusing on relevance drives out discussions of broader IT issues and concepts. So those forms of IT education may not occur. In short, says Gibson, the most effective executive education these days is "issues-based education," where the educators identify with executives' current needs and design the education to address those needs.

There is quite a range of executive education programs in companies. We see three general types that have proven successful. They are categorized by degree of formality:

- Informal programs
- Semiformal programs
- Formal programs

Of the three types of programs, the most prevalent today are generally a mix of informal and semiformal.

Informal Programs. These are programs where education is done by the executives themselves as a part of staying up-to-date. They most often use four methods.

- Learn by doing
- Reading publications
- Through subordinates
- Individual demonstrations

Learn by doing. Gibson notes that more and more companies may follow the example of Charlie Feld when he was CIO at Frito Lay. He knew he had to implement a very large IT infrastructure in order to deliver an executive information system to the company. He also knew he had to do it in cost-justifiable pieces. Feld formed an alliance with the sales department to deliver hand-held computers to route salespeople. This cost-justifiable project included a big part of building the data infrastructure. When it was ready to show to the executives, he was able to find an advocate for the EIS among the executive ranks. In his advocacy role, this executive became information literate. He learned by doing. It took a long time and it required a deeper understanding than most executives obtain, but it can be accomplished if the steps are each made to pay off and learning occurs by doing.

Reading publications. In a similar vein, just reading can provide informal IT education. Publications aimed at executives are carrying more and more articles on IT. For years, *Business Week* has had a section on information processing. *Fortune, Forbes,* and *Newsweek* regularly have special advertising sections on various IT topics, with commentaries by leading consulting firms. *The Wall Street Journal* and *The New York Times* also have a growing number of articles on IT.

Through subordinates. Another informal program is to educate executives through their subordinates. One highly progressive company regularly introduces its secretaries to new equipment and products, knowing that they will spread the word to their bosses (and in some cases will try to sell them on acquiring the new products). In another company, where management is more conservative, the subordinates do not try to sell their bosses on a new system; they simply use it themselves to demonstrate the benefits.

Individual demonstrations. In a fourth informal approach, the information systems director keeps top executives up-to-date by inviting them to see demonstrations of new equipment and discussing possible uses and implications.

These informal approaches seem to work best in two types of companies: (1) very progressive companies where the executives keep themselves abreast of new developments, and (2) companies where the executives are not yet ready for highly visible organizationwide information systems. These executives more readily accept implicit means of education than outright educational programs.

Semiformal Programs. These programs are organized but not lengthy. They are often used to introduce new technologies. Here, we have found three methods in practice:

- Executive briefings
- Brown bag theaters
- Short seminars

Executive briefings. Short briefings, coordinated with management meetings, are a widely used executive education technique, as Gibson pointed out. In some cases, IS teams brief a high-level committee on a technology, such as the Internet or groupware, before requesting project funding.

Brown bag theaters. A brown bag theater is where the training department presents a series of video tapes, outside speakers, or even company employees speaking about their work at lunch time. Attendance is voluntary, and the presentation generally has a wide audience appeal—not too technical, people oriented, and entertaining. If a video is shown, it may be followed by a company expert who answers questions.

Short seminars. More formal than the brown bag theater is the short seminar, which lasts one to three hours. Attendance is also voluntary. The seminar topic is chosen for a narrower audience. This has become a very common approach used by vendors to introduce a new technology and their offerings.

Formal Programs. This form of education is designed to quickly introduce executives to new technology and the state of the art. These programs are therefore intensive, generally lasting one to three days, depending on the number of subjects covered. As Gibson pointed out earlier, formal programs have become much less popular for educating general management about IT due to time constraints. However, when custom tailored and made relevant, they do play an important role in educating managers. Of particular value is learning more about the IS job and the CIO role because more and more CIOs are coming from non-IS ranks. We will discuss this subject shortly, but first, there are two variations of a formal program:

- A single one- to three-day session
- A series of short sessions

A single session. For many companies, the first concern in executive education is *getting management's attention.* Executives often need to be away from their office work for a day before they can concentrate on the material being presented. Thus, the best approach is to hold the seminar off-site. This approach can work well, but it requires top management's conviction that the subject is important and deserves their time. This is the approach used by university executive education courses, many of which are held in the summer.

A series of shorter sessions. A second approach is to spread the presentation over several short sessions. Several years ago, an IT training resource company used this approach in an interesting way. It created a three-part program. The first part was a one-day seminar led by an authority in the field who talked about future computer systems. The purpose of this portion was to expose the top executives to a knowledgeable professional who spoke their language. Following his formal talk, the consultant answered questions. The following day the consultant gave a similar seminar for the information system executives of the same companies.

The second part of the program consisted of video tapes that presented an executive overview. Some of these tapes showed the consultant discussing future systems. The training company believed that once the executives had spent a day listening to the consultant, they would be willing to hear more on the subject. Video tapes allowed them to do this at their own convenience.

The third part of the program was a video teleconference between the participants and the consultant. The purpose of this third portion was to give the executives a chance to hear some of the consultant's newer ideas and to ask the consultant more in-depth questions.

As an example of how one company has educated its executives on IT by making that education relevant to topics under discussion, consider Teradyne. This case is based on a case study written by Charles Osborne of Babson College [6].

CASE EXAMPLE: Teradyne

Teradyne began in 1960 making automated circuit test equipment for components, thus giving electronics manufacturers a way to economically ensure the reliability of the parts they installed in computers and electronic equipment. Teradyne sold its expensive test equipment first to semiconductor manufacturers, then to computer and electronics manufacturers, and then to any company that relied on chips and microprocessors for product performance.

In 1992, the company returned to profitability following a deep, multiyear recession in the semiconductor industry. For the previous few years, the entire company, the data services division included, had focused on cost control and centralized system efficiency. But with profits recovering, top management realized that IT was going to play an increasingly important role in allowing Teradyne to grow at above-market rates. Thus, the Information Systems Steering Committee (ISSC) was formed to coordinate and integrate all Teradyne IT activities. Its work was viewed as critical to the future health of Teradyne.

The committee consisted of six managers: the CFO, two division managers, a manufacturing manager, an MIS manager, corporate controller, and Chuck Gibson, who had extensive experience in IT strategy and education. Two of the committee members were members of the Teradyne's management committee, so they ensured a companywide perspective. Another member presented the important engineering view, and another was widely respected and influential. Meetings were held about every six weeks, six hours at a time.

Early on, the ISSC recognized that one of its roles was to educate the organization on (1) a new strategic direction and (2) the potentials and pitfalls of new information technologies. Therefore, it set aside two hours of every six-hour meeting for presentations on specific technologies. The topics chosen were: strategic systems, IS values, client/server, object-oriented systems, system development (make or buy), infrastructure, operating systems, business reengineering, database technology, management metrics, and data warehousing. For each presentation, the committee heard from an outside expert on the topic. And the committee invited Teradyne business managers and IS staff who were working on major projects to attend. In general, some 25 to 30 people were at each session.

In addition, each meeting had two other components: review of current projects and work on the IS principles; the latter would provide the ground rules for choosing the technologies to be deployed across the organization. ISSC decided Teradyne needed IS principles in five areas: (1) strategy, organization, and management practice, (2) hardware and operating system software, (3) networking, (4) application software, and (5) data access management and security. Working groups were established to develop principles in these areas; their members had attended the technology education sessions so there was a high level of shared knowledge among them as well as the ISSC members.

In short, Teradyne educated its senior management as an adjunct to its IT strategy planning sessions, targeting IT subjects that were the most relevant to the discussions at hand.

Educating Future CIOs

If the educator's dream was fulfilled and executives became information literate and aware of the important issues surrounding IT, in many cases, we would still face a major gap between CIOs' traditional competencies and CEOs' expectations. In almost all the companies Gibson was consulting with at the time, yet another turnover of CIOs was taking place. Why? Gibson believes the problem is that CIOs have done a good job at controlling costs, and they are getting better at implementing major and competitively important systems. They are even trying to do a good job investing in infrastructure to stay ahead. And they have acknowledged that computing and information management are activities that take place throughout the corporation. However, they are now dragging their feet on the IT uses that bring CEOs to the table, such as the Internet, how IT is to be used for e-commerce, new and powerful desktop software, and outsourcing. Furthermore, CIOs are not exhibiting the ability to sit at the table with the executive committee, says Gibson.

As more and more CIOs report higher in the organization, to the COO or CEO, there almost invariably needs to be a new person in the job. Part of this change is due to the CEO's perception that although the technically trained CIO did a good job and won the previous war, the company is no longer fighting that war. So someone else is needed.

For example, says Gibson, the CEO and top executives in a traditional manufacturer are extremely aware of the importance of using information to deal with retail customers, and of having direct links to cash registers. The CIO, while having been good at developing an infrastructure and applications, is not conversant with the top brass. The CIO knows the technology but cannot communicate that technology to this peer group. So the manufacturer, like a number of other companies, is looking for a CIO who is a business executive and has technicians reporting to him or her.

John Rockart, director of MIT's Center for Information Systems Research, reiterates Gibson's point by noting in the *HBR* article [5] that companies that use IT most effectively have two things in common. First, they have line managers who understand their responsibility for implementing IT (rather than delegating that responsibility to the IS department). And second, they have a CIO with a deep understanding of the business who is able to build strong working relationships with line management. Such relationships give the CIO enough credibility to influence the company's future technical direction. For Rockart, choice of a business-savvy, relationship-building CIO is now critical.

Where can companies find such CIOs, asks Gibson? If they must be businesspeople first and comfortable with technology second, then maybe they can be executives plucked from the line and given a crash course in IT, such as the summer IT executive education courses given at leading universities and colleges. These formal, intensive programs may play a growing role in educating future CIOs.

HELPING LINE MANAGERS MANAGE INFORMATION TECHNOLOGY

Information systems executives now realize that line managers play a pivotal role in the successful implementation of IT because they can nurture or kill a new system, consciously or unconsciously, by their support or resistance. As the use of IT spreads, the responsibility for its correct use shifts to line managers. So they need to be comfortable managing the transition from a traditional work environment to one that has a more IT-based organizational structure and culture. The psychological changes can be significant. And finally, line managers need to be looking for ways to leverage IT for their organizational unit. In many cases, that may mean creating a knowledge-sharing culture.

So two areas that are important to middle management are (1) managing technological change and (2) championing IT projects. We deal with these two subjects here.

Managing Technological Change

Change management is the process of assisting people in making major changes in their working environment. In this case, the change is caused by the introduction of a new computer system, and line managers are the ones who need to manage this change. The management of change has often not been handled methodically, so choosing a change management methodology and training managers to use it is a step toward successfully introducing new computer systems.

Change disrupts peoples' frame of reference if it presents a future where past experiences do not hold true, according to ODR, a change management firm in Atlanta, Georgia [7]. People resist change, especially technological change, when they view it as a crisis. They cope by trying to maintain control. In the case of an impending new computer system, such as a groupware system, which people do not understand fully or are not prepared to handle, they may react in several ways. They may deny the change, they may distort information they hear about it, or they may try to convince themselves, and others, that the new system really will not change the status quo. These are forms of resistance.

ODR offers a methodology to help companies manage technological change. It uses three terms from the field of organizational development to describe the types of people involved in a change project. The *sponsor* is the person or group that legitimizes the change. In most cases, this group must contain someone in top management who is highly respected by the targeted user group. The *change agent* is the person or group who causes the change to happen. The *target* is the person or group who is being expected to change, and at whom the change is aimed. ODR recommends a four-step approach for describing and assessing the change:

- Describe the change.
- Assess the sponsors' commitment to the project.
- Evaluate the support or resistance of the targets.
- Assess the change agents' skills.

The purpose of these initial evaluations is to determine whether or not the change can be made successfully with the current scope, sponsors, change agents, and targets. By evaluating each area, the change agent can see where more education or a new approach is needed to make the project more likely to succeed. One organization that is training its managers to use this approach is the First National Bank of Atlanta.

CASE EXAMPLE: First National Bank of Atlanta

First National Bank of Atlanta, a regional bank with headquarters in Atlanta, Georgia, is a full-service bank with some 100 branches throughout the state and a large computer/communication network connecting these branches. The bank's executives are taking a market-driven approach to offering products. Therefore, in the deregulated financial services field, managing change has become an increasingly important talent they want to nurture in their middle managers. In particular, implementing new computer systems is one type of change that the bank's people need to learn to manage.

To teach the bank's managers to manage change better, the executive vice president of operations brought in a course entitled "Managing Organizational Change," developed by ODR. Initially taught by ODR, this three-day course is now taught by the bank's organizational development staff.

The executive vice president sees this course as creating the bank's framework for evaluating the impact of new computer systems on bank personnel and on bank operations. The course sensitizes attendees to change and how change can be managed by describing the stages in the change process, presenting the uses and misuses of power and influence, and pointing out the various ways people resist change, accept change, and commit to change, both consciously and unconsciously. Also, attendees learn about the three roles people play in a change process—sponsor, change agent, and target.

The attendees leave the workshop with an organizational change implementation planning kit that they can use on their own whenever they plan a major change project. The manager of organizational development told us that she is impressed with how many managers use the questionnaires in their planning work. After completing them, they often ask her to assess the objectivity of their answers.

The executive vice president's belief in the importance of managing change is also affecting how IT projects are managed. The bank includes this change management methodology in its system development procedures. Once a manager has assessed the readiness for change, project teams work on managing the resistance they have uncovered. They involve users as much as possible in system development to ensure that when the system is installed, the users will feel that they are its owners.

"Championing" Information Technology Projects

As the rate of change in the IT field has increased, we have heard IS executives say that they can no longer be "close followers" of competitors because they are likely to be left behind. They used to be able to catch up with an innovative competitor; today, that luxury is not always available.

How does a firm *smartly* stay at the forefront of technology? One answer is to encourage IT experimentation, especially by people in the operating units. Here are the ideas of two researchers and one user company on how to do that—by supporting information technology "champions." These champions they support are likely to be line managers.

Cynthia Beath and Blake Ives [8] note that the literature on strategic uses of IT points out the crucial importance of a "champion"—someone who has a vision and gets it implemented by obtaining the funding, pushing the project over hurdles, putting his or her reputation on the line, and taking on the risk of the project. Beath and Ives ask, "How does an IS executive seek out and encourage such IT champions?"

The first step in encouraging champions, say Beath and Ives, is to be able to recognize these people. They are likely to be people you already know about, and they may be doing things that make you uncomfortable. For instance, they are probably already circumventing established project approval processes, they are creating isolated information systems, and they may be using nonstandard equipment. They may already be pursuing a vision of how IT can help their business, whether systems people help them or not.

These people are opinion leaders, and they have a reputation for creative ideas or being involved with innovations. They also have developed strong ties to others in their organization, and they command respect within the firm. They have the organizational power to get strategic innovations implemented.

Information systems champions need three things from information systems management, say the authors: information, resources, and support.

They Need Information. Championing an IT innovation is an information-intensive activity, note Beath and Ives. Therefore, champions need information—facts and expertise—for persuading others that the technology will work. Information systems people can help champions gather and assess information about a technology's capabilities, its costs, risks of operation, and how it might be used in an experiment. Information systems staff also can help by sharing their expertise and by putting champions in contact with other experts, such as vendors or users of a new technology.

Information systems staff can assist champions in understanding current applications and data relevant to their project. Finally, they can help champions understand how the company manages change because systems people are continually involved in implementing system changes throughout the enterprise.

They Need Resources. The authors cite Rosabeth Kanter, author of *ChangeMasters* [9], who says what champions need most is staff time. Giving champions "free" staff time is especially helpful during the evaluation and persuasion portions of a project, say Beath and Ives. But systems management can go even further by assigning, say, information center consultants to help champions.

In addition to staff time, champions are likely to need material resources, such as hardware and software. These can be loaned to them free of charge or provided in some other way.

They Need Support. Finally, champions need supporters—people who approve of what they are doing and give legitimacy to their project. It is important that information systems management corroborate statements made about the technology by the champion, say Beath and Ives. The champion does not need to know how the technology works, only how it might be used. The systems department should handle the technical aspects. Beath and Ives urge demonstrating the champion's claims about the technology, and promoting the technology to build enthusiasm for it and to win support from others.

Finally, IS management can help a champion win the endorsement of upper management, say Beath and Ives, by helping to create the plans for introducing the new technology. The systems department can assist by contacting vendors and assisting in choosing an appropriate implementation approach. All these will improve the quality of the proposal and strengthen it in the eyes of management.

Beath and Ives encourage information systems management to make it easier for IT champions to arise and succeed. One company that has successfully supported champions is Aetna Life and Casualty. Here is what this company is doing.

CASE EXAMPLE: Aetna Life and Casualty

Aetna Life and Casualty, a financial services company with headquarters in Hartford, Connecticut, sells employee benefit and pension programs to large companies, commercial insurance, and personal insurance—health, life, automobile, and home.

Much of the IT work has been decentralized; therefore, the corporate administration department focuses on three functions, which it calls "plan, build, and run." The operations group runs data center and telecommunication operations. The corporate technology services group assists divisions in selecting, building, and implementing computer systems. The people and technology group also helps divisions build and implement successful systems; they emphasize the human perspective.

The "plan" function is the responsibility of the corporate technology planning group, which is meant to be a catalyst for introducing new technology. Its charter is to help Aetna understand and use "breakthrough" technologies throughout the company, meaning those technologies that will increase performance by at least 100 percent. "We constantly seek to make the future credible by encouraging innovation, experimentation, and evaluation," a member of this group told us. Group members see their job as encouraging end users to talk about new technologies and test them out in real-life situations. The corporate technology planning group fosters discussions and experimentation in three ways.

They Seek Out Business Champions. The group tests technologies by cosponsoring end user projects, acting as a "magnet" to attract people who want to experiment with a technology. The group holds workshops on specific technologies, publishes one-page issue papers describing certain technologies, and talks to people in a wide number of functions.

The group's goal is to find end user champions who think a technology might solve their business problem. These people also need to be willing to share the funding and direction of a pilot project using that technology. The users agree to let the planning group study their use and write about it. So, for a project to be funded, it must have a business champion and be aimed at solving a business problem.

In several cases, the group has found champions who recognize the need to test several technologies—some with expected results and others that might change future work life dramatically. These are "smart champions" because they see the value of investing in a portfolio of new technologies.

They Study Pilot Projects. In one pilot project of a 500-user communication system, the planning group did systematic research during this pilot, using before-and-after questionnaires to measure how attitudes changed. They looked to see if "telephone tag" increased or decreased. They held focus group discussions. And they had some users keep daily diaries of their activities.

Based on this research, they concluded that the system would benefit a majority of employees. To then promote its use, they created a brochure and video tapes, which they handed off to the corporate operations group for the marketing and management of the system.

They Establish Steering Committees. Steering committees can be surrogate champions to guide and build support for a new technology. When the corporate technology group sees a technology that appears interesting, it may hold a one-day "magnet" session to find champions. Sometimes the technology group finds steering committees rather than individual champions when a topic is really "hot." In one case, 200 people volunteered to do pilot projects. Since that was too large a group, a smaller steering committee was formed. It put on four seminars, got end users thinking about how they might use the technology, and oversaw some projects.

Challenges They Have Encountered. The technology planning group has encountered the following three challenges.

One is simply getting people's attention. When a technology is not immediately available, people do not want to take any action. But many technologies require a learning curve. Even when a technology is not readily available, people should be experimenting with it, so that the company has in-house knowledge when products do begin to appear. So, making a future technology credible to people today is one hurdle.

Keeping people in an experimental mode is another challenge. Once people are funded for a pilot, they want to do it right. They do not want to create a quick-and-dirty system; they want to create a production-quality system. It is hard to get people to create only quick, experimental systems.

The third challenge is making sure that use will really pay off. The planning group does not want small productivity improvements; they want orders-of-magnitude improvements—at least two-to-one to three-to-one payoffs. So the planning group must constantly ask users: How do you know you will get this payback?

The group's goals are education and action. They want end users to be comfortable using future technologies and achieve a good payback at the same time. For more ideas on how to stimulate innovation, see *Managing Organizational Innovation* [10].

How does such an approach make a company more technologically mature? By putting the company in a position to more likely spot new opportunities, experiment with them, and put them into widespread use before its competitors. In a fast-changing world, nimbleness is a sign of maturity. Becoming comfortable with current technology is not enough; being open to accepting emerging technologies is needed.

TRAINING END USERS ON TECHNOLOGY

In general, the emphasis with end users has been on training, that is, learning skills and know-how, rather than on education, which deals with concepts and understanding. End user training has focused on how to use computers or applications directly. But with the advent of Web browsers, which will become the common way to access more and more applications, once users have learned to use the browser, they have had much of the basic training they need.

Beyond that, to use a system competently, they need to understand the structure of the Web, information access and processing concepts, remote teamwork social protocols, and such—education, not training. The president of a company that sells computer training courses told us that companies generally order hands-on training courses for their users first. But then they discover they should have ordered the computing concepts courses first because the users did not understand the basic concepts about computers. Thus, end user training involves both education and training. To illustrate this point even more graphically, consider the following research study.

CASE EXAMPLE: Factors Influencing EDI Implementation

At the second Association of Information Systems (AIS) conference, Matthew McGowan of Bradley University in Peoria, Illinois, and Gregory Madey of Kent State, in Kent, Ohio [11], described the results of their study of the organizational factors that influenced the implementation of EDI. They were interested in both *breadth* of implementation (the number of different kinds of EDI transactions used in a company, which indicates how widespread EDI use is) and *depth* of implementation (the extent to which one particular type of EDI transaction is done via EDI rather than other means). They studied the effect of 12 organizational characteristics on EDI usage (shown in Figure 17-1) by conducting a U.S. survey; they received 235 usable responses.

They found that, indeed, organizational size correlated very strongly with breadth of implementation and fairly strongly with depth; the larger the organization, the more the use of EDI—no surprise. But surprisingly, top-management support of EDI was only weakly related to breadth and depth, and top-management support of the IS department was not related at all. The next two items, attitude toward risk and functional differentiation, both correlated only to breadth (how many EDI transactions were used) and not to depth (how often a specific transaction, such as invoicing, was used).

Existence of a champion in the organization implementing EDI correlated to both breadth and depth; again, no surprise. However, IS department advocacy of EDI related only to depth (extensive use of one transac-

Figure 17-1   Organizational Characteristics Studied in EDI Research
(from McGowan and Madey [10])

- **Organization size:** Past research showed that large manufacturing firms were more likely to use EDI than smaller ones.
- **Top-management support for EDI:** Past research showed that top-management support correlated to the extent of implementation of innovation, in general, and that this support was the most frequently cited factor aiding EDI implementation.
- **Top-management support for MIS:** McGowan and Madey decided to also look at this more general form of support.
- **Risk attitude:** Past research showed that the amount of risk that top management was willing to accept correlated to adoption of customer-oriented interorganizational systems.
- **Functional differentiation:** More functional differentiation (i.e., more subunits) should provide more opportunity to deploy EDI.
- **External communications:** Past research showed that explaining an innovation to others outside IS was important in getting it implemented.
- **Presence of a champion:** Past research showed that existence of a champion within the business correlated with implementation of an innovation.
- **MIS advocacy for EDI:** Past research showed that advocacy from IS was a factor in implementing EDI.
- **EDI planning:** Past research suggested that EDI planning complemented top-management support in prompting use of EDI.
- **EDI training:** Past research showed a correlation between availability of EDI training and extent of EDI implementation.
- **Technical expertise:** Past research showed a correlation between the existence of technical expertise and adoption of an innovation as well as greater levels of innovation use.
- **EDI knowledge:** McGowan and Madey wanted to see the importance of this factor on EDI implementation depth and breadth.

tion type) and not to breadth (wider use of several transaction types), which was just the opposite of what McGowan and Madey had expected. Likewise, EDI planning only related to depth and not to breadth.

Finally (and pertinent to this section of the book), availability of training related to both depth and breadth, which might mean that training stimulates use, or, on the other hand, more training might be required due to greater levels of implementation. McGowan and Madey do not assume causality, only correlation. Also interestingly, technical expertise did not relate to depth or breadth. This suggests that the technical issues of EDI implementation are not significant. On the other hand, EDI knowledge in the organization was highly correlated to both depth and breadth. McGowan and Madey, therefore, speculate that organizations that know about the benefits of EDI will use it more; but again, they cannot prove causality, only correlation.

Based on these results, McGowan and Madey recommend that organizations increase use of EDI primarily by increasing users' knowledge of EDI and providing EDI training because these two organizational factors appeared to have the greatest correlation to EDI use.

Computer-Based Training

Computer-based training has been around for years, and its success rate has been mixed. Obviously, it permits a very different training environment from traditional classrooms. The training can be on demand, interactive, specific to the immediate interests of the student, performed where and when the student desires, and (to a great extent) not requiring a human instructor to be active in the process. As the field has evolved, the following forms of computer-based training have evolved:

- *CAI. Computer-assisted instruction* (CAI), sometimes called computer-assisted learning (CAL), is where the computer first delivers the material to be learned and then tests the student's grasp of the subject with questions. Depending on the correctness of the answers, it then selects the next section to be presented.

- *CMI. Computer-managed instruction* (CMI) does not necessarily deliver the material via computer; often, conventional methods are used—classes, books, workbooks, films, video tapes, audio tapes, and so on. Instead, CMI tests the student on what has been learned, evaluates whether or not learning has been satisfactory, prescribes corrective action if not, and controls the student's progress.

- *CBT. Computer-based training* (CBT) includes both presenting the material via the computer and managing the administration of the courses using the computer. However, the administrative portion does not appear to be of great interest in end user training.

- *IPSS. Integrated performance support systems* (IPSS) are the newest advance in computer-assisted training. An IPSS is a training system embedded in a worker's workstation—in the factory or in the office or conceivably on the Web. It generally combines all the help and training facilities a person needs in "on-demand" or "just-in-time" training. One example is a "proof of concept" client/server-based

IPSS [12] built by an insurance company for its property analysis underwriters. The system contains a reference manual, training demos, and a expert system-like coaching module for the underwriters.

End User Training Needs

End users need five types of training:

1. Information systems concepts
2. Quick start
3. Refresher aids
4. Explanation of assumptions
5. Help in overcoming difficulties

Information Systems Concepts. Although training is skills oriented, some conceptual background is usually needed before skills can be learned. A major focus of concepts training is literacy—learning how things are done by computers. Examples include creating data files, sending electronic messages, transferring files over the Internet, and backing up data—all simple concepts that end users need to know. As noted earlier, people need to understand these mechanics, especially with regard to the Internet, so that they understand what is easy and what is hard for a computer—something that is often not intuitively obvious. It greatly helps to have a mental picture of the way communication is handled on the Net, the role of servers, and the various uses of computers in accessing information, locating people, contacting people, joining communities, keeping up with events, and using the resources of another computer by logging onto it.

Quick Start. End users need a way of quickly learning how to use a new machine, application, or service. As we noted earlier, the arrival of Web browsers is hoped to obviate some of the need for end user training because more and more applications will use the browser on the front-end. Gloria Gery [13], who has been in various aspects of the training field for over 20 years, told us that an ideal quick-start facility would first give users a mental picture of the organization of the entire system. Then it would present "global" procedures—ones that can be used throughout the system in a consistent manner. Once the size and usefulness of the system are made apparent to users, they can choose what they want to learn. But without this global view, they will not understand the capabilities and limitations of the system.

Refresher Aids. Since many end users will not be doing the same tasks every day, they may forget how to perform some operations. For these circumstances, they need to refresh their memory quickly and on-line. This facility should be easy to initiate and should allow users to choose the topics they want to review. Most software packages these day have embedded help, which can be retrieved by clicking on the icon that is not understood. Packages generally also come with tutorials or demo programs, which a user can rerun to remember forgotten procedures.

Explanation of Assumptions. People who create forecasts and projections using modeling packages must understand the assumptions underlying the models, or else they may use the packages incorrectly. Most CBT products that deal with models present some basic concepts, but they may not explain under which circumstances the model could produce misleading information. Newer modeling packages often have a parameter screen or assumption list that acts as an assumption review, as well as a device for controlling the package.

Help in Overcoming Difficulties. There are times when all users run into a situation for which they cannot find an explanation. These days, with people working at all hours of the day or night, many companies have gone to round-the-clock help desks, staffed by people who rely on systems with answers to FAQ (frequently asked questions). And if help is needed to use the Web, there are numerous FAQ sites to help.

Organizational Learning

These then are the kinds of information end users may need when doing their work via computer. But that's just on the surface, at the individual level. What about deeper at the organizational level? It seems to us that this topic of education and learning also has a lot to do with "remembering," specifically, organizational memory. As Mark Ackerman of the University of California at Irvine and Tom Malone of MIT point out [14], organizations encounter many, many instances when people need questions answered, and they cannot find the answers. Some have nothing to do with computers, some are all about using a computer system, and still others have to do with managing computers. For instance, as the original signers of an outsourcing contract leave the organization, there is often no record of the assumptions underlying the contract. With this loss of memory of the original intent, the foundation of the alliance may veer off course.

To deal with one aspect of organizational memory, Ackerman and Malone developed Answer Garden at MIT, which consists of databases of commonly asked questions that can grow organically as new questions arise and are answered. When no answer is present, the system sends the question to the appropriate expert, who can then insert an answer into the appropriate branch of the database. In this way, Answer Garden builds organizational memory, and helps people either find the information they need or find the right expert.

A person uses Answer Garden by selecting a use, such as "ask question," which brings up diagnostic questions about the subject at hand, such as, "Are you having a problem using such-and-such application, finding information about X, programming with X, and so on?" Selecting one box leads to the next level of questions, and so on, until the system can present specific answers to questions. Or sophisticated users can ask to view the entire tree of branching questions and select the one they want answered. If users do not understand a question or cannot find the answer to their question, they can select the "I'm unhappy" button and an e-mail window appears for them to ask their question. That question is then sent to the appropriate expert (anonymous to the user) along with the history of the user's search, so that the expert can see where the user has been. In answering the question, if the expert believes it is a commonly asked question, he or she can also insert it into the database.

As Ackerman points out [15], Answer Garden is not only useful for getting answers to questions, it is potentially even more useful in finding the right people who have the answers. We found this type of system of great potential importance in the growing world of knowledge management, which is discussed throughout this text. We expect to see much more discussion about both subjects—organizational memory and knowledge management—in the coming years.

RESKILLING SYSTEMS STAFF FOR THE FUTURE

A new word in the education and training arena for the 1990s has become reskilling. And it is not simply a word change, it is a change in philosophy. In the past, training pertained to jobs. Today, companies no longer focus on jobs, they focus on skills, hence, reskilling, especially in IT, where we have gone through two revolutions (client/server and the Web) in less that five years. The other change in philosophy has been from careers to employability, which has shifted the initiative for receiving training from employers to employees. It is now up to IS staff, not the company, to search out reskilling opportunities. And yet a third shift has been in gauging results, from counting the number of students taking a class to assessing performance in the new skill. All three have led to a "revolution" in the training arena.

Tony Brewer [16], a researcher at Wentworth Research, studied IS reskilling and points out that competency is "the ability to perform a task effectively" and it depends on the combination of skills, knowledge, and attitude. Skills are the *know-how* of competency, he notes. They include task skills, process skills, and interpersonal skills; updating skills is a shared responsibility between employer and employee, believes Brewer. Knowledge is the *know-what* of competency—the information resource needed to know which skills to apply to a task; updating knowledge is the employee's responsibility, he notes. And finally, attitude is the *know-why* of competency—the way people think and feel about their work; attitude is the responsibility of the employer.

Companies now begin reskilling, says Brewer, by identifying the competencies they will need. For the 1990s, he identified ten generic competencies that IS staff will need. These are listed in Figure 17-2.

Once these competencies have been tailored to the IS department's specific needs, yielding a set of 12 to 15, the department can create a competency profile. It shows which competencies are needed in each job or role within the department. Then the current competencies of the staff are assessed, the gaps identified, and a strategy for bridging the gaps devised—hopefully striking a balance between recruiting, training, coaching, outsourcing, and outplacement. Since change is likely to continue in IT, competency development should not be seen as a one-time event, says Brewer, by employer or employee. It is a continuing need.

As an example of a company with an exemplary reskilling program, consider American Express Financial Advisors. This case is based on the Sourcebook that accompanied Brewer's IT Management Programme report, "Reskilling for the Information Age."

Figure 17-2   Generic IS Competencies for the 1990s
(from Wentworth Research [15])

Managing change

Envision results, challenge status quo, catalyze action, assemble resources, foster effective processes, monitor progress, behave flexibly, anticipate and resolve obstacles, design effective working environments.

Behaving commercially

Orient to results, understand business practices, understand the organization in its business context, focus on customers, be profit and cash conscious, understand electronic commerce.

Managing relationships

Understand "win-win," negotiate and commit to results, monitor performance, confront shortcomings, build trust, accept mutual dependency.

Working with others

Communicate clearly (verbally *and* in writing), advocate causes and influence outcomes, be alert and aware, be sympathetic and encouraging, behave reliably, provide feedback, be adaptable and resilient, tolerate stress.

Applying systems thinking

Understand concepts, analyze and solve problems, think creatively, recognize systemic patterns, synthesize components into a whole, understand processes, learn from experience.

Exploiting information

Manage data quality, share data, understand the impact of context, practice semiotic analysis, make assumptions explicit, surface tacit knowledge, understand external sources.

Exercising general management skills

Think strategically, lead and inspire, be assertive, exercise judgment and take decisions, control budgets, manage resources, manage quality, resolve conflict, empower and facilitate staff, take risks and manage outcomes, be energetic, set an example.

Applying information technology

Design technical architecture, integrate existing systems, develop applications, understand structured development methods, understand emerging technologies, manage data and application security.

CASE EXAMPLE: American Express Financial Advisors

The American Express Financial Advisors (formerly IDS Financial Services Inc.) group, headquartered in Minneapolis, Minnesota, offers more than 100 financial products and services to individuals and businesses. The firm has over 5,000 employees in its corporate office, 900 of whom are IS people who handle all IT functions for the corporation. Additionally, 12,000 independent financial advisors rely on IS to provide financial systems and applications to support their work.

When IS began its reskilling project in 1992, the focus was on jobs. Now, the focus is on identifying the work that needs to be done, which ties retraining to business strategy and business goals. IS therefore places less emphasis on job profiles and more emphasis on project-specific role profiles. This shift from career development to skills development is an important shift because skills relate to a person, not to a job. IS encourages its staff to see their skills as assets, which they, themselves, need to develop and market.

IS is taking an overall developmental approach to reskilling, rather than treating it solely as training. This holistic view treats project resourcing and staff transitioning as integral to reskilling. Thus, whenever IS brings in external contractors, it pairs them with high-potential staff for on-the-job training. Contractors are used only to "jump start" projects, not to replace staff. The main challenges in retraining have been to plan for staff transitions, assess skill gaps, retrain, and assure staff that they will not be left behind.

The retraining project began with the IS training department defining a retraining process based on the firm's strategic technology plan. Skills were prioritized by the firm's technology steering committee. Taking a business view of IS, the committee concluded that the staff's core competencies should be project management, business process reengineering, system analysis and design, and business knowledge. Combined with the firm's technical direction—client/server and object-oriented application development—these provided the basis for determining each project's skills requirements.

All IS project plans contain detailed resource plans, including number of staff needed to complete the work, skills needed by the team, and so on. Projects are staffed in three ways:

- The first staff assigned to a project are those who have the required skills and who can mentor others.
- The second employees assigned are staff members who do not have the skills but need to be groomed for future assignments. Skills development plans are created to help them bridge their skills gaps.
- If it is not possible to staff a project internally, the company hires external contractors, selecting people who can mentor the firm's less experienced team members.

IS staff members are expected to take the initiative in learning new skills. While the company pays tuition and provides learning opportunities, the staff members must undertake these on their own time. In return, the company draws on these employees first when selecting and training for a new project. Thus, employees expect that once they have learned on their own, they will be put on a project quickly and will soon receive skill-specific training.

While reskilling began as a training department project, it now has been institutionalized. Funding comes from IS functional areas and functional managers are held accountable for successfully reskilling their staff through performance goals. For example, they are required to transition and train a given percentage of their staff from legacy systems to client/server. IS managers receive one-on-one coaching and are taught how to plan for, budget, and implement training for their staff.

In conclusion, the IS training department discovered that proactive reskilling has led to better-planned projects. There is enough lead time to select and train staff properly and prepare them for coaching. Furthermore, managers and employees know everyone is accountable for results, not just for receiving training.

CONCLUSION

With the growing importance of IT to business success, the IS department has a major share of the responsibility for helping the firm to increase its technological maturity—by helping executives, line managers, end users, and systems staff be more comfortable with the technology. In this chapter we have described how this is being done in practice today.

QUESTIONS AND EXERCISES

REVIEW QUESTIONS

1. What is a technologically mature organization?
2. Why do corporate executives need computer education?
3. Name four types of informal executive education programs. In which circumstances are they most appropriate?
4. When are formal executive education programs appropriate?
5. According to Gibson, how might business executives be educated to be future CIOs?
6. What does change management have to do with information technology? Why should middle managers have change management training?
7. If a line manager becomes a champion of an information technology project, what does he or she need?
8. How does Aetna Life and Casualty encourage information technology champions?
9. What did the McGowan and Madey study conclude?
10. According to Brewer, what are the ten competencies needed by IS staff?
11. How does American Express Financial Advisors staff its projects?

DISCUSSION QUESTIONS

1. The typical approach for using this (or another) textbook is for professors to assign a chapter for students to read and then discuss that chapter in class. Some say this is an effective way to educate students. Do you agree or disagree? What other methods of presenting this material would be more effective for you?
2. Education and training approaches are becoming too technology driven and they leave out the human touch. Do you agree or disagree? Where do you see human interaction needed in the learning process?
3. Capturing organizational memory is a mirage. It cannot be done well because it can not be kept up-to-date. Do you agree or disagree? Discuss your reasoning.

EXERCISES

1. Explore a FAQ (frequently asked questions) site on the Web. What did you learn from using it? What were its strengths? What were its weaknesses?
2. Visit a local company that provides computer education for its executives, managers, and/or end users. Describe some of the course offerings. What is the company's training strategy? How is it reskilling IS staff?
3. Read five articles on IT training or education. What new ideas did you pick up? Briefly describe them to the class.

REFERENCES

1. GILDER, GEORGE, speech at the Aspen Institute, July 18, 1996, broadcast on C-SPAN in August 1996. Gilder is a columnist and author of *Life After Television*.
2. NOLAN, RICHARD, and CHUCK GIBSON, "Managing the Four Stages of EDP Growth," *Harvard Business Review*, January-February 1974, Reprint No. 74104.
3. MCFARLAN, F. WARREN and JAMES MCKENNEY, "The Information Archipelago: Maps and Bridges," *Harvard Business Review,* September-October 1982, pp. 109-119, and "The Information Archipelago: Plotting a Course," January-February 1983, pp. 145-156.
4. GIBSON, CHUCK, Gibson and Associates, P.O. Box 428, Concord, MA 01742.
5. "THE END OF DELEGATION? INFORMATION TECHNOLOGY AND THE CEO," *Harvard Business Review*, September-October 1995, pp. 161-172.
6. OSBORN, CHARLES, "Teradyne, Inc.: The Information Systems Steering Committee," Babson College, Babson Park, MA.
7. ODR, 2900 Chamblee-Tucker Road, Building 16, Atlanta, GA 30341.
8. BEATH, CYNTHIA, and BLAKE IVES, "The Information Technology Champion: Aiding and Abetting, Care and Feeding," *Proceedings of the 21st Annual Hawaii International Conference on System Sciences*, Vol. IV, pp. 115-123, IEEE Computer Society. (Volume IV has ten papers, case studies, and abstracts from the conference sessions on strategic and competitive information systems.)
9. KANTER, ROSABETH, *ChangeMasters*, Simon & Schuster, NY, 1983, 432 pages.
10. JOHNSON, BONNIE and RON RICE, *Managing Organizational Innovation,* Columbia University Press (136 S. Broadway, Irvington-on-Hudson, NY 10533), June 1987.
11. MCGOWAN, MATTHEW and GREGORY MADEY, "Organizational Factors Influencing the Implementation of EDI," *Proceedings of 1996 AIS Conference,* August 1996, pp. 131-133; mmcgowan@bradley.edu and gmadey@synapse.kent.edu.
12. BOOKER, ELLIS, "Training on Thin Ice," *Computerworld*, October 11, 1993, pp. 81-84.
13. GERY, GLORIA, Gery Associates, P.O. Box 851, East Otis, MA 01029.
14. ACKERMAN, MARK and THOMAS MALONE, "Answer Garden: A Tool for Growing Organizational Memory," *Proceedings of the ACM Conference on Office Information Systems*, ACM, 1990, pp. 31-39.
15. ACKERMAN, MARK, "Answer Garden and the Organization of Expertise," Center for Coordination Science Technical Report #127, MIT Sloan School, Room E40-179, January 1992.
16. BREWER, TONY, "Reskilling for the Information Age," IT Management Programme, Wentworth Research, Park House, Wick Road, Egham, England, TW20 OHW; http://www.wentworth.co.uk, March 1995.

EIGHTEEN

Creating the New Work Environment

INTRODUCTION

It is obvious to all of us that we are in the midst of a business revolution. The business world is just not the same as it was, even five years ago. As a result, companies around the world are in the throes of redefining their work environment—a tumultuous proposition, at best—without any true guidance. Their goal is to either simply survive in the new business climate or to thrive in it. In this chapter we address this current and most challenging task by assembling a collage of opinions about the goals of the new work environment as well as describe various kinds of organizational environments that are being tried.

Goals of the New Work Environment

Why is this huge amount of change taking place? It appears to us it is because of the computer and its ability to leverage people's brain power, not just their muscle power. This new capability is causing companies to compete in new ways, and forcing them to organize in new ways. We see the following overarching goals for thriving in the new work environment:

- Leverage knowledge globally.
- Organize for complexity.
- Work electronically.
- Handle continuous and discontinuous change.

Leverage Knowledge Globally. The newly recognized asset, the new form of capital, in companies is knowledge. Not "knowledge" in an expert system or a Notes database, but knowledge in people's head. Knowledge they "know" but cannot really explain to others. This is called "tacit" knowledge (as opposed to "explicit" explainable knowledge) and companies that are able to leverage it globally will be very successful—provided, of course, its use is directed by a sound strategy.

Brook Manville, director of knowledge management, and Nathaniel Foote, director of knowledge and practice development, at McKinsey & Company [1] point out that in the current knowledge economy, knowledge-based strategies begin with strategy, not knowledge. This new form of intellectual capital is meaningless unless companies have the corporate fundamentals in place, such as knowing what kind of value they want to provide and to whom.

They also point out, and we enthusiastically concur, that executing a knowledge-based strategy is not about managing knowledge; it's about nurturing people with knowledge, tapping into the knowledge that is locked in their experience. And while companies have numerous systems in place to share explicit knowledge, the key to unlocking tacit knowledge is a work environment in which people "want" to share.

As Manville and Foote point out, a manufacturer that tried to foster greater "knowledge transfer" while downsizing discovered that the combination was impossible. Why would employees share what they know when the bosses were looking for ways to consolidate expertise in order to eliminate jobs?

The means for tapping tacit knowledge is by fostering sharing in the work environment, supported by the technological means to share. E-mail and groupware can be the interconnect means to the end, but the culture is the driving force. When people want to share, say Manville and Foote, they form "worknets"—informal groups whose collective knowledge is used to accomplish a specific task. So sharing and leveraging knowledge happens through organizational "pull"—people needing help from others to solve a problem—rather than organizational "push"—overloading people with information. So leveraging knowledge is all about raising the aspirations of each individual, say Manville and Foote. We will have more to say about an approach to achieving this "leverage knowledge" goal shortly.

Organize for Complexity. A second overarching goal of companies, whether they recognize it or not, is to be able to handle complexity. Why? One reason is because the world has become so interconnected that simple solutions no longer solve a problem. Corporate decisions can have an environmental impact, human resources impact, economic impact, and even ethical impact. The issues are systemic. Furthermore, capturing market share today oftentimes requires allying with others who have complementary knowledge. Alliances increase complexity. So does specialization. Have you bought shampoo, crackers, or tires lately? Those used to be fairly straightforward decisions. Today, the choices are so numerous that consumers can spend an inordinate amount of time making a selection. To thrive in the current information age, companies need to be organized to handle complexity. We have more to say about this shortly.

Work Electronically. Taking advantage of the Internet, and networks in general, is a third major goal of enterprises these days. The work*place* is moving to the work*space*. But just as the move from horse-and-buggy to train to automobile to jet plane was not simply a change in speed but a change in kind, so too is the move to working in a "space" rather than a "place" a change in kind. It requires different organizing principles, compensation schemes, office structures, and so on. It also changes how organizations interact with others, such as their customers.

George Gilder [2], columnist and author, addressed this issue in a speech at the Aspen Institute. He noted that an industrial era is defined by the plummeting price of the key factor of production. During the industrial era, this key factor was the plummeting price of horsepower, as defined in kilowatt-hours, which dropped from many dollars to 7.5 cents. For the past 30 years, the driving force of economic growth has been the plummeting price of transistors, translated into MIPS and bits of semiconductor memory. The latter has fallen 68 percent a year, from $7 some 35 years ago to a millionth of a cent today. Today, however, we are approaching yet another "historic cliff of cost" in a new factor of production: bandwidth. "If you thought the price of computing dropped rapidly in the last decade, just wait until you see what happens with communications bandwidth," said Gilder, referencing a remark by Andy Grove, CEO of Intel.

Up to this point, we have used MIPS and bits to compensate for the limited availability of bandwidth. But as we move into an era of bandwidth abundance, the entire economy will change. The microchip moved power within companies, allowing people to vastly increase their ability to master bodies of specialized learning. Microchips both flattened corporations and increased the ability to launch new corporations. Bandwidth, on the other hand, moves power all the way to the customer. That's the big revolution of the Internet, he said, and that's why there is the move to "relationship marketing" with customers.

This creates a different world. For example, TV is based on a top-down hierarchical model, with a few broadcast stations (transmitters) and millions of passive broadcast receivers (televisions). The result is "lowest common denominator" entertainment, like what we get from Hollywood. The Internet, on the other hand, is a "first-choice" culture, much like a bookstore, where you walk in and you can get your first-choice book. First-choice culture is vastly different from lowest-common-denominator culture, says Gilder. As the Internet spreads, there will be a movement from "what we have in common" to a culture which allows us to explore our individual aspirations, hobbies, and interests.

Handle Continuous and Discontinuous Change. Finally, to keep up, companies will need to innovate, continually—something most have generally not been organized to do. But continual innovation does not mean continuously steady innovation. There are fits and starts. As we have noted several times, there are two kinds of change: continuous change (the kind espoused by total quality management techniques) and discontinuous change (the kind espoused by reengineering). When a product or process is just fine but needs some tuning, continuous change is needed to improve efficiency. But when it is not fine, discontinuous change is needed to move to an entirely new way of working. The two often form a cycle. Companies need to be able to handle both for both their products and processes.

These, then, are four major goals that we believe will underlie the new work environment. Using these as a basis, we now explore some of the alternative forms or approaches organizations are proposing and developing.

ORGANIZING PRINCIPLES

This section of the book is potentially the most exciting because we are in a time of such grand exploration—a new economy is being born. But it is equally the most frustrating because the tenets of this new economy are so different that the rules have not been defined—and may not be defined for quite some time. The following is the most exciting, and most promising, new thinking on how to organize work that we have encountered. Although many of us might like neat, clean distinctions, the following categories slop over into one another.

Processes Rather Than Functions

In his follow-up book to *Reengineering the Corporation,* which is entitled *Beyond Reengineering*, Michael Hammer [3] notes that the key point in the reengineering movement was not that changes needed to be dramatic (that is, in terms of orders of magnitude), but that they needed to be made from a process-centered viewpoint rather than the existing task-centered view. The industrial revolution deconstructed processes into specialized tasks, and the business world has focused on improving tasks ever since. Tasks are about individuals; processes are about groups.

All our current organizational problems are process based, he contends. They center around how the specialized tasks fit together. Simple jobs require management and complex processes to get work done. When companies try to simplify these complex processes, they find that simplifying a process can only be done by creating complex jobs. A typical reengineering case in point is the move from a sequential work flow (where five people each perform just one or a few parts of a job) to a case management approach (where one person performs the entire work flow). With no more hand-offs, there is no need for a supervisor. The employees manage themselves. Working and managing become part of everyone's job in a process-centered structure. Only process-centered organizations can address today's organizational issues, says Hammer, because solutions require shifting perspective from tasks to process. A number of leading-edge companies are now taking the process-centered approach, he notes, with the emphasis on teams.

The shift to processes has a number of ramifications. One is the need for a new position, such as a process owner. In every process, virtually every department is involved. But there is no one person with end-to-end responsibility. This needs to be rectified. Rather than managing the people, the process owner provides the knowledge of the process. He or she owns the design of the process. Since most organizational processes have just grown from the inside, rather than having been designed from the customer's perspective, process design is a new job. This is also true for process improvement, which, says Hammer, becomes the essence of management in a process-centered organization.

The move to a process-centered structure also requires measures of processes, which are very different from measures of tasks, says Hammer. When you measure a process (how long it takes to complete the process, its accuracy rate, its cost, etc.), you measure an outcome from the customer's point of view, says Hammer. Instead of measuring how many calls a customer service rep handles each hour (a task metric), the process metric might be the percentage of problems (calls) handled completely on the first call—the outcome (a process metric).

Yet another ramification of process centering is a sense of urgency and intensity. Teams are more intense. This gives less slack time. Work tends to be full-steam all day, all week, all year long. This tends to wear down nerves and increase stress.

Process centering also turns people into professionals rather than workers, says Hammer, if you define a professional as someone who is responsible for achieving results rather than performing a task. The professional is responsible to customers, solving their problem by producing results. To do so means performing the entire process, doing what it takes. A worker, on the other hand, aims to please the boss, keeping busy with lots of activity, to perform what he or she is told to do. He or she is not to be concerned with the totality of the work. The shift to professional from worker is profound. It makes factory employees concerned with customer satisfaction rather than number of parts produced per hour. It requires a more holistic view by all those involved and greater knowledge.

Given this brief description of some of the principles underlying a process-centered organization, what would one look like? Hammer suggests a football team.

CASE EXAMPLE: A Football Team

A football team is a good example of a process-centered organization, says Hammer [3]. It has two processes: offense and defense. It has process owners: offense coordinators and defense coordinators who select the players, train them, design plays, and script them; their concern is the performance of the process.

The team also has "position coaches," such as line coaches, who train and develop the athletes for specific tasks, acting as counselors and mentors; their concern is the performance of the players.

Finally, the team has a head coach, the leader, who creates the organization, names the coordinators and coaches (and then manages them), creates the team's culture and values, motivates the players to peak performance, and calls the plays during the game. But once on the field, the team is self-directed. It adapts to the unfolding play.

Self-Organizing Rather Than Designed

Some of the most stimulating discussions about the form of future organizations are those centered around chaos theory, ecology, and biology, that is, nature and how it organizes itself. Meg Wheatley's highly influential book, *Leadership and the New Science* [4], and Kevin Kelly's mind-opening *Out of Control* [5] are just two examples. The basic tenet is that nature provides a very good model for future organizations, especially organizations that must deal with complexity, share information and knowledge, and cope with continuous and discontinuous change. In seeming chaos, we can get order for free, both say. As with natural phenomena, enterprises will do much better if they are self-organizing (or emergent) rather than designed. Since it is easiest to illustrate these principles by example, we start there.

Examples of Self-Organization. Kevin Kelly, executive editor of *Wired* magazine, gives many, many examples of the self-organizing principle in *Out of Control*. Here are just two. The first concerns the movie *Batman Returns,* in which computer-generated bats were to flock through Gotham City. One computer-generated bat was created and allowed to automatically flap its wings. Then it was replicated, by the dozens, until there was a mob. Each was instructed to move on its own following just three rules: Don't bump into another bat, keep up with your neighbors, and don't stray too far away. When the computer simulation of the mob of bats was run, they flocked just like real bats! Craig Reynolds had discovered the flocking rules, writes Kelly, and they are very simple. So while the bats were seemingly out of anyone's control, they flocked. The same happened with the marching mob of penguins in the same movie, which also drew on a simple Reynolds algorithm. Kelly says this kind of behavior has taught that order can be achieved from chaos in any distributed organic or man-made system.

In an equally striking example, Kelly describes how Loren Carpenter, a graphics expert, demonstrated a similar kind of order-among-chaos in an auditorium with 5,000 computer graphics conferees. Each one had a cardboard wand, red on one side, green on the other. At the back of the auditorium a computer scanned the wands when they were held up high, picking up the color on each wand. At the front of the auditorium was a huge screen that displayed the sea of wands, like a candlelight parade. Attendees could find themselves in the sea, and change their color on the screen by flipping their wand.

Carpenter then projected the game Pong on the screen, telling the audience that those on the left controlled the left paddle, those on the right the right paddle. Within moments, the 5,000 were playing a pretty good game of Pong, with the movement of the paddle being the average of the several thousand players' intentions. When Carpenter speeded up the game, the crowd adjusted, almost instantly.

When an airplane flight simulator was projected on the screen, Carpenter told the audience that the left side of the room controlled the roll and the right controlled pitch. In essence, the pilot became 5,000 novices. They became silent as they studied the controls in the cockpit, wrote Kelly. The plane was headed for a landing, yet it pitched left and right because the signal was latent and the crowd continually overcompensated. When it was obvious that they would arrive wing first on the landing strip, they somehow pulled up the plane and turned it around, even though no one gave a command. They acted as one mind, turned wide, and tried a second landing. But again, the plane was not straight, so in unison, and again without verbal communication, they pulled up. On the way up, the plane rolled a bit, then a bit more, and then, "at some magical moment" the same thought seemed to occur to everyone, "I wonder if we can do a 360?" In unison, without speaking, they rolled the jet, fairly gracefully, and then gave themselves a standing ovation. Kelly notes that the conferees did just what the birds did: they flocked.

The Self-Organizing Point of View. Wheatley and Kellner-Rogers, explain in their book, *A Simpler Way* [6], that organizations, like many natural phenomena, can be self-organizing. They believe this requires taking the perspective of "organizing-as-a-process" rather than "organization-as-an-object." Processes can do their own work, they write; just supply what the processes need to begin: resources, information, and access to new people.

Self-organizing systems create their own structure, patterns of behavior, and processes to accomplish the work. People within the processes design what is necessary to do the work and agree on the relationships that make sense to them. Systemwide stability depends on the ability of the members to change. Change occurs, at all times, as conditions change. As a result, write Wheatley and Kellner-Rogers, we do not have to plans things into existence, we only need to work with the unknowns, and their organization will emerge. Systems are relationships that we observe as structures, but those relationships cannot be structured, they can only emerge. As the individuals explore their needs, webs develop, if they are free to create the relationships they need. Freedom and trust are paramount for the system to thrive. And systems are healthiest when they are open to including diversity; it gives them strength and resiliency.

Kelly believes that the only way to create truly complex systems is to use biology's logic of self-governance, self-replication, partial learning, and some self-repair. He believes that the mechanical and biological worlds are merging, leading to bionic systems, which he calls vivisystems. For control (as needed in a nation's flight control system), we need mechanical clockwork systems, but when we need adaptability, we need systems that act as "swarms," like a hive of bees. Kelly notes that when bees swarm (that is, move en masse to a new hive), the process is not command controlled. Instead, a few scouts check out possible new hive locations and report back to the swarm by dancing. The more theatrical a scout bee's dance, the better the bee liked the site, says Kelly. Deputy bees then check out one of the competing sites based on the dance that attracts them the most. If a scout concurs with the dancing bee's choice, the scout joins the dance. This induces others to check out the site and then join the dance, if they concur. Thus, in this democracy, the favorite sites get more visitors, and, following the law of increasing returns, they get more dancing votes, and the others get fewer. In the end, one large snowballing dancing swarm dominates, and flies off to the new site, taking the queen bee with it.

Is there an example of an organization with such a self-organizing principle? From our research, the one we would choose is Semco of Brazil.

CASE EXAMPLE: Semco S.A.

In his book, *Maverick: The Success Story Behind the World's Most Unusual Workplace* [7], Ricardo Semler, CEO of Semco, describes how his company, a Brazilian manufacturer of industrial equipment, moved from fifty-sixth place to fourth place in its industry. To survive with Brazil's crippling inflation rate, Semler felt he had to "break all the rules" to reduce costs and raise productivity.

As a result, factory workers at times set their own production quotas, help redesign products, formulate marketing plans, and even choose their own bosses. Bosses set their own salaries, yet everyone knows what they are because workers have unlimited access to Semco's one set of books. And they've all been taught how to read balance sheets and cash flow statements. Finally, on the big decisions, such as relocating a factory, everyone decides. In one case, a factory was shut down for one day and buses took the employees to all three possible sites. Then the workers decided—on a site that management would not have chosen.

There are no receptionists or secretaries, no perks, and Semler really does not know how many employees he has because some of his employees work part-time for him and part-time for competitors, others are contractors, and still others are vendor employees. When Semler took over the company after the death of his father, he threw out the rules because they discouraged flexibility and condoned complacency. So for travel, for example, there are no travel rules; people are to spend whatever they think they should, as if it were their own money. The rationale: "If we're afraid to let people decide in which section of the plane to sit or how many stars their hotels should have, we shouldn't be sending them abroad to do business in our name, should we?" writes Semler. Employees are considered partners; they are self-managing and self-governing. They even vote on how the profit-sharing pot will be split each year.

Things are rather messy around Semco, writes Semler. Machines are not in neat rows. They are set at odd angles, where the team that assembles a complete product puts them. Most workers do several jobs on a team, not just one, with the backing of the unions. And team members do not have to show up for work at the same time, but they do coordinate their schedules so as not to disrupt production. As the workers assumed more responsibility for their work, the number of supervisors decreased—as did corporate staff. Semco does not even have IS, training, or quality control departments. There are three layers of management (there used to be twelve) and those three are represented by three concentric circles.

Furthermore, departments can buy from whomever they choose. This competition keeps them on their toes. Management even encourages employees to start their own companies, even to the point of leasing Semco machinery to these startups at favorable rates. These companies sell to Semco and competitors. This strategy keeps Semco lean and agile.

The story goes on and on. The changes have been rough and not undertaken in an orderly or coherent fashion, as Semler recounts, but the radical change to a far more democratic workplace allowed Semco to grow 600 percent at the same time that Brazil's economy was faltering. It's a very dramatic story, and illustrative of the benefits of self-organization.

Communities Rather Than Groups

Another organizing principle for new organizations is the formation of communities rather than groups. We distinguish between the two by saying that communities form of their own volition. Groups, on the other hand, are formed by design; their members are designated a priori, perhaps by a project manager, a select committee, or an executive.

"Communities of practice" are espoused by the Institute for Research on Learning in Menlo Park, California, a spin-off of Xerox PARC [8]. As described by John Seely Brown, director of Xerox PARC, and Estee Solomon Gray, a founder of Congruity, a consulting firm [9], a community of practice is a small group of people (rarely more than 50) that has worked together for a period of time, but not necessarily in an organized fashion. They may perform the same job or collaborate on a shared task or a product. They have complementary talents and expertise, and they are held together by a common purpose and a need to know what the others know. Most people belong to several communities of practice, and most important work in companies is done through them.

Communities are the critical building blocks of a knowledge-based company, state Brown and Solomon Gray, for three reasons. One, people, not processes, do the work. There are big gaps between official work processes and real-world practices (how things actually get done). These informal, perhaps impromptu, ways that people solve problems cannot be anticipated. And when companies compete on knowledge, the name of the game is improvisation. The challenge is to keep processes elegantly minimal, so that they give room for local interpretation and improvisation, that is, for grassroots practices.

The second reason communities of practice are important is that learning is about work, work is about learning, and both are social. The crucial, unappreciated ingredient in companies is tacit knowledge—intuition, judgment, and common sense—which cannot be explained. Within groups, tacit knowledge exists in practices and relationships based on people working together over time. When people recognize the importance of tacit and collective dimensions of work, they realize that learning has to do with being part of a community rather than absorbing information.

Third, communities of practice are important because organizations are webs of participation. When the patterns of participation change, the organization changes. Participation is the core of the twenty-first century company. Only people who make a commitment to their colleagues can create a winning company. Companies that realize the power of communities and adopt minimal processes that allow communities to emerge are moving toward being a twenty-first century company.

CASE EXAMPLE: National Semiconductor

National Semiconductor has gone the furthest in promoting communities of practice, according to John Seely Brown and Estee Solomon Gray [9]. The company began encouraging such communities in 1991, after its business model—to build low-margin, commodity chips—collapsed. The new CEO restructured and rationalized the company, then put it on a growth path and changed its model to product leadership. Part of the strategy is to build a core competence in mixed signal technology, where chips function as the electronic interface between the "real world" of voice/video and the digital world of computing/communications.

Communities of practice are central to this plan. They energize and mobilize the firm's engineers. They even shape strategy and then enact it. A community of practice on signal processing, for example, grew slowly over 18 months. It includes engineers from numerous product lines and is now influential in strategy decisions.

Another community of practice has grown up around phase lock loops (PLL), a technology critical in some important company products. For 20 years, PLL designers swapped ideas, insights, and solutions to problems, even though they worked in different business units that did not interact. Within this loose community, a group of PLL engineers began reviewing new chip designs. When product groups around National Semiconductor heard about these reviews, they informally brought their designs to the group for advice. The more reviews the group did, the more effective it became, and earned a reputation for excellence.

These engineers cannot publish their design criteria nor teach others how to do design reviews nor create a library of design because their knowledge is embedded within their experience as a community of practice. The only way someone can learn how to critique a design is to become part of that community and interact with it.

In 1994, this PLL community of practice was formally recognized as such and adopted a charter: To make its design know-how accessible, make successes and failures known, and continue to build the firm's PLL competence. This community does not report to anyone; it is "run" by its members. It provides a means of collaboration among National engineers concerning their PLL designs. It even received funding to develop two advanced PLL prototypes outside any National product line. And it has created a "PLL place"—a lab that houses the equipment it buys.

National is extending communities of practice by formally recognizing them, offering funding for their projects, and handing out a toolkit to help people form their own communities of practice. And it encourages them to create home pages on the World Wide Web to communicate.

Virtual Rather Than Physical

The virtual organization has come to be the popular description of a new organizational form. The underlying principle is that time and space are no longer the organizing foundations that they once were. A virtual organization does not exist in one place, or perhaps even in one time. It exists whenever and wherever the participants happen to be "there." As described in Chapter 3, First Virtual Holdings began as a virtual corporation, with the founders working wherever they were when they were working. But today's organizations may actually have virtual organizations inside them, just as they have communities of practice. But, in most cases, neither is formally recognized. As an example of a virtual organization within an existing company, consider Sun Microsystems.

CASE EXAMPLE: Sun Microsystems

John Gage, chief scientist of Sun Microsystems, gives an intriguing description of virtual organizations within existing companies [10]. He says that the network creates the company. "Your e-mail flow determines whether you're really part of the organization; the mailing lists you're on say a lot about the power you have." For example, he had been part of the Java group at Sun for four or five years, when his name mistakenly was taken off. His flow of information stopped; he stopped being part of that organization. He got back on in a hurry, he says.

Gage notes that he used Sun's alias file (the master list of its e-mail lists) to know what was going on at Sun. No one needed to tell him when a new project had started, he would just see a new e-mail list. And when he saw a list balloon from, say, 35 to 200, he knew something was happening.

People even create their own aliases, Gage says. His own alias is his personal view of the company's power structure on projects, such as Java, no matter where the members work. The organization chart does not reflect the same list. These personal aliases have a secondary effect, too, says Gage. They let others know who you are keeping informed. In essence, each alias is a virtual organization. Web technology extends e-mail, says Gage, because it allows people to send "live" messages with embedded hyperlinks. So, rather than try to persuade someone, you can just show them.

The Learning Organization

Peter Senge, director of the Systems Thinking and Organizational Learning Program at MIT's Sloan School of Management, wrote the influential book, *The Fifth Discipline: The Art and Practice of the Learning Organization* [11]. No list of organizing principles for the new work environment would be complete without including his ideas.

Senge begins his book by noting that most organizations live only 40 years—that is, one-half the life of a person. The reason, he says, is because they have learning disabilities. In children, learning disabilities are tragic, he says. In organizations, they are fatal. Therefore, he believes organizations will have to become learning organizations to survive.

Organizational learning disabilities are obvious, notes Senge. Here are just three. First, enterprises move forward by looking backward in that they rely on learning from experience. This approach means that companies end up solving the same problems over and over. Second, organizations fixate on events—budget cuts, monthly sales, competitors' new announcements. Yet the real threats come from gradual processes that move so slowly that no one notices them. Third, teamwork is not optimal, which is contrary to current belief. Team-based organizations operate below the lowest I.Q. on the team, leading to skilled incompetence.

In the 1990s, organizations that can learn faster than their competitors will survive, notes Senge. In fact, this is the only sustainable advantage. To become a learning organization, an enterprise must create new learning and thinking behaviors in its people. That is, the organization and its people must master the following five basic learning disciplines:

- Systems thinking
- Personal mastery
- Mental models
- Shared vision
- Team learning

Systems Thinking. We live in a world of systems. To understand systems, people need to understand the underlying patterns. For example, people can only understand the system of a corporation by contemplating its whole, not its parts. Today's complex corporations are best viewed by looking for the patterns and understanding the whole. Systems thinking is a conceptual framework for making complete patterns clearer. Using and understanding systems thinking can help people see how to change the patterns effectively.

Personal Mastery. There is a special level of proficiency that people can reach where they live creatively, striving for the results that matter the most to them. In essence, their life turns into lifelong learning, in which they continually clarify and deepen their personal vision, focus their energies, and see reality objectively. This is personal mastery and it forms the spiritual foundation for the learning organization. Unfortunately, few enterprises foster such aspirations; they are not committed to the full development of their people. Therefore, they foster burnout rather than creativity.

Mental Models. Peoples' mental models are the deeply ingrained assumptions, generalizations, and images that influence how they see the world and what actions they take. Senge notes that Royal Dutch Shell was one of the first organizations to understand the importance of mental models—that is, how its managers viewed the world and the oil industry. Shell learned how to surface its managers' assumptions and challenge their inaccurate mental models. Shell was able to accelerate its organizational learning process and spur the managers to investigate alternative futures by using scenarios. Then, when the 1974 oil crisis hit, its managers were able to react more appropriately than competitors because they had already explored the possibility of such a crisis and the best steps to take if one did occur.

To change mental models, people must look inwardly—something few organizations encourage. But those that do realize that they have a powerful tool for fostering institutional learning.

Shared Vision. A shared vision is an organization's view of its purpose; it is its calling. It provides the common identity by which its employees and others view it. Senge notes that Apple's shared vision has been to build computers for the rest of us. IBM's shared vision was exemplary service. A shared vision is vital to a learning organization because it provides the overarching goal as well as the rudder for the learning process. It becomes the force in people's hearts. It is the answer to: "What do we want to create?" Organizations with shared visions are powerful organizations.

Team Learning. When teams learn, they produce extraordinary results. One of the major tools for team learning is "dialog," where people essentially think together. Senge distinguishes discussions from dialogs by saying that discussions occur when people try to convince others of their point of view. Dialogs, on the other hand, occur when people explore their own and others' ideas—without being defensive—in order to arrive at the best solution. Few teams dialog; most discuss, so they do not learn.

Team learning, rather than individual learning, is essential in the learning organization, because teams are the fundamental unit of the modern organization. If teams do not learn, neither does the organization.

Of these five disciplines, Senge believes that systems thinking is the cornerstone. It is the fifth discipline. Until organizations look inwardly at the basic kinds of thinking and interacting they foster, they will not be able to learn faster than their competitors.

What stands out for us in this discussion of the organizing principles that have been put forth by leading thinkers in the mid-1990s is the repeated emphasis on naturally forming relationships. They talk about people-to-people contact rather than technology. They talk about natural phenomenon rather than man-made structures. They dwell on how to develop relationships that help people work effectively. That's the key, not technology. Technology is the support structure that allows some of these relationships to take place. But, as Gage's example illustrates, IT can play a major role in implementing these organizing principles.

THE HIGH-TECH SIDE OF THE NEW WORK ENVIRONMENT

John Seely Brown and Estee Solomon Gray [9] ask, "How can communities of practice leverage themselves to affect the fortune of the giant corporation in which they exist—a corporation such as National Semiconductor with annual sales of $2.5 billion and over 20,000 employees worldwide?" They believe the answer is technology, specifically information technology. They believe we are entering a new era of "social computing," where IT is used to help communities form and communicate. Specifically, they believe communities need communication technologies that allow "rich, focused" interactions. An example is Project Jupiter, a "community-based system" under development at Xerox PARC.

CASE EXAMPLE: Project Jupiter

As described by Debra Feinstein [12], Project Jupiter connects some 60 people at three Xerox research sites, Xerox PARC in Palo Alto, California, Grenoble, France, and Rochester, New York. It is a social system, a "network place," a virtual social reality where colleagues can share ideas. They work in virtual offices, walk down virtual halls, and write on a virtual whiteboard, says Feinstein.

It is led by Pavel Curtis, who did groundbreaking work on MUDs (Multi-User Dungeons) and created LambdaMOO (a MUD, Object-Oriented) on the Internet. In MUDs, people build their own electronic worlds and own electronic identities to play interactive adventure games.

Project Jupiter, like MUDs and MOOs, exists via computer screens. It looks a bit like the TV show *Hollywood Squares* with each square occupied by a colleague, sitting in his or her office, talking on the phone, working at a workstation. Via Jupiter, these colleagues can hold one-on-one informal discussions in their offices, or a group discussion in a virtual lab, or have a chance meeting in "the lounge." Each square also contains an icon that shows how accessible that colleague is, at the moment. For example, an open door says they are accessible, just double click and enter. A locked door, on the other hand, means do not disturb. So the system contains social protocols, which John Seely Brown believes are very important.

An important feature of Project Jupiter is that it provides context as well as content. The different "rooms" and "objects" in the system are programmable to evoke different behaviors. It is intended as a place where people interact as a community.

The system also has virtual equivalents of familiar office tools—whiteboards, fax machines, tape recorders, even Post-It notes. For example, seeing a colleague on the phone, a researcher can post a note asking, "Is it convenient to talk in 10 minutes?" The colleague receives the note on his or her screen and can gesture an answer while still talking on the phone.

Unfortunately, many computer systems have not been designed with communities of practice, or even individual needs, in mind. Many companies have viewed improved productivity, rather than increased effectiveness, as the main goal. They have designed jobs to resemble factory assembly-line jobs, with people doing the same thing, over and over, all day long, with more and more information available to them at their fingertips. This can run counter to their needs. Thus, we believe it is important to get employee participation in the design of their jobs; otherwise, the following could happen.

Jon Turner of New York University [13] reported on a study conducted at the U.S. Social Security Administration (SSA) that concerned the use of two systems and their effect on the claims representatives of the SSA who used them. These claims representatives conduct face-to-face and telephone interviews with claimants from the general public, assisting them in completing their applications and submitting the necessary evidence for entitlement to social security benefits. The claims representatives access the SSA's central claim information system. In the older system, the claims representatives submitted requests for claimant information and received an answer in from 10 minutes to 8 hours. In the newer system, response was almost immediate. So the only differences were in the "front-end" that the claims representatives used and the response time.

The results of the research were surprising. Mental strain and absenteeism increased and job satisfaction decreased with the new system. Although the researchers did not find a fully satisfactory explanation, Turner speculates that the new system allowed the claims representatives to deal with more people per day. Since many SSA claimants tend to be unhappy (because they feel they will not get all they should receive from SSA, or are having trouble getting their claims approved), this meant that the claims representatives dealt with more unhappy people per day and, hence, their mental strain went up. That factor, speculates Turner, apparently was more detrimental than the frustration of using the older, slower system.

The point is that job design is a complex issue. If attention is paid only to the technical and economic issues, such as faster access to data, increased productivity, and so on, the side effects can be quite different from what is anticipated. Hence, now we turn to the high-touch side of creating the new work environment.

THE HIGH-TOUCH SIDE OF THE NEW WORK ENVIRONMENT

As we noted earlier, the encouraging aspect of the organizing principles explored earlier is that they dwell so heavily on the human side of work—the high-touch side. In this section we explore approaches to redesigning work to be more fulfilling. We look at two aspects: individuals and groups. We begin by looking at what motivates individuals on the job, specifically IS professionals.

The Job Diagnostic Survey

J. Daniel Couger, a professor at the University of Colorado, in Colorado Springs, Colorado, has conducted national and international research in the area of motivating and managing computer personnel. His early work [14], done with Robert Zawacki, was a national survey of IT personnel and their attitudes about the job. Couger replicated the study ten years later, and then began similar studies in the international arena [15, 16].

The research was motivated by perceptions of the problems in managing computer personnel. For their survey, they used the Job Diagnostic Survey (JDS), developed J. R. Hackman (University of Illinois) and G. R. Oldham (Yale University). Hackman and Oldham established the validity and accuracy of their model of human motivation (Figure 18-1) by testing more than 6,000 people who were performing more than 500 different jobs at more than 50 organizations.

In short, the model says that positive outcomes occur when employees experience meaningfulness in their work. Meaningfulness occurs when people need to use a number of different skills and talents (*skill variety*), when their work involves completing a whole and identifiable piece of work (*task identity*), when the work has a substantial impact on the lives or work of other people (*task significance*), when people have freedom in accomplishing the tasks (*autonomy*), and when the job provides some built-in feedback or reward (*feedback*).

Their Job Diagnostic Survey consists of a series of questions that employees answer anonymously. Some questions are

- How much independence and freedom do you have in the way your carry out your work assignments?
- How effective is your manager in providing feedback on how well you are performing your job?
- To what extent does your job require you to use a number of complex or high-level skills?

Figure 18-1   A Model of Human Motivation
Used by the Hackman/Oldham JDS

Five core job dimensions
1. Skill variety
2. Task identity
3. Task significance
4. Autonomy
5. Feedback from the job itself

Three critical psychological states
1. Experienced meaningfulness of work
2. Experienced responsibility for outcomes of the work
3. Knowledge of the actual results of the work activities

Leading to personal and work outcomes (when the above are "right")
1. High internal work motivation
2. High-quality work performance
3. High satisfaction with the work
4. Low absenteeism and turnover

Employees answer each question by selecting a number from 1 (low) to 7 (high). Only the average scores of a group of people doing the same work are meaningful; individual scores are not. Furthermore, employees are likely to answer with their true feelings only if they believe the results will not be used against them personally, which argues for complete anonymity. The JDS should *not* be used for placement purposes or in diagnosing jobs of individuals. The average values ("scores") on each question are then used for analyzing employee perceptions about the job.

The JDS also includes questions about the employee to help in matching the person to a job type. One of the computed measures is *growth-need strength*, which is determined by averaging employee answers for the questions having to do with personal growth and development. A high growth need strength indicates that the people in a group have a high need for personal growth and development. They will become internally motivated if their jobs have a high motivating potential.

Another computed measure is *social-need strength*. It is obtained from questions having to do with interacting with other people. A high group score in this metric indicates that the people in the group have a strong desire to interact with others; a low score indicates that they prefer to work alone.

A third important computed measure for this discussion is the *motivating potential score* of the job, which is computed from the questions that measure the five core job dimensions—skill variety, task identity, task significance, autonomy, and feedback from the job itself.

Gauging IT Staff. Couger and Zawacki's initial survey included some 2,500 persons from 50 organizations. The database now contains information on more than 18,000 Americans and 19,500 people from other countries. The U.S. data shows that programmers and analysts have the highest growth-need strength of any job category that has been analyzed using the JDS. In a sense, this result is not surprising; IS management has long known that systems professionals want to work on the latest technology, both hardware and software. However, their high growth-need strength means that their managers must continually provide them with new challenges to keep them motivated.

Another survey finding for the U.S. computer professionals has serious implications for systems management. Programmers and analysts have the *lowest* social-need strength of any of the 500 occupations measured by the Job Diagnostic Survey. People with a high social need utilize meetings as a prime device for fulfilling their social need. "Programmers and analysts don't need meetings," says Couger, "and users don't understand why systems personnel show frustration at lengthy or frequent meetings."

The same point applies to project or department meetings, notes Couger. "Programmers and analysts are not antisocial; they will participate actively in meetings that are meaningful to them. But their high growth need also causes intolerance for group activities that are not well organized and conducted efficiently."

Couger, in a discussion, pointed out another factor that IS management must consider. System analysts are expected to interact extensively with users. If they come from the ranks of system developers, they probably want as little interaction with users as possible, and tend to rush through whatever interactions they do have. "Might this be why the study of user requirements has often been so incomplete?" asks Couger.

When he initiated his international studies, Couger hypothesized that the survey responses from people from different cultures would be significantly different. His surveys covered such diverse cultures as Taiwan, Hong Kong, Singapore, Australia, Israel, Finland, South Africa, and Austria. The surprising result was that IT professionals in these countries also exhibit high growth-need strength and low social-need strength. The IT profession appears to attract people with similar characteristics, irrespective of their culture. So the approaches to improving motivation would be similar for all these employees, when there is a mismatch between growth-need strength and the job's motivating potential.

Improving the Maintenance Job. In many of the organizations surveyed, both nationally and internationally, low job satisfaction generally occurred in pockets—the developers in one unit or the analysts in another. To correct the problem, isolate it. It is typically one or more of the five core job dimensions—skill variety, task identity, task significance, autonomy, or feedback from the job. Use an approach to achieve a satisfactory match between growth-need strength and motivating potential score. The following examples come from a study that concentrated on maintenance programmers, conducted by Couger and Colter [17].

Skill variety is the dimension that most often causes IT professionals to perceive maintenance work as less challenging, say Couger and Colter. This job dimension contains two elements: (1) the variety of skills needed to carry out the tasks, and (2) the variety of tasks. When the variety of skills is constrained, such as confinement to maintaining a legacy application when the person has the skills to do client/server or Web work, task variety should be emphasized. An illustration is assigning two people to jointly maintain two systems instead of requiring each to specialize on one system.

Task variety is thereby enhanced for both employees. *Task identity* can be enhanced in a different manner. Lack of task identity can occur when an individual is working on a module with little awareness of how it relates to the whole system or to the company's work. Supervisors could place more emphasis on these relationships, thus enhancing task identity.

The other component of task identity is completing a whole and identifiable piece of work. An example is working with the user to define the needed changes, revising the program, testing, and then implementing the changes. If the maintenance programmer can be given an entire job instead of only portions of this sequence, task identity would increase.

In several of the surveyed organizations, maintenance programmers were quite removed from the users, so little interaction occurred between the two. In such situations, the importance of the work—*the task significance*—was not conveyed to the programmers. This could be improved by asking users to make presentations to the programmers who are maintaining their systems, stressing the importance of their work, or by moving the maintenance people out to the user area.

Another job core dimension that is often rated low for maintenance jobs is *autonomy*. This is not because the supervisors do not give maintenance programmers freedom to operate but because the procedures or policies provide little flexibility. The legacy systems they maintain often provide the constraints, such as a specific language. These lower the programmer's autonomy. One way supervisors can enhance autonomy is by encouraging participative goal setting and then not supervising the programmers too closely in the activities required to attain these goals.

In the study, maintenance personnel saw "compliance with schedule" as the most important evaluation factor for their promotion. This factor also illustrates *feedback from the job*. Companies that provide good project management systems, which emphasize that the information is primarily for the programmers and secondarily for the supervisors, are enhancing feedback from the job. Some companies go a step farther by providing the reports to team members several days before supervisors receive them.

This discussion and these examples illustrate how the Job Diagnostic Survey can reveal the need to better match jobs with the types of people who fill them. By analyzing both the activities and the employee, individuals can be matched with tasks, according to their growth need. A proper matching leads to higher motivation and better productivity.

As noted earlier, there are two aspects to redesigning jobs, individuals, and groups. We turn now to groups.

The Sociotechnical System Approach

In the group redesign arena, we have been most impressed by the sociotechnical system (STS) approach because it deals with the social and human aspects, as well as the technical aspects of work. We briefly mentioned STS in Chapter 14 as the method used by the successful NYNEX reengineering project to create a community of practice for requisitioning T1 lines; the other ten projects used different methods and were not completed. Due to its successful use in practice, and its applicability to teams, groups, and communities, we discuss it in more depth here.

The intent of STS is to design systems to accomplish work effectively and, at the same time, provide jobs where the employees have more say about how they perform their work. Sociotechnical analysis is most applicable where there is concern over specific problems in a work group and where the jobs within the group need to be redefined. It is not aimed at redesigning an individual job.

To illustrate this approach to redesigning jobs, consider the work of Dr. James Taylor, while he was at the center for the Quality of Working Life at the University of California, Los Angeles [18]. In Taylor's work (as in the NYNEX instance as well), the STS design work is generally performed by a team of employees from the work group, under the guidance of an STS consultant. The approach has been successfully implemented in both blue-collar and white-collar environments; also, some of the employees used computers while others did not. Following is how Taylor recommends approaching job design.

Step 1: Scanning the Work Group. The STS approach begins with an examination of the purpose of the work group: What exactly does the group produce? This evaluation defines the boundaries of the group (the points where it relates to other work groups), the inputs the group receives, the product(s) it produces, the staff within the group, and their reporting relationships.

Step 2: Technical Analysis. In the first portion of this step, the group's work process is dissected into the changes that take place in the product as it moves from raw material (say, a customer order received) to finished product (say, the shipping orders produced). One change in this particular example is receipt of a completed customer order. Another change is storage of that order in its proper file. Still another is approval (or disapproval) of the customer's request for credit. And so on.

In the second part of this step, the design team identifies the technical requirements of the process and the major deviations (key variances) that occur during the process. Key variances are very important because they are the aspects of the process that must be controlled, in one way or another, to ensure product quality, quantity, and low cost. For example, if the customer order has been only partially filled out, then some of the necessary data is missing. That is a key variance that someone must handle.

Step 3: Variance Control. In this step, the design team determines how each key variance is currently being controlled. For example, who finds the missing data for the incomplete customer order? The team also identifies alternative means for handling these variances for future use during the job redesign phase. During this step, the team often finds that variances are not controlled where they originate. Supervisors are often responsible for controlling them—either by directing a subordinate to handle the problem or by coordinating with other supervisors. One goal of STS is to eliminate the need for supervisors to intervene in the work group's handling of key variances.

Step 4: Social System Analysis. "Social system" means the work-related interactions among people, not the friendship system within a company. It is the coordination needed within a process that makes the technical process actually work under constantly changing situations.

The first portion of this step is to examine each person's role in the work process under study. The process's boundaries, which were identified in the first step, are important here, because often variances occur in one work group but are handled in another. How these two groups coordinate with each other is an important social relationship that needs to be identified.

The second portion of this step examines the relationship of this work group to other work groups—for receiving needed information and supplying information to others. The group's end product, say, the approval for payment of a supplier's invoice, may be the input to another department, such as the accounting department, where the invoice payments are actually made.

The third portion of this step seeks to discover from the employees themselves how they feel about their current jobs. A process that looks fine on paper may actually be stressful due to physical separation of people who need to communicate often, unnecessary fragmentation or duplication of work, and so on.

Step 5: The Sociotechnical Design. Once the elements of the technical and social aspects of the work process have been separated (in the previous steps), they can be recombined in a new way to keep control of variances within a group. The objective is to allow the group to determine how it will handle variance control itself. For example, one possible key variance is an uneven workload—one day one person is swamped with work and the next day has little to do. If the employees are given the authority to schedule their own work within the group, they can balance the workload, rather than have it assigned by a supervisor. The goal is to place variance control at the earliest possible point in the process and with the fewest number of people involved. Variance control should not involve passing the work from one person to the supervisor, then to another supervisor, and then to a subordinate in another group, unless absolutely necessary.

STS studies often result in pushing decision making down to lower levels within an organization. Typically, the group members, not the supervisor, decide how to handle problems. This changes supervisory jobs more to training, coaching, and coordinating with other supervisors.

Taylor has several hints for improving the likelihood of a successful job redesign effort. First of all, top management must actively support the STS approach and understand the possibility of changes in organizational reporting relationships, levels of authority, and decision making. This support must be communicated to other employees in the organization, says Taylor, especially middle and first-line managers.

Second, management must plan for the consequences of a successful STS project. Failures are generally the result of management's reluctance to make the recommended changes. Therefore, management needs to plan beyond the first successful project by placing it in the context of a larger organizational change. If management does not plan beyond the first project, that project often appears as a threat to other employees rather than a successful model for change, says Taylor.

Self-Managed Work Groups

As we noted earlier, briefly, employees at Semco operate in unusual ways. In many cases, they work as self-managed work groups, which has significantly reduced the number of supervisory and management jobs. As at other companies that have implemented self-managed work groups, work flow redesign accompanies these changes; work is performed in work cells instead of assembly lines. Rather than split a series of work steps among the group so that each person specializes in one step, the entire job process (or much of it) is performed by each person for a segment of the workload.

Cells appeared first in manufacturing; they have now spread to the service industry. We have heard of work cells for handling mortgage loans, processing insurance claims, and even caring for patients in hospitals—hospitals-within-a-hospital, where each one specializes in specific diagnoses and clusters staff, services, and resources close to the patients. The goal is to both increase healthcare quality—by providing more continuous personal care—and reduce costs—by eliminating non-value-added work, such as moving patients around a large hospital.

Henry Sims and Charles Manz [19] studied a number of self-managed work groups at a small southern U.S. manufacturing plant of 320 employees, organized into three levels of teams. At the top level are the managers. Their role is to support the people actually doing the work. The middle managers in the second level (who would traditionally be supervisors and technicians) act as coordinators and advisers to the operating groups. At the operating third level are 33 teams of natural work units. The assembly-line groups are responsible for many duties that are traditionally performed by supervisors and managers. Sims and Manz observed how these functions were carried out, based on the groups' formal and informal conversations. Here are some of their observations.

Groups Hand Out Rewards and Reprimands. Team members often compliment each other on their work or thank each other for specific jobs they have done. But team members also reprimand each other for actions that have adversely affected the group. In one instance, Sims and Manz observed a group resolving the poor attendance record of one of its members. The group leader recounted the record to the offending employee and stated that it was unacceptable. The employee agreed to change his behavior or face formal disciplinary action.

Groups Assign Tasks and Schedule Work. Sometimes, say Sims and Manz, the work assignments are essentially permanent. Other times they rotate, on an hourly, daily, or weekly basis. Task assignment is important to some group members, so they "negotiate" with others on work allocation.

In addition, the groups are responsible for production scheduling. At the time Sims and Manz were studying them, there was a decreased demand for the plant's products. Rather than reduce the labor force, the groups decided to reduce production, reduce unnecessary labor hours, and divert time to needed repair and construction. This led to less flexibility in scheduling, but the groups' hour-by-hour and day-to-day decisions saved the company a significant amount of money.

Teams Perform Production Goal Setting and Performance Feedback. Plant production is determined at the corporate level; however, the local groups determine how these goals are to be met. They have the authority to shift product mixes within certain time limits. The authors also found that the groups discussed quality control, goal setting, and how they would meet their goals. The teams also received much quantitative feedback—daily, weekly, monthly, and quarterly. These reports were on production quantity, quality, and safety. In fact, the authors noted that "there were charts everywhere"; feedback to employees was important at this plant.

Teams Handle Announcements and Problem Resolution. Routine announcements were frequently heard in the groups' everyday conversations. Problem-solving conversations and meetings were also common. In one incident, a coordinator presented members of two teams with a quality control problem. Some members from the two teams met to discuss the problem. The coordinator, who would be a supervisor in a traditional setting, sat in on the meeting and encouraged people to talk. In the end, several problems were identified as the likely causes of the quality control problem, and the members of the groups took it upon themselves to solve those problems.

Teams Handle Communications Problems. When there are difficulties between teams, the teams themselves generally handle the problem. Sometimes, they exchange team members for a short time in order to increase the understanding of all concerned.

Groups Evaluate Themselves and Choose Their Membership. Sims and Manz did not observe conversations about compensation evaluations; however, they did hear employees ask other team members to evaluate them on a task performance demonstration. At the plant, wages are based on a "pay by knowledge" scale. Employees are paid for what they are capable of doing, rather than what they are doing at the moment. An employee must demonstrate competence on all tasks on two different teams to qualify for a pay advancement; this is where the task performance demonstrations are important. Advancement typically takes two years. This method of pay promotes flexibility among employees, say the authors, and it fosters unusual appreciation for "the other fellow's problems."

Teams also determine their membership. When production was reduced, as mentioned earlier, the teams had to decide which of their members would be assigned to the "temporary construction team" to perform repair and cleanup work. In one group, the members first suggested that the person with least seniority go. But that person objected, so another person, who wanted to work outside and do craft work, volunteered.

Sims and Manz were impressed with how well the teams handled the more difficult problems they faced—reprimanding a team member, reducing team size, and resolving problems with other teams. All was not tranquil and harmonious on the teams, they stressed, but overall they found the employees' motivation and commitment to be higher than they had observed elsewhere.

Comparable benefits from job redesign are occurring in offices, with new information systems supporting and even permitting the new work processes. More meaningful and complete jobs do not automatically "fall out" of new systems; good job redesign and more attention to the human aspects of the work make the difference.

CONCLUSION

Information technology professionals have always been enamored with the technical portions of computer systems; the human side has been of less interest. But it is people who make or break a system, through their use or disuse of it. In this chapter we have dealt with the human side of systems by looking at the new work environment, both its technical side (briefly) and its human social side.

While the new work environment is undoubtedly going to rely heavily on IT, it is the social relationships, such as the communities of practice, that are the driving force. IT now allows such relationships to transcend time and space, and with the appearance of cost-justifiable long-distance video, people will be able to communicate in richer ways across greater distances. In so doing, the foundations of past ways of working must change. That is the exciting exploration that is going on right now as managers, researchers, and consultants grapple with creating the new work environment.

QUESTIONS AND EXERCISES

REVIEW QUESTIONS

1. What are the four goals of the new work environment?
2. According to Gilder, what effects do microchips and bandwidth have? And how does TV differ from bookstores?
3. What are the four organizing principles of the new work environment?
4. According to Hammer, how does measurement of a task differ from measurement of a process?
5. What are the elements of a football team that make it a process-centric organization?

6. According to Kelly, what were the three rules given to the computer-generated bats in *Batman Returns?* What was the effect of these rules?
7. According to Kelly, what is the only way to create truly complex systems?
8. List some of the ways Semco operates differently from most companies.
9. According to Brown and Solomon Gray, why are communities the building blocks of knowledge-based companies?
10. What is a community of practice? And what has National Semiconductor done to encourage them?
11. According to Gage, how does he really know the "hot" work being performed at Sun?
12. According to Peter Senge, what are the five attributes of a learning organization?
13. What are the five core job dimensions in the job diagnostic survey? What recommendations do Couger and Colter have for improving the job of the maintenance programmer?
14. What are the goals of the sociotechnical system approach to job redesign? Briefly describe the steps in this approach.
15. What kinds of supervisory and managerial tasks do self-managed work groups perform themselves?

DISCUSSION QUESTIONS

1. Giving employees and small work groups the authority to make most of their own decisions seems to be of obvious benefit to companies. Why do you think this type of on-the-job self-management is not more prevalent?
2. Although we have talked about the benefits of job redesign from the employees' point of view, we have not discussed it from management's point of view. Give some reasons why you think management would be for or against such job redesign. What types of managers do you think would be more likely (or less likely) to accept a new environment where they do less supervising and more training and coordinating?
3. Peter Senge's ideas are too complex to be practical. Organizations cannot make such radical changes in the way their people think and interact. Do you agree or disagree? Describe your reasoning.
4. Likewise, the ideas of Kelly, Wheatley, and Kellner-Rogers about self-organizing systems will not work in organizations. Organizations need defined structure, defined jobs, and limits. Do you agree or disagree? Describe your reasoning.

EXERCISES

1. Read several articles or scan several books on the new work environment. What management issues do these present with respect to work redesign? What potential roadblocks do they discuss?
2. Visit a local company and talk to an information systems executive about the company's employment policies. (a) Does the company regularly survey employees' attitudes about their work? (b) Are jobs redesigned when new technology is introduced? If so, ask for one or two examples of redesigned work. If not, ask what would be required in order to redesign the work. (c) If a work redesign methodology has been used, briefly describe it and its use through an example.
3. Describe your personal vision for your life. If you work, write the shared vision you believe your organization presents to the outside world. Present both to the class.
4. Describe the work environment in which you would like to work. Present it to the class. How might you achieve such a goal?

REFERENCES

1. MANVILLE, BROOK and NATHANIEL FOOTE, "Strategy As If Knowledge Mattered," *Fast Company*, 1996, http://fastcompany.com.

2. GILDER, GEORGE, speech to The Aspen Institute, July 18, 1996, broadcast on C-SPAN during August 1996.

3. HAMMER, MICHAEL, *Beyond Reengineering: How the Process-Centered Organization Is Changing Our Work and Our Lives*, Harper-Collins Publishers, New York, NY, 1996.

4. WHEATLEY, MARGARET, *Leadership and the New Science: Learning about Organizations from an Orderly Universe,* Berrett-Koehler Publishers, San Francisco, CA, 1994.

5. KELLY, KEVIN, *Out of Control: The New Biology of Machines, Social Systems, and the Economic World*, Addison-Wesley Publishing, Reading, MA, 1994.

6. WHEATLEY, MARGARET, and MYRON KELLNER-ROGERS, *A Simpler Way,* Berrett-Koehler Publishers, San Francisco, CA, 1996.

7. SEMLER, RICARDO, *Maverick: The Success Story Behind the World's Most Unusual Workplace,* Warner Books, New York, NY, 1993.

8. INSTITUTE FOR RESEARCH ON LEARNING, 66 Willow Place, Menlo Park, CA.

9. BROWN, JOHN SEELY, and ESTEE SOLOMON GRAY, "The People Are the Company," *Fast Company*, Premier Issue, 1995.

10. RAPAPORT, RICHARD, "The Network Is the Company: An Interview with John Gage," *Fast Company,* 1996.

11. SENGE, PETER, *The Fifth Discipline: The Art and Practice of the Learning Organization,* Doubleday, New York, NY, 1990.

12. FEINSTEIN, DEBRA, "Computing for the People," *Fast Company,* Premier Issue, 1995.

13. TURNER, JON A., "Computer Mediated Work: The Interplay Between Technology and Structured Jobs," *Communications of the ACM* (1515 Broadway, New York, NY 10036), December 1984.

14. COUGER, J. D. and R. A. ZAWACKI, *Motivating and Managing Computer Personnel,* John Wiley and Sons (605 Third Ave., New York, NY 10016), 1980.

15. COUGER, J. D. and R. O'CALLAGHAN, "Comparing the Motivation of Spanish and Finnish Computer Personnel with Those of the United States," *European Journal of Information Systems*, Vol. 3, No. 4, 1994, pp. 285-291.

16. COUGER, J. D., "Comparisons of Motivation Norms for Programmer/Analysts in the Pacific Rim and the U.S.," *International Information Systems*, July 1992, pp. 16-30.

17. COUGER, J. D., and M. A. COLTER, *Maintenance Programming: Improved Productivity Through Motivation*, Prentice-Hall, Englewood Cliffs, NJ 07632, 1985.

18. TAYLOR, JAMES, All Types Publications, Box 998, El Segundo, CA 90245.

19. SIMS, H. P., JR., and C. C. MANZ, "Conversations Within Self-Managed Work Groups," *National Productivity Review* (33 W. 60 St., New York, NY 10023), Summer 1982, pp. 261-269.

Glossary

TERMS

Abend—An abnormal ending of a software program, which is when it stops running because it encounters an error condition (p. 233).

Advanced Technology Group—A group within the IS department that is responsible for spotting and evaluating new technologies, often by conducting pilot projects (p. 495).

Affinity Diagram—Clustering Post-It notes of items (such as business activities) on a wall under headings (such as business processes) to show groupings (p. 122).

Agent—An electronic entity that performs tasks, either on its own or at the request of a person or a computer (p. 330).

Alias—Master list of e-mail lists (p. 518).

Applets—Small single-function applications, often written in Java, that are pulled from the Internet when needed (p. 155).

Application Programming Interface (API)—An interface created for a product that is like a standard because it allows programmers to write to that interface and thus utilize that product in their applications (p. 281).

Architecture—A blueprint that shows how the overall system, house, vehicle, or thing will look and how the parts interrelate (p. 133).

Artificial Intelligence (AI)—The group of technologies that attempt to mimic our senses or emulate certain aspects of human behavior, such as reasoning (p. 423).

Authentication—Assuring that the digital signature of the user is valid (p. 248)

Avatar—A virtual persona that is taken on by a person in a chat room or MUD on the Internet (p. 336).

Back-End Tools—Tools, such as code generators, in computer-aided software engineering suites that automatically generate source code (p. 270).

Backbone Systems—Mainline corporate transaction processing systems (p.305).

Brown Bag Theater—Where the training department presents a series of video tapes, outside speakers, or even company employees speaking about their work during lunch time to educate IS staff on the business or new technologies (p. 488).

Business Process Redesign/Reengineering (BPR)—Significantly restructuring the operational business processes in a firm (p. 64).

Cache—Fast memory used for temporary storage (p. 212).

Case-Based Reasoning—A form of knowledge representation in expert systems that draws inferences by comparing a current problem with hundreds or thousands of similar past cases (p. 429).

Case Management—A way to organize work where each person (or team) handles a customer (a case) or a set of customers from beginning to end rather than each doing a part of the work then passing it to others for further work (p. 69).

Champion—A person inside or outside IS who has a vision and gets it implemented by obtaining the funding, pushing the project over hurdles, putting his or her reputation on the line, and taking on the risk of the project (p. 494).

Chaos Theory—As applied to business, a theory that states that "order is free" when groups and organizations are allowed to be self-organizing because, as in scientific chaos theory, randomness (chaos) works within boundaries, which are called strange attractors. As a result, there is order in chaos (p. 512).

Chief Information Officer (CIO)—The executive who provides the leadership of the IS function, who must be high enough in the organization to influence organizational goals and have enough credibility to lead the harnessing of IT to pursue those goals. (p. 16).

Cleansed Data—Data processed to make it usable for decision support; referred to in conjunction with data warehouses (p. 370).

Cleartext—Non-encrypted versions of passwords and messages (p. 248).

Client/Server—Splitting the computing workload between the "client," which is a computer used by the user and can sit on the desktop or be carried around, and the "server," which houses the sharable resources (p. 149).

Closed Network—A network that is offered by one supplier which uses the proprietary protocols of that supplier (p. 177).

Communities of Practice—Networks of people who work together in an unofficial way to get work accomplished using unofficial procedures that may be outside the company's formal corporate culture (p. 515).

Concept-Based Retrieval—A text retrieval system that allows searching on concepts—such as poor quality, inadequate

product functionality, or obsolescence—rather than words (p. 454).

Connectivity—Allowing users to communicate up, down, across, and out of an organization via a network (p. 93).

Cooperative Processing—A computer system with various components cooperating with each other to perform a task. The components may span several business functions within the organization or even link to other organizations (p. 144).

Corporate Memory—The knowledge or information accumulated by a business that is often stored in its software, databases, patents, and business processes (p. 357).

Creative Problem Solving (CPS)—Procedures and techniques designed to solve complete problems in creative ways; CPS techniques can enhance IS planning (p. 117).

Critical Success Factors (CSF)—The few key areas of an executive's job where things must go right in order for the organization to flourish (p. 104).

Cybermall—A virtual mall on the World Wide Web; it exists in time but not in physical space (p. 6).

Cyberspace—A "space" on the Internet where people "exist" in a virtual world (p. 172).

Cycle Time—The amount of time it takes to accomplish a complete cycle, such as the time from getting an idea to turning it into a product or service (p. 7).

Data—Electronic information that is comprised of facts and devoid of meaning (p. 61).

Data Dictionary—The main tool with which data administrators control a company's standard data definitions to make sure that corporate policy is being followed (p. 201).

Data Integrity—Data that maintains its integrity because it cannot be modified in transit or in storage (p. 200).

Data Mining—Exploring huge repositories of data to uncover patterns, trends, or anomalies (p. 208).

Data Warehouse—A repository of data from many sources that is used for decision making, not for handling operational transactions (p. 370).

Decentralization—Moving the processing or storage of data out from a central site, often with little or no coordination with that central site (p. 8).

Decision Support Systems (DSS) or Decision Support Applications (DSA)—Computer applications used to support decision making (p. 9).

Desktop clients—Desktop machines used in a client/server system environment to make requests of shared servers (p. 9).

Dirty Data—Data from different databases that does not match, has different names, uses different time frames, etc. (p. 198).

Distributed System—A computer system that has components physically distributed around a company or among companies (p. 8).

Document—A unit of recorded information structured for human consumption (p. 453).

Downsizing—Reducing the size of a company workforce via layoffs (p. 64).

Dribbling Data—Obtaining data for a new application from data in an existing application (p. 198).

Dumb Terminals—Desktop machines without processing or storage capabilities (p. 134).

Eavesdropping—Intercepting messages on a computer network (p. 248).

Electronic Data Interchange (EDI)—Business transactions, such as orders, that cross company boundaries electronically via a network using carefully defined protocols and data formats (p. 85).

Electronic Market—A computerized marketplace with several buyers and several sellers where a third party generally acts as the market intermediary (p. 95).

Electronic Vaulting—An off-site data storage facility used by organizations for backing up data to prevent loss in case of a disaster at a main processing site (p. 252).

Encapsulation—Combining data and procedures in an object (p. 273).

Encryption—Coding text into an unintelligible form so that it cannot be understood by people (p. 248)

Enterprise Modeling (EM)—Diagramming an organization using a specific methodology (p. 119).

Ethernet—A network protocol used in many local area networks that broadcasts messages across the network and rebroadcasts if a collision of messages occurs (p. 181).

Executive Information System (EIS)—A computer system specially built for executives to assist them in making decisions (p. 19).

Expert System—A computer system that houses experts' knowledge about a subject, such as how to make a batch of tomato soup (p. 424).

Extended Enterprise Networks—Interconnected single-organization networks that are not limited by industry and permit a type of electronic information consortium (p. 173).

External Document-Based Information—Electronic information that is available outside an organization and is text based, rather than alphanumeric (p. 216).

External Operational Measures—Measures of computer operational performance that users can see, such as system and network uptime (or downtime), response time, turnaround time, and program failures. These directly relate to customer satisfaction (p. 229).

External Record-Based Information—Electronic information that is available outside an organization and is alphanumeric, rather than text based. (p. 216).

Extract file—A file extracted from a company's transaction database and placed in a decision support database or a data warehouse where it can be queried by end users (p. 370).

Extranet—A portion of an intranet that is made available to outsiders, often suppliers, customers, or subscribers (p. 62).

Failure Impact —The cost or damage that could occur from a failure (p. 302).

Federated Databases—A way of organizing databases where each retains its autonomy, where its data is defined independently of the other databases, and where its database management system takes care of itself while retaining rules for others to access its data (p. 212).

Filtering—Using a software program (a filter) to automatically route messages or documents according to their content (p. 429).

Firewall—Software on Internet servers to keep the public from accessing the company's intranet (p. 189).

Fourth Generation Language—A computer programming language used by end users, as opposed to COBOL (a third generation language), or Assembler (a second generation language), or programming via plug boards (first generation programming) (p. 265).

Frame Relay—A newly emerging fast communication protocol for data networks that uses variable-length packets rather than fixed-length packets (p. 182).

Frame—A way of storing knowledge in computers using containers that have slots for information, values, rules and procedural code that can redirect the query until the correct answers or solutions are found (p. 428).

Front-end Tools—Tools in a computer-aided software engineering suite that are used by analysts and designers to create the design of a computer system (p. 270).

Fuzzy Logic—An AI technology that allows computers to handle concepts and fuzzy notions, thus allowing computer systems to more closely work the way people talk and think (p. 430).

Gateway—A data network connection that connects unlike networks (p. 145).

Goal-Based Systems—Systems that support work activities that do not follow the same or similar process every time and with

information and knowledge that is not easily encapsulated (p. 14–15).

Greenfield Approach—A term used in business process reengineering that means "starting from scratch" (p. 69).

Groupware—Software and systems designed specifically to aid group communication, coordination, and decision making (p. 394).

Heuristics—Rules that draw upon experience, common sense, ways of doing business, and even rules and regulations (p. 427).

Hierarchical Database Model—A database model where each data element is subordinate to another in a strict hierarchy, like the boxes on an organization chart (p. 205).

Home Page—A person's or organization's base page on the World Wide Web (p. 6).

Hoshin Planning Interrelationship Digraph— A diagram showing the information that flows between business processes or business segments to illustrate the relationships between them (p. 123).

Hypertext—A style of presenting text in computer systems or networks where the reader can click on a highlighted word and jump to a related thought or site. Hypermedia uses the same technique to link graphical items, as on the World Wide Web (p. 330).

Inference Engine—The software within an expert system that contains the reasoning methods used to search the knowledge base and solve the problem (p. 427).

Information—Data in context, where the meaning depends on the surrounding circumstances or usage (p. 161).

Information Architecture—A blueprint of stable definitions of corporate data—such as customers, products, and business transactions—that can be specified ahead of time and used consistently across the firm (p. 133).

Information Repository—The heart of a computer-aided software engineering system that stores and organizes all information needed to create, modify, and develop a software system (p. 270).

Information Resources—The intangible information assets of a firm, including data, information, knowledge, processes, patents, and so on (p. 197).

Infrastructure—The physical manifestation of an architecture. An IS infrastructure includes the hardware, software, databases, networks, and system-wide rules that underlie a company's electronic means of working (p. 163).

Inheritance—In object-oriented programming, allowing an object to inherit characteristics from the class of objects of which it is a member (p. 274).

Institutional DSS—A decision support system built by DSS professionals using a DSS language that is intended to be used for the long term to support the organization's operations rather than to support an individual or small group for a short time (p. 372).

Internal Document-Based Information—Information that is available in-house and is text based, such as internal reports, memos, and so forth (p. 216).

Internal Operational Measures—Metrics of the performance of the computer operations group that are of interest to IS people, such as computer usage as a percentage of capacity, availability of mainline systems, disk storage utilized, job queue length, number of jobs run, number of jobs rerun due to problems, age of applications, and number of unresolved problems (p. 229).

Internal Record-Based Information—Information that is available in-house and is alphanumeric rather than textual (p. 216).

Interoperability—Ability for different products to work together; driven by the open systems movement (p. 193).

Interorganizational Systems (IOS)—Systems where at least two parties with different objectives have collaborated on the development and operation of the system (p. 85).

Intranet—An internal company network that uses the Internet's and Web's infrastructure, telecommunication protocols, and browsers (p. 176).

Investment Strategy Analysis—An analysis technique used by IS management to determine which computer applications to build next (p. 105).

Issues-Based Education—Where the educators identify executives' current needs and design the education to address those needs (p. 486).

Knowledge—Information with direction or intent; it facilitates a decision or an action (p. 161).

Knowledge Base—The portion of an expert system that contains the facts and data relevant to a specific problem (p. 427).

Knowledge Management—Managing the intellectual capital of the organization; some believe knowledge can reside in machines, others believe it only resides in people's heads (p. 10–11).

Legacy Systems—Mainframe computer applications that handle the day-to-day transactions of the company in an old, centralized style, rather than a distributed manner (p. 306).

Line Executive—A business executive who manages a profit-oriented business unit, such as manufacturing, rather than a supporting staff unit, such as finance (p. 50).

Linkage Analysis Planning—A planning approach that studies the links between an organization and its suppliers and customers (p. 113).

Mail-Enabled Application—The use of application programming interfaces (APIs) for electronic mail systems that allow applications to interact with each other using the mail systems as the communication links (p. 327).

Mainframe—A huge, very fast computer that is capable of handling all the computing for a large organization (p. 9).

Marketspace—A non-physical marketplace where information substitutes for physical products and physical location (p. 80).

Metadata—Information about a data entity, such as its definition, how it was calculated, its source, when it is updated, who is responsible for it, etc. (p. 201).

Mid-Tier Servers—A network topology that has several tiers of servers, such as local work group servers, departmental servers, and an enterprise server (the corporate mainframe) (p. 149).

Middleware—Software that eases connection between clients and servers in a client/server system (p. 281).

Mosaic Messages—Electronic mail messages that contain former messages to show the flow of the discussion (p. 413).

Multimedia—The combination of text, graphics, sound, data, animation, and perhaps video in a message, a document, or at a Web site (p. 329).

Netizens—People who frequently use the Internet and consider themselves citizens of the Net's culture (p. 335).

Network Computer (NC)—A computer that is used much like a telephone; it has no hard disk or house applications, but rather just a browser, memory, keyboard, and a modem to pull applications off the Internet (p. 9).

Network Database Model—A database model that allows each data item to have more than one parent. Assembly parts illustrate this structure, where the same part can be used in more than one assembly (p. 206).

Neural Networks—A type of artificial intelligence that uses networks that contain links (synapses) and nodes that fire signals between each other; some consider them more 'intelligent' than other AI techniques because they can learn (p. 431).

Object Oriented Programming—A style of programming that encapsulates data and the operations that work on that data within an object, thus increasing the reusability of the code (as an object) and

reducing the propagation of errors among objects (p. 273).

Object—In object oriented programming, functions are packaged with data so that the two can be reused. These reusable components are called "classes," whereas at run time, each class can produce instances called "objects." Objects hold all the code and data in an object-oriented system (p. 273).

On-Line Analytical Processing (OLAP)—managers and professionals doing decision support analyses without help from intermediaries or information systems professionals (p. 370).

Open Network or Open System—A network (or system) based on national or international standards so that the products of many manufacturers work with each other (p. 177).

Optical Fiber—Tiny glass fibers that use light to transmit voice or data signals (p. 166).

Outsourcing—Contracting with another firm to perform work that had previously been performed in-house, generally requiring a multi-year contract and generally for "non-core" work (p. 236).

Paradigm Shift—A significant shift in viewpoint, such as shifting from seeing the mainframe as the center of computing to seeing the desktop or the Internet as the center of computing (p. 43).

Partnering—Allying with another organization that has different core competencies, often on a strategic alliance basis, for mutual benefit, such as when Visa partnered with United Airlines to offer the First Card credit card (p. 7).

Password Sniffing—Attempting to unveil passwords to gain access to a system (p. 248).

Peer Level Systems—Systems that allow each unit to communicate directly with each other rather than go through a higher intermediary, such as a mainframe or a central server (p. 184).

Performance Systems—Computer applications that are intended to increase job performance by embedding training so that users can get just-in-time training when they need it (p. 499).

Piggybacking—Loading two truck trailers on a railroad flat car and shipping them to their destination (p. 268).

Planning Tree Diagram—Arranging an affinity diagram into a hierarchy (p. 122).

Power User—Someone who takes the initiative to learn how to use computer applications in their work (p. 347).

Process Centering—An approach to designing an organization where business processes (rather than functions) are the main organizational structures (p. 510).

Prototype—A computer program that is used to test a new computing concept, such as distributed Java applets, for learning and experimentation purposes. (p. 267).

Quality Systems—Computer systems that do not break down, do the work intended, and are easy to maintain (p. 301).

Quick-Hit DSS—A system that is quite limited in scope, is developed and put into use quickly, and helps a manager come to a decision. The term "ad hoc" has also been used to distinguish from institutional DSS, although some quick-hit systems become regularly used (p. 374).

Rapid Application Development (RAD)—An approach to developing systems quickly using prototyping and dividing development into small modules that can be quickly built (pp. 270-71).

Reengineering—Not to be confused with the term "business process reengineering," this term means extracting the data elements from an existing file and the business logic from an existing system and moving them to new hardware platforms (p. 300).

Referential integrity—Adhering to complex relationship rules in a database (p. 203).

Relational Database Model—Databases that store data in tables where the relationships between the data are based on values in specific fields, not pointers, as in hierarchical and network models. Good for ad hoc querying (p. 206).

Replication Software—Software that duplicates (replicates) data, e-mail, or other items among databases, computers, or networks (p. 210).

Repudiation—Refusing a computer-based transaction, such as when one party reneges on an agreement after the fact, so that the other party is not left paying for the processing of that failed transaction (p. 248).

Rules—The most common way to represent knowledge in an expert system. Rules generally are if-then statements (p. 427).

Rummler-Brache Approach—An approach to business process reengineering that looks at the "as is" structure and then designs a "to be" structure using hierarchical lines and boxes (p. 399).

Scenario—A way to manage planning assumptions by creating a speculation of what the future will be like drawing on trends, events, environmental factors, and the relationships among them (p. 108).

Self-Managed Work Teams—Teams of people who represent all the necessary functions to serve one set of customers. The team makes most of its own decisions rather than looking for guidance from a supervisor (p. 139).

Semantic Network—A network whose nodes are concepts and whose links are relationships between the concepts (p 295, 427).

Social Computing—Where IT is used to help electronic communities to form and communicate (p. 520).

Spaghetti Code—The way code in many legacy systems appears to a programmer because it has been patched so many times that the logic of the application weaves in and out like a plate of spaghetti (p. 307).

Spiral Approach to System Development—A way of viewing the application development process as a spiral, as opposed to a waterfall (p. 263).

Spoofing—Masquerading as another party on a network, such as a storefront to collect thousands (or millions) of credit card numbers and other information from naive consumers (p. 248).

Support Systems—Systems that can help white collar workers perform goal-based work (p. 363).

System Integration—The process of piecing together hardware components, software packages, database engines, and network products from numerous vendors into a single, cohesive system; most often used to refer to the way client/server systems are built today. Also known as component-based development (pp. 278–79).

System-Wide Rules—An operating discipline for distributed systems that is enforced at all times and governs security, communication between nodes, data accessibility, program and file transfers, and common operating procedures (p. 135).

Tacit Knowledge—Knowledge "known" but not easily explained to others (p. 222, 306).

Technology Camel—A way to distinguish levels of comfort with any technology using five clusters, which, when graphed on a chart, look a lot like a two-humped camel (p. 342).

Telecommunications—The sending of information in any form from one place to another, electronically (p. 171).

Thin Clients—Network computers that are used much like telephones; they have no hard disk or applications, but rather just a browser, memory, keyboard, and a modem (p. 9).

Third Generation Language—A programming language, such as COBOL, used by a professional programmer (p. 262).

Timebox—A methodology for building a system in which the developers promise to deliver specific portions of the system within a specific timeframe (a timebox);

the intent is to better control project delivery schedules (p. 270).

Total Quality Management—A management technique that focuses on managing the quality of a service or product, often through statistical quality control techniques, in order to achieve higher customer satisfaction and reduce costs as well (p. 5).

Transitional Outsourcing—The outsourcing of the maintenance of legacy systems so that the in-house staff can focus on developing replacement client/server systems. Also known as transformational outsourcing (pp. 238, 307).

Tuple—A row in a relational database that represents an individual entity, such as a person, part, or account. Columns in the table represent attributes of the entities (p. 206).

Value Chain—A technique for describing a chain of business processes from product/service conception through cessation of the product/service, where each of the processes adds some kind of value (p. 82).

Vision—A statement of how someone wants the future to be or believes it will be; it is used to set direction for an organization. (p. 41).

Visual Programming—A technique for programming, such as creating a graphical user interface, by pointing and clicking on generic items—menus, dialog boxes, radio buttons, and other components of graphical displays—and then arranging them to create a screen (p. 275).

Waterfall Approach to System Development—A way to view the system development process as a series of steps that, when diagrammed, appear as a waterfall (p. 262).

Web Site—A personal or organizational site on the World Wide Web (p. 71).

Workscape—The virtual workplace, which includes the Internet (p. 61).

Workstation—A high-powered desktop or portable computer (p. 9).

ACRONYMS AND ABBREVIATIONS

2D/3D—Two dimensional, three dimensional

4GLs—Fourth Generation Languages

ACM—Association for Computing Machinery

AIS—Association for Information Systems

AI—Artificial Intelligence

AMA—American Medical Association

AmEx—American Express

AM—Amplitude Modulation

ANSI—American National Standards Institute

AOL—America Online

API—Application Programming Interface

ARPANET—Advanced Research Projects Agency Network

AS/400—Advanced System/400 (An IBM midrange computer)

ASCII—American Standard Code for Information Interchange

AT&T—American Telephone and Telegraph

ATM—Asynchronous Transfer Mode

BPR—Business Process Redesign/Reengineering

C/C++—Programming languages used with UNIX

CACM—*Communications of the ACM* magazine

CAD/CAM—Computer-Aided Design/Computer-Aided Manufacturing

CAI—Computer-Assisted Instruction

CALS—Computer-aided Acquisition and Logistic Support

CAL—Computer-Assisted Learning

CASE—Computer-Aided Software Engineering

CBR—Case-Based Reasoning

CBT—Computer-Based Training

CCITT—Consultive Committee for International Telegraphy and Telephony

CD-ROM—Compact Disc—Read Only Memory

CEO—Chief Executive Officer

CFO—Chief Financial Officer

CGM—Computer Graphics Metafile

CIO—Chief Information Officer

CMI—Computer-Managed instruction

COBOL—Common Business Oriented Language

COM—Computer Output Microfilm

COO—Chief Operations Officer

CPS—Creative Problem Solving

CSF—Critical Success Factor

CTO—Chief Technology Officer

DASD—Direct Access Data Storage

DB2—Database 2 (an IBM product)

DBMS—Database Management System

DDM—Dialog, Data, and Modeling

DEC—Digital Equipment Corporation

DGMS—Dialog Generation and Management System

DOS—Disk Operating System

DPI—Dots Per Inch

DSS—Decision Support Systems

E-mail—Electronic Mail

E-zines—Electronic magazines

EDI—Electronic Data Interchange

EDM—Electronic Document Management

EDP—Electronic Data Processing

EDS—Electronic Data Systems

EIS—Executive Information System

EM—Enterprise Modeling

EPRI—Electric Power Research Institute

EPSS—Electronic Performance Support System

ERD—Enterprise Reference Data

ESOP—Employee Stock Ownership Plan

ESS—Executive Support System

EUC—End User Computing

EwIM—Enterprise-wide Information Management

FAQ—Frequently Asked Questions
Fax—Facsimile
FDA—U.S. Food and Drug Administration
FDDI—Fiber Distributed Data Interface
FTP—File Transfer Protocol
GDSS—Group Decision Support Systems
GOSIP—Government Standard Internet Protocol
GTE—General Telephone Company
HBO—Home Box Office
***HBR**—Harvard Business Review*
HDTV—High Definition Television
HPT—Hoshin Planning Techniques
HTML—HyperText Markup Language
HTTP—HyperText Transfer Protocol
IBM —International Business Machines Corporation
ICIS—International Conference on Information Systems
IDC—International Data Corporation
IDMS—Integrated Data Management System
IDS—Integrated Data Store
IEA—Information Engineering Associates
IFTF—Institute for the Future
IGES—Initial Graphics Exchange Specification
IMS—Integrated Management System
IOS—Interorganizational System
IPng—Internet Protocol next generation
IPSS—Integrated Performance Support System
IP—Internet Protocol
ISDN—Integrated Services Digital Network
ISO—International Standards Organization
ISSC—Information Systems Steering Committee
ISSC—Integrated Systems Services Corporation
ITMP—Information Technology Management Programme
IT—Information Technology

JAD—Joint Application Design
JDS—Job Diagnostic Survey
JIT—Just-In-Time
Kbps—Kilobytes per second
LAN—Local Area Network
LN—Local Network
LTL—Less-Than-Truckloads
MANs—Metropolitan Area Networks
MBMS—Model Base Management System
Mbps—Megabytes per second
MGM—Metro-Goldwyn-Mayer
MIDS—Management Information and Decision Support System
MIPS—Millions of Instructions Per Second
MIS—Management Information Systems
MIT—Massachussetts Institute of Technology
MOO—MUD, Object-Oriented
MUD—Multi-User Dungeon/Dimension
MU—Multiple-User system
MVS—Multiple Virtual System
NASA—National Aeronautics and Space Administration
NC—Network Computer
Net—The Internet
NNC—Nolan, Norton & Co.
NT—Network Technology
NYNEX—New York National Exchange
ODA—Office Document Architecture
OLAP—On-Line Analytical Processing
OLTP—On-Line Transaction Processing
OR/MS—Operations Research/Management Science
OSI—Open System Interconnection
PARC—Xerox's Palo Alto Research Center
PBX—Private Branch Exchange
PCCA—Plains Cotton Cooperative Association
PCS—Personal Communication Service
PC—Personal Computer
PDA—Personal Digital Assistant
PDES—Project Data Exchange Specification

PIN—Personal Identification Number

PL/1—Programming Language 1

PRA—Passenger Revenue Accounting

PROFS—Professional Office System

PTT—Postal, Telephone, and Telegraph Authority

R&D—Research and Development

RAD—Rapid Application Development

RF—Radio Frequency

RISC—Reduced Instruction Set Computer

RN—Remote Network

ROI—Return On Investment

RPG—Remote Programming Generator

RU—Remote Utility system

SEC—U.S. Securities and Exchange Commission

SET—Secure Electronic Transactions

SGML—Standard Generalized Markup Language

SNA—System Network Architecture

SOFFEX—Swiss Options and Financial Futures Exchange

SPARC—Standards, Planning and Requirements Committee

SQL—Structured Query Language

SSA—U.S. Social Security Administration

SSL—Secure Sockets Layer

STS—Sociotechnical System

SUMURU—Single User, Multiple User, Remote Utility

SU—Single-User system

TCMP—Telecom Management Programme

TCP/IP—Transmission Control Protocol/Internet Protocol

Telecom—Telecommunications

TSC—Technology Solutions Corporation

UCLA—University of California, Los Angeles

UNIX—"Unics" operating system—an attempt at a pun

UPS—United Parcel Service

UTC—United Technologies Corporation

UTMC—United Technologies Microelectronics Center

VLSI—Very Large System Integration

VSAT—Very Small Aperture Terminal

WAN—Wide Area Network

Web—The World Wide Web

WYSIWYG—What You See Is What You Get

Index